Lecture Notes in Computer Science

Lecture Notes in Artificial Intelligence 16014
Founding Editor

Jörg Siekmann

Series Editors

Randy Goebel, *University of Alberta, Edmonton, Canada*
Wolfgang Wahlster, *DFKI, Berlin, Germany*
Zhi-Hua Zhou, *Nanjing University, Nanjing, China*

The series Lecture Notes in Artificial Intelligence (LNAI) was established in 1988 as a topical subseries of LNCS devoted to artificial intelligence.

The series publishes state-of-the-art research results at a high level. As with the LNCS mother series, the mission of the series is to serve the international R & D community by providing an invaluable service, mainly focused on the publication of conference and workshop proceedings and postproceedings.

Rita P. Ribeiro · Bernhard Pfahringer ·
Nathalie Japkowicz · Pedro Larrañaga ·
Alípio M. Jorge · Carlos Soares ·
Pedro H. Abreu · João Gama
Editors

Machine Learning and Knowledge Discovery in Databases

Research Track

European Conference, ECML PKDD 2025
Porto, Portugal, September 15–19, 2025
Proceedings, Part II

 Springer

Editors
Rita P. Ribeiro
University of Porto
Porto, Portugal

Nathalie Japkowicz
American University
Washington, D.C., WA, USA

Alípio M. Jorge
University of Porto
Porto, Portugal

Pedro H. Abreu
University of Coimbra
Coimbra, Portugal

Bernhard Pfahringer
University of Waikato
Hamilton, Waikato, New Zealand

Pedro Larrañaga
Technical University of Madrid
Boadilla del Monte, Madrid, Spain

Carlos Soares
University of Porto
Porto, Portugal

João Gama
University of Porto
Porto, Portugal

ISSN 0302-9743 ISSN 1611-3349 (electronic)
Lecture Notes in Artificial Intelligence
ISBN 978-3-032-05980-2 ISBN 978-3-032-05981-9 (eBook)
https://doi.org/10.1007/978-3-032-05981-9

LNCS Sublibrary: SL7 – Artificial Intelligence

© The Editor(s) (if applicable) and The Author(s), under exclusive license
to Springer Nature Switzerland AG 2026

This work is subject to copyright. All rights are solely and exclusively licensed by the Publisher, whether the whole or part of the material is concerned, specifically the rights of translation, reprinting, reuse of illustrations, recitation, broadcasting, reproduction on microfilms or in any other physical way, and transmission or information storage and retrieval, electronic adaptation, computer software, or by similar or dissimilar methodology now known or hereafter developed.
The use of general descriptive names, registered names, trademarks, service marks, etc. in this publication does not imply, even in the absence of a specific statement, that such names are exempt from the relevant protective laws and regulations and therefore free for general use.
The publisher, the authors and the editors are safe to assume that the advice and information in this book are believed to be true and accurate at the date of publication. Neither the publisher nor the authors or the editors give a warranty, expressed or implied, with respect to the material contained herein or for any errors or omissions that may have been made. The publisher remains neutral with regard to jurisdictional claims in published maps and institutional affiliations.

This Springer imprint is published by the registered company Springer Nature Switzerland AG
The registered company address is: Gewerbestrasse 11, 6330 Cham, Switzerland

If disposing of this product, please recycle the paper.

Preface

The 2025 edition of the European Conference on Machine Learning and Principles and Practice of Knowledge Discovery in Databases (ECML PKDD 2025) was held in the vibrant city of Porto, Portugal on September 15–19, 2025. This marks a significant return of the conference to Porto, following successful editions in 2005 and 2015, underscoring the city's enduring appeal as a hub for scientific exchange.

The annual ECML PKDD conference stands as a premier worldwide platform dedicated to showcasing the latest advancements and fostering insightful discussions in the fields of machine learning and knowledge discovery in databases. Held jointly since 2001, ECML PKDD has firmly established its reputation as the leading European conference in these disciplines. It provides researchers and practitioners with an unparalleled opportunity to exchange knowledge, share innovative ideas, and explore the latest technical advancements. Furthermore, the conference deeply values the synergy between foundational theoretical advances and groundbreaking practical data science applications, actively encouraging contributions that demonstrate how Machine Learning and Data Mining are being effectively employed to address complex real-world challenges.

A Hub for Responsible AI and Cutting-Edge Research

As the technological landscape continues to evolve and societal needs shift, the conference remains committed to adapting to and reflecting these dynamic changes. This year's event saw a robust engagement from the global research community with a substantial increase in the number of submissions.

The three main conference days were organised into five distinct tracks:

- The Research Track received an impressive number of 924 submissions, with 226 papers ultimately accepted, reflecting a highly competitive acceptance rate of 24.5%.
- The Applied Data Science Track received a total of 299 submissions, accepting 74 papers, resulting in an acceptance rate of 24.7%.
- The Journal Track continued to bridge the gap between conference and journal publications, accepting 43 papers (27 for the Machine Learning journal and 16 for the Data Mining and Knowledge Discovery journal) out of 297 submissions.
- The Nectar Track, focusing on recent scientific advances at the frontier of machine learning and data mining, received 30 submissions.
- The Demo Track showcased practical applications and prototypes, accepting 15 papers from a total of 30 submissions.

These proceedings cover the papers accepted in the Research and Applied Data Science tracks.

The high quality and diversity of the accepted papers across all tracks underscore the continued vitality and intellectual breadth of the machine learning and data mining communities. We extend our sincere gratitude to all authors for their valuable contributions, to the program committee members and reviewers for their diligent efforts in ensuring the rigorous double-blind review process, and to the organising committee for their tireless work in making ECML PKDD 2025 a resounding success. We believe these proceedings will serve as a valuable resource, inspiring future research and innovation in these rapidly advancing fields.

This year's conference featured seven insightful keynote talks that focused on crucial and emerging areas within Responsible AI, including trustworthy AI, interpretability, and explainability. The keynotes also explored fundamental theoretical issues, covering causality, neural-symbolic systems, large language models (LLMs), and AI for science. We were honoured to host leading experts who shared their valuable perspectives:

- Cynthia Rudin (Duke University) presented on "Many Good Models Lead to …";
- Elias Bareinboim (Columbia University) discussed "Towards Causal Artificial Intelligence";
- Francisco Herrera (University of Granada) addressed "Not Just a Trend: Institutionalizing XAI for Responsible and Compliant AI Systems";
- Mirella Lapata (University of Edinburgh) explored "Compositional Intelligence: Coordinating Multiple LLMs for Complex Tasks";
- Nuria Oliver (ELLIS Alicante Foundation, Spain) spoke on "Towards a Fairer World: Uncovering and Addressing Human and Algorithmic Biases";
- Pedro Domingos (University of Washington) shared insights on "A Simple Unification of Neural and Symbolic AI"; and
- Sašo Džeroski (Jožef Stefan Institute, Slovenia) presented on "Artificial Intelligence for Science".

Fostering Diversity and Inclusion

Our Diversity and Inclusion initiative proudly awarded 10 scholarship grants of €500 to early-career researchers. These grants enabled individuals from developing countries and communities underrepresented in science and technology to attend the conference, present their work, and become integral members of the ECML PKDD community.

Acknowledging Our Contributors and Supporters

We extend our sincere gratitude to everyone who contributed to making ECML PKDD 2025 such a success. Our heartfelt thanks go to the authors, workshop and tutorial organisers, and all participants for their valuable scientific contributions.

An outstanding conference program would not be possible without the immense dedication and substantial time investment from our area chairs, program committee, and organising committee. The smooth execution of the event was also largely due to the hard work of our many volunteers and session chairs. A special acknowledgement goes to the local organisers for meticulously handling every detail, making the conference a truly memorable experience.

Finally, we are incredibly grateful for the generous financial support from our wonderful sponsors. We also appreciate Springer's ongoing support and Microsoft's provision of their CMT software for conference management, as well as their continued assistance. Our sincere thanks also go to the ECML PKDD Steering Committee for their invaluable advice and guidance over the past two years.

September 2025

João Gama
Pedro H. Abreu
Alípio M. Jorge
Carlos Soares
Rita P. Ribeiro
Pedro Larrañaga
Nathalie Japkowicz
Bernhard Pfahringer
Inês Dutra
Mykola Pechenizkiy
Sepideh Pashami
Paulo Cortez

Organization

Honorary Chair

Pavel Brazdil — University of Porto, Portugal

General Chairs

João Gama — University of Porto, Portugal
Pedro H. Abreu — University of Coimbra, Portugal
Alípio M. Jorge — University of Porto, Portugal
Carlos Soares — University of Porto, Portugal

Research Track Program Chairs

Bernhard Pfahringer — University of Waikato, New Zealand
Nathalie Japkowicz — American University, USA
Pedro Larrañaga — Technical University of Madrid, Spain
Rita P. Ribeiro — University of Porto, Portugal

Applied Data Science Track Program Chairs

Inês Dutra — University of Porto, Portugal
Mykola Pechenisky — TU Eindhoven, The Netherlands
Paulo Cortez — University of Minho, Portugal
Sepideh Pashami — Halmstad University, Sweden

Journal Track Chairs

Ana Carolina Lorena — Instituto Tecnológico de Aeronáutica, Brazil
Arlindo Oliveira — Instituto Superior Técnico, Portugal
Concha Bielza — Technical University of Madrid, Spain
Longbing Cao — Macquarie University, Australia
Tiago Almeida — Federal University of São Carlos, Brazil

Nectar Track Chairs

Ricard Gavaldà Amalfi Analytics, Spain
Riccardo Guidotti University of Pisa, Italy

Demo Track Chairs

Arian Pasquali Faktion, Belgium
Nuno Moniz University of Notre Dame, USA

Local Chairs

Bruno Veloso University of Porto, Portugal
Rita Nogueira INESC TEC, Portugal
Shazia Tabassum INESC TEC, Portugal

Workshop Chairs

Irena Koprinska University of Sydney, Australia
João Mendes Moreira University of Porto, Portugal
Paula Branco University of Ottawa, Canada

Tutorial Chairs

Alicia Troncoso Universidad Pablo de Olavide, Spain
Nikolaj Tatti University of Helsinki, Finland

PhD Forum Chairs

Raquel Sebastião Polytechnic Institute of Viseu, Portugal
Yun Sing Koh University of Auckland, New Zealand

Awards Committee Chairs

André CarvalhoUniversity of São Paulo, Brazil
Amparo Alonso-BetanzosUniversity of A Coruña, Spain
Katharina MorikTU Dortmund, Germany
Vítor Santos CostaUniversity of Porto, Portugal

Proceedings Chairs

João VinagreEuropean Commission (JRC), Spain
Miriam SantosUniversity of Porto, Portugal
Shazia TabassumINESC TEC, Portugal

Diversity and Inclusion Chairs

Inês SousaFraunhofer, Portugal
Zahraa AbdallahUniversity of Bristol, UK

Discovery Challenge Chairs

Carlos FerreiraPolytechnic Institute of Porto, Portugal
Peter van der PuttenLeiden University, The Netherlands
Rui CamachoUniversity of Porto, Portugal

Panel Chairs

Pedro H. AbreuUniversity of Coimbra, Portugal
Paula BritoUniversity of Porto, Portugal

Publicity Chair

Carlos FerreiraPolytechnic Institute of Porto, Portugal

Sponsorship Chairs

Mariam Berry	BNP Paribas, France
Nuno Moutinho	University of Porto, Portugal
Rui Teles	Accenture, Portugal

Social Media Chairs

Luis Roque	ZAAI.ai, Portugal
Ricardo Pereira	University of Coimbra, Portugal
Dalila Teixeira	Creative Matter, USA

Web Chair

Thiago Andrade	University of Porto, Portugal

Senior Program Committee – Research Track

Adam Jatowt	University of Innsbruck, Austria
Andrea Passerini	University of Trento, Italy
Anthony Bagnall	University of Southampton, UK
Arno Knobbe	Leiden University, Netherlands
Arno Siebes	Universiteit Utrecht, Netherlands
Arto Klami	University of Helsinki, Finland
Bernhard Pfahringer	University of Waikato, New Zealand
Bettina Berendt	TU Berlin, Germany
Celine Robardet	INSA Lyon, France
Celine Vens	KU Leuven, Belgium
Cesar Ferri	Universitat Politècnica Valencia, Spain
Charalampos Tsourakakis	Boston University, USA
Chedy Raissi	Inria, France
Chen Gong	Nanjing University of Science and Technology, China
Danai Koutra	University of Michigan, USA
Dimitrios Gunopulos	University of Athens, Greece
Donato Malerba	Università degli Studi di Bari Aldo Moro, Italy
Dragi Kocev	Jožef Stefan Institute, Slovenia
Dunja Mladenic	Jožef Stefan Institute, Slovenia
Eirini Ntoutsi	Universität der Bundeswehr München, Germany

Emmanuel Müller	TU Dortmund, Germany
Ernestina Menasalvas	Universidad Politécnica de Madrid, Spain
Esther Galbrun	University of Eastern Finland, Finland
Evaggelia Pitoura	University of Ioannina, Greece
Evangelos Papalexakis	University of California, Riverside, USA
Fabio A. Stella	University of Milano-Bicocca, Italy
Fabrizio Costa	Exeter University, UK
Fragkiskos Malliaros	CentraleSupélec, France
Georg Krempl	Utrecht University, Netherlands
Georgiana Ifrim	University College Dublin, Ireland
Gustavo Batista	University of New South Wales, Australia
Heikki Mannila	Aalto University, Finland
Hendrik Blockeel	KU Leuven, Belgium
Henrik Bostrom	KTH Royal Institute of Technology, Sweden
Henry Gouk	University of Edinburgh, UK
Ioannis Katakis	University of Nicosia, Cyprus
Jan N. Van Rijn	LIACS, Leiden University, Netherlands
Jefrey Lijffijt	Ghent University, Belgium
Jerzy Stefanowski	Poznań University of Technology, Poland
Jesse Davis	KU Leuven, Belgium
Jesse Read	Ecole Polytechnique, France
Jessica Lin	George Mason University, USA
Jesus Cerquides	IIIA-CSIC, Spain
Jilles Vreeken	CISPA Helmholtz Center for Information Security, Germany
João Gama	INESC TEC - LIAAD, Portugal
Jörg Wicker	University of Auckland, New Zealand
José Hernández-Orallo	Universitat Politècnica de Valencia, Spain
Junming Shao	University of Electronic Science and Technology of China, China
Kai Puolamaki	University of Helsinki, Finland
Manfred Jaeger	Aalborg University, Denmark
Marius Kloft	TU Kaiserslautern, Germany
Marius Lindauer	Leibniz University Hannover, Germany
Mark Last	Ben-Gurion University of the Negev, Israel
Matthias Renz	University of Kiel, Germany
Matthias Schubert	Ludwig-Maximilians-Universität München, Germany
Michele Lombardi	University of Bologna, Italy
Michèle Sebag	LISN CNRS, France
Nathalie Japkowicz	American University, USA
Paolo Frasconi	Università degli Studi di Firenze, Italy

Parisa Kordjamshidi	Michigan State University, USA
Pasquale Minervini	University of Edinburgh, UK
Pauli Miettinen	University of Eastern Finland, Finland
Pedro Larrañaga	Technical University of Madrid, Spain
Peer Kroger	Christian-Albrechts-Universität Kiel, Germany
Peter Flach	University of Bristol, UK
Ricardo B. Prudencio	Universidade Federal de Pernambuco, Brazil
Rita P. Ribeiro	University of Porto and INESC TEC, Portugal
Salvatore Ruggieri	University of Pisa, Italy
Sebastijan Dumancic	TU Delft, Netherlands
Sibylle Hess	TU Eindhoven, Netherlands
Sicco Verwer	Delft University of Technology, Netherlands
Siegfried Nijssen	Université catholique de Louvain, Belgium
Sophie Fellenz	RPTU Kaiserslautern-Landau, Germany
Stefano Ferilli	University of Bari, Italy
Stratis Ioannidis	Northeastern University, USA
Szymon Jaroszewicz	Polish Academy of Sciences, Poland
Tijl De Bie	Ghent University, Belgium
Ulf Brefeld	Leuphana University of Lüneburg, Germany
Varvara Vetrova	University of Canterbury, New Zealand
Wannes Meert	KU Leuven, Belgium
Wei Ye	Tongji University, China
Wenbin Zhang	Florida International University, USA
Willem Waegeman	Universiteit Gent, Belgium
Wouter Duivesteijn	Technische Universiteit Eindhoven, Netherlands
Xiao Luo	University of California, Los Angeles, USA
Yun Sing Koh	University of Auckland, New Zealand
Zied Bouraoui	CRIL CNRS and Université d'Artois, France

Senior Program Committee – Applied Data Science Track

Albrecht Zimmermann	Université de Caen Normandie, France
Andreas Hotho	University of Würzburg, Germany
Anirban Dasgupta	IIT Gandhinagar, India
Anna Monreale	University of Pisa, Italy
Annalisa Appice	University of Bari Aldo Moro, Italy
Bruno Cremilleux	Université de Caen Normandie, France
Carlotta Domeniconi	George Mason University, USA
Dejing Dou	BCG, USA
Fabio Pinelli	IMT Lucca, Italy
Fuzhen Zhuang	Beihang University, China

Gabor Melli	PredictionWorks, USA
Giuseppe Manco	ICAR-CNR, Italy
Glenn Fung	Independent Researcher, USA
Grzegorz Nalepa	Jagiellonian University, Poland
Hui Xiong	Hong Kong University of Science and Technology (Guangzhou), China
Inês Dutra	University of Porto, Portugal
Ioanna Miliou	Stockholm University, Sweden
Ira Assent	Aarhus University, Denmark
Jiayu Zhou	Michigan State University, USA
Jiliang Tang	Michigan State University, USA
Jingrui He	University of Illinois at Urbana-Champaign, USA
João Gama	INESC TEC - LIAAD, Portugal
Jose A. Gamez	Universidad de Castilla-La Mancha, Spain
Ke Liang	National University of Defense Technology, China
Kurt Driessens	Maastricht University, Netherlands
Lars Kotthoff	University of Wyoming, USA
Liang Sun	Alibaba Group, China
Martin Atzmueller	Osnabrück University and DFKI, Germany
Michael R. Berthold	KNIME, Germany
Michelangelo Ceci	University of Bari, Italy
Min-Ling Zhang	Southeast University, China
Mykola Pechenizkiy	TU Eindhoven, Netherlands
Myra Spiliopoulou	Otto-von-Guericke-Universität Magdeburg, Germany
Niklas Lavesson	Blekinge Institute of Technology, Sweden
Nikolaj Tatti	Helsinki University, Finland
Panagiotis Papapetrou	Stockholm University, Sweden
Paolo Frasconi	Università degli Studi di Firenze, Italy
Paulo Cortez	University of Minho, Portugal
Peggy Cellier	INSA Rennes, IRISA, France
Rayid Ghani	Carnegie Mellon University, USA
Sahar Asadi	King (Microsoft), UK
Sandeep Tata	Google, USA
Sepideh Pashami	Halmstad University, Sweden
Slawomir Nowaczyk	Halmstad University, Sweden
Sriparna Saha	IIT Patna, India
Thomas Liebig	TU Dortmund, Germany
Thomas Seidl	LMU Munich, Germany
Tom Diethe	AstraZeneca, UK
Tony Lindgren	Stockholm University, Sweden

Vincent S. Tseng — National Yang Ming Chiao Tung University, Taiwan
Vítor Santos Costa — Universidade do Porto, Portugal
Xingquan Zhu — Florida Atlantic University, USA
Yi Chang — Jilin University, China
Yinglong Xia — Meta, USA
Yongxin Tong — Beihang University, China
Yun Sing Koh — University of Auckland, New Zealand
Zhaochun Ren — Shandong University, China
Zheng Wang — Alibaba DAMO Academy, China
Zhiwei (Tony) Qin — Lyft, USA

Program Committee – Research Track

Christoph Bergmeir — Monash University, Australia
A. K. M. Mahbubur Rahman — Independent University, Bangladesh
Abdulhakim Qahtan — Utrecht University, Netherlands
Abhishek A. — Fujitsu Research, India
Acar Tamersoy — Microsoft, USA
Ad Feelders — Universiteit Utrecht, Netherlands
Adam Goodge — I2R, A*STAR, Singapore
Adele Jia — China Agricultural University, China
Adem Kikaj — KU Leuven, Belgium
Aditya Mohan — Leibniz Universität Hannover, Germany
Ajay A. Mahimkar — AT&T, USA
Akka Zemmari — Université de Bordeaux, France
Akshay Sethi — MasterCard, USA
Alborz Geramifard — Meta, USA
Alessandro Antonucci — IDSIA, Switzerland
Alessandro Melchiorre — Johannes Kepler University Linz, Austria
Alexander Dockhorn — Leibniz University Hannover, Germany
Alexander Schiendorfer — Technische Hochschule Ingolstadt, Germany
Alexander Schulz — CITEC, Bielefeld University, Germany
Alexandre Termier — Université de Rennes 1, France
Alexandre Verine — Ecole Normale Supérieure - PSL, France
Alexandru C. Mara — Ghent University, Belgium
Ali Ayadi — University of Strasbourg, France
Ali Ismail-Fawaz — IRIMAS, Université de Haute-Alsace, France
Alicja Wieczorkowska — Polish-Japanese Academy of Information Technology, Poland
Alipio M. G. Jorge — INESC TEC/University of Porto, Portugal

Alireza Gharahighehi	KU Leuven, Belgium
Alistair Shilton	Deakin University, Australia
Alneu A. Lopes	University of São Paulo, Brazil
Alper Demir	Izmir University of Economics, Turkey
Alvaro Figueira	CRACS and Universidade do Porto, Portugal
Amal Saadallah	TU Dortmund, Germany
Aman Chadha	Stanford University and Amazon, USA
Amer Krivosija	TU Dortmund, Germany
Amir H. Payberah	KTH Royal Institute of Technology, Sweden
Ammar Shaker	NEC Laboratories Europe, Europe
Ana Rita Nogueira	INESC TEC, Portugal
Anand Paul	Louisiana State University HSC, USA
Anastasios Gounaris	Aristotle University of Thessaloniki, Greece
Andre V. Carreiro	Fraunhofer Portugal AICOS, Portugal
André C. P. L. F. de Carvalho	University of São Paulo, Brazil
Andrea Cossu	University of Pisa, Italy
Andrea Mastropietro	University of Bonn, Germany
Andrea Pugnana	University of Trento, Italy
Andrea Tagarelli	DIMES - UNICAL, Italy
Andreas Bender	LMU Munich, Germany
Andreas Nürnberger	Otto-von-Guericke-Universität Magdeburg, Germany
Andreas Schwung	Fachhochschule Südwestfalen, Germany
Andrei Paleyes	University of Cambridge, UK
Andrzej Skowron	University of Warsaw, Poland
Andy Song	RMIT University, Australia
Angelica Liguori	ICAR-CNR, Italy
Anirban Dasgupta	IIT Gandhinagar, India
Anke Meyer-Baese	Florida State University, USA
Anna Beer	University of Vienna, Austria
Anna Krause	Universität Wurzburg and Chair X Data Science, Germany
Anna Monreale	University of Pisa, Italy
Annelot W. Bosman	Universiteit Leiden, Netherlands
Antoine Caradot	Hubert Curien Laboratory, France
Antonio Bahamonde	University of Oviedo, Spain
Antonio Mastropietro	Università di Pisa, Italy
Antonio Pellicani	Università degli Studi di Bari, Aldo Moro, Italy
Antonis Matakos	Aalto University, Finland
Antti Laaksonen	University of Helsinki, Finland
Aomar Osmani	LIPN-UMR CNRS, France
Aonghus Lawlor	University College Dublin, Ireland

Aparna S. Varde	Montclair State University, USA
Apostolos N. Papadopoulos	Aristotle University of Thessaloniki, Greece
Aritra Konar	KU Leuven, Belgium
Arjun Roy	Freie Universität Berlin, Germany
Arthur Charpentier	UQAM, Canada
Arunas Lipnickas	Kaunas University of Technology, Lithuania
Atsuhiro Takasu	National Institute of Informatics, Japan
Aurora Esteban	University of Cordoba, Spain
Baosheng Zhang	Tsinghua University, China
Barbara Toniella Corradini	University of Florence and University of Siena, Italy
Bardh Prenkaj	Technical University of Munich, Germany
Barry O'Sullivan	University College Cork, Ireland
Beilun Wang	Southeast University, China
Benjamin Halstead	University of Auckland, New Zealand
Benjamin Paassen	Bielefeld University, Germany
Benjamin Quost	Université de Technologie de Compiègne, France
Benoit Frenay	University of Namur, Belgium
Bernardo Moreno Sanchez	University of Helsinki, Finland
Bernhard Pfahringer	University of Waikato, New Zealand
Bertrand Cuissart	University of Caen, France
Bin Liu	Chongqing University of Posts and Telecommunications, China
Bin Shi	Xi'an Jiaotong University, China
Bin Wu	Zhengzhou University, China
Bin Zhou	National University of Defense Technology, China
Bitao Peng	Guangdong University of Foreign Studies, China
Bo Kang	Ghent University, Belgium
Bogdan Cautis	Université Paris-Saclay, France
Bojan Evkoski	Central European University, Hungary
Boshen Shi	Institute of Computing Technology, Chinese Academy of Sciences, China
Boualem Benatallah	Dublin City University, Ireland
Brandon Gower-Winter	Utrecht University, Netherlands
Bunil K. Balabantaray	NIT Meghalaya, India
Carlos Ferreira	INESC TEC, Portugal
Carlos Monserrat-Aranda	Universitat Politècnica de Valencia, Spain
Carson K. Leung	University of Manitoba, Canada
Catarina Silva	University of Coimbra, Portugal
Cecile Capponi	Aix-Marseille University, France
Celine Rouveirol	LIPN Université de Sorbonne Paris Nord, France

Cesar H. G. Andrade	Porto University, Portugal
Chandrajit Bajaj	University of Texas, Austin, USA
Chang Rajani	University of Helsinki, Finland
Charlotte Laclau	Polytechnique Institute, Télécom Paris, France
Charlotte Pelletier	Université de Bretagne du Sud, France
Chen Wang	DATA61, CSIRO, Australia
Cheng Cheng	Carnegie Mellon University, USA
Cheng Xie	Yunnan University, China
Chenglin Wang	East China Normal University, China
Chenwang Wu	University of Science and Technology of China, China
Chiara Pugliese	IIT Institute of National Research Council, Italy
Chien-Liang Liu	National Chiao Tung University, Taiwan
Chihiro Maru	Chuo University, Japan
Chongsheng Zhang	Henan University, China
Christian Beecks	FernUniversität in Hagen, Germany
Christian M. M. Frey	University of Technology Nuremberg, Germany
Christian Hakert	TU Dortmund, Germany
Christine Largeron	LabHC Lyon University, France
Christophe Rigotti	INSA Lyon, France
Christophe Rodrigues	DVRC Pôle universitaire Léonard de Vinci, France
Christos Anagnostopoulos	University of Glasgow, UK
Christos Diou Harokopio	University of Athens, Greece
Chuan Qin	Chinese Academy of Sciences, China
Chunchun Chen	Tongji University, China
Chunyao Song	Nankai University, China
Claire Nedellec	INRAE, MaIAGE, France
Claudio Borile	CENTAI Institute, Italy
Claudio Gallicchio	University of Pisa, Italy
Claudius Zelenka	Kiel University, Germany
Colin Bellinger	NRC and Dalhousie University, Canada
Collin Leiber	Aalto University, Finland
Cong Qi	New Jersey Institute of Technology, USA
Congfeng Cao	University of Amsterdam, Netherlands
Corrado Loglisci	Università degli Studi di Bari, Aldo Moro, Italy
Cuicui Luo	University of Chinese Academy of Sciences, China
Cuneyt G. Akcora	University of Central Florida, USA
Cynthia C. S. Liem	Delft University of Technology, Netherlands
Dalius Matuzevicius	Vilnius Gediminas Technical University, Lithuania

Dan Li	Sun Yat-sen University, China
Danai Koutra	University of Michigan, USA
Dang Nguyen	Deakin University, Australia
Daniel Neider	TU Dortmund, Germany
Daniel Schlor	Universität Würzburg, Germany
Danil Provodin	TU Eindhoven, Netherlands
Danyang Xiao	Sun Yat-sen University, China
Dario Garcia-Gasulla	Barcelona Supercomputing Center (BSC), Spain
Dario Garigliotti	University of Bergen, Norway
Darius Plonis	Vilnius Gediminas Technical University, Lithuania
Dariusz Brzezinski	Poznań University of Technology, Poland
David Gomez	Universidad Politecnica de Madrid, Spain
David Holzmüller	University of Stuttgart, Germany
David Q. Sun	Apple, USA
Davide Evangelista	University of Bologna, Italy
Debo Cheng	University of South Australia, Australia
Deepayan Chakrabarti	University of Texas at Austin, USA
Deng-Bao Wang	Southeast University, China
Denilson Barbosa	University of Alberta, Canada
Denis Huseljic	University of Kassel, Germany
Denis Lukovnikov	Ruhr-Universität Bochum, Germany
Destercke Sebastien	UTC, France
Di Jin	TikTok, USA
Di Wu	Chongqing Institute of Green and Intelligent Technology, Chinese Academy of Sciences, China
Diana Benavides Prado	University of Auckland, New Zealand
Dianhui Wang	Independent Researcher, Australia
Diego Carrera	STMicroelectronics, Switzerland
Diletta Chiaro	Università degli Studi di Napoli Federico II, Italy
Dimitri Staufer	TU Berlin, Germany
Dimitrios Katsaros	University of Thessaly, Greece
Dimitrios Rafailidis	University of Thessaly, France
Dino Ienco	INRAE, France
Dmitry Kobak	University of Tübingen, Germany
Domenico Redavid	University of Bari, Italy
Dominik M. Endres	Philipps-Universität Marburg, Germany
Dominique Gay	Université de La Réunion, France
Dong Li	Baylor University, USA
Duarte Folgado	Fraunhofer Portugal AICOS, Portugal
Duo Xu	Georgia Institute of Technology, USA

Edoardo Serra	Boise State University, USA
Edouard Fouche	Karlsruhe Institute of Technology (KIT), Germany
Eduardo F. Montesuma	Université Paris-Saclay, France
Edward Apeh	Bournemouth University, UK
Edwin Simpson	University of Bristol, UK
Ehsan Aminian	INESC TEC, Portugal
Ekaterina Antonenko	Mines Paris - PSL, France
Eliana Pastor	Politecnico di Torino, Italy
Emanuela Marasco	George Mason University, USA
Emilio Dorigatti	LMU Munich, Germany
Emilio Parrado-Hernandez	Universidad Carlos III de Madrid, Spain
Emmanouil Krasanakis	CERTH, Greece
Emmanouil Panagiotou	Freie Universität Berlin, Germany
Emre Gursoy	Koc University, Turkey
Engelbert Mephu Nguifo	Université Clermont Auvergne, CNRS, LIMOS, France
Eran Treister	Ben-Gurion University of the Negev, Israel
Erasmo Purificato	Otto-von-Guericke Universität Magdeburg, Germany
Erik Novak	Jožef Stefan Institute, Slovenia
Erwan Le Merrer	Inria, France
Esra Akbas	Georgia State University, USA
Esther-Lydia Silva-Ramirez	Universidad de Cadiz, Spain
Evaldas Vaičiukynas	Kaunas University of Technology, Lithuania
Evangelos Kanoulas	University of Amsterdam, Netherlands
Evelin Amorim	INESC TEC, Portugal
Fabian C. Spaeh	Boston University, USA
Fabio Fassetti	Università della Calabria, Italy
Fabio Fumarola	Prometeia, Italy
Fabio Mercorio	University of Milan-Bicocca, Italy
Fabio Vandin	University of Padova, Italy
Fandel Lin	University of Southern California, USA
Federica Granese	Inria, Université Côte d'Azur, France
Federico Baldo	University of Bologna, Italy
Federico Sabbatini	National Institute for Nuclear Physics (INFN), Italy
Feifan Zhang	China Agricultural University, China
Felipe Kenji Nakano	KU Leuven, Belgium
Fernando Martinez-Plumed	Universitat Politècnica de Valencia, Spain
Filipe Rodrigues	Technical University of Denmark (DTU), Denmark

Flavio Giobergia	Politecnico di Torino, Italy
Florent Masseglia	Inria, France
Florian Beck	JKU Linz, Austria
Florian Lemmerich	University of Passau, Germany
Francesca Naretto	University of Pisa, Italy
Francesco Piccialli	University of Naples Federico II, Italy
Francesco Renna	Universidade do Porto, Portugal
Francisco Pereira	DTU, Denmark
Franco Raimondi	Gran Sasso Science Institute, Italy
Frederic Koriche	Université d'Artois, CRIL CNRS, France
Frederic Pennerath	CentraleSupélec - LORIA, France
Furong Peng	Shanxi University, China
Gabriel Marques Tavares	LMU Munich, Germany
Gabriele Sartor	University of Turin, Italy
Gabriele Venturato	KU Leuven, Belgium
Gaetan De Waele	Ghent University, Belgium
Gaia Saveri	University of Trieste, Italy
Gang Li	Deakin University, Australia
Gaoyuan Du	Amazon, USA
Gavin Smith	University of Nottingham, UK
Geming Xia	National University of Defense Technology, China
Geng Zhao	Heidelberg University, Germany
Gennaro Vessio	University of Bari Aldo Moro, Italy
Geoffrey I. Webb	Monash, Australia
Georgia Baltsou	Centre for Research & Technology, Greece
Geraldin Nanfack	Concordia University, Canada
Germain Forestier	University of Haute Alsace, France
Gerrit Grossmann	DFKI, Germany
Gerrit J. J. van den Burg	Alan Turing Institute, UK
Gherardo Varando	Universitat de Valencia, Spain
Giacomo Medda	University of Cagliari, Italy
Gilberto Bernardes	INESC TEC and University of Porto, Portugal
Giorgio Venturin	University of Padova, Italy
Giovanna Castellano	University of Bari Aldo Moro, Italy
Giovanni Ponti	ENEA, Italy
Giovanni Stilo	Università degli Studi dell'Aquila, Italy
Gisele Pappa	UFMG, Brazil
Giuseppe Manco	ICAR-CNR, IT, Italy
Gizem Gezici	Scuola Normale Superiore, Italy
Gjergji Kasneci	TU Munich, Germany
Goreti Marreiros	ISEP/GECAD, Portugal

Graziella De Martino	University of Bari, Aldo Moro, Italy
Grazina Korvel	Vilnius University, Lithuania
Grigorios Tsoumakas	Aristotle University of Thessaloniki, Greece
Guangyin Jin	National University of Defense Technology, China
Guangzhong Sun	University of Science and Technology of China, China
Guanjin Wang	Murdoch University, Australia
Guilherme Weigert	Cassales University of Waikato, New Zealand
Guillaume Derval	UC Louvain - ICTEAM, Belgium
Guorui Quan	University of Manchester, UK
Guoxi Zhang	Beijing Institute of General Artificial Intelligence, China
Gustau Camps-Valls	Universitat de Valencia, Spain
Gustav Sir	Czech Technical University, Czech Republic
Gustavo Batista	University of New South Wales, Australia
Hachem Kadri	Aix-Marseille University, France
Hadi Asghari	Humboldt Institute for Internet and Society, Germany
Haifeng Sun	University of Science and Technology of China, China
Haihui Fan	Institute of Information Engineering, Chinese Academy of Sciences, China
Haizhou Du	Shanghai University of Electric Power, China
Hajer Salem	AUDENSIEL, France
Hakim Hacid	TII, United Arab Emirates
Hamid Bouchachia	Bournemouth University, UK
Han Wang	Xidian University, China
Hang Yu	Shanghai University, China
Hanna Sumita	Institute of Science Tokyo, Japan
Hao Niu	KDDI Research, Japan
Hao Xue	University of New South Wales, Australia
Hao Yan	Carleton University, Canada
Haowen Zhang	Zhejiang Sci-Tech University, China
Harsh Borse	IIT Kharagpur, India
Heitor M. Gomes	Victoria University of Wellington, New Zealand
Helder Oliveira	FCUP and INESC TEC, Portugal
Helge Langseth	Norwegian University of Science and Technology, Norway
Hendrik Blockeel	KU Leuven, Belgium
Henrique O. Marques	University of Southern Denmark, Denmark
Henryk Maciejewski	Wroclaw University of Science and Technology, Poland

Hideaki Ishibashi	Kyushu Institute of Technology, Japan
Hilde J. P. Weerts	Eindhoven University of Technology, Netherlands
Holger Froening	University of Heidelberg, Germany
Holger Karl	HPI, Germany
Hongbo Bo	University of Bristol, UK
Hongyang Chen	Zhejiang Lab, China
Hua Chu	Xidian University, China
Huaiyu Wan	Beijing Jiaotong University, China
Huaming Chen	University of Sydney, Australia
Huandong Wang	Tsinghua University, China
Huanlai Xing	Southwest Jiaotong University, China
Hui Ji	University of Pittsburgh, USA
Hui (Wendy) Wang	Stevens Institute of Technology, USA
Huiping Chen	University of Birmingham, UK
Humberto Bustince	Universidad Publica de Navarra, Spain
Huong Ha	RMIT University, Australia
Idir Benouaret	Epita Research Laboratory, France
Ines Sousa	Fraunhofer AICOS, Portugal
Ingo Thon	Siemens AG, Germany
Inigo Jauregi Unanue	University of Technology Sydney, Australia
Ioannis Sarridis	Centre for Research & Technology, Greece
Issam Falih	Université Clermont Auvergne, CNRS, LIMOS, France
Ivan Vankov	iris.ai, Norway
Ivor Cribben	University of Alberta, Canada
Jaemin Yoo	KAIST, South Korea
Jakir Hossain	University at Buffalo, USA
Jakub Klikowski	Wroclaw University of Science and Technology, Poland
Jalaj Bhandari	Columbia University, USA
Jaleed Khan	University of Oxford, UK
James Goulding	University of Nottingham, UK
Jan Kalina	Czech Academy of Sciences, Czech Republic
Jan P. Mielniczuk	Polish Academy of Sciences, Poland
Jan Ramon	Inria, France
Jan Verwaeren	Ghent University, Belgium
Jannis Brugger	TU Darmstadt, Germany
Jean-Marc Andreoli	Naverlabs Europe, Netherlands
Jedrzej Potoniec	Poznań University of Technology, Poland
Jeronimo Arenas-Garcia	Universidad Carlos III de Madrid, Spain
Jhony H. Giraldo	Télécom Paris, Institut Polytechnique de Paris, France

Jia Cai	Guangdong University of Finance and Economics, China
Jiahui Jin	Southeast University, China
Jiang Zhong	Independent Researcher, China
Jianwu Wang	University of Maryland, Baltimore County, USA
Jiawei Chen	Tianjin University, China
Jiaxin Ding	Shanghai Jiao Tong University, China
Jidong Yuan	Beijing Jiaotong University, China
Jie Song	Zhejiang University, China
Jie Wu	Fudan University, China
Jie Yang	University of Wollongong, China
Jimeng Shi	Florida International University, USA
Jin Chen	Hong Kong University of Science and Technology, China
Jin Liang	South China Normal University, China
Jing Ren	NUDT, China
Jing Wang	Amazon, USA
Jinghui Zhong	South China University of Technology, China
Jingtao Ding	Tsinghua University, China
Jinli Zhang	Beijing University of Technology, China
Jiri Sima	Czech Academy of Sciences, Czech Republic
João Gama	University of Porto, Portugal
Joao Mendes-Moreira	University of Porto, Portugal
Joao Vinagre	European Commission (JRC), Spain
Joaquim Silva	NOVA LINCS, Universidade Nova de Lisboa, Portugal
Jochen De Weerdt	KU Leuven, Belgium
Joe Mellor	University of Edinburgh, UK
Johanne Cohen	LISN-CNRS, France
Johannes Jakubik	IBM Research, USA
John W. Sheppard	Montana State University, USA
Jonata Tyska Carvalho	Federal University of Santa Catarina, Brazil
Jordi Guitart	Barcelona Supercomputing Center (BSC), Spain
Joris Mattheijssens	Ghent University, Belgium
Jose M. Costa Pereira	University of Porto, Portugal
Jose Oramas	University of Antwerp, sqIRL/IDLab, imec, Belgium
Jose Tomas Palma	University of Murcia, Spain
Joydeep Chandra	Indian Institute of Technology, Patna, India
Juan A. Botia	University of Murcia, Spain
Juan Rodriguez	Universidad de Burgos, Spain
Jukka Heikkonen	University of Turku, Finland

Julien Delaunay	Inria, France
Julien Ferry	Polytechnique Montreal, Canada
Julien Perez	EPITA, France
Jun Zhuang	Boise State University, USA
Jun Yu Hou	Nanjing University, China
Junbo Zhang	JD Intelligent Cities Research, USA
Junze Liu	University of California, Irvine, USA
Jurgita Kapočiūtė-Dzikienė	Tilde SIA, University of Latvia and Tilde IT, Vytautas Magnus University, Lithuania
Justina Mandravickaitė	Vytautas Magnus University, Lithuania
Kamil Adamczewski	Max Planck Institute for Intelligent Systems, Germany
Kamil Michal Ksiazek	Jagiellonian University, Poland
Karim Radouane	Université Sorbonne Paris Nord, France
Kary Framing	Umeå University, Sweden
Katerina Taskova	University of Auckland, New Zealand
Katharina Dost	Jožef Stefan Institute, Slovenia
Kaushik Roy	University of South Carolina, USA
Kejia Chen	Nanjing University of Posts and Telecommunications, China
Ken Kobayashi	Tokyo Institute of Technology, Japan
Khaled Mohammed Saifuddin	Northeastern University, USA
Khalid Benabdeslem	Université de Lyon 1, France
Kim Thang Nguyen	LIG, University Grenoble-Alpes, France
Kira Maag	Heinrich-Heine-Universität Düsseldorf, Germany
Koji Maruhashi	Fujitsu Research, Japan
Koyel Mukherjee	Adobe Research, USA
Kristen M. Scott	KU Leuven, Belgium
Krzysztof Ruda	Polish Academy of Sciences, Poland
Krzysztof Slot	Lodz University of Technology, Poland
Kuldeep Singh	Cerence, Germany
Kushankur Ghosh	University of Alberta, Canada
Lamine Diop	EPITA, France
Latifa Oukhellou	IFSTTAR, France
Laurence Park	Western Sydney University, Australia
Laurens Devos	KU Leuven, Belgium
Len Feremans	Universiteit Antwerpen, Belgium
Lena Wiese	Goethe University Frankfurt, Germany
Lenaig Cornanguer	CISPA Helmholtz Center for Information Security, Germany
Lennert De Smet	KU Leuven, Belgium
Lev Reyzin	University of Illinois at Chicago, USA

Li Wang	National University of Defense Technology, China
Liang Du	Shanxi University, China
Lianyong Qi	China University of Petroleum (East China), China
Lijie Hu	King Abdullah University of Science and Technology, Saudi Arabia
Lijing Zhu	Bowling Green State University, USA
Lingling Zhang	Capital Normal University, China
Lingyue Fu	Shanghai Jiao Tong University, China
Linh Le Pham Van	Deakin University, Australia
Livio Bioglio	University of Turin, Italy
Lixing Yu	Yunnan University, China
Liyan Song	Harbin Institute of Technology, China
Longlong Sun	Chang'an University, China
Luca Corbucci	University of Pisa, Italy
Luca Ferragina	University of Calabria, Italy
Luca Romeo	University of Macerata, Italy
Lucas Pereira	LARSyS, Tecnico Lisboa, Portugal
Luciano Caroprese	ICAR-CNR, Italy
Ludovico Boratto	University of Cagliari, Italy
Luis Rei	Jožef Stefan Institute, Slovenia
Mahardhika Pratama	University of South Australia, Australia
Maiju Karjalainen	University of Eastern Finland, Finland
Makoto Onizuka	Osaka University, Japan
Manali Sharma	Samsung, South Korea
Maneet Singh	MasterCard, India
Manuel M. Garcia-Piqueras	Universidad de Castilla La Mancha, Spain
Manuele Bicego	University of Verona, Italy
Mao A. Cheng	University of California, Berkeley, USA
Marc Plantevit	EPITA, France
Marc Tommasi	Lille University, France
Marcel Wever	Leibniz University Hannover, Germany
Marcilio de Souto	LIFO/Université d'Orleans, France
Marco Lippi	University of Florence, Italy
Marco Loog	Radboud University, Netherlands
Marco Mellia	Politecnico di Torino, Italy
Marco Podda	University of Pisa, Italy
Marco Polignano	Università di Bari, Italy
Marco Viviani	Università degli Studi di Milano Bicocca, Italy
Maria Vasconcelos	Fraunhofer Portugal AICOS, Portugal
Maria Sofia Bucarelli	Sapienza University of Rome, Italy

Mariana Oliveira	Universidade do Porto, Portugal
Mariana Vargas Vieyra	MostlyAI, Austria
Marielle Malfante	CEA, France
Marina Litvak	Shamoon College of Engineering, Israel
Mario Antunes	Universidade de Aveiro, Portugal
Mario Andres Munoz	University of Melbourne, Australia
Marius Koppel	Johannes Gutenberg University Mainz, Germany
Mark Junjie Li	Shenzhen University, China
Marko Robnik-Sikonja	University of Ljubljana, Slovenia
Marta Soare	Université d'Orleans, France
Martin Holena	Czech Academy of Sciences, Czech Republic
Martin Pilat	Charles University, Czech Republic
Martino Ciaperoni	Aalto University, Finland
Marwan Hassani	TU Eindhoven, Netherlands
Masahiro Suzuki	University of Tokyo, Japan
Massimo Guarascio	ICAR-CNR, Italy
Matej Mihelcic	University of Zagreb, Croatia
Mathias Verbeke	KU Leuven, Belgium
Mathieu Lefort	Université de Lyon, France
Matteo Francobaldi	University of Bologna, Italy
Matteo Riondato	Amherst College, USA
Matteo Salis	University of Turin, Italy
Matthew B. Middlehurst	University of Southampton, UK
Matthia Sabatelli	University of Groningen, Netherlands
Mattia Cerrato	JGU Mainz, Germany
Mattia Setzu	University of Pisa, Italy
Mattis Hartwig	German Research Center for Artificial Intelligence, Germany
Matyas Bohacek	Stanford University, USA
Maximilian T. Fischer	University of Konstanz, Germany
Maximilian Münch	University of Applied Sciences, Würzburg-Schweinfurt, Germany
Maximilian Stubbemann	University of Hildesheim, Germany
Maximilian Thiessen	TU Wien, Austria
Maximilian von Zastrow	Southern Denmark University, Denmark
Megha Khosla	TU Delft, Netherlands
Meiyun Zuo	Renmin University of China, China
Meng Liu	National University of Defense Technology, China
Mengying Zhu	Zhejiang University, China
Michael Granitzer	University of Passau, Germany
Michael B. Ito	University of Michigan, USA

Michael G. Madden	National University of Ireland, Galway, Ireland
Michal Wozniak	Wroclaw University of Science and Technology, Poland
Michele Fontana	Università di Pisa, Italy
Michiel Stock	Ghent University, Belgium
Miguel Rocha	University of Minho, Portugal
Miguel Silva	INESC TEC, Portugal
Mike Holenderski	Eindhoven University of Technology, Netherlands
Milos Savic	University of Novi Sad, Serbia
Mina Rezaei	LMU Munich, Germany
Minh P. Nguyen	University of Texas, Austin, USA
Minyoung Choe	Korea Advanced Institute of Science and Technology, South Korea
Minyu Chen	Shanghai Jiaotong University, China
Miquel Perello-Nieto	University of Bristol, UK
Mira Kristin Jurgens	Ghent University, Belgium
Miriam Santos	University of Porto, Portugal
Mirko Bunse	TU Dortmund, Germany
Mirko Polato	University of Turin, Italy
Mitra Baratchi	LIACS, University of Leiden, Netherlands
Mohammed Elbamby	Telefonica Scientific Research, Spain
Moises Rocha dos Santos	University of Porto, Portugal
Monowar Bhuyan	Umeå University, Sweden
Morteza Rakhshaninejad	Ghent University, Belgium
Mounim A. El Yacoubi	Télécom SudParis, France
Muhammad Rajabinasab	University of Southern Denmark, Denmark
Muhao Guo	Arizona State University, USA
Mustapha Lebbah	Paris Saclay University-Versailles, France
Nabeel Hussain Syed	Rheinland-Pfälzische Technische Universität, Kaiserslautern-Landau, Germany
Nandyala Hemachandra	Indian Institute of Technology Bombay, India
Nannan Wu	Tianjin University, China
Nanqing Dong	Shanghai Artificial Intelligence Laboratory, China
Naresh Manwani	International Institute of Information Technology, Hyderabad, India
Natan Tourne	Ghent University, Belgium
Nate Veldt	Texas A&M, USA
Nathalie Japkowicz	American University, USA
Natthawut Kertkeidkachorn	Japan Advanced Institute of Science and Technology (JAIST), Japan
Ngoc-Son Vu	ENSEA, France
Nhat-Tan Bui	University of Arkansas, USA

Nian Li	Tsinghua University, China
Nick Lim	University of Waikato, New Zealand
Nico Piatkowski	Fraunhofer IAIS, Germany
Nicolas Roque dos Santos	University of São Paulo, Brazil
Niklas A. Strauss	LMU Munich, Germany
Nikolaj Tatti	Helsinki University, Finland
Nikolaos Nikolaou	University College London, UK
Nikolaos Stylianou	Information Technologies Institute, Greece
Nikos Kanakaris	University of Southern California, USA
Ning Xu	Southeast University, China
Nripsuta Saxena	University of Southern California, USA
Nuwan Gunasekara	Halmstad University, Sweden
Olga Kurasova	Vilnius University, Lithuania
Olga Slizovskaia	AstraZeneca, UK
Olivier Teste	IRIT, University of Toulouse, France
Oswald C	NIT Trichy, India
Oswaldo Solarte-Pabon	Universidad del Valle, Colombia
Ozge Alacam	University of Bielefeld, Germany
P. S. Sastry	Indian Institute of Science, India
Pablo Olmos	Universidad Carlos III de Madrid, Spain
Panagiotis Karras	University of Copenhagen, Denmark
Panagiotis Symeonidis	University of the Aegean, Greece
Pance Panov	Jožef Stefan Institute, Slovenia
Paolo Bonetti	Politecnico di Milano, Italy
Paolo Merialdo	Università degli Studi Roma Tre, Italy
Paolo Mignone	University of Bari Aldo Moro, Italy
Pascal Welke	TU Wien, Austria
Patrick Y. Wu	American University, USA
Paul Caillon	LAMSADE Université Paris Dauphine - PSL, France
Paul Davidsson	Malmo University, Sweden
Paul Prasse	University of Potsdam, Germany
Paulo J. Azevedo	Universidade do Minho, Portugal
Pawel Teisseyre	Warsaw University of Technology, Poland
Pawel Zyblewski	Wroclaw University of Science and Technology, Poland
Pedro G. Ferreira	University of Porto, Portugal
Pedro Larrañaga	Technical University of Madrid, Spain
Pedro Ribeiro	University of Porto, Portugal
Pedro H. Abreu	CISUC, Portugal
Peijie Sun	Tsinghua University, China
Peng Wu	Shanghai Jiao Tong University, China

Pengpeng Qiao	Institute of Science Tokyo, Japan
Peter Karsmakers	KU Leuven, Belgium
Peter Schneider-Kamp	SDU, Denmark
Peter van der Putten	Leiden University, Netherlands
Petia Georgieva	University of Aveiro, Portugal
Philipp Vaeth	Technical University of Applied Sciences Würzburg-Schweinfurt and Universität Bielefeld, Germany
Philippe Preux	Inria, France
Phung Lai	SUNY-Albany, USA
Pierre Geurts	Montefiore Institute, University of Liège, Belgium
Pierre Monnin	Université Côte d'Azur, Inria, CNRS, I3S, France
Pierre Schaus	UC Louvain, Belgium
Pierre Wolinski	Paris Dauphine University - PSL, France
Pieter Robberechts	KU Leuven, Belgium
Pietro Sabatino	ICAR-CNR, Italy
Pingchuan Ma	HKUST, China
Piotr Habas	Amazon, USA
Piotr Lipinski	University of Wroclaw, Poland
Piotr Porwik	University of Silesia, Katowice, Poland
Prithwish Chakraborty	IBM Corporation, USA
Lucie Flek	Marburg University, Germany
Przemyslaw Biecek	Warsaw University of Technology, Poland
Qiang Sheng	Institute of Computing Technology, Chinese Academy of Sciences, China
Qiang Zhou	Nanjing University of Aeronautics and Astronautics, China
Rafet Sifa	Fraunhofer IAIS, Germany
Raha Moraffah	Arizona State University, USA
Raivydas Simanas	Vilnius University, Lithuania
Rajeev Rastogi	Amazon, USA
Ranya Almohsen	Baylor College of Medicine, USA
Raphael Romero	Ghent University, Belgium
Raquel Sebastiao	ESTGV-IPV & IEETA-UA, Portugal
Ravi Kolla	Sony Research India, India
Raza Ul Mustafa	Loyola University, USA
Remy Cazabet	Université de Lyon 1, France
Renhe Jiang	University of Tokyo, Japan
Reza Akbarinia	Inria, France
Ricardo P. M. Cruz	University of Porto (FEUP), Portugal
Ricardo B. Prudencio	Universidade Federal de Pernambuco, Brazil
Ricardo Rios	Federal University of Bahia, Brazil

Ricardo Santos	Fraunhofer Portugal AICOS, Portugal
Riccardo Guidotti	University of Pisa, Italy
Robertas Damasevicius	Vytautas Magnus University, Lithuania
Roberto Corizzo	American University, USA
Roberto Interdonato	CIRAD, France
Rocio Chongtay	University of Southern Denmark, Denmark
Rohit Babbar	University of Bath, UK and Aalto University, Finland
Romain Tavenard	Université de Rennes, LETG/IRISA, France
Rosana Veroneze	LBiC, Italy
Ruggero G. Pensa	University of Turin, Italy
Rui Meng	BNU-HKBU United International College, USA
Rui Yu	University of Louisville, USA
Ruixuan Liu	Emory University, USA
Runqun Xiong	Southeast University, China
Runxue Bao	University of Pittsburgh, USA
Ruochun Jin	National University of Defense Technology, China
Ruta Juozaitiene	Vytautas Magnus University, Lithuania
Rytis Maskeliunas	Polsl, Poland
Salvatore Ruggieri	University of Pisa, Italy
Sam Verboven	Vrije Universiteit Brussel, Belgium
Sangkyun Lee	Korea University, South Korea
Sara Abdali	University of California, Riverside, USA
Sarah Masud	LCS2, IIIT-D, India
Sarwan Ali	Georgia State University, USA
Satoru Koda	Fujitsu Limited, Japan
Sebastian Buschjager	Lamarr Institute for ML and AI, Germany
Sebastian Jimenez	Ghent University, Belgium
Sebastian Meznar	Jožef Stefan Institute, Ljubljana, Slovenia
Sebastian Ventura Soto	University of Cordoba, Spain
Sebastien Razakarivony	Safran, France
Selpi Selpi	Chalmers University of Technology, Sweden
Sergio Greco	University of Calabria, Italy
Sergio Jesus	Feedzai, Portugal
Sha Lu	University of South Australia, Australia
Shalini Priya	Indian Institute of Technology Patna, India
Shanqing Guo	Shandong University, China
Shaofu Yang	Southeast University, China
Shazia Tabassum	INESCTEC, Portugal
Shengxiang Gao	Kunming University of Science and Technology, China

Shichao Pei	University of Massachusetts, Boston, USA
Shin Matsushima	University of Tokyo, Japan
Shin-ichi Maeda	Preferred Networks, Japan
Shiwen Ni	Chinese Academy of Sciences, China
Shiyou Qian	Shanghai Jiao Tong University, China
Shu Zhao	Anhui University, China
Shuai Li	University of Cambridge, UK and University of Tokyo, Japan, Tsinghua University, China
Shuang Cheng	Institute of Computing Technology, Chinese Academy of Sciences, China
Shubhranshu Shekhar	Brandeis University, USA
Shurui Cao	Carnegie Mellon University, USA
Shuteng Niu	Mayo Clinic, USA
Siamak Ghodsi	Leibniz University of Hannover, Germany
Sihai Zhang	University of Science and Technology of China, China
Silvia Chiusano	Politecnico di Torino, Italy
Silviu Maniu	Université de Grenoble Alpes, France
Simon Gottschalk	L3S Research Center, Leibniz Universität Hannover, Germany
Simona Nistico	University of Calabria, Italy
Simone Angarano	Politecnico di Torino, Italy
Sinong Zhao	Nankai University, China
Siwei Wang	Intelligent Game and Decision Lab, China
Sofoklis Kitharidis	LIACS, Netherlands
Songlin Du	University of Melbourne, Australia
Songlin Du	Southeast University, China
Soumyajit Chatterjee	Nokia Bell Labs, USA
Sourav Dutta	Huawei Research Centre, China
Stefan Duffner	University of Lyon, France
Stefan Heindorf	Paderborn University, Germany
Stefan Kesselheim	Forschungszentrum Jülich, Germany
Stefano Bortoli	Huawei Research Center, China
Stefanos Vrochidis	Information Technologies Institute, CERTH, Greece
Steffen Thoma	FZI Research Center for Information Technology, Germany
Stephan Doerfel	Kiel University of Applied Sciences, Germany
Steven D. Prestwich	University College Cork, Ireland
Suman Banerjee	IIT Jammu, India
Sunil Aryal	Deakin University, Australia
Surabhi Adhikari	Columbia University, USA

Susan McKeever	TU Dublin, Ireland
Swati Swati	Universität der Bundeswehr München, Germany
Szymon Wojciechowski	Wroclaw University of Science and Technology, Poland
Talip Ucar	AstraZeneca, UK
Taro Tezuka	University of Tsukuba, Japan
Tatiana Passali	Aristotle University of Thessaloniki, Greece
Tatiane Nogueira Rios	UFBA, Brazil
Telmo M. Silva Filho	University of Bristol, UK
Teng Lin	Hong Kong University of Technology (Guangzhou), China
Teng Zhang	Huazhong University of Science and Technology, China
Thach Le Nguyen	Insight Centre, Ireland
Thang Duy Dang	Fujitsu Limited, Japan
Thanh-Son Nguyen	A*STAR, Singapore
Theresa Eimer	Leibniz University Hannover, Germany
Thiago Andrade	INESC TEC & University of Porto, Portugal
Thomas Bonald	Telecom Paris, France
Thomas Guyet	Inria, Centre de Lyon, France
Thomas Lampert	University of Strasbourg, France
Thomas L. Lee	University of Edinburgh, UK
Thomas Mortier	Ghent University, Belgium
Tianyi Chen	Boston University, USA
Tie Luo	University of Kentucky, USA
Tiehang Duan	Mayo Clinic, USA
Tijl De Bie	Ghent University, Belgium
Timilehin B. Aderinola	University College Dublin, Ireland
Timo Bertram	Johannes-Kepler Universität, Germany
Timo Ropinski	Ulm University, Germany
Tobias A. Hille	University of Kassel, Germany
Tom Hanika	University of Hildesheim, Germany
Tomas Kliegr	University of Economics, Prague, Czech Republic
Tomasz Michalak	University of Warsaw and Ideas NCBiR, Poland
Tomasz Walkowiak	Wroclaw University of Science and Technology, Poland
Tommaso Zoppi	University of Florence, Italy
Tong Li	Hong Kong University of Technology, China
Tong Mo	Peking University, China
Tongya Zheng	Hangzhou City University, China
Tonio Weidler	Maastricht University, Netherlands
Tony Lindgren	Stockholm University, Sweden

Tsunenori Mine	Kyushu University, Japan
Tuan Le	New Mexico State University, USA
Tuwe Lofstrom	Jönköping University, Sweden
Ulf Johansson	Jönköping University, Sweden
Vadim Ermolayev	Ukrainian Catholic University, Ukraine
Vahan Martirosyan	CentraleSupélec, Belgium
Vana Kalogeraki	Athens University of Economics and Business, Greece
Vanessa Gomez-Verdejo	Universidad Carlos III de Madrid, Spain
Vasileios Iosifidis	SCHUFA Holding, Germany
Vasilis Gkolemis	ATHENA RC, Greece
Victor Charpenay	Mines Saint-Etienne, France
Vincent Derkinderen	KU Leuven, Belgium
Vincent Lemaire	Orange Research, France
Vincenzo Pasquadibisceglie	University of Bari, Aldo Moro, Italy
Virginijus Marcinkevicius	Vilnius University, Lithuania
Vitor Cerqueira	University of Porto, Portugal
Vivek Kumar	Universität der Bundeswehr München, Germany
Vivek Srikumar	University of Utah, USA
Wagner Meira Jr.	UFMG, Brazil
Wei Wu	Ben Gurion University of the Negev, Israel
Weichen Li	RPTU Kaiserslautern-Landau, Germany
Weifeng Xu	Independent Researcher, China
Weike Pan	Shenzhen University, China
Weiwei Jiang	Beijing University of Posts and Telecommunications, China
Weiwei Sun	Carnegie Mellon University, USA
Weiwei Yuan	Nanjing University of Aeronautics and Astronautics, China
Weixiong Rao	Tongji University, China
Wen-Bo Xie	Southwest Petroleum University, China
Wenhao Li	Tongji University, China
Wenhao Zheng	Shopee, Singapore
Wenjie Feng	National University of Singapore, Singapore
Wenjie Xi	George Mason University, USA
Wenshui Luo	Nanjing University of Science and Technology, China
Wentao Yu	Nanjing University of Science and Technology, China
Wenzhe Yi	Wuhan University, China
Wenzhong Li	Nanjing University, China
Wojciech Rejchel	Nicolaus Copernicus University, Torun, Poland

Xi Jiang	Southern University of Science and Technology, China
Xiang Li	East China Normal University, China
Xiang Lian	Kent State University, USA
Xiao Ma	Beijing University of Posts and Telecommunications, China
Xiao Zhang	Shandong University, China
Xiaobing Zhou	Yunnan University, China
Xiaofeng Cao	University of Technology Sydney, Australia
Xiaofeng Gao	Shanghai Jiaotong University, China
Xiaojun Chen	Institute of Information Engineering, Chinese Academy of Sciences, China
Xiao-Jun Zeng	University of Manchester, UK
Xiaoming Zhang	Beihang University, China
Xiaoting Zhao	Etsy, USA
Xiaowei Mao	Beijing Jiaotong University, China
Xiaoyu Shi	Chinese Academy of Sciences, China
Xin Du	University of Edinburgh, UK
Xin Qin	California State University, Long Beach, USA
Xing Tang	Tencent, China
Xing Xing	Tongji University, China
Xinning Zhu	Beijing University of Posts and Telecommunications, China
Xinpeng Lv	National University of Defense Technology, China
Xintao Wu	University of Arkansas, USA
Xinyang Zhang	University of Illinois at Urbana-Champaign, USA
Xinyu Guan	Xi'an Jiaotong University, China
Xixun Lin	Chinese Academy of Sciences, China
Xiyue Zhang	University of Bristol, UK
Xuan-Hong Dang	IBM T.J. Watson Research Center, USA
Xue Li	University of Queensland, Australia
Xue Yan	Institute of Automation, Chinese Academy of Sciences, China
Xuefeng Chen	Chongqing University, China
Xuemin Wang	Guilin University of Electronic Technology, China
Yachuan Zhang	East China University of Science and Technology, China
Yan Zhang	Peking University, China
Yang Li	University of North Carolina at Chapel Hill, USA
Yang Shu	East China Normal University, China
Yang Wei	Nanjing University of Science and Technology, China

Yanhao Wang	East China Normal University, China
Yanmin Zhu	Shanghai Jiao Tong University, China
Yansong Y. L. Li	University of Ottawa, Canada
Yao-Xiang Ding	Nanjing University, China
Yaqi Xie	Carnegie Mellon University, USA
Yasutoshi Ida	NTT, Japan
Yaying Zhang	Tongji University, China
Ye Zhu	Deakin University, Australia
Yeon-Chang Lee	Ulsan National Institute of Science and Technology, South Korea
Yexiang Xue	Purdue University, USA
Yi Wang	Xinjiang Technical Institute of Physics and Chemistry, Chinese Academy of Sciences, China
Yifeng Gao	University of Texas, Rio Grande Valley, USA
Yilun Jin	Hong Kong University of Science and Technology, China
Yin Zhang	University of Electronic Science and Technology of China, China
Ying Chen	RMIT University, Australia
Yinsheng Li	Fudan University, China
Yong Li	Huawei European Research Center, China
Yongyu Wang	JD Logistics, China
Youhei Akimoto	University of Tsukuba/RIKEN AIP, Japan
You-Wei Luo	Sun Yat-sen University and Jiaying University, China
Yuchen Li	Baidu, China
Yuchen Yang	Harbin Institute of Technology, China
Yudi Zhang	Eindhoven University of Technology, Netherlands
Yuhao Li	University of Melbourne, Australia
Yuheng Jia	Southeast University, China
Yujia Zheng	CMU, USA
Yulong Pei	TU Eindhoven, Netherlands
Yuncheng Jiang	South China Normal University, China
Yuntao Shou	Xi'an Jiaotong University, China
Yunyun Wang	Nanjing University of Posts and Telecommunications, China
Yutong Ye	East China Normal University, China
Yuzhou Chen	University of California, Riverside, USA
Zahraa Abdallah	University of Bristol, UK
Zaineb Chelly Dagdia	UVSQ, Paris-Saclay, France
Zehua Cheng	University of Oxford, UK
Zeyu Chen	University of Auckland, New Zealand

Zhaocheng Ge	Huazhong University of Science and Technology, China
Zhe Yang	Soochow University, China
Zhen Liu	Guangdong University of Foreign Studies, China
Zheng Chen	Osaka University, Japan
Zhenghao Liu	Northeastern University, China
Zhenyu Yang	Macquarie University, Australia
Zhi Li	Tsinghua University, China
Zhichao Han	ETHZ, Switzerland
Zhihui Wang	Fudan University, China
Zhilong Shan	South China Normal University, China
Zhipeng Yin	Florida International University, USA
Zhipeng Zou	Nanjing University of Science and Technology, China
Zhiwen Xiao	Southwest Jiaotong University, China
Zhiwen Zhang	LocationMind, Japan
Zhixin Li	Guangxi Normal University, China
Zhiyong Cheng	Shandong Academy of Sciences, China
Zhong Chen	Southern Illinois University, USA
Zhong Li	Leiden University, Netherlands
Zhong Zhang	Tsinghua University, China
Zhongjing Yu	Peking University, China
Zhuang Liu	Dongbei University of Finance and Economics, China
Zhuo Cao	Forschungszentrum Jülich, Germany
Zhuoming Xie	Guangdong University of Technology, China
Zhuoqun Li	Louisiana State University, USA
Zicheng Zhao	Nanjing University of Science and Technology, China
Zichong Wang	Florida International University, USA
Zifeng Ding	University of Cambridge, UK
Ziheng Chen	Walmart, USA
Zijie J. Wang	Georgia Tech, USA
Zirui Zhuang	Beijing University of Posts and Telecommunications, China
Zixing Song	Chinese University of Hong Kong, China
Ziyu Wang	University of Tokyo, Japan
Ziyue Li	University of Cologne, Germany
Zongxia Xie	Tianjin University, China
Zongyue Li	LMU Munich, Germany
Zuojin Tang	Zhejiang University, China

List of Editors

Bernhard Pfahringer University of Waikato, New Zealand
Nathalie Japkowicz American University, USA
Pedro Larrañaga Technical University of Madrid, Spain
Rita P. Ribeiro University of Porto, Portugal
Alípio M. Jorge University of Porto, Portugal
Carlos Soares University of Porto, Portugal
João Gama University of Porto, Portugal
Pedro H. Abreu University of Coimbra, Portugal

Program Committee – Applied Data Science Track

Nasrullah Sheikh IBM Research, USA
Aakarsh Malhotra MasterCard, USA
Aakash Goel Amazon, USA
Abdoulaye Sakho Artefact, France
Abhijeet Pendyala Ruhr-Universität Bochum, Germany
Abu Shad Ahammed University of Siegen, Germany
Adi Lin Didi, China
Aditya Gautam Meta, USA
Ahmed K. Mohamed Meta, USA
Akihiro Yoshida Kyushu University, Japan
Akshay Sethi MasterCard, USA
Alejandro Kuratomi Stockholm University, Sweden
Alessandro Gambetti Nova School of Business and Economics, Portugal
Alessandro Leite INSA Rouen, Inria, France
Alessio Russo Politecnico di Milano, Italy
Alex Beeson University of Warwick, UK
Alexander Galozy Halmstad University, Sweden
Alexander Karlsson University of Skovde, Sweden
Alexander Kovalenko Czech Technical University in Prague, Czech Republic
Alexey Zaytsev Skoltech, Russia
Alina Bazarova Forschungszentrum Jülich, Germany
Alix Lheritier Amadeus SAS, France
Allan Tucker Brunel University London, UK
Alvaro Figueira CRACS and Universidade do Porto, Portugal
Aman Gulati Amazon, USA
Amira Soliman Halmstad University, Sweden

Ana Gjorgjevikj	Jožef Stefan Institute, Slovenia
Anders Holst	RISE SICS, Sweden
André C. P. L. F. de Carvalho	University of São Paulo, Brazil
Andrea Seveso	University of Milan-Bicocca, Italy
Andreas Bender	LMU Munich, Germany
Andreas Henelius	Independent Researcher, Finland
Andreas Holzinger	University of Natural Resources and Life Sciences, Vienna, Austria
Andrei Shelopugin	Independent Researcher, Brazil
Angelo Impedovo	Niuma, Italy
Aniket Chakrabarti	Amazon, USA
Animesh Prasad	Roku, USA
Anisio Lacerda	UFMG, Brazil
Anli Ji	Georgia State University, USA
Antoine Doucet	La Rochelle Université, France
Anton Borg	Blekinge Institute of Technology, Sweden
Antonio Bevilacqua	Meetecho, Italy
Antonis Klironomos	University of Mannheim, Germany
Aron Henriksson	Stockholm University, Sweden
Artur Chudzik	Polish-Japanese Academy of Information Technology, Poland
Arun Venkitaraman	EPFL, Switzerland
Arunabha Choudhury	ASML, Netherlands
Asem Omari	Higher Colleges of Technology, UAE
Ashman Mehra	Birla Institute of Technology and Science, India
Ashwani Rao	Amazon, USA
Asier Rodriguez	BBVA, Spain
Asma Atamna	Ruhr-Universität Bochum, Germany
Atiye Sadat Hashemi	Halmstad University, Sweden
Atul Anand Gopalakrishnan	SUNY Buffalo, USA
Avani Wildani	Emory University, USA
Aviv Rovshitz	Ben-Gurion University of the Negev, Israel
Axel Brando	Barcelona Supercomputing Center (BSC) and Universitat de Barcelona (UB), Spain
Azadeh Alavi	RMIT University, Australia
Beihong Jin	Institute of Software, China
Benoit Frenay	University of Namur, Belgium
Berkay Aydin	Georgia State University, USA
Bijaya Adhikari	University of Iowa, USA
Bin Li	Alibaba Group, China
Bo Pang	University of Auckland, New Zealand
Bogdan Ruszczak	Opole University of Technology, Poland

Bohao Qu	Agency for Science, China
Bruno Veloso	INESC TEC, FEP-UP, Portugal
Buyue Qian	Xi'an Jiaotong University, China
Camille Kurtz	Université Paris Cité, France
Cangbai Li	Guangdong University of Technology, China
Carlo Metta	ISTI CNR, Italy
Carlos N. Silla	Pontifical Catholic University of Paraná (PUCPR), Brazil
Cecile Bothorel	IMT Atlantique, France
Cesar Ferri	Universitat Politècnica Valencia, Spain
Chang Li	Apple, USA
Chang-Dong Wang	Sun Yat-sen University, China
Chaofan Li	Karlsruhe Institute of Technology, Germany
Chaoyuan Zuo	Nankai University, China
Chen Gao	Tsinghua University, China
Chen Li	Computer Network Information Center, China
Chen Zhao	Baylor University, USA
Chen-Wei Chang	Virginia Tech, USA
Chenxi Xue	Nanjing Normal University, China
Chongke Bi	Tianjin University, China
Christian M. Adriano	Hasso-Plattner Institute, Germany
Christophe Rodrigues	DVRC Pôle universitaire Léonard de Vinci, France
Chuan Li	Sorbonne University, LIPADE, France
Chunhui Zhang	Dartmouth College, USA
Cristina Soguero Ruiz	Rey Juan Carlos University, Spain
Daheng Wang	Amazon, USA
Daifeng Li	Sun Yat-sen University, China
Damien Fay	HPE Labs, Ireland
Dania Herzalla	Technology Innovation Institute, UAE
Daniel Lemire	University of Quebec (TELUQ), Canada
Daniel Trejo Banos	SDSC, USA
Daochen Zha	Rice University, USA
Dawei Cheng	Tongji University, China
Dayne Freitag	SRI International, USA
Di Yao	Institute of Computing Technology, China
Dimitris Nick Dimitriadis	Aristotle University of Thessaloniki, Greece
Diogo F. Soares	Universidade de Lisboa, Portugal
Dirk Pflueger	University of Stuttgart, Germany
Doheon Han	University of Notre Dame, USA
Dongxiang Zhang	Zhejiang University, China
Dongxiao Yu	Shandong University, China

Dugang Liu	Guangdong Laboratory of Artificial Intelligence and Digital Economy (Shenzen), China
Ece Calikus	Uppsala University, Sweden
Edwyn Brient	Thales LAS/Mines Paris PSL, France
Efstathios Stamatatos	University of the Aegean, Greece
Elaine Faria	UFU, Brazil
Elio Masciari	University of Naples, Italy
Emilie Devijver	Université Grenoble Alpes, Inria, CNRS, Grenoble INP, LIG, France
Emmanuelle Claeys	IRIT, France
Enayat Rajabi	Halmstad University, Sweden
Enda Barrett	University of Galway, Ireland
Enyan Dai	Hong Kong University of Science and Technology (Guangzhou), China
Eric Peukert	ScaDS.AI, Germany
Eric Sanjuan	Avignon University, France
Erik Frisk	Linköping University, Sweden
Eui-Hong (Sam) Han	The Washington Post, USA
Eunil Park	Sungkyunkwan University, South Korea
Fabio Carrara	CNR-ISTI, Italy
Fabiola Pereira	Federal University of Uberlandia, Brazil
Fan Yang	Rice University, USA
Fangzhao Wu	MSRA, China
Fangzhou Shi	Didi Chuxing, China
Fathima Nuzla Ismail	State University of New York, USA
Flavio Bertini	University of Parma, Italy
Francesco Dente	EURECOM, France
Francesco Guerra	University of Modena e Reggio Emilia, Italy
Francesco Scala	CNR-ICAR, Italy
Francesco Spinnato	University of Pisa, Italy
Francesco Paolo Nerini	Sapienza University of Rome, Italy
Francisco P. Romero	UCLM, Spain
Franco Maria Nardini	ISTI-CNR, Italy
Francois Schwarzentruber	ENS Lyon, France
Fudong Lin	University of Delaware, USA
Gabriel Augusto Pinheiro	UNIFESP, Brazil
Gan Sun	South China University of Technology, China
Gargi Srivastava	Rajiv Gandhi Institute of Petroleum Technology Jais, India
Giacomo Boracchi	Politecnico di Milano, Italy
Giuseppe Garofalo	DistriNet, KU Leuven, Belgium
Giuseppina Andresini	University of Bari Aldo Moro, Italy

Goran Falkman	University of Skovde, Sweden
Grzegorz Nalepa	Jagiellonian University, Poland
Guanggang Geng	Jinan University, China
Guojun Liang	Halmstad University, Sweden
Haifang Li	Baidu, China
Haina Tang	University of Chinese Academy of Sciences, China
Hancheng Ge	Amazon, USA
Hao Li	National University of Defense Technology, China
Haohui Chen	CSIRO, Australia
Haomin Yu	Aalborg University, Denmark
Haoyi Xiong	Baidu, China
Hiba Najjar	DFKI, Germany
Hillol Kargupta	Agnik, USA
Hong Zhou	Meta, USA
Hongbin Pei	Xi'an Jiao Tong University, China
Hou-Wan Long	Chinese University of Hong Kong, China
Hua Wei	Arizona State University, USA
Huaiyuan Yao	Xi'an Jiaotong University, China
Huan Song	Amazon, USA
Hubert Baniecki	University of Warsaw, Poland
Hyunsung Kim	KAIST, Fitogether, South Korea
Ibtihal El Mimouni	Inria, France
Ildar Baimuratov	L3S Research Center, Germany
Ilir Jusufi	Blekinge Institute of Technology, Sweden
Inaam Ashraf	Bielefeld University, Germany
Ines Sousa	Fraunhofer AICOS, Portugal
Iris Heerlien	Saxion, Netherlands
Isak Samsten	Stockholm University, Sweden
Ishan Verma	TCS Research, India
Ismail Hakki Toroslu	METU, Turkey
Ivan Carrera	EPN, Ecuador
Jaakko Hollmen	Stockholm University, Sweden
Jairo Cugliari	Laboratoire ERIC, France
Jakub Nalepa	Silesian University of Technology, Poland
Jelica Vasiljeivić	Hoffmann-La Roche, Switzerland
Jens Lundstrom	Halmstad University, Sweden
Jesse Davis	KU Leuven, Belgium
Jiahui Bai	Meta, USA
Jiajun Gu	Carnegie Mellon University, USA
Jiali Pan	Department of Information Management, USA

Jian Yu	Auckland University of Technology, New Zealand
Jiangbin Zheng	Westlake University, China
Jianhua Yin	Shandong University, China
Jingbo Zhou	Baidu, China
Jingjing Liu	MD Anderson Cancer Center, USA
Jingwen Shi	Michigan State University, USA
Jingxuan Wei	University of Chinese Academy of Sciences, China
Jinyoung Han	Sungkyunkwan University, South Korea
Jiue-An Yang	City of Hope Beckman Research Institute, USA
Joao R. Campos	University of Coimbra, Portugal
Jochen De Weerdt	KU Leuven, Belgium
Joe Tekli	Lebanese American University, Lebanon
Joel Ky	University of Lorraine, CNRS, Inria, France
John McCall	Robert Gordon University, UK
John Mitros	University College Dublin, Ireland
Jonas Fischer	Ruhr-Universität Bochum, Germany
Jonas Nordqvist	Linnaeus University, Sweden
Joydeep Chandra	Indian Institute of Technology Patna, India
Julian Martin Rodemann	LMU Munich, Germany
Jun Shen	University of Wollongong, Australia
Junichi Tatemura	Google, USA
Junxuan Li	Microsoft, USA
Jyun-Yu Jiang	Amazon Science, USA
Kai Wang	Shanghai Jiao Tong University, China
Kaiping Zheng	National University of Singapore, Singapore
Kaiwen Dong	University of Notre Dame, USA
Katarzyna Bozek	University of Cologne, Germany
Katerina Schindlerova	UniVie, Austria
Katharina Dost	Jožef Stefan Institute, Slovenia
Katsiaryna Mirylenka	Zalando SE, Germany
Keith Burghardt	ISI, Germany
Klaus Brinker	Hamm-Lippstadt University of Applied Sciences, Germany
Koki Kawabata	Osaka University, Japan
Korbinian Randl	Stockholm University, Sweden
Krzysztof Krawiec	Poznań University of Technology, Poland
Krzysztof Kutt	Jagiellonian University, Poland
Kwan Hui Lim	Singapore University of Technology and Design, Singapore
Lamija Lemes	University of Zenica, Bosnia & Herzegovina
Le Nguyen	University of Oulu, Finland

Lei Li	Hong Kong University of Science and Technology (Guangzhou), China
Lei Liu	York University, Canada
Li Liu	Chongqing University, China
Li Zhang	University College London, UK
Liang Tang	Google, USA
Liang Tong	NEC Labs America, USA
Liang Wang	Alibaba Group, China
Lina Yao	University of New South Wales, Australia
Lingxiao Li	Michigan State University, USA
Lingyang Chu	McMaster University, Canada
Lixin Zou	Wuhan University, China
Lluis Garcia-Pueyo	Meta, USA
Lou Salaun	Nokia Bell Labs, USA
Luca Corbucci	University of Pisa, Italy
Luca Pappalardo	ISTI, Italy
Luca Romeo	University of Macerata, Italy
Luis Ferreira	Olympus Medical Products Portugal, Portugal
Luis Miguel Matos	ALGORITMI Centre, Portugal
Lukas Grasmann	TU Wien, Austria
Lukas Pensel	Johannes Gutenberg University Mainz, Germany
Maciej Grzenda	Warsaw University of Technology, Poland
Maciej Piernik	Poznań University of Technology, Poland
Madiraju Srilakshmi	Dream Sports, India
Mads C. Hansen	A.P. Moller-Maersk, Denmark
Mahardhika Pratama	University of South Australia, Australia
Mahmoud Rahat	Halmstad University, Sweden
Man Tianxing	Jilin University, China
Manish Gupta	Microsoft, USA
Manos Papagelis	York University, Canada
Manuel Lopes	Instituto Tecnico Superior, Portugal
Manuel Portela	Universitat Pompeu Fabra, Spain
Marc Tommasi	Lille University, France
Marco Fisichella	Leibniz Universität, Hannover, Germany
Maria Riveiro	Jonkoping University, Sweden
Maria Ulan	RISE Research Institutes of Sweden, Sweden
Marian Scuturici	LIRIS, France
Marianne Clausel	IECL, France
Mario Doller	University of Applied Sciences, Kufstein, Austria
Marius Schwammle	DLR/BT, Germany
Markus Gotz	Karlsruhe Institute of Technology (KIT), Germany

Markus Leyser	Technische Universität Dresden, Germany
Martin Boldt	Blekinge Institute of Technology, Sweden
Martin Mladenov	Google, USA
Martin Vita	Institute of Physics, Czech Academy of Sciences, Czech Republic
Matthias Demant	Fraunhofer ISE, Germany
Matthias Galipaud	SDSC, Switzerland
Matthias Petri	Amazon, USA
Matthieu Latapy	CNRS, France
Maurice Van Keulen	University of Twente, Netherlands
Maxime Cordy	University of Luxembourg, Luxembourg
Maxwell J. Jacobson	Purdue University, USA
Md Nahid Hasan	Miami University, USA
Md Zia Ullah	Edinburgh Napier University, UK
Mehtab Alam Syed	CIRAD, France
Melanie Neubauer	University of Leoben, Austria
Meng Chen	Shandong University, China
Mengxuan Zhang	Australian National University, Australia
Miao Fan	NavInfo, China
Michael Bain	University of New South Wales, Australia
Michele Bernardini	Uni eCampus.It, Italy
Michiel Dhont	EluciDATA Lab of Sirris, Belgium
Mickael Coustaty	L3i Laboratory, France
Miguel Couceiro	LORIA, France
Mihaela Mitici	Utrecht University, Netherlands
Min Lee	Singapore Management University, Singapore
Min Hun Lee	Singapore Management University, Singapore
Mina Rezaei	LMU Munich, Germany
Ming Ma	Inner Mongolia University, China
Minghao Chen	Tencent, China
Mirco Nanni	CNR-ISTI Pisa, Italy
Mirjam Wattenhofer	Google, USA
Mirko Marras	University of Cagliari, Italy
Mitra Heidari	University of Melbourne, Australia
Modesto Castrillon-Santana	Universidad de Las Palmas de Gran Canaria, Spain
Mohammadmehdi Saberioon	German Research Centre for Geosciences, Germany
Mohammed Amer	Fujitsu Research of Europe, Germany
Mohammed Ghaith Altarabichi	Halmstad University, Sweden
Mojgan Kouhounestani	University of Melbourne, Australia
Moonki Hong	Sogang University, South Korea

Munira Syed	Procter & Gamble, USA
Nan Li	Microsoft, USA
Narendhar Gugulothu	TCS Research, India
Nedra Mellouli	LIASD, Portugal
Ngoc Son Le	University of Hildesheim, Germany
Niklas Lavesson	Blekinge Institute of Technology, Sweden
Niraj Kumar	Fujitsu, Japan
Nitish Kumar	MasterCard, USA
Nuno Cruz Garcia	FCUL, Portugal
Nuno R. P. S. Guimaraes	INESC TEC, University of Porto, Portugal
Nuwan Gunasekara	Halmstad University, Sweden
Pablo Picazo-Sanchez	Halmstad University, Sweden
Pablo Torrijos Arenas	Universidad de Castilla-La Mancha, Spain
Pablo Jose Del Moral Pastor	Ekkono.ai, Finland
Pan He	Auburn University, USA
Panagiotis Kanellopoulos	University of Essex, UK
Panagiotis Papadakos	FORTH-ICS, Greece
Pandey Shourya Prasad	International Institute of Information Technology, Bangalore, India
Panpan Xu	Amazon AWS, USA
Paola Velardi	Sapienza University of Rome, Italy
Paolo Cintia	Kode, Italy
Pascal Plettenberg	Intelligent Embedded Systems, Italy
Paul Boniol	Inria, France
Pavel Blinov	Sber AI Lab, Russia
Pawel Parczyk	Wroclaw University of Science and Technology, Poland
Pedro M. Ferreira	University of Lisbon, Portugal
Pedro Seber	MIT, USA
Peng Qiao	NUDT, China
Pengyuan Wang	University of Georgia, USA
Petr Olegovich Sokerin	Skoltech, Russia
Philipp Bach	University of Hamburg, Germany
Philipp Froehlich	TU Darmstadt, Germany
Philipp Schmidt	Amazon Research, USA
Philipp Zech	University of Innsbruck, Austria
Pinar Karagoz	Middle East Technical University (METU), Turkey
Ping Luo	Chinese Academy of Sciences, China
Po Yang	University of Sheffield, UK
Pop Petrica	Technical University of Cluj-Napoca, Romania
Prathap Manohar Joshi R	Zoho Corporation, India

Praveen Borra	Florida Atlantic University, USA
Praveen Paruchuri	IIIT Hyderabad, India
Qian Li	Curtin University, Australia
Qihang Yao	Georgia Institute of Technology, USA
Qiwei Han	Nova School of Business and Economics, Portugal
Quentin Duchemin	Université Gustave Eiffel, France
Radu Tudor Ionescu	University of Bucharest, Romania
Rafal Kucharski	Jagiellonian University, Poland
Rafet Sifa	Fraunhofer IAIS & University of Bonn, Germany
Ramasamy Savitha	I2R A*STAR, Singapore
Ran Yu	DSIS Research Group, Singapore
Ranga Raju Vatsavai	North Carolina State University, USA
Raphael Couturier	University of Bourgogne Franche-Comte (UBFC), France
Renato M. Assuncao	ESRI, USA
Renaud Lambiotte	University of Oxford, UK
Reuben Kshitiz Borrison	ABB, Switzerland
Reza Shirvany	Zalando SE, Germany
Ricardo R. Pereira	Feedzai, Portugal
Riccardo Rosati	Università Politecnica delle Marche, Ancona, Italy
Richard Allmendinger	University of Manchester, UK
Richard Nordsieck	XITASO GmbH IT and Software Solutions, Germany
Richi Nayak	Queensland University of Technology, Australia
Roberto Trasarti	CNR, Italy
Rogerio Luis de C. Costa	Polytechnic of Leiria, Portugal
Romain Ilbert	Huawei Paris Research Center, France
Roy Ka-Wei Lee	Singapore University of Technology and Design, Singapore
Ruilin Wang	University of Aberdeen, UK
Sabrina Gaito	Università degli Studi di Milano, Italy
Sai Karthikeya Vemuri	Computer Vision Group Jena, Italy
Saisubramaniam Gopalakrishnan	Quantiphi, USA
Sajjad Shumaly	Max-Planck-Institut for Polymer Research, Germany
Salvatore Rinzivillo	KDD Lab, ISTI, CNR, Italy
Samaneh Shafee	LASIGE, Portugal
Sandra Wissing	Fachhochschule Münster, Germany
Sarwan Ali	Georgia State University, USA
Sebastian Becker	Fraunhofer ISST, Germany

Sebastian Honel	Linnaeus University, Sweden
Selin Colakhasanoglu	Saxion University of Applied Sciences, Netherlands
Senzhang Wang	Central South University, China
Sepideh Nahali	York University, Canada
Shahrooz Abghari	Blekinge Institute of Technology, Sweden
Shahroz Tariq	CSIRO, Australia
Shang Yanlei	BUPT, China
Shen Liang	Paris Cité University, France
Shengheng Liu	Southeast University, China
Shereen Elsayed	University of Hildesheim, Germany
Shi-ting Wen	NingboTech University, China
Shiv Krishna Jaiswal	Walmart Global Tech, USA
Shoujin Wang	Macquarie University, Australia
Shuai Li	University of Cambridge, UK and University of Tokyo, UK
Shuchu Han	Capital One Financial Group, Japan
Simon F. Weinberger	EssilorLuxottica, France
Siyuan Chen	Guangzhou University, China
Snehanshu Saha	BITS Pilani Goa Campus, India
Souhaib Ben Taieb	University of Mons, Abu Dhabi
Sriparna Saha	IIT Patna, India
Stefan Rueping	Fraunhofer IAIS, Germany
Stephane Chretien	Université Lyon 2, France
Sunil Aryal	Deakin University, Australia
Susana Ladra	University of A Coruña, Spain
Szymon Bobek	Jagiellonian University, Poland
Szymon Jaroszewicz	Institute of Computer Science, Poland
Szymon Wilk	Poznań University of Technology, Poland
Tanel Tammet	Tallinn University of Technology, Estonia
Thanh Thi Nguyen	Monash University, Australia
Thiago Zangato	Université Sorbonne Paris Nord, France
Theodora Tsikrika	Information Technologies Institute, Greece
Thibault Girardin	Université Jean Monnet, France
Thomas Czernichow	Darwinlabs, Portugal
Thorsteinn Rognvaldsson	Halmstad University, Sweden
Tiago Mendes-Neves	FEUP/INESC TEC, Portugal
Tianshu Yu	Chinese University of Hong Kong (Shenzhen), China
Ting Su	Imperial College London, UK
Tingrui Qiao	University of Auckland, New Zealand
Tobias Glasmachers	Ruhr-Universität Bochum, Germany

Tomas Olsson — RISE SICS, Sweden
Tome Eftimov — Jožef Stefan Institute, Slovenia
Topon Paul — Toshiba Corporation, Japan
Tsuyoshi Okita — Kyushu Institute of Technology, Japan
Unmesh Padalkar — Dream Sports, India
Vahid Shahrivari Joghan — Utrecht University, Netherlands
Valerio Bonsignori — Unipisa, Italy
Vanessa Borst — University of Würzburg, Germany
Venkata Sai Prakash Mukkamala — Quantiphi Analytics, USA
Veselka Boeva — Blekinge Institute of Technology, Sweden
Viacheslav Komisarenko — University of Tartu, Estonia
Vikas Gupta — HPCL, India
Vinayak Gupta — University of Washington, Seattle, USA
Vincent Auriau — Artefact Research Center, France
Vincenzo Pasquadibisceglie — University of Bari, Aldo Moro, Italy
Vincenzo Scotti — KASTEL, Germany
Vinothkumar Kolluru — Stevens Institute of Technology, USA
Vladimir Mic — Aarhus University, Denmark
Wang-Zhou Dai — Nanjing University, China
Wee Siong Ng — Institute for Infocomm Research, Singapore
Wei Cheng — NEC Laboratories America, USA
Wei Li — Harbin Engineering University, China
Wei Wang — Tsinghua University, China
Wei-Peng Chen — Fujitsu Research of America, USA
Wentao Wang — Michigan State University, USA
Wentao Wu — Microsoft Research, USA
Wray Buntine — VinUniversity, Vietnam
Xianchao Wu — Nvidia, USA
Xiang Lian — Kent State University, USA
Xianli Zhang — Xi'an Jiaotong University, China
Xiaobo Jin — Xi'an Jiaotong-Liverpool University, China
Xiaofei Zhou — University of Chinese Academy of Sciences, China
Xiaofeng Gao — Shanghai Jiaotong University, China
Xiaolin Han — Northwestern Polytechnical University, China
Xin Huang — Hong Kong Baptist University, China
Xin Liu — East China Normal University, China
Xing Tang — Tencent, China
Xiuqiang He — Tencent, China
Xiuyuan Hu — Tsinghua University, China
Xueping Peng — University of Technology Sydney, Australia
Yanchang Zhao — CSIRO, Australia

Yang Guo	Xidian University Hangzhou Institute of Technology, China
Yang Song	Apple, USA
Yijun Zhao	Fordham University, USA
Yinghui Wu	Case Western Reserve University, USA
Yingzhen Lin	Harbin Institute of Technology (Shenzhen), China
Yintao Yu	University of Illinois at Urbana-Champaign, USA
Yixiang Fang	Chinese University of Hong Kong, China
Yixuan Cao	Institute of Computing Technology, China
Yizheng Huang	York University, Canada
Yongchao Liu	Ant Group, China
Yu Huang	Indiana University, USA
Yu Wang	University of Oregon, USA
Yuantao Fan	Halmstad University, Sweden
Yucheng Zhou	University of Macau, China
Yue Shi	Meta, USA
Yueyuan Zheng	Beihang University, China
Yunchuan Shi	University of Sydney, Australia
Yunjun Gao	Zhejiang University, China
Yuting Ding	Southeast University, China
Yuzhuo Li	University of Auckland, New Zealand
Zahra Kharazian	Stockholm University, Sweden
Zahra Taghiyarrenani	Halmstad University, Sweden
Zahraa Abdallah	University of Bristol, UK
Zeyi Wen	Hong Kong University of Science and Technology (Guangzhou), China
Zeyu Zhu	National University of Defense Technology, China
Zhanyu Liu	Shanghai Jiao Tong University, China
Zhaogeng Liu	Jilin University, China
Zhaohui Liang	National Library of Medicine, USA
Zhen Zhang	Shandong University, China
Zhendong Chu	Squirrel Ai Learning, China
Zheng Zhang	University of California, USA
Zhengze Li	University of Göttingen, Germany
Zhibin Gu	Hebei Normal University, China
Zhuang Liu	Dongbei University of Finance and Economics, China
Ziyu Guan	Xidian University, China
Zoltan Miklos	Université de Rennes, France
Zunlei Feng	Zhejiang University, China

Program Committee – Demo Track

Andrzej Wójtowicz	Adam Mickiewicz University, Poznań, Poland
Anna Sokol	University of Notre Dame, USA
Arian Pasquali	Faktion AI, Belgium
Bruno Veloso	INESC TEC - FEP-UP, Portugal
Chongsheng Zhang	Henan University, China
Christos Doulkeridis	University of Piraeus, Greece
Danqing Zhang	PathOnAI.org, USA
Fátima Rodrigues	INESC TEC, Portugal
Grigorii Khvatskii	University of Notre Dame, USA
Joe Germino	University of Notre Dame, USA
Jungwon Seo	University of Stavanger, Norway
Ke Li	University of Exeter, England
Manfred Jaeger	Aalborg University, Denmark
Marcin Luckner	Warsaw University of Technology, Poland
Mehwish Alam	Institut Polytechnique de Paris, France
Nuno Moniz	University of Notre Dame, USA
Tânia Carvalho	FCUP, Portugal
Vitor Cerqueira	FEUP, Portugal
Wei-Wei Du	National Yang Ming Chiao Tung University, Taiwan

Additional Reviewers

Andrea D'Angelo	Antonia Hain
Patrick Altmeyer	Md Athikul Islam
Guiseppina Adresini	Michael Ito
Vedangi Bengali	Philipp Jahn
Michele Bernardini	Rahul Kumar
Zhi Cao	Bishal Lakha
Louis Carpentier	Yuwen Liu
Alessio Cascione	Jerry Lonlac
Lilia Chebbah	Shijie Luo
Meng Ding	Francesca Naretto
Roberto Esposito	Navid Nobani
Alina Fastowski	Diego Coello de Portugal
Roger Ferrod	Joana Santos
Michele Fontana	Francesco Scala
Chang Gong	Richard Serrano
Michal Grzejdziak-Zdziarski	Nuno Silva
Paul Hahn	Francesco Spinnato

Pedro C. Vieira
Xiao Wang
Yunyun Wang
Qi Wen
Jianye Xie

Huaiyuan Yao
Yutong Ye
Obaidullah Zaland
Efstratios Zaradoukas
Nan Zhang

Sponsors

Diamond

Platinum

Gold

Silver

Bronze

Other Sponsors

Partners

AI-BOOST

Keynotes

Many Good Models Leads to ...

Cynthia Rudin

Duke University, USA

Abstract. As it turns out, many good models leads to amazing things! The Rashomon Effect, coined by Leo Breiman, describes the phenomenon that there exist many equally good predictive models for the same dataset.

This phenomenon happens for many real datasets, and when it does it sparks both magic and consternation, but mostly magic. In light of the Rashomon Effect, my collaborators and I propose to reshape the way we think about machine learning, particularly for tabular data problems in the nondeterministic (noisy) setting. I'll address how the Rashomon Effect impacts (1) the existence of simple-yet-accurate models, (2) flexibility to address user preferences, such as fairness and monotonicity, without losing performance, (3) uncertainty in predictions, fairness, and explanations, (4) reliable variable importance, (5) algorithm choice, specifically, providing advanced knowledge of which algorithms might be suitable for a given problem, and (6) public policy. I'll also discuss a theory of when the Rashomon Effect occurs and why: interestingly, noise in data leads to a large Rashomon Effect. My goal is to illustrate how the Rashomon Effect can have a massive impact on the use of machine learning for complex problems in society.

Towards Causal Artificial Intelligence

Elias Bareinboim

Columbia University, USA

Abstract. While a significant portion of AI scientists and engineers believe we are on the verge of achieving highly general forms of AI, I offer a critical appraisal of this view through a causal lens. In particular, building on foundational developments in the field, I will present my perspective on the relationship between intelligence and causality – and the central role of the latter in building intelligent systems and advancing credible data science.

I frame this discussion in terms of five core capabilities that we should expect from an intelligent AI system: performing causal reasoning and articulating explanations; making precise, surgical, and sample-efficient decisions; generalizing across changing conditions and environments; generating and simulating in a causally consistent manner; and learning causal structures and variables.

In this talk, I will elaborate on this perspective and share current progress toward building causally intelligent AI systems. A more detailed discussion of this thesis is provided in my forthcoming textbook, a draft of which is available here: https://causalai-book.net/.

Not Just a Trend: Institutionalizing XAI for Responsible and Compliant AI Systems

Francisco Herrera

Granada University, Spain

Abstract. As artificial intelligence (AI) systems increasingly mediate decisions in high-stakes domains – from healthcare and finance to public policy – the demand for explainable AI (XAI) has grown rapidly. Yet many current XAI approaches remain disconnected from the practical needs of stakeholders and the requirements of emerging regulatory frameworks. This talk argues that XAI must not be treated as a passing trend or optional technical add-on, but as a foundational principle in the design and deployment of AI systems. We critically examine the state of the field, exposing the gap between model-centric explainability and stakeholder-centric accountability. In response, we propose a framework that aligns explainability with legal, ethical, and social responsibilities, emphasizing co-design with affected users, sensitivity to institutional contexts, and governance over opacity. Our goal is to advance XAI from superficial compliance toward deeply integrated transparency that fosters trust, accountability, and responsible innovation.

Compositional Intelligence: Coordinating Multiple LLMs for Complex Tasks

Mirella Lapata

University of Edinburgh, UK

Abstract. Recent years have witnessed the rise of increasingly larger and more sophisticated language models (LMs) capable of performing every task imaginable, sometimes at (super)human level. In this talk, I will argue that in many realistic scenarios, solely relying on a single general-purpose LLM is suboptimal. A single LLM is likely to underrepresent real-world data distributions, heterogeneous skills, and task-specific requirements. Instead, I will discuss multi-LLM collaboration as an alternative to monolithic generative modeling. By orchestrating multiple LLMs, each with distinct roles, perspectives, or competencies, we can achieve more effective problem-solving while being more inclusive and explainable. I will illustrate this approach through two case studies: narrative story generation and visual question answering, showing how a society of agents can collectively tackle complex tasks while pursuing complementary subgoals. Additionally, I will explore how these agent societies leverage reasoning to improve performance.

Towards a Fairer World: Uncovering and Addressing Human and Algorithmic Biases

Nuria Oliver

ELLIS Alicante Foundation, Spain

Abstract. In my talk, I will first briefly present ELLIS Alicante1, the only ELLIS unit that has been created from scratch as a non-profit research foundation devoted to responsible AI for Social Good. Next, I will provide an overview of AI with a focus on the ethical implications and limitations of today's AI systems, including algorithmic discrimination and bias. On this topic, I will present a few examples of our work on uncovering and mitigating both human and algorithmic biases with AI.

On the human front, I will present the body of work that we have carried out in the context of AI-based beauty filters that are so popular on social media. On the algorithmic front, I will explain the main approaches to address algorithmic discrimination and I will present three novel methods to achieve fairer decisions.

Tensor Logic: A Simple Unification of Neural and Symbolic AI

Pedro Domingos

University of Washington, USA

Abstract. Deep learning has achieved remarkable successes in language generation and other tasks, but is extremely opaque and notoriously unreliable. Both of these problems can be overcome by combining it with the sound reasoning and transparent knowledge representation capabilities of symbolic AI. Tensor logic accomplishes this by unifying tensor algebra and logic programming, the formal languages underlying respectively deep learning and symbolic AI. Tensor logic is based on the observation that predicates are compactly represented Boolean tensors, and can be straightforwardly extended to compactly represent numeric ones. The two key constructs in tensor logic are tensor join and project, numeric operations that generalize database join and project. A tensor logic program is a set of tensor equations, each expressing a tensor as a series of tensor joins, a tensor project, and a univariate nonlinearity applied elementwise. Tensor logic programs can succinctly encode most deep architectures and symbolic AI systems, and many new combinations.

In this talk I will describe the foundations and main features of tensor logic, and present efficient inference and learning algorithms for it. A system based on tensor logic achieves state-of-the-art results on a suite of language and reasoning tasks. How tensor logic will fare on trillion-token corpora and associated tasks remains an open question.

Artificial Intelligence for Science

Sašo Džeroski

Jožef Stefan Institute, Slovenia

Abstract. Artificial intelligence is already transforming science, with its future impact expected to be even greater. Realizing this potential requires addressing key scientific challenges, such as ensuring explainability (of models and their predictions), learning effectively from limited data, and integrating data with prior domain knowledge. It also requires the provision of support for open and reproducible science through formalizing and sharing scientific knowledge.

I will present an overview of my research on the development of AI methods suitable for use in science. These include methods for explainable machine learning – including multi-target prediction and relational learning – that deliver accurate yet interpretable models suitable for complex scientific domains. These methods have been applied in environmental science, life science and materials science. Learning from limited data is critical in science. I will discuss two complementary approaches: semi-supervised learning, which leverages unlabeled data directly, together with labeled data, and foundation models, which use representations learned from vast unlabeled data to support downstream tasks with minimal supervision, i.e., limited amounts of labeled data. Both paradigms expand AI's reach into data-scarce scientific problems.

I will then present our work on automated scientific modeling, where we learn interpretable models of dynamical systems – such as process-based models and differential equations – from time series data and domain knowledge. Finally, I will highlight the role of ontologies and semantic technologies in experimental computer science, including machine learning and optimization. In these areas, we have developed ontologies for the representation and annotation of both data and other artefacts produced by science, such as algorithms, models, and results of experiments.

Contents – Part II

Data Challenges

Safe Screening Rules for Group SLOPE 3
    Runxue Bao, Quanchao Lu, and Yanfu Zhang

Efficient Bayesian Updates for Deep Active Learning via Laplace
Approximations 20
    *Denis Huseljic, Marek Herde, Lukas Rauch, Paul Hahn, Zhixin Huang,
Daniel Kottke, Stephan Vogt, and Bernhard Sick*

Bayesian Active Learning for Censored Regression 36
    *Frederik Boe Hüttel, Christoffer Riis, Filipe Rodrigues,
and Francisco Pereira*

An (ϵ, δ)-Accurate Level Set Estimation with a Stopping Criterion 52
    Hideaki Ishibashi, Kota Matsui, Kentaro Kutsukake, and Hideitsu Hino

Self-improvement for Computerized Adaptive Testing 70
    Yannick Rudolph, Kai Neubauer, and Ulf Brefeld

Voronoi Diagram Encoded Hashing 87
    Yang Xu and Kai Ming Ting

Adaptive Multi-space Defense Framework Against Adversarial Attacks 104
    Xiaohui Yu and Qiao Yan

How to RETIRE Tabular Data in Favor of Discrete Digital Signal
Representation 119
    Paweł Zyblewski and Szymon Wojciechowski

Diffusion Models

Diffusion Model with Selective Attention for Temporal Knowledge Graph
Reasoning 139
    Rushan Geng, Ge Chen, and Cuicui Luo

Topology-Aware Hierarchical Graph Diffusion Model for Molecular
Graph Generation 156
    *Rongshen He, Abubakar Zakari, Qinru Yang, Jiaqi Luo,
and Changsheng Ma*

Single-Fold Distillation for Diffusion Models 173
Chi Hong, Jiyue Huang, Robert Birke, Dick Epema, Stefanie Roos, and Lydia Y. Chen

Loss Functions in Diffusion Models: A Comparative Study 190
Dibyanshu Kumar, Philipp Väth, and Magda Gregorová

Diffusion Classifier Guidance for Non-robust Classifiers 206
Philipp Vaeth, Dibyanshu Kumar, Benjamin Paassen, and Magda Gregorová

Improving Discriminator Guidance in Diffusion Models 222
Alexandre Verine, Ahmed Mehdi Inane, Florian Le Bronnec, Benjamin Negrevergne, and Yann Chevaleyre

JKDM: A Joint Structural and Semantic Diffusion-Generated Knowledge Completion Model 239
Wendong Zhang, Haoqi Chen, and Song Yu

Ensemble Learning

EM-SEC: Efficient Multi-head Set-Valued Evidential Classification 259
Grigor Bezirganyan, Sana Sellami, Laure Berti-Équille, and Sébastien Fournier

A Complementarity-Enhanced Mixture of Human-AI Teams for Decision-Making 278
Hefei Liang, Jiaqi Liu, Bin Guo, and Zhiwen Yu

MEAN: Multi-Expert Adaptive Network For Customer Lifetime Value Prediction 294
Kelin Liu, Yao Zhou, Bin Liu, Hanjing Su, and Shouzhi Chen

Enabling ControlNet to follow Localized Descriptions Using Cross-Attention Control 310
Denis Lukovnikov and Asja Fischer

Federated Learning

FedCluLearn: Federated Continual Learning Using Stream Micro-cluster Indexing Scheme 331
Milena Angelova, Veselka Boeva, Shahrooz Abghari, Selim Ickin, and Xiaoyu Lan

FedRNL: Federated Rationalization with Soft Parameter Sharing 350
   Lingxiao Kong, Jiahui Jiang, Haozhao Wang, Lei Wu, and Ruixuan Li

Bkd-FedGNN: A Benchmark for Classification Backdoor Attacks
on Federated Graph Neural Network 367
   Fan Liu, Siqi Lai, Yansong Ning, and Hao Liu

Federated Time Series Generation on Feature and Temporally Misaligned
Data 384
   Zhi Wen Soi, Chenrui Fan, Aditya Shankar, Abel Malan, and Lydia Y. Chen

Graph Neural Networks

Distribution Matching for Graph Quantification Under Structural
Covariate Shift 403
   Clemens Damke and Eyke Hüllermeier

Understanding and Improving Laplacian Positional Encodings
for Temporal GNNs 420
   Yaniv Galron, Fabrizio Frasca, Haggai Maron, Eran Treister, and Moshe Eliasof

REDELEX: A Framework for Relational Deep Learning Exploration 438
   Jakub Peleška and Gustav Šír

Localized Heat Kernel for Graph Neural Networks 457
   Taoyang Qin, Ke-Jia Chen, and Zheng Liu

Graph Neural Network Leveraging Higher-Order Class Label Connectivity
for Heterophilous Graphs 474
   Takuto Takahashi, Itsuki Nakayama, Takahiro Mitani, Ryosuke Kikuchi, Yuya Sasaki, and Makoto Onizuka

A QUBO Framework for Team Formation 492
   Karan Vombatkere, Theodoros Lappas, and Evimaria Terzi

Enhancing Graph Transformers with SNNs and Mutual Information 511
   Ziyu Wang

PipeQS: Pipeline-Based Adaptive Quantization and Staleness-Aware Distributed GNN Training System 527
Donghang Wu, Lian Shen, Changzhi Jiang, Yanhao Li, and Xiangrong Liu

Author Index 545

Data Challenges

Safe Screening Rules for Group SLOPE

Runxue Bao[1](✉), Quanchao Lu[2], and Yanfu Zhang[3]

[1] University of Pittsburgh, Pittsburgh, PA 15260, USA
runxue.bao@pitt.edu
[2] Georgia Institute of Technology, Atlanta, GA 30332, USA
qlu43@gatech.edu
[3] The College of William and Mary, Williamsburg, VA 23185, USA
yzhang105@wm.edu

Abstract. Variable selection is a challenging problem in high-dimensional sparse learning, especially when group structures exist. Group SLOPE performs well for the adaptive selection of groups of predictors. However, the block non-separable group effects in Group SLOPE make existing methods either invalid or inefficient. Consequently, Group SLOPE tends to incur significant computational costs and memory usage in practical high-dimensional scenarios. To overcome this issue, we introduce a safe screening rule tailored for the Group SLOPE model, which efficiently identifies inactive groups with zero coefficients by addressing the block non-separable group effects. By excluding these inactive groups during training, we achieve considerable gains in computational efficiency and memory usage. Importantly, the proposed screening rule can be seamlessly integrated into existing solvers for both batch and stochastic algorithms. Theoretically, we establish that our screening rule can be safely employed with existing optimization algorithms, ensuring the same results as the original approaches. Experimental results confirm that our method effectively detects inactive feature groups and significantly boosts computational efficiency without compromising accuracy.

Keywords: Safe Screening Rules · Group SLOPE · Feature Selection

1 Introduction

Group structures are ubiquitous in many high-dimensional problems with massive correlated and superfluous features. To obtain more stable and interpretable models with better prediction performance, many sparse learning models with grouping structures were proposed and achieved great success in many real-world applications. Group Lasso [39] and its variants, including Sparse Group Lasso [30], composite absolute penalties [41], tree Lasso [22], and Overlapping Group Lasso [18,19], are the most popular ones for group feature selection, which encourages structured sparsity with the prior information of feature group structures.

In this paper, we focus on the adaptive group feature selection model - Group SLOPE [10,15,16]. Let design matrix $X = [x_1, \ldots, x_n]^\top \in \mathbb{R}^{n \times d}$ have n observations and d variables and $y \in \mathbb{R}^n$ denote the measurement vector. Given I is a

Table 1. Representative safe screening algorithms.

Problem	Reference	Group-wise	Inseparability	Group Effects	Dynamic
Lasso	[13]	✗	✗	✗	Singly
Logistic Regression	[34]	✗	✗	✗	✗
Proximal Weighted Lasso	[28]	✗	✗	✗	Singly
SLOPE	[23]	✗	✓	✗	Singly
Group Lasso	[9]	✓	✗	✗	Singly
Sparse Group Lasso	[32]	✓	✗	✗	Singly
Tree Structured Group Lasso	[33]	✓	✗	✗	✗
Sparse-group Lasso	[26]	✓	✗	✗	Singly
Group SLOPE	Ours	✓	✓	✓	Doubly

partition of the set $\{1,\ldots,d\}$ and W is a diagonal matrix with $W_{i,i} := w_i$ for $i = 1,\ldots,m$, $X_{I_i} \in \mathbb{R}^{n \times |I_i|}$ denotes a partition of the matrix X and $[\![\beta]\!]_{X,I} := (\|X_{I_1}\beta_{I_1}\|_2, \ldots, \|X_{I_m}\beta_{I_m}\|_2)^\mathsf{T}$ denotes the group effects, Group SLOPE can be formulated as follows:

$$\min_{\beta} P_\lambda(\beta) := \frac{1}{2}\|y - X\beta\|_2^2 + J_\lambda(W[\![\beta]\!]_{X,I}), \tag{1}$$

where $\beta \in \mathbb{R}^d$ denotes the unknown coefficient vector and $\lambda = [\lambda_1, \ldots, \lambda_m]$ is a nonnegative regularization parameter vector of m non-increasing weights that $\lambda_1 \geq \ldots \geq \lambda_m$. The term $J_\lambda(b)$ denotes the ordered weighted l_1-norm as $J_\lambda(b) = \sum_{i=1}^m \lambda_i |b|_{[i]}$ where $b_{[1]} \geq \ldots \geq b_{[m]}$ are the ordered terms.

Group SLOPE penalty $J_\lambda(W[\![b]\!]_{X,I})$ adaptively penalizes the group effects based on the magnitude. Thus, Group SLOPE can simultaneously encourage the group effects to be equal and sparse, which is helpful to denoise and improve the prediction. [10] provided both nice empirical results and theoretical analysis for Group SLOPE on the adaptive selection of groups of predictors. In general, Group SLOPE can achieve the exact minimax estimation without any knowledge of coefficients sparsity and control the group false discovery rate at a specific level [10, 15]. The attractive properties above, which do not simultaneously exist in other models such as Group Lasso and SLOPE [8], had made Group SLOPE an effective method for the analysis in the high-dimensional setting [10, 15, 16]. Please note that Group SLOPE includes a broad set of sparse learning models. For example, Group SLOPE reduces to Group Lasso when $\lambda_1 = \ldots = \lambda_m$ and $w_i = \sqrt{|I_i|}$. Group SLOPE reduces to SLOPE when each group only has one variable and X is standardized to have unit column norms. Besides, Group SLOPE certainly includes Lasso, weighted Lasso [7] and L_∞-norm regression. Also, Group SLOPE can be easily extended to the logistic loss for classification tasks.

From an optimization perspective, the block-nonseparable group effects render the coordinate descent algorithm for Group Lasso ineffective. To address the computational challenges of Group SLOPE, proximal gradient methods have been introduced [10]. However, these methods encounter significant computational and memory challenges, particularly in high-dimensional settings. This is primarily because the algorithm processes all data points at each iteration, even when group coefficients are zero.

Various screening rules have been developed to speed up the training of sparse learning models by eliminating inactive features. [24] introduced a static safe screening rule for l_1-regularized problems, which eliminates features before the optimization process. Relaxing the constraints of the safe rule, [31] introduced a strong rule for Lasso that employs heuristic strategies through an active set method. However, this approach may mistakenly discard features. Additionally, the sequential safe rule presented in [35, 37] relies on the exact dual optimal solution, making it potentially time-consuming. More recently, [13] proposed a dynamic screening rule for Lasso, which is applied throughout the learning process, based on the duality gap, offering provable safety and improved speed compared to previous rules. This has led to the development of many dynamic screening rules for various sparse learning models [2–5, 26, 28, 29], all aimed at enhancing training efficiency. Thus, improving the efficiency of solving Group SLOPE via dynamic screening rules becomes both important and promising. Moreover, by reducing the number of model parameters, such techniques can also enhance inference performance, similar to the benefits observed with pruning methods [14, 17, 25, 36].

The goal of this research is to expedite the training process of Group SLOPE models through the application of safe screening techniques, enabling the secure exclusion of inactive groups whose parameters are guaranteed to be zeros during training. Table 1 outlines various representative safe screening algorithms, highlighting that such rules have been developed to boost the efficiency of training algorithms across numerous sparse learning models. However, the complex penalty structure of Group SLOPE, characterized by its block-nonseparable nature in relation to group effects, has so far hindered the development of safe screening rules for this model. The challenges can be summarized as follows: Firstly, unlike other models that penalize coefficients directly, Group SLOPE penalizes group effects $\|X\beta\|_2$, which does not directly enforce coefficient sparsity. Secondly, while other models are restricted to either feature-wise or separable group-wise penalties, Group SLOPE introduces the first non-separable group-wise feature selection method, with all hyperparameters for each group remaining unfixed during the training process—unlike in models such as Group Lasso or Sparse Group Lasso, where hyperparameters are predetermined before optimization.

In response to these challenges, this paper introduces a doubly dynamic safe screening rule tailored to the general Group SLOPE models. This represents, to our knowledge, the first safe screening rule specifically designed for adaptive group feature selection models. In high-dimensional settings where many groups have zero-valued coefficients, our screening rule efficiently identifies and excludes these inactive groups, thereby accelerating the original algorithms. Our approach begins by decoupling the design matrix to manage the block non-separable group effects. We then establish a doubly dynamic screening rule featuring a decreasing left bound and an increasing right bound, resulting in an expanding safe region. Crucially, the proposed screening rule is solver-independent and can be seamlessly integrated into existing iterative algorithms. Empirical evaluations on four benchmark datasets confirm that our approach yields significant computational advantages.

2 Safe Screening Rules for Group SLOPE

In this section, we first decouple the over-complex group effect penalty and then propose a doubly dynamic safe screening rule for Group SLOPE.

2.1 Decoupling the Group Effect Penalty

Different from other models, Group SLOPE penalizes group effects $\|X\beta\|_2$ directly. To propose a screening rule for Group SLOPE, we first derive an equivalent formulation of (1), which decomposes the design matrix as an orthogonal matrix and a corresponding full-row rank matrix. Specifically, by representing $X_{I_i} = U_i R_i$ where U_i is any matrix with $|I_i|$ orthogonal columns and R_i is the corresponding full-row rank matrix, we can obtain:

$$X\beta = \sum_{i=1}^{m} X_{I_i}\beta_{I_i} = \sum_{i=1}^{m} U_i R_i \beta_{I_i} = \tilde{X}\eta, \tag{2}$$

$$\|X_{I_i}\beta_{I_i}\|_2 = \|R_i\beta_{I_i}\|_2 = \|\eta_{I_i}\|_2, \tag{3}$$

where $\tilde{X}_{I_i} = U_i$ and $\eta_{I_i} := R_i\beta_{I_i}$ for $i = 1, \ldots, m$. Thus, the decoupled version of Problem (1) can be equivalently presented as:

$$\min_{\eta} \frac{1}{2}\|y - \tilde{X}\eta\|_2^2 + J_\lambda(W[\![\eta]\!]_\mathbb{I}), \tag{4}$$

where $[\![\eta]\!]_\mathbb{I} := \left(\|\eta_{I_1}\|_2, \|\eta_{I_2}\|_2, \ldots, \|\eta_{I_m}\|_2\right)^\top$.

Considering the diagonal matrix W with $W_{i,i} = w_i$ for $i = 1, \ldots, m$, define Z as a diagonal matrix with $Z_{i,i} := 1/w_j$ for $i \in I_j$ where $i = 1, \ldots, d$ and $j = 1, \ldots, m$, we have $J_\lambda(W[\![\eta]\!]_\mathbb{I}) = J_\lambda([\![Z^{-1}\eta]\!]_\mathbb{I})$. Further, defining $b = Z^{-1}\eta$, we have $\eta = Zb$. Thus, denoting $\hat{X} = \tilde{X}Z$, we can formulate (4) as

$$\min_{\eta} \frac{1}{2}\|y - \tilde{X}\eta\|_2^2 + J_\lambda(W[\![\eta]\!]_\mathbb{I})$$

$$= \min_{b} \frac{1}{2}\|y - \tilde{X}\eta\|_2^2 + J_\lambda([\![Z^{-1}\eta]\!]_\mathbb{I})$$

$$= \min_{b} \frac{1}{2}\|y - \tilde{X}Zb\|_2^2 + J_\lambda([\![b]\!]_\mathbb{I})$$

$$= \min_{b} \frac{1}{2}\|y - \hat{X}b\|_2^2 + J_\lambda([\![b]\!]_\mathbb{I}). \tag{5}$$

That is to say, by the equivalent transformation above, the next step to achieve our aim is to propose a safe screening rule for Problem (5).

2.2 Dual Formulation and Screening Test

Problem (5) can be formulated as follows:

$$b = \arg\min_{b \in \mathbb{R}^d} P_\lambda(b) := F(b) + J_\lambda([\![b]\!]_\mathbb{I}), \tag{6}$$

where loss $F(b) = \sum_{i=1}^{n} f_i(x_i^\top b)$, $f_i : \mathbb{R} \to \mathbb{R}_+$ is the squared loss. Generally, (6) is convex, non-smooth, and non-separable.

We initiate the derivation of the screening test by reformulating the primal objective (6) into its dual. Leveraging insights from the dualization of l_1-regularized models as outlined in [21], the resulting dual problem takes the form:

$$\min_b F(b) + J_\lambda(\llbracket b \rrbracket_\mathbb{I})$$

$$= \min_b \sum_{i=1}^{n} f_i(x_i^\top b) + J_\lambda(\llbracket b \rrbracket_\mathbb{I})$$

$$= \min_b \sum_{i=1}^{n} f_i^{**}(x_i^\top b) + \sum_{i=1}^{m} \lambda_i \|b_{I_{[i]}}\|_2$$

$$= \min_b \sum_{i=1}^{n} \max_{\theta_i} [\beta x_i \theta_i - f_i^*(\theta_i)] + \sum_{i=1}^{m} \lambda_i \|b_{I_{[i]}}\|_2$$

$$= \min_b \max_\theta - \sum_{i=1}^{n} f_i^*(\theta_i) + \beta^\top X^\top \theta + \sum_{i=1}^{m} \lambda_i \|b_{I_{[i]}}\|_2$$

$$= \max_\theta - \sum_{i=1}^{n} f_i^*(\theta_i) + \min_b \beta^\top X^\top \theta + \sum_{i=1}^{m} \lambda_i \|b_{I_{[i]}}\|_2$$

$$= \max_{\theta \in \Delta} D(\theta) := \sum_{i=1}^{n} -f_i^*(\theta_i), \tag{7}$$

where $\theta \in \mathbb{R}^n$ is the solution of the dual problem. Note f_i^* is the convex conjugate of function f_i as

$$f_i^*(\theta_i) = \max_{z_i \in \mathbb{R}} \theta_i z_i - f_i(z_i). \tag{8}$$

Let us define $\widetilde{\theta} := \left(\|X_{I_1}^\top \theta\|_2, \ldots, \|X_{I_m}^\top \theta\|_2 \right)^\top$. Under this definition, the constraint $\theta \in \Delta$ in (7) can be equivalently expressed as $\sum_{j \leq i} \widetilde{\theta}_{[j]} \leq \sum_{j \leq i} \lambda_j$ for all $i = 1, \ldots, m$. We next apply the optimality condition associated with the minimization part in the penultimate expression of (7):

$$\min_b \beta^\top X^\top \theta + \sum_{i=1}^{m} \lambda_i \|b_{I_{[i]}}\|_2. \tag{9}$$

This optimality condition naturally leads to the constraint structure previously introduced in (7), thereby finalizing the dual reformulation of (6).

Leveraging the Fermat rule [6], we obtain

$$- X^\top \theta^* \in \partial J_\lambda(\llbracket b \rrbracket_\mathbb{I}), \tag{10}$$

where θ^* denotes the dual optimum solution and $\partial J_\lambda(\llbracket b \rrbracket_\mathbb{I})$ represents the subdifferential of the regularizer $J_\lambda(\llbracket b \rrbracket_\mathbb{I})$.

Let $\widetilde{\mathcal{A}}^*$ be the index corresponding to inactive groups at optimality. The conditions for the partition $\mathcal{A}^*$ and $\widetilde{\mathcal{A}}^*$ of problems (9) can be separately expressed as:

$$-X_{I_{\mathcal{A}^*}}^\top \theta^* \in \partial J_{\lambda_{\mathcal{A}^*}}(\llbracket b \rrbracket_{\mathrm{I}}), \tag{11}$$

$$-X_{I_{\widetilde{\mathcal{A}}^*}}^\top \theta^* \in \partial J_{\lambda_{\widetilde{\mathcal{A}}^*}}(\llbracket b \rrbracket_{\mathrm{I}}). \tag{12}$$

For any group $i \in \mathcal{A}^*$, we have $b_{I_i}^* \neq 0$, it holds that

$$\|X_{I_i}^\top \theta^*\|_2 \in [\min_{j \in \mathcal{A}^*} \lambda_j, \max_{j \in \mathcal{A}^*} \lambda_j]. \tag{13}$$

Assuming both primal and dual optimal solutions are available, one can derive a safe screening rule for each group based on the following condition:

$$\|X_{I_i}^\top \theta^*\|_2 < \lambda_{|\mathcal{A}^*|} \implies b_{I_i}^* = 0, \tag{14}$$

which implies that such a group can be safely discarded without affecting the final solution. This enables subsequent training stages to proceed with a significantly reduced parameter space, leading to faster training while preserving accuracy.

Nevertheless, the main difficulty lies in the fact that the screening conditions (14) necessitate prior knowledge of both the dual optimum and the order structure of the primal optimum, which can only be obtained after the full training process has been completed. As a result, these screening conditions cannot be utilized to enhance optimization during the training phase.

Therefore, our objective is to devise a screening rule capable of identifying as many inactive variables (i.e., those with coefficients that should be zero) as possible, using the screening test (14) without knowing the dual optimum or the order structure of the primal optimum during the optimization process. To this end, we can formulate safe screening rules by defining a screening region that is as large as possible, characterized by smaller lower bounds and larger upper bounds derived from the screening conditions (14).

2.3 Upper Bound for the Left Term

It is worth noting that the lower bound of the screening region corresponds to the upper bound of $\|X_{I_i}^\top \theta^*\|_2$. To this end, we focus on deriving a tight upper estimate for $\|X_{I_i}^\top \theta^*\|_2$ by monitoring the intermediate duality gap $G(b, \theta)$ throughout the training iterations.

Utilizing the triangle inequality, we have:

$$\|X_{I_i}^\top \theta^*\|_2 \leq \|X_{I_i}^\top \theta\|_2 + \|X_{I_i}\|_2 \|\theta - \theta^*\|_2. \tag{15}$$

Since each $f_i^*(\theta_i)$ in the dual is known to be strongly convex (see Proposition 3.2 in [21]), the overall dual objective $D(\theta) := \sum_{i=1}^n -f_i^*(\theta_i)$ inherits strong concavity w.r.t. θ. As a direct implication, we obtain the following upper bound:

$$D(\theta) \leq D(\theta^*) - \mathrm{tr}(\nabla D(\theta^*)^\top (\theta^* - \theta)) - \frac{1}{2}\|\theta - \theta^*\|_2^2. \tag{16}$$

This inequality enables us to derive a bound on the distance between any feasible dual iterate θ and the optimal dual solution θ^* based on the first-order condition summarized in Corollary 1

Corollary 1. *For any dual feasible point θ, the following estimate holds:*

$$\|\theta - \theta^*\|_2 \leq \sqrt{2G(b,\theta)}, \tag{17}$$

where $G(b,\theta) = P(b) - D(\theta)$ denotes the intermediate duality gap at training.

Proof. We begin by applying the first-order optimality condition to the strongly concave dual objective $D(\theta)$, yielding:

$$\text{tr}(\nabla D(\theta^*)^\top (\theta^* - \theta)) \geq 0. \tag{18}$$

Combining this with inequality (16), we obtain:

$$\|\theta - \theta^*\|_2 \leq \sqrt{D(\theta^*) - D(\theta)}. \tag{19}$$

Under the assumption of strong duality, which ensures $P(b) \geq D(\theta^*)$, we replace the intractable term with a computable surrogate:

$$\|\theta - \theta^*\|_2 \leq \sqrt{2(P(b) - D(\theta))}. \tag{20}$$

This concludes the proof.

Based on the upper bound derived in Corollary 1, we substitute the quantity $\|\theta - \theta^*\|_2$ in the right-hand side of Inequality (15). This leads to an improved safe screening condition given by:

$$\|X_{I_i}^\top \theta\|_2 + \|X_{I_i}\|_2 \sqrt{2G(b,\theta)} < \lambda_{|\mathcal{A}^*|} \Rightarrow b_{I_i}^* = 0. \tag{21}$$

The duality gap $G(b,\theta)$ can be efficiently evaluated using the primal-dual variables b and θ, both of which are directly available during each iteration of standard proximal gradient methods.

As training proceeds and the gap between the primal and dual objectives narrows, the upper estimate of $\|X_{I_i}^\top \theta^*\|_2$ is reduced accordingly. This results in a progressively tighter screening threshold over time.

2.4 Lower Bound for the Right Term

In contrast, the upper limit of the screening region aligns with the minimal value of $\lambda_{|\mathcal{A}^*|}$. Therefore, our objective in this section is to derive a sharp lower estimate for this critical quantity.

To effectively compute this bound amidst numerous unspecified hyperparameters, we design an iterative scheme that tackles the challenges introduced by the non-separability of the penalty term. This is achieved by exploiting the unknown order structure embedded in the primal solution of (14). In its general form, our screening criterion can be formulated as:

$$\|X_{I_i}^\top \theta\|_2 + \|X_{I_i}\|_2 \sqrt{2G(b,\theta)} < \lambda_{|\mathcal{A}|} \Rightarrow b_{I_i}^* = 0. \tag{22}$$

At the initial stage, we assume all m groups are active, and hence the screening is applied with respect to λ_m:

$$\|X_{I_i}^\top \theta\|_2 + \|X_{I_i}\|_2 \sqrt{2G(b,\theta)} < \lambda_m \Rightarrow b_{I_i}^* = 0. \tag{23}$$

As training proceeds and only m_k groups remain active, the set $\mathcal{A}$ is updated to size m_k. The remaining $m - m_k$ groups can then be assigned any permutation of $\lambda_{m_k+1}, \ldots, \lambda_m$—the smallest parameters—without affecting the final result. This reveals that the ranks of the $m - m_k$ zero-valued coefficients are deterministically among the lowest values in the λ sequence. Accordingly, the screening test is adapted and evaluated at λ_{m_k}:

$$\|X_{I_i}^\top \theta\|_2 + \|X_{I_i}\|_2 \sqrt{2G(b,\theta)} < \lambda_{m_k} \Rightarrow b_{I_i}^* = 0, \tag{24}$$

yielding an updated active group set $\mathcal{A}$ of size m'_k, where $m'_k \leq m_k$. The $m_k - m'_k$ newly deactivated groups are again assigned the next smallest unused λ values.

This iterative refinement continues until convergence—i.e., when the active set stabilizes. Crucially, each iteration involves only a single hyperparameter, ensuring computational efficiency even when Group SLOPE involves a large number of tuning parameters.

Throughout this process, as the active set $\mathcal{A}$ shrinks and due to the monotonicity of λ, the corresponding $\lambda_{|\mathcal{A}|}$ increases. This raises the lower bound of $\lambda_{|\mathcal{A}^*|}$ and in turn, enlarges the screening threshold.

In summary, by jointly updating the upper and lower bounds across iterations, the screening region continuously expands, enabling more inactive groups to be excluded and improving overall algorithmic efficiency.

For the computation of the screening rule, the dual f_i^* for Group SLOPE can also be calculated as $f_i^*(\theta_i) = \frac{1}{2}\theta_i^2 + \theta_i y_i$. Using this screening rule, inactive feature groups can be eliminated during the training process.

3 Proposed Algorithms

In this section, we begin by applying the safe screening rules to proximal gradient algorithms, specifically focusing on the APGD algorithm for batch settings and the SPGD algorithm for stochastic settings. We then delve into the theoretical analysis of our unified safe screening rules, highlighting their properties in terms of safeness, convergence, and screening capability.

3.1 Algorithms

Coordinate descent and block coordinate descent methods are efficient for solving Lasso and Group Lasso problems. However, due to the challenges posed by the non-separable penalty, these algorithms are highly efficient but not practical for solving

Group SLOPE. To address this issue, accelerated proximal gradient descent (APGD) methods have been proposed, as seen in works like [10, 16].

Since Group SLOPE is generally used in high-dimensional settings, all the proximal algorithms mentioned above face significant computational and memory challenges when dealing with large feature sizes. Therefore, accelerating the training of Group SLOPE through the use of screening techniques for proximal algorithms becomes both important and promising.

For the APGD algorithm in batch settings, our approach involves repeatedly performing the screening test and updating the active set $\mathcal{A}$. If $\mathcal{A}$ is updated during this iteration, we set the step size $t_k = t_1$. From this point onward, the procedure mirrors that of the original APGD algorithm, using the current active set $\mathcal{A}$. This process is detailed in Algorithm 1.

Algorithm 1. APGD Algorithm with Our Safe Screening Rules

Input: $b^0, \hat{b}^1 = b^0, t_1 = 1$
1: **for** $k = 1, 2, \ldots$ **do**
2:    **repeat**
3:        Apply the safe screening from (22)
4:        Update the active group set $\mathcal{A}$
5:    **until** $\mathcal{A}$ remains unchanged
6:    **if** $\mathcal{A}$ was updated **then**
7:        $t_k = t_1$
8:    **end if**
9:    $b^k = prox_{t_k, \lambda}(\hat{b}^k - t_k \nabla F(\hat{b}^k))$
10:   $t_{k+1} = \frac{1}{2}(1 + \sqrt{1 + 4t_k^2})$
11:   $\hat{b}^{k+1} = b^k + \frac{t_k - 1}{t_{k+1}}(b^k - b^{k-1})$
12: **end for**
Output: Coefficient b

Moreover, as each update in Algorithm 1 relies on all samples, the per-iteration cost of the APGD algorithm can be substantial in large-scale learning because it necessitates full gradient computations. To mitigate this, the stochastic proximal gradient descent (SPGD) algorithm, as introduced in [38] and building on [20], serves as an efficient alternative in the stochastic setting, requiring only mini-batch gradient calculations.

In applying our screening rule to the SPGD algorithm for stochastic settings, we similarly repeat the screening test and update $\mathcal{A}$ in the outer loop before proceeding with the standard SPGD algorithm steps using the newly obtained active set. This procedure is outlined in Algorithm 2.

Interestingly, the duality gap, which represents the main time-consuming aspect of our screening rule, has already been computed in the original APGD and SPGD algorithms. Furthermore, as inactive variables are continually screened during optimization, and given that the active set size for iteration k is d_k, the computational complexity of the screening rule for this iteration is only $O(d_k)$, which is even less than the complexity of the original stopping criterion evaluation $O(d)$. Consequently, the complexity

Algorithm 2. SPGD Algorithm with Our Safe Screening Rules
___
Input: b^0, l.
1: **for** $k = 1, 2, \ldots$ **do**
2:   **repeat**
3:     Apply the safe screening from (22)
4:     Update the active group set $\mathcal{A}$
5:   **until** $\mathcal{A}$ remains unchanged
6:   $b = b^{k-1}$
7:   $\tilde{v} = \nabla F(b)$
8:   $\tilde{b}^0 = b$
9:   **for** $t = 1, 2, \ldots, T$ **do**
10:     Pick mini-batch $I_t \subseteq X$ of size l
11:     $v_t = (\nabla F_{I_t}(\tilde{b}^{t-1}) - \nabla F_{I_t}(b))/l + \tilde{v}$
12:     $\tilde{b}^t = prox_{\gamma, \lambda}(\tilde{b}^{t-1} - \gamma v_t)$
13:   **end for**
14:   $b^k = \tilde{b}^T$
15: **end for**
Output: Coefficient b
___

$O(d_k(n + \log d_k))$ and $O(d_k(n + Tl + T \log d_k))$ for each iteration of the APGD and SPGD algorithms, respectively, can be reduced to $O(d_k)$ for analysis purposes.

We further examine the overall complexity of our algorithms, focusing on both the per-iteration cost and the number of iterations. For per-iteration cost, if the algorithm has d_k active variables at iteration k, our Algorithm 1 requires only $O(d_k(n + \log d_k))$, which is less than the original APGD algorithm's complexity of $O(d(n + \log d))$. Regarding the number of iterations, since the optimal solution for the inactive features screened at iteration k must be zeros, removing these inactive features beforehand either keeps the objective function the same or decreases it. Thus, our Algorithm 1 will converge to the same stopping criterion with at most the same (and usually fewer) iterations compared to the original APGD algorithm. With fewer or the same iterations and lower per-iteration costs, our proposed algorithm is more efficient. Similarly, our Algorithm 2 requires $O(d_k(n+Tl+T \log d_k))$ for the main loop k, whereas the original SPGD algorithm's complexity is $O(d(n + Tl + T \log d))$. Since our algorithm also requires fewer or the same iterations and lower per-iteration costs, the overall complexity is reduced compared to the original SPGD algorithm.

More precisely, the computational advantage of our methods hinges on the sparsity of the final model. The training process gains more from the screening rule when dealing with sparser models. In cases where $n < d$, the final model becomes very sparse, leading to $d_k \ll d$ during training. Consequently, our method is particularly well-suited for high-dimensional settings. It is evident that the proposed algorithms consistently outperform the original ones in terms of speed. Additionally, it's important to note that our method also applies to datasets where $n > d$. Assuming the presence of sparsity, our screening rule will effectively identify inactive features, enabling our algorithms to determine the final active set in a finite number of iterations. As a result, we still achieve $d_k < d$ during training, and the per-iteration cost of our algorithm remains lower than the original one. Therefore, with fewer or an equivalent number of iterations and reduced per-iteration costs, the proposed algorithms remain faster than the original ones for $n > d$.

The following part provides the theoretical analysis of our screening rules, highlighting their safeness, convergence, and screening ability.

Property 1. (Safeness) The proposed screening rule retains all relevant groups throughout the entire optimization trajectory of Group SLOPE, irrespective of the specific iterative method employed.

Property 2. (Convergence) Our screening rule can be seamlessly embedded into a wide range of iterative algorithms, such as APGD, SPGD, and their derivatives, without disrupting convergence guarantees.

Theorem 1. *Let i denote any group that belongs to the final active set $\mathcal{A}^*$. Then $\|X_{I_i}^\top \theta^*\|_2 \in [\min_{j \in \mathcal{A}^*} \lambda_j, \max_{j \in \mathcal{A}^*} \lambda_j]$. As algorithm Ψ converges, there exists a finite iteration number $K_0 \in \mathbb{N}$ s.t. $\forall k \geq K_0$, any group $i \notin \mathcal{A}^*$ will be successfully discarded by the screening rule.*

Proof. From the strong concavity of the dual problem, it follows that the optimal dual variable θ^* is unique. Moreover, θ converges to θ^* as b converges to b^*. Thus, for any given $\epsilon > 0$, one can find an index K_0 s.t. $\forall k \geq K_0$: $\|\theta^k - \theta^*\|_2 \leq \epsilon$, $\sqrt{2G(b^k, \theta^k)} \leq \epsilon$. Then, for any group $i \notin \mathcal{A}^*$, we can bound the screening condition as:

$$\|X_{I_i}^\top \theta^k\|_2 + \|X_{I_i}\|_2 \sqrt{2G(b^k, \theta^k)}$$
$$\leq \|X_{I_i}\|_2 \|\theta^k - \theta^*\|_2 + \|X_{I_i}^\top \theta^*\|_2 + \|X_{I_i}\|_2 \sqrt{2G(b^k, \theta^k)}$$
$$\leq 2\|X_{I_i}\|_2 \epsilon + \|X_{I_i}^\top \theta^*\|_2. \tag{25}$$

Since $i \notin \mathcal{A}^*$ implies $\lambda_{|\mathcal{A}^*|} - \|X_{I_i}^\top \theta^*\|_2 > 0$, choosing $\epsilon < \frac{\lambda_{|\mathcal{A}^*|} - \|X_{I_i}^\top \theta^*\|_2}{2\|X_{I_i}\|_2}$, ensures $\|X_{I_i}^\top \theta^k\|_2 + \|X_{I_i}\|_2 \sqrt{2G(b^k, \theta^k)} < \lambda_{|\mathcal{A}^*|}$, which triggers our screening condition.

Theorem 1 highlights the strong screening performance of the proposed rules. As the iterative solver progresses and the duality gap narrows, the rule becomes increasingly effective: the upper bound on the left-hand side tightens, while the right-hand side's lower bound increases. This progressively improves the chances of filtering out inactive groups. Ultimately, every group $i \notin \mathcal{A}^*$ will be accurately screened and discarded in a finite number of iterations.

4 Experiments

In this section, we outline our experimental setup and subsequently present the results and discussions.

4.1 Experimental Setup

Design of Experiments. We empirically evaluated our method on real-world benchmark datasets under the Group SLOPE framework, highlighting its computational advantages and its capability to reliably discard irrelevant groups.

To assess the efficiency of our algorithms in reducing computation time, we compared the runtime of our proposed algorithms against other competitive algorithms for solving Group SLOPE under various conditions. Given that the APGD algorithm is well-suited for scenarios where $n \ll p$ in the batch setting, and the SPGD algorithm is tailored for large-scale learning where n is large in stochastic settings, we evaluated the runtime across both batch and stochastic setups using different datasets. The algorithms compared in batch and stochastic settings are summarized as follows:

- Batch setting
    - APGD: Accelerated proximal gradient descent algorithms as presented in [10, 16].
    - APGD + Screening: Accelerated proximal gradient descent algorithms enhanced with our safe screening rules.
- Stochastic setting
    - SPGD: Stochastic proximal gradient descent algorithm adopted from [38].
    - SPGD + Screening: Stochastic proximal gradient descent algorithm integrated with our safe screening rules.

Table 2. The descriptions of benchmark datasets used in our experiments.

Dataset	Sample size	Attribute
Duke Breast Cancer (DBC)	44	7129
Colon Cancer (CC)	62	2000
IndoorLoc (IL)	21048	520
SenseIT Vehicle (SV)	78823	100

To further confirm the effectiveness of our algorithms in filtering inactive variables, we evaluated the screening rate at each iteration of the algorithms with our screening rules applied to Group SLOPE, tested in both batch and stochastic setups across various datasets during the training process.

Datasets. Table 2 provides an overview of the benchmark datasets utilized in our experiments. Duke Breast Cancer, Colon Cancer, and SenseIT Vehicle datasets are from the LIBSVM repository [11], which can be accessed at https://www.csie.ntu.edu.tw/~cjlin/libsvmtools/datasets/. IndoorLoc dataset is obtained from the UCI benchmark repository [12], available at https://archive.ics.uci.edu/ml/datasets.php. IndoorLoc dataset includes 2 tasks: IndoorLoc Latitude and IndoorLoc Longitude.

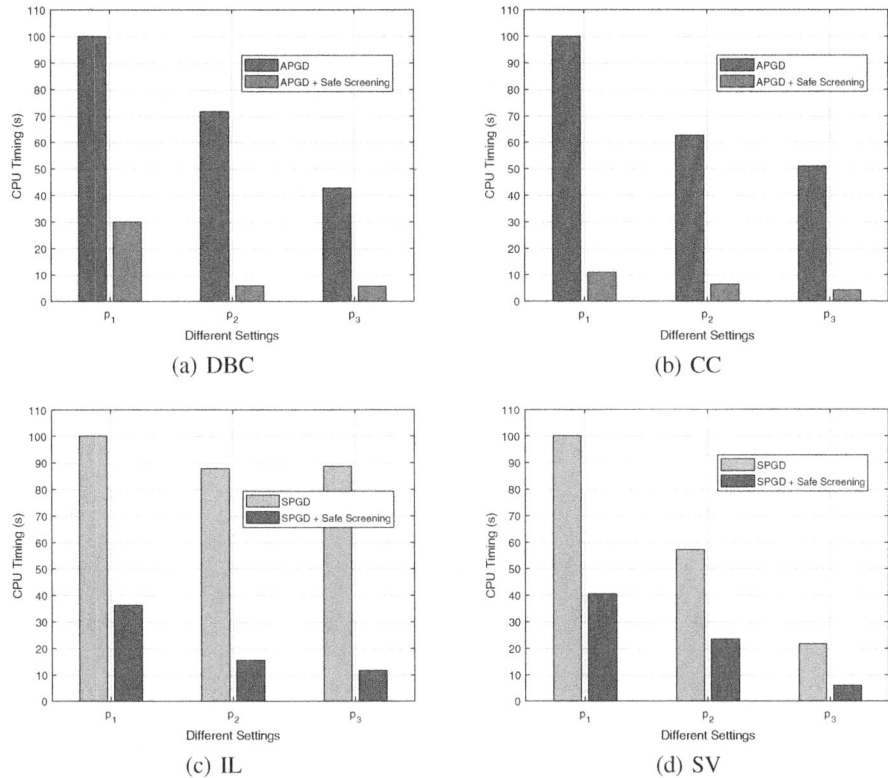

Fig. 1. Running time of the algorithms without and with safe screening for Group SLOPE.

Implementation Details. We implemented all the algorithms using MATLAB and compared the average CPU time across different algorithms on a 2.70 GHz machine over 5 trials. We adhered to the basic setup described in [10] and set the tolerance for the duality gap and the dual infeasibility to 10^{-6}. To ensure fairness in comparisons, the experimental configurations for Algorithm 1 and 2 followed the original APGD and SPGD algorithms, maintaining consistent hyperparameters across all setups. In the stochastic setting, the mini-batch size and the number of inner loop iterations were set to 30 or 40, depending on the dataset. The step size γ was selected from a range of 10^{-8} to 10^{-5}. Initially, the APGD algorithms exhibited a large duality gap, offering minimal benefit from our screening rule, so we first ran the algorithms without screening and later applied our screening rule with a warm start. For ease of comparison, the CPU time of each algorithm is presented as a percentage relative to the runtime of the first configuration for each dataset.

The OSCAR hyperparameter setting, which is commonly used (see [1,27,40,42]), was applied in all our experiments:

$$\lambda_i = \alpha_1 + \alpha_2(m - i), \tag{26}$$

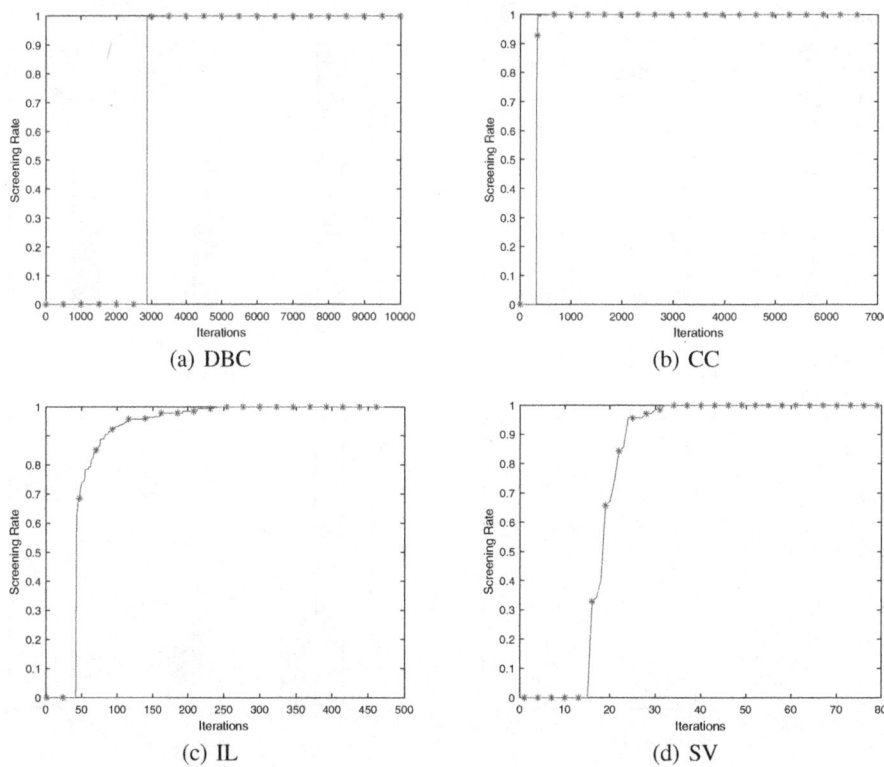

Fig. 2. Screening rate of our screening rule in both batch and stochastic settings for Group SLOPE.

where $\alpha_1 = p_i \|X^\top y\|_\infty$ and $\alpha_2 = \alpha_1/d$ for Group SLOPE. For a fair comparison, the factor p_i is used to control sparsity. In our experiments, we set $p_i = i * e^{-\tau}, i = 1, 2, 3$.

For Group SLOPE, batch algorithms were applied to the Duke Breast Cancer and Colon Cancer datasets, while stochastic algorithms were run on the SenseIT and IndoorLoc Longitude datasets, with τ set to 2 for IndoorLoc Longitude and 3 for the other datasets. We duplicate each feature i to form the feature group I_i with size $|I_i| \sim U(1, s)$ where U is the discrete uniform distribution and choose $s = 10$ for Duke Breast Cancer and Colon Cancer datasets and $s = 40$ for IndoorLoc Latitude and SenseIT Vehicle datasets.

To assess the screening rate of our algorithms, it was calculated as the proportion of inactive partitions of groups screened by our method to the total number of inactive groups at the optimal solution. We used the p_1 setting for this evaluation.

4.2 Experimental Results and Discussions

Figures 1(a)–(d) present the average runtime comparisons of the proposed algorithms with and without the safe screening technique applied to Group SLOPE, under both batch and stochastic optimization frameworks across multiple experimental settings. In cases where the sample size is much smaller than the number of features ($n \ll d$), the APGD method achieves acceleration ratios between 3× and 14× when integrated with our screening approach. For large-scale problems, incorporating the screening rule into the SPGD variant leads to speed improvements ranging from 2.5× to 8× compared to its unscreened counterpart. These observations consistently validate the substantial efficiency gains attained by augmenting Group SLOPE solvers—both batch and stochastic—with our screening mechanism. The primary contributor to this acceleration is the effective early-stage exclusion of inactive feature groups, which lowers the computational complexity throughout training. Notably, the improvements become even more pronounced as the data dimensionality increases and sparsity intensifies.

Figures 2(a)–(d) depict the screening rates of our algorithms in both batch and stochastic settings for Group SLOPE, highlighting the effectiveness and characteristics of our screening rule. The data support the conclusion that our algorithm can successfully eliminate most inactive feature groups at an early stage, converge on the final active set, and ultimately screen nearly all inactive features within a finite number of iterations. This effectiveness is due to the tight upper and lower bounds of the screening test's left and right terms, respectively, which allow for more efficient screening of inactive variables as the optimization algorithm progresses. Specifically, as the algorithm converges, the duality gap narrows, leading to a continuously decreasing upper bound for the left term of the screening test, while the iterative strategy increasingly solidifies the order structure of variables, thus continuously increasing the lower bound for the right term.

5 Conclusion

In this paper, we introduced a safe variable screening rule for Group SLOPE, addressing the challenges posed by the non-separable group effects. This approach significantly speeds up the training process by eliminating unnecessary computations for inactive variables. Our screening rule is uniquely dynamic, featuring a decreasing left term through tracking the intermediate duality gap, and an increasing right term by iteratively assessing the order of the primal solution, considering the unknown order structure. Importantly, the proposed rules are seamlessly integrable into existing iterative optimization methods, applicable in both batch and stochastic settings, such as the APGD and SPGD algorithms. We have theoretically proven that our screening rule remains safe when applied to these algorithms, ensuring no loss in accuracy. Extensive empirical results on real-world benchmark datasets demonstrate that our algorithms provide substantial computational benefits while maintaining accuracy in both batch and stochastic learning contexts by effectively screening out inactive variables.

Acknowledgement. This work is supported in part by the National Science Foundation (NSF) grant IIS-2451436 and Commonwealth Cyber Initiative grant HC-4Q24-059.

References

1. Bao, R., Gu, B., Huang, H.: Efficient approximate solution path algorithm for order weight l_1-norm with accuracy guarantee. In: 2019 IEEE International Conference on Data Mining (ICDM), pp. 958–963. IEEE (2019)
2. Bao, R., Gu, B., Huang, H.: Fast OSCAR and OWL regression via safe screening rules. In: International Conference on Machine Learning, pp. 653–663. PMLR (2020)
3. Bao, R., Gu, B., Huang, H.: An accelerated doubly stochastic gradient method with faster explicit model identification. In: Proceedings of the 31st ACM International Conference on Information & Knowledge Management, pp. 57–66 (2022)
4. Bao, R., Lu, Q., Zhang, Y.: Safe screening rules for group owl models. arXiv preprint arXiv:2504.03152 (2025)
5. Bao, R., Wu, X., Xian, W., Huang, H.: Doubly sparse asynchronous learning. In: The 31st International Joint Conference on Artificial Intelligence (IJCAI 2022) (2022)
6. Bauschke, H.H., Combettes, P.L., et al.: Convex Analysis and Monotone Operator Theory in Hilbert Spaces, vol. 408. Springer, Cham (2011). https://doi.org/10.1007/978-3-319-48311-5
7. Bergersen, L.C., Glad, I.K., Lyng, H.: Weighted lasso with data integration. Stat. Appl. Genet. Mol. Biol. **10**(1) (2011)
8. Bogdan, M., Van Den Berg, E., Sabatti, C., Su, W., Candès, E.J.: Slope–adaptive variable selection via convex optimization. Ann. Appl. Stat. **9**(3), 667–698 (2015)
9. Bonnefoy, A., Emiya, V., Ralaivola, L., Gribonval, R.: Dynamic screening: accelerating first-order algorithms for the lasso and group-lasso. IEEE Trans. Signal Process. **63**(19), 5121–5132 (2015)
10. Brzyski, D., Gossmann, A., Su, W., Bogdan, M.: Group slope-adaptive selection of groups of predictors. J. Am. Stat. Assoc. **114**(525), 419–433 (2019)
11. Chang, C.C., Lin, C.J.: LIBSVM: a library for support vector machines. ACM Trans. Intell. Syst. Technol. (TIST) **2**(3), 1–27 (2011)
12. Dua, D., Graff, C.: UCI machine learning repository (2017)
13. Fercoq, O., Gramfort, A., Salmon, J.: Mind the duality gap: safer rules for the lasso. In: International Conference on Machine Learning, pp. 333–342 (2015)
14. Frankle, J., Carbin, M.: The lottery ticket hypothesis: finding sparse, trainable neural networks. In: International Conference on Learning Representations (2018)
15. Gossmann, A., Cao, S., Brzyski, D., Zhao, L.J., Deng, H.W., Wang, Y.P.: A sparse regression method for group-wise feature selection with false discovery rate control. IEEE/ACM Trans. Comput. Biol. Bioinf. **15**(4), 1066–1078 (2017)
16. Gossmann, A., Cao, S., Wang, Y.P.: Identification of significant genetic variants via slope, and its extension to group slope. In: Proceedings of the 6th ACM Conference on Bioinformatics, Computational Biology and Health Informatics, pp. 232–240 (2015)
17. Han, S., Pool, J., Tran, J., Dally, W.: Learning both weights and connections for efficient neural network. Adv. Neural Inf. Process. Syst. **28** (2015)
18. Jacob, L., Obozinski, G., Vert, J.P.: Group lasso with overlap and graph lasso. In: Proceedings of the 26th Annual International Conference on Machine Learning, pp. 433–440 (2009)
19. Jenatton, R., Audibert, J.Y., Bach, F.: Structured variable selection with sparsity-inducing norms. J. Mach. Learn. Res. **12**, 2777–2824 (2011)
20. Johnson, R., Zhang, T.: Accelerating stochastic gradient descent using predictive variance reduction. In: Advances in Neural Information Processing Systems, pp. 315–323 (2013)
21. Johnson, T., Guestrin, C.: BLITZ: a principled meta-algorithm for scaling sparse optimization. In: International Conference on Machine Learning, pp. 1171–1179 (2015)

22. Kim, S., Xing, E.P.: Tree-guided group lasso for multi-task regression with structured sparsity. In: Proceedings of the 27th International Conference on International Conference on Machine Learning, pp. 543–550 (2010)
23. Larsson, J., Bogdan, M., Wallin, J.: The strong screening rule for slope. Adv. Neural. Inf. Process. Syst. **33**, 14592–14603 (2020)
24. El Ghaoui, L., Vivian Viallon, T.R. Safe feature elimination in sparse supervised learning. Pac. J. Optim. **8**, 667–698 (2012)
25. Lu, L., et al.: All-in-one tuning and structural pruning for domain-specific LLMs. arXiv preprint arXiv:2412.14426 (2024)
26. Ndiaye, E., Fercoq, O., Gramfort, A., Salmon, J.: Gap safe screening rules for sparse-group lasso. In: Advances in Neural Information Processing Systems, pp. 388–396 (2016)
27. Oswal, U., Cox, C., Lambon-Ralph, M., Rogers, T., Nowak, R.: Representational similarity learning with application to brain networks. In: International Conference on Machine Learning, pp. 1041–1049 (2016)
28. Rakotomamonjy, A., Gasso, G., Salmon, J.: Screening rules for lasso with non-convex sparse regularizers. In: International Conference on Machine Learning, pp. 5341–5350 (2019)
29. Shibagaki, A., Karasuyama, M., Hatano, K., Takeuchi, I.: Simultaneous safe screening of features and samples in doubly sparse modeling. In: International Conference on Machine Learning, pp. 1577–1586 (2016)
30. Simon, N., Friedman, J., Hastie, T., Tibshirani, R.: A sparse-group lasso. J. Comput. Graph. Stat. **22**(2), 231–245 (2013)
31. Tibshirani, R., et al.: Strong rules for discarding predictors in lasso-type problems. J. R. Stat. Soc. Ser. B Stat. Methodol. **74**(2), 245–266 (2012)
32. Wang, J., Ye, J.: Two-layer feature reduction for sparse-group lasso via decomposition of convex sets. In: Advances in Neural Information Processing Systems, pp. 2132–2140 (2014)
33. Wang, J., Ye, J.: Multi-layer feature reduction for tree structured group lasso via hierarchical projection. In: Advances in Neural Information Processing Systems, pp. 1279–1287 (2015)
34. Wang, J., Zhou, J., Liu, J., Wonka, P., Ye, J.: A safe screening rule for sparse logistic regression. In: Advances in Neural Information Processing Systems, pp. 1053–1061 (2014)
35. Wang, J., Zhou, J., Wonka, P., Ye, J.: Lasso screening rules via dual polytope projection. In: Advances in Neural Information Processing Systems, pp. 1070–1078 (2013)
36. Wu, X., et al.: Auto-train-once: controller network guided automatic network pruning from scratch. In: Proceedings of the IEEE/CVF Conference on Computer Vision and Pattern Recognition, pp. 16163–16173 (2024)
37. Xiang, Z.J., Wang, Y., Ramadge, P.J.: Screening tests for lasso problems. IEEE Trans. Pattern Anal. Mach. Intell. **39**(5), 1008–1027 (2016)
38. Xiao, L., Zhang, T.: A proximal stochastic gradient method with progressive variance reduction. SIAM J. Optim. **24**(4), 2057–2075 (2014)
39. Yuan, M., Lin, Y.: Model selection and estimation in regression with grouped variables. J. R. Stat. Soc. B Stat. Methodol. **68**(1), 49–67 (2006)
40. Zhang, D., Wang, H., Figueiredo, M., Balzano, L.: Learning to share: Simultaneous parameter tying and sparsification in deep learning (2018)
41. Zhao, P., Rocha, G., Yu, B.: The composite absolute penalties family for grouped and hierarchical variable selection. Ann. Stat. **37**(6A), 3468–3497 (2009)
42. Zhong, L.W., Kwok, J.T.: Efficient sparse modeling with automatic feature grouping. IEEE Trans. Neural Netw. Learn. Syst. **23**(9), 1436–1447 (2012)

Efficient Bayesian Updates for Deep Active Learning via Laplace Approximations

Denis Huseljic[✉], Marek Herde, Lukas Rauch, Paul Hahn, Zhixin Huang, Daniel Kottke, Stephan Vogt, and Bernhard Sick

Intelligent Embedded Systems, University of Kassel, Kassel, Germany
dhuseljic@uni-kassel.de

Abstract. Deep active learning (AL) selects batches of instances for annotation to avoid retraining deep neural networks (DNNs) after each new label. Employing a naive top-b selection can result in a batch of redundant (similar) instances. To address this, various AL strategies employ clustering techniques that ensure diversity within a batch. We approach this issue by substituting the costly retraining with an efficient Bayesian update. Our proposed update represents a second-order optimization step using the Gaussian posterior from a last-layer Laplace approximation. Thereby, we achieve low computational complexity by computing the inverse Hessian in closed form. We demonstrate that in typical AL settings, our update closely approximates retraining while being considerably faster. Leveraging our update, we introduce a new framework for batch selection through sequential construction, updating the DNN after each label acquisition. Furthermore, we incorporate our update into a look-ahead selection strategy as a feasible upper baseline approximating optimal batch selection. Our results highlight the potential of efficient updates to advance deep AL research.

Keywords: Deep Active Learning · Batch Selection · Bayesian Updates

1 Introduction

Active Learning (AL) sequentially selects instances for annotation by human experts, aiming to maximize model performance while minimizing labeling efforts. When combined with deep neural networks (DNNs), AL typically selects instances in batches rather than one at a time. The reason for this is that retraining DNNs after each label acquisition is computationally expensive, and delay can lead to additional costs since annotators' time is valuable [18].

In a naive top-b batch selection, a batch of b instances with the highest scores is chosen based on an informativeness measure. However, when many similar instances are present, this approach can result in significant redundancy within the batch (similar instances have a similar score). Many selection strategies have

---

Supplementary Information The online version contains supplementary material available at https://doi.org/10.1007/978-3-032-05981-9_2.

been developed to replace this naive selection [15]. These strategies often employ clustering techniques to ensure diverse batches, ensuring that instances within a batch are dissimilar to one another [15]. While effective in reducing redundancy, clustering does not guarantee optimal selection due to its heuristic motivation.

Orthogonal to these strategies, we explore the concept of efficient "retraining" in deep AL. If retraining were computationally feasible, researchers could place greater emphasis on the development of theoretically sound informativeness measures instead of using heuristic clustering approaches to ensure diversity. Additionally, selection strategies that aim to maximize future performance–strategies that have been shown to be near-optimal in traditional AL [34]–could be made feasible with DNNs. Therefore, we examine the concept of updating DNNs through a single optimization step as a proxy for retraining and explore its potential to enhance the AL process.

To underscore the requirements of such an update, consider strategies designed to maximize future performance. Typically, these use a look-ahead to select instances that significantly change model predictions. Specifically, they examine how adding unlabeled instances to the labeled pool and retraining the model affects predictions [34]. However, with a large number of unlabeled instances and the costly retraining process of DNNs, this approach becomes infeasible in deep AL. Therefore, instead of retraining, a highly efficient update method is required. The only work to realize this with DNNs is by [39], which employ an ensemble of DNNs combined with Monte Carlo (MC) updates via Bayes' theorem. Although this update makes a look-ahead feasible, it remains suboptimal for several reasons: (i) the update requires an ensemble of DNNs, making the actual retraining time and memory demands inefficient; (ii) the update does not accurately reflect the performance of full retraining; and (iii) the updating process becomes inefficient with an increasing number of ensemble members.

In this article, we propose an efficient update method for DNNs in the context of AL for classification. Specifically, we transform an arbitrary DNN into a Bayesian neural network (BNN) by employing a last-layer Laplace approximation (LA) [8]. While the closed-form expression of the posterior allows us to leverage second-order optimization techniques, we ensure low computational complexity by computing the required inverse Hessian analytically. Unlike the MC-based update used in [39], our approach does not require an ensemble of DNNs, making it easily applicable and both memory- and training-efficient [8]. Additionally, as we utilize a single DNN, we can leverage pretrained foundation models [30], which are an essential part of modern AL strategies [14,15]. The resulting update is fast and closely matches the performance of full retraining. Extensive studies across different data modalities demonstrate that our updates outperform the typically employed MC-based ones [39] in terms of speed and performance. Furthermore, we examine the proposed update in two distinct AL scenarios:

1. **Enhancing Existing Strategies with Immediate Label Utilization:** We propose a simple framework to improve existing strategies by immediately making use of acquired labels through the proposed updates. Rather than

selecting the top-b highest-scoring instances simultaneously, we iteratively select the highest-scoring instance b times *but* update the model between each selection. This simple strategy, which approximates single-instance AL during batch construction, performs surprisingly well, outperforming naive top-b selection as well as selection strategies that employ clustering.
2. **Optimal AL with Look-Ahead Selection:** We investigate the potential of our update with a look-ahead selection strategy in an optimal AL setting. Specifically, we approximate an optimal selection strategy that maximizes future performance. Instead of retraining, we ensure computational feasibility by employing our update. The resulting strategy outperforms all competitors, showcasing that currently employed selection strategies have much potential for improvement.

Summary of Contributions

Efficient DNN Update: We propose an efficient update method for DNNs that employs a Laplace approximation and second-order optimization techniques. We enable low computational complexity through closed-form computation of the inverse Hessian.

Comprehensive Evaluation: We perform an extensive evaluation across data modalities, demonstrating that our update outperforms MC-based updates in both speed and accuracy.

Immediate Label Utilization: We develop a simple framework that employs our update to immediately incorporate acquired labels, improving existing selection strategies by updating the model during batch construction.

Optimal AL with Look-Ahead: We study our update in an optimal AL setting, making a near-optimal selection strategy as an upper baseline computationally feasible.

---

2 Related Work

Pool-based deep AL strategies can be divided into three types. Uncertainty-based methods, such as margin sampling [3,37] and BALD [13], assume that instances with high predictive uncertainty are most informative. When selecting batches, these strategies pick the top-b highest-scoring instances, leading to redundancy. In contrast, diversity-based approaches like Core-Set [36] aim to select a diverse batch of instances by considering the feature representations of labeled and unlabeled data. In practice, *hybrid strategies*, a combination of both types, have been shown to work well. BatchBALD [20] extends BALD by reducing redundant information within a batch. Badge [1] selects instances with high gradient norms and ensures diversity by employing k-MEANS++ in the gradient space. Typiclust [15] replaces the notion of uncertainty with typicality and selects typical instances from clusters obtained through k-MEANS.

Look-ahead strategies [34] remain underexplored in deep AL. They aim to select instances expected to improve the model's performance the most by retraining for all possible candidate instances. In non-deep settings, such approaches have been shown to achieve near-optimal selection [34] while offering convergence guarantees [45]. However, adapting these strategies to deep AL is challenging due to the computational cost of retraining. To the best of our knowledge, BEMPS [39] is the only strategy to implement a look-ahead mechanism in deep AL. They employ deep ensembles and MC-based updates via Bayes' theorem (see Sect. 3). while this update is computationally efficient, we show that its performance falls short compared to full model retraining.

Continual learning [9] updates models by only using new data, retaining knowledge from the previous one. Related techniques [17,33] use conventional first-order optimization methods, deriving regularization terms from an LA that penalizes large deviations from prior knowledge. Unlike our method, these approaches require training over multiple epochs for the regularization term to have an impact. Used as an update (i.e., single optimization step), these strategies simplify to a first-order gradient step. Additionally, they assume large amounts of new data per task (thousands of instances), whereas our update method is designed batch construction in AL, ranging from a single to hundreds of instances. For example, a typical benchmark is to extend a dataset with a task consisting of all instance-label pairs of a new class (ca. 5,000 in MNIST).

More closely related to our work is **online learning** [16], which aims to sequentially and efficiently update models from incoming data streams. Traditional approaches often focus on linear [46] or shallow [21] models with maximum-margin classification. However, applying online learning to DNNs remains difficult due to issues such as convergence, vanishing gradients, and large model sizes [35,43]. [35] proposed a method that modifies a DNN's architecture to facilitate updates. We argue that this is restrictive in state-of-the-art settings, given the increasing reliance on pretrained foundation models [10,30]. Recently, [19] proposed Bayesian online inference, which is also used in [39]. This method samples hypotheses (e.g., via MC-Dropout) from a BNN's posterior and weights them by the likelihood for new arriving data. However, the empirical results raise concerns about its feasibility in high-dimensional parameter spaces. We refer to these as MC-based updates.

BNNs [40] induce a prior distribution on parameters of a DNN and learn a posterior distribution given data. MC-Dropout [12] uses dropout to obtain a distribution over predictions. While it is simple to use, its inference is inefficient, and it provides suboptimal uncertainty estimates [31]. Deep ensembles [23] are known for their superior uncertainty estimates but are train and memory inefficient [31]. LAs [8] approximate the posterior as a Gaussian, with the MAP estimate as the mean and the inverse Hessian as the covariance. As computing this Hessian is expensive for large DNNs, LA is often used only in the last layer [8].

Finally, we consider related approaches focusing on the **efficiency of AL**. Prior work [6] shows that smaller more efficient proxy models can be used for AL selection with minimal performance loss. Building on this, [44] employed the last layer of a DNN as a proxy model in their benchmark. Other efforts to improve efficiency revolve around sub-sampling strategies with warm starts [7].

In contrast, rather than improving efficiency of the AL cycle, we update the DNN *while constructing the batch*, immediately incorporating label information that guides the construction process.

3 Fast Bayesian Updates for Deep Neural Networks

In this section, we first introduce the general concept of Bayesian updates together with the variant MC-based updates [19,39]. Afterward, we propose our novel method focusing on an efficient update of the Gaussian posterior distribution via last-layer LAs. For an introduction to LA, we refer to [8].

3.1 Bayesian Updates

We focus on classification problems with instance space $\mathcal{X}$ and label space $\mathcal{Y} = \{0, \ldots, K-1\}$. The primary goal in our setting is to efficiently incorporate the information of new instance-label pairs $\mathcal{D}^\oplus = \{(\boldsymbol{x}_n, y_n)\}_{n=1}^N \subset \mathcal{X} \times \mathcal{Y}$ into a DNN trained on dataset $\mathcal{D} \subset \mathcal{X} \times \mathcal{Y}$. Retraining the entire network on the extended dataset $\mathcal{D} \cup \mathcal{D}^\oplus$ results in high computational cost for a large dataset $\mathcal{D}$. Conversely, using the new data solely can cause catastrophic forgetting [33].

For this purpose, we employ BNNs with Bayesian updates as an efficient alternative to retraining. The main idea of BNNs is to estimate the posterior distribution $p(\boldsymbol{\omega}|\mathcal{D})$ over the parameters $\boldsymbol{\omega} \in \Omega$ given the observed training data $\mathcal{D}$ using Bayes' theorem. The obtained posterior distribution over the parameters can then be used to specify the predictive distribution over a new instance's class membership via marginalization:

$$p(y|\boldsymbol{x}, \mathcal{D}) = \mathbb{E}_{p(\boldsymbol{\omega}|\mathcal{D})}[p(y|\boldsymbol{x}, \boldsymbol{\omega})] = \int p(y|\boldsymbol{x}, \boldsymbol{\omega}) p(\boldsymbol{\omega}|\mathcal{D}) \, d\boldsymbol{\omega}. \tag{1}$$

Thereby, the likelihood $p(y|\boldsymbol{x}, \boldsymbol{\omega}) = [\mathrm{softmax}(f^\omega(\boldsymbol{x}))]_y$ denotes the probabilistic output of a DNN with parameters $\boldsymbol{\omega}$, where $f^\omega : \mathcal{X} \to \mathbb{R}^K$ is a function outputting class-wise logits.[1]

The formulation in Eq. 1 provides a theoretically sound way to obtain updated predictions. In particular, this is because the probabilistic outputs $p(y|\boldsymbol{x}, \boldsymbol{\omega})$ do not directly depend on the training data $\mathcal{D}$. Consequently, to obtain an updated predictive distribution, we do not need to update the parameters $\boldsymbol{\omega}$ directly but only the posterior distribution $p(\boldsymbol{\omega}|\mathcal{D})$. The updated posterior distribution $p(\boldsymbol{\omega}|\mathcal{D}, \mathcal{D}^\oplus)$ is found through Bayes' theorem, where the current posterior distribution $p(\boldsymbol{\omega}|\mathcal{D})$ is considered the prior and multiplied with the likelihood $p(y|\boldsymbol{x}, \boldsymbol{\omega})$ per instance-label pair $(\boldsymbol{x}, y) \in \mathcal{D}^\oplus$. As instances in $\mathcal{D}$ and $\mathcal{D}^\oplus$ are assumed to be independently distributed, we can simplify the likelihood and reformulate the parameter distribution as follows[2]:

$$p(\boldsymbol{\omega}|\mathcal{D}^\oplus, \mathcal{D}) \propto p(\boldsymbol{\omega}|\mathcal{D}) p(\mathcal{D}^\oplus|\mathcal{D}, \boldsymbol{\omega}) \stackrel{\text{i.i.d.}}{=} p(\boldsymbol{\omega}|\mathcal{D}) p(\mathcal{D}^\oplus|\boldsymbol{\omega}) = p(\boldsymbol{\omega}|\mathcal{D}) \prod_{(\boldsymbol{x}, y) \in \mathcal{D}^\oplus} p(y|\boldsymbol{x}, \boldsymbol{\omega}). \tag{2}$$

We refer to Eq. 2 as the *Bayesian update*.

---

[1] We denote the i-th element of a vector $\boldsymbol{b}$ as $[\boldsymbol{b}]_i = b_i$.
[2] We denote $p(y_1, \ldots, y_N \mid \boldsymbol{x}_1, \ldots, \boldsymbol{x}_N, \boldsymbol{\omega})$ with $\mathcal{D} = \{(\boldsymbol{x}_n, y_n)\}_{n=1}^N$ as $p(\mathcal{D}|\boldsymbol{\omega})$.

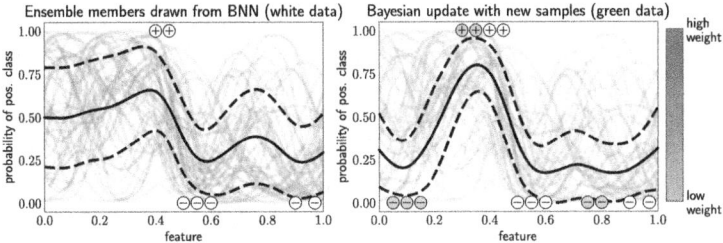

Fig. 1. The left plot shows the predicted probabilities of the positive class for each hypothesis (colored lines) drawn from a BNN as well as the mean (black solid line) and standard deviation (black dashed line) of its predictive distribution. The right plot shows updated weights for each hypothesis and the predictive distribution after observing additional instances (green). (Color figure online)

The most common realization [19,39] of this update is through MC-based BNNs, such as MC-Dropout and deep ensembles. These BNNs rely on samples (or hypotheses) $\omega_1, \ldots, \omega_M$ drawn from an approximate posterior $q(\omega|\mathcal{D})$. Research [19,39] assumes that all hypotheses are equally likely to explain the observed data and have the same probability before updating. By updating the posterior distribution through Eq. (2), they weigh more likely hypotheses given the new data higher. We refer to these as MC-based updates with a formal definition given in Appendix A. Figure 1 illustrates this concept where different hypotheses $\omega_1, \ldots, \omega_M \sim q(\omega|\mathcal{D})$ are shown. Each hypothesis represents a possible true solution for the learning task (white instances). When new data (green instances) arrives, we weigh each hypothesis by its likelihood of explaining the new data and obtain an updated prediction without retraining. This results in an updated predictive distribution, as seen in bold in Fig. 1 (right).

3.2 Fast Approximations of Bayesian Updates for Deep Neural Networks

Our update method is based on a combination of two concepts. First, instead of MC-based BNNs, we suggest using LAs on the last layer of a DNN. Second, we directly modify the approximate posterior distribution of the LA, providing a much more flexible way to adapt it to new data than reweighting. In the following, we explain each component in detail. For now, we focus on binary classification with $K = 2$, and refer to Appendix C for an extension to multi-class classification.

Last-Layer LA: LAs approximate the (intractable) posterior distribution $p(\omega|\mathcal{D})$ with a Gaussian centered on the maximum a posteriori (MAP) estimate with a covariance equal to the negative Hessian of the log posterior [8]. We denote this approximate distribution as

$$q(\omega|\mathcal{D}) = \mathcal{N}(\omega|\hat{\mu}, \hat{\Sigma}) \propto q(\omega) \prod_{(x,y) \in \mathcal{D}} p(y|x, \omega), \quad (3)$$

where $q(\boldsymbol{\omega})$ is a Gaussian prior distribution. The MAP estimate $\hat{\boldsymbol{\mu}}$ results from training on $\mathcal{D}$ with conventional gradient optimization techniques. The covariance matrix $\hat{\boldsymbol{\Sigma}}$ is the inverse Hessian of the negative log posterior evaluated at the MAP estimate $\hat{\boldsymbol{\mu}}$ given training data $\mathcal{D}$. We model the posterior distribution only on the last layer of a DNN to ensure fast inference.

The benefits of using a last-layer LA are manifold. Given access to $q(\boldsymbol{\omega}|\mathcal{D})$ through a Gaussian, we enable *more flexible updates* compared to MC-based ones, as we can directly modify the mean and covariance. In contrast, MC-based updates only change the approximate distribution by reweighting hypotheses, leading to a strong dependency on the samples $\boldsymbol{\omega}_1, \ldots, \boldsymbol{\omega}_M$. Last-layer LAs can be *integrated seamlessly* into nearly all DNNs, including pretrained models, as only the covariance has to be computed to obtain $q(\boldsymbol{\omega}|\mathcal{D})$. This is particularly important in deep AL, where recent findings highlight self-supervised learning as a crucial factor in selecting informative instances [14,15]. Finally, compared to deep ensembles and MC-Dropout, last-layer LAs introduce *minimal computational overhead*. While deep ensembles require longer training and MC-dropout impairs the inference time, LAs simply need to calculate a covariance matrix after training and allow fast inference through techniques such as mean-field approximation [27].

Second-Order Update: The second concept focuses on the update step of the Gaussian distribution. Observing new data, we follow the same approach as in Eq. 3, but with $q(\boldsymbol{\omega}|\mathcal{D})$ as our prior:

$$q(\boldsymbol{\omega}|\mathcal{D}, \mathcal{D}^{\oplus}) = \mathcal{N}(\boldsymbol{\omega}|\hat{\boldsymbol{\mu}}^{\text{upd}}, \hat{\boldsymbol{\Sigma}}^{\text{upd}}) \propto q(\boldsymbol{\omega}|\mathcal{D}) \prod_{(\boldsymbol{x},y)\in\mathcal{D}^{\oplus}} p(y|\boldsymbol{x},\boldsymbol{\omega}), \quad (4)$$

where $\hat{\boldsymbol{\mu}}^{\text{upd}}$ and $\hat{\boldsymbol{\Sigma}}^{\text{upd}}$ represent the updated mean and covariance, respectively. The resulting updated posterior $q(\boldsymbol{\omega}|\mathcal{D}, \mathcal{D}^{\oplus})$ is non-Gaussian due to $p(y|\boldsymbol{x},\boldsymbol{\omega})$ being a categorical likelihood. Consequently, the closed-form computation of the integral in Eq. (1) becomes intractable. The basic idea of our update is to approximate the new posterior $q(\boldsymbol{\omega}|\mathcal{D}, \mathcal{D}^{\oplus})$ by first applying a second-order optimization step via Gauss-Newton and then estimating the new covariance at that point. Thus, the updated mean and covariance are given by:

$$\hat{\boldsymbol{\mu}}^{\text{upd}} = \hat{\boldsymbol{\mu}} - \gamma \boldsymbol{H}^{-1}(\hat{\boldsymbol{\mu}}, \hat{\boldsymbol{\Sigma}}, \mathcal{D}^{\oplus}) \sum_{(\boldsymbol{x},y)\in\mathcal{D}^{\oplus}} (p_{\boldsymbol{x}} - y)\boldsymbol{h}_{\boldsymbol{x}}, \quad (5)$$

$$\hat{\boldsymbol{\Sigma}}^{\text{upd}} = \boldsymbol{H}^{-1}(\hat{\boldsymbol{\mu}}^{\text{upd}}, \hat{\boldsymbol{\Sigma}}, \mathcal{D}^{\oplus}), \quad (6)$$

where $\boldsymbol{h}_{\boldsymbol{x}}$ denotes the representation of $\boldsymbol{x}$ at the penultimate layer, $p_{\boldsymbol{x}} = \text{sigmoid}(\boldsymbol{h}_{\boldsymbol{x}}^{\text{T}}\boldsymbol{\mu})$ is the probability for the positive class, and γ is a factor controlling the step size. The required updated Hessian can be computed efficiently in closed form following [38] by

$$\boldsymbol{H}^{-1}(\boldsymbol{\mu}, \boldsymbol{\Sigma}, \mathcal{A}) = \boldsymbol{\Sigma} - \sum_{(\boldsymbol{x},y)\in\mathcal{A}} \frac{p_{\boldsymbol{x}}(1-p_{\boldsymbol{x}})}{1 + \overline{\sigma}_{\boldsymbol{x}} \cdot p_{\boldsymbol{x}}(1-p_{\boldsymbol{x}})} (\boldsymbol{\Sigma}\boldsymbol{h}_{\boldsymbol{x}})(\boldsymbol{\Sigma}\boldsymbol{h}_{\boldsymbol{x}})^{\text{T}}, \quad (7)$$

where $\overline{\sigma}_{\boldsymbol{x}} = \boldsymbol{h}_{\boldsymbol{x}}^{\text{T}}\boldsymbol{\Sigma}\boldsymbol{h}_{\boldsymbol{x}}$ is the predictive variance. The derivation can be found in Appendix D.

The idea behind using second-order optimization techniques is that they are more robust than first-order gradient optimization techniques due to the incorporation of curvature information of the log posterior. This results in a more accurate representation of the loss landscape, enabling more efficient and robust parameter updates that are less sensitive to hyperparameter choices. A critical aspect of our method's efficiency is that we do not need to recompute the Hessian from scratch. Instead, our updates leverage the covariance available through LAs and use the Woodbury identity [42] for closed-form inversion, significantly reducing computational overhead. Further, a common problem with last-layer LAs is that the Hessian can become a bottleneck when dealing with a large number of classes. To address this, we can approximate the Hessian in Eq. (7) by considering a Gaussian likelihood instead of a multi-class one, as also done in [25]. Lastly, we want to highlight that an assumption of an LA is that we are at the mode of a distribution, and adding more data violates this assumption. As we focus on AL and only update with a few (up to hundreds) instances at a time, this issue is less severe.

4 Bayesian Updating Experiments

In this section, we evaluate the efficiency of the proposed update by comparing it against competitors on various benchmark datasets for image and text classification. Our code is publicly available at https://github.com/dhuseljic/dal-toolbox.

4.1 Experimental Setup

Our **experimental design** is based on the work of [19]. First, we train a DNN on the training dataset $\mathcal{D}$ (baseline). We then use this baseline DNN to evaluate a last-layer LA and related Bayesian updates on additional instance-label pairs $\mathcal{D}^\oplus$ and compare these results to retraining the DNN on the complete dataset $\mathcal{D} \cup \mathcal{D}^\oplus$. We evaluate (i) the influence of the step size γ on chosen validation datasets, (ii) the impact of our update at different learning stages of the DNN, (iii) the impact of our update with increasing sizes of new arriving datasets, and (iv) the time efficiency of our update by considering the speed-up factor against retraining. For comparison, we consider MC-based updates by sampling 10k hypotheses from the approximate Gaussian posterior $q(\omega|\mathcal{D})$ and the less complex first-order updates only considering gradients. Note that the latter is equivalent to the continual learning strategy of [33], as we demonstrate in Appendix A. Since first-order updates do not use the Hessian, this comparison also allows us to assess the benefits of using second-order optimization. We exclude retraining solely on $\mathcal{D}^\oplus$, as we empirically found that it leads to catastrophic forgetting [17]. All performance metrics are averaged across 10 repetitions. For visual clarity, we do not report standard errors.

The datasets $\mathcal{D}$ and $\mathcal{D}^\oplus$ are randomly sampled from real-world datasets. We use three image and three text **benchmark datasets** commonly used in

Table 1. Overview of datasets.

Type	Dataset	# classes
Image	Cifar-10 [22]	10
	Snacks [28]	20
	DTD [5]	47
Text	DBPedia [2]	14
	Banking-77 [4]	77
	Clinc-150 [24]	150

literature [15, 32] with varying complexity reflected through different numbers of classes. Table 1 gives an overview. A detailed summary for each dataset is provided in Appendix E.

The goal of an update method is to ensure both effectiveness and speed. To assess this, we use different **performance metrics**. To evaluate *effectiveness*, or how well an update or retraining generalizes, we measure accuracy. When experimenting with hyperparameters, accuracy is assessed on a 10% validation split. Otherwise, it is measured on the test dataset. An optimal update method should achieve the same performance as completely retraining the DNN with $\mathcal{D} \cup \mathcal{D}^\oplus$. To assess the *speed* of an update, we report the speed-up factor compared to retraining by dividing the time required for retraining by the time required for updating (Eq. (6) and 7). Retraining and updating times were recorded on an NVIDIA RTX 4090 GPU and an AMD Ryzen 9 7950X CPU, respectively.

We choose common pretrained DNN **architectures** from the literature [14, 15]. For image datasets, we employ a Vision Transformer (ViT) [11] with pretrained weights via self-supervised learning, complemented by a randomly initialized fully connected layer. Specifically, we use the DINOv2-ViT-S/14 model [30] with a feature dimension of $D = 384$ in its final hidden layer. For text datasets, we employ the transformer-based pretrained language model BERT [10]. We utilize BERT-BASED-UNCASED from the Huggingface library [41] with a feature dimension of $D = 768$ and a maximum sequence length of 512. We train each DNN by finetuning for 200 epochs, employing the Rectified Adam optimizer [26] with a training batch size of 64, a learning rate of 0.01 for images and 0.1 for text, and weight decay of 0.0001. In addition, we utilize a cosine annealing learning rate scheduler. These hyperparameters were determined empirically to be effective across all datasets by investigating the loss convergence on validation splits.

4.2 Experiments

Hyperparameter Ablation: In Eq. 6, we introduced the hyperparameter γ, which controls the step size of our update. Intuitively, this factor determines the extent to which the DNN is influenced by the new dataset $\mathcal{D}^\oplus$. This factor is essential to control the update process and avoid issues such as catastrophic forgetting. Similarly, first-order and MC-based updates also utilize this factor to mitigate such problems. For further details, we refer to Appendix A.

To investigate the influence of γ and determine a suitable value for all subsequent experiments, we conduct a simple ablation study on two datasets. The results of our update are shown here, while the results for first-order and MC-based updates can be found in Appendix B. We determine the value of γ in this manner since an extensive hyperparameter search for update methods is typically impractical in an online setting [9]. Hence, fixing a value beforehand is necessary. We randomly sample an initial dataset $\mathcal{D}$ of 50 instances and train our baseline DNN. Subsequently, updates and retraining are performed on randomly sampled datasets $|\mathcal{D}^\oplus| \in \{1, \ldots, 10\}$, and the accuracy is computed on a validation split. We repeat this process for different values of γ.

The resulting curves in Fig. 2 indicate that our update with $\mathcal{D}^\oplus$ consistently achieves better performance than the baseline DNN that is only trained on $\mathcal{D}$. For both CIFAR-10 and DBPedia, updating with $\gamma = 1$ does not yield accuracies close to retraining, suggesting that the update is too weak. By increasing γ, we observe accuracies much closer to complete retraining, with $\gamma = 10$ being sufficient for CIFAR-10 and DBPedia. For CIFAR-10, we also notice that a very high value, i.e., $\gamma = 30$, can lead to worse performance, likely due to catastrophic forgetting. To ensure effective updates across all datasets, we will be using $\gamma = 10$ in all subsequent experiments. While this may not be optimal for some datasets, it should ensure a consistently working update in all cases.

Different Learning Stages: To investigate how our update behaves at different stages of learning, we train the baseline DNN on varying sizes of initial datasets $\mathcal{D}$ and update it with a new dataset of fixed size $|\mathcal{D}^\oplus| = 10$. To better visualize the differences, we report accuracy improvement of updated/retrained DNNs relative to the baseline in Fig. 3. The results demonstrate that our updates provide the highest accuracy improvements across all datasets, highlighting the effective and consistent performance improvements of our update at different learning stages. While first-order and MC-based updates are also effective in earlier stages (when $|\mathcal{D}| < 50$), they tend to be less effective and even deteriorate accuracy in later stages. Compared to the first-order update, our update consistently enhances performance due to including the Hessian. As the Hessian considers curvature information about the posterior, the update is more robust regarding the choice of γ.

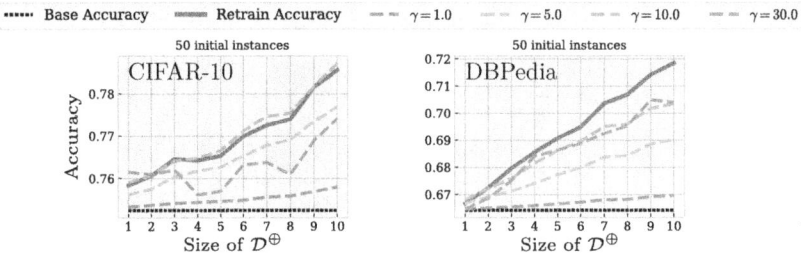

Fig. 2. Accuracies after updating with different values for γ in comparison to the baseline DNN and retraining.

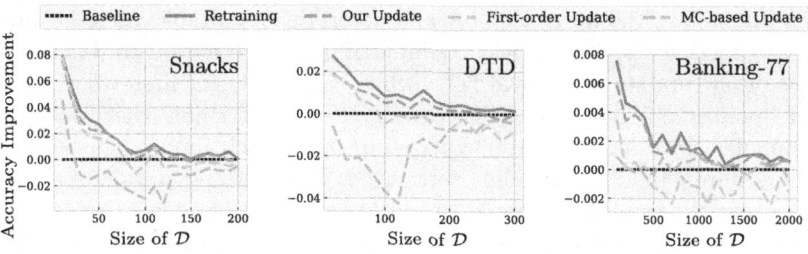

Fig. 3. Accuracy improvement curves for benchmark datasets, showing the difference in accuracy between retrained and updated DNNs for varying sizes of $\mathcal{D}$.

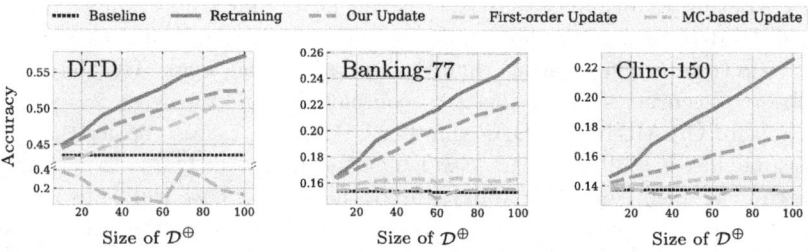

Fig. 4. Accuracy curves for three benchmark datasets after updating and retraining DNNs for varying sizes of $\mathcal{D}^\oplus$.

Varying Size of $\mathcal{D}^\oplus$: To investigate our update's behavior with an increasing number of new data points in $\mathcal{D}^\oplus$, we train a baseline DNN with a fixed initial dataset $|\mathcal{D}| = 100$ and vary the size of the new dataset $|\mathcal{D}^\oplus| \in \{10, 20, \ldots, 100\}$. We report the results for the most complex datasets DTD, Banking-77, and Clinc-150. In Fig. 4, we observe that as the size of $\mathcal{D}^\oplus$ increases, the accuracy of retraining, our update, and the first-order update consistently improves. In contrast, MC-based updates result in worse accuracies than the baseline, indicating that it is not suited for an increasing size of $\mathcal{D}^\oplus$. Considering our update, we see that it consistently achieves better accuracies compared to competitors, regardless of the complexity of the dataset. Moreover, first-order updates seem to be

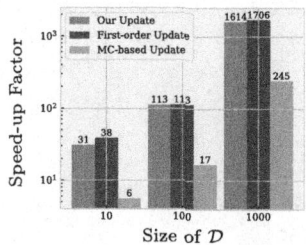

Fig. 5. Speed-up of update methods compared to retraining.

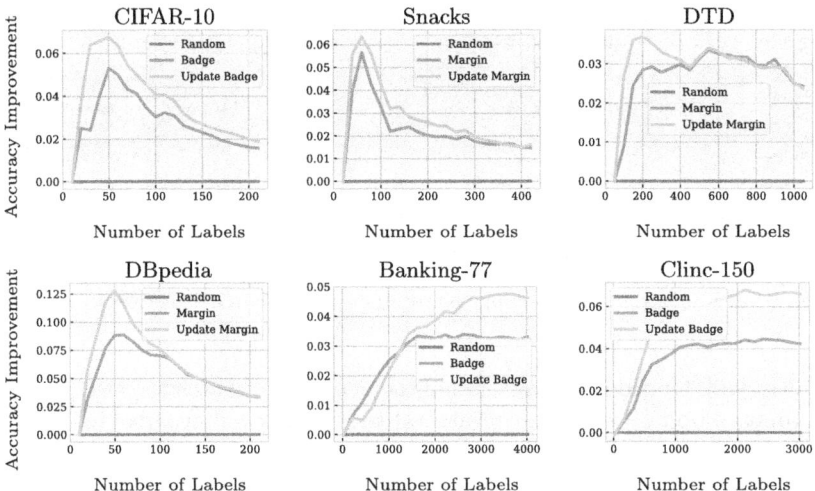

Fig. 6. Accuracy improvement curves for different datasets showing the accuracy difference between the respective selection strategy and random instance selection.

less effective on the more complex datasets such as Banking-77 and Clinc-150, highlighting the importance of the Hessian.

Time Comparison: Finally, to evaluate the speed of updates, we fix the size of the new dataset to $|\mathcal{D}^\oplus| = 10$ and compute the speed-up relative to retraining by varying the initial dataset size $|\mathcal{D}|$. Figure 5 presents the speed-up factors on CIFAR-10. All update methods are faster than retraining, with the first-order update being the fastest. For example, with an initial dataset of $|\mathcal{D}| = 1000$, the first-order update is about 1700 times faster than retraining. Notably, our update provides a similar speed-up factor while yielding more effective updates by using the closed-form Hessian update. Compared to MC-based updates, both the first-order and our update are significantly faster.

5 Deep Active Learning

In this section, we examine the proposed update in AL. First, we introduce a new framework that uses our updates to exploit label information during batch construction. Essentially, this approach mimics single instance AL, in which the model is retrained after each label acquisition. Next, we employ our update to approximate an optimal look-ahead strategy. Instead of obtaining future performance of the DNN with expensive retraining, we realize this through our update. Here, we average metrics over 30 repetitions to account for reproducibility challenges in AL [29]. Labeling budgets and acquisition sizes differ based on the complexity of a dataset. A more detailed experimental setup and all learning curves, including ones that report absolute values, are available in Appendix F.

Improved Batch Selection via Updates: A naive and suboptimal way of using sequential selection strategies for batch selection is to use the top-b scoring

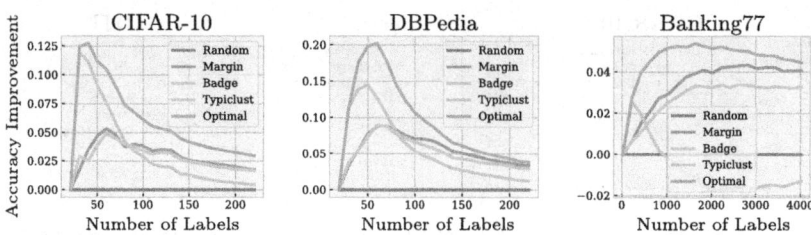

Fig. 7. Accuracy improvement over random selection of popular selection strategies compared to our upper baseline approximating optimal batch selection.

instances [18]. Our idea is to overcome the necessity of batch strategies by using the proposed update with sequential strategies as a fast alternative to retraining. Thus, we iteratively select the highest-scoring instance b times and update the DNN between each selection. After acquiring b labels, we retrain the DNN similar to batch selection strategies. An algorithm can be found in Appendix F.

The hypothesis is that already well-performing sequential selection strategies [37] can simply be used in a batch setting and that our framework can achieve higher performance compared to selecting the top-b instances. Here, we consider the widely used strategy Margin, which has proven to be effective in several studies [3]. Additionally, we are interested in whether this idea can also replace the diversity component of a batch selection strategy. Therefore, we also evaluate the popular strategy Badge [1] in combination with our updates.

Figure 6 shows the accuracy improvement curves relative to a random instance selection. The query strategies using our updates outperform the respective top-b selection strategies. Specifically, we see improved performance in early stages when redundancy within a batch plays an important role. Moreover, combining our update with Badge also results in improved accuracy. This indicates that *selecting a single instance and updating the DNN* leads to a more effective selection than using the k-MEANS++ algorithm as proposed in Badge.

Updating in Look-Ahead Strategies: The idea of look-ahead strategies is to select instances that, once labeled and added to the labeled pool, maximize the performance of the model [34]. Unlike uncertainty- or diversity-based approaches, look-ahead strategies select instances based on an optimal criterion: the model's actual performance. However, they are often neglected in deep AL due to the high computational requirements. One of the biggest bottlenecks in the selection is retraining. DNNs are not well-suited for this due to their long training process. For this reason, we employ our proposed update to make this feasible.

Here, we consider a near-optimal strategy with access to ground truth information, including labels and validation datasets. It can be considered as an upper baseline in deep AL research. For the selection, we randomly sample 2000 subsets, each with a size equal to the acquisition size, and assess how their addition to the labeled pool affects the performance. The batch leading to the highest performance gain is selected. While this approach would traditionally require 2000 times of retraining our update enables the efficient use of this strategy.

We also include the recently proposed Typiclust strategy, which demonstrated strong performance [15], especially in early stages of AL. Figure 7 presents the resulting accuracy improvement compared to random instance selection. Our optimal strategy, using updates rather than full retraining, performs exceptionally well, consistently outperforming all competitors. Based on these results, we can see that the current selection strategies still have much potential for improvement. Interestingly, we can see that Typiclust's selection in the early stages of AL seems to be close to an optimal selection but declines in effectiveness in later stages.

6 Conclusion

We proposed an efficient second-order update for DNNs in AL using the Gaussian posterior of a last-layer LA. It achieves low computational complexity through a closed-form computation of the required inverse Hessian. An extensive experimental evaluation showed that the proposed update provides an efficient alternative to retraining. Based on this, we introduced a new batch selection framework by sequentially updating the DNN after each label, offering a new perspective on constructing batches without resorting to heuristics such as clustering. Additionally, we realized a look-ahead strategy as a feasible upper baseline approximating optimal batch selection, highlighting the great potential for improvement in current research on batch selection strategies. In future work, we plan to utilize the proposed updates to enhance look-ahead selection strategies [34] in deep AL. As these strategies are based on decision-theoretic principles, they naturally balance explorative and exploitative instance selection, a key challenge in AL.

References

1. Ash, J.T., Zhang, C., Krishnamurthy, A., Langford, J., Agarwal, A.: Deep batch active learning by diverse, uncertain gradient lower bounds. In: ICLR (2020)
2. Auer, S., Bizer, C., Kobilarov, G., Lehmann, J., Cyganiak, R., Ives, Z.: DBpedia: a nucleus for a web of open data. In: ISWC, pp. 722–735 (2007)
3. Bahri, D., Jiang, H., Schuster, T., Rostamizadeh, A.: Is margin all you need? an extensive empirical study of active learning on tabular data. arXiv preprint arXiv:2210.03822 (2022)
4. Casanueva, I., Temčinas, T., Gerz, D., Henderson, M., Vulić, I.: Efficient intent detection with dual sentence encoders. In: NLP4ConvAI, pp. 38–45 (2020)
5. Cimpoi, M., Maji, S., Kokkinos, I., Mohamed, S., Vedaldi, A.: Describing textures in the wild. In: CVPR, pp. 3606–3613 (2014)
6. Coleman, C., et al.: Selection via proxy: efficient data selection for deep learning. In: ICLR (2020)
7. Das, A.M., Bhatt, G., Bhalerao, M.M., Gao, V.R., Yang, R., Bilmes, J.: Accelerating batch active learning using continual learning techniques. TMLR (2023)
8. Daxberger, E., Kristiadi, A., Immer, A., Eschenhagen, R., Bauer, M., Hennig, P.: Laplace redux-effortless Bayesian deep learning. In: NeurIPS (2021)
9. De Lange, M., et al.: A continual learning survey: defying forgetting in classification tasks. TPAMI **44**(7), 3366–3385 (2021)

10. Devlin, J., Chang, M.W., Lee, K., Toutanova, K.: BERT: pre-training of deep bidirectional transformers for language understanding. In: NAACL (2019)
11. Dosovitskiy, A., et al.: An image is worth 16x16 words: transformers for image recognition at scale. In: ICLR (2021)
12. Gal, Y., Ghahramani, Z.: Dropout as a Bayesian approximation: representing model uncertainty in deep learning. In: ICML, pp. 1050–1059 (2016)
13. Gal, Y., Islam, R., Ghahramani, Z.: Deep Bayesian active learning with image data. In: ICML, pp. 1183–1192 (2017)
14. Gupte, S.R., Aklilu, J., Nirschl, J.J., Yeung-Levy, S.: Revisiting active learning in the era of vision foundation models. TMLR (2024)
15. Hacohen, G., Dekel, A., Weinshall, D.: Active learning on a budget: opposite strategies suit high and low budgets. In: ICML, pp. 8175–8195 (2022)
16. Hoi, S.C.H., Sahoo, D., Lu, J., Zhao, P.: Online learning: a comprehensive survey. Neurocomputing **459**, 249–289 (2021)
17. Kirkpatrick, J., et al.: Overcoming catastrophic forgetting in neural networks. PNAS **114**(13), 3521–3526 (2017)
18. Kirsch, A., Farquhar, S., Atighehchian, P., Jesson, A., Branchaud-Charron, F., Gal, Y.: Stochastic batch acquisition: a simple baseline for deep active learning. TMLR (2023)
19. Kirsch, A., Kossen, J., Gal, Y.: Marginal and joint cross-entropies & predictives for online bayesian inference, active learning, and active sampling. arXiv preprint arXiv:2205.08766 (2022)
20. Kirsch, A., Van Amersfoort, J., Gal, Y.: BatchBALD: efficient and diverse batch acquisition for deep Bayesian active learning. In: NeurIPS (2019)
21. Kivinen, J., Smola, A., Williamson, R.C.: Online learning with kernels. In: NeurIPS (2001)
22. Krizhevsky, A.: Learning multiple layers of features from tiny images. Master's thesis, University of Toronto (2009)
23. Lakshminarayanan, B., Pritzel, A., Blundell, C.: Simple and scalable predictive uncertainty estimation using deep ensembles. In: NeurIPS (2017)
24. Larson, S., Mahendran, A., et al.: An evaluation dataset for intent classification and out-of-scope prediction. In: EMNLP, pp. 1311–1316 (2019)
25. Liu, J.Z., et al.: A simple approach to improve single-model deep uncertainty via distance-awareness. JMLR **24**(42), 1–63 (2023)
26. Liu, L., et al.: On the variance of the adaptive learning rate and beyond. In: ICLR (2019)
27. Lu, Z., Ie, E., Sha, F.: Mean-field approximation to Gaussian-softmax integral with application to uncertainty estimation. arXiv preprint arXiv:2006.07584 (2020)
28. Matthijs: Snacks dataset. https://huggingface.co/datasets/Matthijs/snacks (2021). Accessed 20 May 2024
29. Munjal, P., Hayat, N., Hayat, M., Sourati, J., Khan, S.: Towards robust and reproducible active learning using neural networks. In: CVPR, pp. 223–232 (2022)
30. Oquab, M., et al.: DINOv2: learning robust visual features without supervision. TMLR (2023)
31. Ovadia, Y., et al.: Can you trust your model's uncertainty? Evaluating predictive uncertainty under dataset shift. In: NeurIPS (2019)
32. Rauch, L., Assenmacher, M., Huseljic, D., Wirth, M., Bischl, B., Sick, B.: ActiveGLAE: a benchmark for deep active learning with transformers. In: ECML (2023)
33. Ritter, H., Botev, A., Barber, D.: Online structured Laplace approximations for overcoming catastrophic forgetting. In: NeurIPS (2018)

34. Roy, N., McCallum, A.: Toward optimal active learning through sampling estimation of error reduction. In: ICML, pp. 441–448 (2001)
35. Sahoo, D., Pham, Q., Lu, J., Hoi, S.C.: Online deep learning: learning deep neural networks on the fly. In: IJCAI, pp. 2660–2666 (2018)
36. Sener, O., Savarese, S.: Active learning for convolutional neural networks: a core-set approach. In: ICLR (2018)
37. Settles, B.: Active learning literature survey. Computer Sciences Technical Report 1648, University of Wisconsin–Madison (2009)
38. Spiegelhalter, D.J., Lauritzen, S.L.: Sequential updating of conditional probabilities on directed graphical structures. Networks **20**(5), 579–605 (1990)
39. Tan, W., Du, L., Buntine, W.: Diversity enhanced active learning with strictly proper scoring rules. In: NeurIPS (2021)
40. Wang, H., Yeung, D.Y.: A survey on Bayesian deep learning. CSUR **53**(5), 1–37 (2020)
41. Wolf, T., et al.: Transformers: state-of-the-art natural language processing. In: EMNLP, pp. 38–45 (2020)
42. Woodbury, M.A.: Inverting modified matrices. Princeton University, Department of Statistics (1950)
43. Yoon, J., Yang, E., Lee, J., Hwang, S.J.: Lifelong learning with dynamically expandable networks. In: ICLR (2018)
44. Zhang, J., et al.: LabelBench: a comprehensive framework for benchmarking adaptive label-efficient learning. DMLR (2024)
45. Zhao, G., Dougherty, E., Yoon, B.J., Alexander, F., Qian, X.: Uncertainty-aware active learning for optimal Bayesian classifier. In: ICLR (2021)
46. Zinkevich, M.: Online convex programming and generalized infinitesimal gradient ascent. In: ICML, pp. 928–936 (2003)

Bayesian Active Learning for Censored Regression

Frederik Boe Hüttel, Christoffer Riis, Filipe Rodrigues[(✉)],
and Francisco Pereira

Technical University of Denmark, Kongens Lyngby, Denmark
rodr@dtu.dk

Abstract. Bayesian active learning is based on information theoretical approaches that focus on maximising the information that new observations provide to the model parameters. This is commonly done by maximizing the Bayesian Active Learning by Disagreement (BALD) acquisition function. However, it is challenging to estimate BALD when the new data points are subject to censorship, where only clipped values of the targets are observed. To address this, we derive the entropy and the mutual information for right-censored distributions and derive the BALD objective for active learning in censored regression ($\mathcal{C}$-BALD). We propose a novel modeling approach to estimate the $\mathcal{C}$-BALD objective and use it for active learning in the censored setting. Across a wide range of datasets and models, we demonstrate that $\mathcal{C}$-BALD outperforms other Bayesian active learning methods in censored regression.

1 Introduction

Active learning is a framework where a model learns from a small amount of labeled data and chooses the data it wants to acquire a label for [43]. This acquisition of new data points is done iteratively to improve the model's predictive performance and reduce model uncertainty [33]. This naturally poses the challenge: which new data points can improve the model the most? Information theoretical approaches are often the basis to solve this challenge by reasoning about the information that new labels can provide to the model's parameters [34]. A widely used strategy in active learning is the Bayesian Active Learning by Disagreement (BALD) acquisition function, which identifies new data points by estimating the mutual information between the model parameters and the acquired labels [17]. BALD has demonstrated effectiveness across various domains such as computer vision [8], natural language processing [45], and survival analysis [37]. However, applying BALD to censored regression tasks introduces unique challenges, where labels are only partially observed due to censoring.

Supplementary Information The online version contains supplementary material available at https://doi.org/10.1007/978-3-032-05981-9_3.

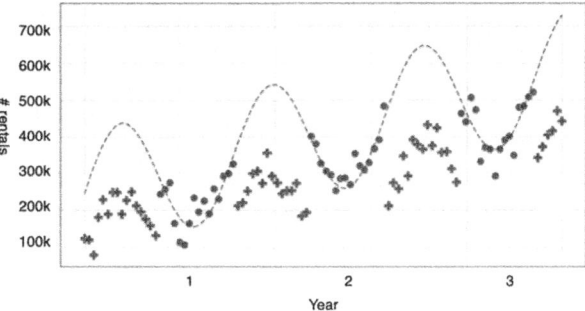

Fig. 1. Evolving shared bikes demand over a 3-year period. The dashed black line represents the (unobserved) true demand. The blue circles denote non-censored observations and the blue crosses represent censored observations (due to limited supply). In the context of bike-sharing network expansion, obtaining new observations of demand in an arbitrary location is expensive since it may involve buying new equipment. (Color figure online)

Censored data arises in scenarios where certain observations are incomplete or "clipped" due to limitations in the measurement process [4]. This phenomenon has substantial implications across multiple critical real-world domains. A particularly important context where censoring plays a key role is the ubiquitous predict-then-optimize framework, where systematic bias introduced by censorship can lead to suboptimal decision-making. Let us illustrate this problem through an application from the transportation domain. Consider the synthetic dataset shown in Fig. 1 mimicking bike sharing rentals (demand) for an expanding network of docking stations through time, where the blue markers represent the number of observed rentals (censored observations), and the dashed line represents the unobserved "true demand". Every year, the number of users increases in the population, albeit with seasonal fluctuations. However, the available bicycles (supply) are limited and their number often reaches zero in certain locations, thus resulting in censored observations of the "true demand" as studied, for example, in [20]. In the context of this application, the predict-then-optimize cycle consists of periodically re-estimating the demand and placing new bikes (or docking stations) in areas to minimize the difference between predicted demand and supply. Although costly, additional supply can be placed in areas with high uncertainty to "probe" the demand, i.e., uncover unobserved demand, thus resulting in an active learning setup.

Another example with important real-world implications in the energy domain is electrical vehicle charging infrastructure expansion [11]. The decision of where to place new infrastructure, such as additional fixed or mobile chargers, hinges on these censored observations, aiming to minimize the mismatch between predicted demand and available supply. Obtaining new observations (e.g., via placing new infrastructure) can aid in uncovering the spatio-temporal distribution of the true (uncensored) demand, but it can be extremely costly.

The predict-then-optimize framework is common across various domains with real-world applications, often involving censored data and requiring strategic decision-making under uncertainty. For instance, sensor networks in environmental monitoring, such as oceanography and forestry, face limitations where data collection is constrained by device capabilities. In these cases, models optimize sensor placement in dynamic environments to maximize information gain despite censored/noisy observations. [38] explore Bayesian Gaussian processes for processing sensor data in real-time, accounting for the censoring inherent in environmental or technical constraints. Similarly, [35] examines optimal sensing policies for dynamic decisions based on censored or incomplete data. [12] discuss strategies in cognitive radio systems, where censorship arises from bandwidth limitations or interference, affecting the system's ability to observe the full environment. Emergency response logistics face similar challenges, where resources like medical supplies or personnel must be deployed based on censored demand data. During natural disasters or pandemics, real-time demand for critical resources is often unobserved due to limited availability, creating uncertainty in supply chain optimization. [32] apply Bayesian methods to update demand information, while [49] focus on optimizing emergency logistics in epidemics by accounting for demand urgency.

Common for all these applications is the high cost associated with gathering new data or labels, while maintaining good estimates of the true targets. For instance, in the case of electric vehicle charging networks, obtaining additional observations implies moving or building new infrastructure. Similarly, in online advertisement bidding systems, exploring new strategies comes with a trade-off: the cost of exploration versus the potential gains from exploitation. This balance between acquiring more information and managing costs is crucial across various domains, influencing decision-making under uncertainty and resource constraints. Therefore, this work introduces a novel approach to Bayesian active learning in the context of censored regression. We extend the BALD acquisition function to handle censored observations, formulating the Censored-BALD ($\mathcal{C}$-BALD) acquisition function. This function quantifies the mutual information between censored data points and the model parameters, allowing us to efficiently select the most informative observations, even when they are subject to censoring. By explicitly modeling the censoring process and incorporating it into the active learning framework, we aim to reduce uncertainty in censored regression tasks, providing a principled method to address these complex real-world problems.

2 Background and Setting

We are interested in the supervised learning of a probabilistic regression model, $p(y_i^*|\mathbf{x}_i, \theta)$, where $\mathbf{x}_i \in \mathcal{X} \subseteq \mathbb{R}^d$ for $d \geq 1$, $y_i^* \in \mathcal{Y}^* \subseteq \mathbb{R}$, and θ is a set of stochastic model parameters. We assume that we can sample a set of model parameters, θ, from the posterior distribution $p(\theta|\mathcal{D})$. We consider the special regression case, where y_i^* is subject to censoring, meaning that for some observations in our dataset, y_i^* is unknown. Specifically, we consider *right-censored* data, which means that instead of observing y^*, we observe $y_i = \min(y_i^*, z_i)$, where $z_i \in \mathcal{Z} \subseteq \mathbb{R}$ is a threshold value of y_i. In addition, we also observe a censoring indicator $\ell_i = \mathbb{1}\{y_i^* \leq z_i\}$, which indicates whether y_i is censored or not. A censored dataset of size n can thus be denoted $\mathcal{D} = \{\mathbf{x}_i, y_i, \ell_i\}_{i=1}^n$.

In the case of censored regression, the objective is to infer the true distribution $p(y_i^*|\mathbf{x}_i, \theta)$ and the model parameters, θ, based on the censored dataset $\mathcal{D}$. In censored regression, one typically assumes that the distributions of $p(y_i^*|\mathbf{x}_i)$ and $p(z_i|\mathbf{x}_i)$ are independent given the covariates, $\mathbf{x}_i$ [46]. This assumption is more general than other assumptions, such as fixed-value censoring, i.e., $z_i = $ constant, $\forall i$ [40]. We formally state this assumption as follows:

Assumption 1. *(Independent censoring) Conditioned on the covariates, $\mathbf{x}_i$, the censoring distribution and the true distribution of the target are independent. That is $y_i^* \perp z_i | \mathbf{x}_i$.*

Under Assumption 1, we obtain the following densities for $p(y^*)$ and $p(y)$,

$$p(y^*|\mathbf{x}, \theta) = \varphi(y^*|\mathbf{x}, \theta), \tag{1}$$

$$p(y|\ell, \mathbf{x}, \theta) = \varphi(y|\mathbf{x}, \theta)^\ell (1 - \Phi(y|\mathbf{x}, \theta))^{(1-\ell)}, \tag{2}$$

where Φ is the Cumulative Distribution Function (CDF) and φ is the Probability Density Function (PDF) of $p(y^*|\mathbf{x}, \theta)$. Since we do not have access to the non-censored dataset, y^*, we can only estimate θ through their censored counterparts, y. Equation 2, also known as Tobit likelihood [46], thus models the joint distribution of censored ($\ell = 1$) and censored data points ($\ell = 0$). The corresponding log-likelihood loss function for right-censored models simplifies to:

$$\mathcal{L}_C(\theta) = -\sum_{i \in \mathcal{D}} \Big(\underbrace{\ell_i \log(\varphi(y_i|\mathbf{x}_i, \theta))}_{\text{Observed loss}} + \underbrace{(1 - \ell_i) \log(1 - \Phi(y_i|\mathbf{x}_i, \theta))}_{\text{Censored loss}} \Big), \tag{3}$$

While we focus on right-censoring, left-censoring (i.e. $y_i = \max(y_i^*, z_i)$) can be handled by inverting $y_i, \forall i$.

We will assume $p(y_i^*|\mathbf{x}_i, \theta)$ to be Gaussian, such that $p(y_i^*|\mathbf{x}_i, \theta) = \mathcal{N}(\mu_i^*, \sigma_i^{2*}|\mathbf{x}_i, \theta)$. As a consequence, $p(y|\ell, \mathbf{x}_i, \theta)$ will be a mixture model that reduces to a Gaussian when all $\ell = 1$.

Using the loss in Eq. 3 we can fit a model of $p(y_i^*|\mathbf{x}_i, \theta)$, as long as its PDF φ and CDF Φ are well-defined. Since our focus is on Bayesian active learning, and concretely BALD, we consider the broad class of Bayesian models. Common choices include deep ensembles [28] and neural networks with stochastic parameters [7,44].

2.1 Active Learning

In the supervised regression setting, active learning involves selecting which labels to acquire during training to increase the model performance [34,43].

It maximizes an acquisition function, which captures the utility of acquiring the label for a given input [26]. We are interested in such settings, but where the data points are subject to censoring. Typically, one starts with a small training dataset, $\mathcal{D}^{\text{train}} = \{(\mathbf{x}_i, y_i, \ell_i)\}_{i=1}^{n}$, which is used to train a probabilistic model with likelihood $p(y_i^* | \mathbf{x}_i, \theta)$. Then, from a larger (finite or infinite) pool of future unlabelled data, $\mathcal{D}^{\text{pool}} = \{\mathbf{x}_i\}_{t=1}^{m}$, the model is used to actively select $\mathbf{x}_i$ to acquire a label for [26]. Once the label is acquired, the sample is added to the training set. In the pool, $\mathcal{D}^{\text{pool}}$, the censorship status of new observations is *unknown*, i.e., during acquitions of new observations, both y_i and ℓ_i are unknown [37]. Thus, acquiring new labels involves obtaining its label y_i alongside its censorship status ℓ_i [48].

2.2 Bayesian Experimental Design

Bayesian experimental design is a formal framework for quantifying the information gained from an experiment [31]. In active learning, we can view the input $\mathbf{x}_i$ as the design of an experiment and the acquired label y_i as the experiment's outcome and formalize the information gained from observing y_i [2]. Let θ be the quantity we are trying to infer. Given a prior (or the most recent knowledge), $p(\theta)$, and a likelihood function, $p(y_i | \mathbf{x}_i, \theta)$, then we can quantify the information gain (IG) in θ due to an acquisition of $(\mathbf{x}_i, y_i)$, as the reduction in Shannon entropy in θ that results from observing $(\mathbf{x}_i, y_i)$:

$$\text{IG}_\theta(\mathbf{x}_i, y_i) = \text{H}[p(\theta)] - \text{H}[p(\theta | \mathbf{x}_i, y_i)]. \tag{4}$$

Since y_i is a random variable, the expected information of y_i can be computed across multiple simulated outcomes using

$$p_\theta(y_i | \mathbf{x}_i) = \mathbb{E}_{p(\theta)}[p(y_i | \mathbf{x}_i, \theta)], \tag{5}$$

which leads to the expected information gain,

$$\text{EIG}_\theta(\mathbf{x}_i) = \mathbb{E}_{p_\theta(y_i | \mathbf{x}_i)} \left[\text{H}\left[p(\theta)\right] - \text{H}\left[p(\theta | \mathbf{x}_i, y_i)\right] \right]. \tag{6}$$

This is the expected reduction in uncertainty of θ after conditioning on $(\mathbf{x}_i, y_i)$. Equivalently, it is the mutual information between θ and y_i given $\mathbf{x}_i$, denoted $\text{I}[y_i, \theta | \mathbf{x}_i]$ [2].

2.3 Bayesian Active Learning

The expected information gain has often been the basis for Bayesian active learning, seeking to acquire data points that provide high information gain in the model parameters θ. This acquisition function is referred to as the *Bayesian Active Learning by Disagreement* (BALD) [17]:

$$\begin{aligned}
\text{BALD}(\mathbf{x}_i) &= \mathbb{E}_{p_\theta(y_i | \mathbf{x}_i)}[\text{H}[p(\theta)] - \text{H}[p(\theta | \mathbf{x}_i, y_i)]] \\
&= \mathbb{E}_{p(\theta)}[\text{H}[p(y_i | \mathbf{x}_i)] - \text{H}[p(y_i | \mathbf{x}_i, \theta)]] \\
&= \text{H}[p(y_i | \mathbf{x}_i)] - \mathbb{E}_{p(\theta)}[\text{H}[p(y_i | \mathbf{x}_i, \theta)]],
\end{aligned} \tag{7}$$

where the unconditional entropy is obtained by marginalizing over the parameters θ,

$$\mathrm{H}[p(y_i|\mathbf{x}_i)] = \mathrm{H}[\mathbb{E}_{p(\theta)}[p(y_i|\mathbf{x}_i, \theta)]]. \tag{8}$$

The BALD score is often used when the update to the model parameters is non-Bayesian, for example, when applying Monte Carlo dropout in a neural network [8], which we use to approximate the marginalizing over the parameters θ in Eq. 8. For Bayesian active learning without censoring, the BALD acquisition function can be used for classification and regression methods, as the entropies are well-defined for these tasks [8,21].

3 Censoring and Information

Ideally, we would still like to use the BALD objectives for active learning in the censored data case. However, we must consider that, for a new observation $\mathbf{x}_i$ in the pool, the corresponding label y_i can provide a varying amount of information for the distribution of y_i and θ depending on the censorship status of the label [1,14–16]. To use the EIG and BALD acquisition functions, we will derive the information (Shannon entropy) for a model trained with Eq. 3. Using the derived entropy, we extend the BALD objective to the censored case and use this as an acquisition function for Bayesian active learning in this setting. For the entropy equations in the following, we omit the dependency on $\mathbf{x}_i$, i, and θ for readability.

3.1 Censored Information

In the case of non-censorship, the amount of information that y provides to the continuous distribution $p(y)$ corresponds to the Shannon differential entropy, defined as,

$$\mathrm{H}[p(y)] = -\int p(y) \log p(y) dy = -\mathbb{E}_{y \sim p(y)}[\log p(y)]. \tag{9}$$

If we consider the density of a (right) censored distribution introduced in Eq. 2, we can formulate the entropy for a censored distribution into the following entropy,

$$\mathrm{H}[p(y|\ell)] = -\mathbb{E}_{y \sim p(y|\ell)}[\ell \log \varphi(y) + (1 - \ell) \log(1 - \Phi(y))]. \tag{10}$$

This entropy naturally reflects our assumption of censored observations that the reduction in entropy from observing y is conditioned on its censorship status. Using the fact that if y is censored, then $y = z$ and if y is not censored, $y = y^*$, then we can reformulate the entropy as,

$$\mathrm{H}[p(y|\ell)] = -\mathbb{E}_{y \sim p(y|\ell)}[\ell \log \varphi(y^*) + (1 - \ell) \log(1 - \Phi(z))]. \tag{11}$$

However, the censoring information (both z and ℓ) is *unknown* during acquisitions of new data points. To use this entropy for active learning, we propose

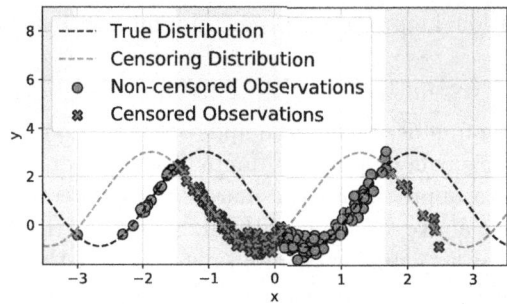

Fig. 2. Illustration of a 1-dimensional censored dataset, in which the dashed black line represents the underlying function that generated the data. The (blue) circles denote non-censored observations, while the (green) crosses represent observations that have been censored. The grey background indicates areas where the observations are censored. (Color figure online)

treating the indicator variable ℓ as a binary random variable. Later, we describe our approach to modeling ℓ. Having a model of $p(\ell)$, we propose to approximate Eq. 11 with its expectation with respect to $p(\ell)$:

$$\begin{aligned} \mathrm{H}[p(y|\ell)] &\approx \mathbb{E}_{p(\ell)}\left[\mathrm{H}[p(y|\ell)]\right] \\ &= -\mathbb{E}_{y \sim p(y|\ell)}[p(\ell) \log \varphi(y^*) + (1-p(\ell)) \log(1-\Phi(z))] \,. \end{aligned} \quad (12)$$

3.2 Expected Information Gain in Censored Acquisitions

We can use the derived entropy to calculate the information that newly observed targets y_i will provide to the parameters of a Bayesian model. However, the acquisition of new labels not only requires obtaining new values of y_i, but it also involves acquiring new censoring indicators ℓ_i [37]. Consequently, it is necessary to account for the mutual information between y_i and θ and consider the information provided by ℓ_i. As a result, we jointly compute the mutual information between the set (y_i, ℓ_i) and θ. This leads to the following mutual information (derivation in Appendix A.1),

$$\begin{aligned} \mathcal{C}\text{-BALD}(\mathbf{x}_i) &= \mathrm{I}\left[(y_i, \ell_i), \theta | \mathbf{x}_i\right] \\ &= \mathbb{E}_{p(\theta)}[\mathrm{H}[p_\theta(y_i, \ell_i|\mathbf{x}_i)] - \mathrm{H}[p(y_i, \ell_i|\mathbf{x}_i, \theta)]] \,. \\ &= \mathrm{I}\left[y_i, \theta | \ell_i, \mathbf{x}_i\right] + \mathrm{I}\left[\ell_i, \theta | \mathbf{x}_i\right] \,. \end{aligned} \quad (13)$$

Therefore, in the censored regression case, the information gained from observing y_i and ℓ_i is the information provided by observing the label y_i given the censoring indicator ℓ_i, plus the information from observing the censoring indicator ℓ_i. The mutual information criteria can be computed similarly to the BALD objective using the derived entropies,

$$\begin{aligned} \mathrm{I}\left[y_i, \theta | \ell_i, \mathbf{x}_i\right] &= \mathbb{E}_{p(\theta)}[\mathrm{H}[p_\theta(y_i|\ell_i, \mathbf{x}_i)] - \mathrm{H}[p(y_i|\ell_i, \mathbf{x}_i, \theta)]], \\ \mathrm{I}\left[\ell_i, \theta | \mathbf{x}_i\right] &= \mathbb{E}_{p(\theta)}[\mathrm{H}[p_\theta(\ell_i|\mathbf{x}_i)] - \mathrm{H}[p(\ell_i|\mathbf{x}_i, \theta)]] \,. \end{aligned} \quad (14)$$

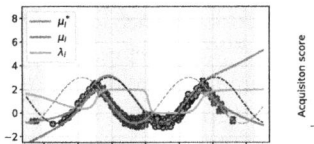 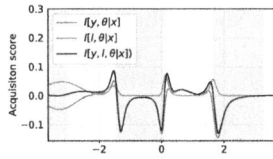 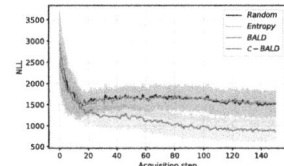

Fig. 3. Left): Overview of the fit of the proposed modeling approach on the 1-D synthetic dataset. Red: Estimated distribution of the true function, $p(y_i^*|\mathbf{x}_i,\theta)$. Blue: Estimated distribution of the observed values, $p(y_i|\mathbf{x}_i,\theta)$. Orange: Estimated probability of being censored, $p_\theta(\ell_i|\mathbf{x}_i)$ (scaled between 0 and 2 for illustration purposes). **Middle)**: The mutual information calculations for the label y and the censoring status. Grey areas indicate areas with complete censoring. Most information comes from the cross-over point between the censored and non-censored values. **Right)**: The right censored NLL for the models across different acquisition functions on the synthetic dataset (mean ± standard error). $\mathcal{C}$-BALD achieves the best overall fit on the test set.

4 Information Gain in $\mathcal{C}$-BALD

A fundamental challenge of $\mathcal{C}$-BALD for active learning is that the censored regression model, estimated using the censored loss function from Eq. 3, only approximates the parameters for the distribution of y_i^*, and its corresponding PDF φ and CDF Φ. This means that during acquisition, there is no knowledge of the potential censoring status of new observations ℓ_i, which is required to compute the mutual information (Eq. 13), and there is no knowledge of the potential censoring threshold z_i, which is required to compute the entropy of y_i (Eq. 12). Therefore, applying $\mathcal{C}$-BALD in practice is not straightforward. To overcome these challenges, we propose explicitly modeling the probability of being censored ℓ_i and the censoring threshold z_i as described below.

Modeling of ℓ_i: Recall that the censoring indicator $\ell_i = \mathbb{1}\{y_i^* \leq z_i\}$ is observed for each data point in a censored dataset. It is a binary indicator of whether the observations are censored or not. Using a neural network, we propose to fit the distribution of $p(\ell_i|\mathbf{x}_i,\theta)$. Concretely, we parameterise $p(\ell_i|\mathbf{x}_i,\theta)$ as a Bernoulli distribution $\text{Ber}(\lambda_i|\mathbf{x}_i,\theta)$, and infer the parameters θ using the binary cross entropy loss ($\mathcal{L}_{\text{BCE}}(\theta)$). Consequently, this explicit modeling of ℓ_i allows us to approximate the mutual information $\text{I}[\ell_i,\theta|\mathbf{x}_i]$ required for Eq. 13 ($\mathcal{C}$-BALD).

Modelling of z_i and y_i: Explicit modeling of z_i is more challenging, as it is not fully observed (similarly to y_i^*). However, notice that for computing the conditional entropy in Eq. 12, we are only interested in the value of z_i for the case when $\mathbf{x}_i$ is subject to censoring, i.e. $\ell_i = 0$, in which case $y_i = z_i$. This implies that we directly observe the true values of z_i when we have censored data points. Therefore, we propose to also explicitly model y_i using a standard Gaussian distribution, $\tilde{p}(y_i|\mathbf{x}_i,\theta) = \mathcal{N}(\mu_i,\sigma_i^2|\mathbf{x}_i,\theta)$, estimated with the maximum likelihood (with loss $\mathcal{L}_{\text{GAUSS}}(\theta))$[1]. Notice that $\tilde{p}(y_i|\mathbf{x}_i,\theta)$ represents the distribution of the observations regardless of censorship, while $p(y_i^*|\mathbf{x}_i,\theta)$ represents that actual latent distribution we are trying to model. By explicitly modelling both $\tilde{p}(y_i|\mathbf{x}_i,\theta_i)$ and $p(\ell_i|\mathbf{x}_i,\theta)$, for censored observations (when $\ell_i = 0$), $\mathbb{E}[y_i] = \mu_i$ provides an estimate of z_i, while for uncensored observations $\mathbb{E}[y_i^*] = \mu^*$. This approach thus allows us to estimate z_i for censored cases, which is crucial for the entropy calculations described in Eq. 12. An example of this can be seen in Fig. 3, where $\tilde{p}(y_i|\mathbf{x}_i,\theta_i)$ follows the data points, also for censored observations, thereby estimating z_i.

Entropy Estimation: With this explicit modeling approach, we can approximate information that new observations provide to the parameters of the censored model.

$$\mathrm{H}[p(y_i)] \approx - \mathbb{E}_{y_i \sim p(y_i)}[p_\theta(\ell_i|\mathbf{x}_i) \log \varphi(y_i) + (1 - p_\theta(\ell_i|\mathbf{x}_i)) \log(1 - \Phi(\mu_i))]. \tag{15}$$

4.1 Summary and Implementation Details

We want to use the mutual information between observations of (y_i, ℓ_i) and the model parameters θ to acquire new labels to reduce model uncertainty about y_i^*. Since the distribution of y^* is not fully observed, we use the entropy defined in Eq. 12 to compute the mutual information. However, the entropy relies on the knowledge of unknown variables z_i and ℓ_i. We propose explicitly modeling them using neural networks, thus resulting in the estimated entropy of Eq. 15.

Implementation: We will use Gaussian distributions for y_i^* and y_i and a Bernoulli distribution for ℓ_i. We enforce the constraint that σ_i^* and σ_i should be positive by applying the softplus activation function on these parameters. To summarise,

$$\begin{aligned} p(y_i^*|\mathbf{x}_i,\theta) &\sim \underbrace{\mathcal{N}(\mu_i^*, \sigma_i^{2*}|\mathbf{x}_i,\theta)}_{\text{True distribution of } y_i^*} \\ p(y_i|\mathbf{x}_i,\theta) &\sim \underbrace{\mathcal{N}(\mu_i, \sigma_i^2|\mathbf{x}_i,\theta)}_{\text{Dist. of observed values } y_i}, \\ p(\ell_i|\mathbf{x}_i,\theta) &\sim \underbrace{\text{Ber}(\lambda_i|\mathbf{x}_i,\theta)}_{\text{Distribution of } \ell_i}. \end{aligned} \tag{16}$$

We model all these distributions with a single Bayesian neural network with stochastic parameters. The outputs of the Bayesian neural network are the parameters of the distributions $p(y_i^*|\mathbf{x}_i,\theta)$, $p(y_i|\mathbf{x}_i,\theta)$ and $p(\ell_i|\mathbf{x}_i,\theta)$, i.e. five outputs neurons for the set $\{\mu_i^*, \sigma_i^*, \mu_i, \sigma_i, \lambda_i\}$. The latter can then be used to

---

[1] Note that this distribution is different from Eq. 2, where we fit a distribution for y using a Tobit likelihood.

Table 1. Overview of the various datasets used in this analysis, including the number of features and the percentage of censorship in $\mathcal{D}^{\text{pool}}$. We also include n_0 as the initial data points in $\mathcal{D}^{\text{train}}$

NAME	NUM. FEATURES	CENSORSHIP	n_0	ACQUISITION SIZE	STEPS	REPETITIONS	$\mathcal{D}^{\text{POOL}}$	$\mathcal{D}^{\text{VAL}}$	$\mathcal{D}^{\text{TEST}}$
SYNTHETIC	1	44%	10	3	150	50	9000	250	500
BREASTMSK	5	77%	5	3	150	50	1285	183	366
METABRIC	9	42%	5	3	150	50	1523	76	305
WHAS	6	58%	5	3	150	50	1310	65	263
GBSG	7	37%	5	3	150	50	1546	137	549
SUPPORT	14	32%	5	3	150	50	7098	355	1420
CHURN	26	53%	5	3	150	50	1276	136	546
CREDIT RISK	47	30%	5	3	150	50	650	70	280
SURVMNIST	28 × 28	53%	100	5	100	25	60000	5000	5000

compute the conditional entropy in Eq. 15 as highlighted by the respective colors. The parameters of the neural network, θ, are inferred using the total loss from the maximum likelihood estimation of all these distributions,

$$\mathcal{L}(\theta) = \mathcal{L}_\mathcal{C}(\theta) + \mathcal{L}_{\text{GAUSS}}(\theta) + \mathcal{L}_{\text{BCE}}(\theta). \tag{17}$$

Figure 3 shows the fit of the proposed model for all the different distributions on a synthetic dataset. Using all the explicit models of y_i^*, y_i and ℓ_i, we can compute the $\mathcal{C}$-BALD objective (Eq. 13) and use it as an acquisition function in active learning.

5 Experiments

In this section, we present the results of the proposed acquisition function with multiple experiments on synthetic and real-world datasets. Source code for reproducing the experiments is available at: https://github.com/fbohu/Censored-Active-Learning.

Models: We implement the Bayesian Neural Network with stochastic parameters using Monte Carlo Dropout [7]. We use three layers, 128 hidden units, a dropout probability of 0.25, and the ADAM optimizer with a learning rate of $0.3 \cdot 10^{-3}$ [23] and the ReLU activation function[2].

Baselines: We compare the proposed acquisition function with the following baselines: **Random** acquisitions, which randomly acquires data points in $\mathcal{D}^{\text{pool}}$, the **Entropy** (Entropy) of Bayesian neural networks, which is proportional to variance between the individual's models in the sampled ensemble, $\text{Var}_{\theta \sim p(\theta|\mathcal{D})}[p(y_i|\mathbf{x}_i)]$, and the **BALD** objective from Eq. 7.

Evaluation: To quantify the performance of the acquisition function, we evaluate the relative decrease in the area under the curve (RD-AUC) across the entire

---

[2] In Appendix C, we experiment with different model architectures.

active learning experiment [41]. We compare the relative decrease to a baseline acquisition function (Random) and evaluate the models' right censored negative log-likelihood (NLL) on a test set ($\mathcal{D}^{\text{test}}$). Since the NLL is not bounded by 0, we use the lowest NLL obtained across all the acquisition functions as a lower bound for the metric. We compute the average across all the number of acquisitions, N_{Acq}. The RD-AUC is defined as follows:

$$\text{RD-AUC} = \frac{1}{N_{\text{Acq}}} \sum_{i=0}^{N_{\text{Acq}}} \left(\frac{NLL_{\text{Random}} - NLL_s}{NLL_{\text{Random}}} \right), \quad (18)$$

where NLL_s is the negative log-likelihood of the model with the acquisition function s and NLL_{Random} is the negative log-likelihood of from Random acquisition.

Synthetic Data: We begin our empirical evaluation of the proposed acquisition by considering the following 1D synthetic dataset, with $x_i = \mathcal{N}(5,1)$, and,

$$y_i^* = \frac{1}{2}\sin(2x_i) + 2 + \varepsilon_i \qquad z_i = \frac{1}{2}\cos(2x_i) + 2 + \varepsilon_i, \quad (19)$$

$y_i = \min(y_i^*, z_i)$, and $\ell_i = \mathbb{1}\{y_i^* \leq z_i\}$ and $\varepsilon_i \sim \mathcal{N}(0, 0.01|x_i|)$. The dataset can be seen in Fig. 2 and our proposed modeling fit in Fig. 3. We generate a small pool of labelled data points ($n_0 = 10$), a larger set of unlabelled data points $|\mathcal{D}^{\text{pool}}| = 9000$, and a $|\mathcal{D}^{\text{test}}| = 500$. We train a model of the small pool of labeled data and acquire three new data points with labels every iteration. During each training step, we use a small validation set $\mathcal{D}^{\text{val}}$ with 250 observations to evaluate the models and apply early stopping on the right censored maximum likelihood.

Figure 3 shows the $\mathcal{C}$-BALD scores across the entire range of x. $\mathcal{C}$-BALD assigns a high mutual information value in regions where the censoring status changes, i.e. when the model is uncertain about the information that new samples will provide. In the right of Fig. 3, we show the right censored negative log-likelihood for the different acquisition functions. We find that $\mathcal{C}$-BALD achieves the best overall fit of the data with the lowest NLL, which shows that it identifies which data point provides the most information to the model.

Real Datasets: We test the proposed functions on seven real-world datasets: five from a biomedical context [22] and two from a predictive analytics context [6]. Three datasets focus on estimating the survival time for various types of cancer patients (**BreastMSK, METABRIC,** and **GBSG**), one dataset for modeling the survival time of myocardial infarction (**WHAS**), and the last dataset estimates the survival time for critically-ill hospital patients (**SUPPORT**). For the predictive analytics datasets, we focus on predicting the time customers remain subscribed to a service (**Churn**) and the other on estimating the time for borrowers to repay their credit (**Credit Risk**)[3].

Table 1 summarises the datasets used in the experiments, including the number of features, the percentage of censored observations, and the total number of

---
[3] A more extensive summary of these datasets can be found in Appendix B.3.

Table 2. Relative decrease in the area under the curve (RD-AUC) compared to the Random scoring function. A higher value in the table represents better performance, with the best performance highlighted in **bold**.

Dataset	Entropy	BALD	C-BALD
Synthetic	8.65 ± 0.42	−0.12 ± 0.14	**33.49 ± 1.11**
BreastMSK	8.21 ± 1.43	−1.89 ± 0.66	**8.75 ± 1.42**
Metabric	−0.67 ± 0.39	2.25 ± 0.34	**18.26 ± 0.94**
whas	0.42 ± 0.27	**1.68 ± 0.17**	0.26 ± 0.32
GBSG	−0.81 ± 0.05	−0.04 ± 0.05	**5.58 ± 0.05**
support	0.70 ± 0.02	−0.53 ± 0.01	**4.55 ± 0.02**
churn	5.14 ± 0.31	0.17 ± 0.21	**32.75 ± 0.87**
credit risk	−0.72 ± 0.36	−0.17 ± 0.33	**22.11 ± 0.64**
Survmnist	−0.05 ± 0.28	1.06 ± 0.30	**13.47 ± 0.66**

observations. Additionally, it includes a summary of the parameters used for the active learning experiments for each dataset. The results reported are averages over the number of repetitions for each dataset and acquisition function (mean ± standard error). Table 2 reports the RD-AUC compared across the different scoring functions. Figure 4 shows the right-censored NLL across the different runs for two real-world datasets. We find that the proposed acquisition function leads to better acquisition of new data points by obtaining a superior fit on the test set compared to the baselines.

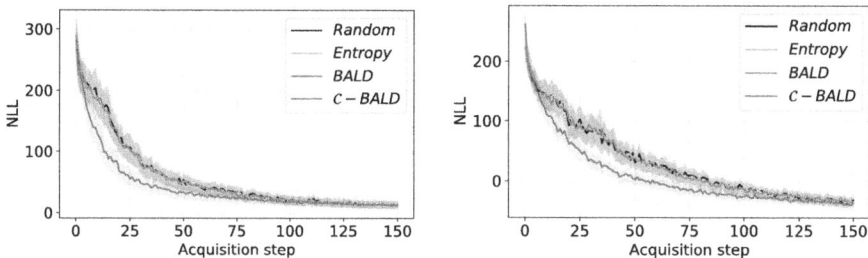

Fig. 4. Results of the real-world experiments on two of the seven datasets, namely the METABRIC and CREDIT RISK datasets, respectively. The figure shows the NLL (mean ± standard error) across the multiple repetitions of the experiment.

High-Dimensional Data: Lastly, we evaluate the performance of our proposed scoring functions with Bayesian convolutional neural networks on the **SurvM-NIST** dataset [10]. In SurvMNIST, each label is replaced with a random draw from a Gamma distribution, with different distributional parameters across the labels [39]. The observations in the dataset are censored uniformly, between the minimum and the 90th percentile in the training set [10]. The initial training set contains ten samples from each class in the dataset[4]. The experiment on the SurvMNIST dataset shows that the proposed scoring functions outperformed the baseline functions, as shown in Table 2.

6 Related Work

The study of the information that an experiment or observation provides was introduced by [31] and has often been the basis for new acquisition functions in active learning [33,34]. The study of information in censored experiments has traditionally focused on survival experiments, where observations are studied over time [14,16]. In survival experiments, an individual is observed for an amount of time and is considered censored if the person drops out of the experiment [15]. For the discrete and continuous case, the entropy calculations come down to the integral over the time an individual was observed [1], and entropy decreases after observations are censored [15]. In these and other settings with censored data, such as transportation systems [18,20], subscription-based businesses [3,5,36], and in health survival applications [30,37], data can be expensive to collect and label, necessitating the need for active learning in this context. Despite the challenges of censored data, there is limited research on active learning in this context. Two notable exceptions from the survival analysis literature include the work of [48], who proposed a query strategy based on discriminative gradients to identify the most informative points, and the work of [37], who suggested a query strategy for acquiring data points with the highest expected performance increase if their labels were known. A popular approach is Bayesian Active Learning with the BALD objective [17], specifically with its ability to work in conjunction with deep neural networks [8] and extensions to batch-acquisitions [25]. In the Deep Bayesian active learning, the BALD objective has primarily been used for classification tasks with MC Dropout models but has recently seen applications for deep regression tasks, such as estimating causal treatment effects [21] and for black-box models [24]. While plenty of research has focused on the BALD objective, to our knowledge, we are the first to explore the BALD objective in censored regression.

As previously mentioned, this work is motivated by predict-then-optimize scenarios, often involving dynamic feedback between supply and demand, which aligns with exploration/exploitation approaches as in Bayesian Optimization (BO) and Reinforcement Learning (RL), however in our work, we not focused on optimization, but increase the predictive quality of the censored regression models, used in these contexts. This is an important distinction, as supply is often limited and needs proper allocation, which is often done by optimizing a utility function, such as profit or cost [11]. While BO extensions for censored data (e.g. [19]) exist that handle uncertainty from censoring, focusing on active learning allows for the separation between learning from optimization, thus allowing for

---

[4] The details of the gamma distributions and the model architecture can be found in Appendix B.4.

greater flexibility in applying and comparing different optimization techniques. For instance, [11] shows that a Chance Constrained Mixed Integer Programming approach outperforms a BO baseline when censoring is not modeled. In contrast, while RL has been studied in the context of censored data (e.g., [9,47]), it is less suited to the type of problems targeted by our work due to the high cost of acquiring new data (e.g., deploying infrastructure). This restricts the extensive exploration typically needed in RL, making it impractical for real-world applications with tight exploration budgets.

7 Conclusion

This paper studies Bayesian active learning for censored regression problems. This problem is prevalent in many fields, such as engineering, marketing, finance, and medicine, where datasets often contain censored observations and obtaining new observations can be costly, thus constraining the learning process of the true underlying uncensored distribution and requiring careful strategic decision-making under uncertainty. Motivated by this challenge, we derive the entropy for censored distributions and propose the $\mathcal{C}$-BALD acquisition function, which accounts for censored observations. Empirically, across various synthetic and real datasets, we show that $\mathcal{C}$-BALD outperforms BALD on synthetic and real-world datasets.

References

1. Baxter, L.A.: A note on information and censored absolutely continuous random variables. Stat. Risk Model. **7**(1–2), 193–198 (1989)
2. Bickford Smith, F., Kirsch, A., Farquhar, S., Gal, Y., Foster, A., Rainforth, T.: Prediction-oriented bayesian active learning. In: Proceedings of The 26th International Conference on Artificial Intelligence and Statistics, pp. 7331–7348 (2023)
3. Chandar, P., et al.: Using survival models to estimate user engagement in online experiments, pp. 3186–3195 (2022)
4. Cox, D.R.: Regression models and life-tables. J. Royal Stat. Soc. Ser. B (Methodol.) **34**(2), 187–220 (1972)
5. Fader, P.S., Hardie, B.G.: How to project customer retention. J. Interact. Mark. **21**(1), 76–90 (2007)
6. Fotso, S., et al.: PySurvival: open source package for survival analysis modeling (2019)
7. Gal, Y., Ghahramani, Z.: Dropout as a bayesian approximation: representing model uncertainty in deep learning. In: Proceedings of The 33rd International Conference on Machine Learning, pp. 1050–1059 (2016)
8. Gal, Y., Islam, R., Ghahramani, Z.: Deep Bayesian active learning with image data. In: Proceedings of the 34th International Conference on Machine Learning, pp. 1183–1192 (2017)
9. Goldberg, Y., Kosorok, M.R.: Q-learning with censored data. Ann. Stat. **40**(1), 529 (2012)

10. Goldstein, M., Han, X., Puli, A., Perotte, A., Ranganath, R.: X-CAL: explicit calibration for survival analysis. In: Advances in Neural Information Processing Systems, vol. 33, pp. 18296–18307 (2020)
11. Golsefidi, A.H., Hüttel, F.B., Peled, I., Samaranayake, S., Pereira, F.C.: A joint machine learning and optimization approach for incremental expansion of electric vehicle charging infrastructure. Transp. Res. Part A Policy Pract. **178**, 103863 (2023)
12. Haghighi, K., Ström, E.G., Agrell, E.: Sensing or transmission: causal cognitive radio strategies with censorship. IEEE Trans. Wireless Commun. **13**(6), 3031–3041 (2014)
13. Hendrycks, D., Gimpel, K.: Gaussian error linear units (GELUs). arXiv preprint arXiv:1606.08415 (2016)
14. Hollander, M., Proschan, F., Sconing, J., Florida State Univ Tallahassee Dept of Statistics: Information in censored models. FSU Stat. Rep. M **701** (1985)
15. Hollander, M., Proschan, F., Sconing, J.: Measuring information in right-censored models. Naval Res. Logist. (NRL) **34**(5), 669–681 (1987)
16. Hollander, M., Proschan, F., Sconing, J.: Information, censoring, and dependence. Lect. Notes-Monogr. Ser. **16**, 257–268 (1990)
17. Houlsby, N., Huszár, F., Ghahramani, Z., Lengyel, M.: Bayesian active learning for classification and preference learning (2011)
18. Hüttel, F.B., Rodrigues, F., Pereira, F.C.: Mind the gap: modelling difference between censored and uncensored electric vehicle charging demand. Transp. Res. Part C Emerg. Technol. **153**, 104189 (2023)
19. Hutter, F., Hoos, H., Leyton-Brown, K.: Bayesian optimization with censored response data. arXiv preprint arXiv:1310.1947 (2013)
20. Hüttel, F.B., Peled, I., Rodrigues, F., Pereira, F.C.: Modeling censored mobility demand through censored quantile regression neural networks. IEEE Trans. Intell. Transp. Syst. **23**(11), 21753–21765 (2022)
21. Jesson, A., Tigas, P., van Amersfoort, J., Kirsch, A., Shalit, U., Gal, Y.: Causal-bald: deep bayesian active learning of outcomes to infer treatment-effects from observational data. In: Advances in Neural Information Processing Systems. Curran Associates, Inc. (2021)
22. Katzman, J.L., Shaham, U., Cloninger, A., Bates, J., Jiang, T., Kluger, Y.: Deep-Surv: personalized treatment recommender system using a cox proportional hazards deep neural network. BMC Med. Res. Methodol. **18**(1), 24 (2018)
23. Kingma, D.P., Ba, J.: Adam: a method for stochastic optimization. arXiv preprint arXiv:1412.6980 (2014)
24. Kirsch, A.: Black-box batch active learning for regression. Trans. Mach. Learn. Res. (2023). Expert Certification
25. Kirsch, A., van Amersfoort, J., Gal, Y.: BatchBALD: efficient and diverse batch acquisition for deep bayesian active learning. In: Advances in Neural Information Processing Systems, vol. 32. Curran Associates, Inc. (2019)
26. Kirsch, A., Gal, Y.: Unifying approaches in active learning and active sampling via fisher information and information-theoretic quantities. Trans. Mach. Learn. Res. (2022). Expert Certification
27. Knaus, W., et al.: The support prognostic model. objective estimates of survival for seriously ill hospitalized adults. Study to understand prognoses and preferences for outcomes and risks of treatments. Ann. Internal Med. **122**, 191–203 (1995)
28. Lakshminarayanan, B., Pritzel, A., Blundell, C.: Simple and scalable predictive uncertainty estimation using deep ensembles. In: Advances in Neural Information Processing Systems, vol. 30 (2017)

29. Lemeshow, S., May, S., Hosmer Jr, D.W.: Applied Survival Analysis: Regression Modeling of Time-to-Event Data. Wiley, Hoboken (2011)
30. Lian, J., et al.: Imaging-based deep graph neural networks for survival analysis in early stage lung cancer using CT: a multicenter study. Front. Oncol. **12** (2022)
31. Lindley, D.V.: On a measure of the information provided by an experiment. Ann. Math. Stat. **27**(4), 986–1005 (1956)
32. Liu, N., Ye, Y.: Humanitarian logistics planning for natural disaster response with Bayesian information updates. J. Ind. Manag. Optim. **10**(3), 901–919 (2014)
33. MacKay, D.J.C.: The evidence framework applied to classification networks. Neural Comput. **4**(5), 720–736 (1992)
34. MacKay, D.J.C.: Information-based objective functions for active data selection. Neural Comput. **4**(4), 590–604 (1992)
35. Mahajan, A.: Structure of optimal policies in active sensing. In: 2012 IEEE International Conference on Acoustics, Speech and Signal Processing (ICASSP), pp. 5265–5268. IEEE (2012)
36. Maystre, L., Russo, D.: Temporally-consistent survival analysis. In: Advances in Neural Information Processing Systems (2022)
37. Nezhad, M.Z., Sadati, N., Yang, K., Zhu, D.: A deep active survival analysis approach for precision treatment recommendations: application of prostate cancer. Expert Syst. Appl. **115**, 16–26 (2019)
38. Osborne, M.A., Roberts, S.J., Rogers, A., Jennings, N.R.: Real-time information processing of environmental sensor network data using Bayesian Gaussian processes. ACM Trans. Sens. Netw. (TOSN) **9**(1), 1–32 (2012)
39. Pearce, T., Jeong, J.H., Jia, Y., Zhu, J.: Censored quantile regression neural networks for distribution-free survival analysis. In: Advances in Neural Information Processing Systems (2022)
40. Powell, J.L.: Censored regression quantiles. J. Econom. **32**(1), 143–155 (1986)
41. Riis, C., Antunes, F., Hüttel, F.B., Azevedo, C.L., Pereira, F.C.: Bayesian active learning with fully Bayesian gaussian processes. In: Advances in Neural Information Processing Systems (2022)
42. Schumacher, M., et al.: Randomized 2 x 2 trial evaluating hormonal treatment and the duration of chemotherapy in node-positive breast cancer patients. German breast cancer study group. J. Clin. Oncol. **12**(10), 2086–2093 (1994)
43. Settles, B.: Active learning literature survey (2009)
44. Sharma, M., Farquhar, S., Nalisnick, E., Rainforth, T.: Do bayesian neural networks need to be fully stochastic? In: Proceedings of the 26th International Conference on Artificial Intelligence and Statistics, vol. 206, pp. 7694–7722 (2023)
45. Shen, Y., Yun, H., Lipton, Z.C., Kronrod, Y., Anandkumar, A.: Deep active learning for named entity recognition. In: International Conference on Learning Representations (2018)
46. Tobin, J.: Estimation of relationships for limited dependent variables. Econometrica **26**(1), 24–36 (1958)
47. Tornede, A., Bengs, V., Hüllermeier, E.: Machine learning for online algorithm selection under censored feedback. In: Proceedings of the AAAI Conference on Artificial Intelligence, vol. 36, pp. 10370–10380 (2022)
48. Vinzamuri, B., li, Y., Reddy, C.: Active learning based survival regression for censored data. In: Proceedings of the 2014 ACM International Conference on Information and Knowledge Management, pp. 241–250 (2014)
49. Zhang, J., Huang, J., Wang, T., Zhao, J.: Dynamic optimization of emergency logistics for major epidemic considering demand urgency. Systems **11**(6), 303 (2023)

An (ϵ, δ)-Accurate Level Set Estimation with a Stopping Criterion

Hideaki Ishibashi[1]($\boxtimes$), Kota Matsui[2,4], Kentaro Kutsukake[2], and Hideitsu Hino[3]

[1] Kyushu Institute of Technology, Kitakyushu, Fukuoka 808-0196, Japan
ishibashi@brain.kyutech.ac.jp
[2] Nagoya University, Nagoya Aichi 464-8601, Japan
{matsui.kota.x3,kutsukake.kentaro.c3}@f.mail.nagoya-u.ac.jp
[3] The Institute of Statistical Mathematics, Tachikawa, Tokyo 190-0014, Japan
hino@ism.ac.jp
[4] RIKEN AIP, Chuo Tokyo 103-0027, Japan

Abstract. The level set estimation problem seeks to identify regions within a set of candidate points where an unknown and costly to evaluate function's value exceeds a specified threshold, providing an efficient alternative to exhaustive evaluations of function values. Traditional methods often use sequential optimization strategies to find ϵ-accurate solutions, which permit a margin around the threshold contour but frequently lack effective stopping criteria, leading to excessive exploration and inefficiencies. This paper introduces an acquisition strategy for level set estimation that incorporates a stopping criterion, ensuring the algorithm halts when further exploration is unlikely to yield improvements, thereby reducing unnecessary function evaluations. We theoretically prove that our method satisfies ϵ-accuracy with a confidence level of $1 - \delta$, addressing a key gap in existing approaches. Furthermore, we show that this also leads to guarantees on the lower bounds of performance metrics such as F-score. Numerical experiments demonstrate that the proposed acquisition function achieves comparable precision to existing methods while confirming that the stopping criterion effectively terminates the algorithm once adequate exploration is completed.

Keywords: Level set estimation · Stopping criterion · Gaussian process · Adaptive experimental design

1 Introduction

Adaptive experimental design is a data-driven approach to planning experiments that determines the next experimental conditions based on data obtained so far. It is applied in various fields of experimental sciences such as drug discovery [20]

Supplementary Information The online version contains supplementary material available at https://doi.org/10.1007/978-3-032-05981-9_4.

and the development of new materials [47]. For example, in manufacturing industries, identifying defective areas where the physical properties of materials do not meet the desired quality is a crucial issue. Such defective areas are often determined by measuring the physical properties, using techniques like X-ray diffraction, in various parts of refined materials and determining whether they exceed acceptable lower limits. This problem can be formulated as a *Level Set Estimation* (LSE) by considering a black-box function that takes the coordinates of measurement locations as input and outputs the physical properties at each measurement location. LSE is a problem aimed to identify regions on the input space where the output values of a black-box function are greater (or smaller) than a certain threshold, and active learning (AL; [44]) approach has been proposed specifically to perform LSE with as few experimental iterations as possible [9,12,18,51].

In practical scenarios of adaptive experimental design, determining "when to stop the experiment" is crucially important. If stopping is not done appropriately, it can lead to wasteful experiments and the squandering of various costs. In experimental sciences, there are situations where an upper limit on the number of experiments that can be conducted. A naïve approach often involves conducting experiments up to such a "budget limit" and then stopping. For LSE, few theoretical guarantees exist on the consistency [7] or sample complexity [5], and there also exist some theoretical results on the finite-time guarantee of LSE [18,36], but to the best of the authors' knowledge, research on the stopping criterion for LSE is limited, with one example being the F-score sampling criterion [42]. This method stops when the 5th percentile of the sampled F-scores exceeds the desired F-score, and it allows for intuitive parameter setting and can be applied to a wide range of acquisition functions. However, in many applications, it is often unclear what is the maximum possible F-score for the problem, and the actual F-score at the stopping point may not exceed the desired F-score, making it difficult to stop the LSE procedure by specifying the F-score.

Contributions. In this paper, we propose an acquisition function for LSE based on the distribution of a random variable that represents the difficulty of classification. The proposed acquisition function entails a natural stopping criterion, probabilistically ensuring that the algorithm can be appropriately stopped when the LSE is accurately performed when used with the proposed acquisition function. Furthermore, our method probabilistically guarantees the lower bounds of performance metrics such as the F-score, accuracy, recall, precision, and specificity. Experiments using test functions and real-world data on the quality of silicon ingots demonstrate that the proposed method performs at least as well as existing methods in terms of the F-score, and can stop the algorithm when sufficient estimation accuracy is achieved.

Related Works. For active learning, stopping criteria based on various perspectives have been proposed. For example, it is investigated in [48] that the use of classifier confidence to determine that there are no informative instances remaining in the candidate point set and to stop AL. In [40], an intrinsic stopping criterion based on the exhaustiveness of the candidate point set is proposed, that does not depend on a predefined threshold parameter. A stopping criteria based on *Stabilizing Predictions* is proposed in [11], that checks the stability of the current model's predictions on the validation set and decides whether to stop the AL. In [2,10,29], stopping criterion based on the change in the F-score is considered. Criteria called *TotalConf* and *LeastConf* are proposed in [37], which stop the AL based on the amount of change in the classification confidence (i.e., prediction uncertainty) for unlabeled data. A method to stop AL based on upper bound of the generalization error is proposed in [24]. For Bayesian optimization (BO), stopping criteria based on regret have been proposed [25,33,50]. Note that each of these studies concerns stopping criteria for active learning and adaptive experimental design for classification, regression and optimization tasks, and are not directly applicable to the LSE problem.

Similar to the LSE problem, the estimation of the excursion set (which is also known as the probability of failure of a system in the industrial world) has also been considered, and different approaches such as sequential experimental design and kriging have been employed to tackle it with criteria targeted to reduce the uncertainty about the level set [3,8,15]. Contour finding, which identifies the contour where a black-box function equals a given threshold, has been developed independently of LSE but is closely related to it [17,31,35]. Several extensions of LSE to various situations are also considered, such as LSE under input uncertainty [16,23,26], heavy-tailed output noise [32] or heteroscedasticity of outputs [52], settings that aim at distributionally robust LSE [22], dealing with Bernoulli observations [30], considering control over type-I and type-II errors [4], and the setting where the input is composed of both deterministic and uncertain parts [1].

2 Level Set Estimation

Consider an unknown function $f : \mathcal{X} \to \mathbb{R}$ where $\mathcal{X}$ is a finite set of input $\mathbf{x}$. This is a so-called pool-based problem. The objective of LSE is to classify, given a threshold $\theta \in \mathbb{R}$, whether the outputs $\{f(\mathbf{x}) \mid \mathbf{x} \in \mathcal{X}\}$ corresponding to a given candidate point set $\mathcal{X}$ exceed θ, using as few datasets as possible. The upper/lower level sets are defined as $H_\theta = \{\mathbf{x} \in \mathcal{X} \mid f(\mathbf{x}) > \theta\}$ and $L_\theta = \{\mathbf{x} \in \mathcal{X} \mid f(\mathbf{x}) \leq \theta\}$, respectively. In LSE, the following procedure is iteratively performed to achieve this objective: i) Estimate the surrogate function $\hat{f}$ from the obtained dataset. ii) Utilize the surrogate function to classify each candidate point into any one of the upper-level set, the lower-level set, or the undetermined set. iii) Select the next search point based on the surrogate function. iv) Query the oracle for the corresponding output of the selected point. v) Add the obtained point to the dataset.

The surrogate function is often modeled by the Gaussian process regression (GPR; [49]). Consider a set of input-output pairs $S_N = \{(\mathbf{x}_n, y_n)\}_{n=1}^N$. In GPR, we assume that the function $\hat{f}$ is generated by a Gaussian process (GP) with a mean function $m(\mathbf{x})$ and a covariance function $k(\mathbf{x}, \mathbf{x}')$. Additionally, the observed output y is assumed to have Gaussian noise with precision parameter λ added to the generated function $\hat{f}$. Therefore, in GPR, we consider the following generative model: $\hat{f}(\mathbf{x}) \sim \mathcal{N}(m(\mathbf{x}), k(\mathbf{x}, \mathbf{x}'))$, and $y \mid \mathbf{x} \sim \mathcal{N}(\hat{f}(\mathbf{x}), \lambda^{-1})$. Denoting $\mathbf{y} := (y_1, y_2, \ldots, y_N)$, the joint distribution of $\mathbf{y}$ and the output $\hat{f}(\mathbf{x}^*)$ for a new input $\mathbf{x}^*$ can be expressed by the following equation.

$$\begin{bmatrix} \mathbf{y} \\ \hat{f}(\mathbf{x}^*) \end{bmatrix} \sim \mathcal{N}\left(\begin{bmatrix} \mathbf{m} \\ m(\mathbf{x}^*) \end{bmatrix}, \begin{bmatrix} \tilde{\mathbf{K}} & \mathbf{k}(\mathbf{x}^*) \\ \mathbf{k}^\mathrm{T}(\mathbf{x}^*) & k(\mathbf{x}^*, \mathbf{x}^*) \end{bmatrix} \right), \tag{1}$$

where $\tilde{\mathbf{K}} = \mathbf{K} + \lambda^{-1}\mathbf{I}$, $[\mathbf{K}]_{i,j} = k(\mathbf{x}_i, \mathbf{x}_j)$, $\mathbf{k}(\mathbf{x}^*) = (k(\mathbf{x}_n, \mathbf{x}^*))_{n=1}^N \in \mathbb{R}^N$, and $\mathbf{m} = (m(\mathbf{x}_n))_{n=1}^N \in \mathbb{R}^N$. Therefore, the posterior distribution when observing the dataset S_N is given by $p(\hat{f}(\mathbf{x}^*) \mid \mathbf{y}) = \mathcal{N}(\hat{f}(\mathbf{x}^*) \mid \mu_N(\mathbf{x}^*), \sigma_N^2(\mathbf{x}^*))$. Here,

$$\mu_N(\mathbf{x}^*) = m(\mathbf{x}^*) + \mathbf{k}^\mathrm{T}(\mathbf{x}^*)\tilde{\mathbf{K}}^{-1}(\mathbf{y} - \mathbf{m}), \tag{2}$$

$$\sigma_N^2(\mathbf{x}^*) = k(\mathbf{x}^*, \mathbf{x}^*) - \mathbf{k}^\mathrm{T}(\mathbf{x}^*)\tilde{\mathbf{K}}^{-1}\mathbf{k}(\mathbf{x}^*). \tag{3}$$

In LSE using GPR, the next exploration point is determined based on the posterior distribution. Specifically, if we define the acquisition function $\alpha : \mathcal{X} \to \mathbb{R}$ parameterized by $p(\hat{f} \mid \mathbf{y})$, the next exploration point is determined by $\mathbf{x}^{\mathrm{new}} = \arg\max_{\mathbf{x} \in \mathcal{X}} \alpha(\mathbf{x}; p(\hat{f} \mid \mathbf{y}), \theta)$. Although there are various types of acquisition functions, such as those based on confidence bounds [18] and expected improvement for level set estimation [51], we focus on a typical approach based on misclassification probability [14]. Assuming that the true function f is generated from the posterior distribution $p(\hat{f} \mid \mathbf{y})$, the probability $\Pr(\mathbf{x} \in L_\theta)$ can be expressed as follows, where $\Phi(\cdot)$ denotes the cumulative distribution function of the standard Gaussian:

$$\Pr(\mathbf{x} \in L_\theta) = \int_{-\infty}^{\theta} p(\hat{f}(\mathbf{x}) \mid \mathbf{y}) d\hat{f}(\mathbf{x}) = \Phi\left(\frac{\theta - \mu_N(\mathbf{x})}{\sigma_N(\mathbf{x})} \right). \tag{4}$$

Similarly, $\Pr(\mathbf{x} \in H_\theta) = 1 - \Pr(\mathbf{x} \in L_\theta)$. Then, $p^{\min}(\mathbf{x}) = \min\{\Pr(\mathbf{x} \in H_\theta), \Pr(\mathbf{x} \in L_\theta)\}$ represents the difficulty of classifying the candidate point $\mathbf{x}$; hence we call this "misclassification probability" [14]. Similarly, we call $p^{\max}(\mathbf{x}) = \max\{\Pr(\mathbf{x} \in H_\theta), \Pr(\mathbf{x} \in L_\theta)\}$ "classification probability". Therefore, the following acquisition function selects the candidate points that are difficult to classify as the next points of evaluation:

$$\mathbf{x}^{\mathrm{new}} = \arg\max_{\mathbf{x} \in \mathcal{X}} p^{\min}(\mathbf{x}). \tag{5}$$

When classifying candidate points, the standard method is the classification rule based on confidence intervals proposed by [18]. Let $\tilde{H}_\theta$ and $\tilde{L}_\theta$ be estimated upper-level set and lower-level set, respectively. We further introduce an undetermined set $\tilde{U}_\theta$. Then, a candidate point $\mathbf{x}$ is classified according to the following classification rule:

$$\tilde{H}_\theta = \{\mathbf{x} \mid \mathbf{x} \in \mathcal{X}, \mu_N(\mathbf{x}) - \beta\sigma_N(\mathbf{x}) > \theta\}, \tag{6}$$

$$\tilde{L}_\theta = \{\mathbf{x} \mid \mathbf{x} \in \mathcal{X}, \mu_N(\mathbf{x}) + \beta\sigma_N(\mathbf{x}) < \theta\}, \tag{7}$$

$$\tilde{U}_\theta = \mathcal{X} \setminus \{\tilde{H}_\theta \cup \tilde{L}_\theta\}, \tag{8}$$

where β is the parameter that controls the exploration-exploitation trade-off in the acquisition function.

3 Proposed Acquisition Function and Stopping Criterion

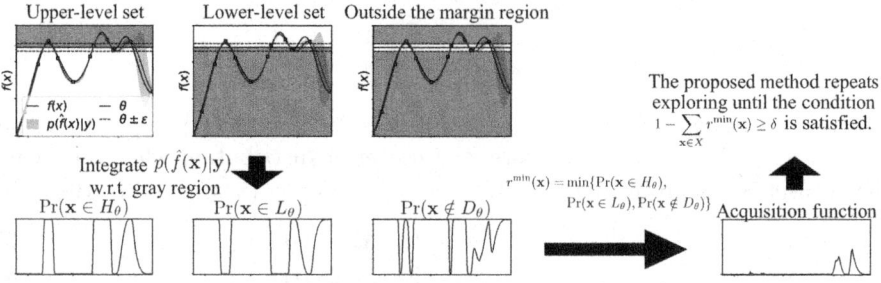

Fig. 1. The proposed method selects a candidate point that is difficult to classify and has a low probability of containing the true function value in the margin region and stops LSE when the condition is satisfied.

This section describes the acquisition function for LSE proposed in this paper and its stopping criterion. The pseudocode of the proposed LSE procedure is shown in Appendix B.2.

3.1 Proposed Acquisition Function

The acquisition function based on misclassification probability (5) is an intuitive and natural choice, where points with Bernoulli distribution parameters close to 0.5, and therefore difficult to classify, are selected as candidates for the next observation. In this formulation, noting that the cumulative distribution function of the standard Gaussian is $\Phi(0) = 0.5$, Eq. (4) suggests two possible scenarios for the selected candidate points. The first case occurs when the true function value at the candidate point is far from the threshold, but due to insufficient data observed near the candidate point, the posterior distribution's variance is large, making classification difficult ($\Phi\left(\frac{\theta - \mu_N(\mathbf{x})}{\sigma_N(\mathbf{x})}\right) \to 0.5$ as $\sigma_N(\mathbf{x}) \to \infty$). In this case, exploring the candidate point reduces the variance of the posterior distribution and increases the classification probability, making it less likely to be explored in subsequent searches. This is the case the exploration offers reasonable information.

On the other hand, the second case is problematic. The acquisition function (5) would select points at which the true function values are close to the threshold ($\Phi\left(\frac{\theta - \mu_N(\mathbf{x})}{\sigma_N(\mathbf{x})}\right) \to 0.5$ as $\mu_N(\mathbf{x}) \to \theta$). In this scenario, the same candidate point is repeatedly explored while other candidate points are ignored. For this issue, the previous study has heuristically used the product of the misclassification probability and the posterior variance as the acquisition function [14].

In this study, we assume that a margin $\epsilon > 0$ is given[1], which indicates a tolerance of the accuracy of estimation. If the gap between the true func-

---

[1] Here, the margin is assumed to be given, but a method for setting the margin based on the observed data are discussed in Appendix. B.1.

tion value $f(\mathbf{x})$ and threshold θ for a candidate point $\mathbf{x}$ lies within the range $\mathcal{E} := (-\epsilon/2, \epsilon/2]$, it is considered as a difficult to classify, and that exploring this candidate point will not increase certainty about the classification, and thus the point is removed from the candidate point set. To put it another way, for candidate points that are difficult to classify, we decide to make a concession and perform an ϵ-accurate classification. The notion of the margin is essentially equivalent to ϵ-accuracy introduced in [12], but we explicitly utilize it as information for determining the next experimental condition. The difficult-to-classify set is defined as $U_\theta = \{\mathbf{x} \in \mathcal{X} \mid (f(\mathbf{x}) - \theta) \in \mathcal{E}\}$, and the solution triplet $(\tilde{H}_\theta, \tilde{L}_\theta, \tilde{U}_\theta)$ is ϵ-accurate if $\forall \mathbf{x} \in \tilde{H}_\theta$ is in H_θ, $\forall \mathbf{x} \in \tilde{L}_\theta$ is in L_θ, and $\forall \mathbf{x} \in \tilde{U}_\theta$ is in U_θ.

The probability of $\mathbf{x} \in U_\theta$ is given by

$$\Pr(\mathbf{x} \in U_\theta) = \int_{\theta-\epsilon/2}^{\theta+\epsilon/2} p(\hat{f}(\mathbf{x}) \mid \mathbf{y}) d\hat{f}(\mathbf{x})$$

$$= \Phi\left(\frac{\theta + \epsilon/2 - \mu_N(\mathbf{x})}{\sigma_N(\mathbf{x})}\right) - \Phi\left(\frac{\theta - \epsilon/2 - \mu_N(\mathbf{x})}{\sigma_N(\mathbf{x})}\right).$$

Similarly, $\Pr(\mathbf{x} \notin U_\theta) = 1 - \Pr(\mathbf{x} \in U_\theta)$. Then, with $r^{\min}(\mathbf{x}) := \min\{\Pr(\mathbf{x} \in H_\theta), \Pr(\mathbf{x} \in L_\theta), \Pr(\mathbf{x} \notin U_\theta)\}$, we redefine the acquisition function as

$$\mathbf{x}^{\text{new}} = \arg\max_{\mathbf{x} \in \mathcal{X}} r^{\min}(\mathbf{x}). \tag{9}$$

As shown in Fig. 1, this acquisition function evaluates not only the probability that a candidate point belongs to the upper/lower level sets but also the probability $\Pr(\mathbf{x} \notin U_\theta)$ that the gap does not fall within the range $\mathcal{E}$. For a candidate point $\mathbf{x}$ where the gap $f(\mathbf{x}) - \theta$ is within $\mathcal{E}$, if the area around the candidate point has not been well explored, $\Pr(\mathbf{x} \notin U_\theta)$ increases, and if $p^{\min}(\mathbf{x})$ is also large, then $r^{\min}(\mathbf{x})$ increases, leading to the selection of $\mathbf{x}$. Conversely, if the area around the candidate point has been thoroughly explored, the posterior variance decreases, thus increasing the probability that the gap $f(\mathbf{x}) - \theta$ falls within $\mathcal{E}$ and decreasing $\Pr(\mathbf{x} \notin U_\theta)$. Therefore, even if $p^{\min}(\mathbf{x})$ is large and classification is difficult, $r^{\min}(\mathbf{x})$ becomes small, making it less likely to be chosen as the next point of evaluation.

As similar approaches to the misclassification-based approach, there are entropy-based and variance-based approaches [14,17]. These acquisition functions share the fundamental idea with the one in (5) and therefore inherit similar issues to those mentioned at the beginning of this section regarding (5). Several studies have discussed approaches to address the issues of these acquisition functions [35,41], but none provide theoretical guarantees on stopping performance, leaving the evaluation of this aspect to empirical analysis. In contrast, our acquisition function addresses the aforementioned issues while also providing theoretical guarantees on stopping performance, as discussed in the next section.

3.2 Classification Rule and Stopping Criterion

We describe the classification rule and stopping method for LSE using the acquisition function Eq. (9). Letting $r^{\max}(\mathbf{x}) := \max\{\Pr(\mathbf{x} \in H_\theta), \Pr(\mathbf{x} \in L_\theta), \Pr(\mathbf{x} \in U_\theta)\}$, the proposed classification rule is as follows:

$$\tilde{H}_\theta := \{\mathbf{x} \mid \mathbf{x} \in \mathcal{X}, r^{\max}(\mathbf{x}) = \Pr(\mathbf{x} \in H_\theta)\}, \tag{10}$$

$$\tilde{L}_\theta := \{\mathbf{x} \mid \mathbf{x} \in \mathcal{X}, r^{\max}(\mathbf{x}) = \Pr(\mathbf{x} \in L_\theta)\}, \tag{11}$$

$$\tilde{U}_\theta := \{\mathbf{x} \mid \mathbf{x} \in \mathcal{X}, r^{\max}(\mathbf{x}) = \Pr(\mathbf{x} \in U_\theta)\}. \tag{12}$$

As will be discussed later, this classification rule can be considered equivalent to the classification rule of Eqs. (6), (7), and (8) under certain conditions.

The proposed stopping criterion uses a confidence parameter δ ($0 < \delta < 1$) as a threshold, and LSE is stopped when the following inequality is satisfied:

$$1 - \sum_{\mathbf{x} \in \mathcal{X}} r^{\min}(\mathbf{x}) \geq \delta. \tag{13}$$

That is, LSE is stopped when the sum of the acquisition function values for all candidate points becomes small enough. At the point of stopping LSE, the following probability inequality holds:

Theorem 1. *If we assume that $\tilde{H}_\theta, \tilde{L}_\theta$ and $\tilde{U}_\theta$ are determined by using the classification rule of Eqs. (10),(11) and (12), then the following inequality holds:*

$$\Pr((\tilde{H}_\theta, \tilde{L}_\theta, \tilde{U}_\theta) \text{ is } \epsilon\text{-accurate}) \geq 1 - \sum_{\mathbf{x} \in \mathcal{X}} r^{\min}(\mathbf{x}). \tag{14}$$

The proof is shown in Appendix A. From this theorem, when Eq. (13) is satisfied, stopping LSE guarantees that $(\tilde{H}_\theta, \tilde{L}_\theta, \tilde{U}_\theta)$ is ϵ-accurate with a probability of at least δ. Therefore, we refer to the LSE that uses the combination of the proposed acquisition function and stopping criterion as the (ϵ, δ)-*accurate* LSE. Since the left-hand side of Eq. (14) can be evaluated by sampling functions according to the GP posterior distribution, we provide the tightness of the proposed lower bound in the Appendix C.1.

By using Theorem 1, we can also guarantee the lower bound of performance measures. Here, we present only the lower bound of the F-score as follows.

Proposition 1. *If we assume that $\tilde{H}_\theta, \tilde{L}_\theta$ and $\tilde{U}_\theta$ are determined by using the classification rule of Eqs. (10),(11) and (12), then the inequality*

$$F\text{-score} \geq \frac{2|\tilde{H}_\theta|}{2|\tilde{H}_\theta| + |\tilde{U}_\theta|}$$

holds with probability $1 - \sum_{\mathbf{x} \in \mathcal{X}} r^{\min}(\mathbf{x})$.

The lower bound of other performance measures such as accuracy, recall, precision, and specificity, and their proofs are shown in Appendix A. In [43], the lower bound of the F-score could not be analytically computed, so it is estimated using sampling. In contrast, our method provides lower bounds for the various measures such as F-score.

The standard classification rule and the proposed classification rule can be considered the same under certain conditions. The standard classification rule can be interpreted as follows: $\mathbf{x}$ is classified into upper-level set when $\Pr(\mathbf{x} \in H_\theta) > \Phi(\beta)$ is satisfied, $\mathbf{x}$ is classified into lower-level set when $\Pr(\mathbf{x} \in L_\theta) > \Phi(\beta)$ is satisfied, and $\mathbf{x}$ is classified into undetermined set when the both of conditions are not satisfied. Regarding $\Pr(\mathbf{x} \in U_\theta)$ as $\Phi(\beta)$, the standard classification is equivalent to the proposed classification rule under the assumption that $\Phi(\beta) > 0.5$[2].

By using the above relationship, we can show that the triplet $(\tilde{H}_\theta, \tilde{L}_\theta, \tilde{U}_\theta)$ is ϵ-accurate in the case of the standard classification rule. Here, β in the standard classification rule and ϵ in the proposed classification rule can be mutually converted. Note that β also changes for each $\mathbf{x}$ in general even if ϵ is common to all $\mathbf{x}$ since $\Pr(\mathbf{x} \in U_\theta)$ varies depending on $\mathbf{x}$. We denote $\Pr(\mathbf{x} \in U_\theta)$ as $g(\epsilon \mid \mathbf{x})$, then there is an inverse mapping of $g(\epsilon \mid \mathbf{x})$ because $g(\cdot \mid \mathbf{x}) : \mathbb{R}^+ \to (0,1)$ is a strictly increasing function with respect to $\epsilon \in \mathbb{R}^+$. Therefore, the following mutual conversions between ϵ and β hold:

$$\beta = \Phi^{-1}\left(g(\epsilon \mid \mathbf{x})\right), \quad \epsilon = g^{-1}(\Phi(\beta) \mid \mathbf{x}).$$

With these conversions, we can show that the triplet $(\tilde{H}_\theta, \tilde{L}_\theta, \tilde{U}_\theta)$ is ϵ-accurate when we use the standard classification rule as follows:

Corollary 1. *We assume that $\tilde{H}_\theta, \tilde{L}_\theta$ and $\tilde{U}_\theta$ are determined by using the classification rule of Eqs. (6), (7), and (8) with β and $\Phi(\beta) > 0.5$. Let $\tilde{r}^{\min}(\mathbf{x}) = \min\{\Pr(\mathbf{x} \in H_\theta), \Pr(\mathbf{x} \in L_\theta), 1 - \Phi(\beta)\}$. Then, the following inequality holds:*

$$\Pr((\tilde{H}_\theta, \tilde{L}_\theta, \tilde{U}_\theta) \text{ is } g^{-1}(\Phi(\beta) \mid \mathbf{x}) \text{ -accurate}) \geq 1 - \sum_{\mathbf{x} \in \mathcal{X}} \tilde{r}^{\min}(\mathbf{x}). \qquad (15)$$

The proof is shown in Appendix A.

3.3 Choice of ϵ and δ

We explain how to determine the parameters ϵ and δ, and its sensitivity. Regarding δ, the proposed lower bound tends to increase monotonically, and the bound becomes tighter as the true probability of ϵ-accuracy approaches 1 as shown in Appendix. C.1. Therefore, we just have to set δ close to 1, such as $\delta = 0.99$. Since the stopping time does not change significantly when δ is close to 1, we can say that the stopping timing tends to be insensitive to the choice of δ.

---

[2] The condition $\Phi(\beta) > 0.5$ is added because in the standard classification rule, when $\Phi(\beta) \leq 0.5$, there is a possibility that $\mathbf{x}$ belongs to both the upper-level and lower-level sets. The standard classification rule often uses values such as $\beta = 1.96$, which corresponds to $\Phi(\beta) = 0.975$, implicitly assuming $\Phi(\beta) > 0.5$.

On the other hand, it is difficult to set ϵ appropriately, since it depends on the range of the objective function and the noise variance. In this study, instead of determining ϵ directly, we determine ϵ as follows:[3]

$$\epsilon(\mathbf{x}) = 2\sqrt{\frac{\lambda^{-1}k(\mathbf{x},\mathbf{x})}{\lambda^{-1}+Lk(\mathbf{x},\mathbf{x})}}\Phi^{-1}\left(1-\frac{1-\delta}{2|\mathcal{X}|}\right), \qquad (16)$$

where L is a parameter set by the user instead of ϵ, and it can be interpreted as the minimum number of observations required per candidate point, even in cases where classification is not possible. As shown in the Appendix. C.3, L is less sensitive to the range of the function and the noise variance than directly specifying ϵ, making it a more robust parameter.

3.4 Computational Cost

The proposed stopping criterion only requires the cumulative distribution function (CDF) of the standard normal distribution, and it does not require any sampling. Since the CDF of the standard normal distribution can be efficiently computed using libraries, the computational cost increases only linearly with the number of candidate points. In contrast, F-scores sampling (FS) [43] requires sampling functions from the posterior distribution, resulting in a quadratic increase in computational cost with respect to the number of candidate points. Therefore, compared to FS, the proposed stopping criterion remains computationally feasible even as the number of candidate points increases.

4 Experimental Results

In this section, we demonstrate the effectiveness of the proposed acquisition function using both synthetic data and a practical application for estimating the red zone in silicon ingots.[4] In all experiments, the threshold θ that defines the level set is a pre-fixed value, but the results of setting θ to several different values are also shown in the Appendix C.7. Note that consistent results are obtained even when different thresholds are used.

4.1 LSE for Test Functions

Aiming at demonstrating the applicability of the proposed method across functions with various shapes, we evaluate the proposed method using test functions commonly used as benchmarks in the study of optimization algorithms. The test functions employed in this experiment are the **Rosenbrock**, **Branin**, and

---

[3] When using a stationary kernel, ϵ is independent of $\mathbf{x}$. Please refer to the Appendix. B.1 for the detailed derivation of this equation.

[4] In these experiments, we use a Macbook Pro with Apple M1 Max (10-core CPU, 32-core GPU and 32GB memory), and implemented with Python and library GPy [19]. The code is available at https://github.com/hideaki-ishibashi/stopping_LSE.

Cross in tray functions[5], each representing a different landscape: one with a single local minimum with a spherical vicinity, one with a valley-like structure, and one with multiple local minima. Additional results are discussed in the Appendix C.3. For each function, thresholds are set, and candidate points exceeding these thresholds are considered part of the true upper set, while those below are viewed as the true lower set. The thresholds are set as follows: $\theta = 100$ for the Rosenbrock function and the Branin function, $\theta = -1.5$ for the Cross in tray function. Although these test functions have continuous domains, they are discretized into a grid of $20 \times 20 = 400$ points, which serve as observation candidates. In the Appendix C.2, we show that the stopping timing of the proposed method tends not to change even if the number of candidate points increases. Any of these points may be selected by acquisition functions, and repeated selections of the same points is allowed. Gaussian noise is added to the observations, with standard deviations set according to the range of each test function: $\sigma_{\text{noise}} = 30$ for the Rosenbrock function, $\sigma_{\text{noise}} = 20$ for the Branin function, and $\sigma_{\text{noise}} = 0.01$ for the Cross in tray function.

The proposed method is evaluated based on both the performance of the acquisition function and the efficiency achieved by early stopping. Generally, the performance of the LSE acquisition function is assessed using the F-score, which compares the predicted upper/lower level sets to the true upper/lower level sets over the candidate points. Not all candidate points may be classified in every search due to the classification rules. For the evaluation purpose, unclassified candidate points are assigned to the upper or lower level sets only for the F-score calculation if the posterior mean of GP exceeds or falls below the threshold, respectively. The performance of the acquisition function is evaluated based on the mean and variance of the convergence speed of the F-score when the LSE algorithm is executed using five randomly selected initial points. On the other hand, the effectiveness of the stopping criterion is evaluated based on the stopping time and the F-score at that moment. In other words, a good stopping criterion allows the algorithm to stop with fewer observations while achieving a high F-score.

Comparison Methods. The level set estimation problem is also related to Bayesian optimization [38] and bandit problems [46], and its applications range from brain science [34] to astronomy [6,39] for example. Various algorithms (acquisition functions) have been proposed, but in this study, we compare those that are considered particularly major types and important in terms of practical performance: in addition to uncertainty sampling (US), which selects points that maximize the predictive variance of the Gaussian process as a baseline, we consider Straddle [14], MILE [18], RMILE [18], and MELK [36], which is a recently proposed sampling method based on experimental design. Although many other methods exist, they do not consistently outperform those mentioned here. It should also be noted that the main focus of this paper is the proposal of an acquisition function equipped with a stopping criterion. In these acqui-

---

[5] https://www.sfu.ca/~ssurjano/optimization.html.

sition functions, candidate points are classified according to Eqs. (6), (7), and (8), where $\beta = 1.96$. On the other hand, in the proposed method, candidate points are classified according to Eqs. (10), (11), and (12). The same value of $\beta = 1.96$ is used for Straddle, MILE, and RMILE. MELK assumes that candidate points are not reclassified and that multiple points are sampled simultaneously. Following the settings of the previous study [36], MELK samples 10 points at a time without reclassifying candidate points. In contrast, other methods reclassify candidate points and sample one point at a time. RMILE's robust adjustment parameter ν is set to $\nu = 0.1$ according to the previous studies [22,51]. The proposed acquisition function also requires setting a parameter L, which is conservatively set to $L = 5$ to address the complex shape function based on the experimental results in Appendix C.6. The threshold for the proposed stopping criterion is set at $\delta = 0.99$. To evaluate the stopping criterion of the proposed method, we consider two stopping criteria. One is a standard stopping criterion which stops LSE when all candidate points are classified' (we call this the *fully classified (FC)* criterion), and the other is a stopping criteria based on sampling F-scores [43] (the criterion referred to as F-score Sampling (FS)). The stopping times of these stopping criteria are compared with the stopping times when using the proposed acquisition function and stopping criterion. In the FS criterion, as hyperparameters, we need to set the desired F-score and the probability of exceeding that F-score. In this experiment, we set the desired F-score and the probability to 0.95 and 95% (that is, 5th percentile).

Hyper-Parameter Setting. In this experiment, we consider a GP with the mean function set to θ and the covariance function defined by a Gaussian kernel $k(\mathbf{x}, \mathbf{x}') = \rho \exp(-\frac{1}{2l^2}\|\mathbf{x} - \mathbf{x}'\|^2)$. The mean function is set to θ to ensure that, in the absence of any observed data, the probability of unobserved candidate points being classified into either the upper or lower level set is 50%. This setting can be adjusted based on any prior knowledge available in real applications. The variance ρ of the Gaussian kernel, the kernel width l, and the noise precision λ are hyperparameters, which are estimated by maximizing the marginal likelihood of the observed data each time a search is conducted using LSE. To prevent large fluctuations in the hyperparameters with each search, gamma priors are placed on ρ and l. Additionally, the noise precision λ is constrained within the range $[10^{-6}, 10^6]$ to prevent it from becoming infinite.

Results. The F-scores for each acquisition function and the respective stopping timings are shown in Figs. 2. Although there are slight differences between individual test functions, no acquisition function, including the proposed method, significantly outperforms the baseline US or is markedly inefficient. Thus, it is crucial to stop LSE at the right moment when the F-scores have converged to enhance the efficiency of LSE. Regarding the stopping timings, the fully classified criterion often fails to stop the LSE even when the budget is fully utilized except for MELK in Cross in tray function. The inability of the FC criterion to stop is due to the occurrence of difficult-to-classify candidate points when function values at candidate points equal the threshold, and classification becomes more

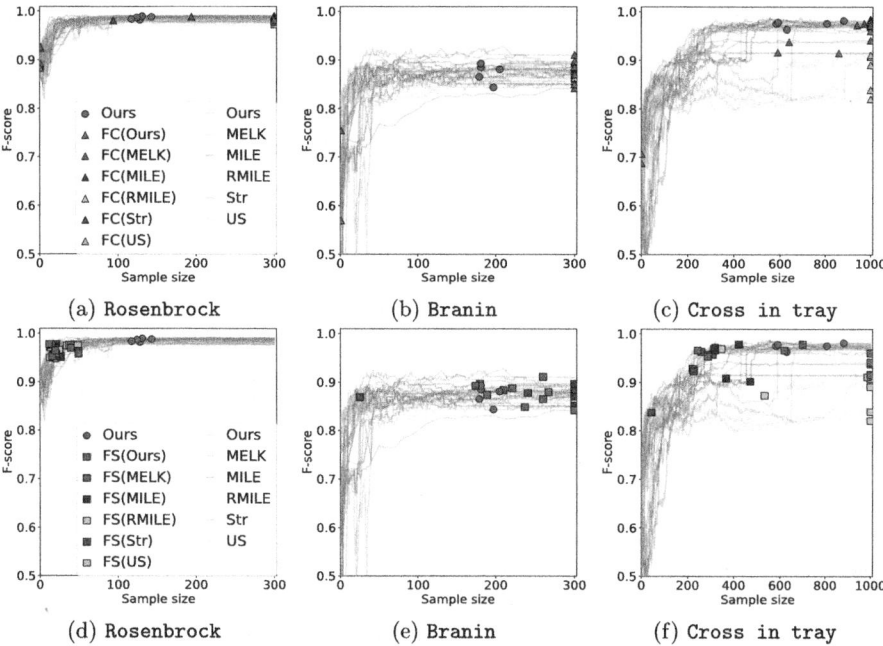

Fig. 2. F-scores using each acquisition function and stoped timings with the proposed (Ours), F-score sampling (FS) and fully classified (FC) criteria for test functions. (a)–(c) Stopping time of FC and Ours. (d)–(f) Stopping times of FS and Ours.

challenging as noise is added to the data, distancing the function values from the threshold. In MELK, it is sometimes possible to stop LSE even when the fully classified stopping criteria are used, as shown in Fig. 2(c), since it does not reclassify candidate points. However, the F-score of MELK may be lower than that of other methods, as it cannot correct candidate points that have been misclassified. In the FS criterion, as shown in Fig. 2(d), when the F-score converges, LSE can be stopped regardless of the acquisition function used. However, as shown in Fig. 2(f), despite the F-score not having converged, FS stops LSE. This is because the desired F-score is set to 0.95 in this experiment. This value was suitable when the F-score converged to 1, as in case Rosenbrock. However, it was not suitable when the noise was high, and the F-score did not converge to 1, as in cases of Branin function. Moreover, when noise was low, FS stopped LSE before the F-score converged to 1. Therefore, it is necessary to set the appropriate desired F-score according to the situation in the FS. Furthermore, under the FS criterion, despite setting the desired threshold to 0.95, the actual F-scores at the stopping time tend to be lower than 0.95 as shown in Fig. 2(e) and (f). Therefore, in practical applications, the desired value should be set higher than expected. In contrast, the proposed method, despite using the same parameters, can stop at the time when convergence occurs, regardless of where the F-score converges. This demonstrates that, compared to FS, the proposed method does not require the parameters of the stopping criterion to be finely tuned to the specific problem.

4.2 Red-Zone Estimation of Silicon Ingots

We demonstrate the effectiveness of the proposed method when using LSE to estimate the red zone in silicon ingots used in solar cells. The objective in this problem is to estimate regions contaminated with impurities (called the red zone) that are unsuitable for solar cell production. Typically, red zone estimation is performed through spatial mapping with measurement points placed in a regular grid, which is very time-consuming. Recently, the efficiency of red zone estimation using LSE has been proposed [21]. The data used in the experiments consist of lifetime measurements taken at grid points on two different types of silicon ingots, with each ingot measured at a grid of 161 × 121 points [28]. Hereinafter, the lifetime data from the first silicon ingot will be referred to as Lifetime1, and from the second ingot as Lifetime2. In both cases, the threshold is set to $\theta = 230$.

The performance of LSE methods are evaluated, in the similar manner to the test functions, by observing the F-scores, and the F-score at the stopping timing, with initial values changed randomly five times. The same methodology as for the test functions was used for comparison, but once a candidate point is selected, it is not selected again to estimate the noise because we have only one observation for each point. The parameters of the acquisition functions, the GP prior, and the hyperparameter estimation method were employed in the same manner as for the test functions.

As shown in Fig. 3, the transition of the F-score shows no significant differences regardless of the acquisition function used, except for MELK. In MELK, the F-score tends to converge to a low value. This is because MELK does not reclassify candidate points. In the perspective of the stopping timings, the FC stopping criterion fails to stop even after the entire budget is used. On the other hand, the proposed criterion allows for early stopping once the F-scores converge. This is likely due to measurement noise, leading to difficult-to-classify candidate points. Thus, the proposed method effectively stops the LSE in red zone estimation. FS criterion stops LSE earlier than the proposed criterion. However, the F-score continues to gradually increase even after FS stops, and the appropriate stopping point varies depending on the situation.

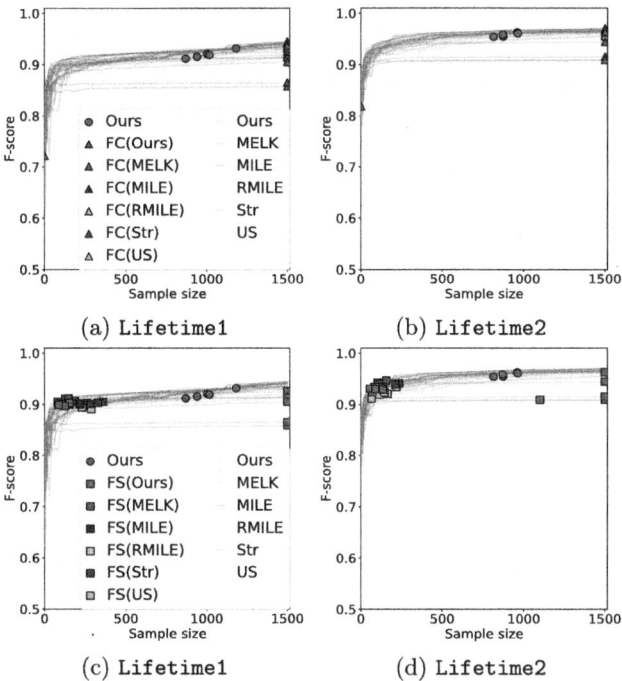

Fig. 3. F-scores using each acquisition function and stoped timings with the proposed (Ours), F-score sampling (FS) and fully classified (FC) criteria for red zone estimation. (a), (b) Stopping time of FC and Ours. (c), (d) Stopping times of FS and Ours. (Color figure online)

5 Discussion and Conclusion

In this paper, we proposed an acquisition function for level set estimation by directly modeling the difficulty of classifying into upper/lower sets. The proposed acquisition function is based on the notion of the ϵ-accuracy [12], and an adaptive determination method of the ϵ parameter is proposed. A stopping criterion for the algorithm was also proposed. When applied to both synthetic and real data, the proposed method performed comparably to existing methods in terms of acquisition function performance and was able to stop the algorithm early, even in the presence of observation noise. Empirically, the proposed method tends to be conservative. This behavior can be beneficial in some cases but harmful in others. Balancing theoretical guarantees with more aggressive stopping remains an open problem for future work. Another direction for future work is extending the method to query-based problems where evaluation points are selected from a continuous domain [45]. Additionally, extending the method to high-dimensional problems is also an important issue.

Acknowledgments. This work was supported by Grants-in-Aid from the Japan Society for the Promotion of Science (JSPS) for Scientific Research (KAKENHI grant nos. JP23K28146 and JP24K20836 to K.M., JP24K15088 to H.I., and JP23K24909, 25H01494 and JPMJMI21G2 to H.H.).

References

1. Ait Abdelmalek-Lomenech, R., Bect, J., Chabridon, V., Vazquez, E.: Bayesian sequential design of computer experiments for quantile set inversion. Technometrics, pp. 1–10 (2024). https://doi.org/10.1080/00401706.2024.2394475
2. Altschuler, M., Bloodgood, M.: Stopping active learning based on predicted change of f measure for text classification. In: 2019 IEEE 13th International Conference on Semantic Computing (ICSC), pp. 47–54 (2019). https://doi.org/10.1109/ICOSC.2019.8665646
3. Azzimonti, D., Bect, J., Chevalier, C., Ginsbourger, D.: Quantifying uncertainties on excursion sets under a Gaussian random field prior. SIAM/ASA J. Uncert. Quant. **4**(1), 850–874 (2016). https://doi.org/10.1137/141000749
4. Azzimonti, D., Ginsbourger, D., Chevalier, C., Bect, J., Richet, Y.: Adaptive design of experiments for conservative estimation of excursion sets. Technometrics J. Stat. Phys. Chem. Eng. Sci. **63**(1), 13–26 (2021). https://doi.org/10.1080/00401706.2019.1693427
5. Bachoc, F., Cesari, T., Gerchinovitz, S.: The sample complexity of level set approximation. In: The 24th International Conference on Artificial Intelligence and Statistics, AISTATS 2021, April 13-15, 2021, Virtual Event. Proceedings of Machine Learning Research, vol. 130, pp. 424–432. PMLR (2021)
6. Beaky, M.M., Scherrer, R.J., Villumsen, J.V.: Topology of large-scale structure in seeded hot dark matter models. Astrophys. J. **387**, 443 (1992). https://doi.org/10.1086/171097
7. Bect, J., Bachoc, F., Ginsbourger, D.: A supermartingale approach to Gaussian process based sequential design of experiments. Bernoulli **25**(4A), 2883–2919 (2019). https://doi.org/10.3150/18-BEJ1074
8. Bect, J., Ginsbourger, D., Li, L., Picheny, V., Vazquez, E.: Sequential design of computer experiments for the estimation of a probability of failure. Stat. Comput. **22**, 773–793 (2012)
9. Bichon, B.J., Eldred, M.S., Swiler, L.P., Mahadevan, S., McFarland, J.M.: Efficient global reliability analysis for nonlinear implicit performance functions. AIAA J. **46**(10), 2459–2468 (2008). https://doi.org/10.2514/1.34321
10. Bloodgood, M., Grothendieck, J.: Analysis of stopping active learning based on stabilizing predictions. In: Proceedings of the Seventeenth Conference on Computational Natural Language Learning, pp. 10–19. Association for Computational Linguistics, Sofia, Bulgaria (Aug 2013)
11. Bloodgood, M., Vijay-Shanker, K.: A method for stopping active learning based on stabilizing predictions and the need for user-adjustable stopping. In: Proceedings of the Thirteenth Conference on Computational Natural Language Learning (CoNLL-2009), pp. 39–47. Association for Computational Linguistics, Boulder, Colorado (2009)
12. Bogunovic, I., Scarlett, J., Krause, A., Cevher, V.: Truncated variance reduction: a unified approach to Bayesian optimization and level-set estimation. In: Advances in Neural Information Processing Systems, vol. 29. Curran Associates, Inc. (2016)

13. Brooks, S.P., Gelman, A.: General methods for monitoring convergence of iterative simulations. J. Comput. Graph. Stat. **7**(4), 434–455 (1998). https://doi.org/10.1080/10618600.1998.10474787
14. Bryan, B., Nichol, R.C., Genovese, C.R., Schneider, J., Miller, C.J., Wasserman, L.: Active learning for identifying function threshold boundaries. Adv. Neural Info. Process. Syst. **18** (2005)
15. Chevalier, C., Bect, J., Ginsbourger, D., Vazquez, E., Picheny, V., Richet, Y.: Fast parallel kriging-based stepwise uncertainty reduction with application to the identification of an excursion set. Technometrics J. Stat. Phys. Chem. Eng. Sci. **56**(4), 455–465 (2014). https://doi.org/10.1080/00401706.2013.860918
16. Chevalier, C., Ginsbourger, D., Bect, J., Molchanov, I.: Estimating and quantifying uncertainties on level sets using the Vorob EV expectation and deviation with Gaussian process models. In: Contributions to Statistics, pp. 35–43. Contributions to statistics, Springer International Publishing, Heidelberg (2013) https://doi.org/10.1007/978-3-319-00218-7_5
17. D. Austin Cole, Robert B. Gramacy, J.E.W.G.F.B.P.E.L., Leser, W.P.: Entropy-based adaptive design for contour finding and estimating reliability. J. Qual. Technol. **55**(1), 43–60 (2023). https://doi.org/10.1080/00224065.2022.2053795
18. Gotovos, A., Casati, N., Hitz, G., Krause, A.: Active learning for level set estimation. In: Proceedings of the Twenty-Third International Joint Conference on Artificial Intelligence. AAAI Press (2013)
19. GPy: GPy: A Gaussian Process Framework in Python. http://github.com/SheffieldML/GPy (2012)
20. Griffiths, R.R., Hernández-Lobato, J.M.: Constrained Bayesian optimization for automatic chemical design using variational autoencoders. Chem. Sci. **11**(2), 577–586 (2020)
21. Hozumi, S., Kutsukake, K., Matsui, K., Kusakawa, S., Ujihara, T., Takeuchi, I.: Adaptive defective area identification in material surface using active transfer learning-based level set estimation. ArXiv **abs/2304.01404** (2023)
22. Inatsu, Y., Iwazaki, S., Takeuchi, I.: Active learning for distributionally robust level-set estimation. In: International Conference on Machine Learning, pp. 4574–4584. PMLR (2021)
23. Inatsu, Y., Karasuyama, M., Inoue, K., Takeuchi, I.: Active learning for level set estimation under input uncertainty and its extensions. Neural Comput. **32**(12), 2486–2531 (2020)
24. Ishibashi, H., Hino, H.: Stopping criterion for active learning based on deterministic generalization bounds. In: The 23rd International Conference on Artificial Intelligence and Statistics, AISTATS 2020, 26-28 August 2020, Online [Palermo, Sicily, Italy]. Proceedings of Machine Learning Research, vol. 108, pp. 386–397. PMLR (2020)
25. Ishibashi, H., Karasuyama, M., Takeuchi, I., Hino, H.: A stopping criterion for bayesian optimization by the gap of expected minimum simple regrets. In: International Conference on Artificial Intelligence and Statistics, pp. 6463–6497. PMLR (2023)
26. Iwazaki, S., Inatsu, Y., Takeuchi, I.: Bayesian experimental design for finding reliable level set under input uncertainty. IEEE Access **8**, 203982–203993 (2020)
27. Kish, L.: Survey Sampling. Wiley (1965)
28. Kutsukake, K., Deura, M., Ohno, Y., Yonenaga, I.: Characterization of silicon ingots: mono-like versus high-performance multicrystalline. Jpn. J. Appl. Phys. **54**(8S1), 08KD10 (2015). https://doi.org/10.7567/JJAP.54.08KD10

29. Laws, F., Schütze, H.: Stopping criteria for active learning of named entity recognition. In: Proceedings of the 22nd International Conference on Computational Linguistics, vol. 1, pp. 465–472. Association for Computational Linguistics, Morristown, NJ, USA (2008). https://doi.org/10.3115/1599081.1599140
30. Letham, B., Guan, P., Tymms, C., Bakshy, E., Shvartsman, M.: Look-ahead acquisition functions for Bernoulli level set estimation. In: AISTATS. Proceedings of Machine Learning Research, vol. abs/2203.09751, pp. 8493–8513. PMLR (2022). https://doi.org/10.48550/arXiv.2203.09751
31. Li, J., Li, J., Xiu, D.: An efficient surrogate-based method for computing rare failure probability. J. Comput. Phys. **230**(24), 8683–8697 (2011). https://doi.org/10.1016/j.jcp.2011.08.008
32. Lyu, X., Binois, M., Ludkovski, M.: Evaluating Gaussian process metamodels and sequential designs for noisy level set estimation. Stat. Comput. **31**(4), 1–21 (2021). https://doi.org/10.1007/s11222-021-10014-w
33. Makarova, et al.: Automatic termination for hyperparameter optimization. In: International Conference on Automated Machine Learning, pp. 1–7. PMLR (2022)
34. Marchini, J., Presanis, A.: Comparing methods of analyzing FMRI statistical parametric maps. Neuroimage **22**(3), 1203–1213 (2004). https://doi.org/10.1016/j.neuroimage.2004.03.030
35. Marques, A., Lam, R., Willcox, K.: Contour location via entropy reduction leveraging multiple information sources. In: Advances in Neural Information Processing Systems, vol. 31. Curran Associates, Inc. (2018)
36. Mason, B., Jain, L., Mukherjee, S., Camilleri, R., Jamieson, K.G., Nowak, R.D.: Nearly optimal algorithms for level set estimation. In: International Conference on Artificial Intelligence and Statistics, AISTATS 2022, 28-30 March 2022, Virtual Event. Proceedings of Machine Learning Research, vol. 151, pp. 7625–7658. PMLR (2022)
37. McDonald, G., Macdonald, C., Ounis, I.: Active learning stopping strategies for technology-assisted sensitivity review. In: Proceedings of the 43rd International ACM SIGIR Conference on Research and Development in Information Retrieval, pp. 2053–2056. SIGIR '20, Association for Computing Machinery, New York, NY, USA (2020). https://doi.org/10.1145/3397271.3401267
38. Nguyen, Q.P., Low, B.K.H., Jaillet, P.: An information-theoretic framework for unifying active learning problems. arXiv [cs.LG] (2020)
39. Nikakhtar, F., Ayromlou, M., Baghram, S., Rahvar, S., Rahimi Tabar, M.R., Sheth, R.K.: The excursion set approach: stratonovich approximation and Cholesky decomposition. Mon. Not. R. Astron. Soc. **478**(4), 5296–5300 (2018). https://doi.org/10.1093/mnras/sty1415
40. Olsson, F., Tomanek, K.: An intrinsic stopping criterion for committee-based active learning. In: Proceedings of the Thirteenth Conference on Computational Natural Language Learning, pp. 138–146. CoNLL '09, Association for Computational Linguistics, Stroudsburg, PA, USA (2009)
41. Picheny, V., Ginsbourger, D., Roustant, O., Haftka, R.T., Kim, N.H.: Adaptive designs of experiments for accurate approximation of a target region. J. Mech. Des. (New York, N.Y.: 1990) **132**(7), 071008 (2010). https://doi.org/10.1115/1.4001873
42. Qing, J., Knudde, N., Garbuglia, F., Spina, D., Couckuyt, I., Dhaene, T.: Adaptive sampling with automatic stopping for feasible region identification in engineering design. Eng. Comput. **38**(Suppl 3), 1955–1972 (2022). https://doi.org/10.1007/s00366-021-01341-7

43. Qing, J., Knudde, N., Garbuglia, F., Spina, D., Couckuyt, I., Dhaene, T.: Adaptive sampling with automatic stopping for feasible region identification in engineering design. Eng. Comput. **38**(3), 1955–1972 (2022). https://doi.org/10.1007/s00366-021-01341-7
44. Settles, B.: Active learning literature survey. Mach. Learn. **15**(2), 201–221 (2010). 10.1.1.167.4245
45. Shekhar, S., Javidi, T.: Multiscale gaussian process level set estimation. In: Proceedings of the Twenty-Second International Conference on Artificial Intelligence and Statistics. Proceedings of Machine Learning Research, vol. 89, pp. 3283–3291. PMLR (2019)
46. Srinivas, N., Krause, A., Kakade, S., Seeger, M.: Gaussian process optimization in the bandit setting: no regret and experimental design. In: Proceedings of the 27th International Conference on International Conference on Machine Learning, pp. 1015–1022. ICML'10, Omnipress, Madison, WI, USA (2010)
47. Ueno, T., Rhone, T.D., Hou, Z., Mizoguchi, T., Tsuda, K.: Combo: an efficient Bayesian optimization library for materials science. Mater. Dis. **4**, 18–21 (2016)
48. Vlachos, A.: A stopping criterion for active learning. Comput. Speech Lang. **22**(3), 295–312 (2008). https://doi.org/10.1016/j.csl.2007.12.001
49. Williams, C., Rasmussen, C.: Gaussian processes for regression. In: Advances in Neural Information Processing Systems, vol. 8, pp. 514–520. MIT Press (1995)
50. Wilson, J.: Stopping Bayesian optimization with probabilistic regret bounds. In: Advances in Neural Information Processing Systems, vol. 37, pp. 98264–98296. Curran Associates, Inc. (2024)
51. Zanette, A., Zhang, J., Kochenderfer, M.J.: Robust super-level set estimation using gaussian processes. In: Machine Learning and Knowledge Discovery in Databases: European Conference, ECML PKDD 2018, Dublin, Ireland, September 10–14, 2018, Proceedings, Part II 18, pp. 276–291. Springer (2019)
52. Zhang, Y., Chen, X.: Sequential metamodel? Based approaches to level?set estimation under heteroscedasticity. Stati. Anal. Data Min. **17**(3) (2024). https://doi.org/10.1002/sam.11697

Self-improvement for Computerized Adaptive Testing

Yannick Rudolph[✉], Kai Neubauer, and Ulf Brefeld

Leuphana University, 21335 Lüneburg, Germany
{yannick.rudolph,kai.neubauer,ulf.brefeld}@leuphana.de

Abstract. Computerized adaptive testing (CAT) allows for assessing latent traits and abilities of students with fewer items and in less time due to an individualized item selection algorithm based on previous responses. Following recent machine learning solutions to CAT, we study learning both the underlying response model for cognitive diagnosis and a policy for the item selection algorithm jointly from offline training data. While the task of the response model is to predict performances on all unseen items for a user, the goal of the policy is to select the subset of items which maximizes information for the response model. Since subset selection is a combinatorial problem, we propose to leverage an iterative self-improvement approach to policy learning from the field of neural combinatorial optimization while accounting for interdependencies between response model and policy. We specifically focus on the generalization capabilities of transformer-based models and, in contrast to related work, do not rely on optimization of local variables during inference. We report on empirical results.

Keywords: Educational data mining · Computerized adaptive testing · Neural combinatorial optimization · Self-improvement

1 Introduction

Classical test theory [26,37] focuses on estimating latent traits and abilities of students by observing their responses in tests. In computerized adaptive testing (CAT), questions are adaptively selected according to a student's performance on previously seen items. Due to this personalization, selected questions are on average better suited to assess latent traits compared to classical test theory, rendering adaptive tests more accurate and shorter in terms of test length and time [42,43]. The theoretical foundation of CAT is closely related to item response theory (IRT) [19,23,29] that introduces a large family of models to estimate latent traits of students. Traditional CAT approaches use IRT-based models to estimate latent abilities of students and difficulties of questions to predict future responses on unseen questions and to guide item selection.

Y. Rudolph and K. Neubauer—Contributed equally to this work.

Recent machine learning approaches to CAT proposed to employ learned policies for question selection [10,51] and have framed CAT as an iterative subset selection problem [52] while deep learning architectures such as the neural cognitive diagnosis model (CDM) [45] have been proposed to replace classical IRT-based response models.

In this paper, we leverage the observation that the CAT setting is related to problem settings and solutions from the field of neural combinatorial optimization (NCO), where NCO is concerned with learning policies to obtain generalizable solutions to combinatorial problems [16]. Specifically, we propose novel response and policy models that build upon transformer- [40] and NCO-architectures [2,41], and adapt a self-improvement training approach to policy learning for NCO [28] for CAT.

The remainder is structured as follows: Sect. 2 introduces the problem setting. We present our main contribution in Sect. 3 and report on experiments in Sect. 4. Section 5 briefly reviews related work, and Sect. 6 concludes.

2 Preliminaries

The goal in computerized adaptive testing (CAT) is to assess latent traits and abilities of students as accurately as possible by individually selecting questions for every student. CAT models thus consist of (i) a *response model* for cognitive diagnosis to estimate student abilities and (ii) a *policy* that iteratively adapts the selection of questions to a given student. In practice, both models are trained on the outcomes of a calibration pre-study and then applied to test unseen students.

Given a calibration study where N students answered K questions.[1] The calibration study is represented by N sets $\mathcal{Q}^n$, $1 \leq n \leq N$, of cardinality K. Every element of $\mathcal{Q}^n$ is a tuple (q_k^n, r_k^n), consisting of the k-th question that has been answered by the n-th student. The binary response variable r_k^n indicates whether her answer was correct ($r_k^n = 1$) or incorrect ($r_k^n = 0$). In the remainder, $\mathcal{Q}^n$ is also referred to as the *question bank* of the n-th student.

Similar to [52], we phrase learning the policy as a subset selection task: For the n-th student, we *iteratively* aim to select the subset $S \subset \mathcal{Q}^n$ with $|S| = T \leq K$ questions that provides maximal information about her latent ability θ_{true}^n. Note that selecting the subset iteratively is key to the CAT setting as this allows us to update the response model with observed responses. Initializing the subset at $t = 0$ with $S_0^n = \emptyset$, we proceed as follows. At time $0 < t \leq T$, we have selected t questions $S_t^n = \{(q_1^n, r_1^n), ..., (q_t^n, r_t^n)\}$.[2] A straightforward way to learn

---

[1] Without loss of generality, we do not assume that all students answer the same K questions; every student may actually have answered a different number of questions. To not clutter notation, we ignore extra indices and write K for all students.

[2] The selection of questions induces a partial permutation of elements in $\mathcal{Q}^n$ forming the set S_t^n. As above, we prefer not to clutter notation and refrain from defining a proper permutation operator and simply enumerate the tuples by their time index t. That is, we lose a clear identifier and simply consider elements $(q_j, r_j) \in S_t^n$ and $(q_j, r_j) \in \mathcal{Q}^n$ as being different. It should be clear from the context whether we refer to the numbering in S_t^n or $\mathcal{Q}^n$.

the latent ability θ_t^n of the n-th student is offered by minimizing

$$\theta_t^n = \arg\min_{\theta^n} \sum_{(q,r) \in S_t^n} \ell(r, p_\psi(q; \theta^n)), \quad (1)$$

where $\ell(\cdot, \cdot)$ is an appropriate loss (e.g., binary cross entropy), and $p_\psi(\cdot)$ a response model estimating the probability of a correct response, e.g., a neural cognitive diagnosis [10] or Rasch model [29], with global parameters ψ. In practice, these parameters are often fixed and, for example, correspond to item difficulties in IRT [29]. The underlying assumption is that a well-estimated response model is able to predict student performance accurately, resulting in a small loss on the subset S_t^n.

Our approach grounds on the idea that the performance of the n-th student on question bank $\mathcal{Q}^n$ serves as a good proxy for her true but unknown latent abilities θ_{true}^n. This can be shown in the limit by assuming a consistent estimator of latent abilities and a question bank with infinite cardinality [52]. Hence, given a learnable policy π_ϕ with parameters ϕ, we formalize our selection algorithm as

$$q_{t+1}^n \sim \pi_\phi(\theta_t^n; \mathcal{Q}^n \setminus S_t^n, p_\psi),$$

and minimize the empirical risk jointly over parameters ϕ and ψ on so far *unused* (i.e., not yet contained in S_t^n) elements of the question bank $\mathcal{Q}^n$. We arrive at the following optimization problem,

$$\min_{\psi, \phi} \frac{1}{N} \sum_n \sum_{(q,r) \in \mathcal{Q}^n \setminus S_t^n} \ell(r, p_\psi(q|\theta_t^n)) \quad (2)$$

$$\text{s.t.} \quad \theta_t^n = \arg\min_{\theta^n} \sum_{(q,r) \in S_t^n} \ell(r, p_\psi(q; \theta^n)),$$

where subsets S_t^n are sampled autoregressively from policy π_ϕ.

An alternative to learning a policy has been introduced by uncertainty sampling [18,33]. The idea of uncertainty sampling is to select at every time the question that the response model is most uncertain about. That is, at time $t+1$, uncertainty sampling chooses the question q for which holds

$$q = \arg\min_{q_m} |p_\psi(q_m|\theta_t^n) - 0.5|. \quad (3)$$

This strategy relies on a well-calibrated response model. Proposition 1 shows that uncertainty sampling is optimal if the response model is optimal as well.

Proposition 1. *A perfectly calibrated response model for which*

$$p_\psi(q|\theta_{t_0}^n) = \mathbb{E}\left[r|q, \theta_{\text{true}}^n\right]$$

holds for all $(q, r) \in \mathcal{Q}^n$ and $1 \leq n \leq N$ renders the uncertainty baseline in Eq. (3) an optimal policy given the learning task as introduced above.

Proof. Assume the response model $p_\psi(q|\theta_t^n)$ converges after an update $t_0 \in \{1,\ldots,T\}$ to the optimal model for student n and the remaining items of the question bank $\mathcal{Q}^n \backslash S_{t_0}^n$. This directly implies that $\forall (q,r) \in \mathcal{Q}^n : p_\psi(q|\theta_{t_0}^n) = p_\psi(q|\theta_{t \geq t_0}^n)$ and hence also $p_\psi(q|\theta_{t \geq t_0}^n) \equiv \mathbb{E}[r|q, \theta_{\text{true}}^n]$. Thus, for all $t \geq t_0$, uncertainty sampling in Eq. (3) trivially picks the question that leads to the largest minimization of the loss in Eq. (2) as all other remaining questions in $\mathcal{Q}^n \backslash S_{t \geq t_0}^n$ are closer to the expected response and realize smaller losses in expectation. In turn, the policy is optimal for $\mathcal{Q}^n \backslash S_{t \geq t_0}^n$. □

Uncertainty sampling is a greedy heuristic and can lead to suboptimal results in practice. While the proposition above provides a motivation for its application, in practice the learned response model will hardly be perfect due to noisy data (e.g., guessing and slip probabilities or miscalibration). Conditioning the response model on previously seen question-response tuples in S_t^n should increase the quality of the model, since asking more questions should lead to an improvement of predictive accuracies. That is, we have $p_\psi(q|S_t^n) \neq p_\psi(q|S_{t+1}^n)$ in general.

3 Toward Self-improvement Training for CAT

We now propose a deep learning approach that relies on strong generalization properties of modern deep learning architectures to solve the optimization problem in Eq. (2). Specifically, we develop novel response and policy models for CAT that leverage the encoder-decoder structure of transformers. Further, we adapt self-improvement training [28] to learn the policy, leveraging similarities between our subset selection problem and neural combinatorial optimization.

3.1 Amortized Student Representation

Instead of local variable optimization per student, we consider the student representation θ_t^n to be an encoded representation of S_t^n given by

$$\theta_t^n = p_\psi^{\text{enc}}(S_t^n),$$

as obtained by a transformer encoder-like self-attention architecture. The encoder $p_\psi^{\text{enc}}(S_t^n)$ itself is part of a response model $p_\psi(q|p_\psi^{\text{enc}}(S_t^n)) = p_\psi(q|S_t^n)$ that operates on the observed subsets S_t^n of questions and responses for student n at time t. We argue as follows: if we can learn the encoder on calibration data such that it generalizes well on unseen examples, we may discard local parameter optimization per student since all relevant individual traits are already captured by the encoded representations. Additionally, we can also base the policy model on the encoded student representation, with parameters either optimized independently or shared with the encoder. Thus, incorporating an encoder-like self-attention architecture allows us to discard learning the latent abilities via Eq. (1) and simplify the optimization problem in Eq. (2) as

$$\min_{\psi,\phi} \frac{1}{N} \sum_n \sum_{(q,r) \in \mathcal{Q}^n \backslash S_t^n} \ell(r, p_\psi(q|S_t^n)), \quad (4)$$

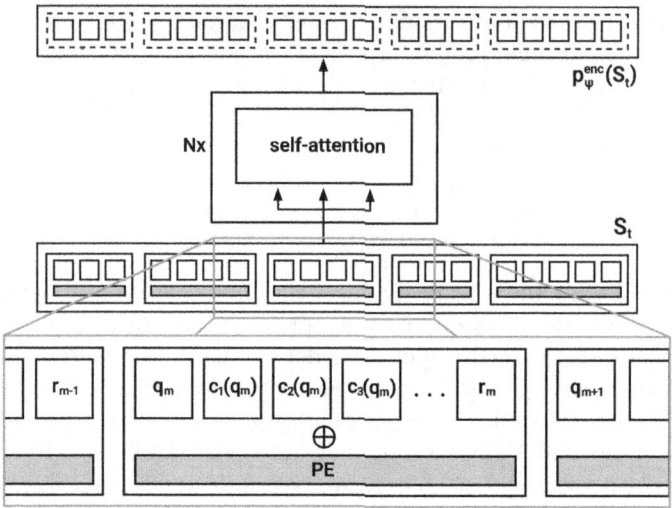

Fig. 1. Sketch of our student representation, where $c_i(q)$ denote question features

where subsets S_t^n of questions-response tuples for student n are sampled from policy π_ϕ and ψ and ϕ are global parameters as before. Trusting global parameters and learned representations to be sufficient for generalization resembles the idea of *amortized inference* [49] prominent in variational autoencoders [14,30].

In comparison to classical IRT models [29], however, we lose interpretability by discarding the explicit representation of the latent student traits θ_{true}^n. Instead, we trade interpretability for a better response model. In cases where interpretability is necessary, we could either train additional response models or apply post-hoc and model-agnostic strategies [8,31]. We consider both ideas straightforward additions to our contribution but focus on the predictive performance that is integral to personalization in CAT at test time.

Another advantage of our approach is the ability to process possibly rich feature representations of questions and responses. Recall that the input to the student encoder is the set S_t^n of question-response tuples which could be represented in the form of sets of features. The encoder then operates on a *set of sets*, given that the features are discretely tokenizable. To showcase the benefit of this extension, we experimentally include knowledge components that describe skills that are necessary to solve a particular question as part of a domain model. Our approach allows to include any number of descriptive features for questions, responses, and also students.

Since self-attention is position-agnostic, we apply positional encoding (PE) to link question-response tuples to the tokenized features (here and elsewhere we apply PE by element-wise addition denoted by $\oplus$). In addition, we include learnable *start tokens* that enable us to learn a student representation for S_0. The encoder architecture follows a stack of standard transformer encoder layers [40] comprised of multi-head self-attention, residual connections [11], dropout

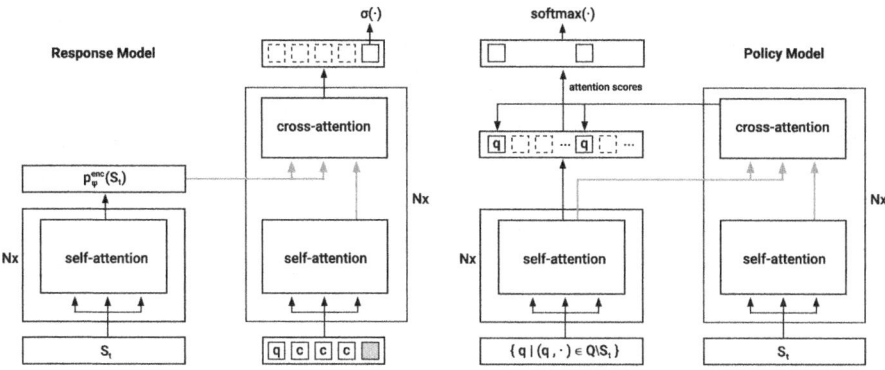

Fig. 2. Sketch of proposed response and policy models

[38], layer normalization [1], and feed-forward neural networks. Since attention in the transformer architecture scales quadratically [15], our student representation can be computed in $\mathcal{O}((f_q + f_r + f_n)^2)$ where $f_{(\cdot)}$ denotes the number of tokens in question (f_q), response (f_r), and student representations (f_n) up to time t. Figure 1 visualizes the model for the student representation.

3.2 Response and Policy Models

The response and policy models are both based on standard transformer encoder-decoder architectures [40] where only positional encoding, problem specific masking in self- and cross-attention and classifier architectures are adjusted. We present both models in the following sections; see Fig. 2 for a visualization of the two architectures.

Response Model. The task of the response model is to estimate the probability that a student answers a question correctly. The model is conditioned on all previously observed question-response tuples, so that, after having asked t questions, we can estimate the probability $\hat{r} = p_\psi(q|p_\psi^{\text{enc}}(S_t))$, for every unseen question $q \in \{q|(q,\cdot) \in \mathcal{Q}\backslash S_t\}$.

To compute these probabilities, we pass the set of features for a desired question q as well as a learnable *query token* into a transformer decoder, where the self-attention layers operate on question features and the query token. The cross-attention layers attend from the decoder question representation to the encoded student representation. The response can be predicted by applying a binary classifier to the transformed representation of the query token.

Different from standard decoder layers of the transformer architecture, there is no masking involved, as all tokens representing question q are allowed to attend to the full representation as obtained via $p_\psi^{\text{enc}}(S_t)$. During training and inference we repeat the encoded student representation $p_\psi^{\text{enc}}(S_t^n)$ for each question in $\mathcal{Q}^n\backslash S_t^n$ for efficiency. At time t, self-attention in the decoder scales with

$\mathcal{O}\left(f_q^2\right)$, while cross-attention scales with $\mathcal{O}\left(f_{S_t} \times f_q\right)$, where f_{S_t} extracts the number of tokens in the subset S_t; it usually holds that $f_q < f_{S_{t>0}}$.

Policy Model. The encoder of the policy model transforms the set of sets of tokenized features of available questions $q \in \{q|(q,\cdot) \in \mathcal{Q}\}$, where we apply positional encoding to inform the transformer about the association between tokens and questions, i.e. we apply the same positional information to tokens from the same interaction. The student representation as presented in Sect. 3.1 results from the application of self-attention in the decoder, which operates on S_t ($\oplus$ PE). In the cross-attention layers, student representations obtained via self-attention on S_t attend to the candidate questions $q \in \{q|(q,\cdot) \in \mathcal{Q}\backslash S_t\}$ as transformed by the encoder. To obtain a probability distribution over all candidate questions at timestep $t+1$, we apply a softmax to the final cross-attention scores.[3] To efficiently train the model via teacher forcing, we train on all $q \in \{q|(q,\cdot) \in \mathcal{Q}\}$ and the complete subset S_T, which we treat as a sequence of question-response tuples with appropriate autoregressive block-structured masking applied in the self-attention (where all tokens from tuple (q_t, r_t) can only attend to tokens from $S_{\leq t}$). In the cross-attention, we mask out all question tokens already included in S_t. Self-attention in the encoder scales with $\mathcal{O}(f^2_{|\{q|(q,\cdot)\in\mathcal{Q}\}|})$, self-attention in the decoder with $\mathcal{O}(f^2_{S_T})$, while cross-attention scales with $\mathcal{O}(f_{S_T} \times f_{\{q|(q,\cdot)\in\mathcal{Q}\}})$. Within our approach this renders the policy model the component with the highest computational and memory complexity.

Since response and policy models operate on either the same or similar tokens, we experimented with weight sharing within and between both models. We finally settled on sharing weights in the encoder and decoder for self-attention in both, response and policy model (cf. [32]) but dropped sharing parameters between response and policy model for a lack of noticeable improvements.

3.3 Self-improvement Training

In this section, we describe a method to train the policy model on previously recorded calibration data. Instead of applying reinforcement learning, we choose to adapt a recent self-improvement training approach proposed for neural combinatorial optimization [28] and language models [12]. The idea of this strategy is to train a model on its own output in a supervised fashion.

Given a trained response model, we sample multiple subsets S_T^n for every student from a randomly initialized policy model. To induce a learning signal, we focus for each student on the sampled subset that achieves the lowest average binary-cross entropy loss after predicting response probabilities for all unseen questions. The *best* subsets are now used as target sequences for training the policy model in a supervised fashion. When the performance of the policy improves (as measured by the accuracy of the response model with subsets sampled greedily from the policy), the response model is finetuned on subsets sampled from

---

[3] We average over attention heads in our implementation.

Algorithm 1. Self-improvement training for CAT

Require: Offline train and validation data $\mathcal{D}_{\text{train}} = \{\mathcal{Q}^n\}_{n=1}^{N_{\text{train}}}$ and $\mathcal{D}_{\text{val}} = \{\mathcal{Q}^n\}_{n=1}^{N_{\text{val}}}$
Require: Response model p_ψ pretrained on random subsets S_T
1: Randomly initialize policy π_ϕ and set $\pi_{\text{best}} \leftarrow \pi_\phi$
2: **for** each epoch **do**
3:     **for** each $n \in \{1, ..., N_{\text{train}}\}$ **do**
4:         Sample m subset candidates $S_{\text{candidates}}^n := \{S_T^{n,1}, ..., S_T^{n,m}\} \sim \pi_{\text{best}}$
5:         Set $S_T^n = \arg\min_{S_T \in S_{\text{candidates}}^n} \sum_{(q,r) \in \mathcal{Q}^n \setminus S_T} \ell(r, p_\psi(q|S_T))$
6:     **end for**
7:     **for** each batch **do**
8:         Sample tuples $(\mathcal{Q}^n, S_T^n)$ of question bank and corresponding subset
9:         Update π_ϕ with gradient optimizing next-step prediction
10:    **end for**
11:    **if** greedy performance of π_ϕ on $\mathcal{D}_{\text{val}}$ better than π_{best} **then**
12:        $\pi_{\text{best}} \leftarrow \pi_\phi$
13:        Finetune p_ψ on $S_T^n \sim \pi_{\text{best}}$
14:    **end if**
15: **end for**

the new policy. We then continue to sample subsets from the best policy to train both the policy and finetune the response model in an alternating fashion.

Algorithm 1 sketches the complete training loop. In contrast to [28], we do not have a fixed objective function but alternate between training policy and response model. This scheme is motivated by policy-induced shifts in the distribution of subsets S_T selected during adaptive testing, which can be accounted for by finetuning the response model by training on subsets S_T selected by the policy. We alternate between training both models, since finetuning the response model will in principle affect the optimal policy. The initial response model is trained on randomly sampled subsets. We use early stopping on validation data for training and finetuning the response model as well as for training the policy.

Neural combinatorial optimization deals for example with synthetic traveling salesman instances and millions of training examples [28]. By contrast, calibration studies in CAT are usually orders of magnitude smaller than that. Thus, we need to adapt the strategies used in neural combinatorial optimization to cope with overfitting and small sample sizes. During training on all student question banks, we sample sequences anew in every epoch while [28] reuse sampled sequences. We also optimize the policy with respect to the complete subset instead of optimizing a single timestep as is done in [28], who argue in favor of a more expressive model that does not support teacher forcing.

4 Experiments

In this section, we empirically evaluate our approach on real world data, support the design choices in our student representation and response model on a standardized benchmark, and shed light on the interplay between response model, learned policies and the uncertainty policy on artificially generated data.

4.1 Computerized Adaptive Testing

We evaluate the performance of our approach on a real CAT problem from the NeurIPS 2020 Education Challenge [46]. We train, validate and test on all 6148 available students in 5-folds (training on 60% of the students, using different 20% for validation and testing in each fold). Following related work from neural combinatorial optimization, we restrict the question bank of each student to contain maximally 100 questions each, covering all 948 questions in the dataset.

In absence of the true latent abilities of the involved students, we need to resort to a proxy for a quantitative evaluation and compute predictive performances on unseen test questions instead [10,52]. In our evaluation we resort to calculate mean accuracy and AUC for N^{test} students who are not present in the training data using questions given by $\mathcal{Q}^n \backslash S_T^n$. This out-of-sample evaluation directly addresses the desired goal of having every student answer every question in her question bank, but in practice being able to ask her only T questions and estimating the remaining responses as best as possible.

We compare three versions of our model: a random question selection and an uncertainty sampling policy, both using the learned response model, as well as the full model trained with self-improvement. We further compare against an implementation of BECAT [52][4], applied to a standard IRT [23,29] model, as well as baseline policies based on maximum Fisher and Kullback-Leibler information [3,24]. Our implementations build upon the code provided by [19][5]. The neural CDM [45] did not achieve comparable performances and stayed significantly below the results of the IRT model with a random policy. This is most likely caused by difficulties in optimizing the neural CDM itself. In the experiments with our approach we relied on standard ancestral sampling to optimize policy and response models. Further implementation details are provided in our code repository for this paper.[6]

Tables 1 and 2 show the resulting accuracies and AUCs for test lengths of $T \in \{5, 10, 20\}$, following the experiment protocol in [52].[7] Compared to adaptive question selection with BECAT, our policy model enables significantly faster inference by a factor of over 20. Accuracy and AUC results show that methods building upon our student representation and response model generally outperform the baseline policies with an IRT model. Overall, uncertainty sampling with our response model performs best. Although self-improvement training achieves comparable performance on a test length of 5 the uncertainty sampling policy performs better with longer test lengths. Under the assumption that our response model performs well, the results are in line with the intuition provided by Proposition 1. We will address this observation again in Sect. 4.4.

---

[4] BECAT's results are significantly better than other recent CAT approaches [10,51], especially on longer test lengths, according to [52].
[5] Code available at https://github.com/bigdata-ustc/EduCAT.
[6] Experiments in this paper can be reproduced with code and hyperparameters provided at https://github.com/kainbr/cat_self_improvement.
[7] Our experiments differ from [52] and results are not directly comparable.

Table 1. Accuracies on the NeurIPS 2020 Education Challenge. Markers ∗, ∘ and •
indicate whether our method with self-improvement is statistically superior, equal or
inferior to baselines, using a paired t-test at the 0.01 significance level.

Metric@Step	Accuracy@5	Accuracy@10	Accuracy@20
IRT w/Random	0.6538 ± 0.0047 ∗	0.6693 ± 0.0063 ∗	0.6798 ± 0.0089 ∗
IRT w/MFI	0.6669 ± 0.0021 ∗	0.6815 ± 0.0015 ∗	0.6915 ± 0.0026 ∗
IRT w/KLI	0.6626 ± 0.0016 ∗	0.6787 ± 0.0011 ∗	0.6891 ± 0.0021 ∘
IRT w/BECAT	0.6533 ± 0.0010 ∗	0.6727 ± 0.0031 ∗	0.6885 ± 0.0017 ∗
Our w/Random	0.6649 ± 0.0023 ∗	0.6781 ± 0.0047 ∘	0.6912 ± 0.0019 ∗
Our w/Uncertainty	**0.6758** ± 0.0034 ∘	**0.6959** ± 0.0033 •	**0.7239** ± 0.0047 •
Our w/Self-Improv.	<u>0.6753</u> ± 0.0030	<u>0.6855</u> ± 0.0027	<u>0.6967</u> ± 0.0034

Table 2. AUC results on the NeurIPS 2020 Education Challenge.

Metric@Step	AUC@5	AUC@10	AUC@20
IRT w/ Random	0.7128 ± 0.0049 ∗	0.7304 ± 0.0068 ∗	0.7403 ± 0.0093 ∗
IRT w/ MFI	0.7273 ± 0.0022 ∗	0.7466 ± 0.0022 ∘	0.7615 ± 0.0032 ∘
IRT w/ KLI	0.7235 ± 0.0013 ∗	0.7443 ± 0.0011 ∘	0.7597 ± 0.0016 ∘
IRT w/ BECAT	0.7116 ± 0.0017 ∗	0.7363 ± 0.0030 ∗	0.7547 ± 0.0028 ∘
Our w/ Random	0.7256 ± 0.0019 ∗	0.7446 ± 0.0026 ∗	0.7576 ± 0.0025 ∘
Our w/ Uncertainty	<u>0.7363</u> ± 0.0039 ∘	**0.7589** ± 0.0037 •	**0.7843** ± 0.0043 •
Our w/ Self-Improv.	**0.7372** ± 0.0032	<u>0.7490</u> ± 0.0035	<u>0.7637</u> ± 0.0041

4.2 Performance of the Response Model

In this section, we focus on the evaluation of the student representation and
response model on a related educational task, namely knowledge tracing (KT,
[7]). The task in KT is to predict binary responses of a student interacting
sequentially with an intelligent tutoring system: After observing t question-
response tuples, we aim to predict the student's response for question q_{t+1}. A
key difference to CAT is the assumption that the knowledge of a student may
change over time. Nevertheless, knowledge tracing constitutes a sequential prediction task where a response model is learned on a fixed and fully observable
policy.

Differences to the CAT task are for example that question-response tuples in
the student representation are treated as a sequence instead of a set. We thus
need to adapt the handling of positional encoding which should now reflect temporal relations. To that end, we employ a rotary embedding [39], which is useful
in conveying relational positional information to the transformer architecture.
For efficiency, we employ an encoder only architecture with an autoregressive
mask applied to the student representation, such that tokens corresponding to
features of question q_t can only attend to tokens corresponding to $q_{\leq t}$ and $r_{<t}$.

Table 3. Results for the knowledge tracing task on the Ednet dataset. Markers ∗, ◦ and • indicate whether our method is statistically superior, equal or inferior to baselines, respectively, using a paired t-test at the 0.01 significance level.

	AUC	Accuracy
simpleKT [20]	0.6593 ± 0.0041 ∗	0.6565 ± 0.0029 ∗
SAINT [5]	0.6598 ± 0.0023 ∗	0.6511 ± 0.0039 ∗
AKT [9]	0.6705 ± 0.0024 ∗	0.6645 ± 0.0035 ∗
DTransformer [48]	0.6719 ± 0.0037 ∗	0.6656 ± 0.0032 ∗
FoLiBiKT [13]	0.6721 ± 0.0018 ∗	0.6666 ± 0.0028 ∗
DIMKT [34]	0.6748 ± 0.0030 ∗	0.6700 ± 0.0038 ∗
HawkesKT [44]	0.6815 ± 0.0041 ∗	0.6905 ± 0.0025 ∗
qDKT [36]	0.6986 ± 0.0006 ∗	0.6922 ± 0.0005 ∗
QIKT [4]	0.7260 ± 0.0013 ∗	0.7077 ± 0.0014 ∗
IEKT [22]	0.7301 ± 0.0012 ∗	0.7106 ± 0.0018 ◦
LPKT [35]	<u>0.7340 ± 0.0007</u> ◦	<u>0.7128 ± 0.0004</u> ◦
Our	**0.7355 ± 0.0006**	**0.7134 ± 0.0005**

In combination with teacher forcing, these changes enable us to efficiently train a knowledge tracing model based on our student representation.

We experiment on large-scale student data provided with Ednet [6], which includes learning data from 784,309 students. The *pykt*-benchmark [21] enables standardized comparison against several recent KT models. In Table 3 we provide an evaluation of our model against the best performing baselines.[8] The KT model based on our student representation achieves significantly better performance than all but one baselines and is on par with the remaining one. We conjecture that the excellent performance of our (adapted) response model can be taken as an indicator of the predictive accuracy of our response model in the CAT setting.

4.3 Uncertainty Sampling

Proposition 1 suggests that uncertainty sampling provides a strong baseline given a good response model. We have observed good performance of uncertainty sampling in the CAT experiment in Sect. 4.1 and provided empirical evidence that our response model architecture is highly competitive on the CAT related knowledge tracing task in Sect. 4.2. We now investigate the interplay between response model, learned policy and uncertainty sampling for CAT tasks with uncalibrated questions in the question bank.

We generate artificial students as follows: Every student has a question bank of the same 50 candidate questions that are equally distributed in five groups.

---

[8] We report on the eleven baselines achieving the best AUC out of 22 total comparisons.

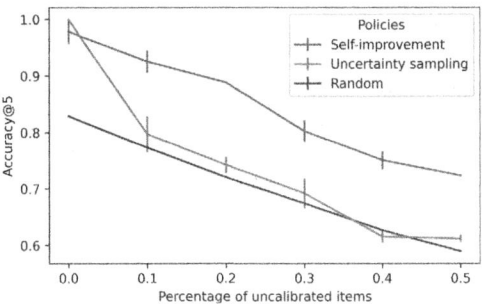

Fig. 3. Performance of different policies on artificially generated CAT tasks with differing proportions of uncalibrated items; error bars indicate standard error.

Within a group, a student either answers all questions correctly or incorrectly. This setting resembles questions belonging to knowledge components that are either fully understood or completely unknown to the student. Whether a student has mastered a group is determined randomly by a coin flip. In addition, we include *uncalibrated* questions that are answered randomly according to a coin flip as well, but that are not linked to any group and for which the policy cannot acquire any information. We experiment with different percentages of these uncalibrated questions in the question bank. We train on 500 students and validate and test on 1000 students. We report on averages over five repetitions.

Figure 3 shows the results for test length $T = 5$. As expected, uncertainty sampling achieves perfect results in the absence of uncalibrated questions, by picking one question of every group each, thereby reducing the uncertainty of the response model towards that group. However, as soon as we observe uncalibrated questions, uncertainty sampling deteriorates and self-improvement dominates in terms of predictive accuracy.

4.4 Discussion

We conclude that our student representation and response model lead to accurate predictions and is well suited for question selection algorithms in CAT-based learning tasks. However, under optimal conditions, a simple uncertainty sampling based policy is sufficient to achieve perfect results, as we have shown theoretically in Proposition 1 and experimentally on artificial data. Hence, our response model together with uncertainty sampling should be sufficient for adaptive testing in ideal settings. If, however, calibration tests result in a suboptimal question bank due to non-trivial student guessing and slip probabilities, a learned policy can improve predictive accuracies. With self-improvement training to jointly learn deep response and policy models, we provide a strong solution to CAT under suboptimal conditions.

5 Related Work

Early on, computerized adaptive testing (CAT) allowed for large-scale personalized tests [43] and is closely related to item response theory (IRT, [23,29]). While CAT can reduce test lengths by assessing students with fewer items and in shorter time due to an item selection algorithm based on previous responses, IRT provides the foundation of explicitly modeling latent abilities of students. Recent approaches to policy learning for CAT include reinforcement learning; for example [10] propose shallow feed-forward neural networks as their policy model and [51] employ an attention based neural network architecture, where optimization is based on the score function estimator [47] and deep Q-learning [25], respectively. Formulating CAT as a subset selection problem, [52] propose a greedy algorithm based on the approximation of expected gradient differences. Response models are either based on IRT, simple feed-forward neural networks or on a neural cognitive diagnosis model (CDM) as proposed in [45] and account for explicit modeling of latent student skills. For a more comprehensive survey on modern CAT approaches see [19].

Without an explicit focus on interpretability, our student representation and response model are more closely related to recent deep learning approaches to knowledge tracing (KT, [7]), a related educational field which is concerned with reasoning about changes in students' knowledge and enabling the adaptation of learning materials. Transformer-based KT models include for example [5,9,20,27]. Closely related to our response model is [50], who also consider an alternating sequence of question and response embedding as model input. Different from our approach, their sequential model includes question features (such as knowledge components) only indirectly via optimization of auxiliary prediction tasks.

Besides training with self-improvement [28], the design of our policy model is further related to recent work in the field of neural combinatorial optimization. Specifically, [41] introduced classification based on cross-attention scores for sequential combinatorial problems where the target dictionary size depends on the input at the current time step. The idea has since successfully been applied to policy learning for combinatorial optimization via reinforcement learning [16]. Our policy architecture is closely related to the traveling salesman problem (TSP) transformer [2], which provides a similar architecture to the one proposed in this paper. However, we operate on sets of sets of tokens rather than only a set of tokens like the TSP transformer and we allow for different features in encoder and decoder, corresponding to questions and question-response tuples, respectively.

6 Conclusion

We studied computerized adaptive testing (CAT) as an iterative subset selection problem, learning both the underlying response model for cognitive diagnosis and a policy for question selection jointly from offline training data (e.g., a calibration pre-study). We leveraged the close relation of CAT to neural combinatorial optimization (NCO), proposed novel response and policy models, and adapted a recent self-improvement training approach to CAT policy learning, relying on strong generalization properties of deep learning models.

Our proposed response model empirically outperformed baselines in CAT as well as in related knowledge tracing tasks. We further provided theoretical and empirical evidence that our response model can be combined successfully with uncertainty sampling-based policies in scenarios where the response model can be learned (almost) perfectly. Our results also show that scenarios with imperfect response models (e.g., due to higher guess and slip probabilities) clearly favor jointly learning both a response and policy model via self-improvement training as proposed in this paper.

Avenues for future work include (i) exploiting the novel student representation by introducing more descriptive features to CAT, (ii) exploring more sampling schemes [17, 28] for self-improvement training in CAT, and (iii) combining our approach with interpretable models or post-hoc interpretability methods [8, 31].

Acknowledgments. We thank Laurin Luttmann for discussions on advances in NCO. We thank the Joachim Herz Foundation for their support and funding as part of the ALEE project. Infrastructure used in this project was funded in parts by the European Union (EFRE/85202549).

Disclosure of Interests. The authors have no competing interests to declare.

References

1. Ba, J.L., Kiros, J.R., Hinton, G.E.: Layer normalization. arXiv preprint arXiv:1607.06450 (2016)
2. Bresson, X., Laurent, T.: The transformer network for the traveling salesman problem. arXiv preprint arXiv:2103.03012 (2021)
3. Chang, H.H., Ying, Z.: A global information approach to computerized adaptive testing. Appl. Psychol. Meas. **20**(3), 213–229 (1996)
4. Chen, J., Liu, Z., Huang, S., Liu, Q., Luo, W.: Improving interpretability of deep sequential knowledge tracing models with question-centric cognitive representations. In: Proceedings of the AAAI Conference on Artificial Intelligence, vol. 37, pp. 14196–14204 (2023)
5. Choi, Y., et al.: Towards an appropriate query, key, and value computation for knowledge tracing. In: Proceedings of the Seventh ACM Conference on Learning @ Scale (2020)
6. Choi, Y., et al.: EdNet: a large-scale hierarchical dataset in education. In: Bittencourt, I.I., Cukurova, M., Muldner, K., Luckin, R., Millán, E. (eds.) AIED 2020. LNCS (LNAI), vol. 12164, pp. 69–73. Springer, Cham (2020). https://doi.org/10.1007/978-3-030-52240-7_13
7. Corbett, A.T., Anderson, J.R.: Knowledge tracing: Modeling the acquisition of procedural knowledge. User Model. User-Adap. Inter. **4**, 253–278 (1994)
8. Gervet, T., Koedinger, K., Schneider, J., Mitchell, T., et al.: When is deep learning the best approach to knowledge tracing? J. Educ. Data Mining **12**(3), 31–54 (2020)

9. Ghosh, A., Heffernan, N., Lan, A.S.: Context-aware attentive knowledge tracing. In: Proceedings of the 26th ACM SIGKDD SIGKDD Conference on Knowledge Discovery & Data Mining, pp. 2330–2339 (2020)
10. Ghosh, A., Lan, A.: Bobcat: Bilevel optimization-based computerized adaptive testing. In: International Joint Conference on Artificial Intelligence (2021)
11. He, K., Zhang, X., Ren, S., Sun, J.: Deep residual learning for image recognition. In: IEEE Conference on Computer Vision and Pattern Recognition (2016)
12. Huang, J., Gu, S.S., Hou, L., Wu, Y., Wang, X., Yu, H., Han, J.: Large language models can self-improve. In: Conference on Empirical Methods in Natural Language Processing (2023)
13. Im, Y., Choi, E., Kook, H., Lee, J.: Forgetting-aware linear bias for attentive knowledge tracing. In: Proceedings of the 32nd ACM International Conference on Information and Knowledge Management, pp. 3958–3962 (2023)
14. Kingma, D.P., Welling, M.: Auto-Encoding Variational Bayes. In: International Conference on Learning Representations (2014)
15. Kitaev, N., Kaiser, Ł., Levskaya, A.: reformer: the efficient transformer. In: International Conference on Learning Representations (2020)
16. Kool, W., Van Hoof, H., Welling, M.: Attention, learn to solve routing problems! In: International Conference on Learning Representations (2019)
17. Kool, W., Van Hoof, H., Welling, M.: Stochastic beams and where to find them: the gumbel-top-k trick for sampling sequences without replacement. In: International Conference on Machine Learning, pp. 3499–3508. PMLR (2019)
18. Lewis, D.D.: A sequential algorithm for training text classifiers: corrigendum and additional data. In: Acm Sigir Forum, vol. 29, pp. 13–19 (1995)
19. Liu, Q., et al.: Survey of computerized adaptive testing: A machine learning perspective. arXiv preprint arXiv:2404.00712 (2024)
20. Liu, Z., Liu, Q., Chen, J., Huang, S., Luo, W.: simpleKT: a simple but tough-to-beat baseline for knowledge tracing. In: International Conference on Learning Representations (2023)
21. Liu, Z., Liu, Q., Chen, J., Huang, S., Tang, J., Luo, W.: pyKT: a python library to benchmark deep learning based knowledge tracing models. In: Advances in Neural Information Processing Systems, vol. 35, pp. 18542–18555 (2022)
22. Long, T., Liu, Y., Shen, J., Zhang, W., Yu, Y.: Tracing knowledge state with individual cognition and acquisition estimation. In: Proceedings of the 44th International ACM SIGIR Conference on Research and Development in Information Retrieval, pp. 173–182 (2021)
23. Lord, F.: A theory of test scores. Psychometric monographs (1952)
24. Lord, F.M.: Applications of item response theory to practical testing problems. Routledge (2012)
25. Mnih, V., et al.: Human-level control through deep reinforcement learning. Nature **518**(7540), 529–533 (2015)
26. Novick, M.R.: The axioms and principal results of classical test theory. J. Math. Psychol. **3**(1), 1–18 (1966)
27. Pandey, S., Karypis, G.: A self-attentive model for knowledge tracing. In: 12th International Conference on Educational Data Mining, EDM 2019, pp. 384–389. International Educational Data Mining Society (2019)
28. Pirnay, J., Grimm, D.G.: Self-improvement for neural combinatorial optimization: Sample without replacement, but improvement. Trans. Mach. Learn. Res. (2024)
29. Rasch, G.: Probabilistic models for some intelligence and attainment tests. Danmarks Paedagogiske Institut (1960)

30. Rezende, D.J., Mohamed, S., Wierstra, D.: Stochastic backpropagation and Approximate Inference in Deep Generative Models. In: International Conference on Machine Learning, pp. 1278–1286 (2014)
31. Rodrigues, T.B., de Souza, J.F., Bernardino, H.S., Baker, R.S.: Towards interpretability of attention-based knowledge tracing models. In: Anais do XXXIII Simpósio Brasileiro de Informática na Educação, pp. 810–821. SBC (2022)
32. Rothe, S., Narayan, S., Severyn, A.: Leveraging pre-trained checkpoints for sequence generation tasks. Trans. Assoc. Comput. Linguist. **8**, 264–280 (2020)
33. Settles, B., T. LaFlair, G., Hagiwara, M.: Machine learning-driven language assessment. Trans. Assoc. Comput. Linguist. **8**, 247–263 (2020)
34. Shen, S., Huang, Z., Liu, Q., Su, Y., Wang, S., Chen, E.: Assessing student's dynamic knowledge state by exploring the question difficulty effect. In: Proceedings of the 45th international ACM SIGIR Conference on Research and Development in Information Retrieval, pp. 427–437 (2022)
35. Shen, S., et al.: Learning process-consistent knowledge tracing. In: Proceedings of the 27th ACM SIGKDD Conference on Knowledge Discovery & Data Mining, pp. 1452–1460 (2021)
36. Sonkar, S., Waters, A.E., Lan, A.S., Grimaldi, P.J., Baraniuk, R.G.: qDKT: question-centric deep knowledge tracing. In: 13th International Conference on Educational Data Mining (2020)
37. Spearman, C.: 'General intelligence', objectively determined and measured. Am. J. Psychol. **15**(2), 201–293 (1904)
38. Srivastava, N., Hinton, G., Krizhevsky, A., Sutskever, I., Salakhutdinov, R.: Dropout: a simple way to prevent neural networks from overfitting. J. Mach. Learn. Res. **15**(1), 1929–1958 (2014)
39. Su, J., Ahmed, M., Lu, Y., Pan, S., Bo, W., Liu, Y.: Roformer: enhanced transformer with rotary position embedding. Neurocomputing **568**, 127063 (2024)
40. Vaswani, A., Shazeer, N., Parmar, N., Uszkoreit, J., Jones, L., Gomez, A.N., Kaiser, Ł., Polosukhin, I.: Attention Is All You Need. In: Advances in Neural Information Processing Systems, pp. 5998–6008 (2017)
41. Vinyals, O., Fortunato, M., Jaitly, N.: Pointer Networks. In: Advances in Neural Information Processing Systems, pp. 2692–2700 (2015)
42. Wainer, H., Dorans, N.J., Flaugher, R., Green, B.F., Mislevy, R.J.: Computerized adaptive testing: A primer. Routledge (2000)
43. Wainer, H., Kiely, G.L.: Item clusters and computerized adaptive testing: A case for testlets. J. Educ. Meas. **24**(3), 185–201 (1987)
44. Wang, C., Ma, W., Zhang, M., Lv, C., Wan, F., Lin, H., Tang, T., Liu, Y., Ma, S.: Temporal cross-effects in knowledge tracing. In: Proceedings of the 14th ACM International Conference on Web Search and Data Mining. pp. 517–525 (2021)
45. Wang, F., Liu, Q., Chen, E., Huang, Z., Chen, Y., Yin, Y., Huang, Z., Wang, S.: Neural cognitive diagnosis for intelligent education systems. In: Proceedings of the AAAI Conference on Artificial Intelligence. vol. 34, pp. 6153–6161 (2020)
46. Wang, Z., et al.: Results and Insights from Diagnostic Questions: The NeurIPS 2020 Education Challenge. In: NeurIPS 2020 Competition and Demonstration Track, pp. 191–205. PMLR (2021)
47. Williams, R.J.: Simple statistical gradient-following algorithms for connectionist reinforcement learning. Mach. Learn. **8**, 229–256 (1992)
48. Yin, Y., et al.: Tracing knowledge instead of patterns: Stable knowledge tracing with diagnostic transformer. In: Proceedings of the ACM Web Conference 2023, pp. 855–864 (2023)

49. Zhang, C., Bütepage, J., Kjellström, H., Mandt, S.: Advances in variational inference. IEEE Trans. Pattern Anal. Mach. Intell. **41**(8), 2008–2026 (2019)
50. Zhou, H., Rong, W., Zhang, J., Sun, Q., Ouyang, Y., Xiong, Z.: AAKT: enhancing knowledge tracing with alternate autoregressive modeling. IEEE Trans. Learn. Technol. (2024)
51. Zhuang, Y., Liu, Q., Huang, Z., Li, Z., Shen, S., Ma, H.: Fully adaptive framework: Neural computerized adaptive testing for online education. In: Proceedings of the AAAI Conference on Artificial Intelligence. vol. 36, pp. 4734–4742 (2022)
52. Zhuang, Y., et al.: A bounded ability estimation for computerized adaptive testing. In: Advances in Neural Information Processing Systems, vol. 36, pp. 2381–2402 (2023)

Voronoi Diagram Encoded Hashing

Yang Xu and Kai Ming Ting[(✉)]

National Key Laboratory for Novel Software Technology, Nanjing University,
Nanjing 210023, China
xuyang@lamda.nju.edu.cn, tingkm@nju.edu.cn

Abstract. The goal of learning to hash (L2H) is to derive data-dependent hash functions from a given data distribution in order to map data from the input space to a binary coding space. Despite the success of L2H, two observations have cast doubt on the source of the power of L2H, i.e., learning. First, a recent study shows that even using a version of locality sensitive hashing functions without learning achieves binary representations that have comparable accuracy as those of L2H, but with less time cost. Second, existing L2H methods are constrained to three types of hash functions: thresholding, hyperspheres, and hyperplanes only. In this paper, we unveil the potential of Voronoi diagrams in hashing. Voronoi diagram is a suitable candidate because of its three properties. This discovery has led us to propose a simple and efficient no-learning binary hashing method, called Voronoi Diagram Encoded Hashing (VDeH), which constructs a set of hash functions through a data-dependent similarity measure and produces independent binary bits through encoded hashing. We demonstrate through experiments on several benchmark datasets that VDeH achieves superior performance and lower computational cost compared to existing state-of-the-art methods under the same bit length. Our code is available at: https://github.com/Phantom-Det/VDeH/tree/main.

Keywords: Learning to hash · Binary representation · Voronoi diagram

1 Introduction

For decades, hashing techniques have been one of the most effective tools commonly used to compress data for fast access, analysis, and learning [5,6,36]. Hashing techniques are popular for their simplicity and offer significant advantages in data processing and security [2,16]. Their primary strength lies in the ability to efficiently map arbitrary-sized input data to fixed-size embeddings, known as hash values. This process is deterministic, meaning the same input always yields the same output, ensuring data consistency. These attributes facilitate a wide range of applications, including data integrity verification, data indexing, blockchain technology, and distributed systems [3,25,26,29].

Learning to hash (L2H) [22,31,35], a prominent subfield within hashing techniques, aims to map data from the input space to a binary coding space, in which the Hamming distance well approximates the distance (e.g., ℓ_p norm) in input space. Then, efficient retrieval and learning can be performed in the binary coding space. The general problem in L2H is to learn long binary codes that approximate the input distance[1].

Given input data of size N with dimensionality d, the core task of L2H is to construct binary hash functions that map the data into L-bit binary codes. Broadly, existing L2H methods can be categorized into three classes: thresholding [9,10,32,34,35], hyperspheres [15], and hyperplanes [4,17,22,37]. Thresholding-based methods initiate the process by transforming distance or similarity relationships from the input space into a new matrix of size $N \times L$ through metric learning [32,35] or PCA-based methods [9,10,34]. Then, matrix values are binarized based on a given threshold. Hypersphere and hyperplane-based methods construct hash functions by partitioning the input space. Points falling within the same partition are mapped to identical binary code values. Due to randomness in the partitioning process, these methods typically improve binary codes performance by learning the partitioning strategy to achieve a uniform distribution of points across distinct partitions [15,22].

Despite the success of L2H, the following two observations cast doubt on the source of the power of methods, i.e., learning:

1. Existing L2H methods all claim that their learning process (in optimizing some defined objective) plays a crucial role in obtaining effective binary codes. Yet, a recent study [4] shows that even using brLSH, a version of locality-sensitive hashing [5] without learning, achieves binary codes that have comparable performance as those of L2H methods, but with less computation cost.
2. They are constrained to three types of hash functions. Learning is required in order to ensure that these functions satisfy three key properties for effective binary codes [10,15,17,22,32,34], i.e., (a) *full space coverage*: each hash function covers the entire space; (b) *entropy maximization*: each hash function covers approximate the same number of points from the input data, such that the total set of hash functions maximizes information entropy; and (c) *bit independence*: all hash functions have mutually independent hash bits. Their importance will be discussed in detail in Sect. 3.

In this work, we provide the insight that Voronoi diagram is a suitable alternative to L2H, attributed to its three properties: first, a Voronoi diagram naturally covers the entire input space; second, for a given dataset, every Voronoi cell

---

[1] Note that another related area called *deep hashing* [24,28] conducts a similar task but with a totally different goal: generating short compact binary codes, where proximate or identical binary codes represent semantic (categorical) similarity between instances, while distant binary codes represent semantic dissimilarity. However, deep hashing is specifically designed for datasets with explicit categorical information, notably image data [11,14,33], and is incompatible with datasets lacking this information, including extensive text and tabular data. Besides, these short binary codes do not adequately approximate the input distance. Existing studies demonstrate that achieving an effective approximation of the input distance through binary codes requires a code length of $\mathcal{O}(d)$, where d is the input dimensionality [9,22,34,35].

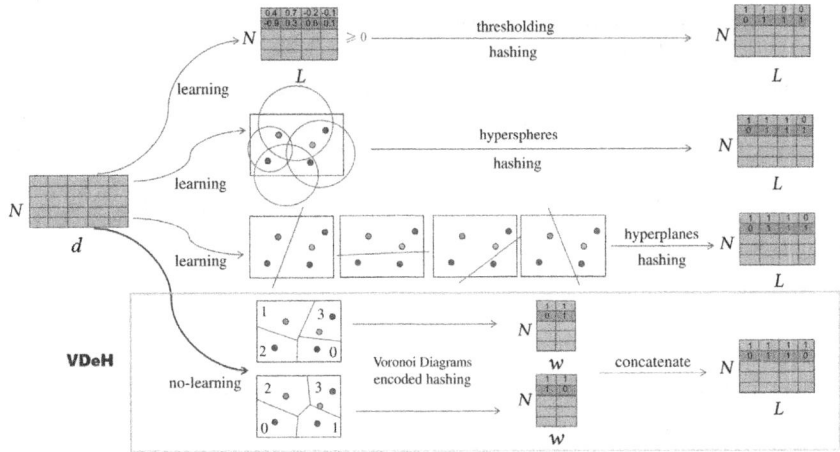

Fig. 1. An illustrative comparison of VDeH using Voronoi diagram and three existing types of hash functions (thresholding, hyperspheres and hyperplanes). The parameters $N = 5$, $d = 5$, $L = 4$, and $w = 2$ are used in this example.

in a Voronoi diagram covers approximately the same number of points [7]; third, it is feasible to transform a Voronoi diagram into a set of hash functions, which generates mutually independent bits (hash values). Unlike existing L2H methods, all these properties are obtained in Voronoi diagrams without any extra learning process.

Voronoi diagrams facilitate the generation of *data-dependent* hash functions, as these hash functions are derived by samples from a given dataset and are dependent on the distribution of the data. Specifically, they yield small Voronoi cells in areas of high densities, while large Voronoi cells are produced in areas of low densities [7,30]. This discovery has led us to propose a simple and effective no-learning approach called Voronoi Diagram Encoded Hashing (VDeH), which is the first data-dependent binary hashing scheme based on Voronoi diagram already used in a kernel. Figure 1 shows an illustrative comparison of VDeH using Voronoi diagram and three existing types of hash functions.

Our main contributions are summarized as follows:

- Providing the insight that Voronoi diagram can be leveraged to realize a family of data-dependent hash functions, without learning.
- Creating a new definition of hashing scheme derived directly from a kernel based on Voronoi diagrams.
- Proposing VDeH, which creates the first kernel-based implementation of a data-dependent binary hashing scheme, and formulating a binary distance function intrinsic to VDeH. We have theoretically proved that VDeH is capable of generating mutually independent binary bits.
- Conducting comprehensive empirical comparisons and analyses between VDeH and existing state-of-the-art L2H methods to demonstrate the effectiveness and efficiency of VDeH.

2 Background and Related Work

With the emergence of large-scale data, numerous learning to hash (L2H) methods have been developed [12,22,31]. The generic binary hashing problem is the following. Given N data points $\mathcal{X} = [\mathbf{x}_1, \ldots, \mathbf{x}_N] \in \mathbb{R}^{d \times N}$, generate L hash functions to map a data point $\mathbf{x}$ into a L-bit binary hash code $\mathcal{B}(\mathbf{x}) = [h_1(\mathbf{x}), h_2(\mathbf{x}), \ldots, h_L(\mathbf{x})]$ where $h_l(\mathbf{x}) \in \{0,1\}$ is the l-th hash function.

For the linear binary projection-based hashing [9,22,35]:

$$h_l(\mathbf{x}) = sgn(F(\mathbf{R}_l\mathbf{x} + t_l)),$$

where $\mathbf{R}_l \in \mathbb{R}^{L \times d}$ is the projection matrix, $sgn(\cdot)$ is a binary map, and t_l is the intercept. Different hashing methods aim at finding different F, $\mathbf{R}_l$ and t_l with respect to different objective functions.

Existing L2H methods seek to ensure that the Hamming distance of generated binary codes closely approximates the input distance by imposing specific constraints on these codes. For example, given $b_i \in \{0,1\}^L$, Spectral Hashing (SH) [32] aims to minimize the average Hamming distance between similar neighbors, represented by $\sum_{ij} W_{ij}||b_i - b_j||^2$, where W_{ij} is the similarity between points i and j as measured by Gaussian kernel, and $||b_i - b_j||^2$ is the Hamming distance between binary codes b_i and b_j. SH uses two constraints: (i) $\sum_i b_i = \frac{1}{2}$ to ensure entropy maximization, and (ii) $\frac{1}{n}\sum_i b_i b_i^T = I$ to guarantee bit independence. In addition, Spherical Hashing (SpH) [15] generates hash functions by partitioning the input space using hyperspheres. SpH achieves bit independence by ensuring that each hashing function has an equal probability of output 0 and 1. To achieve entropy maximization, it requires each hypersphere to contain an approximately equal number of points. Since hyperspheres do not cover the entire input space, SpH increases the radius of the hyperspheres to cover at least all training data, thus ensuring full space coverage. It is worth noting that most existing methods explicitly or implicitly ensure the three key properties: full space coverage, entropy maximization, and bit independence by constructing similar constraints. Methods operated on spatial partitioning necessitate that the hash functions provide complete coverage of the input space [4,15,17,22,37]. Besides, existing methods ensure entropy maximization by explicitly constraining each bit to have a half probability of being 0 or 1, while maintaining the independence of each bit's output [9,10,15,17,22,32,34,35,37]. The detailed explanations of how these methods guarantee these properties and their categorizations can be found in comprehensive survey papers [24,31].

The three properties have been demonstrated to be crucial for effective binary codes in existing methods. However, these methods invariably require a learning process to gain these properties, as their employed hash functions, including those based on thresholding, hyperspheres, and hyperplanes, do not naturally possess these properties.

Table 1. Key notations used.

Notation	Definition
$\mathcal{X}$	Input dataset with N points in $\mathbb{R}^d$
$\mathcal{D}$	A set of ψ points randomly sampled from $\mathcal{X}$ to generate a Voronoi diagram
$\mathcal{B}$	L-bit binary codes correspond to all points in $\mathcal{X}$
H	A set of hash functions derived from a Voronoi diagram
κ	kernel $\kappa(x,y)$, where $x, y \in \mathbb{R}^d$
s	A similarity function defined in $\mathbb{R}^d$
w	The number of bits generated by encoded hashing over a Voronoi diagram
$\mathcal{H}$	A hashing scheme consisting of a family of hash functions.
$P_{\mathcal{H}}$	Distribution over a family of hash functions $\mathcal{H}$

3 Insight: Voronoi Diagram is a Suitable Candidate for Binary Hashing

The key notations used in this paper are provided in Table 1.

Given a point $\mathbf{x} \in \mathbb{R}^d$, a hashing scheme of a family H of hash functions $h \in H$, where $h(\mathbf{x}) \in \{0, 1\}$, must have the following three properties: full space coverage, entropy maximization, and bit independence.

Full Space Coverage. All $h \in H$ cover the entire $\mathbb{R}^d$, i.e., $\forall \mathbf{x} \in \mathbb{R}^d, \exists h \in H$ s.t. $h(\mathbf{x}) = 1$. The failure to achieve this coverage can severely impair retrieval effectiveness. Two possible current treatments of this shortcoming are unsatisfactory: (a) All points outside the covered regions have no binary code representations, rendering them irretrievable. (b) Using a common binary mapping to all points outside the covered regions risks conflating vastly distant points in the input space with a same binary code. This issue is particularly pronounced when adopting hypersphere-based hashing strategies [15]. Therefore, ensuring that hash functions cover the entire space is a critical aspect of maintaining high retrieval accuracy in binary hashing-based information retrieval systems. This coverage guarantees that every point $\mathbf{x} \in \mathbb{R}^d$ can be effectively indexed and retrieved, thereby maximizing the utility of binary hashing in real-world applications.

Entropy Maximization. For a given dataset $\mathcal{X} \subset \mathbb{R}^d$ with N points, every hash function $h \in H$ shall cover approximately the same number of points $x \in \mathcal{X}$, i.e., uniformly distributed over all hash functions:

$$\forall h \in H, \left||h(\mathcal{X})| - \frac{N}{|H|}\right| \leq \varepsilon,$$

where $|H|$ denotes the total number of hash functions in H and ε is a predefined non-negative small number indicating the tolerance level for the approximation. This is to ensure that there are no under-utilized hash functions. This uniform coverage can be understood as maximizing the information entropy of the resulting binary codes [21], where high information entropy is indicative of a rich, diverse representation of the dataset. It avoids the scenario where a large proportion of the dataset is lumped in a few binary codes only.

Bit Independence. All hash functions in H are mutually independent. This means that for any pair of distinct hash functions $h_i \neq h_j \in H$, and for any point $\mathbf{x} \in \mathbb{R}^d$, the outputs $h_i(\mathbf{x})$ and $h_j(\mathbf{x})$ are statistically independent. It has been proven to be indispensable for optimizing performance [13,15,18,32]. This independence ensures that each hash function contributes uniquely to the hashing process, thereby eliminating potential redundancy in the generated binary bits. When hash functions are not mutually independent, the resulting binary representations suffer from information redundancy, which in turn, dilutes the effectiveness of the binary hashing scheme, leading to poor retrieval efficiency. Such redundancy also inflates the storage requirements unnecessarily.

It is interesting to note that none of the existing hash functions (i.e., thresholding, hyperspheres and hyperplanes) have the three properties naturally. That is the reason why learning has been employed to ensure that the final hash functions satisfy the three properties.

Here we have the insight that Voronoi diagrams is a suitable candidate for hash functions because they have the following properties, without learning:

1. A Voronoi diagram naturally covers the entire input space.
2. For a given dataset, every Voronoi cell in a Voronoi diagram covers approximately the same number of points. This occurs when a set of points, that represents the data distribution, is used to construct the Vonoroi diagram. And it can be easily achieved through a random Voronoi partition created by a set of points drawn independently and randomly from the dataset [7].
3. It is feasible to transform a Voronoi diagram into a set of mutually independent hash functions (see the analysis in Sect. 4.3).

This insight has led us to propose a no-learning data-dependent hashing scheme based on Voronoi diagrams, described in the next section.

4 Proposed Approach

Here we give the formal definition of our proposed binary hashing method called Voronoi Diagram Encoded Hashing (VDeH), which is the first binary hashing scheme based on a data-dependent similarity using Voronoi diagram partitioning.

4.1 A New Definition of Hashing

A kernel based on Voronoi diagrams called Isolation Kernel [30] is defined as:

$$\kappa(\mathbf{x},\mathbf{y}|\mathcal{H}(\mathcal{X})) = \mathbb{E}_{H \sim \mathcal{H}(\mathcal{X})}[\mathbb{1}(\mathbf{x},\mathbf{y} \in \theta \mid \theta \in H)],$$

where each Voronoi diagram H has cells θ, and $\mathbb{1}(\cdot)$ is an indicator function.

By re-writing each cell θ as a hash function h, it can be re-expressed as:

$$\kappa(\mathbf{x},\mathbf{y}|\mathcal{H}(\mathcal{X})) = \mathbb{E}_{H \sim \mathcal{H}(\mathcal{X})}[\mathbb{1}(h(\mathbf{x}) = h(\mathbf{y}) = 1 \mid h \in H)].$$

The above revelation, together with the three properties of Voronoi diagram (stated in Sect. 3), prompt us to propose a new definition of hashing. Given a dataset $\mathcal{X} \subset \mathbb{R}^{d \times N}$, the proposed VDeH scheme is defined as follows:

Definition 1. *The VDeH scheme is a family $\mathcal{H}(\mathcal{X})$ of hash functions created by Voronoi diagrams associated with a distribution $P_\mathcal{H}$ over $\mathcal{H}(\mathcal{X})$ generated from a dataset $\mathcal{X}$ such that it satisfies*

$$Pr_{h\in H\in\mathcal{H}(\mathcal{X})}[h(\mathbf{x}) = h(\mathbf{y}) = 1] = \kappa(\mathbf{x},\mathbf{y}|\mathcal{H}(\mathcal{X})), \quad (1)$$

where $\kappa(\mathbf{x},\mathbf{y}|\mathcal{H}(\mathcal{X}))$ is derived from Voronoi diagrams generated from $\mathcal{X}$; and H is a set of all hash functions h derived from a Voronoi diagram.

This definition makes the implementation of VDeH extremely simple because the hashing functions can be obtained with a simple additional encoding from the Voronoi diagrams already used in Isolation Kernel. Unlike existing hashing methods, VDeH needs no special design or learning of hash functions to gain the three properties mentioned in Sect. 3.

4.2 Implementation Details of VDeH

Given a subset $\mathcal{D} = \{\mathbf{s}_1,\ldots,\mathbf{s}_\psi\} \subset \mathcal{X}$ with ψ randomly selected points. A Voronoi diagram H, created by $\mathcal{D}$, partitions the $\mathbb{R}^d$ space into ψ Voronoi cells, where $\mathbf{s}_i$ is at the center of Voronoi cell i. Let a set of hash functions created by $\mathcal{D}$ be $H = \{h_1, h_2, \ldots, h_\psi\}$. For any $\mathbf{x} \in \mathbb{R}^d$, $h_i(\mathbf{x})$ is defined as:

$$h_i(\mathbf{x}) = \begin{cases} 0 & \text{if } dist(\mathbf{x},\mathbf{s}_i) > dist(\mathbf{x},\mathcal{D}) \\ 1 & \text{if } dist(\mathbf{x},\mathbf{s}_i) = dist(\mathbf{x},\mathcal{D}), \end{cases} \quad (2)$$

where $dist(\mathbf{x},\mathbf{s}_i) = \|\mathbf{x} - \mathbf{s}_i\|$ denotes the ℓ_2 distance between $\mathbf{x}$ and $\mathbf{s}_i$; and $dist(\mathbf{x},\mathcal{D}) = \min_{\mathbf{y}\in\mathcal{D}/\{\mathbf{x}\}} \|\mathbf{x} - \mathbf{y}\|$. When a point is located on a boundary, it is randomly assigned to any one of the cells sharing that boundary.

Given a fixed length of binary bits, existing studies have established that ensuring independence among generated binary bits is key to effective binary hashing. However, directly converting Voronoi cells into hash functions results in dependencies between them, due to the fact:

$$\forall h \in H, \forall \mathbf{x} \in \mathbb{R}^d, \sum_{i\in[1,\psi]} \mathbb{1}[h_i(\mathbf{x}) = 1] = 1. \quad (3)$$

This dependency arises because if $\mathbf{x}$ belongs to the i-th Voronoi cell, indicating $h_i(\mathbf{x}) = 1$, then $\mathbf{x}$ can not fall into other regions, hence $h(\mathbf{x}) = 0$ for those. As a result, any $h(\mathbf{x})$ is influenced by other hash functions.

To address this issue, we have adopted a simple encoded hashing mechanism to generate mutually independent binary bits. Let $\psi = 2^w$, and as 2^w Voronoi cells can be encoded with a binary code of w mutually independent bits, a L-bit code of the VDeH scheme represents $L/w \times 2^w$ hash functions (the proof is presented in the Sect. 4.3).

The process for generating a binary code corresponding to a point $\mathbf{x} \in \mathbb{R}^d$ via VDeH is outlined as follows:

1. Given a dataset $\mathcal{X}$, we randomly sample ψ points to form a set $\mathcal{D}$, and generate the set of Voronoi diagram hash functions $H = \{h_1, h_2, \ldots, h_\psi\}$. According to Eq. (3), there is one and only one $h_i(\mathbf{x}) = 1$ for any point $\mathbf{x}$, and $\forall u \neq i, h_u(\mathbf{x}) = 0$.
2. The above 'raw' ψ-bit vector $[h_1(\mathbf{x}), h_2(\mathbf{x}), \ldots, h_\psi(\mathbf{x})]$ can then be encoded as w-bit vector $b(\mathbf{x}) = [e_1(\mathbf{x}), e_2(\mathbf{x}), \ldots, e_w(\mathbf{x})]$, where $\psi \leqslant 2^w$, through the following encoded hashing function:

$$e_j(\mathbf{x}) = \begin{cases} 0 & \text{if } \lfloor \frac{\arg_{i \in [1,\psi]} h_i(\mathbf{x})=1}{2^{j-1}} \rfloor \mod 2 = 0 \\ 1 & \text{if } \lfloor \frac{\arg_{i \in [1,\psi]} h_i(\mathbf{x})=1}{2^{j-1}} \rfloor \mod 2 \neq 0, \end{cases} \quad (4)$$

where $j = 1, 2, \ldots, w$.
3. After repeating the above two steps L/w times, we concatenate all w-bit vectors $b(\mathbf{x})$ to formulate a L-bit code $\mathcal{B}(\mathbf{x}) = [b^1(\mathbf{x}), \ldots, b^{L/w}(\mathbf{x})]$ for any point $\mathbf{x}$.

It is interesting to note that this simple encoding is not applicable to existing L2H methods where a L-bit code could represent L hash functions only. In short, the VDeH scheme represents $(\frac{\psi}{w} - 1)L$ more hash functions than existing L2H methods when both have codes of the same number of L bits. This is a key to VDeH's better performance over existing L2H methods. Also note that the Voronoi diagram does not necessarily have to have 2^w Voronoi cells. It is simply a convenience for a binary encoded hashing with mutually independent bits.

The Time Complexity of VDeH. VDeH has a linear time complexity with respect to the size of the dataset, denoted as N, and the dimensionality of the data, denoted as d. A detailed analysis of the time complexity of VDeH is presented as follows: to convert a dataset $\mathcal{X}$ of N points of d dimensions, VDeH first finds the nearest neighbor of each point in $\mathcal{X}$ from the set $\mathcal{D}$ of ψ points (or Voronoi cells), resulting in a complexity of $\mathcal{O}(\psi N d)$. This process is repeated L/w times, leading to a total complexity of $\mathcal{O}(\frac{\psi L N d}{w})$. VDeH then uses the encoded hash functions h to generate L-bit binary codes for all N points, resulting in a complexity of $\mathcal{O}(LN)$. Thus, the overall time complexity for VDeH's 'training' process is $\mathcal{O}(\frac{\psi L N d}{w})$, which is linear to the dataset size N and the input dimensionality d.

4.3 Distance Measure for VDeH Codes

Hamming distance, renowned for its simplicity and efficiency, is predominantly employed in the comparison of binary codes due to its methodological advantage of merely counting the differing bits between two codes, thereby circumventing the necessity for intricate arithmetic operations such as multiplication and square root calculations. This stands in stark contrast to the computationally more demanding Euclidean distance.

For VDeH, the measurement of similarity between any two points is conducted by calculating the probability that both points fall into the same regions across all generated Voronoi cells. To fully utilize the three properties of the Voronoi diagram hashing functions, we propose the following distance metric, VDeH distance ($d_V(\mathcal{B}_i, \mathcal{B}_j)$), between two binary codes $\mathcal{B}_i$ and $\mathcal{B}_j$ generated by VDeH:

$$d_V(\mathcal{B}_i, \mathcal{B}_j) = \frac{w}{L} \sum_{k=1}^{L/w} \mathbb{1}(b_i^k \neq b_j^k), \tag{5}$$

where $\mathcal{B}_i = [b_i^1, \ldots, b_i^{L/w}]$ and $\mathcal{B}_j = [b_j^1, \ldots, b_j^{L/w}]$. Then, for any given query point $\mathbf{q}$, after computing its binary code $\mathcal{B}(\mathbf{q})$ through VDeH and its distance to every point in the dataset can be calculated using Eq. (5), the retrieval process returns a point in the dataset having the shortest distance to the query point $\mathbf{q}$.

4.4 Independence Among VDeH Bits

The importance of independence among hash bits are mentioned in existing studies [13,18,32]. It can be defined as follows:

Definition 2 *(Independence among hash bits)*. *Given a family of hash functions $\{h_1, h_2, \ldots, h_L\}$, for any $\mathbf{x} \in \mathbb{R}^d$, $h_1(\mathbf{x}), h_2(\mathbf{x}), \ldots, h_L(\mathbf{x})$ are said to be mutually independent for $\forall \mathbf{x}$ if for any set of values $v_1, v_2, \ldots, v_L \in \{0, 1\}$, it holds that:*

$$Pr(h_1(\mathbf{x}) = v_1, h_2(\mathbf{x}) = v_2, \ldots, h_L(\mathbf{x}) = v_L) = $$
$$Pr(h_1(\mathbf{x}) = v_1) \cdot Pr(h_2(\mathbf{x}) = v_2) \cdot \cdots \cdot Pr(h_L(\mathbf{x}) = v_L).$$

This means that the value of one hash bit does not influence the value of another hash bit. Although directly converting regions generated by Voronoi diagrams into hash functions results in dependencies between them based on the Eq. (3), we prove that the encoded hashing enables the achievement of such independence among hash bits. VDeH generates mutually independent binary bits through encoded hashing, as demonstrated by the following theorem.

Lemma 1. *Let $\mathcal{D} = \{\mathbf{s}_1, \mathbf{s}_2, \ldots, \mathbf{s}_\psi\} \sim G^\psi$ be a dataset, where every $\mathbf{s}_i$ is i.i.d drawn from an unknown probability distribution G on the input space Ω. Let $\mathcal{D}$ forms its Voronoi cells $V_i \subset \Omega$, the probability that $\mathbf{s}_i$ is the nearest neighbor of any $\mathbf{x} \in \Omega$ in $\mathcal{D}$ is given as: $Pr(\mathbf{x} \in V_i) = 1/\psi$, for every $i = 1, 2, \ldots, \psi$.*

Proof. Let $R(\mathbf{x}) = \{\mathbf{y} \in \Omega \mid dist(\mathbf{x}, \mathbf{y}) \leq r\}$ be r-neighborhood region of $\mathbf{x}$, and $\Delta R(\mathbf{x}) = \{\mathbf{y} \in \Omega \mid r \leq dist(\mathbf{x}, \mathbf{y}) \leq r + \Delta r\}$ be Δr incremental r-neighborhood region of x. Let ρ_G be the probability density of G, for $\Delta r > 0$, $f = \int_{R(\mathbf{x})} \rho_G(\mathbf{y}) d\mathbf{y}$ and $\Delta f = \int_{\Delta R(\mathbf{x})} \rho_G(\mathbf{y}) d\mathbf{y}$.

Then, let two events T and Q be as follows:

$$T \equiv \mathbf{s}_k \notin R(\mathbf{x}) \text{ for all } \mathbf{s}_k \in \mathcal{D}(k = 1, 2, \ldots, \psi), \text{ and}$$

$$Q \equiv \begin{cases} \mathbf{s}_i \in \Delta R(\mathbf{x}) \text{ for } \mathbf{s}_i \in \mathcal{D}, \text{ and} \\ \mathbf{s}_k \notin \Delta R(\mathbf{x}) \text{ for all } \mathbf{s}_k \in \mathcal{D} \ (k = 1, 2, \ldots, \psi, i \neq k). \end{cases}$$

Next, the probability $Pr(T \wedge Q) = Pr(T)Pr(Q \mid T)$ denotes that $\mathbf{s}_i$ is the nearest neighbor of $\mathbf{x}$ in $\mathcal{D}$, i.e., $\mathbf{x} \in V_i$, where

$$Pr(T) = (1-f)^{\psi}, \text{ and}$$

$$Pr(Q \mid T) = \frac{\Delta f}{1-f} \left\{ 1 - \frac{\Delta f}{1-f} \right\}^{\psi-1}.$$

By letting Δf be infinite decimal df, $\Delta f/(1-f) \to df/(1-f)$ and $\{1-\Delta f/(1-f)\} \to 1$. Thus, we obtain the following total probability that $\mathbf{s}_i$ is the nearest neighbor of $\mathbf{x}$ in $\mathcal{D}$, i.e., $\mathbf{x} \in V_i$, by integrating $Pr(T \wedge Q)$ on $f \in [0,1]$ for every $i = 1, 2, \ldots, \psi$.

$$Pr(\mathbf{x} \in V_i) = \int_0^1 (1-f)^{\psi} \frac{df}{1-f} = \frac{1}{\psi}.$$

Theorem 1. *Let a L-bit code vector $\mathcal{B}(\mathbf{x}) = [b_1(\mathbf{x}), b_2(\mathbf{x}), \ldots, b_T(\mathbf{x})]$ denote the VDeH encoded binary vector for any point $\mathbf{x}$, where $T = L/w$ is the number of Voronoi diagrams generated and every $b_i(\mathbf{x})$ is the w-bit vector generated by the i-th VDeH encoded hashing. When each Voronoi diagram has 2^w regions, every bit in $\mathcal{B}(\mathbf{x})$ is mutually independent.*

Proof. For any two bits $\alpha, \beta \in \mathcal{B}(\mathbf{x})$ located at different Voronoi cells, there are the following two cases:

Case 1: α and β are generated by the different encoded hashing.

Let $\alpha \in b_j$ and $\beta \in b_k$ ($1 \leq j < k \leq T$). Given that Voronoi diagrams generated in each random sampling are mutually independent, the bits obtained from each encoded hashing are also mutually independent. Consequently, it follows that:

$$Pr(b_j = s_j, b_k = s_k) = Pr(b_j = s_j) \cdot Pr(b_k = s_k),$$

where $s_j, s_k \in \{0,1\}^w$. Moreover, for the bits $\alpha \in b_j$ and $\beta \in b_k$

$$Pr(\alpha = v_\alpha, \beta = v_\beta) = Pr(\alpha = v_\alpha) \cdot Pr(\beta = v_\beta),$$

where $v_\alpha, v_\beta \in \{0,1\}$.

Case 2: α and β are generated by the same encoded hashing.

Let $\alpha, \beta \in b_i$ ($1 \leq i \leq T$), $b_i = [e_1, e_2, \ldots, e_w]$, and $\mathcal{B}$ denote a set of ψ different w-bit binary codes correspond to the ψ distinct Voronoi cells.

When $\psi = 2^w$, $\mathcal{B}$ exhaustively represents all probable w-bit binary codes corresponding to ψ Voronoi cells. Let $v_\alpha, v_\beta \in \{0,1\}$, then we have $\sum \mathbb{1}[\alpha = v_\alpha] = \frac{\psi}{2}$, and $\sum \mathbb{1}[\alpha = v_\alpha, \beta = v_\beta] = \frac{\psi}{4}$. Based on Lemma 1, it follows that

$$\begin{aligned} Pr(\alpha = v_\alpha, \beta = v_\beta) &= \sum_{i=1}^{\psi} (Pr(\mathbf{x} \in V_i) \mathbb{1}[\alpha = v_\alpha, \beta = v_\beta]) \\ &= \frac{1}{\psi} \sum_{i=1}^{\psi} \mathbb{1}[\alpha = v_\alpha, \beta = v_\beta] \\ &= \frac{\sum_{i=1}^{\psi} \mathbb{1}[\alpha = v_\alpha]}{\psi} \times \frac{\sum_{i=1}^{\psi} \mathbb{1}[\beta = v_\beta]}{\psi} \\ &= \sum_{i=1}^{\psi} (Pr(\mathbf{x} \in V_i) \mathbb{1}[\alpha = v_\alpha]) \times \sum_{i=1}^{\psi} (Pr(\mathbf{x} \in V_i) \mathbb{1}[\beta = v_\beta]) \\ &= Pr(\alpha = v_\alpha) \cdot Pr(\beta = v_\beta). \end{aligned}$$

Consequently, in all cases, α and β are mutually independent. Since α and β are arbitrary bits in $\mathcal{B}$, when each Voronoi diagram has 2^w regions, every bit in $\mathcal{B}(\mathbf{x})$ generated by VDeH is mutually independent.

5 Experiment

5.1 Datasets and Settings

To evaluate the proposed Voronoi diagram encoded hashing, we conducted experiments on four public datasets, including two image datasets and two text datasets. It is important to note that existing studies mainly evaluate their performance on image datasets [9,10,15,22,32,34,35], our work extends the evaluation to text datasets for a more comprehensive analysis. Unlike images, which have obviously discriminating features and can be easily identified to guide retrieval tasks, text data presents a greater challenge due to its inherent complexity. The datasets vary in size and dimensionality: CIFAR-10 [20] contains 60,000 images (512 dimensions), GIST [19] contains one million images represented by 960-dimensional descriptors, Nytimes [27] includes 290,000 articles (256 dimensions), and Kosarak [8] includes 74,962 click-stream news (27,983 dimensions).

Following existing studies [15,17,22], we use 10,000 randomly sampled instances for training. We then randomly sample 500 instances, different from the training set as queries. The retrieval performance is assessed using two frequently used evaluation metrics, i.e., mean average precision (mAP) and the precision-recall curve (PR curve). We compared the performance of VDeH with the three types of state-of-the-art methods, i.e., (1) thresholding-based methods: spectral hashing (SH), circulant binary embedding (CBE), iterative quantization (ITQ), bilinear projections (BP), and sparse projections (SP); (2) hyperspheres-based method: spherical hashing (SpH); (3) hyperplanes-based methods: density sensitive hashing (DSH), sparse embedding and least variance encoding (SELVE), and refining codes for locality sensitive hashing (rcLSH). The parameters within each hashing method were assigned to default or suggested values by authors. For VDeH, the parameter ψ is searched in $\{2^2, 2^3, \ldots, 2^8\}$. All experiments are executed on a Linux CPU machine: AMD 128-core CPU with each core running at 2 GHz and 1T GB RAM.

5.2 Results and Discussion

Comparing to the State-of-the-Art. Table 2 presents the mAP scores of our proposed VDeH and the competing hashing methods conducted on the benchmark datasets. VDeH has the best results, compared with all the state-of-the-art methods, across all the tested number of hash bits ranging from 128 bits to 2048 bits. The mAP of VDeH increases consistently as the number of hash bits increases. Overall, only DSH demonstrated comparable performance across all datasets, positioning it as VDeH's closest contender. Among existing methods, rcLSH exhibited the best performance on image datasets. Notably, many existing methods showed a marked decrease in performance on the text datasets as

Table 2. The mAP scores on four datasets with different number of hash bits. The highest score in each row is marked with bold font.

Dataset	bits	VDeH	rcLSH	SH	CBE	ITQ	BP	SP	DSH	SELVE	SpH
CIFAR-10	128	**0.366**	0.283	0.117	0.315	0.355	0.344	0.352	0.318	0.199	0.242
	256	**0.438**	0.351	0.153	0.342	0.377	0.343	0.370	0.372	0.176	0.289
	512	**0.468**	0.392	0.193	0.396	0.389	0.339	0.397	0.401	0.167	0.304
	1024	**0.501**	0.412	0.201	0.401	0.398	0.332	0.407	0.429	0.169	0.314
	2048	**0.525**	0.432	0.214	0.407	0.401	0.335	0.426	0.457	0.169	0.321
GIST	128	**0.664**	0.582	0.338	0.617	0.644	0.645	0.604	0.501	0.430	0.222
	256	**0.714**	0.631	0.454	0.644	0.650	0.641	0.614	0.580	0.399	0.223
	512	**0.763**	0.651	0.501	0.656	0.654	0.634	0.638	0.618	0.402	0.232
	1024	**0.774**	0.659	0.514	0.657	0.657	0.642	0.638	0.610	0.399	0.233
	2048	**0.793**	0.687	0.532	0.662	0.663	0.644	0.641	0.621	0.398	0.242
Nytimes	128	**0.116**	0.017	0.033	0.022	0.023	0.023	0.022	0.016	0.003	0.100
	256	**0.165**	0.026	0.055	0.029	0.029	0.029	0.027	0.033	0.004	0.110
	512	**0.340**	0.028	0.160	0.026	0.030	0.026	0.029	0.185	0.004	0.146
	1024	**0.348**	0.103	0.295	0.108	0.104	0.008	0.106	0.339	0.006	0.088
	2048	**0.376**	0.113	0.310	0.100	0.097	0.008	0.100	0.326	0.008	0.089
Kosarak	128	**0.457**	0.235	0.375	0.255	0.261	0.254	0.258	0.368	0.203	0.256
	256	**0.603**	0.271	0.512	0.286	0.293	0.295	0.304	0.494	0.226	0.296
	512	**0.607**	0.308	0.571	0.301	0.298	0.346	0.341	0.437	0.279	0.346
	1024	**0.615**	0.307	0.569	0.300	0.302	0.351	0.357	0.415	0.289	0.372
	2048	**0.638**	0.313	0.579	0.309	0.312	0.359	0.369	0.412	0.300	0.381

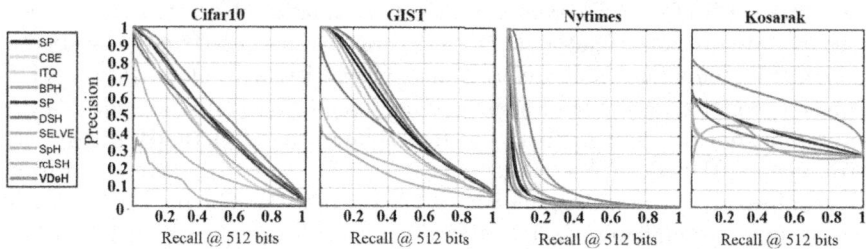

Fig. 2. PR curves on four datasets with the 512-bit binary codes

the hash bits increases, except VDeH, SH, and DSH. This is probably because text data have complex density variations. DSH and SH are adapted by using more hash functions in dense distribution and fewer in sparse distribution; while VDeH naturally adapts because it creates smaller Voronoi cells in dense distribution and larger ones in sparse distribution [7,30]. In addition, Fig. 2 provides the PR curves of VDeH and the competing hashing methods, when the number of hash bits is 512. We can observe that the VDeH curve (in red) consistently dominates the curves of other methods across all datasets, demonstrating its superior precision and recall scores. For the cases with different hash bits, similar results can be observed (not presented due to lack of space).

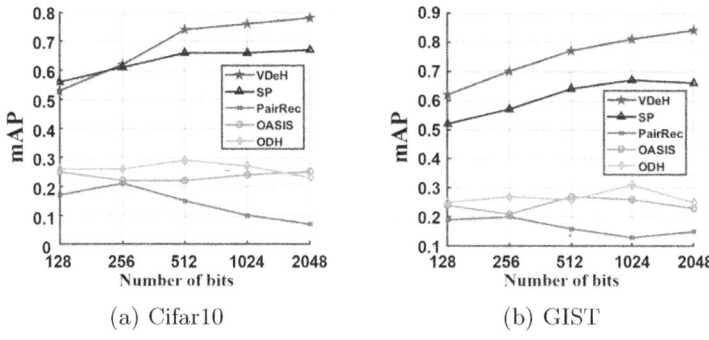

Fig. 3. The mAP scores comparison for five methods on image datasets.

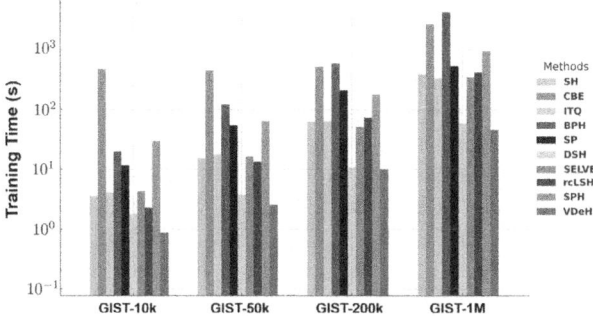

Fig. 4. Training time comparison on GIST dataset with the 512-bit binary codes.

Comparing to the Deep Hashing Methods. Deep hashing is known for its high accuracy in semantic-based image retrieval [24]. However, deep hashing methods cannot accurately retrieve input distance similarities, even after extracting semantic information from images. To show this, we use CIFAR-10 and GIST datasets, which possess semantic information in images. Initially, we utilized ResNet18 to extract embeddings from these two datasets. Since the Euclidean distance between the obtained embeddings can reflect the semantic information between images, we used the Euclidean distances derived from these embeddings as ground truth to test the performance of VDeH and SP, as well as three deep hashing methods PairRec [11], OASIS [33] and ODH [14]. The comparison results are shown in Fig. 3. We can observe that typical L2H methods can effectively preserve the Euclidean distances between instances, whereas deep methods lack this capability. This is due to the fact that deep methods incorporate labels as part of their loss function during training, aiming to map instances with the same label to close hash codes, rather than being designed to preserve the input distance similarities between instances.

Training Time Comparison. Unlike existing hashing methods that rely on optimization for learning hash functions, VDeH's training process is straightfor-

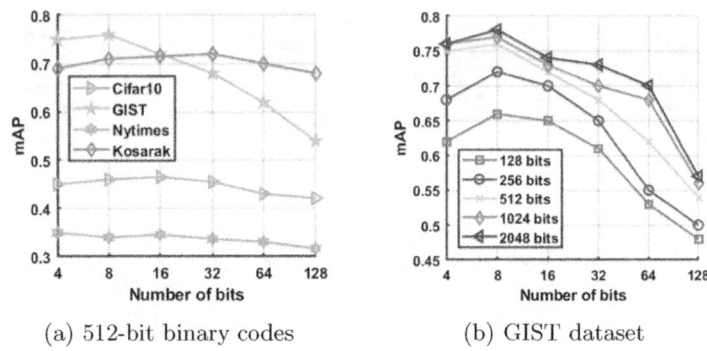

Fig. 5. The impact of Parameter ψ: (a) testing on different datasets with 512-bit binary codes; (b) Testing on GIST dataset with different number of hash bits.

ward, requiring only the random sampling of a given number of points from the training data, each corresponding to a nearest-neighbor-based hash function (as shown in Eq. 2). Note that all methods require the transformation of training data into binary codes via hash functions. We tested the training time of various methods on the GIST dataset, shown in Fig. 4. VDeH took the shortest time for every training data size, from 10k to 1M, demonstrating its efficiency superiority over other methods. This is because VDeH needs no learning, but all other existing methods must perform learning.

Effects of Hyper-parameter ψ. Figure 5 illustrates the impact of the parameter ψ on the performance of the proposed VDeH method across different datasets and binary code lengths. In subfigure (a), we observe that only the GIST dataset shows a degree of sensitivity to ψ, while Cifar10, Nytimes, and Kosarak show relatively stable mAP scores across the different ψ values. Subfigure (b) further explores this by examining VDeH's mAP scores on the GIST dataset with varying binary code lengths. We can observe that the optimal ψ value remains consistent regardless of the number of hash bits, ranging from 128 to 2048 bits. This suggests that the optimal selection of ψ is intrinsic to the characteristics of the specific dataset, rather than the code length.

6 Discussion

We acknowledge that the integration of Voronoi diagrams with hashing techniques is not an entirely novel concept [1,23]. However, our proposed VDeH distinguishes itself from existing works through its unique mechanism for generating data-dependent hash functions and its redefinition of the hashing process. Prior approaches, such as VLSH by Loi *et al.* [23], use Voronoi regions to primarily localize and adapt standard Locality Sensitive Hashing (LSH); its core hashing still relies on LSH's random projection-based mechanism within these regions. Similarly, the work by Ajani & Wanjari combines Voronoi clustering with hash indexing, where hash indexing serves to optimize their k-means clustering algorithm for uncertain data rather than generating binary codes for similarity search. In contrast, VDeH directly derives hash functions from the partitions of Voronoi diagrams themselves. The goal of VDeH is to generate highly efficient binary representations for large-scale datasets, thereby enabling rapid similarity search and retrieval. The main novelty of VDeH lies in its utilization of Voronoi diagrams as the core data-dependent hash function generator. It proposes a method that can achieve key hashing properties, including full space coverage, entropy maximization, and bit independence, without resorting to complex learning procedures, notably through its specifically defined encoded hashing mechanism.

7 Conclusion

We introduce VDeH, a novel no-learning data-dependent method for binary hashing. VDeH distinguishes itself from L2H methods in three aspects. First, VDeH employs the unique space partitioning of Voronoi diagrams, leveraging its three previously concealed properties that match perfectly those required for hashing. Second, VDeH is an implementation of a new definition of hashing which equates the probability of some hashed condition to a similarity function. The definition enables Voronoi diagrams, already used to compute the similarity of Isolation Kernel, to construct hash functions easily without much effort. No existing L2H methods have used a similar definition as far as we know. Third, the integration of encoded hashing enables VDeH to generate mutually independent binary bits, which could not be utilized by existing methods because they have already employed independent hash functions. Our experiments show that VDeH exhibits superior performance with lower computational cost compared to the state-of-the-art methods.

Acknowledgments. We thank the anonymous reviewers for their valuable comments. This work was supported in part by the National Natural Science Foundation of China (Grant No. 92470116).

References

1. Ajani, S., Wanjari, M.: An efficient approach for clustering uncertain data mining based on hash indexing and Voronoi clustering. In: 2013 5th International Conference and Computational Intelligence and Communication Networks, pp. 486–490. IEEE (2013)
2. Al-Odat, Z.A., Ali, M., Abbas, A., Khan, S.U.: Secure hash algorithms and the corresponding FPGA optimization techniques. ACM Comput. Surv. (CSUR) **53**(5), 1–36 (2020)
3. Borthwick, A., Ash, S., Pang, B., Qureshi, S., Jones, T.: Scalable blocking for very large databases. In: Koprinska, I., et al. (eds.) ECML PKDD 2020. CCIS, vol. 1323, pp. 303–319. Springer, Cham (2020). https://doi.org/10.1007/978-3-030-65965-3_20

4. Cai, D.: A revisit of hashing algorithms for approximate nearest neighbor search. IEEE Trans. Knowl. Data Eng. **33**(6), 2337–2348 (2021)
5. Charikar, M.S.: Similarity estimation techniques from rounding algorithms. In: Proceedings of the Thirty-Fourth Annual ACM Symposium on Theory of Computing, pp. 380–388 (2002)
6. Chi, L., Zhu, X.: Hashing techniques: a survey and taxonomy. ACM Comput. Surv. (CSUR) **50**(1), 1–36 (2017)
7. Devroye, L., Györfi, L., Lugosi, G., Walk, H.: On the measure of Voronoi cells. J. Appl. Probab. **54**(2), 394–408 (2017)
8. FIMI: FIMI datasets (2017). http://fimi.ua.ac.be/data/. Accessed 2 Jan 2017
9. Gong, Y., Kumar, S., Rowley, H.A., Lazebnik, S.: Learning binary codes for high-dimensional data using bilinear projections. In: Proceedings of the IEEE Conference on Computer Vision and Pattern Recognition (2013)
10. Gong, Y., Lazebnik, S., Gordo, A., Perronnin, F.: Iterative quantization: a procrustean approach to learning binary codes for large-scale image retrieval. IEEE Trans. Pattern Anal. Mach. Intell. **35**(12), 2916–2929 (2013)
11. Hansen, C., Hansen, C., Simonsen, J.G., Alstrup, S., Lioma, C.: Unsupervised semantic hashing with pairwise reconstruction. In: Proceedings of the 43rd International ACM SIGIR Conference on Research and Development in Information Retrieval (2020)
12. Haq, I.U., Caballero, J.: A survey of binary code similarity. ACM Comput. Surv. (CSUR) **54**(3), 1–38 (2021)
13. He, J., Chang, S.-F., Radhakrishnan, R., Bauer, C.: Compact hashing with joint optimization of search accuracy and time. In: Proceedings of the IEEE Conference on Computer Vision and Pattern Recognition, pp. 753–760 (2011)
14. He, L., et al.: One-bit deep hashing: towards resource-efficient hashing model with binary neural network. In: Proceedings of the 32nd ACM International Conference on Multimedia, pp. 7162–7171 (2024)
15. Heo, J.-P., Lee, Y., He, J., Chang, S.-F., Yoon, S.-E.: Spherical hashing: binary code embedding with hyperspheres. IEEE Trans. Pattern Anal. Mach. Intell. **37**(11), 2304–2316 (2015)
16. Hu, D., Chen, Z., Wu, J., Sun, J., Chen, H.: Persistent memory hash indexes: an experimental evaluation. Proc. VLDB Endowment **14**(5), 785–798 (2021)
17. Jin, Z., Li, C., Lin, Y., Cai, D.: Density sensitive hashing. IEEE Trans. Cybern. **44**(8), 1362–1371 (2014)
18. Joly, A., Buisson, O.: Random maximum margin hashing. In: Proceedings of the IEEE Conference on Computer Vision and Pattern Recognition (2011)
19. Jégou, H., Douze, M., Schmid, C.: Product quantization for nearest neighbor search. IEEE Trans. Pattern Anal. Mach. Intell., 117–128 (2011)
20. Krizhevsky, A.: Learning multiple layers of features from tiny images. Technical report from the Department of Computer Science at the University of Toronto (2009)
21. Li, Y., van Gemert, J.: Deep unsupervised image hashing by maximizing bit entropy. In: Proceedings of the AAAI Conference on Artificial Intelligence, vol. 35, no. 3, pp. 2002–2010 (2021)
22. Liu, H., Zhou, W.H., Wu, Z., Zhang, S.C., Li, G., Li, X.L.: Refining codes for locality sensitive hashing. IEEE Trans. Knowl. Data Eng., 1–11 (2023)
23. Loi, T.L., Heo, J.-P., Lee, J., Yoon, S.-E.: VLSH: Voronoi-based locality sensitive hashing. In: 2013 IEEE/RSJ International Conference on Intelligent Robots and Systems, pp. 5345–5352. IEEE (2013)
24. Luo, X., et al.: A survey on deep hashing methods. ACM Trans. Knowl. Discov. Data **17**(1), 1–50 (2023)

25. Mao, J.-Y., Pan, Q.-K., Miao, Z.-H., Gao, L., Chen, S.: A hash map-based memetic algorithm for the distributed permutation flowshop scheduling problem with preventive maintenance to minimize total flowtime. Knowl.-Based Syst. **242**, 108413 (2022)
26. Min, X., et al.: SepHash: a write-optimized hash index on disaggregated memory via separate segment structure. Proc. VLDB Endowment **17**(5), 1091–1104 (2024)
27. Pham, N., Liu, T.: Falconn++: a locality-sensitive filtering approach for approximate nearest neighbor search. In: Proceedings of the 36th Annual Conference on Neural Information Processing Systems (2022)
28. Singh, A., Gupta, S.: Learning to hash: a comprehensive survey of deep learning-based hashing methods. Knowl. Inf. Syst. **64**(10), 2565–2597 (2022)
29. Thangavel, M., Varalakshmi, P.: Enabling ternary hash tree based integrity verification for secure cloud data storage. IEEE Trans. Knowl. Data Eng. **32**(12), 2351–2362 (2019)
30. Ting, K.M., Zhu, Y., Zhou, Z.-H.: Isolation kernel and its effect on SVM. In: Proceedings of the 24th ACM SIGKDD International Conference on Knowledge Discovery and Data Mining (2018)
31. Wang, J., Zhang, T., Song, J., Sebe, N., Shen, H.T.: A survey on learning to hash. IEEE Trans. Pattern Anal. Mach. Intell. **13**(9) (2017)
32. Weiss, Y., Torralba, A., Fergus, R.: Spectral hashing. In: Proceedings of the 21st Annual Conference on Neural Information Processing Systems, pp. 1753–1760 (2008)
33. Wu, X.-M., Luo, X., Zhan, Y.-W., Ding, C.-L., Chen, Z.-D., Xu, X.-S.: Online enhanced semantic hashing: towards effective and efficient retrieval for streaming multi-modal data. In: AAAI Conference on Artificial Intelligence, pp. 4263–4271 (2022)
34. Xia, Y., He, K., Kohli, P., Sun, J.: Sparse projections for high-dimensional binary codes. In: Proceedings of the 2015 IEEE Conference on Computer Vision and Pattern Recognition, pp. 3332–3339 (2015)
35. Yu, F.X., Kumar, S., Gong, Y., Chang, S.-F.: Circulant binary embedding. In: Proceedings of the 31st International Conference on Machine Learning (2014)
36. Zhu, L., Zheng, C., Guan, W., Li, J., Yang, Y., Shen, H.T.: Multi-modal hashing for efficient multimedia retrieval: a survey. IEEE Trans. Knowl. Data Eng. **36**(1), 239–260 (2023)
37. Zhu, X., Zhang, L., Huang, Z.: A sparse embedding and least variance encoding approach to hashing. IEEE Trans. Image Process. (2014)

Adaptive Multi-space Defense Framework Against Adversarial Attacks

Xiaohui Yu and Qiao Yan[✉]

Shenzhen University, Shenzhen, China
yanq@szu.edu.cn

Abstract. Graph Neural Networks (GNNs) are vulnerable to adversarial attacks, leading to a significant performance degradation. Many current methods guide graph purification or graph structure learning through predefined robust properties. However, attackers can also apply the same constraints to these properties, rendering the defenses ineffective. This paper proposes an adaptive multi-sapce defense framework that enhances the robustness of GNNs without relying on prior knowledge. The core idea is to generate an estimated graph using clean attribute information and then apply graph convolution to both the perturbed graph and the estimated graph to obtain their respective node embeddings. Common embeddings between the estimated graph and the perturbed graph is then captured through shared parameters, and an attention mechanism is utilized to learn the weights of the three spaces. Extensive experiments demonstrate that our method extracts the information most relevant to classification performance where both attack methods and perturbation rates are unknown, resulting in significant improvements in both classification accuracy and performance stability.

Keywords: Adversarial robustness · Representation learning · Graph convolutional networks

1 Introduction

Graph Neural Networks (GNNs) effectively combine attribute and structural information within graphs, demonstrating superior performance in node classification, graph classification, and link prediction tasks. They are widely applied to recommender systems [1], traffic networks [2], and financial transactions [3]. However, GNNs are vulnerable to adversarial attacks, where small perturbations mislead the model into making incorrect predictions [4]. For instance, in social networks, attackers can manipulate the network structure by adding or removing a small number of edges (social relationships), causing the GNN to misidentify communities or influence propagation paths. This vulnerability of GNNs in many critical applications can have serious consequences. Therefore, developing robust GNN models to defend against adversarial attacks is crucial.

Given the complexity of structural information, the majority of existing adversarial attacks on graph data have focused on modifying graph structure,

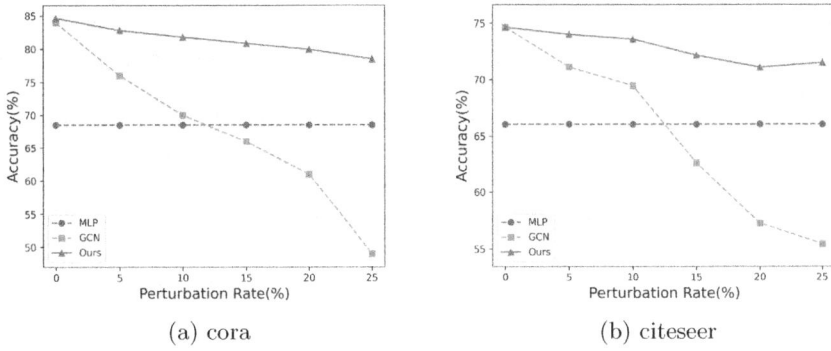

Fig. 1. Performance under Metattack with a perturbation rate of 20%

especially adding/deleting/rewiring edges [5]. Thus, in this work, we aim to defend against the most common setting of adversarial attacks on graph data, i.e., poisoning adversarial attacks on graph structure.

There is a significant amount of research addressing the issue of adversarial robustness, among which defense methods based on graph purification are very effective. These methods eliminate adversarial edges or relearn the graph structure through intrinsic properties of the graph (low-rank property [9,11], feature similarities [6,7,11]). However, these methods have two significant drawbacks: (1) attackers can also impose the same constraints on these predefined robust properties during the attack process, rendering the defense ineffective; (2) a large amount of valid information still exists in the perturbed original graph, which is very important for GNNs, but these methods ignore the structure of the original graph. To address these issues, we attempt to design an end-to-end defense method that does not rely on artificially defined properties and can retain the valid information of the original graph.

Figure 1 shows the node classification accuracy of GCN and MLP on the Cora and Citeseer datasets at different perturbation rates. When the perturbation rate is low, the performance of GCN is significantly higher than that of MLP, indicating that there is still a large amount of useful information in the structural information despite being contaminated. When the perturbation rate is very high, MLP, which only uses the attribute information of the graph data, performs better than GCN in classification. Therefore, when the perturbation rate is unknown, classification performance may be related to the original graph, the attribute graph, or a combination of them. Therefore, we designed an adaptive multi-space defense framework that uses graph convolutional networks to automatically capture task-relevant node representations in the graph and can adaptively adjust the weights of the original graph, attribute graph, and combined parts regardless of the perturbation rate. The results in the figure show that the method in this paper can maintain excellent performance at all perturbation rates.

Specifically, we proposed an **A**daptive multi-**S**pace defense framework, ASGCN. We use MLP to generate an estimated graph from clean node attributes. Then, we use two graph convolution modules to extract personalized representations from the two graphs that are beneficial for classification. Considering the common features between the two graphs, we designed a general convolution module with a shared parameter strategy to extract the common embeddings they share. We further utilize an attention mechanism to automatically learn the importance weights of different embeddings, thereby adaptively fusing them. In this way, node labels can supervise the learning process, adaptively adjust weights, and extract information most relevant to task performance.

Our contributions can be summarized as follows:

(1) We investigated the contributions of the original perturbed graph and the attribute graph under different perturbation rates, and concluded that task performance may be related to the perturbed graph, the attribute graph, or a combination thereof.
(2) We proposed an adaptive multi-space defense framework, ASGCN. Combined with an attention mechanism, two specific GCNs and a common GCN extract task-relevant information from the original perturbed graph, the attribute estimation graph, and their combination, respectively.
(3) Our method does not rely on manually defined graph intrinsic properties as prior knowledge, enabling end-to-end learning.
(4) Our extensive experiments on a series of benchmark datasets clearly show that MS-GCN outperforms the state-of-the-art GCNs. Furthermore, when the graph is heavily poisoned, MS-GCN can still maintain excellent classification performance.

2 Related Work

In recent years, adversarial defense research for GNNs has received increasing attention. Graph purification-based defense methods identify normal or adversarial edges based on the intrinsic properties of the graph. Jaccard-GCN [6] and GNNGuard [7] rely on the homophily assumption, with the former calculating the Jaccard similarity between node pairs and removing edges below a certain threshold, and the latter using cosine similarity to filter adversarial edges during message aggregation. STABLE [8] utilizes a similar idea of calculating similarity based on unsupervised representations instead of features. SVD-GCN [9] recognizes that Nettack [10] tends to attack high-frequency components in graph data. Therefore, it replaces the adjacency matrix with a low-rank approximation, reducing the impact of adversarial attacks while preserving important information about the structure of the graph. Graph structure learning-based methods impose regularization terms based on inherent graph properties, constraining the generated graph structure to conform to standard patterns. ProGNN [11] discovers that real-world graphs are often low-rank and sparse, with adjacent nodes having similar features. Consequently, it uses these three properties as regularization terms to constrain graph structure generation. TGNN [12] points out that previous methods ignore the connections and balance between different graph properties, proposing a tensor-based GNN framework that fuses multiple properties. RGCN [19] also relies on the intrinsic properties of the graph to adaptively weight edges, using low weights to penalize adversarial edges. DualRGNN [13] incorporates a node-similarity-preserving graph refining (SPGR) module, where these node representations contain the similarity relationships of the original nodes, thereby weakening the poisoning effect of graph adversarial attacks on graph data. Adversarial training does not rely on prior knowledge, but GOOD-AT [20] points out that it can lead to models learning incorrect information. It uses adversarial examples to define an out-of-distribution (OOD) detector as a classifier to optimize the graph structure. D4A [14] proposes smooth-less message passing to enhance the tolerance with respect to structure perturbations.

3 Preliminaries

3.1 Notations

We consider an undirected graph $G = (V, E)$, where V is the set of N nodes, where $V = \{v_1, v_2, \ldots, v_n\}$ and $E = \{e_{ij}\}$ are the set of nodes and edges. We use matrix $A \in \{0,1\}^{N \times N}$ to denote the adjacency matrix of G. Furthermore, we use $X = [x_1, x_2, \ldots, x_n] \in R^{N \times d}$ to denote the node feature matrix where d is the dimension of the node feature vectors. $Y = [y_1, y_2, \ldots, y_n]$ are the labels corresponding to each node. In this work, we focus on the semi-supervised node classification, where the model f_θ is trained with labeled nodes $V_L \subset V$ to classify the other unlabeled nodes $V_U = V/V_L$.

3.2 A General Form of Poisoning Attacks

In poisoning attacks, attackers minimize an attack loss to cause incorrect final classification results. A general form of the objective for adversarial attacks can be stated as:

$$\arg\min_{\mathcal{A} \in \phi(\mathcal{A})} L_{attack}(f(\mathcal{A}, X; \theta^*), y) \quad \text{s.t.} \quad \theta^* = \arg\min_\theta L_{predict}(f(\mathcal{A}, X; \theta), y) \tag{1}$$

where y denotes ground-truth labels, L_{attack} denotes the attacker's loss function, and L_{predict} denote GNN's loss. A' is the perturbed adjacency matrix, and $\phi(A)$ is a set of adjacency matrices that satisfy the unnoticeability: $\|A' - A\|_0 \leq \Delta$ in which Δ is budget to constrain the number of perturbed edges.

4 Methodology

The overall architecture of the proposed ASGCN framework is shown in Fig. 2.

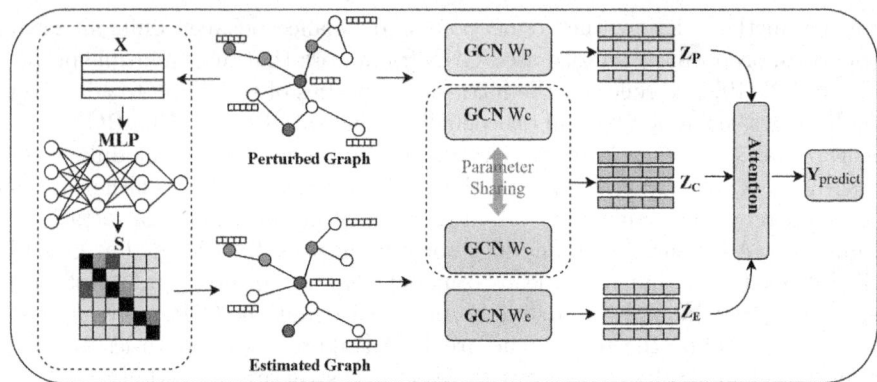

Fig. 2. The framework of the proposed ASGCN. (1) Generating an estimated graph from clean attributes using an MLP. (2) Extracting embeddings Z_P, Z_E, and Z_C from the perturbed graph, estimated graph, and a combination respectively, using two individual GCNs and one common GCN. (3) The attention mechanism assigns weights to the three spaces.

4.1 Attribute-Estimated Graph Generation

After a graph suffers a structural attack, its edges are perturbed, leading to significant noise. However, attribute information remains unaffected. We apply a multi-layer perceptron (MLP) to generate an estimated graph. The $l-th$ layer of the MLP is defined as:

$$Z_m^{(l)} = \sigma \left(Z_m^{(l-1)} W_m^{(L)} \right) \quad (2)$$

where $Z_m^{(0)} = X$, $W_m^{(l)}$ is the learnable weight matrix for MLP, and σ is activation function. Denote the output of the final layer of MLP as Z_m, then we can obtain the soft assignment matrix $B \in R^{n \times C}$ as follows:

$$B = \text{soft max}\,(Z_m) \quad (3)$$

The element in matrix B represents the probability that the $i-th$ node belongs to class c. All parameters θ_{mlp} of the MLP are optimized using the labels from the dataset, and the loss function is defined as follows:

$$\theta_{mlp}^* = \arg\min_{\theta_{mlp}} L_{mlp} = \arg\min_{\theta_{mlp}} \frac{1}{|V_L|} \sum_{v_a \in V_L} J(b_a^{mlp}, y_a) \quad (4)$$

where b_a^{mlp} is the predicted labels of node v_a by MLP. Based on matrix B, the probability of two nodes belonging to the same class can be calculated as follows:

$$S = BB^T \quad (5)$$

The element S_{ij} in matrix $S \in R^{n \times n}$ represents the probability that node i and node j belong to the same class. Finally, we set a threshold τ to generate the estimated graph G_e as follows:

$$G_e(ij) = \begin{cases} 0, S_{ij} < \tau, \\ 1, S_{ij} \geq \tau, \end{cases} \tag{6}$$

When the value of S_{ij} is greater than τ an edge is formed in the estimated graph. After calculating this for all node pairs, we obtain the adjacency matrix A_e corresponding to the estimated graph, while the feature matrix remains X.

4.2 Specific Convolution Module

Convolutional graph neural networks obtain high-quality node representations by aggregating neighbor information. Both the perturbed graph and the estimated graph contain substantial information beneficial for node classification. In this paper, we use two GCNs [16] to obtain node representations from the perturbed graph and the estimated graph, respectively. The $l-th$ layer output in the estimated graph can be represented as

$$Z_e^{(l)} = ReLU(\widetilde{D}_e^{-\frac{1}{2}} \widetilde{A}_e \widetilde{D}_e^{-\frac{1}{2}} Z_e^{(l-1)} W_e^{(l)}) \tag{7}$$

Here, $\widetilde{A}_e = A_e + I$ is the adjacency matrix of the estimated graph G_e with added self-connections. I is the identity matrix, $\widetilde{D}_e$ is the diagonal degree matrix of $\widetilde{A}_e$, where $\widetilde{D}_e(ii) = \sum_j \widetilde{A}_e(ij)$. $W_e^{(l)}$ is the weight matrix of the $l-th$ layer in GCN. $RuLU$ is the activation function and $Z_e^{(0)} = X$. Following the same calculation method, the output embedding for the perturbed graph after graph convolution is:

$$Z_p^{(l)} = ReLU(\widetilde{D}_p^{-\frac{1}{2}} \widetilde{A}_p \widetilde{D}_p^{-\frac{1}{2}} Z_p^{(l-1)} W_p^{(l)}) \tag{8}$$

4.3 Common Convolution Module

Perturbed graph and estimated graphs contain a significant amount of correlated information relevant to node classification tasks, and this correlation is often difficult to know in advance. Therefore, in addition to capturing the individual representations of perturbed graph and estimated graph, it is also necessary to capture the common information present in both graphs. We designed a Common-GCN with a parameter sharing strategy to obtain an embedding shared between the two graphs. First, we utilize Common-GCN to extract the node embedding $Z_{cp}^{(l)}$ from perturbed graph (A_p, X) as follows:

$$Z_{cp}^{(l)} = ReLU(\widetilde{D}_p^{-\frac{1}{2}} \widetilde{A}_p \widetilde{D}_p^{-\frac{1}{2}} Z_{cp}^{(l-1)} W_c^{(l)}) \tag{9}$$

where $W_C^{(l)}$ is the $l-th$ layer weight matrix of Common-GCN, and $Z_{cp}^{(l)}$, $Z_{cp}^{(l-1)}$ are the node representations of the perturbed graph in the $l-th$ and $(l-1)-th$ layers of Common-GNN, respectively. For estimated graph (A_e, X), we share the same weight matrix $W_C^{(l)}$ for every layer of Common-GCN as follows:

$$Z_{ce}^{(l)} = ReLU(\widetilde{D}_e^{-\frac{1}{2}} \widetilde{A}_e \widetilde{D}_e^{-\frac{1}{2}} Z_{ce}^{(l-1)} W_c^{(l)}) \tag{10}$$

Then we can get the $l-th$ common embedding $Z_c^{(l)}$ of the two graphs is:

$$Z_c^{(l)} = \frac{Z_{cp}^{(l)} + Z_{ce}^{(l)}}{2} \tag{11}$$

Sharing weights allows the two networks to focus more on the common information in the data. The node representations obtained from the common convolutional module can filter out the shared characteristics from the two graphs.

4.4 Attention Mechanism

We now have two specific embeddings Z_P and Z_E, and one common embedding Z_C. Under different perturbation rates, the contributions of the three inputs to the classification performance are different. We use the attention mechanism $att(Z_P, Z_E, Z_C)$ to learn their corresponding importance $(\lambda_p, \lambda_e, \lambda_c)$ as follows:

$$(\lambda_p, \lambda_e, \lambda_c) = att(Z_P, Z_E, Z_C) \tag{12}$$

Here $a_p, a_e, a_c \in \mathbb{R}^{n \times 1}$ indicate the attention values of n nodes with embeddings Z_P, Z_E, Z_C respectively. Taking the embedding Z_P in the perturbed graph as an example, the representation of node i is $z_p^i \in \mathbb{R}^{1 \times n}$. First, a non-linear transformation is performed. Then, the node attention value ξ_p^i is obtained after the operation with the attention vector $q \in \mathbb{R}^{h \times 1}$. The calculation method is as follows:

$$\xi_p^i = q^T \cdot \tanh(W \cdot (z_p^i)^T + b) \tag{13}$$

Using the method in formula (13), we can successively obtain the attention coefficients ξ_p^i, ξ_e^i of node i in Z_P, Z_E, Z_C. Using the softmax function to normalize, we obtain the weights $\lambda_p^i, \lambda_e^i, \lambda_c^i$ of the node i in Z_P, Z_E, Z_C. After the above calculation steps, each node obtains the weights on each channel. The embedding on the three channels are weighted and summed to obtain the final representation of the node:

$$Z = \lambda_p \cdot Z_P + \lambda_E \cdot Z_E + \lambda_C \cdot Z_C \tag{14}$$

4.5 Classifier

The final node representations obtained from the previous three parts are used for node classification. We employ the softmax function to compute the predicted label probabilities for each node and use the cross-entropy loss to optimize the model parameters.

$$\hat{y}_i = \text{softmax}(Z) \tag{15}$$

$$L_{loss} = -\frac{1}{|V_L|} \sum_{v_i \in V_L} Y_i \log(\hat{y}_i) \tag{16}$$

$Y_i, \hat{y}_i \in R^{|c|}$ is the one-hot embedding of label and the predicted label of i respectively.

5 Experiments

5.1 Experimental Setup

Dataset. We conduct extensive experiments on four widely used [8,11,13] graph datasets, including Cora, Citeseer, Pubmed [17], and Polblogs [18]. The Cora, Citeseer, and Pubmed datasets are citation graphs, in which each node represents scientific literature, and the edges between nodes represent the citation relationship of scientific literature. The Polblogs dataset is a blog graph, in which each edge represents the link between blogs. Note that there are no node features available in the Polblogs dataset, so following the previous work [11,13], we set the feature matrix to be a $N \times N$ identity matrix, where N is the number of nodes. More details of these datasets are summarized in Table 1.

Table 1. Datasets statistics

Datasets	Nodes	Edges	Features	Classes	Feature type
Cora	2485	5096	1433	7	Binary
Citeseer	2110	3668	3703	6	Binary
Pubmed	19717	44338	500	3	Continuous
Polblogs	1222	16714	/	2	/

Baseline. To highlight the outstanding performance in resisting various graph adversarial attacks of our method, we compare the DualRGNN with representative and state-of-the-art graph neural networks and robust graph neural network models. More detailed descriptions of the baselines are as follows:

- **GCN-Jaccard** [6]. GCN-Jaccard purifies the graph structure by calculating the Jaccard similarity of node features and removing edges below a similarity threshold.
- **RGCN** [19]. RGCN models the $l-th$ layer hidden representation of nodes as a Gaussian distribution and applies an attention mechanism to penalize nodes with high variance.
- **GCN-SVD** [9]. Enhancing the robustness of GCNs by low-rank approximation of perturbed graphs is also a strategy to defend against adversarial attacks through preprocessing.
- **GNNGuard** [7]. GNNGuard employs the theory of network homophily to assign higher scores to edges connecting similar nodes while pruning edges between unrelated nodes.
- **ProGNN** [11]. ProGNN generates a clean graph structure using three constraints: low-rank, sparsity, and feature similarity of neighboring nodes.
- **STABLE** [8]. STABLE utilizes a similar idea of calculating similarity based on unsupervised representations instead of features.
- **Good-AT** [20]. Good-AT defines an OOD detector as a classifier to filter adversarial edges using adversarial examples.

Parameter Settings. We randomly choose 10% of nodes for training, 10% of nodes for validation and the remaining 80% of nodes for testing. To obtain the three representations in our model, we simultaneously train three 2-layer GCNs. These GCNs share the same hidden layer dimension (nhid1) and the same output dimension (nhid2), where $nhid1 \in \{512, 768\}$ and $nhid2 \in \{32, 128, 256\}$. The MLP pre-training was performed for 100 epochs, with a single hidden layer of size nhid = nhid2. We explore weight decay in $\{5e - 3, 5e - 4\}$ and use a dropout rate of 0.5. The learning rate is searched within the range of 0.01 to 0.05. τ is an important parameter in the ASGCN. Too large a value will cause the estimated graph to be too dense, while too small a value will lead to underlearning. In this paper, based on the number of edges in each dataset, the (n * number of edges) node pairs with the greatest similarity, S_{ij}, are chosen to form edges. n is searched in $\{0.5, 1.0, 1.5, 2.0, 2.5, 3.0\}$. To ensure a fair comparison with the baseline methods, we adopt the same set of hyperparameters as recommended by their respective authors across all our models. All results were performed five times, and the results were averaged.

5.2 Performance on Clean Graph

Excellent defense methods should not only demonstrate robustness on perturbed graphs but also maintain comparable performance on clean graph data. Table 2 shows the classification results of baselines and our proposed method on clean datasets. The results demonstrate that our method maintains competitive performance across all four datasets, indicating that it does not sacrifice excessive original data accuracy in order to improve robustness against adversarial attacks. This is because, even when the data is unperturbed, our method can adaptively adjust the weights of the three representations to obtain the most task-relevant information.

Table 2. Performance on clean graph. The top two performances are highlighted in **bold** and underline.

Datasets	GCN-Jaccard	RGCN	GCN-SVD	GNNGuard	ProGNN	STABLE	Good-AT	Ours
Cora	82.45 ± 0.32	83.09 ± 0.15	80.63 ± 0.46	79.51 ± 0.30	83.45 ± 0.41	83.54 ± 0.40	84.30 ± 0.16	**84.65 ± 0.15**
Citeseer	72.43 ± 0.24	71.20 ± 0.31	70.65 ± 0.19	71.83 ± 0.45	73.87 ± 0.31	73.95 ± 0.37	74.08 ± 0.28	**74.64 ± 0.12**
PubMed	85.06 ± 0.08	85.16 ± 0.06	83.44 ± 0.14	83.88 ± 0.05	**87.24 ± 0.13**	85.79 ± 0.04	84.14 ± 0.08	86.24 ± 0.06
Polblogs	–	94.79 ± 0.15	**95.06 ± 0.20**	–	94.68 ± 0.19	94.96 ± 0.07	93.79 ± 0.20	94.46 ± 0.16

5.3 Defense Performance

5.3.1 Against Non-targeted Adversarial Attacks.
The goal of non-targeted attack is to degrade the overall performance of GNNs on the whole graph. We use Mettack [21] to perform non-targeted poisoning attacks, which is an effective attack method. Mettack needs to compute meta-gradients, which

Table 3. Node classification performance under non-targeted attack (metattack). The top two performances is highlighted in **bold** and underline.

Datasets	Ptb Rate	GCN-Jaccard	RGCN	GCN-SVD	GNN Guard	ProGNN	STABLE	Good-AT	Ours
Cora	5%	79.13	77.42	78.39	78.27	<u>82.27</u>	81.49	79.82	**82.80**
	10%	75.16	72.22	71.47	78.03	79.03	<u>80.06</u>	70.26	**81.79**
	15%	71.03	66.82	66.69	78.18	76.40	<u>78.45</u>	67.80	**80.84**
	20%	65.71	59.27	58.94	77.15	73.32	<u>78.01</u>	55.60	**79.93**
	25%	60.82	50.51	52.06	<u>76.34</u>	69.72	71.22	51.23	**78.47**
	Avg.	70.37	65.25	65.51	77.59	76.15	<u>77.85</u>	64.94	**80.77**
Citeseer	5%	70.51	70.50	68.84	71.32	73.09	<u>73.61</u>	72.39	**73.99**
	10%	69.54	67.71	68.87	<u>70.86</u>	72.51	73.13	69.46	**73.58**
	15%	65.95	65.69	63.26	70.83	72.03	<u>72.13</u>	66.78	**72.15**
	20%	59.30	62.49	58.55	70.97	70.02	<u>72.43</u>	60.27	**71.09**
	25%	59.89	55.35	57.18	<u>71.08</u>	68.95	70.21	57.90	**71.50**
	Avg.	65.04	64.35	63.34	71.01	71.32	<u>72.30</u>	65.36	**72.46**
PubMed	5%	85.44	82.51	83.64	84.24	<u>87.23</u>	**87.32**	84.02	86.36
	10%	85.26	80.36	82.31	84.10	**87.21**	<u>87.16</u>	83.87	85.82
	15%	84.72	75.84	82.26	84.14	<u>87.20</u>	**87.24**	83.07	85.75
	20%	83.65	71.24	83.07	84.22	**87.15**	<u>87.04</u>	82.41	85.18
	25%	83.74	70.12	81.88	84.12	<u>86.76</u>	**87.15**	82.00	85.54
	Avg.	84.56	76.01	82.63	84.16	<u>87.11</u>	**87.18**	83.07	85.73
Polblogs	5%	-	74.34	89.09	-	<u>93.29</u>	93.21	91.45	**93.33**
	10%	-	71.04	81.24	-	89.42	**92.14**	87.26	<u>91.92</u>
	15%	-	67.28	68.10	-	86.04	<u>90.23</u>	80.88	**93.76**
	20%	-	59.86	57.33	-	79.56	<u>88.43</u>	74.14	**92.84**
	25%	-	56.02	48.66	-	63.18	<u>84.56</u>	69.51	**90.69**
	Avg.	-	65.71	68.88	-	82.30	<u>89.71</u>	80.65	**92.51**

requires huge memory space to store the computation graphs in all iterations, so we only use the perturbed graphs provided by ProGNN [11]. We vary the perturbation rate, i.e., the ratio of changed edges, from 0 to 25% with a step of 5%. Due to the node features being unavailable on the Polblogs dataset, it is no means of evaluating the baselines methods Jaccard-GCN and GNNGuard on this dataset. The defense results are shown in Table 3, we have the following observations:

- Our method consistently outperforms all baseline methods across different perturbation rates on the Cora, Citeseer, and Polblogs datasets, while also achieving competitive performance on the PubMed dataset.
- Our method exhibits stable performance across varying attack rates. Across the four datasets, as the perturbation rate increases from 5% to 25%, our method's performance decreases by only 4.33%, 2.49%, 0.57%, and 0.79%, respectively. In contrast, ProGNN [11] performs well at low perturbation rates but experiences a sharp decline in performance as the perturbation rate increases. GNNGuard [7] and STABLE [8] demonstrate good defense

stability, but their accuracy is lower than that of our method. This indicates that our method is insensitive to the perturbation rate and can adaptively regulate the coefficients of the three convolutional layers in scenarios where the perturbation rate is unknown, consistently identifying the most beneficial components for classification.
- Even when the graph is heavily poisoned, our method maintains superior classification performance. For example, on the Cora dataset at a 25% perturbation rate, our method achieves a node classification accuracy of 78.47%, significantly higher than Good-AT [20] (51.23%) and RGCN [19] (50.51%). This demonstrates the robustness of our approach under varying levels of adversarial perturbations.

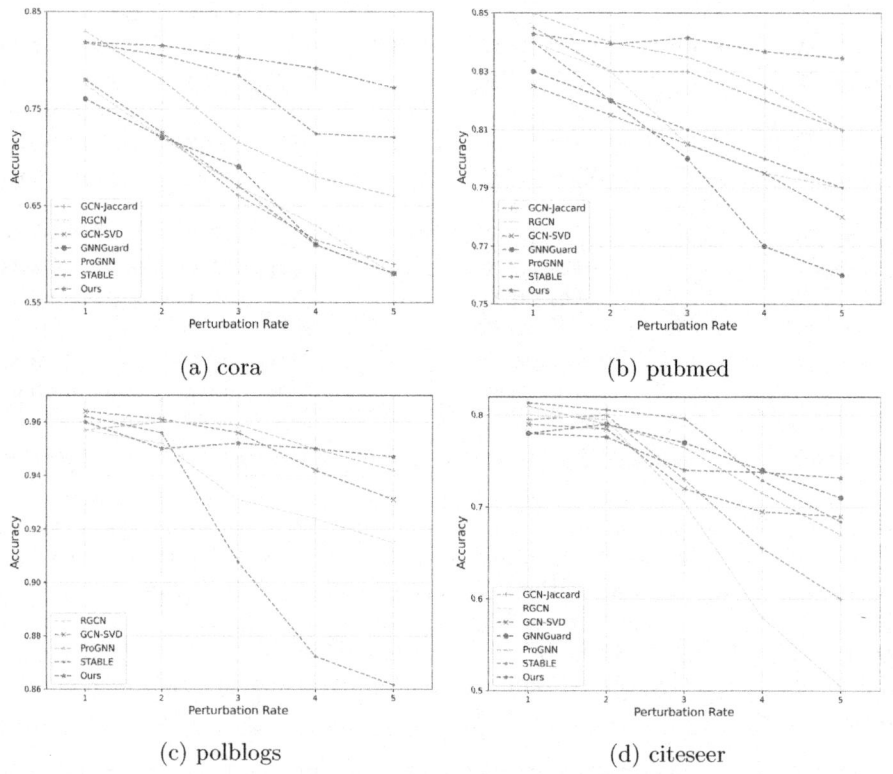

Fig. 3. Results of different models under nettack

5.3.2 Against Targeted Adversarial Attacks. Targeted attack generates attacks on specific nodes and aims to fool GNNs on these target nodes. We employ Nettack [10] as the target graph adversarial attack method, and we follow the default parameter settings in the authors' original implementation. Following [11,13], we set the number of perturbations made on every targeted node from 0 to 5 with a step size of 1. The nodes in the test set with a degree larger than 10 are treated as target nodes. Figure 3 presents the node classification results under different perturbation rates. From the results, we can make a few observations as follows:

- On the Cora and Pubmed datasets, our ASGCN method can effectively defend against targeted graph adversarial attacks, outperforming all baseline methods in most cases. Compared to the ProGNN [11] and STABLE [8] methods, ASGCN achieves higher semi-supervised node classification accuracy. Furthermore, at perturbation rates of 4 and 5, ASGCN maintains performance of 79.18% and 77.16% on the Cora dataset, significantly exceeding other baseline methods.
- On the Citeseer and Polblogs datasets, ASGCN does not outperform certain baseline methods on perturbed graphs. However, the overall performance of ASGCN remains comparable to most baseline methods, particularly when the perturbation rate is 5, where ASGCN still exhibits the best performance.

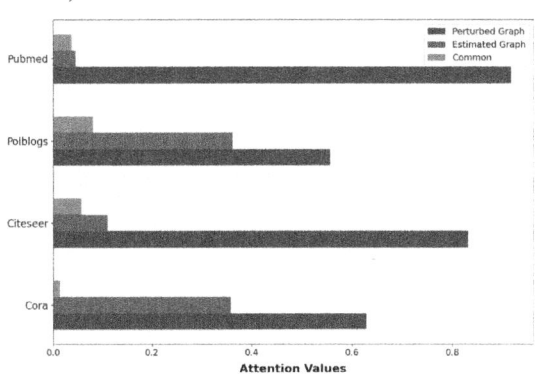

Fig. 4. Attention values under metattack (20% perturbation)

5.4 Analysis of Attention Mechanism

To investigate our proposed model's ability to adaptively learn the weights assigned to the perturbed graph, the estimated graph, and the common space – under perturbations with arbitrary attack rates – we observed the attention value distribution across these three components for all datasets under metattack with a 20% perturbation rate. As illustrated in Fig. 5, the attention distribution differs for the three spaces in each dataset. For the PubMed dataset, the information contribution from the perturbed graph is significantly greater than that

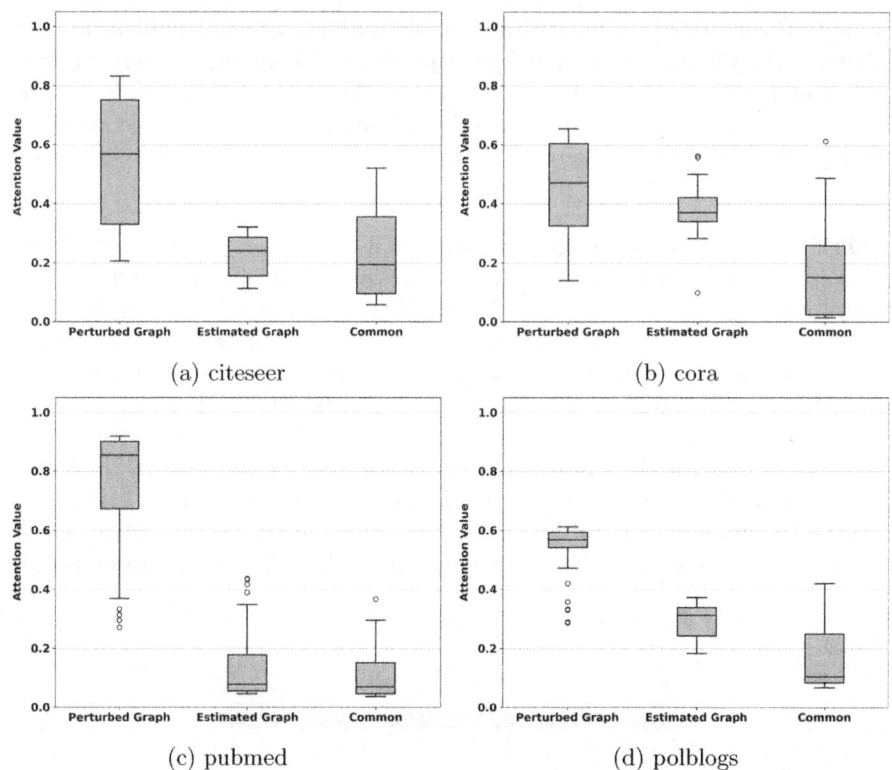

Fig. 5. Attention distribution under metattack with a perturbation rate of 20%

of the other two spaces. In the Cora dataset, the contributions of the perturbed graph and the estimated graph are comparable.

Furthermore, Fig. 4 illustrates the attention values for the three spaces (original graph, estimated graph, and common space) when each dataset achieves its best classification accuracy under Metattack with a 20% perturbation rate. In Pubmed, the original perturbed graph still provides the most useful information. However, in Cora and Polblogs, the attention values for the estimated graph increase. Across all datasets, the common space values are the lowest, but they are also distinct for each dataset. In summary, the experiment demonstrates that our proposed ASGCN is able to adaptively assign a larger attention value to the more important information.

6 Conclusion

In this paper, we investigate the limitations of methods relying on predefined robust properties. To address these limitations, we propose an adaptive multi-space defense framework that leverages the original graph structure to varying degrees. By incorporating an attention mechanism, two specific convolution modules, and one common convolution module, we can capture task-relevant information. Through extensive experiments, we validate the adversarial robustness of ASGCN against poisoning attacks. Furthermore, even when the graph is heavily poisoned, ASGCN can still maintain excellent performance.

References

1. Guo, Q., et al.: A survey on knowledge graph-based recommender systems. IEEE Trans. Knowl. Data Eng. **34**(8), 3549 (2021)
2. Jiang, W., Luo, J.: Graph neural network for traffic forecasting: a survey. Exp. Syst. Appl. **207** (2022)
3. Wang, J., Zhang, S., Xiao, Y., Song, R.: A review on graph neural network methods in financial applications. CoRR abs/2111.15367 (2021)
4. Xu, K., et al.: Topology attack and defense for graph neural networks: an optimization perspective. In: International Joint Conference on Artificial Intelligence, pp. 3961–3967 (2019)
5. Xu, H., Ma, Y., Liu, H.C., Deb, D., Liu, H.: Adversarial attacks and defenses in images, graphs and text: a review. arXiv preprint arXiv:1909.08072 (2019)
6. Wu, H., Wang, C., Tyshetskiy, Y., Docherty, A., Lu, K., Zhu, L.: Adversarial examples on graph data: deep insights into attack and defense. In: International Joint Conference on Artificial Intelligence (2019)
7. Zhang, X., Zitnik, M.: GNNGuard: defending graph neural networks against adversarial attacks. In: Neural Information Processing Systems (2020)
8. Li, K., et al.: Reliable representations make a stronger defender: unsupervised structure refinement for robust GNN. In: Proceedings of the 28th ACM SIGKDD Conference on Knowledge Discovery and Data Mining, pp.925–935 (2022)
9. Entezari, N., Al-Sayouri, S.A., Darvishzadeh, A., Papalexakis, E.E.: All you need is low (rank): defending against adversarial attacks on graphs. In: International Conference on Web Search and Data Mining (2020)
10. Zügner, D., Akbarnejad, A., Günnemann, S.: Adversarial attacks on neural networks for graph data. In: ACM SIGKDD (2018)
11. Jin, W., Ma, Y., Liu, X., Tang, X., Wang, S., Tang, J.: Graph structure learning for robust graph neural networks. In: ACM SIGKDD (2020)
12. Zhang, J., Hong, Y., Cheng, D., Zhang, L., Zhao, Q.: Defending adversarial attacks in graph neural networks via tensor enhancement. Pattern Recogn. **158** (2025)
13. Qian, T., Jianpeng, L., Enze, Z., Lusi, L., et al.: A dual robust graph neural network against graph adversarial attacks. Neural Netw. **175** (2024)
14. Li, X., Gan, Z., Bai, Y., et al.: D4A: an efficient and effective defense across agnostic adversarial attacks. Neural Netw. **183** (2025)
15. Mujkanovic, F., Geisler, S., Günnemann, S., Bojchevski, A.: Are defenses for graph neural networks robust? In: Advances in Neural Information Processing Systems, vol. 35 (2022)
16. Kipf, T.N., Welling, M.: Semi-supervised classification with graph convolutional networks. In: International Conference on Learning Representations (2017)
17. Sen, P., Namata, G.M., Bilgic, M., Getoor, L., Gallagher, B., Eliassi-Rad, T.: Collective classification in network data. AI Mag. **29**(3), 93–106 (2008)
18. Adamic, L.A., Glance, N.: The political blogosphere and the 2004 U.S. election: divided they blog. Association for Computing Machinery, New York, NY, USA (2005)

19. Zhu, D., Zhang, Z., Cui, P., Zhu, W.: Robust graph convolutional networks against adversarial attacks. In: ACM SIGKDD, pp. 1399–1407 (2019)
20. Li, K., et al.: Boosting the adversarial robustness of graph neural networks: an OOD perspective. In: International Conference on Learning Representations (2024)
21. Zügner, D., Günnemann, S.: Adversarial attacks on graph neural networks via meta learning. In: 7th International Conference on Learning Representations. OpenReview.net (2019)

How to RETIRE Tabular Data in Favor of Discrete Digital Signal Representation

Paweł Zyblewski(✉) and Szymon Wojciechowski

Department of Systems and Computer Networks, Faculty of Information and Communication Technology, Wrocław University of Science and Technology, Wybrzeże Wyspiańskiego 27, 50-370 Wrocław, Poland
{pawel.zyblewski,szymon.wojciechowski}@pwr.edu.pl

Abstract. The successes achieved by deep neural networks in computer vision tasks have led in recent years to the emergence of a new research area dubbed *Multi-Dimensional Encoding* (MDE). Methods belonging to this family aim to transform tabular data into a homogeneous form of discrete digital signals (images) to apply convolutional networks to initially unsuitable problems. Despite the successive emerging works, the pool of *multi-dimensional encoding* methods is still low, and the scope of research on existing modality encoding techniques is quite limited. To contribute to this area of research, we propose the *Radar-based Encoding from Tabular to Image REpresentation* (RETIRE), which allows tabular data to be represented as radar graphs, capturing the feature characteristics of each problem instance. RETIRE was compared with a pool of *state-of-the-art* MDE algorithms as well as with *XGBoost* in terms of classification accuracy and computational complexity. In addition, an analysis was carried out regarding transferability and explainability to provide more insight into both RETIRE and existing MDE techniques. The results obtained, supported by statistical analysis, confirm the superiority of RETIRE over other established MDE methods.

Keywords: Multi-Dimensional Encoding · Modality Encoding · Tabular data representation · Data visualization · Convolutional neural networks

1 Introduction

Even though current technological developments are leading to a continuous increase in the amount of data in text or discrete digital signal form, tabular modality is still considered the most popular form of data [23], commonly found in tasks such as medical diagnosis [26], recommendation systems [30], cybersecurity [4] or psychology [27]. This information is essential because, despite the increasing proliferation of deep learning methods that excel at computer vision tasks or audio and text analysis, it is tabular data that provides enough of a challenge for it to be called the "last unconquered castle" for deep neural networks

[12]. This is due to the heterogeneous nature of tabular data, which, unlike text, discrete digital signals or acoustic signals – which are inherently homogeneous in nature – can contain different feature types. In brief, the literature currently identifies four significant challenges in analyzing tabular data: **(i)** Low-Quality Training Data, **(ii)** Missing or Complex Irregular Spatial Dependencies, **(iii)** Dependency on Preprocessing, and **(iv)** Importance of Single Features [3].

Due to these difficulties, using deep learning for tabular data analysis is currently an important and rapidly growing area of research. At present, a taxonomy of approaches to the application of deep learning for tabular data distinguishes three main paths: **(i)** Data Transformation Methods, **(ii)** Specialized Architectures, and **(iii)** Regularization Models [3]. While the vast majority of work in this area focuses on specialized network architectures or dedicated tabular data regularization mechanisms, this article focuses on data transformation methods, specifically *Multi-Dimensional Encoding* (MDE) techniques. While *Single-Dimensional Encoding* methods, such as ordinal or label encoding, are dedicated to transforming categorical variables into real numbers, MDE aims to turn entire feature vectors into image representation in order to facilitate employing convolutional neural networks for initially unsuitable problems. The upside of such approaches is the ability to leverage existing architectures without modification, as well as the potential benefit of *transfer learning* [32].

As already mentioned, *multi-dimensional encoding* methods, despite offering a highly intriguing way of dealing with tabular data and presenting potentially valuable results, are a definite minority in the pool of scientific articles addressing the application of deep learning in this area. As a result, the number of available MDE methods is relatively low, and their potential is still under-researched. In an effort to take the next step towards filling this gap in the literature and expanding the field of *multi-dimensional encoding*, this paper introduces the *Radar-based Encoding from Tabular to Image REpresentation* (RETIRE) method. RETIRE allows individual instances of tabular datasets to be depicted in the form of radar diagrams, capturing the characteristics of their feature values. The proposed method has been compared based on a robust experimental protocol with MDE algorithms known from the literature in order to determine which image representation offers the highest generalization ability while employing the *ResNet18* [10] as the architecture of choice. In addition, the *XGBoost* [5] algorithm was used as a strong baseline for tabular data classification tasks. In order to gain better insight into the interaction of selected MDE methods with convolutional networks, an attempt was made to analyze them in terms of transferability and explainability.

In brief, the main contributions of this article are as follows:

- The introduction of a novel *Radar-based Encoding from Tabular to Image REpresentation* (RETIRE) *multi-dimensional* encoding method.
- Extensive experimental evaluation of RETIRE on 22 benchmark datasets, including selected modality encoding methods and the *XGBoost* algorithm.
- Analysis of selected *state-of-the-art multi-dimensional encoding* methods and RETIRE in terms of transferability, explainability and computational complexity.

2 Related Works

This chapter briefly introduces existing approaches to applying deep neural networks to the task of tabular data classification, with an emphasis on multidimensional encoding methods. In addition, to highlight the research area's potential and the scientific community's interest, the *Sentence Space* approach, which is similar to MDE but applied to textual modality, is described.

2.1 Deep Neural Networks for Tabular Data

As already mentioned, the taxonomy for employing deep learning for tabular data distinguishes three groups: **(i)** Data Transformation Methods, **(ii)** Specialized Architectures, and **(iii)** Regularization Models [3]. While the *multidimensional encoding* methods are the main focus of this article, which is described in a separate section, the other approaches are briefly introduced below.

Specialized architectures, the largest group of approaches, focus on developing deep neural network structures dedicated to tabular data and considering its heterogeneous nature. The literature here distinguishes two subgroups: **(i)** Hybrid models and **(ii)** Transformer-based models. Solutions from the hybrid models group combine canonical machine learning algorithms with neural networks and include both fully and partly differentiable models. The Network-On-Network (NON) classification model by Luo et al. [18] consists of a fieldwise network containing unique deep networks for each problem feature, a cross-field network choosing optimal operations for a given dataset, and an operation fusion network, allowing for nonlinearities by connecting selected operations. In contrast, Ke et al. proposed the *DeepGBM* model, which combines neural networks with the preprocessing capability of gradient-boosted decision trees. *DeepGBM* consists of two networks, one dealing with dense numerical features and the other with sparse categorical features [13]. A subgroup of transformer-based approaches is inspired by transformers' successes in text and image data tasks [14]. One of the most popular examples of a model in this category is *TabNet*, introduced by Arik and Pfister [2], consisting of multiple sequential hierarchical subnetworks, where each corresponds to a single decision step.

Regularization models are based on the assumption that in the case of heterogeneous tabular data, the flexibility of neural networks can be an obstacle, and strong regularization of parameters is needed. Kadra et al. [12] have shown that a multilayer perceptron using a set of 13 different regularization methods can outperform *state-of-the-art* tabular data classification methods at the cost of increased time.

Single-Dimensional Encoding, which belongs to the Data Transformation methods group, focuses on dealing with categorical features by encoding them into a form suitable for deep neural networks [9]. *Ordinal encoding*, *label encoding*, and *one-hot encoding* are among the most popular approaches. We can also distinguish *leave-one-out encoding*, which replaces each category with the target variable's average value, and *hash-based encoding*, which transforms each category using a hash function to a fixed-size value.

2.2 Multi-dimensional Encoding

Numerous scientific articles attest to the effectiveness of convolutional networks in both unimodal and multimodal scenarios for natural language analysis [8] and image, video, and audio classification (e.g., in spectrogram form) [21]. Additionally, deep networks facilitate *transfer learning*, which enables models to apply previously learned information to the current challenge [32]. As a result of these achievements, a new field of study known as *Multi-Dimensional Encoding* [3] was created that focuses on converting tabular data into a more uniform form of digital discrete signals.

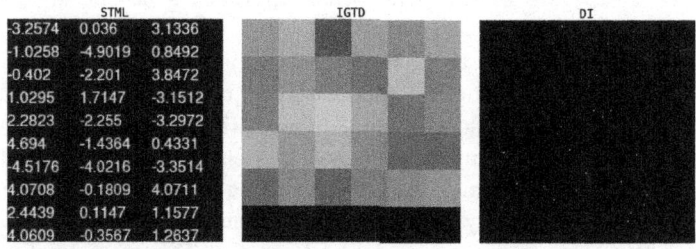

Fig. 1. An example of encoding a single sample of a synthetically generated tabular problem with 30 features, into a two-dimensional discrete digital signal using STML, IGTD and DI techniques.

This idea is best shown by *Super Tabular Machine Learning* (STML) approach, proposed by Sun et al. [25], which projects the feature values of a given problem instance onto the image. The *Image Generator for Tabular Data* (IGTD) [31] created by Zhu et al. offers an alternative approach. By minimizing the discrepancy between the ranking of distances among features and the ranking of distances between their corresponding pixels in the image, the algorithm looks for an optimal mapping. Damri et al. proposed *Feature Clustering-Visualization* (*FC-Viz*) [6] approach, where each instance of tabular data is converted into a 2D pixel-based representation, where pixels representing strongly correlated and interacting features are located in close proximity of each other. *SuperTML-Clustering*, as proposed by Zhang and Ding, embeds the indices of clustered continuous feature values onto an image [29]. *DeepInsight* (DI) by Sharma et al. [22] allows for the collective utilization of neighboring elements by arranging different elements or features farther away and similar elements or features closer together. The exemplary results of employing selected multi-dimensional encoding methods to tabular data is shown in Fig. 1. It is also worth noting that recently, there have been first works successfully employing MDE in data stream classification tasks while demonstrating relatively low computation time [33].

Although *multi-dimensional encoding* methods were developed to convert heterogeneous tabular data into homogeneous discrete digital signals, similar approaches have also been successfully applied to inherently homogeneous text modality with remarkable results. Such techniques are usually based on *Sentence Space*, which is a reference to the method presented by Kim [15], in which text data is converted into an image with embeddings of individual words in each row. While these methods are not the subject of this article, and we will not describe them in depth, they undoubtedly provide evidence of the scientific community's interest in MDE methods and their derivatives.

3 Radar-Based Encoding from Tabular to Image REpresentation (RETIRE)

The RETIRE algorithm is inspired by radar charts – a form of graphical representation of an instance's attributes. It can be often seen in cases where one need to compare available options with each other based on their properties. A radar chart is constructed by drawing a polygon over coordinates in a polar coordinate system. Such a figure has N vertices (same as object attributes), which coordinates (r - radius, ϕ - angle) can be determined as:

$$r_n = f_n, \quad \phi_n = (n-1) \times \frac{2\pi}{N} \tag{1}$$

where f_n is the value of an n-th attribute. Obviously, for the chart to be readable, values have to be relatable to each other. To achieve that, the scaling function S is often used so that $\{S(f_n) \mid l <= S(f_n) <= u\}$ where l and u is a set parameter (usually $l = 0, u = 1$).

The radar charts often include the axis grid and labels. The figure can also introduce colors if used to compare multiple samples. The goal of the encoding algorithm, however, is to create a representation in the shortest possible time, so the RETIRE algorithm extracts only the binarized shape of the sample and a border indicating the upper limit of the value. An example of the original graph and the corresponding representation is presented in Fig. 2a.

Of course, there can be many modifications to the proposed method, which are the parameters of the algorithm. The very important one is assumed scaling. In this work, S will be function applied to each features as:

$$S(x_f) = \frac{(x_f - min(X_f))}{(max(X_f) - min(X_f))} \times (u - l) + l \tag{2}$$

where X is the full set of observations and x is a single sample. As can be seen, the scaling requires obtaining minimum and maximum values of X. Those have to be determined during the learning process – which indicates that RETIRE requires training before being applied to the dataset.

In addition, u and l are also important scaling parameters. Since the first part of the equation will be in the range of $<0,1>$, setting $l > 0$ and $u < 1$ allows scaling to provide "space" for observations. It is important because when

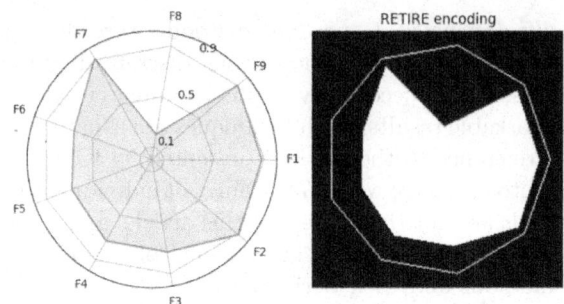

(a) Example of radar chart (left) and RETIRE encoding (right).

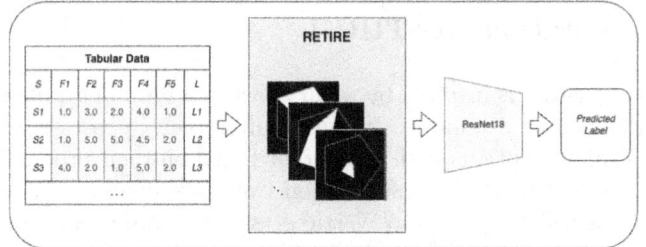

(b) Pipeline for classification system.

Fig. 2. Graphical abstract for the proposed method.

RETIRE is used for test data, values from the test set might be outside the observed min-max range. Finally, an important element is the retained figure outline – it provides a reference point for the maximum observed value. The full pipeline of the proposed method is shown in Fig. 2b.

The image representations obtained utilizing encoding are then used by CNN – in this case, *ResNet18*. It is worth mentioning that although the image created by RETIRE is binarized, CNN uses all color channels as the input. Therefore, the resulting binary image is multiplied to obtain 3 identical color channels.

4 Experimental Evaluation

This section describes in detail the experimental evaluation process conducted to analyze the properties of the proposed RETIRE method. The experiments were designed to answer the following research questions:

- **RQ1** Does the discrete digital signal representation obtained using RETIRE benefits from ImageNet knowledge transfer in terms on *TransRate* metric?
- **RQ2** In the case of the *ResNet18* architecture, does the use of an image representation obtained using RETIRE offers a statistically significantly better balanced accuracy score compared to reference MDE methods?
- **RQ3** Can the RETIRE image representation be interpreted by a human?

- **RQ4** What is the computational complexity of the RETIRE encoding and how it compares with reference methods?

4.1 Set-Up

Data. The experiments were conducted using 22 benchmark datasets originating from the KEEL repository [7]. The datasets can be considered balanced - most have an *Imbalance Ratio* (IR) of less than 1.5, and only in one case the IR exceeds 2. The precise dataset characteristics are shown in Table 1.

Table 1. Datasets characteristics.

Dataset	#Instances	#Features	Dataset	#Instances	#Features
australian	690	14	mammographic	830	5
banknote	1372	4	monk-2	432	6
breastcan	683	9	monkone	556	6
breastcancoimbra	116	9	phoneme	5404	5
bupa	345	6	pima	768	8
cryotherapy	90	6	ring	7400	20
german	1000	24	sonar	208	60
haberman	306	3	spambase	4601	57
heart	270	13	titanic	2201	3
ionosphere	351	34	twonorm	7400	20
liver	345	6	wisconsin	699	9

Experimental Protocol. In order to guarantee a robust experimental protocol, the experiments were carried out using 5-times repeated 2-fold stratified cross-validation. The results were supported by the *Combined* 5×2 *CV F-test* [1] and the *Wilcoxon signed-rank test* [24] with $\alpha = 0.05$ (the higher the rank, the better). *The Combined* 5×2 *CV F-test* was used to examine the statistical correlations between methods within particular datasets, whilst the *Wilcoxon signed-rank test* allowed for a global comparison of the investigated approaches. Although the datasets used have a relatively low IR and can be considered balanced, the classification performance was evaluated based on the *balanced accuracy score* (BAC).

Reference Methods. In the course of the experiments, RETIRE was compared with three state-of-the-art MDE approaches described in Sect. 2: **(i)** *SuperTML*, **(ii)** IGTD, and **(iii)** *DeepInsight*. They were chosen because of the promising results obtained in previous studies and the access to a Python implementation offered by their authors (IGTD and DI). Despite the lack of an official implementation, we implemented STML due to its simplicity. IGTD and DI were used with default parameters. The size of the image representation for STML, DI, and RETIRE multi-dimensional encoding techniques was set to 224 × 224 pixels. The size of images created using IGTD, due to the characteristics of the method, depended on the number of features in each dataset. For each method the resulting representation is multiplied in order to achieve 3 identical color channels.

Regardless of the MDE approach used, the *ResNet18* architecture was chosen as a convolutional network due to its vast popularity and relatively small size. Training lasted for 20 epochs and the batch size was set to 8. An SGD optimizer with a learning rate of 0.001 and momentum of 0.9 was used. Cross-entropy loss was chosen as the loss function.

In addition, the *XGBoost* [5] algorithm with 100 estimators was used as the baseline. The other parameters remained default. This comparison was added to improve the interpretability of the results obtained through experiments, but it should be noted that *XGBoost* is a very strong benchmark and winning against it is not the primary goal of this work.

Reproducibility. All experiments presented in this paper were carried out in *Python* using the *scikit-learn* [20], *PyTorch* [19], and *XGBoost* [5] libraries. The results obtained can be fully replicated using the code located on the *GitHub* repository[1]. The computing platform used in all experiments was Mac Studio with Apple M1 Ultra with 20-core CPU, 64-core GPU, 32-core Neural Engine system, 128 GB RAM.

4.2 Experimental Scenarios

Experiment 1 – Comparative Experimental Evaluation. The purpose of Experiment 1 is to investigate which MDE method achieves statistically significantly the best balanced accuracy score for the 22 selected datasets and how it compares to the results obtained by the *XGBoost* algorithm. This is the main experiment of this paper, and it will allow us to investigate the quality of the image representations offered by each MDE method, thus answering **RQ2**.

Additionally, in order to verify the usefulness of *transfer learning* in conjunction with the studied representations obtained using MDE, all four encoding methods are evaluated in terms of *TransRate* metrics [11] and BAC. The *ResNet18* architecture offers the possibility of using pre-trained weights, but many scientific articles utilize this option without considering the possibility of negative transfer [28]. Since we are concerned with establishing the network's inherent properties, *ResNet18* is not trained or finetuned in any way during this experiment. We only evaluate the initial compatibility of knowledge transfer with individual image representations. The results obtained will make it possible to answer **RQ1**.

Experiment 2 – Explainability. As part of Experiment 2, the performance of the MDE algorithms offering representations potentially understandable to humans, namely STML and RETIRE, will be subjected to explainability methods derived from the SHAP (*SHapley Additive exPlanations*) library [16,17].

---
[1] https://github.com/w4k2/mde-retire.

The results of this analysis will be contrasted with the explained output of the *XGBoost* algorithm in order to investigate whether humans can interpret the images resulting from the MDE and whether the information relevant to the *ResNet18* convolutional network overlaps with that which most influences the decision of the algorithm based solely on tabular data. Based on the observations made, it will be possible to find an answer to **RQ3**.

Experiment 3 – Computational Complexity Analysis. The purpose of the experiment is to study and analyze the computational complexity of selected methods. The main factor subject to this study is to demonstrate the relation of inference time to the dimensionality of the problem. For this experiment, the synthetically generated datasets of a variable number of features will be used. Other parameters will be set as follows: MADELON generator, 100 samples, informative-only features, and random generation seed for each instance. Other parameters remain the default for each instance. The test will include measurement of encoding time and *ResNet18* model inference. To stabilize the results, the measurements will be repeated 100 times. The results obtained in this externality will make it possible to find the answer to **RQ4**.

4.3 Experiment 1 – Comparative Experimental Evaluation

Before the actual comparison experiment, a brief study was conducted to determine whether MDE representations could benefit from knowledge transfer derived from the *ImageNet* dataset. The results obtained in terms of BAC and *TransRate*, which measures the transferability as the mutual information between features of target examples extracted by a pre-trained model and their labels [11], are shown in Fig. 3.

It should be noted that although *TransRate* has a relatively linear relationship to generalization ability, in this case, we are dealing with a random classifier, and BAC values oscillating around 50% regardless of the use of *transfer learning* are expected. This is because, despite the use of *transfer learning*, the images in ImageNet deviate too much from the representations offered by MDE.

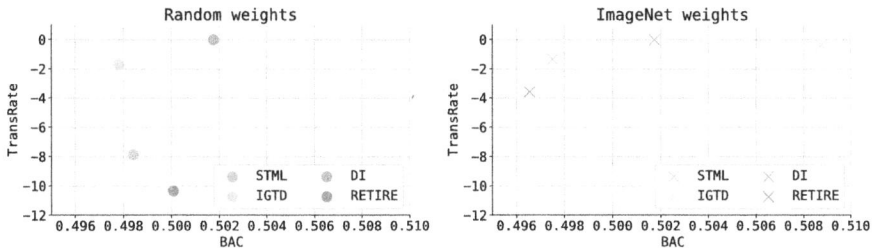

Fig. 3. Results of transferability estimation using the *TransRate* metric. Both BAC and *TransRate* values were averaged for all 22 datasets.

At the same time, interesting conclusions can be drawn from the obtained *TransRate* values, which clearly divide the four analyzed methods into two groups. IGTD and DI theoretically show better compatibility with *ResNet18*, but at the same time, the use of pretreated weights has virtually no effect on them. This is probably due to the abstract nature of the representations they offer, which cannot be compared to the images found in *ImageNet*.

On the other hand, STML and RETIRE, using a less abstract two-dimensional word embedding or geometric shape as the basis for encoding, despite theoretically lower compatibility with *ResNet18*, show significant improvement after using pretreated weights. RETIRE's lower *TransRate* than STML may be explained by its use of encoding based on a single geometric shape, which inherently has a lower level of complexity than directly transcribing feature values onto the image. Without fine-tuning, such representation may carry slightly less information – especially for a large number of features.

Based on these results, we can answer **RQ1** and conclude that the RETIRE representation allows us to benefit from positive knowledge transfer from the *ImageNet* dataset. At the same time, due to the lack of negative transfer in the case of all tested MDE methods, the pre-trained *ResNet18* is used in further research.

The results of the experiment comparing RETIRE with the reference MDE methods and *XGBoost* can be seen in Fig. 4 and in Table 2. The first thing that catches the eye is the relatively low results achieved by IGTD. This is because the images produced by this method are relatively small, and their size depends directly on the number of features. Consequently, the *ResNet18*, adapted initially for 224 × 224 pixels images, is not the optimal solution. However, since the study aimed to evaluate the role of individual image representations in learning one selected architecture, we decided to utilize this method in its original form without any modifications.

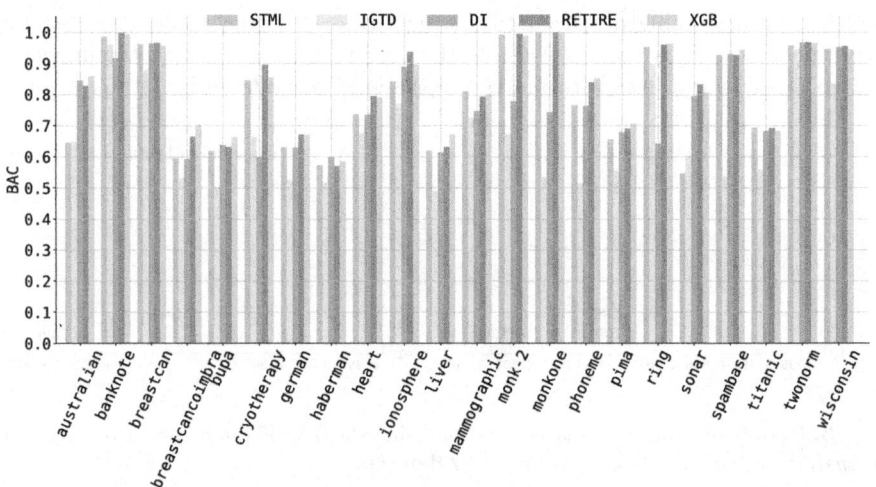

Fig. 4. The results of the experimental evaluation conducted in terms of BAC for each of the 22 datasets.

Table 2. Results of statistical analysis. The first row for each dataset shows the averaged BAC. The indices (by column) of the algorithms from which the given model is statistically significantly better based on the 5×2 *CV F-test* ($\alpha = 0.05$) are given below. The last two rows present the Wilcoxon signed-rank test. The highest BAC or rank values are **bold** or highlighted in red. **Bold** indicates the highest value among MDE methods, and red indicates the highest value overall (including *XGBoost*).

	STML[1]	IGTD[2]	DI[3]	RETIRE[4]	XGB[5]
australian	0.646	0.650	**0.846**	0.829	0.861
	—	—	1, 2	1, 2	1, 2, 4
banknote	0.986	0.962	0.918	0.999	0.994
	2	—	—	1, 2, 5	2
breastcan	0.962	0.880	0.965	0.966	0.957
	—	—	—	—	—
breastcancoimbra	0.594	0.531	0.593	**0.664**	0.703
	—	—	—	2	1, 2, 3
bupa	0.619	0.502	**0.638**	0.631	0.664
	2	—	2	2	1, 2
cryotherapy	0.846	0.664	0.599	0.895	0.857
	2, 3	—	—	2, 3	2, 3
german	0.631	0.525	0.630	0.671	0.671
	2, 3	—	2	2	2, 3
haberman	0.574	0.518	0.599	0.570	0.586
	—	—	—	—	2
heart	0.737	0.676	0.735	0.793	0.790
	—	—	—	1, 2	1, 2
ionosphere	0.843	0.770	0.889	0.937	0.897
	2	—	1, 2	1, 2, 3	1, 2
liver	0.621	0.490	0.614	**0.631**	0.672
	2	—	2	2	2
mammographic	0.811	0.727	0.747	**0.793**	0.802
	—	—	—	—	—
monk-2	0.993	0.672	0.778	0.995	0.990
	2, 3	—	—	2, 3	2, 3
monkone	1.000	0.536	0.743	1.000	0.999
	2, 3	—	—	2, 3	2, 3
phoneme	0.766	0.515	0.764	**0.840**	0.854
	2	—	2	1, 2, 3	1, 2, 3
pima	0.655	0.555	0.679	**0.690**	0.706
	—	—	2	2, 3	1, 2
ring	0.952	0.899	0.643	**0.961**	0.964
	2, 3	3	—	3	2, 3
sonar	0.546	0.605	0.796	0.832	0.807
	—	—	1, 2	1, 2	1, 2
spambase	0.927	0.538	**0.931**	0.927	0.945
	2	—	2	2	2, 3, 4
titanic	0.694	0.560	0.682	0.692	0.684
	2, 5	—	2	—	—
twonorm	0.958	0.947	0.968	0.968	0.966
	2	—	2	2	2
wisconsin	0.947	0.834	0.953	0.956	0.945
	2	—	2	2	2
Mean rank	2.932	1.227	2.682	4.114	4.045
	2	—	2	1, 2, 3	1, 2, 3

Among the other MDE methods, RETIRE shows the highest generalization ability by far. For 17 of the 22 datasets, it achieved the highest BAC value. For 6 datasets, it proved statistically significantly better than STML, and for 7 datasets - than DI. At the same time, none of the reference MDE methods ever obtained a statistically significantly better balanced accuracy score than RETIRE.

It is somewhat of a surprise that RETIRE for 11 datasets obtained a higher average BAC than *XGBoost*. The difference was statistically significantly better in only one case, but these minor differences translated into RETIRE obtaining a higher average rank value than *XGBoost*. At the same time, RETIRE is the only one of the MDE methods studied that, according to the *Wilcoxon signed-rank* test, globally scored statistically comparable to *XGBoost*. Also, like *XGBoost*, RETIRE is globally statistically significantly better than the other reference MDE methods, thus responding to **RQ2**.

4.4 Experiment 2 – Explainability

Figure 5 presents the results of the explainability analysis for the RETIRE, STML, and *XGBoost* algorithms in the form of a SHAP image plot and Waterfall plot. Since the purpose of the analysis was to verify that the features relevant to *ResNet18* in the image representations overlapped with those that determined the *XGBoost* algorithm's decision, the 4 samples analyzed were taken from the *monkone* dataset, for which all three approaches achieved near perfect BAC.

In the case of STML, we can see that regardless of the class, the first row of the image containing *Feature 0* and *Feature 1* values strongly influences the decision. In the case of *Sample 3* and *Sample 4*, *Feature 4*, located in the lower-left corner of the representation, also plays a significant role in making the correct decision. We can see similar correlations in the case of RETIRE, where the first two features (starting from the right and going clockwise) seem to be the most significant. In addition, in the case of *Class 0*, the area belonging to *Feature 4* also plays an important role in the decision-making process. The most significant observation here is that the components of the STML and RETIRE images that *ResNet18* found to be most relevant overlap significantly with the features that have the greatest impact on the decision of the *XGBoost* algorithm, based solely on tabular data. This confirms that despite minor differences due to the characteristics of the individual approaches and differing representations, convolutional networks employing MDE methods (including the proposed RETIRE) make their decisions based on the values of the problem's features in a manner similar to algorithms operating on tabular data. This makes the proposed representation interpretable to humans, thus answering **RQ3**.

4.5 Experiment 3 – Computational Complexity Analysis

The computational complexity experiments were measured separately for data encoding time and model inference time. The results are shown in Fig. 6. As can be seen, the lowest time values are achieved by the RETIRE and DI methods. Both graphs show a linear relationship between embedding preparation time and the

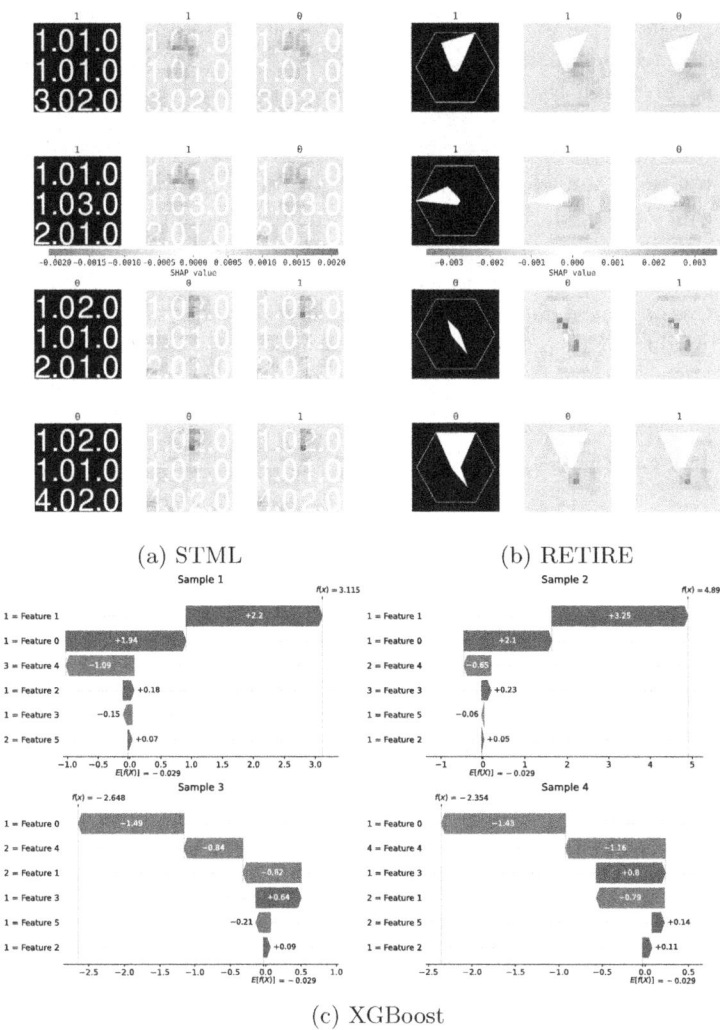

Fig. 5. Explainability of selected data transformation methods applied to the first data fold of the Monkone dataset. The sample numbers in subfigure (c) correspond to the subsequent rows in subfigures (a) and (b). In subfigures (a) and (b), the consecutive columns from the left represent: (i) the original image and its class, (ii) the classifier's decision and the explanation behind it, and (iii) the decision with less support value and its justification.

number of features, although in the case of DI – in the first phases, it is flat. This can be justified by the fact that DI performs optimization (*Asymmetric Greedy Search*), which can reach convergence in the first phases, but not for problems with higher dimensionality. As for RETIRE, this linear time characteristic was an assumed theoretical, computational complexity that responds to **RQ4**. It can be explained that drawing the figure is related to an additional condition check with each new feature. Lastly, the STML also has linear computational complexity, although the time values achieved by the algorithm increase much faster.

An important observation is also the inference time, which, for most cases, is constant and very low when compared to the encoding time. This is an expected behavior since the structure of the CNN remains constant. The only differences are due to the processing time of smaller resolution images, which is relatable for IGTD, although these are not noticeable differences. In addition, IGTD is characterized by exponential computational complexity, which, with a large number of features, might not be feasible for computations.

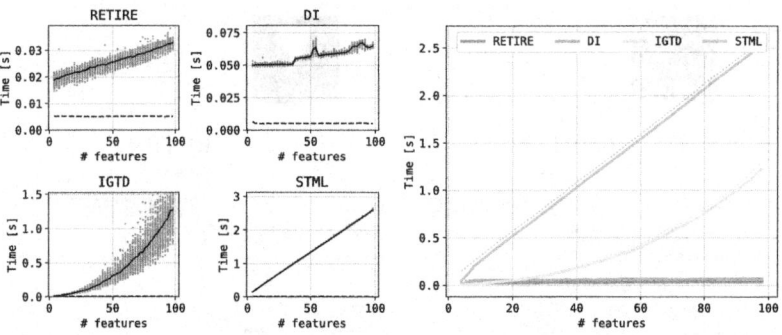

Fig. 6. Time complexity analysis. Results for individual methods on the left and the comparison (with applied Simple Moving Average) on the right.

5 Conclusions

The study aimed to expand the still under-exploited but extremely promising area of data transformation methods for tabular data analysis. This was done by proposing a novel *multi-dimensional encoding* method, namely *Radar-based Encoding from Tabular to Image REpresentation* (RETIRE), which allows obtaining an image representation depicting the characteristics of the features of each problem instance as a single geometric shape.

Extensive comparison experiments have been carried out, showing that the representation obtained using RETIRE in conjunction with the *ResNet18* architecture enables a balanced accuracy score statistically significantly better than *state-of-the-art* MDE methods with publicly available implementations. Most importantly, RETIRE is the only *multi-dimensional encoding* method tested that is not statistically significantly inferior to the *XGBoost* algorithm and even surpasses it in terms of average rank.

Additional strengths of the proposed method are its inherent explainability and relatively low linear computation time when compared to other MDE approaches. Analysis using SHAP confirmed that the features considered most important by *ResNet18* in the RETIRE representation overlap with those that have the greatest impact on the classification results of the *XGBoost* algorithm.

Future work may include a study of the transferability and explainability of MDE methods to provide more insight into the specifics of their work, as well as the use of color in methods so far focused on binary or grayscale images.

Acknowledgments. This work was supported by the statutory funds of the Department of Systems and Computer Networks, Faculty of Information and Communication Technology, Wroclaw University of Science and Technology.

Disclosure of Interests. The authors have no competing interests to declare that are relevant to the content of this article.

References

1. Alpaydm, E.: Combined 5 × 2 CV F test for comparing supervised classification learning algorithms. Neural Comput. **11**(8), 1885–1892 (1999)
2. Arik, S.Ö., Pfister, T.: TabNet: attentive interpretable tabular learning. In: Proceedings of the AAAI Conference on Artificial Intelligence, vol. 35, pp. 6679–6687 (2021)
3. Borisov, V., Leemann, T., Seßler, K., Haug, J., Pawelczyk, M., Kasneci, G.: Deep neural networks and tabular data: a survey. IEEE Trans. Neural Netw. Learn. Syst. (2022)
4. Buczak, A.L., Guven, E.: A survey of data mining and machine learning methods for cyber security intrusion detection. IEEE Commun. Surv. Tutorials **18**(2), 1153–1176 (2015)
5. Chen, T., Guestrin, C.: XGBoost: a scalable tree boosting system. In: Proceedings of the 22nd ACM SIGKDD International Conference on Knowledge Discovery and Data Mining, pp. 785–794 (2016)
6. Damri, A., Last, M., Cohen, N.: Towards efficient image-based representation of tabular data. Neural Comput. Appl., 1–21 (2023)
7. Derrac, J., Garcia, S., Sanchez, L., Herrera, F.: Keel data-mining software tool: data set repository, integration of algorithms and experimental analysis framework. J. Mult. Valued Logic Soft Comput. **17**, 255–287 (2015)
8. Gimenez, M., Palanca, J., Botti, V.: Semantic-based padding in convolutional neural networks for improving the performance in natural language processing. A case of study in sentiment analysis. Neurocomputing **378**, 315–323 (2020)
9. Hancock, J.T., Khoshgoftaar, T.M.: Survey on categorical data for neural networks. J. Big Data **7**(1), 1–41 (2020). https://doi.org/10.1186/s40537-020-00305-w
10. He, K., Zhang, X., Ren, S., Sun, J.: Deep residual learning for image recognition. In: Proceedings of the IEEE Conference on Computer Vision and Pattern Recognition, pp. 770–778 (2016)

11. Huang, L.K., Huang, J., Rong, Y., Yang, Q., Wei, Y.: Frustratingly easy transferability estimation. In: International Conference on Machine Learning, pp. 9201–9225. PMLR (2022)
12. Kadra, A., Lindauer, M., Hutter, F., Grabocka, J.: Well-tuned simple nets excel on tabular datasets. In: Advances in Neural Information Processing Systems, vol. 34, pp. 23928–23941 (2021)
13. Ke, G., Xu, Z., Zhang, J., Bian, J., Liu, T.Y.: DeepGBM: a deep learning framework distilled by GBDT for online prediction tasks. In: Proceedings of the 25th ACM SIGKDD International Conference on Knowledge Discovery & Data Mining, pp. 384–394 (2019)
14. Khan, S., Naseer, M., Hayat, M., Zamir, S.W., Khan, F.S., Shah, M.: Transformers in vision: a survey. ACM Comput. Surv. (CSUR) **54**(10s), 1–41 (2022)
15. Kim, Y.: Convolutional neural networks for sentence classification. arXiv preprint arXiv:1408.5882 (2014)
16. Lundberg, S.M., et al.: From local explanations to global understanding with explainable AI for trees. Nat. Mach. Intell. **2**(1), 2522–5839 (2020)
17. Lundberg, S.M., Lee, S.I.: A unified approach to interpreting model predictions. In: Guyon, I., et al. (eds.) Advances in Neural Information Processing Systems, vol. 30, pp. 4765–4774. Curran Associates, Inc. (2017)
18. Luo, Y., Zhou, H., Tu, W.W., Chen, Y., Dai, W., Yang, Q.: Network on network for tabular data classification in real-world applications. In: Proceedings of the 43rd International ACM SIGIR Conference on Research and Development in Information Retrieval, pp. 2317–2326 (2020)
19. Paszke, A., et al.: Automatic differentiation in PyTorch (2017)
20. Pedregosa, F., et al.: Scikit-learn: machine learning in Python. J. Mach. Learn. Res. **12**, 2825–2830 (2011)
21. Satt, A., Rozenberg, S., Hoory, R., et al.: Efficient emotion recognition from speech using deep learning on spectrograms. In: Interspeech, pp. 1089–1093 (2017)
22. Sharma, A., Vans, E., Shigemizu, D., Boroevich, K.A., Tsunoda, T.: DeepInsight: a methodology to transform a non-image data to an image for convolution neural network architecture. Sci. Rep. **9**(1), 11399 (2019)
23. Shwartz-Ziv, R., Armon, A.: Tabular data: deep learning is not all you need. Inf. Fusion **81**, 84–90 (2022)
24. Stapor, K., Ksieniewicz, P., García, S., Woźniak, M.: How to design the fair experimental classifier evaluation. Appl. Soft Comput. **104**, 107219 (2021)
25. Sun, B., et al.: SuperTML: two-dimensional word embedding for the precognition on structured tabular data. In: Proceedings of the IEEE/CVF Conference on Computer Vision and Pattern Recognition Workshops (2019)
26. Ulmer, D., Meijerink, L., Cinà, G.: Trust issues: uncertainty estimation does not enable reliable OOD detection on medical tabular data. In: Machine Learning for Health, pp. 341–354. PMLR (2020)
27. Urban, C.J., Gates, K.M.: Deep learning: a primer for psychologists. Psychol. Methods **26**(6), 743 (2021)
28. Wang, Z., Dai, Z., Póczos, B., Carbonell, J.: Characterizing and avoiding negative transfer. In: Proceedings of the IEEE/CVF Conference on Computer Vision and Pattern Recognition, pp. 11293–11302 (2019)
29. Zhang, J., Ding, G.: SuperTML-Clustering: two-dimensional word embedding for structured tabular data. In: International Conference on Image, Vision and Intelligent Systems, pp. 600–609. Springer (2023)

30. Zhang, Q., Cao, L., Shi, C., Niu, Z.: Neural time-aware sequential recommendation by jointly modeling preference dynamics and explicit feature couplings. IEEE Trans. Neural Netw. Learn. Syst. **33**(10), 5125–5137 (2021)
31. Zhu, Y., et al.: Converting tabular data into images for deep learning with convolutional neural networks. Sci. Rep. **11**(1), 11325 (2021)
32. Zhuang, F., et al.: A comprehensive survey on transfer learning. Proc. IEEE **109**(1), 43–76 (2020)
33. Zyblewski, P.: Employing two-dimensional word embedding for difficult tabular data stream classification. In: Joint European Conference on Machine Learning and Knowledge Discovery in Databases, pp. 73–89. Springer (2024)

Diffusion Models

Diffusion Model with Selective Attention for Temporal Knowledge Graph Reasoning

Rushan Geng[1], Ge Chen[1], and Cuicui Luo[2(✉)]

[1] School of Computer Science and Technology, University of Chinese Academy of Sciences, Beijing, China
{gengrushan23,chenge221}@mails.ucas.ac.cn
[2] International College, University of Chinese Academy of Sciences, Beijing, China
luocuicui@ucas.ac.cn

Abstract. Temporal knowledge graph reasoning aims to predict missing entities at future time steps, and as a critical task, it has attracted widespread attention in recent years due to its impressive ability to capture historical correlations and forecast future events. Although existing approaches, such as graph learning and logic rules, have partially addressed this problem, they still face limitations in modeling the uncertainty of future events—especially when predicting rare or unseen facts. To address these challenges, we propose a diffusion model based on a selective attention mechanism (DMSA) for temporal knowledge graph reasoning. In our method, the encoder incorporates selective attention to emphasize key information, while the diffusion module introduces noise to enhance the model's capability to predict unseen events. By integrating selective attention with the diffusion module, our model improves both its memory and its ability to predict future, unseen events. Experimental results on five public datasets demonstrate that our proposed model achieves state-of-the-art performance across multiple evaluation metrics.

Keywords: Temporal knowledge graph · Temporal knowledge graph reasoning · Diffusion model · Selective attention

1 Introduction

Knowledge graphs (KGs) record facts about the real world as triples (s, r, o), where entities serve as nodes and relations as edges, forming a graph structure. However, traditional knowledge graphs only capture static facts and cannot reflect the dynamic evolution of events over time. For example, a fact such as (China, visit, USA) may convey significantly different information at different time points. To address this limitation, researchers have gradually incorporated temporal information to construct temporal knowledge graphs (TKGs), which are represented as quadruples (s, r, o, t), where s denotes the subject, r the relation, o the object, and t the timestamp. For instance, (China, visit, USA, 2023-11-15) indicates that China visited the USA on November 15, 2023. TKGs not only maintain the simplicity and accuracy of traditional

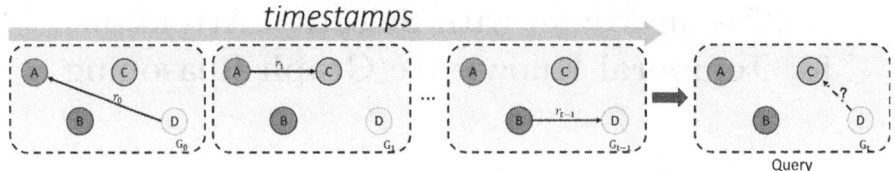

Fig. 1. One example for TKG reasoning.

knowledge graphs but also dynamically capture the time-varying nature of facts, thereby playing an important role in various downstream natural language processing tasks, such as recommendation systems [1], question answering [2], and information retrieval [3].

Due to the inherent incompleteness of TKGs, researchers have been actively developing efficient reasoning methods to fill in missing information. TKG reasoning can typically be categorized into interpolation and extrapolation. Interpolation reasoning aims to predict missing facts within the observed time span—that is, given snapshots from time 0 to t, it predicts events that occurred within that period. In contrast, extrapolation reasoning leverages historical facts to forecast new events at future time steps (where $t_i > t$), as illustrated in Fig. 1. Each snapshot corresponds to the facts occurring at a specific timestamp, and a TKG is composed of many such snapshots. This paper primarily focuses on extrapolation reasoning, which, compared with interpolation, not only poses greater challenges but also offers more practical value by completing future knowledge graphs and predicting emerging events [4].

Current TKG reasoning methods primarily rely on historical information to predict missing entities at future time steps, as illustrated in Fig. 1. For example, many approaches use GNNs to learn the structural information from historical TKG snapshots and RNNs to capture temporal evolution patterns. Since past events often tend to reoccur, these methods have been widely adopted and studied. However, this reliance on historical data makes them less effective at predicting events that have never been observed before. Moreover, using the same historical information for all queries prevents the model from focusing on the most relevant details, as its attention gets dispersed by irrelevant data.

Based on this analysis, we propose DMSA, a diffusion model with selective attention for TKG reasoning, which is built on an encoder–decoder framework. By incorporating Gaussian noise through a diffusion process, DMSA enhances the model's ability to predict unseen events. In addition, a selective attention mechanism is introduced in the encoder to allow the model to autonomously choose the most pertinent information. Specifically, we employ CompGCN [10] as the encoder and integrate Relative Attention to select relation information that is closely linked to the current event. By converting entities, relations, and timestamps into a sequence prediction task based on historical snapshots—and by injecting Gaussian noise into the sequence to introduce uncertainty—we improve the probability of accurately predicting unseen events. Finally, predictions are generated using Time-aware ConvTransE as the decoder. Extensive experiments on five public TKG datasets demonstrate that DMSA significantly outperforms state-of-the-art methods across multiple evaluation metrics.

In summary, the main contributions of this paper are as follows:

- We propose a novel approach that introduces the diffusion process into knowledge graph reasoning to increase the uncertainty in event representations, thereby enhancing the model's ability to predict unseen events.
- We incorporate a selective attention mechanism in the encoder, which enables the model to process information in a targeted manner within each snapshot.
- Extensive experiments on five public datasets show that DMSA significantly outperforms existing methods across multiple evaluation metrics.

2 Related Work

Knowledge graph reasoning can be broadly categorized into static knowledge graph reasoning and temporal knowledge graph reasoning. Below, we briefly discuss some representative methods in each category. Next, we introduce research applications of diffusion models.

2.1 Static Knowledge Graph Reasoning

Static knowledge graph reasoning methods for temporal knowledge graphs generally ignore timestamps and directly process triples, mainly modeling the structural and semantic information of entities. TransE [5] treats relations as translation transformations when projecting entity embeddings into a latent space. They use distance functions (such as L1 and L2 norms) to score factual triples. DistMult [6] and ComplEx [7] represent knowledge graphs as three-dimensional tensors and decompose them into low-dimensional vectors to learn embeddings for entities and relations. Methods like ConvE [8] utilize transformations, bilinear objectives, complex embeddings, and convolutional operations to capture relational semantics. Graph Convolutional Networks (GCNs) are representative methods characterized by their ability to learn structural features of knowledge graphs. R-GCN [9] is a typical graph neural network model that integrates relational information through specialized message passing and aggregation mechanisms, enabling effective capture of complex patterns and dependencies in graph-structured data. CompGCN [10] generalizes several multi-relational GCN methods and employs various composition operations to handle multi-relational graph data.

2.2 Temporal Knowledge Graph Reasoning

Temporal Knowledge Graph (TKG) reasoning models the dynamic evolution of entities and relations over time. Early methods such as TA-DistMult [11] incorporate time embeddings, while TeMP [12] leverages GNNs and RNNs to mitigate temporal sparsity via message passing. Building on these, RE-NET [13] uses an encoder-aggregator structure for fixed-length historical subgraphs, and CyGNet [14] employs a replication-based mechanism to capture repetitive patterns. EvoKG [15], RE-GCN [16], and TiRGN [17] further model dynamic and long-term dependencies through subgraph evolution, temporal gating, and time embeddings. Other approaches, including HGLS [18], SMiFY [19], CENET [20], PLEASING [21], LSEN [22], and HIP [23], enhance reasoning by constructing global graphs, simplifying architectures, or mining both short- and long-term patterns. PPT [24] converts temporal knowledge graph completion into a masked prediction task on pre-trained language models by designing dedicated prompts for entities, relations, and time intervals, enabling explicit modeling of temporal and relational semantics. LLM-DA [25] leverages large language models to extract interpretable temporal logical rules from historical data and dynamically updates these rules with recent events, enabling accurate and adaptive temporal knowledge graph reasoning without fine-tuning the LLMs. Yuan et al. [26] introduces the first explainable temporal reasoning task, accompanied by the ExplainTemp instruction-tuning dataset and the TimeLlaMA model series, enabling large language models to predict future events with step-by-step explanations derived from temporal knowledge graphs.

2.3 Diffusion Models on Discrete Data

Diffusion models were first introduced by [27] and have since been widely applied in generative tasks such as image generation [28] and audio generation [29], where they have demonstrated excellent performance. Diffusion-LM [30] applied diffusion models to text processing tasks, while DiffuSeq [31] introduces partial noise during the forward diffusion process. In the field of named entity recognition, DiffusionNER [32] uses diffusion models by treating the entity recognition task as a boundary denoising process. DiffCLR [33] brings diffusion models into knowledge graph reasoning by leveraging its multi-step generation process to inject uncertainty and generate distributions, thus better capturing the multi-dimensional semantic information in queries. The DiffTGK [34] model redefines temporal knowledge graph reasoning as a sequence prediction task by encoding historical events as conditional inputs and gradually adding Gaussian noise to target facts in the forward process to simulate the uncertainty of future events, followed by restoring the target facts through a reverse denoising process. Although many researchers have started exploring the application of diffusion models in the field of knowledge graphs, effectively integrating diffusion models with historical information remains an important area of study.

3 Preliminaries

3.1 Diffusion Models on Discrete Data

Diffusion models are a type of probabilistic model composed of a forward process and a reverse process. The core idea is to represent the input data x_0 as a Markov chain $\{\mathbf{x}_T, \mathbf{x}_{T-1}, \ldots, \mathbf{x}_0\}$, where each state lies in the real space $\mathbb{R}$ and $\mathbf{x}_T$ follows a Gaussian distribution.

In the forward diffusion process, we first convert w into a continuous embedding $\mathbf{x}_0 \in \mathbb{R}^d$. This is expressed as:

$$\mathbf{x}_0 = \sqrt{\beta_0}\, \text{Embed}(w) + \sqrt{1-\beta_0}\, \epsilon, \tag{1}$$

where $\text{Embed}(\cdot)$ denotes the embedding operation, β_0 controls the amount of noise added in the initial step, and $\epsilon \sim \mathcal{N}(0,1)$ is a random noise drawn from a Gaussian distribution. Then, Gaussian noise is gradually added to the original data $\mathbf{x}_0$ until at diffusion step T the generated sample $\mathbf{x}_T$ approximately follows a Gaussian distribution. Each transition from $\mathbf{x}_{t-1}$ to $\mathbf{x}_t$ in the forward process is given by:

$$\begin{aligned} q\left(\mathbf{x}_t \mid \mathbf{x}_{t-1}\right) &= \mathcal{N}\left(\mathbf{x}_t;\, \sqrt{1-\beta_t}\,\mathbf{x}_{t-1},\, \beta_t \mathbf{I}\right) \\ &= \sqrt{\beta_t}\,\mathbf{x}_{t-1} + \sqrt{1-\beta_t}\,\epsilon, \quad t \in \{1, \cdots, T\}. \end{aligned} \tag{2}$$

In the reverse process, the model starts from the initial state $\mathbf{x}_T$ and uses a neural network to reconstruct the original data $\mathbf{x}_0$. This is expressed as:

$$p_\theta\left(\mathbf{x}_{t-1} \mid \mathbf{x}_t\right) = \mathcal{N}\left(\mathbf{x}_{t-1};\, \mu_\theta(\mathbf{x}_t, t),\, \Sigma_\theta(\mathbf{x}_t, t)\right), \tag{3}$$

where μ_θ and Σ_θ represent the mean and variance parameters computed by a neural network.

Since the parameterization of the forward process $q(\mathbf{x}_t \mid \mathbf{x}_{t-1})$ does not include any trainable parameters, a training objective is needed to allow the model to learn how to reverse this process using the noise data generated in the forward process, thereby reconstructing the original data. The training objective of the diffusion model is to maximize a variational lower bound on the marginal likelihood $\log p_\theta(x_0)$, which can be expressed as:

$$\mathcal{L}_{\text{vlb}}(\mathbf{x}_0) = \mathbb{E}_{q(\mathbf{x}_{1:T}|\mathbf{x}_0)}\left[\log \frac{q(\mathbf{x}_T \mid \mathbf{x}_0)}{p_\theta(\mathbf{x}_T)} + \sum_{t=2}^{T} \log \frac{q(\mathbf{x}_{t-1} \mid \mathbf{x}_0, \mathbf{x}_t)}{p_\theta(\mathbf{x}_{t-1} \mid \mathbf{x}_t)} - \log p_\theta(\mathbf{x}_0 \mid \mathbf{x}_1)\right]. \tag{4}$$

However, in practice, this objective is often unstable, and various optimization techniques are required for convergence. Therefore, Ho et al. [35] proposed a simplified alternative objective by expanding and reweighting the KL divergence terms in L_{vlb}, which is eventually transformed into a mean squared error (MSE) loss:

$$\mathcal{L}_{\text{simple}}(\mathbf{x}_0) = \sum_{t=1}^{T} \mathbb{E}_{q(\mathbf{x}_t|\mathbf{x}_0)} \left\| \mu_\theta(\mathbf{x}_t, t) - \hat{\mu}(\mathbf{x}_t, \mathbf{x}_0) \right\|^2, \tag{5}$$

where $\hat{\mu}(\mathbf{x}_t, \mathbf{x}_0)$ is the mean of the posterior $q(\mathbf{x}_{t-1} \mid \mathbf{x}_0, \mathbf{x}_t)$, and $\mu_\theta(\mathbf{x}_t, t)$ is the mean of $p_\theta(\mathbf{x}_{t-1} \mid \mathbf{x}_t)$. To better suit the task of TKG reasoning, Cai et al. [34] extend this simplified MSE loss to the case where the continuous values of $\mathbf{x}_0$ are approximated or mapped to discrete representations. The objective is expressed as:

$$\mathcal{L}_{\text{simple}}^{\text{e2e}}(\mathbf{x}_0) = \mathbb{E}_{q_\phi(\mathbf{x}_{0:T}|\mathbf{x}_0)} \left[\sum_{t=2}^{T} \|\mathbf{x}_0 - f_\theta(\mathbf{x}_t, t)\|^2 \right]$$
$$+ \mathbb{E}_{q_\phi(\mathbf{x}_{0:1}|\mathbf{x}_0)} \left[\|\mathbf{x}_0 - f_\theta(\mathbf{x}_1, 1)\|^2 - \log p_\theta(\mathbf{w} \mid \mathbf{x}_0) \right], \quad (6)$$

where the first expectation term is used to train the prediction model $f_\theta(\mathbf{x}_t, t)$ to accurately recover $\mathbf{x}_0$ from steps 2 to T, effectively reducing errors in practice; the second expectation term contains two parts: the first part ensures that the predicted $\mathbf{x}_0$ is close to the embedding Embed(w), while the second part focuses on accurately mapping $\mathbf{x}_0$ back to the discrete text w.

3.2 Task Definition

Temporal knowledge graph extrapolation aims to predict entities at future timestamps. Given a query $q = (s, r, ?, t)$, where $q \in \mathcal{Q}_t$, and the event at timestamp t is unknown, the task is formally defined as computing the conditional probability of the missing object o given the known subject s, relation r, timestamp t, and historical information $G_{t_0:t_i}$ before t:$p(o|s, r, t, G_{t_0:t_i})$ where $t_i < t$.

In this paper, we represent a temporal knowledge graph as $G = \{\mathcal{E}, \mathcal{R}, \mathcal{T}, \mathcal{F}\}$, where $\mathcal{E}$, $\mathcal{R}$, $\mathcal{T}$, and $\mathcal{F}$ denote the entity types, relation types, timestamp types, and fact set, respectively. Additionally, a TKG can be viewed as a series of snapshots $\{G_0, G_1, \ldots, G_t, \ldots\}$, where G_t contains all quadruples occurring at timestamp t. The query set is denoted as $\mathcal{Q}$, and a TKG consists of quadruples of the form (s, r, o, t), where $s, o \in \mathcal{E}$, $r \in \mathcal{R}$, and $t \in \mathcal{T}$. The embedding dimension is denoted as d.

4 Methodology

In this section, we provide a detailed description of our DMSA architecture, shown in Fig. 2. It mainly consists of three modules: the Selective Attention with CompGCN module, the diffusion module, and the decoding module. The Selective Attention with CompGCN module uses CompGCN and an attention extraction mechanism to capture information from historical snapshots, with a focus on information that is relevant to the current snapshot. The diffusion module comprises two processes: the forward noise propagation process and the reverse denoising process. The decoder employs Time-aware ConvTransE. In the following, we describe each module in detail.

4.1 Selective Attention with CompGCN

Relying solely on static entity representations in TKG reasoning may cause significant temporal information loss. Inspired by [36], we integrate static and

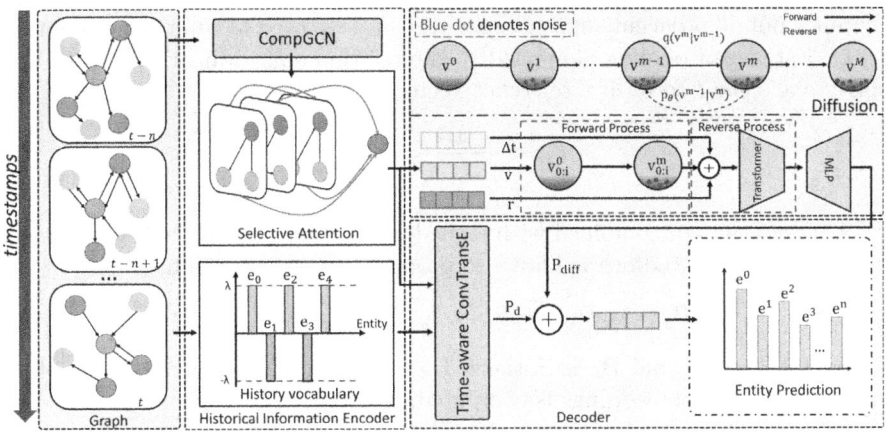

Fig. 2. Overall architecture of DMSA for temporal knowledge graph reasoning. From the input TKG, we first extract the most recent n snapshots as short-term context. Each snapshot is encoded by CompGCN, and Selective Attention filters out irrelevant information. The filtered representations are then combined by the Selective Attention with CompGCN to produce entity and relation embeddings. In parallel, the Diffusion module applies forward noise injection and reverse denoising to model uncertainty in the target entity embedding. Finally, the diffusion-based prediction is concatenated with the Time-aware ConvTransE output, and the fused vector is used for the final fact prediction.

dynamic components using timestamp information. Given a sequence of l temporal snapshots with query timestamp t, the static embedding $\mathbf{e}_t^s$ captures invariant features of entity s, while the dynamic embedding $\mathbf{e}_t^d$ models temporal variations:

$$\mathbf{e}_t^d = \mathbf{W}_1^e t + \sin(2\pi \mathbf{W}_2^e t), \tag{7}$$

where $\mathbf{W}_1^e \in \mathbb{R}^{1 \times d}$ and $\mathbf{W}_2^e \in \mathbb{R}^{1 \times d}$ are learnable parameters capturing linear changes and periodic fluctuations, respectively.

The final entity representation is obtained by concatenating the static and dynamic embeddings and transforming them:

$$\mathbf{e}_t = \mathbf{W}_3^e(\mathbf{e}_t^s \oplus \mathbf{e}_t^d), \tag{8}$$

with $\mathbf{W}_3^e \in \mathbb{R}^{d \times 2d}$ adjusting the balance between the two.

To capture evolution, we process l consecutive snapshots using CompGCN:

$$\mathbf{x}_t = \text{CompGCN}(\mathbf{e}_t, \mathbf{r}), \tag{9}$$

yielding node representations $\{\mathbf{X}_{t-l}, \ldots, \mathbf{X}_t\}$ that reflect changes in entities and relations. A GRU then encodes the temporal sequence to capture hidden dependencies:

$$\mathbf{v}_t = \text{GRU}(\mathbf{x}_t, \mathbf{v}_{t-1}), \tag{10}$$

where $\mathbf{v}_t$ is the updated representation of entity s at timestamp t.

Since not all adjacent snapshots are relevant, we need to filter useful information. First, mean pooling is applied to the relation embeddings associated with entity e at time t to form a reference vector:

$$\mathbf{r}_m = \frac{1}{|\mathcal{R}(e_t)|} \sum_{r \in \mathcal{R}(e_t)} \mathbf{r}. \qquad (11)$$

Then $\mathbf{r}_m$ is then combined with embeddings from the past l timestamps and passed through a feedforward layer to produce attention weights:

$$\mathbf{B}_j = \mathrm{softmax}\left(\mathbf{W}_b\left(\mathbf{v}_{t-j} + \mathbf{r}_m\right)\right), \quad j \in [0, l], \qquad (12)$$

where $\mathbf{W}_b \in \mathbb{R}^{d \times d}$ and $\mathbf{B}_0$ is initialized to zero. Finally, a weighted sum of the current and past embeddings is computed:

$$\mathbf{v}_t^e = \mathbf{B}_0 \mathbf{v}_t + \sum_{j=1}^{l} \mathbf{B}_j \mathbf{v}_{t-j}. \qquad (13)$$

Selective attention with CompGCN effectively combines recent interactions with periodic patterns to refine the entity representation over time.

4.2 Diffusion Module

The diffusion process consists of a forward process and a reverse process. We treat the historical information as input to predict the current missing entity. The representations of entities in the historical snapshots are denoted as $\mathbf{v}_{0:l-1}^e \in \mathbb{R}^{(l-1) \times d}$, and the representation of the target object is denoted as $\mathbf{v}_l^e \in \mathbb{R}^{1 \times d}$. To better capture the time information, we use relative time representations by calculating the time interval between each snapshot in $Q_{0:l-1} = \{(\mathbf{v}_0^e, \mathbf{r}_0, \mathbf{t}_0), \cdots, (\mathbf{v}_{l-1}^e, \mathbf{r}_{l-1}, \mathbf{t}_{l-1})\}$ and the current snapshot, and encoding these intervals with an embedding function.

Forward Process. Following the method in [34], after obtaining the embedding $\mathbf{v}^{e,0}$ of the object sequence, we gradually add randomness to the target object $\mathbf{v}_l^{e,0}$ during the forward process. Specifically, the forward process is constructed as a Markov chain with Gaussian transitions. For each object $\mathbf{v}_i^{e,0}$, we define:

$$q\left(\mathbf{v}_i^{e,m} \mid \mathbf{v}_i^{e,0}\right) = \begin{cases} \mathbf{v}_i^{e,0}, & \text{if } i < l, \\ \sqrt{\bar{\beta}_m}\, \mathbf{v}_i^{e,0} + \sqrt{1 - \bar{\beta}_m}\, \epsilon, & \text{if } i = l, \end{cases} \qquad (14)$$

$$\bar{\beta}_m = 1 - \delta \cdot \left(\beta_{\min} + \frac{m-1}{M-1}(\beta_{\max} - \beta_{\min})\right), \qquad (15)$$

where $\epsilon \sim \mathcal{N}(0, 1)$ is a random Gaussian noise, $\delta \in [0, 1]$ controls the noise scale, and $\bar{\beta}_m$ is the cumulative product that controls the noise level at each diffusion step. The diffusion process is performed for $m \in \{1, 2, \cdots, M\}$, where M is the maximum number of forward steps. $\beta_{\min}$ and $\beta_{\max}$ denote the lower and upper bounds of the noise, respectively, with $\beta_{\min} < \beta_{\max} \in (0, 1)$.

Reverse Process. In the reverse process, we denoise the noisy representation while using the time and relation information from historical snapshots as conditions. Specifically, we incorporate the encoded information of the relations $\mathbf{r}$ and the time intervals Δt into the denoising process, as expressed by:

$$p_\theta\left(\hat{\mathbf{v}}^{m-1} \mid \hat{\mathbf{v}}^m, \mathbf{r}, \mathbf{t}, m\right) = \mathcal{N}(\hat{\mathbf{v}}^{m-1}; \mu_\theta(\hat{\mathbf{v}}^m, \mathbf{r}, \mathbf{t}, m), \Sigma_\theta(\hat{\mathbf{v}}^m, \mathbf{r}, \mathbf{t}, m)), \quad (16)$$

where $\hat{\mathbf{v}}^{m-1} = \mathbf{v}_{0:n-1}^m \oplus \hat{\mathbf{v}}_n^{m-1}$. In the first step of the reverse process, we set $\hat{\mathbf{v}}^m = \mathbf{v}^m$. At this stage, we use a Transformer architecture to compute $\mu_\theta(\hat{\mathbf{v}}^m, \mathbf{r}, \mathbf{t}, m)$ and $\Sigma_\theta(\hat{\mathbf{v}}^m, \mathbf{r}, \mathbf{t}, m)$. This is represented as:

$$\begin{aligned} f_\theta(\hat{\mathbf{v}}^m, \mathbf{r}, \mathbf{t}, m) &= \hat{\mathbf{v}}^0, \\ \bar{\mathbf{v}}^m &= \hat{\mathbf{v}}^m + \mathbf{r} + \mathbf{t} + \mathbf{m}, \end{aligned} \quad (17)$$

where f_θ denotes the Transformer, and $\mathbf{m}$ represents the step embedding used to adjust the impact of different noise levels [31]. Finally, the final prediction is generated through a fully connected layer:

$$P_{\text{diff}} = \text{softmax}((\text{MLP}(\mathbf{v}_t \oplus \mathbf{r} \oplus \bar{\mathbf{v}}^m))\mathbf{V}^\top + \mathbf{H}_{\text{history}}), \quad (18)$$

where $\mathbf{V}^\top$ represents the evolving representations of all entities output by the selective attention with CompGCN at each moments, $\mathbf{H}_{\text{history}}$ is an embedding representation that records the frequency of entity and relation occurrences in the historical data. We assign a value of λ to the subject and relation pairs with a frequency greater than 0, and λ to the subject and relation pairs with a frequency less than 0. This operation is similar to previous methods [20–22].

4.3 Time-Aware ConvTransE

Prior work has shown that Time-aware ConvTransE is effective as a temporal knowledge graph decoder [17]. We thus adopt it as our decoder backbone. Time-aware ConvTransE takes three inputs: entity embeddings, relation embeddings, and timestamp embeddings. Since the entity and relation embeddings come from previous modules, we next introduce the timestamp embedding.

Timestamp Embedding. We represent timestamps by considering both relative and absolute aspects. Specifically, we use a sine function for periodic (relative) changes and a linear function for non-periodic (absolute) changes. These features are fused via element-wise addition:

$$\mathbf{h}_t = \mathbf{h}_t^p + \mathbf{h}_t^{np}, \quad (19)$$

$$\mathbf{h}_t^p = \sin(\mathbf{W}_{1,\omega} t + \mathbf{b}_p), \quad (20)$$

$$\mathbf{h}_t^{np} = \mathbf{W}_{2,\omega} t + \mathbf{b}_{np}, \quad (21)$$

where $\mathbf{W}_{1,\omega} \mathbb{R}^{d \times d}$ and $\mathbf{b}_p$ are learnable parameters for periodic features, and $\mathbf{W}_{2,\omega} \mathbb{R}^{1 \times d}$ and $\mathbf{b}_{np}$ are for non-periodic features. The resulting $\mathbf{h}_t$ is used as the timestamp embedding.

Prediction. We feed the entity embedding $\mathbf{v}_t$, relation embedding $\mathbf{r}_t$, and timestamp embedding $\mathbf{h}_t$ into Time-aware ConvTransE to get:

$$P_\mathrm{d} = \mathrm{softmax}(f(\mathbf{v}_t, \mathbf{r}_m, \mathbf{h}_t)), \tag{22}$$

where $f(\cdot)$ is the mapping function of Time-aware ConvTransE.

To balance the diffusion module and the Time-aware ConvTransE, we fuse their outputs as follows:

$$P = \gamma P_\mathrm{d} + (1-\gamma) P_\mathrm{diff}, \tag{23}$$

where γ is a hyperparameter, and P_diff is the prediction from the diffusion.

4.4 Model Training

The main training goal is to minimize a combined loss:

$$\mathcal{L} = \alpha \mathcal{L}_1 + (1-\alpha)\mathcal{L}_2, \tag{24}$$

where $\alpha \in [0,1]$ balances the losses from the Selective Attention with CompGCN module and the Time-aware ConvTransE. The Selective Attention with CompGCN module minimizes the cross-entropy loss:

$$\mathcal{L}_1 = -\sum_{i=1}^{|\mathcal{Q}(t)|} y_i \log(P_\mathrm{diff}), \tag{25}$$

where $|\mathcal{Q}(t)|$ as the number of queries at timestamp t, y_i the true label for the i-th query, and P_diff the predicted probability.

Similarly, the Time-aware ConvTransE minimizes a cross-entropy loss:

$$\mathcal{L}_2 = -\sum_{i=1}^{|\mathcal{Q}(t)|} y_i \log(P_\mathrm{d}), \tag{26}$$

where P_d as the predicted probability for the target entity. Jointly optimizing these losses allows the model to capture both historical information and unseen events information, enhancing reasoning on temporal knowledge graphs.

5 Experiments

In this section, we present a series of experiments to evaluate the performance of DMSA. We compare DMSA with various state-of-the-art TKG models. Then we conduct an ablation study to evaluate the effectiveness of different components of the model. Lastly, we explore the impact of hyperparameters on the overall model performance.

Table 1. Statistics of the datasets.

Dataset	Entities	Relations	Training	Validation	Test	Time gap	Snapshots
ICEWS14	12,498	260	323,895	-	341,409	1 day	365
ICEWS18	23,033	256	373,018	45,995	49,545	1 day	304
GDELT	7,691	240	1,734,399	238,765	305,241	15 min	2,976
YAGO	10,623	10	161,540	19,523	20,026	1 year	189
WIKI	12,554	24	539,286	67,538	63,110	1 year	232

5.1 Setup

Datasets. We utilize three real-world event-driven temporal knowledge graph datasets—ICEWS14 [11], ICEWS18 [4], and GDELT [37]. Meanwhile, we utilize two widely used public knowledge graph datasets, YAGO [38] and WIKI [39]. ICEWS14 and ICEWS18 are derived from the Integrated Crisis Early Warning System (ICEWS), capturing a wide range of international political events across different periods. GDELT is a dataset sourced from global news media, recording human societal behaviors, while YAGO and WIKI are subsets of YAGO3 and Wikipedia, respectively.

To ensure fair comparisons with baseline models, we follow the dataset partitioning strategies employed in previous studies. For all datasets except ICEWS14, we divide the data into training, validation, and test sets with an 8:1:1 ratio. Since the original ICEWS14 dataset does not provide a validation set, we split it into training and test sets only. The detailed statistics for each dataset are presented in Table 1.

Evaluation Metrics. We employ Mean Reciprocal Rank (MRR) and Hits@N as the evaluation metrics, which are standard indicators used to assess the performance of temporal knowledge graph models. In order to maintain consistency with baseline methods, we adopt the same evaluation standards. MRR calculates the mean reciprocal of the rank of the correct answer, while Hits@N measures the proportion of correct predictions ranked within the top N positions. A higher ranking of the correct entity leads to higher MRR and Hits@N values.

Baselines. We compare DMSA with several recent approaches, which fall into two main categories: static knowledge graph reasoning methods and temporal knowledge graph reasoning methods. The static reasoning methods include TransE [5], DistMult [6], ComplEx [7], ConvE [8], R-GCN [9], and CompGCN [40]. Temporal knowledge graph extrapolation methods include RE-NET [13], xERTE [41], EvoKG [15], CyGNet [14], HIP [23], RE-GCN [16], TiRGN [17], HGLS [18], CENET [20], LSEN [22], SiMFy [19], and PLEASING [21].

Implementation Details. For all experiments, we employ the Adam optimizer with a learning rate of 0.001, a batch size of 1024, and an embedding dimension of 200. A dropout rate of 0.2 is applied uniformly across all modules to mitigate overfitting, while the number of GNN layers is chosen from $\{1, 2, 3, 4\}$

based on validation performance. In line with prior work [20], we constrain the hyperparameter λ to values in $\{2, 3, 4\}$ and set the hyperparameter α to 0.1, and the length of historical information l is set to match the number of diffusion steps M, chosen from $\{1, 2, 4\}$. All experiments are conducted on an NVIDIA Tesla A100 GPU (40 GB) using PyTorch, with 128 GB of memory and 100 GB of storage. Required environments, codes, and details of commands are available at https://github.com/AAristotle/DMSA.

Table 2. Model performance comparison on five TKG datasets. All values are in percentage (%). The best results are in **bold**, and the second-best are underlined.

Model	ICEWS14			ICEWS18			GDELT			YAGO			WIKI		
	MRR	H@1	H@3	MRR	H@1	H@3	MRR	H@1	H@3	MRR	H@1	H@3	MRR	H@1	H@3
TransE	18.65	1.12	31.34	17.56	2.48	26.95	16.05	0.00	26.10	48.97	46.23	62.45	46.68	36.19	49.71
DistMult	19.06	10.09	22.00	22.16	12.13	26.00	18.71	11.59	20.05	59.47	52.97	60.91	46.12	37.24	49.81
ComplEx	24.47	16.13	27.49	30.09	21.88	34.15	22.77	15.77	24.05	61.29	54.88	62.28	47.84	38.15	50.08
ConvE	40.73	33.20	43.92	36.67	28.51	39.80	35.99	27.05	39.32	62.32	56.19	63.97	47.57	38.76	50.10
R-GCN	26.31	18.23	30.43	23.19	16.36	25.34	23.31	17.24	24.96	41.30	32.56	44.44	37.57	28.15	39.66
CompGCN	26.46	18.38	30.64	23.31	16.52	25.37	23.46	16.65	25.54	41.42	32.63	44.59	37.64	28.33	39.87
EvoKG	18.30	6.30	19.43	29.67	12.92	33.08	11.29	2.93	10.84	55.11	54.37	81.38	50.66	12.21	63.84
xERTE	32.92	26.44	36.58	36.95	30.71	40.38	>> 1 day			58.75	58.46	58.85	>>1 day		
RE-NET	45.71	38.42	49.06	42.93	36.19	45.47	40.2	32.43	43.40	65.16	63.29	65.63	51.97	48.01	52.07
CyGNet	48.63	41.77	52.50	46.69	40.58	49.82	50.29	44.53	54.69	63.47	64.26	65.71	45.50	50.48	50.79
RE-GCN	41.61	33.81	44.76	37.92	28.90	41.44	28.66	21.52	30.50	65.69	59.98	68.70	44.86	39.82	46.75
TiRGN	45.13	37.03	48.80	39.58	30.41	43.41	31.58	23.78	33.69	-	-	-	-	-	-
HGLS	40.63	31.97	43.90	39.22	28.96	43.34	>> 1 day			59.02	48.17	65.73	49.63	39.62	55.17
HIP	50.57	45.73	54.28	48.37	43.51	51.32	52.76	46.35	55.31	67.55	66.32	68.49	54.71	53.82	54.73
CENET	53.35	49.61	54.07	51.06	47.10	51.92	58.48	55.99	58.63	84.13	84.03	84.23	68.39	68.33	68.36
LSEN	54.82	51.15	55.53	52.12	48.37	52.95	<u>59.47</u>	<u>57.44</u>	59.38	<u>88.07</u>	<u>86.70</u>	<u>88.61</u>	<u>76.13</u>	<u>74.01</u>	<u>76.82</u>
SiMFy	54.81	47.99	<u>58.54</u>	46.87	39.29	51.00	47.40	40.17	50.81	-	-	-	-	-	-
PLEASING	<u>55.82</u>	<u>51.50</u>	56.99	<u>54.98</u>	<u>50.09</u>	<u>56.66</u>	59.12	55.96	<u>59.85</u>	84.36	84.27	84.38	68.13	67.97	68.28
DMSA	**58.41**	**53.54**	**59.62**	**57.08**	**51.40**	**58.95**	**62.49**	**58.29**	**63.44**	**89.20**	**88.10**	**89.50**	**79.32**	**77.31**	**80.08**

5.2 Results

Table 2 presents the entity prediction results on five TKG datasets, where DMSA outperforms most baselines. Static reasoning methods perform poorly because they cannot effectively model temporal dynamics. Although xERTE offers interpretability, it struggles with computational efficiency on large datasets like GDELT. SiMFy, despite its simple structure and fast convergence, delivers suboptimal overall results. LSEN focuses solely on historical data and thus misses future trends, even though it performs well on GDELT where historical correlations are strong. Notably, DMSA improves MRR by 3.02% on GDELT compared to LSEN. Both CENET and PLEASING achieve excellent results through contrastive learning, but their two-stage training leads to high computational overhead. Compared with PLEASING, DMSA boosts MRR by 2.59% on ICEWS14 and by 2.1% on ICEWS18. On two public TKG datasets (YAGO and WIKI), DMSA achieves the best performance, while CENET and PLEASING show similar results. The YAGO and WIKI datasets rely less on historical snapshots, which poses a challenge for models that depend solely on past data. For example, the low frequency of relevant facts in the WIKI dataset makes it difficult for many models to correctly infer subject entities.

Table 3. Performance comparison on ICEWS14, ICEWS18, YAGO, and WIKI datasets. All values are in percentage. The best score is in bold. w/o denotes without. SA denotes Selective Attention with CompGCN. TC denotes Time-aware ConvTransE.

Model	ICEWS14			ICEWS18			YAGO			WIKI		
	MRR	H@1	H@3	MRR	H@1	H@3	MRR	H@1	H@3	MRR	H@1	H@3
DMSA	**58.41**	**53.54**	**59.62**	**57.08**	**51.40**	**58.95**	**88.14**	**86.80**	**88.59**	**79.32**	**77.31**	**80.04**
-w/o SA	54.22	50.44	54.98	51.61	47.00	53.20	80.66	78.82	81.59	69.04	68.58	69.13
-w/o Diffusion	57.67	52.58	59.02	55.77	49.93	57.71	85.58	84.77	85.49	78.32	76.23	79.13
-w/o TC	50.96	47.95	50.77	45.14	42.48	44.83	84.47	84.21	84.38	68.78	68.39	68.57

5.3 Ablation

Table 3 shows the ablation study results on four datasets. ICEWS18 and ICEWS14 are event-based knowledge graphs, while YAGO and WIKI are public knowledge graphs, each with its own characteristics. We systematically removed key modules from DMSA to assess their contributions, and overall, the removal of any module led to a drop in performance.

Removing the Selective Attention with CompGCN reduced the model's ability to capture recent historical details, which negatively affected its performance in modeling recent events. This module's removal caused the largest drop in performance, highlighting the critical role of historical data in TKG reasoning. Similarly, removing the Diffusion module resulted in only a small overall decrease in MRR; however, its impact was more noticeable on the YAGO and WIKI datasets than on ICEWS14 and ICEWS18. This difference reflects the varying data characteristics of the datasets and supports our design goal of introducing uncertainty to improve the recognition of unseen entities. In addition, removing the Time-aware ConvTransE module significantly hurt DMSA's prediction performance, further confirming its effectiveness.

5.4 Sensitivity Analysis

To explore the importance of historical facts on prediction performance, we conducted a sensitivity analysis. First, we examined the impact of historical information length on model performance (as shown in Fig. 3). The results indicate that, in the YAGO and WIKI datasets, the model's performance significantly

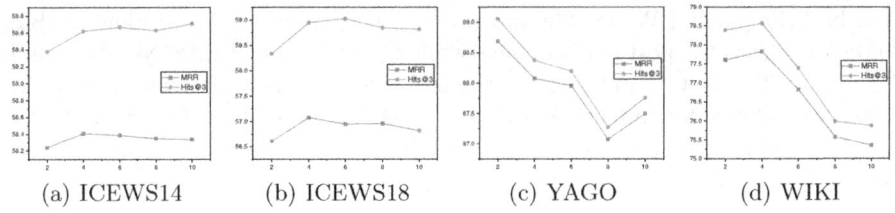

(a) ICEWS14   (b) ICEWS18   (c) YAGO   (d) WIKI

Fig. 3. Performance of DMSA under different length of history length l in terms of MRR and Hits@3 (%).

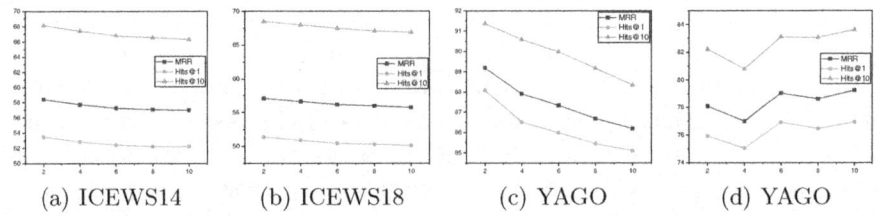

(a) ICEWS14   (b) ICEWS18   (c) YAGO   (d) YAGO

Fig. 4. Performance of DMSA under different length of CompGCN layers in terms of MRR Hits@1 and Hits@10 (%).

declines as the length of historical information increases, while in the ICEWS datasets, performance remains relatively stable with no obvious decline. This suggests that historical information plays a vital role in temporal knowledge graph reasoning.

Next, we analyze the impact of the number of CompGCN layers on model performance, as shown in Fig. 4. As the number of layers increases, the performance of DMSA decreases. This is due to the problem of over-smoothing caused by too many CompGCN layers. On the YAGO dataset, the model performance declines significantly as the number of CompGCN layers increases. In ICEWS18, the performance decreases more slowly. The WIKI dataset requires multiple CompGCN layers to extract features, and as the number of layers increases, performance improves. By adjusting the number of CompGCN layers on the validation set, DMSA can achieve the best performance.

6 Conclusion

In this paper, we propose DMSA, a novel model for temporal knowledge graph reasoning. DMSA leverages historical information and introduces noise to enhance the model's ability to predict unseen facts in knowledge graphs. By incorporating a selective attention mechanism, the model can focus on the historical information that is most relevant to the current query. Entities are predicted through decoding using Time-aware ConvTransE. Experimental results show that DMSA significantly outperforms existing methods, highlighting its promise for advancing temporal knowledge graph reasoning. In future work, we will focus on addressing the uncertainty in entity representations within temporal graphs to better capture event evolution and improve the modeling of unseen events. Additionally, we plan to explore the use of pre-trained language models to further enhance the semantic representation of entities.

Acknowledgments. This work was supported by the National Natural Science Foundation of China under Grant No. 72210107001, the Beijing Natural Science Foundation under Grant No. IS23128, the Fundamental Research Funds for the Central Universities, and the CAS PIFI International Outstanding Team Project (Grant No. 2024PG0013).

References

1. Wang, X., He, X., Cao, Y., Liu, M., Chua, T.-S.: KGAT: knowledge graph attention network for recommendation. In: Proceedings of the 25th ACM SIGKDD International Conference on Knowledge Discovery & Data Mining, pp. 950–958 (2019)
2. Saxena, A., Tripathi, A., Talukdar, P.: Improving multi-hop question answering over knowledge graphs using knowledge base embeddings. In: Proceedings of the 58th Annual Meeting of the Association for Computational Linguistics, pp. 4498–4507 (2020)
3. Zamiri, M., Qiang, Y., Nikolaev, F., Zhu, D., Kotov, A.: Benchmark and neural architecture for conversational entity retrieval from a knowledge graph. In: Proceedings of the ACM Web Conference 2024, pp. 1519–1528 (2024)
4. Jin, W., Qu, M., Jin, X., Ren, X.: Recurrent event network: autoregressive structure inference over temporal knowledge graphs. arXiv preprint arXiv:1904.05530 (2019)
5. Bordes, A., Usunier, N., Garcia-Duran, A., Weston, J., Yakhnenko, O.: Translating embeddings for modeling multi-relational data. In: Advances in Neural Information Processing Systems, vol. 26 (2013)
6. Yang, B., Yih, S.W.-T., He, X., Gao, J., Deng, L.: Embedding entities and relations for learning and inference in knowledge bases. In: Proceedings of the International Conference on Learning Representations (ICLR) 2015 (2015)
7. Trouillon, T., Welbl, J., Riedel, S., Gaussier, É., Bouchard, G.: Complex embeddings for simple link prediction. In: International Conference on Machine Learning. PMLR, pp. 2071–2080 (2016)
8. Dettmers, T., Minervini, P., Stenetorp, P., Riedel, S.: Convolutional 2D knowledge graph embeddings. In: Proceedings of the AAAI Conference on Artificial Intelligence, vol. 32 (2018)
9. Schlichtkrull, M., Kipf, T.N., Bloem, P., van den Berg, R., Titov, I., Welling, M.: Modeling relational data with graph convolutional networks. In: Gangemi, A., et al. (eds.) ESWC 2018. LNCS, vol. 10843, pp. 593–607. Springer, Cham (2018). https://doi.org/10.1007/978-3-319-93417-4_38
10. Vashishth, S., Sanyal, S., Nitin, V., Talukdar, P.P.: Composition-based multi-relational graph convolutional networks. ArXiv abs/1911.03082 (2019). https://api.semanticscholar.org/CorpusID:207847719
11. Garcia-Duran, A., Dumančić, S., Niepert, M.: Learning sequence encoders for temporal knowledge graph completion. In: Proceedings of the 2018 Conference on Empirical Methods in Natural Language Processing, pp. 4816–4821 (2018)

12. Wu, J., Cao, M., Cheung, J.C.K., Hamilton, W.L.: TeMP: temporal message passing for temporal knowledge graph completion. In: Proceedings of the 2020 Conference on Empirical Methods in Natural Language Processing (EMNLP), pp. 5730–5746 (2020)
13. Jin, W., Qu, M., Jin, X., Ren, X.: Recurrent event network: autoregressive structure inference over temporal knowledge graphs. In: Proceedings of the 2020 Conference on Empirical Methods in Natural Language Processing (EMNLP), pp. 6669–6683 (2020)
14. Zhu, C., Chen, M., Fan, C., Cheng, G., Zhang, Y.: Learning from history: modeling temporal knowledge graphs with sequential copy-generation networks. In: Proceedings of the AAAI Conference on Artificial Intelligence, vol. 35, pp. 4732–4740 (2021)
15. Park, N., Liu, F., Mehta, P., Cristofor, D., Faloutsos, C., Dong, Y.: EvoKG: jointly modeling event time and network structure for reasoning over temporal knowledge graphs. In: Proceedings of the Fifteenth ACM International Conference on Web Search and Data Mining, pp. 794–803 (2022)
16. Li, Z., et al.: Temporal knowledge graph reasoning based on evolutional representation learning. In: Proceedings of the 44th International ACM SIGIR Conference on Research and Development in Information Retrieval, pp. 408–417 (2021)
17. Li, Y., Sun, S., Zhao, J.: TiRGN: time-guided recurrent graph network with local-global historical patterns for temporal knowledge graph reasoning. In: IJCAI, pp. 2152–2158 (2022)
18. Zhang, M., Xia, Y., Liu, Q., Wu, S., Wang, L.: Learning long-and short-term representations for temporal knowledge graph reasoning. In: Proceedings of the ACM Web Conference 2023, pp. 2412–2422 (2023)
19. Liu, Z., Tan, L., Li, M., Wan, Y., Jin, H., Shi, X.: SiMFy: a simple yet effective approach for temporal knowledge graph reasoning. In: Findings of the Association for Computational Linguistics: EMNLP 2023, pp. 3825–3836 (2023)
20. Xu, Y., Ou, J., Xu, H., Fu, L.: Temporal knowledge graph reasoning with historical contrastive learning. In: Proceedings of the AAAI Conference on Artificial Intelligence, vol. 37, pp. 4765–4773 (2023)
21. Zhang, J., Sun, M., Huang, Q., Tian, L.: PLEASING: exploring the historical and potential events for temporal knowledge graph reasoning. Neural Netw. **179**, 106516 (2024)
22. Wang, F., Zhu, G., Hou, H., Yuan, C., Huang, Y.: Mining long short-term evolution patterns for temporal knowledge graph reasoning. In: Antonacopoulos, A., Chaudhuri, S., Chellappa, R., Liu, C.L., Bhattacharya, S., Pal, U. (eds.) ICPR 2024. LNCS, vol. 15304, pp. 227–242 Springer, Cham (2024). https://doi.org/10.1007/978-3-031-78128-5_15
23. He, Y., Zhang, P., Liu, L., Liang, Q., Zhang, W., Zhang, C.: HIP network: historical information passing network for extrapolation reasoning on temporal knowledge graph. arXiv preprint arXiv:2402.12074 (2024)
24. Xu, W., Liu, B., Peng, M., Jia, X., Peng, M.: Pre-trained language model with prompts for temporal knowledge graph completion. In: Findings of the Association for Computational Linguistics: ACL 2023, pp. 7790–7803 (2023)
25. Wang, J., et al.: Large language models-guided dynamic adaptation for temporal knowledge graph reasoning. In: Advances in Neural Information Processing Systems, vol. 37, pp. 8384–8410 (2024)
26. Yuan, C., Xie, Q., Huang, J., Ananiadou, S.: Back to the future: towards explainable temporal reasoning with large language models. In: Proceedings of the ACM Web Conference 2024, pp. 1963–1974 (2024)

27. Sohl-Dickstein, J., Weiss, E., Maheswaranathan, N., Ganguli, S.: Deep unsupervised learning using nonequilibrium thermodynamics. In: International Conference on Machine Learning, pp. 2256–2265. PMLR (2015)
28. Ruiz, N., Li, Y., Jampani, V., Pritch, Y., Rubinstein, M., Aberman, K.: DreamBooth: fine tuning text-to-image diffusion models for subject-driven generation. In: Proceedings of the IEEE/CVF Conference on Computer Vision and Pattern Recognition, pp. 22 500–22 510 (2023)
29. Borsos, Z., et al.: AudioLM: a language modeling approach to audio generation. IEEE/ACM Trans. Audio Speech Lang. Process. **31**, 2523–2533 (2023)
30. Li, X., Thickstun, J., Gulrajani, I., Liang, P.S., Hashimoto, T.B.: Diffusion-LM improves controllable text generation. In: Advances in Neural Information Processing Systems, vol. 35, pp. 4328–4343 (2022)
31. Gong, S., Li, M., Feng, J., Wu, Z., Kong, L.: DiffuSeq: sequence to sequence text generation with diffusion models. arXiv preprint arXiv:2210.08933 (2022)
32. Shen, Y., Song, K., Tan, X., Li, D., Lu, W., Zhuang, Y.: DiffusionNER: boundary diffusion for named entity recognition. arXiv preprint arXiv:2305.13298 (2023)
33. Liu, Y., Cao, Y., Wang, S., Wang, Q., Bi, G.: Generative models for complex logical reasoning over knowledge graphs. In: Proceedings of the 17th ACM International Conference on Web Search and Data Mining, pp. 492–500 (2024)
34. Cai, Y., et al.: Predicting the unpredictable: uncertainty-aware reasoning over temporal knowledge graphs via diffusion process. In: Findings of the Association for Computational Linguistics ACL 2024, pp. 5766–5778 (2024)
35. Ho, J., Jain, A., Abbeel, P.: Denoising diffusion probabilistic models. In: Advances in Neural Information Processing Systems, vol. 33, pp. 6840–6851 (2020)
36. Wang, K., Han, S.C., Poon, J.: Re-Temp: relation-aware temporal representation learning for temporal knowledge graph completion. arXiv preprint arXiv:2310.15722 (2023)
37. Leetaru, K., Schrodt, P.A.: GDELT: global data on events, location, and tone, 1979–2012. In: ISA Annual Convention, vol. 2, no. 4, pp. 1–49. Citeseer (2013)
38. Mahdisoltani, F., Biega, J., Suchanek, F.: YAGO3: a knowledge base from multilingual Wikipedias. In: 7th Biennial Conference on Innovative Data Systems Research. CIDR Conference (2014)
39. Leblay, J., Chekol, M.W.: Deriving validity time in knowledge graph. In: Companion Proceedings of the the Web Conference 2018, pp. 1771–1776 (2018)
40. Vashishth, S., Sanyal, S., Nitin, V., Talukdar, P.: Composition-based multi-relational graph convolutional networks. In: International Conference on Learning Representations (2019)
41. Han, Z., Chen, P., Ma, Y., Tresp, V.: Explainable subgraph reasoning for forecasting on temporal knowledge graphs. In: International Conference on Learning Representations (2020)

Topology-Aware Hierarchical Graph Diffusion Model for Molecular Graph Generation

Rongshen He[1], Abubakar Zakari[2], Qinru Yang[1], Jiaqi Luo[1], and Changsheng Ma[1(✉)]

[1] School of Information Science and Engineering, Lanzhou University, Lanzhou, China
{320220940271,320220940961,320220917431,macs}@lzu.edu.cn
[2] Fashable AI, Quinta da Barca, R. Nossa Sra. de Guadalupe 113 Lote 78, Loja 1, 4740-473 Esposende, Portugal
abubakar@fashable.ai

Abstract. This work introduces THGD, a Topology-Aware Hierarchical Graph Diffusion Model designed to address the challenges of generating large, structurally complex molecules. THGD employs a coarse-to-fine framework that decouples global topology preservation from local atomic refinement, enabling precise generative control and efficient exploration of broader chemical spaces without relying on restrictive, predefined motif vocabularies. Extensive experiments underscore THGD's superior performance. It robustly preserves complex structural constraints, achieving up to 2× higher scaffold validity than the previous state-of-the-art model in scaffold-constrained generation task. Furthermore, in molecular generation task, THGD excels in generating large molecules with high distribution fidelity, attaining an FCD score of 80.26 on the challenging GuacaMol dataset, effectively matching the diversity of real-world molecular distributions. These results highlight THGD's potential to advance molecular design for drug discovery and beyond. Our code is available at https://github.com/hers22/THGD.

Keywords: Molecular Generation · Hierarchical Diffusion · Graph Coarsening · Large Molecules

1 Introduction

Modern drug discovery requires the development of advanced machine learning models capable of effectively capturing and sampling from the vast chemical space. This task is both highly challenging and urgent, given the astronomical scale of drug-like compounds, estimated to exceed 10^{60} [18]. Recently, deep

---

Supplementary Information The online version contains supplementary material available at https://doi.org/10.1007/978-3-032-05981-9_10.

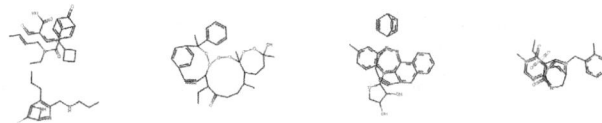

Fig. 1. Visualization results of unreasonable structure generated by atom-based generative methods.

graph generative models, which model the underlying probability distributions of molecular graph structures, enabling the generation of high-quality candidate molecules while avoiding the prohibitive costs associated with exhaustive chemical space searches [6,27], have achieved significant success in this domain, demonstrating their potential to revolutionize molecular design.

Although existing graph generative models have shown promising results, significant challenges remain in generating large and structurally complex molecules. These models can be broadly categorized into two main paradigms: atom-based generative models [21] and motif-based generative models [9]. Atom-based generative models construct molecules at the atom level, treating each atom as a node and each bond as an edge in a graph. While this fine-grained approach allows for precise control over molecular structures, it suffers from scalability issues. As the size of the molecular graph grows, the computational complexity increases drastically due to the quadratic scaling of edges with respect to nodes. This leads to substantial computational overhead, escalating memory requirements, and difficulties in accurately predicting sparse chemical bonds, often resulting in disconnected substructures, implausible ring systems, and invalid valency states, as illustrated in Fig. 1.

On the other hand, motif-based generative models construct molecules by assembling predefined structural motifs, such as functional groups or subgraphs. By leveraging larger building blocks, this approach reduces combinatorial complexity and improves scalability compared to atom-based models. However, these models are constrained by their heavy reliance on predefined motif libraries, which inherently limits the exploration of the chemical space and the ability to generate truly innovative molecules that deviate from predefined patterns. While enlarging the motif library might alleviate this issue, it complicates the modeling of diverse motif graphs due to their permutation-unequivariant nature [24].

To address these challenges, we introduce THGD, a novel topology-aware hierarchical graph diffusion model designed for large molecular graph generation. THGD employs a coarse-to-fine hierarchical diffusion process that decouples global topology preservation from local atomic refinement, enabling precise control over molecular generation while maintaining scalability. The model first generates a coarse graph representation through spectral-preserved graph coarsening, dynamically identifying and partitioning ring structures without relying on predefined motif libraries.

The coarse graph is then refined into detailed atom level structures using a conditioned diffusion process guided by structural type priors, ensuring chemically realistic substructure generation. Extensive experiments conducted on the GuacaMol [2] and MOSES [20] benchmarks demonstrate THGD's superior performance in capturing true dataset distributions and excelling in scaffold-constrained generation tasks. The contributions of this work are as follows:

1. **Novel Hierarchical Framework:** We propose a coarse-to-fine diffusion model that decouples global topology preservation from local atomic refinement, addressing scalability and chemical validity challenges faced by existing methods.
2. **Elimination of Predefined Motif Libraries:** By leveraging spectral-preserved graph coarsening and type-specific marginal priors, THGD eliminates reliance on predefined motif libraries, enhancing flexibility and generalization.
3. **State-of-the-Art Performance:** THGD achieves state-of-the-art results on both generation and scaffold-constrained generation tasks, with an FCD score of 80.26 on GuacaMol and up to 2× higher scaffold validity compared to previous state-of-the-art model.

2 Related Work

Molecule generation remains a cornerstone challenge in drug discovery. Early approaches relied on SMILES-based sequence generation models [3,5,12], which pioneered automated molecular design but struggled to explicitly model chemical topology and valency rules, resulting in limited validity rates for complex molecules. Subsequent research shifted to molecular graph representations, achieving significant progress through GANs [4], VAEs [15], and normalizing flows [27].

Recent breakthroughs in diffusion and score-based models have revolutionized the field. For instance, EDM [7] introduced permutation-equivariant diffusion for 3D molecular conformations, GDSS [11] leveraged stochastic differential equations to model node and edge features, and DiGress [24] advanced discrete diffusion techniques. Building on these foundations, Cometh [22] and DisCo [25] reformulated discrete diffusion modeling using continuous-time Markov chains [1]. While existing methods achieve strong performance in generating small molecules, they exhibit significant limitations in fitting the distribution of large molecules due to combinatorial explosion and strict chemical valence rules, particularly as molecular complexity escalates exponentially.

To address scalability, hierarchical frameworks decompose molecular generation into coarse-to-fine stages. Existing methods such as tree decompositions [9] and atom-motif hierarchies [10] reduce complexity by leveraging predefined structural motifs. However, their reliance on fixed motif libraries restricts the exploration of novel chemical spaces. This limitation is commonly observed in structured data generation tasks, where static prior knowledge hinders adaptability to dynamic patterns [26]. In contrast, our proposed method employs a hierarchical framework that eliminates dependence on predefined vocabularies through spectral-preserved graph coarsening and dynamic structural typing, enabling broader exploration of the chemical space while maintaining scalability and validity.

3 Background

Graph Diffusion Models. Diffusion models [6,23] are probabilistic generative models defined by a forward diffusion process that gradually adds noise to graphs and a reverse denoising process that learns to remove it, enabling sample generation. Formally, the model is expressed as a latent variable model:

$$p_\theta(G_0) := \int p_\theta(G_{0:T}) \, dG_{1:T}. \tag{1}$$

Recent advancements extend denoising diffusion probabilistic models to discrete domains, with DiGress [24] applying this framework to graph G with its nodes V and edges E. Noise is added to graphs using transition matrices Q^t, where $[Q^t]_{ij}$ defines transitions from state i to j. The noisy graph G^t in the forward process is computed as:

$$q(G^t|G_0) = G_0 \bar{Q}^t, \quad \text{with} \quad \bar{Q}^t = \bar{\alpha}_t I + (1 - \bar{\alpha}_t) \mathbf{1} m^\top, \tag{2}$$

where $\bar{\alpha}_t$ controls noise levels, and m approximates the true data distribution $q_V \times q_E$. Transition matrices satisfy:

$$\lim_{T \to \infty} \bar{Q}_T^\top \mathbf{1} = m, \tag{3}$$

ensuring transitions align with training set marginal probabilities.

The reverse process reconstructs the clean graph iteratively using Bayes' theorem:

$$q(G^{t-1}|G^t, G_0) \propto G^t (Q^t)^\top \odot G_0 \bar{Q}^{t-1}, \tag{4}$$

where $(Q^t)^\top$ is the transpose of Q^t, and $\odot$ denotes element-wise multiplication.

A denoising neural network ϕ_θ predicts clean graphs from noisy inputs $G^t = (V^t, E^t)$. It is trained by minimizing the cross-entropy loss between predicted probabilities $\hat{p}^G = (\hat{p}^V, \hat{p}^E)$ and ground truth G:

$$l(\hat{p}^G, G) = \sum_i \text{CE}(v_i, \hat{p}_i^V) + \lambda \sum_{i,j} \text{CE}(e_{ij}, \hat{p}_{ij}^E), \tag{5}$$

where $\lambda \in \mathbb{R}^+$ balances node and edge importance, and CE denotes cross-entropy.

4 Methodology

We propose THGD, a novel hierarchical molecular generation framework that employs a two-stage diffusion process to synthesize molecules at both coarse topological and fine atomic levels. As illustrated in Fig. 2, the first stage trains a discrete diffusion model to generate coarse graphs representing cluster level molecular topologies. The second stage refines these coarse graphs into detailed atom level structures using a conditioned diffusion model. This decomposition enables efficient generation while preserving critical chemical constraints.

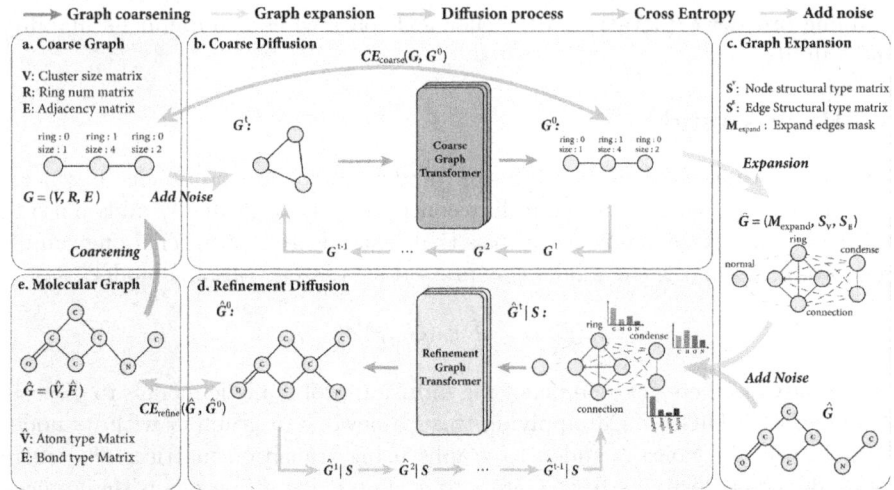

Fig. 2. Architecture of *THGD*: (I) Coarse graph generation via discrete diffusion learns cluster-level topologies; (II) Refined graph generation uses topology-conditioned diffusion to reconstruct atom-level details. Both stages employ graph transformers trained with cross-entropy loss.

4.1 Notation and Definitions

A molecular graph $\hat{G} = (\hat{V}, \hat{E})$ containing $\hat{n}$ atoms also noted as refined graph, represents the original molecular structure. The node features $\hat{V} \in \{0, 1\}^{\hat{n} \times a}$ are one-hot encodings of atom types, where a is the total number of distinct atom types. Similarly, edge features $\hat{E} \in \{0, 1\}^{\hat{n} \times \hat{n} \times b}$ are one-hot encodings of bond types between pairs of atoms, where b is the total number of distinct bond types.

A coarse graph $G = (V, R, E)$ is an abstracted representation of the molecular topology, consisting of n clusters (where $n \leq \hat{n}$). The cluster node features $V \in \{0, 1\}^{n \times c}$ are one-hot encodings representing the number of atoms in each cluster, where c is the maximum number of atoms a single cluster can contain. The cluster ring features $R \in \{0, 1\}^{n \times r}$ are one-hot encodings that represents the number of fused rings within each cluster, where r is the maximum number of fused rings a single cluster can represent. The adjacency matrix $E \in \{0, 1\}^{n \times n}$ encodes inter-cluster connectivity. This abstraction simplifies the molecular graph while preserving its high-level topological structure.

An expanded graph $\tilde{G} = (M_{\text{expand}}, S_V, S_E)$ serves as an intermediate representation during the refinement process, bridging the coarse graph G and the molecular graph $\hat{G}$. It has $\tilde{n}$ nodes, where $\tilde{n} = \hat{n}$ to align with the atom count of the original molecular graph. It employs a connectivity mask $M_{\text{expand}} \in \{0, 1\}^{\tilde{n} \times \tilde{n}}$, which encodes permissible atom-atom connections derived from the expanded clusters, enforcing topological constraints from the coarse graph. Furthermore, it integrates structural matrices $S_V \in \{0, 1\}^{\tilde{n} \times s}$ and $S_E \in \{0, 1\}^{\tilde{n} \times \tilde{n} \times s}$, which are hot encodings that represent the structural types of the nodes and edges derived from the coarse graph, where s denotes the possible structural types and is consistent for both nodes and edges.

4.2 Coarsening and Refinement

Traditional motif-based coarsening methods rely on predefined motif vocabularies, which constrain the exploration of chemical space and impede the generation of innovative molecules. To overcome this limitation, we introduce a novel molecular graph coarsening method that eliminates dependence on fixed motif libraries.

Coarsening: The coarsening stage transforms the original molecular graph $\hat{G}$ into a compact coarse graph G, reducing complexity while retaining key chemical and topological information. The quality of the coarse graph is pivotal, we employ a two-stage strategy (illustrated in Fig. 3):

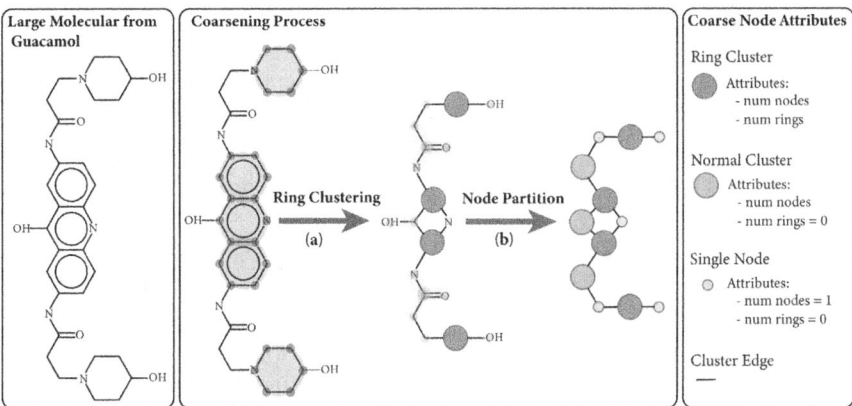

Fig. 3. Illustration of structure preserved coarsening. A large molecule from Guacamol dataset was taken as an example. (a) All nodes in rings are clustered together (highlighted in red), and connected rings were partitioned by splitting rings (split nodes in purple); (b) Remaining nodes (highlighted in yellow) are partitioned by spectrum reduction. (Color figure online)

1. **Ring Identification and Partitioning:** We begin by identifying the rings in the molecular graph, as they contribute significantly to the structure and properties of the molecule. Fundamental ring structures are identified and merged into clusters. Small rings with fewer than 6 atoms or those sharing atoms with neighboring rings are grouped. To manage complexity from very large ring systems (e.g., up to 14 fused rings, details in Appendix A), we partition them by splitting shared atoms, ensuring manageable cluster sizes. (see Fig. 3, "(a) Ring Clustering").

2. **Graph Coarsening:** The remaining non-ring nodes are partitioned into clusters using spectral-preserved techniques [14], leveraging the Laplacian spectrum to maintain the original graph's topology (Fig. 3b). This ensures the coarse graph accurately reflects the molecular structure, and this dynamic, vocabulary-free approach allows for flexible abstraction of diverse chemical entities. (see Fig. 3, "(b) Node Partition").

Refinement: The refinement stage focuses on reconstructing the original molecular graph from the coarse graph G. However, the coarse graph (with n clusters) and the molecular graph $\hat{G}$ (with $\hat{n}$ atoms) exhibit size misalignment, necessitating joint modeling of distributions across different scales. To address this, we introduce an intermediate expanded graph $\tilde{G} = (M_{\text{expand}}, S_V, S_E)$ as a bridge between the abstracted coarse topology and fine-grained molecular details, ensuring size consistency and preserving chemical information via three interconnected mechanisms: (1) **cluster expansion** to align node counts, (2) **edge masking** (M_{expand}) to regulate connectivity, and (3) **structural typing** (S_V, S_E) to enforce chemical constraints.

1. **Cluster Expansion:** The process begins by expanding each cluster $c_p \in G$ into a set of atomic nodes. Specifically, a cluster containing $V[p]$ atoms is mapped to $V[p]$ atomic nodes through the operator $\text{Expand}(c_p)$, defined as:

$$V' = \bigcup_{p=1}^{n} \text{Expand}(c_p), \quad \text{where } |\text{Expand}(c_p)| = V[p] \text{ and } \sum_{p=1}^{n} V[p] = \tilde{n}.$$

Here, $\text{Expand}(c_p)$ represents the operator mapping cluster c_p to $V[p]$ atomic nodes, and V' is the expanded node set with size $\tilde{n} = \hat{n}$, matching the molecular graph. This expansion ensures $|V'| = \hat{n}$, aligning $\tilde{G}$ with the molecular graph size while preserving cluster-level information.

2. **Edge Masking:** To regulate connectivity during refinement, we define a binary mask $M_{\text{expand}} \in \{0,1\}^{\tilde{n} \times \tilde{n}}$. This mask encodes permissible edges as:

$$M_{\text{expand}}^{(i,j)} = \begin{cases} 1, & \text{if } v_i, v_j \text{ belong to the same cluster (intra-cluster)} \\ 1, & \text{if } v_i \in c_p, v_j \in c_q \text{ and } E_{p,q} = 1 \text{ (inter-cluster)} \\ 0, & \text{otherwise.} \end{cases}$$

The mask acts as a structural scaffold: intra-cluster edges preserve local substructures (e.g., aromatic rings), inter-cluster edges enforce connectivity defined in G, and masked regions ($M_{\text{expand}}^{(i,j)} = 0$) prohibit chemically invalid bonds during refinement.

3. **Structural Typing:** To enforce chemical validity, we introduce structural type matrices S_V (nodes) and S_E (edges). The node structural matrix $S_V \in \mathbb{N}^{\tilde{n} \times s}$ assigns each expanded node a type inherited from its parent cluster as:

$$S_V[i] = \begin{cases} \text{NORMAL}, & \text{if } V[p] = 1 \quad \text{(singleton cluster)} \\ \text{CONDENSED}, & \text{if } V[p] > 1 \text{ and } R[p] = 0 \quad \text{(chain/functional group)} \\ \text{RING}_k, & \text{if } R[p] = k \geq 1 \quad \text{(fused ring system).} \end{cases}$$

And the edge structural matrix $S_E \in \mathbb{N}^{\tilde{n} \times \tilde{n} \times s}$ labels edges based on connectivity as:

$$S_E[i,j] = \begin{cases} \text{CONNECTION,} & \text{if } M_{\text{expand}}^{(i,j)} = 1 \text{ and inter-cluster} \\ \text{Inherited from } S_V[i] \text{ or } S_V[j], & \text{if intra-cluster.} \end{cases}$$

Here, s is the number of structural types (NORMAL, CONDENSED, $RING_k$, CONNECTION). These matrices enforce domain-specific constraints. For example, $RING_k$ clusters enforce aromaticity, CONDENSED clusters bias atom types toward chain-appropriate elements, and CONNECTION edges restrict bonds to single/double/triple types.

The expanded graph $\tilde{G}$ guides molecular generation through a conditioned diffusion model that iteratively denoises the noisy molecular graph. This process is guided by structural type priors (S_V, S_E) and the connectivity mask (M_{expand}) derived from the coarse graph. Specifically, S_V/S_E biases atom/bond predictions, while masked regions ($M_{\text{expand}} = 0$) prohibit invalid bonds and enforce valid atom valency during denoising. By decoupling topology preservation from atomic refinement, this hierarchical design ensures alignment with both global molecular topology and local chemical rules, enabling scalable synthesis of complex molecules with chemical validity, as shown in Fig. 4.

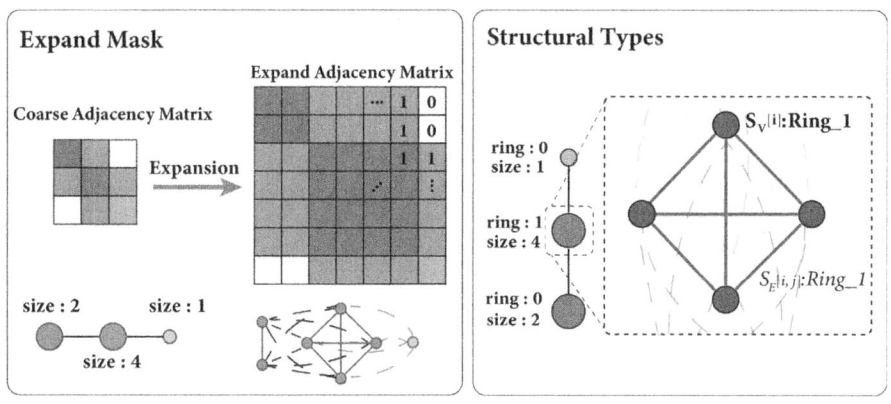

Fig. 4. Illustration of Coarse Graph Expansion.

4.3 Hierarchical Diffusion

Our hierarchical generation process decomposes molecular synthesis into two coupled diffusion stages governed by the joint distribution:

$$q(\hat{G}, G) = \underbrace{q(\hat{G}|G)}_{\text{Atomic Refinement}} \underbrace{q(G)}_{\text{Coarse Topology}} \quad (6)$$

We employ two graph diffusion models to learn both the distribution $q(G)$ of the coarse graph and the conditioned distribution $q(\hat{G} \mid G)$ of the molecular graph.

Coarse Graph Diffusion: Our coarse graph diffusion process is conceptually similar to the approach used in DiGress [24]. Specifically, we model the distribution $q(G)$ of the coarse graph $G = (V, R, E)$ through discrete diffusion over its components. This similarity allows us to directly leverage the established framework of DiGress for learning and sampling coarse graphs, ensuring a solid foundation for our hierarchical generation process.

The training objective for the coarse graph diffusion model is formulated as:

$$L_{\text{coarse}} = \sum_{i=1}^{n} \text{CE}(v_i, \hat{p}_V^i) + \zeta \cdot \text{CE}(r_i, \hat{p}_R^i) + \gamma \cdot \sum_{ij} \text{CE}(e_{ij}, \hat{p}_E^{ij}), \quad (7)$$

where: v_i, r_i, and e_{ij} represent the node features, ring counts, and edge connectivity of the coarse graph, respectively. $\hat{p}_i^V$, $\hat{p}_i^R$, and $\hat{p}_{ij}^E$ are the predicted probabilities for the corresponding attributes. $\zeta \in \mathbb{R}^+$ and $\gamma \in \mathbb{R}^+$ are hyperparameters that balance the importance of ring count prediction, node count prediction, and edge connectivity relative to node attributes.

This formulation ensures that the coarse graph diffusion model effectively captures both the structural and topological characteristics of the molecular graph at the cluster level. By building on the success of DiGress, we achieve robust performance in generating coarse graphs that accurately reflect the underlying molecular topology.

Optimal Marginal Prior Probability: The choice of initial distributions significantly impacts model performance, as demonstrated in DiGress [24], where better priors lead to markedly improved results. We observe a similar phenomenon in our framework: atom and bond types exhibit distinct distributions across different topological structures. For instance, aromatic bonds occur more frequently in ring systems compared to chain structures (see Appendix B for detailed statistics). We compute optimal prior distributions tailored to each structural condition to enhance the discrete diffusion process.

Formally, let M denote the optimal prior distribution for molecular graph generation $q(\hat{V}, \hat{E} \mid S)$, constrained by structural typologies that best approximate the true data distribution. The accumulated node attribute transition matrices $\bar{Q}_T^V$ satisfy:

$$\lim_{T \to \infty} \bar{Q}_T^V \mathbf{1}_a = (S_k^V M^V)^\top, \quad (8)$$

where the structural type matrix $S^V \in \mathbb{N}^{\hat{n} \times s}$ contains node-wise structural types with S_k^V specifying the k-th node's structural type ($k \in [0, \hat{n})$). Here $\mathbf{1}_a$ represents an a-dimensional vector of ones, and $M^V \in \mathbb{R}^{s \times a}$ constitutes the core marginal probability matrix where s enumerates structural categories and a denotes node label cardinality. The probability of transitioning from state i to state j for the k-th refined node is proportional to the marginal probability of M^V selected by the structural type at that node (i.e. $S_k^V M^V$), with a similar formulation applied to edges.

This ensures that the forward process begins closer to the true data distribution, maintaining both unbiased sampling and chemical fidelity throughout the generation process. By incorporating these structure-specific priors, we align the diffusion process with realistic molecular configurations, improving both the quality and efficiency of the generated outputs.

Forward Process: We define a conditional diffusion process in which the coarse graph guides noise injection into the molecular graph. The forward process is formulated as

$$q(\hat{G}_1, \ldots, \hat{G}_T \mid G) = \prod_{t=1}^{T} q(\hat{G}_t \mid \hat{G}_{t-1}, G), \tag{9}$$

where the coarse graph G is then expanded to the expanded graph represented by structural type matrix S that contains topological information and constraints. Consequently, the transition probability can be equivalently written as $q(\hat{G}_t \mid \hat{G}_{t-1}, G) = q(\hat{G}_t \mid \hat{G}_{t-1}, S)$.

For each node of the molecular graph, the forward transition matrix for the k-th entry ($k \in [0, \hat{n})$) is defined as

$$Q_k^t = (1 - \beta_t)I + \beta_t \mathbf{1}_a(S_k M), \tag{10}$$

where I denotes the identity matrix, $\mathbf{1}_a$ is an a-dimensional vector of ones and β_t is a time-dependent parameter controlling the noise level. The cumulative transition matrix over t time steps is given by $\bar{Q}^t = Q^1 Q^2 \cdots Q^t$. A similar formulation is applied to the edge features.

Reverse Process: The reverse diffusion process reconstructs the original molecular graph $\hat{G}_0$ from its noisy counterpart $\hat{G}_T$. By applying Bayes' rule, the conditional probability for the reverse step can be expressed as:

$$q(\hat{G}_{t-1} \mid \hat{G}_t, S) = q(\hat{G}_{t-1} \mid \hat{G}_t, \hat{G}_0, S) \propto q(\hat{G}_t \mid \hat{G}_{t-1}, S) \, q(\hat{G}_{t-1} \mid \hat{G}_0, S), \tag{11}$$

where S is the structural type matrix. In this framework, the only modification compared to the standard reverse process is the explicit conditioning on S, which is integrated into the forward transition matrix Q and the input feature. As a result, the reverse process formulation remains consistent with Eq. 4. The model thus denoises the noisy molecular graph based on the structural types derived from the coarse graph, ensuring the generation of chemically plausible molecules.

Training Refinement Denoising Network: The refinement denoising neural network $\phi_{\theta r}$ parametrized by θr take taking a noisy molecular graph $\hat{G}_t = (\hat{V}, \hat{E})$ at t-th step conditioned on the coarse graph and the structural types matrices (S_V, S_E) as input and aims to predict the clean refined graph $\hat{G}_0 = (\hat{V}, \hat{E})$. It was trained by optimizing the cross-entropy loss l between the predicted probabilities $\hat{p}^{\hat{G}} = (\hat{p}^{\hat{V}}, \hat{p}^{\hat{E}})$ for each node and edge and the true refined graph following [24]. Notably, the refinement is restricted to chemically plausible regions using an expansion mask M_{expand} attained from expanding the coarse graph, the refinement loss then focuses only on mask-valid edges:

$$\mathcal{L}_{\text{refine}} = \sum_{i \in \hat{V}} \text{CE}(v_i, \hat{p}^{\hat{V}}) + \lambda \sum_{(i,j) \in M_{\text{expand}}} \text{CE}(e_{ij}, \hat{p}^{\hat{E}}), \tag{12}$$

where $\lambda \in \mathbb{R}^+$ is a hyperparameter balancing the importance of node attributes relative to edge attributes.

4.4 Model Review

The overall structure of our proposed model is as shown in Fig. 2, which uses a two-stage process: coarse graph generation for high-level structure and expansion for detailed atom-level refinement. Two diffusion models drive these stages, enabling fine-grained control and preserving global structure. Detailed architectures are in Appendix C.

Stage I: Coarse graph generation via discrete diffusion learns cluster-level topologies.

1. **Coarsening:** Abstracts the molecular graph into a coarse graph G^0, where nodes are atom clusters and edges are cluster connections.
2. **Coarse Diffusion Model Training:** Progressively adds noise to G^0 over timesteps, resulting in noisy G^t. A graph transformer then learns to reverse the noise, denoising G^t to predict G^0. Training minimizes cross-entropy loss.
3. **Coarse Diffusion Model Sampling:** Sample a noisy representation G^t from the prior distribution, then progressively remove the noise to G^0 using the learned coarse graph transformer.

Stage II: Refined graph generation uses topology-conditioned diffusion to reconstruct atom-level details.

1. **Expansion and Refinement**: Expand coarse graph nodes into atom clusters with structural types and expand mask.
2. **Refinement Diffusion Model Training:** Progressively adds noise to $\hat{G}$ over timesteps, conditioned by structural types retrieved from expanding G^0. A refinement graph transformer then denoises the expanded graph using structural type information to predict the refined molecular graph. Training minimizes cross-entropy loss under the constrain of expand mask.
3. **Refinement Diffusion Model Sampling:** Sample a noisy representation from the prior distribution conditioned by structural types retrieved from expanding G^0. A refinement graph transformer then progressively removes the noise to $\hat{G}^0$.

This hierarchical approach decomposes molecular generation, allowing THGD to generate complex, valid, and diverse molecules using diffusion models at coarse and fine levels.

4.5 Scaffold Constrained Generation

In drug discovery, generating molecules with specific scaffolds—subgraphs possessing desired chemical properties—is essential. Given a subgraph $S = (V_S, E_S)$ with n_s nodes, the generation process conditioned on S can be achieved by masking the first n_s-th node and edge feature tensors at each reverse iteration step using a permutation-equivariant model [24]. After sampling G^{t-1}, the node and edge features are updated as follows:

$$V^{t-1} = M_V \odot V_s + (1-M_V) \odot V^{t-1}, \quad E^{t-1} = M_E \odot E_s + (1-M_E) \odot E^{t-1}, \quad (13)$$

where $M_V \in \{0,1\}^n$ and $M_E \in \{0,1\}^{n \times n}$ are binary masks that identify the first n_s nodes and their associated edges, ensuring the preservation of the scaffold structure during the generation process. For our case, scaffold masking was applied separately to both the coarse and refined graphs during their respective generation stages.

5 Experiments

This section provides a thorough evaluation of THGD on both molecular graph generation and scaffold-constrained generation.

We evaluate our model on two large-scale molecular datasets: MOSES [20] and GuacaMol [2]. MOSES is a refined subset of the ZINC database, containing 1.9 million molecules, with 1.6 million designated for training, and graph size averaging 21.7 nodes. GuacaMol is a large molecular dataset derived from the ChEMBL database with an average molecular graph size of 27.8 nodes, includes 1.6 million molecules, of which 1.3 million are used for training. For the two datasets, we apply a preprocessing step similar to that of DiGress [24] and FreeGress [19]. Further preprocessing details and dataset statistics can be found in Appendix D.

5.1 Molecular Generation

Setup. We evaluate generation quality using several metrics: Validity measures the percentage of molecules that satisfy basic valency rules. Uniqueness quantifies the proportion of molecules with distinct SMILES strings, indicating non-isomorphic structures. Novelty assesses the fraction of generated molecules absent from the training set. The filter score evaluates the proportion of molecules passing the same filters used to construct the test set. The Fréchet ChemNet Distance (FCD) compares the similarity between training and test set molecules using embeddings learned by a neural network. SNN represents the similarity to the nearest neighbor, measured via Tanimoto distance. Scaffold similarity analyzes the frequency distribution of Bemis-Murcko scaffolds, while KL divergence compares the distributions of various physicochemical descriptors.

Baselines. We compare our THGD with several state-of-the-art molecular graph generative models, including JT-VAE [9] which decomposes molecules into tree-structured motifs for generation, GraphINVENT [17] which constructs molecular graphs through canonical breadth-first search ordering, NAGVAE [13] which encodes substructural patterns of molecular graphs into edge features for scalable generation, MCTS [8] which is enhanced by Monte Carlo tree search for efficient chemical space exploration, as well as DiGress [24], DisCo [25] and Cometh [22] are discrete molecular graph diffusion models, operating in discrete-time, discrete-state, and continuous-time settings, respectively (Tables 1 and 2).

Table 1. Molecular Generation on MOSES. JT-VAE and GraphINVENT have hard-coded rules to ensure high validity, others do not.

Model	Validity(%) ↑	Unique(%) ↑	Novelty(%) ↑	Filter(%) ↑	FCD ↓	SNN ↑
JT-VAE [9]	*100.0*	100.0	*100.0*	97.8	*1.00*	0.53
GraphINVENT [17]	96.4	92.7	–	95.0	1.22	*0.54*
DisCo [25]	88.3	100.0	97.7	95.6	1.44	0.50
Cometh [22]	90.5	100.0	92.6	**99.1**	1.27	**0.54**
DiGress [24]^a	<u>96.5</u>	100.0	<u>95</u>	95.0	<u>1.20</u>	<u>0.51</u>
THGD	**96.8**	100.0	94.2	<u>98.3</u>	**1.17**	**0.54**

^a DiGress is re-run here using the same settings as in the original paper after dataset preprocessing

Table 2. Molecular Generation on GuacaMol. We report scores, higher is better for all metrics. NAGVAE and MCTS are tailored for molecule datasets, which incorporate more in-depth domain knowledge into the model. Others are general graph generation models.

Model	Validity (%) ↑	Unique (%) ↑	Novelty (%) ↑	KLdiv ↑	FCD ↑
NAGVAE [13]	92.9	95.5	*100*	38.4	0.90
MCTS [8]	*100*	*100*	95.4	*82.2*	*1.50*
DiGress [24]	85.2	100	100	92.9	68.00
DisCo [25]	86.6	86.6	86.5	92.6	59.7
Cometh [22]	**98.9**	<u>98.9</u>	97.6	**96.7**	<u>72.7</u>
THGD	<u>94.2</u>	100	<u>99.2</u>	<u>94.4</u>	**80.26**

Results Analysis. THGD demonstrates strong performance in generating diverse and realistic molecules, particularly excelling in distribution fidelity, which measures how closely the generated molecules resemble real-world chemical compounds. On the GuacaMol dataset, THGD achieves a leading Fréchet ChemNet Distance (FCD) score of **80.26** among diffusion-based methods, and similarly obtains the best FCD of **1.17** on MOSES. Lower FCD scores signify a better match to true molecular distributions, indicating THGD's superior ability to learn and replicate these complex patterns. This is further supported by a high KL divergence score of **94.4** (on GuacaMol), showing good agreement with various physicochemical properties of known molecules.

Beyond distributional alignment, THGD consistently generates high-quality structures. It achieves near-perfect chemical validity (the ability to produce chemically correct molecules) with scores of **96.8%** on MOSES and **94.2%** on GuacaMol. Notably, this is achieved without relying on hard-coded chemical rules or domain-specific knowledge, unlike specialized models such as JT-VAE, GraphINVENT, NAGVAE, and MCTS, showcasing its robust learning

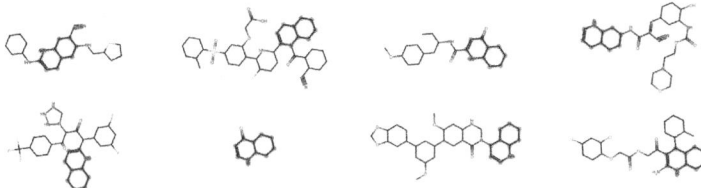

Fig. 5. Scaffold constrained generation result of 1, 3-Dimethylquinolin-4(1H)-one.

capabilities. Furthermore, THGD excels in generating entirely distinct and new molecules (up to **99.2% novelty** on GuacaMol), highlighting its potential for discovering novel chemical entities.

These results validate the effectiveness of our topology-aware hierarchical framework. By integrating spectral-preserved coarsening (to capture global structure) with type-specific marginal priors (to guide local atomic details), THGD ensures chemically realistic substructure generation while mitigating common distributional biases, leading to a better overall generation quality.

5.2 Scaffold-Constrained Generation

Setup. In this section, we evaluate THGD's scaffold-constrained generation capabilities using four diverse scaffold templates, including three medium-sized scaffolds and one large scaffold consisting of 25 atoms, as described by Maziarz et al. [16]. The model is constrained to generate molecules that are at least as large as the given scaffold. Each scaffold was sampled four times with a batch size of 512.

Results Analysis. Table 3 clearly demonstrates THGD's superiority in scaffold-constrained generation. Our model is the first graph diffusion model

Table 3. Scaffold-Constrained Generation. DiGress serves as a baseline, evaluated on the three smaller scaffolds using its publicly available source code and provided checkpoint.

Scaffold	DiGress	THGD	Improvement (%)
1,4-Dihydroquinoline[a]	46.8	**93.0**	98.7
1,3-Dimethylquinolin-4(1H)-one[b]	35.9	**88.7**	147.0
3-(Trifluoromethyl) aniline[c]	32.3	**94.7**	193.2
Modified-Sildenafil[d]	\	**88.6**	-

[a] https://pubchem.ncbi.nlm.nih.gov/compound/1_4-Dihydroquinoline.
[b] https://pubchem.ncbi.nlm.nih.gov/compound/3-_Trifluoromethyl_aniline.
[c] https://pubchem.ncbi.nlm.nih.gov/compound/1_3-Dimethylquinolin-4_1H_-one.
[d] https://pubchem.ncbi.nlm.nih.gov/compound/Sildenafil.

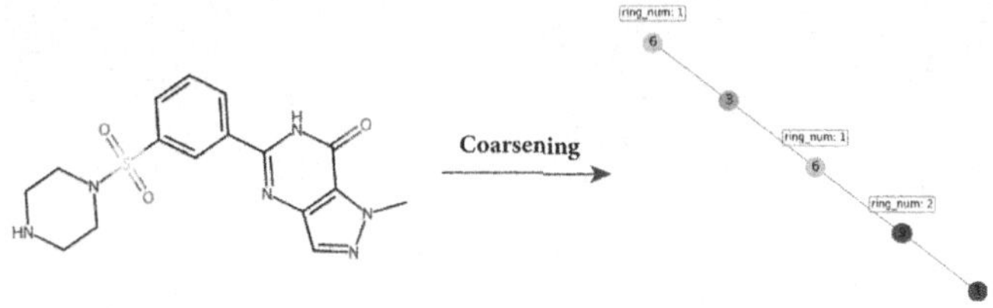

Fig. 6. Modified-Sildenafil and its coarse graph. The scaffold containing 25 atoms, is efficiently represented by only 5 coarse nodes after coarsening.

capable of handling large scaffolds while maintaining high validity. THGD consistently achieves impressive performance with high validity over 88% across all samples, while DiGress struggles with increasingly large scaffolds and fails with the Sildenafil case, underscoring the limitations of atomic-level diffusion in managing long-range dependencies. We further show more examples in Fig. 5.

The key to THGD's success lies in its hierarchical approach, which encodes complex scaffolds into compact coarse graphs with drastically fewer nodes. For example, the modified Sildenafil scaffold, which consists of 25 atoms, is efficiently represented by only 5 coarse nodes, as shown in Fig. 6. This reduction in complexity enables more manageable refinement while preserving scaffold integrity. THGD compactly encodes scaffolds and confines refinement to peripheral regions by adopting a vocabulary-free hierarchical paradigm, ensuring precise structural control and enabling flexible molecular modifications. These capabilities are particularly critical in drug discovery, where maintaining scaffold integrity while exploring chemical diversity is essential for optimizing therapeutic candidates.

6 Conclusion

In this work, we introduced THGD, a Topology-Aware Hierarchical Graph Diffusion Model designed to address the challenges of generating large, structurally complex molecules. Our model innovatively decouples global topology preservation and local atomic refinement through a coarse-to-fine framework, enabling scalable and fine-grained control over molecular graph generation. By leveraging spectral-preserved graph coarsening and type-specific marginal priors, THGD eliminates reliance on predefined motif vocabularies. Experimental results on MOSES and GuacaMol benchmarks demonstrate SOTA performance, achieving an FCD score of 80.26 on GuacaMol and up to 2× higher scaffold validity than previous SOTA model in scaffold-constrained generation tasks. THGD's success highlights the potential of hierarchical diffusion models to revolutionize de novo molecular design, paving the way for more efficient drug discovery pipelines.

Acknowledgments. Thanks to the support of the Super Computing Center of Lanzhou University and Professor Yang Zhang's GPU clusters.

Disclosure of Interests. The authors have no competing interests to declare that are relevant to the content of this article.

References

1. Anderson, W.J.: Continuous-Time Markov Chains: An Applications-Oriented Approach. Springer Science & Business Media (2012)
2. Brown, N., Fiscato, M., Segler, M.H., Vaucher, A.C.: GuacaMol: benchmarking models for de novo molecular design. J. Chem. Inf. Model. **59**(3), 1096–1108 (2019)
3. Dai, H., Tian, Y., Dai, B., Skiena, S., Song, L.: Syntax-directed variational autoencoder for structured data. arXiv preprint arXiv:1802.08786 (2018)
4. De Cao, N., Kipf, T.: MolGAN: an implicit generative model for small molecular graphs. arXiv preprint arXiv:1805.11973 (2018)
5. Gómez-Bombarelli, R., et al.: Automatic chemical design using a data-driven continuous representation of molecules. ACS Cent. Sci. **4**(2), 268–276 (2018)
6. Ho, J., Jain, A., Abbeel, P.: Denoising diffusion probabilistic models. In: Advances in Neural Information Processing Systems, vol. 33, pp. 6840–6851 (2020)
7. Hoogeboom, E., Satorras, V.G., Vignac, C., Welling, M.: Equivariant diffusion for molecule generation in 3D. In: International Conference on Machine Learning, pp. 8867–8887. PMLR (2022)
8. Jensen, J.H.: A graph-based genetic algorithm and generative model/Monte Carlo tree search for the exploration of chemical space. Chem. Sci. **10**(12), 3567–3572 (2019)
9. Jin, W., Barzilay, R., Jaakkola, T.: Junction tree variational autoencoder for molecular graph generation. In: International Conference on Machine Learning, pp. 2323–2332. PMLR (2018)
10. Jin, W., Barzilay, R., Jaakkola, T.: Hierarchical generation of molecular graphs using structural motifs. In: International Conference on Machine Learning, pp. 4839–4848. PMLR (2020)
11. Jo, J., Lee, S., Hwang, S.J.: Score-based generative modeling of graphs via the system of stochastic differential equations. In: International Conference on Machine Learning, pp. 10362–10383. PMLR (2022)
12. Kusner, M.J., Paige, B., Hernández-Lobato, J.M.: Grammar variational autoencoder. In: International Conference on Machine Learning, pp. 1945–1954. PMLR (2017)
13. Kwon, Y., Lee, D., Choi, Y.-S., Shin, K., Kang, S.: Compressed graph representation for scalable molecular graph generation. J. Cheminformatics **12**(1), 1–8 (2020). https://doi.org/10.1186/s13321-020-00463-2
14. Loukas, A.: Graph reduction with spectral and cut guarantees. J. Mach. Learn. Res. **20**(116), 1–42 (2019)
15. Ma, C., Zhang, X.: GF-VAE: a flow-based variational autoencoder for molecule generation. In: Proceedings of the 30th ACM International Conference on Information & Knowledge Management, pp. 1181–1190 (2021)
16. Maziarz, K., et al.: Learning to extend molecular scaffolds with structural motifs. arXiv preprint arXiv:2103.03864 (2021)
17. Mercado, R., et al.: Graph networks for molecular design. Mach. Learn. Sci. Technol. **2**(2), 025023 (2021)
18. Mullard, A., et al.: The drug-maker's guide to the galaxy. Nature **549**(7673), 445–447 (2017)

19. Ninniri, M., Podda, M., Bacciu, D.: Classifier-free graph diffusion for molecular property targeting. In: Joint European Conference on Machine Learning and Knowledge Discovery in Databases, pp. 318–335. Springer (2024)
20. Polykovskiy, D., et al.: Molecular sets (MOSES): a benchmarking platform for molecular generation models. Front. Pharmacol. **11**, 565644 (2020)
21. Simonovsky, M., Komodakis, N.: GraphVAE: towards generation of small graphs using variational autoencoders. In: International Conference on Artificial Neural Networks, pp. 412–422. Springer (2018)
22. Siraudin, A., Malliaros, F.D., Morris, C.: Cometh: A continuous-time discrete-state graph diffusion model. arXiv preprint arXiv:2406.06449 (2024)
23. Sohl-Dickstein, J., Weiss, E., Maheswaranathan, N., Ganguli, S.: Deep unsupervised learning using nonequilibrium thermodynamics. In: International Conference on Machine Learning, pp. 2256–2265. PMLR (2015)
24. Vignac, C., Krawczuk, I., Siraudin, A., Wang, B., Cevher, V., Frossard, P.: DiGress: discrete denoising diffusion for graph generation. arXiv preprint arXiv:2209.14734 (2022)
25. Xu, Z., et al.: Discrete-state continuous-time diffusion for graph generation. arXiv preprint arXiv:2405.11416 (2024)
26. Yang, M., et al.: Echoes of empathy: a symbiotic IoT-based emotion feedback framework for psychological interventions via large language model. IEEE Internet Things J. (2025)
27. Zang, C., Wang, F.: MoFlow: an invertible flow model for generating molecular graphs. In: Proceedings of the 26th ACM SIGKDD International Conference on Knowledge Discovery & Data Mining, pp. 617–626 (2020)

Single-Fold Distillation for Diffusion Models

Chi Hong[1(✉)], Jiyue Huang[1], Robert Birke[2], Dick Epema[1], Stefanie Roos[3], and Lydia Y. Chen[1,4]

[1] TU Delft, Delft, The Netherlands
{c.hong,j.huang-4,D.H.J.Epema}@tudelft.nl, lydiaychen@ieee.org
[2] University of Turin, Turin, Italy
robert.birke@unito.it
[3] RPTU Kaiserslautern-Landau, Mainz, Germany
stefanie.roos@cs.rptu.de
[4] University of Neuchatel, Neuchatel, Switzerland

Abstract. While diffusion models effectively generate remarkable synthetic images, a key limitation is the inference inefficiency, requiring numerous sampling steps. To accelerate inference and maintain high-quality synthesis, teacher-student distillation is applied to compress the diffusion models in a progressive and binary manner by retraining, e.g., reducing the 1024-step model to a 128-step model in 3 folds. In this paper, we propose a single-fold distillation algorithm, SFDDM, which can flexibly compress the teacher diffusion model into a student model of any desired step, based on reparameterization of the intermediate inputs from the teacher model. To train the student diffusion, we minimize not only the output distance but also the distribution of the hidden variables between the teacher and student model. Extensive experiments on four datasets demonstrate that our student model trained by the proposed SFDDM is able to sample high-quality data with steps reduced to less than 1%, thus, trading off inference time. Our remarkable performance highlights that SFDDM effectively transfers knowledge in single-fold distillation, achieving semantic consistency and meaningful image interpolation.

Keywords: knowledge distillation · diffusion models · inference efficiency

1 Introduction

Diffusion models [7,8,23] have emerged as generative models for images of exceptionally high quality without the necessity of conducting adversarial training. A diffusion model constitutes a Markov chain of forward steps of slowly adding random noise to data, followed by a reverse denoising process that gradually reconstructs the data from the noise via trained neural networks. These underlying networks typically use the UNet architecture to better connect the forward steps to the corresponding denoising step. However, such models require large numbers of sampling steps, e.g., 1000 in DDPM [7], which leads to high sampling/inference[1] times, limiting their applications in latency-sensitive applications.

Prior art explored diverse directions to reduce the sampling time of diffusion models and maintain the image synthesis quality. One approach is to reduce the computing complexity by compressing the UNet [11,25] and leverage the acceleration technologies of modern GPUs. Another approach is to reduce the number of sampling steps, i.e., the required UNet inferences. [21] skips intermediate steps by generalizing the original Markovian process via a class of non-Markovian diffusion steps. These two approaches do not change the original training procedure. Differently, progressive distillation [15,19] introduces a teacher-student framework to reduce a trained teacher diffusion model of T steps into a student diffusion of T' steps, where $T' \ll T$, via multiple binary foldings by retraining. For instance, distilling a 1024-step diffusion model into a 128-step model needs first to train a 512-step intermediate model, then a 256-step, to finally arrive to the 128-step model. The distillation objective is to minimize the output differences between the teacher and student models. Progressive distillation better maintains the synthesis quality than step-skipping, but it incurs high distillation time and must comply with specific values of T and T' due to progressive halvings.

Our objective is to design an effective distillation method that achieves high quality in (any) small sampling step and concurrently incurs low distillation time. We propose SFDDM, a single-fold distillation framework able to reduce a T-step teacher diffusion model into a T'-step student diffusion model in a single fold. Thanks to its single-fold nature, SFDDM offers the flexibility to distill the teacher model into a student with any number of steps. To such an end, we first define a new student model, which can extract knowledge of the teacher diffusion model, by an arbitrary steps sub-sequence. Our forward process definition solves the challenge of aligning the variables of teacher and student models, enabling flexible single-fold distillation. Secondly, when training the reverse denoise process of the student model, we minimize not only the difference in the model outputs but also in the hidden variables at each step to better preserve the image synthesis quality.

To demonstrate the effectiveness, we evaluate SFDDM against sampling-skip [21] and progressive distillation [19] on CIFAR-10, CelebA, LSUN-Church, LSUN- Bedroom image datasets and 2D Swiss Roll tabular dataset. We compare their synthesis quality in terms of Fréchet Inception Distance (FID) [6] of distilling a 1024-step diffusion model into 128-step and 16-step models. SFDDM achieves the lowest FID as well as the best perceptual quality, also with flexibility on the numerical relation between the teacher and the student, i.e., works for both 1024 to 128 or 100 steps. Further, the distillation effectiveness is validated on semantic input-output consistency and image interpolation.

We summarize the contributions of this paper as follows:

---

[1] We interchangly use sampling and inference time.

- We propose a novel single-fold distillation algorithm, SFDDM, which can agilely compress teacher diffusion into a student diffusion model of any step in one fold.
- We define a new forward process for student diffusion, which aligns and approximates student and teacher Markovian variables, enabling flexible single-fold distillation.
- We design effective training for student diffusion by minimizing the difference of output and hidden variables with respect to the teacher diffusion.
- We experimentally demonstrate superiority of SFDDM in achieving high-quality sampling data by less than 1% number of steps.

2 Related Studies

Diffusion models [5,7,8,12,17,23] first step-wise destroy in a forward process the training data structure and then learn how to restore the data structure from noise in a reverse process. DDPM [7] proposed the first stable and effective implementation capable of high-quality image synthesis. However, diffusion models, including DDPM, suffer from slow inference stemming from immense intermediate hidden variables, each the size of the synthetic output, as well as the complex architecture. This sparked research on how to accelerate data synthesis with related work exploring three main directions.

Fast Sampling. Diffusion models mostly rely on an UNet [18] architecture combining cross-attention and ResNet blocks for denoising. Fast sampling [11,25] facilitates the reverse process by optimizing the computations of UNets. [11] proposes an efficient UNet by identifying the redundancy of the original model and reducing the computation, while [25] further comprehensively analyzes and simplifies each component. These optimizations are orthogonal to other acceleration techniques.

Sampling Step Skipping. DDIM [21] focuses on generalizing the Markovian diffusion of DDPM via a family of non-Markovian processes. These are deterministic and thus faster. Accordingly, it is able to reduce the required number of sampling steps on the trained DDPM model, without necessity of retraining. A noticeable limitation is that DDIM trades off the quality of generated data. as DDIM sampling approximates the procedure of the original model with skipped intermediate steps.

Knowledge Distillation. Previously explored for GANs [4,13], distillation [1,3] allows to transfer knowledge from a large trained teacher model to a smaller student model for faster inference. To train a student model, progressive distillation [19] halves repeatedly the steps of a teacher model until the desired number of steps has been reached. [15] further extends the folding optimization to classifier-free guided diffusion implementation of Text-to-Image tasks. Although progressive distillation delivers increasingly efficient inference, each halving requires to train a new student model which multiples the training effort and impacts the output quality due to added approximation noise at each folding. Consistency models are proposed to improve the sample quality with few steps [22]. A consistency model can be directly trained or obtained by distilling a trained teacher model.

3 Single-Fold Distillation

We rethink knowledge distillation of diffusion models to reduce the number of sampling steps by proposing single-fold distillation. Instead of progressive multiple folds [19], which introduces distortion and costs extra training effort at each fold, SFDDM directly distills the teacher model to a student model with a given number of steps in a single fold. One crucial challenge is the alignment from the teacher's to the student's hidden variables, as the Markov chain is defined by every two consecutive variables but the student has much fewer steps.

We first introduce the preliminaries of a DDPM model used as a teacher model, including the definition of the forward/reverse process and the training objective. Then we present SFDDM which defines the forward and reverse process of the student by aligning and matching the hidden variables of the teacher. Finally, we design the distillation algorithm for deployment, which shows the training procedure of the student accordingly. For ease of presentation, we set the number of steps in the student model as a divisor of the number of steps in the teacher model, but the method is valid for an arbitrary number of student steps, i.e. fractional teacher/student step ratios.

3.1 Preliminary

DDPM is composed of a reverse (denoising) and a forward (noising) process, through T steps. Its objective is to learn the denoising process via a given forward process.

Reverse Process: The optimization objective of diffusion models [20] is derived by variational inference. Given the observed data $\boldsymbol{x}_0$, the diffusion model is a probabilistic model which specifies the joint distribution $p_\theta(\boldsymbol{x}_{0:T})$, where $\boldsymbol{x}_1, ..., \boldsymbol{x}_T$ are latent variables with the same dimensions as $\boldsymbol{x}_0$, and θ are learnable model parameters. $p_\theta(\boldsymbol{x}_{0:T})$ is a Markov chain that samples from $\boldsymbol{x}_T$ to $\boldsymbol{x}_0$, $p_\theta(\boldsymbol{x}_{0:T}) := p_\theta(\boldsymbol{x}_T) \prod_{t=1}^{T} p_\theta(\boldsymbol{x}_{t-1} \mid \boldsymbol{x}_t)$. DDPM assumes that $p_\theta(\boldsymbol{x}_T) = \mathcal{N}(\boldsymbol{x}_T; \boldsymbol{0}, \boldsymbol{I})$ and

$$p_\theta(\boldsymbol{x}_{t-1} \mid \boldsymbol{x}_t) = \mathcal{N}(\boldsymbol{x}_{t-1}; \boldsymbol{\mu}_\theta(\boldsymbol{x}_t, t), \sigma_t^2 \boldsymbol{I}),$$

where $\sigma_t \in \mathbb{R}_{\geq 0}$. $p_\theta(\boldsymbol{x}_{0:T})$ is called the *reverse process*. It gradually denoises a noise $\boldsymbol{x}_T \sim \mathcal{N}(\boldsymbol{0}, \boldsymbol{I})$.

Forward Process: To derive a lower bound on the log likelihood of the observed data, diffusion models introduce the approximate posterior $q(\boldsymbol{x}_{1:T} \mid \boldsymbol{x}_0)$ which is a Markov chain, $q(\boldsymbol{x}_{1:T} \mid \boldsymbol{x}_0) := \prod_{t=1}^{T} q(\boldsymbol{x}_t \mid \boldsymbol{x}_{t-1})$, that samples from $\boldsymbol{x}_1$ to $\boldsymbol{x}_T$. Then the log data likelihood can be decomposed as

$$\mathbb{E}\left[\log p_\theta(\boldsymbol{x}_0)\right] = \mathbb{E}_q\left[\log \frac{p_\theta(\boldsymbol{x}_{0:T})}{q(\boldsymbol{x}_{1:T} \mid \boldsymbol{x}_0)}\right] + D_{\mathrm{KL}}\left(q(\boldsymbol{x}_{1:T} \mid \boldsymbol{x}_0) \| p_\theta(\boldsymbol{x}_{1:T} \mid \boldsymbol{x}_0)\right).$$

Thus, we have the lower bound $\mathbb{E}\left[\log p_\theta(\boldsymbol{x}_0)\right] \geq \mathbb{E}_q\left[\log \frac{p_\theta(\boldsymbol{x}_{0:T})}{q(\boldsymbol{x}_{1:T} \mid \boldsymbol{x}_0)}\right]$. When training the diffusion model, to maximize $\mathbb{E}\left[\log p_\theta(\boldsymbol{x}_0)\right]$, the parameters θ are learned to minimize the negative evidence lower bound:

$$\arg\min_\theta \mathbb{E}_q\left[\log q(\boldsymbol{x}_{1:T} \mid \boldsymbol{x}_0) - \log p_\theta(\boldsymbol{x}_{0:T})\right]. \tag{1}$$

The Markov chain $q(\boldsymbol{x}_{1:T} \mid \boldsymbol{x}_0)$ is called the *forward process*. It progressively turns the data x_0 into noise. The conditional distribution in each forward step is defined as:

$$q(\boldsymbol{x}_t \mid \boldsymbol{x}_{t-1}) := \mathcal{N}\left(\boldsymbol{x}_t; \sqrt{\frac{\alpha_t}{\alpha_{t-1}}} x_{t-1}, \left(1 - \frac{\alpha_t}{\alpha_{t-1}}\right)\boldsymbol{I}\right), \tag{2}$$

where $\alpha_t \in (0,1]$ and $\alpha_1, ..., \alpha_T$ is a decreasing sequence, which ensures that the values on the diagonal of the covariance matrix are positive. Reparameterizing using the definition in Eq. (2), an important property of the forward process is that:

$$q(\boldsymbol{x}_t \mid \boldsymbol{x}_0) = \mathcal{N}(\boldsymbol{x}_t; \sqrt{\alpha_t}\boldsymbol{x}_0, (1-\alpha_t)\boldsymbol{I}). \tag{3}$$

Training and Sampling: According to the definition of the reverse p and forward q processes, α_t and σ_t for all t are not learnable parameters. Thus, DDPM simplifies Eq. (1) as:

$$\arg\min_\theta \sum_t \mathbb{E}_q[D_{\mathrm{KL}}(q(x_{t-1} \mid \boldsymbol{x}_t, \boldsymbol{x}_0) \| p_\theta(\boldsymbol{x}_{t-1} \mid \boldsymbol{x}_t))]. \tag{4}$$

DDPM further chooses the form of $\boldsymbol{\mu}_\theta(\boldsymbol{x}_t, t)$ to be:

$$\boldsymbol{\mu}_\theta(\boldsymbol{x}_t, t) = \frac{1}{\sqrt{\frac{\alpha_t}{\alpha_{t-1}}}}\left(\boldsymbol{x}_t - \frac{1-\frac{\alpha_t}{\alpha_{t-1}}}{\sqrt{1-\alpha_t}}\epsilon_\theta(\boldsymbol{x}_t, t)\right), \tag{5}$$

where ϵ_θ is a function with trainable parameters θ. According to the above definitions of the forward and reverse processes and applying the parameterization shown in Eq. (5), Eq. (4) can be simplified as $\arg\min_\theta L(\theta)$, where:

$$L(\theta) := \sum_{t=1}^{T} \mathbb{E}_{\boldsymbol{x}_0, \epsilon_t}\left[\gamma_t \left\|\epsilon_t - \epsilon_\theta\left(\sqrt{\alpha_t}\boldsymbol{x}_0 + \sqrt{1-\alpha_t}\epsilon_t, t\right)\right\|^2\right] \tag{6}$$

with $\gamma_t = \frac{(\alpha_{t-1}-\alpha_t)^2}{2\sigma_t^2\alpha_t\alpha_{t-1}(1-\alpha_t)}$ and $\epsilon_t \sim \mathcal{N}(\boldsymbol{0}, \boldsymbol{I})$. It is important to note that when deriving this loss, DDPM reparameterize $\boldsymbol{x}_t$ as

$$\boldsymbol{x}_t = \sqrt{\alpha_t}\boldsymbol{x}_0 + \sqrt{1-\alpha_t}\epsilon_t, \tag{7}$$

using the property in Eq. (3). DDPM further simplifies L by setting $\gamma_t = 1$ independent of $\alpha_{1:T}$.

The number of sampling steps T decides the generalization capability and sampling cost of diffusion models. A big T leads to a reverse process with high generalization capability that better captures the pattern of x_0. However, it also increases the sampling time and makes the sampling from DDPMs significantly slower than other generative models, e.g., GANs. Such inefficiency promotes our design of SFDDM to reduce the number of sampling steps via knowledge distillation.

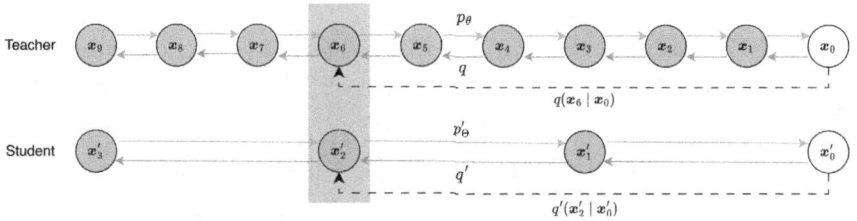

Fig. 1. Single-Fold Distillation of Diffusion Model (SFDDM). The student accelerates the inference by a small number of steps T' instead of a large T. We use $T = 9$ and $T' = 3$ in the figure for readability. To align the teacher and student Markov chains, we propose to match the intermediate hidden variables to make, e.g., $q'(x'_2 = x_6 | x'_0 = x_0)$ equal to $q(x_6 | x_0)$.

3.2 Single-Fold Distilled Diffusion (SFDDM)

Instead of multiple folds like progressive distillation, which introduces distortion at every fold by retraining, we want to extract knowledge from the teacher model through a single fold. The first consideration is aligning steps from a T-step teacher to steps of a given smaller T'-step student. Here, our goal is to distill the knowledge of the teacher model by mimicking its hidden variables $(x_1, ..., x_T)$ by a compressed student model[2] with hidden variables $(x'_1, ..., x'_{T'})$, where $T' \ll T$.

A crucial challenge stems from the need to map a subset of multiple consecutive steps at the teacher into one single step at the student (see Fig. 1). For example, given an index[3] $c \cdot t$, where $c = T/T'$ and $c \in \mathbb{Z}$, according to Sect. 3.1, the distributions we can explicitly obtain from the teacher are $q(x_{c \cdot t} | x_{c \cdot t - 1})$ (see Eq. 2). However, mapping x'_t with $x_{c \cdot t}$ from the student to the teacher does not hold for the next step, i.e., x'_{t-1} does not correspond to $x_{c \cdot t - 1}$, which is supposed to map $x_{c(t-1)}$. Thus, when distilling the DDPM-like Markov chains, it is not reasonable to simply and straightforwardly simulate $q'(x'_t | x'_{t-1})$ as $q(x_{c \cdot t} | x_{c \cdot t - 1})$

---

[2] Hereon we use "'" in symbols to indicate the corresponding student variables.
[3] For simplicity, we assume that T is divisible by T' but this is not necessary (see Sect. 3.6).

while correspondingly estimating $p'_\Theta(x'_t|x'_{t-1})$ as $p_\theta(x_{c\cdot t}|x_{c\cdot t-1})$, where the notations q' and p'_Θ are used to represent the forward process and reverse process of the student model, respectively.

To overcome this challenge, we define a novel student model as follows. Note that the key definition for diffusion models is the forward process, as it determines the variational inference and dominates the training of the model. Therefore, to better distill the knowledge from the teacher, we design the forward process of the student $q'\left(x'_{1:T'} \mid x'_0\right)$ by extracting the teacher's forward process $q\left(x_{1:T} \mid x_0\right)$. Specifically, to ensure correspondence between the latent variables in the two diffusion models, given any $t \in [1, T']$, the proposed distillation algorithm **aims** to make $q'(x'_t = x_{c\cdot t} \mid x'_0 = x_0)$ equal to $q(x_{c\cdot t}|x_0)$, which has a close-form solution (see Eq. 3). After fixing q' by such an approximation in the forward process, the reverse process of the student is constructed accordingly. In the following, we show in detail how to define and train a student model.

3.3 The Forward Process of the Student Model

To distill the DDPM teacher, we also assume that the student model has a Markovian forward process. Thus $q'\left(x'_{1:T'} \mid x'_0\right)$ is a Markov chain that can be factorized as

$$q'\left(x'_{1:T'} \mid x'_0\right) := \prod_{t=1}^{T'} q'\left(x'_t \mid x'_{t-1}\right).$$

As shown in Eq. (2), the forward process of the teacher is defined by a decreasing sequence $\alpha_1, ..., \alpha_T$. As for the student, different from the Gaussian distribution shown in Eq. (2), we set the student's forward process to the following form:

$$q'\left(x'_t \mid x'_{t-1}\right) := \mathcal{N}\left(x'_t; \sqrt{\frac{\alpha_{c\cdot t}}{\alpha_{c\cdot t-c}}} x'_{t-1}, \left(1 - \frac{\alpha_{c\cdot t}}{\alpha_{c\cdot t-c}}\right) I\right), \tag{8}$$

for all $t \in [1, T']$ based on the elements of the sequence $\{\alpha_t\}_{t=1}^T$ (the hyperparameters of the given teacher). Then, according to this forward process definition of the student, we have the property:

$$q'(x'_t \mid x'_0) = \mathcal{N}\left(x'_t; \sqrt{\alpha_{c\cdot t}} x'_0, (1 - \alpha_{c\cdot t}) I\right). \tag{9}$$

This **ensures** that $q'(x'_t = x_{c\cdot t} \mid x'_0 = x_0) = q(x_{c\cdot t}|x_0)$, where x'_t corresponds to $x_{c\cdot t}$. Thus, the student's Markov chain $q'\left(x'_{1:T'} \mid x'_0\right)$ can be regarded as a simplified copy of the teacher's forward process $q\left(x_{1:T} \mid x_0\right)$.

Before introducing the reverse process, we derive some important forward process posteriors. Using Bayes' rule $q'\left(x'_{t-1} \mid x'_t, x'_0\right) = q'\left(x'_t \mid x'_{t-1}, x'_0\right) \frac{q'(x'_{t-1}|x'_0)}{q'(x'_t|x'_0)}$, and the Markov chain property that $q'\left(x'_t \mid x'_{t-1}, x'_0\right) = q'\left(x'_t \mid x'_{t-1}\right)$, we have the posteriors:

$$q'\left(x'_{t-1} \mid x'_t, x'_0\right) = \mathcal{N}(x'_{t-1}; \frac{(1-\alpha_{c\cdot t-c})\sqrt{\alpha_{c\cdot t}}}{(1-\alpha_{c\cdot t})\sqrt{\alpha_{c\cdot t-c}}} x'_t + \frac{\alpha_{c\cdot t-c} - \alpha_{c\cdot t}}{(1-\alpha_{c\cdot t})\sqrt{\alpha_{c\cdot t-c}}} x'_0, \sigma'_t I), \tag{10}$$

where $\sigma'_t = \frac{(1-\alpha_{c\cdot t-c})(\alpha_{c\cdot t-c}-\alpha_{c\cdot t})}{(1-\alpha_{c\cdot t})\alpha_{c\cdot t-c}}$.

3.4 The Reverse Process of the Student Model

In the following, we define the reverse process of the student model according to its forward process. Similarly, it is also a Markov chain represented as $p'_\Theta(x'_{0:T'}) := p'_\Theta(x'_{T'}) \prod_{t=1}^{T'} p'_\Theta(x'_{t-1} \mid x'_t)$, where $p'_\Theta(x'_{T'}) = \mathcal{N}(0, I)$ and Θ represents the learnable parameters of the student.

Then, we decide the form of $p'_\Theta(x'_{t-1} \mid x'_t)$. Referring to Eq. (9), we can reparameterize x'_t as a linear combination of x'_0 and $\epsilon_t \sim \mathcal{N}(0, I)$ that is $x'_t = \sqrt{\alpha_{c \cdot t}} x'_0 + \sqrt{1 - \alpha_{c \cdot t}} \epsilon_t$. Let the model $\epsilon'_\Theta(x'_t, t)$ predict ϵ_t, we have a prediction of x'_0 given x'_t:

$$f^{(t)}_\Theta(x'_t) := \left(x'_t - \sqrt{1 - \alpha_{c \cdot t}} \cdot \epsilon'_\Theta(x'_t, t)\right) / \sqrt{\alpha_{c \cdot t}} \tag{11}$$

According to Eq. (4), we know that in the student diffusion model, $p'_\Theta(x'_{t-1} \mid x'_t)$ is a distribution that predicts $q'(x'_{t-1} \mid x'_t, x'_0)$. Thus, we define that for all $t \in [1, T']$,

$$p'_\Theta(x'_{t-1} \mid x'_t) = q'(x'_{t-1} \mid x'_t, f^{(t)}_\Theta(x'_t)). \tag{12}$$

Then, based on Eq. (10) and Eq. (12), by replacing x'_0 as the predictor $f^{(t)}_\Theta(x'_t)$, we have:

$$p'_\Theta(x'_{t-1} \mid x'_t) = \mathcal{N}(x'_{t-1}; \mu'_\Theta(x'_t, t), \sigma'^2_t I), \tag{13}$$

where the mean is:

$$\mu'_\Theta(x'_t, t) = \frac{(1 - \alpha_{ct-c})\sqrt{\alpha_{ct}}}{(1 - \alpha_{ct})\sqrt{\alpha_{ct-c}}} x'_t + \frac{\alpha_{ct-c} - \alpha_{ct}}{(1 - \alpha_{ct})\sqrt{\alpha_{ct-c}}} f^{(t)}_\Theta(x'_t). \tag{14}$$

3.5 Distillation Procedure

Having defined the forward and reverse processes, here we design the algorithm for training the student model. The reparameterization of $\mu'_\Theta(x'_t, t)$ shown in Eq. (14) can be applied to derive the training loss of the student. For maximizing the log data likelihood of the observed data $\{x'_0\}$ on the student[4], referring to Eq. (4), it is equivalent to minimize the Kullback-Leibler divergence between Eq. (10) and Eq. (13). Then by using Eq. (10), (13), (14) and (11), we have the following loss for training the student:

$$L(\Theta) := \sum_{t=1}^{T} \mathbb{E}_{x'_0, \epsilon'_t} \left[\gamma'_t \left\| \epsilon'_t - \epsilon_\Theta\left(\sqrt{\alpha_{c \cdot t}} x'_0 + \sqrt{1 - \alpha_{c \cdot t}} \epsilon'_t, t\right) \right\|^2 \right], \tag{15}$$

where $\gamma'_t = \frac{(\alpha_{c \cdot t - c} - \alpha_{c \cdot t})^2}{2\sigma'^2_t \alpha_{c \cdot t} \alpha_{c \cdot t - c}(1 - \alpha_{c \cdot t})}$. By the loss (Eq. 15), we can train the defined student model from scratch using the observed data $\{x'_0\}$. However, in order to

---

[4] In distillation, student and teacher observe the same training samples. Thus, x'_0 always equals x_0 and $\{x'_0\}$ is equivalent to $\{x_0\}$. To avoid confusion, we use $\{x'_0\}$ to represent the observed data when training the student.

extract the knowledge from the trained teacher, in the following we connect the training of the student with the trained teacher.

In the derivation of the loss $L(\Theta)$ (Eq. 15), we use the following reparameterization:
$$x'_t = \sqrt{\alpha_{c \cdot t}} x'_0 + \sqrt{1 - \alpha_{c \cdot t}} \epsilon'_t. \tag{16}$$

According to Eq. (7), we know that $x_{c \cdot t} = \sqrt{\alpha_{c \cdot t}} x_0 + \sqrt{1 - \alpha_{c \cdot t}} \epsilon_{c \cdot t}$. In our distillation, we want to make the hidden variable x'_t of the student equal to its corresponding hidden variable $x_{c \cdot t}$ of the teacher. As the student and the teacher use the same observed data, $x'_0 = x_0$, by Eq. (16), if we assume $\epsilon'_t = \epsilon_{c \cdot t}$, then we can have $x'_t = x_{c \cdot t}$. By the training loss of the teacher $L(\theta)$ (Eq. 6), we know that the output $\epsilon_\theta \left(\sqrt{\alpha_{c \cdot t}} x_0 + \sqrt{1 - \alpha_{c \cdot t}} \epsilon_{c \cdot t}, c \cdot t \right)$ from the trained function ϵ_θ of the teacher is a good predictor for $\epsilon_{c \cdot t}$ (also for ϵ'_t). Thus, we naturally rewrite the student loss (Eq. 15) as

$$L(\Theta) := \sum_{t=1}^{T} \mathbb{E}_{x'_0, \epsilon'_t} [\gamma'_t \| \epsilon_\theta \left(\sqrt{\alpha_{c \cdot t}} x'_0 + \sqrt{1 - \alpha_{c \cdot t}} \epsilon'_t, c \cdot t \right) \\ - \epsilon_\Theta \left(\sqrt{\alpha_{c \cdot t}} x'_0 + \sqrt{1 - \alpha_{c \cdot t}} \epsilon'_t, t \right) \|^2]. \tag{17}$$

Training: For distillation, we train the student according to the loss (Eq. 17). During the implementation in Sect. 4, we simplify the loss by setting $\gamma'_t = 1$, a simpler approach shown beneficial for sample quality.

Sampling: We need an input noise $x'_{T'}$ when sampling images from the trained student. The straightforward way is to draw the noise by $x'_{T'} \sim \mathcal{N}(\mathbf{0}, \mathbf{I})$. Reducing the number of sampling steps can negatively impact a model's generalization ability. To avoid the risk of generating poor-quality images from certain input sample points when performing direct random sampling from $\mathcal{N}(\mathbf{0}, \mathbf{I})$, we propose a method to reduce the sampling space of $x'_{T'}$. This approach ensures that the student model maintains strong performance even with fewer sampling steps (e.g., 4 steps), preserving high-quality outputs while improving efficiency. For a distilled student model, a high-quality input noise set $\{\hat{x}'\}$ can be obtained by $\arg\min_{\hat{x}'} \| StudentDiffusion(\hat{x}') - x'_0 \|$. A random linear weighted combination of elements from this set will be used for the random sampling of $x'_{T'}$.

Since the reverse process of the student is defined by Eq. (13), given the input $x'_{T'}$, we can steadily sample all variables from $x'_{T'-1}$ to x'_0. Note that the student model is also a DDPM model. Any sampling algorithm compatible with DDPM can be applied to the distilled student.

3.6 Distillation on Flexible Sub-sequence

In the previous derivation, the student extracts the knowledge from a special variable subset $\{x_{c \cdot t}\}$ of the teacher where $t \in [1, T']$. Indeed, our proposed method can be extended to a more general case where we distill the knowledge from any given subset $\{x_{\phi_0}, ..., x_{\phi_{T'}}\}$ of the teacher where ϕ is an increasing subsequence of $\{0, ..., T\}$, $\phi_0 = 0$ and $\phi_{T'} = T$. In this general case, the Gaussian mean of $p'_\Theta (x'_{t-1} \mid x'_t)$ (see Eq. 13) is

$$\mu'_\Theta (x'_t, t) = \frac{(1-\alpha_{\phi_{t-1}})\sqrt{\alpha_{\phi_t}}}{(1-\alpha_{\phi_t})\sqrt{\alpha_{\phi_{t-1}}}} x'_t + \frac{\alpha_{\phi_{t-1}} - \alpha_{\phi_t}}{(1-\alpha_{\phi_t})\sqrt{\alpha_{\phi_{t-1}}}} \mathcal{F}^{(t)}_\Theta (x'_t),$$

where $\mathcal{F}^{(t)}_\Theta (x'_t) := \left(x'_t - \sqrt{1-\alpha_{\phi_t}} \cdot \epsilon'_\Theta (x'_t, t) \right) / \sqrt{\alpha_{\phi_t}}$ is a prediction of x'_0 given x'_t. Remarkably, T no longer needs to be divisible by T'. This extension is beneficial as it greatly expands the applicability of our distillation under various steps of teacher diffusion models.

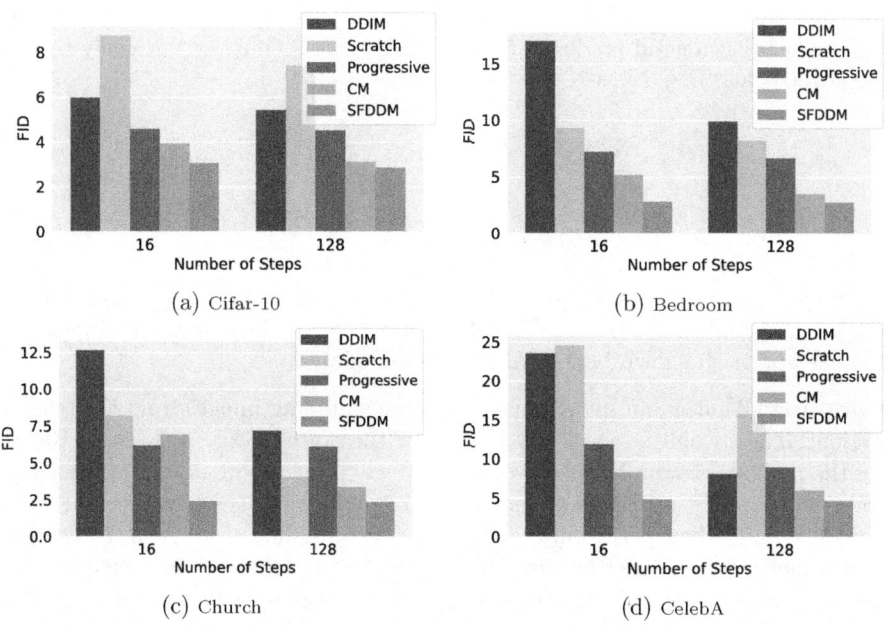

Fig. 2. FID under different number of sampling steps from the teacher $T = 1024$, on four datasets.

4 Evaluation

SFDDM distills the knowledge of any arbitrary DDPM-like teacher models with efficiency and high sampling quality. We demonstrate its effectiveness by four image benchmark datasets: CIFAR-10 [10], CelebA [14], LSUN-Church and LSUN-Bedroom [24], as well as one tabular dataset: 2D Swiss Roll following the diffusion model settings [16]. For each image dataset, we distill the same teacher diffusion model of DDPM into 16, 100, or 128 student steps. Note that although the original DDPM contains 1000 sampling steps, in this paper, we set it as 1024 steps in order to compare with progressive distillation [19], which requires a number of steps that is a power of 2 for progressive halving. For the 2D Swiss Roll dataset, we distill a teacher model with 500 steps into a student with 50 steps by SFDDM. The evaluation metric applied is FID together with perceptual visualization of sampled images.

4.1 Experimental Setups

Our evaluation is carried out by Alienware-Aurora-R13 with Ubuntu 20.04. The machine is equipped with 64G memory, 4× GeForce RTX 3090 GPU and 16-core Intel i9 CPU. Each of the 8 P-cores has two threads, hence each machine contains 24 logical CPU cores in total. We consider various image generation benchmarks (CIFAR-10, CelebA, LSUN-Bedroom, LSUN-Church), with resolution varying from 32×32 to 128×128. All experiments for the teacher diffusion model use the sigmoid schedule, particularly good for large images, following the settings of [9] and all models use a UNet architecture same as DDPM [7]. Our schedule of the student model is defined in Sect. 3.3 accordingly. Our training setup closely matches the open source code by DDPM. For the training of the student model, we choose Adam optimizer with learning rate fixed to 2×10^{-5} while other hyper-parameters remain the same as the default setting of PyTorch Adam. An interesting observation on SFDDM is that experimentally using l_1 norm on L_Θ leads to faster convergence comparing to l_2 norm. FID scores are computed across 10K images.

4.2 Sampling Quality and Efficiency

To demonstrate the quality and efficiency of SFDDM, we report the FID in Fig. 2 on all four image datasets comparing against DDIM, progressive distillation ("Progressive"), Consistency model (CM) [22], and training directly on the smaller model with the same dataset as the teacher model ("From scratch").

In general, our SFDDM achieves the best FID over different datasets and different small T'. From the results, we observe that the sampling data quality increases with the increase of T', as more sampling steps match more hidden variables of the teacher model, better approximating the teacher distributions.

Comparing the baselines, DDIM achieves mostly the lowest quality in sampled images as shown by high FID scores. This stems from the nature that DDIM **does not** retrain a student model but focuses on improving the inference efficiency of the original model. Thus, it benefits from simplicity but falls short in terms of quality, when skipping too many intermediate steps during sampling, e.g., $T' = 16$. On the other hand, training from scratch on a small diffusion model comes in as the second worst in terms of FID, due to the difficulty of capturing image features with a small number of steps. Progressive distillation yields marginal improvement as multiple folding and retraining increases distortion from teacher knowledge due to noises it introduces at each folding. An interesting finding emerges in the context of the LSUN-Church dataset with 128 sampling steps. Here, training from scratch surpasses progressive distillation in FID performance. This can be attributed to the fact that, with a relatively large

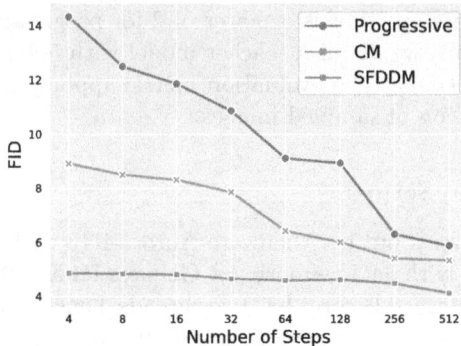

Fig. 3. FID of the methods with different number of sampling steps on CelebA-HQ.

number of steps, direct training exhibits superior quality compared to progressive distillation, where systematic distortion occurs fold by fold. This is consistent with the conclusion in [19]. We also compare the student FID for progressive distillation, CM, and SFDDM with varying sampling steps from 4 to 512 in Fig. 3. Overall, SFDDM consistently outperforms the baselines. We also visualize the corresponding student model output of step 4 and 16 in Fig. 4, demonstrating limited quality loss of small sampling steps by SFDDM.

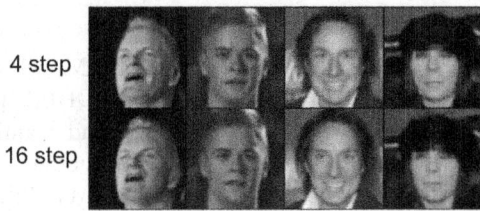

Fig. 4. Visualizied images generated by student model of SFDDM on CelebA-HQ.

4.3 Distillation with Different Sub-sequences

In accordance with Sect. 3.6, our algorithm can be extended to accommodate flexible sub-sequences of the student model. Here, we compare FID values for different choices to demonstrate their impact. Specifically, the different cases of flexible sub-sequence are designed by various degrees of concentration of mapped steps around the midpoint element. We define it by the percentage of elements distributed uniformly within a 5% range near the midpoint element (i.e., 512) while the others are uniformly distributed in the remaining range of steps. Moreover, In our results presented in Tab. 1, we include the concentration degrees of 40%, 20%, plus Scattered. "Scattered" refers to the student model matching a sparse sub-sequence spread across the full teacher Markov chain. Scattered allows to cover more knowledge of the noising/denoising procedure form the teacher. Yet, concentrated choices, in which elements are nearby and centered in a partial part of the teacher chain, are still able to distill high-quality diffusion models, as shown by similarity in FID scores.

Table 1. Distilling the same teacher with different sub-sequences on CelebA-HQ with $T' = 16$.

sub-sequence	Concentrated (40%)	Concentrated (20%)	Scattered
FID	4.85	4.69	4.82

Fig. 5. Consistency on CelebA-HQ, LSUN-Bedroom and LSUN-Church: inputing the same noise.

4.4 Consistency Between Teacher and Student

We zoom into the consistency between images sampled by the teacher and student models when inputting identical noise. It is important to note that for a fair comparison of the distillation results, we use the DDIM sampling method (also applied in Sect. 4.5) for both the DDPM teacher and our SFDDM student. This is because the output of the original DDPM sampling is not solely determined by the input noise, owing to the introduced random factor during the stochastic generative process. In contrast, DDIM sampling ensures pair correspondence, i.e., same input, same output, facilitating a clear and accurate comparison. The outcomes across three distinct datasets are illustrated in Fig. 5. It is noteworthy that we employ different sampling steps for the student among different datasets, thereby validating the flexibility of our approach under varying numbers of subsequences, where the number of steps is not a power of 2. As evidenced by the images, it is clearly observed that inputting identical noise leads to similar outputs, showing our effectiveness in transferring knowledge from the teacher to a student having only approximately 1/10 of the steps.

4.5 Interpolation on the Teacher and the Student

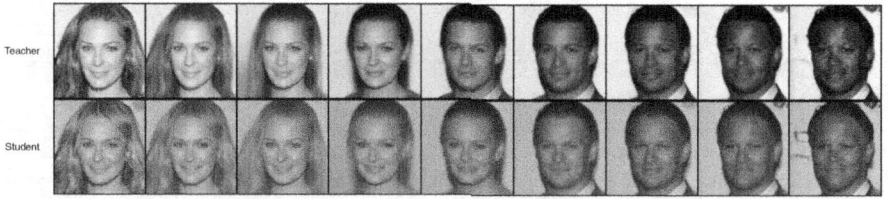

Fig. 6. Interpolation on the distilled student and original teacher.

We further assess the efficacy of knowledge transfer through measuring the similarity of semantic interpolation between the teacher and student models. We evenly interpolate between two given noises to showcase the intermediate sampled data in Fig. 6. The results reveal a stable visual interpolation in the generated images since the input noise encodes distinctive high-level features of the image. Consequently, the interpolation data implicitly captures the features between the two noises into perceptually similar outputs. When comparing the output of the teacher and student, we observe similarity in each interpolation, showcasing the effectiveness of distillation as the student successfully inherits a stable and consistent sampling capability from the teacher.

4.6 Distillating Tabular Data

To assess the generality and applicability of SFDDM among different types of data, we apply SFDDM on the tabular 2D Swiss Roll dataset, visualized in Fig. 7. On this tabular DDPM, the forward process turns Swiss Roll-like points into randomly distributed 2D points. Contrarily, the reverse process constructs a Swiss Roll distribution according to randomly distributed points. Figure 7 presents the forward process of both teacher and student models. The results show that our

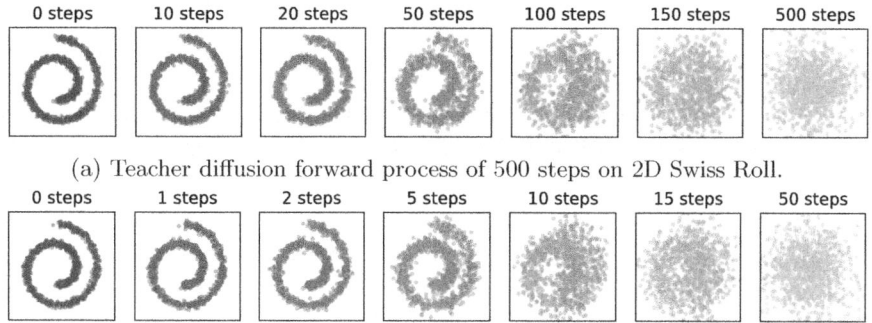

(a) Teacher diffusion forward process of 500 steps on 2D Swiss Roll.

(b) Student diffusion forward process of 50 steps on 2D Swiss Roll.

Fig. 7. Forward process of teacher and SFDDM student model on 2D Swiss Roll dataset.

proposed algorithm SFDDM works on DDPM for distilling the generation of tabular data by demonstrating the similar capability of generating 2D Swiss Roll points with student sampling steps 10x fewer than the teacher diffusion.

5 Conclusion

In this paper, we propose a novel and effective single-fold distillation method for diffusion models, SFDDM. In contrast to the prior study of progressive distillation, SFDDM is able to compress any T-step teacher model into any T'-step student model in single-fold distillation. The key enabling features are (i) new derivation of the forwarding process of the student model, which leverages the reparameterization of the teacher model and approximation of their Markovian states; and (ii) optimization of the denoise process of the student model by minimizing the difference of model outputs and distribution of the hidden variables. Our evaluation results on five datasets show that SFDDM achieves remarkable quality on FID, allowing to strike better quality-compute tradeoffs.

Acknowledgments. This research is part of the Priv-GSyn project, 200021E_229204 of Swiss National Science Foundation and the DEPMAT project, P20-22 / N21022, of the research programme Perspectief which is partly financed by the Dutch Research Council (NWO). This research was partly funded by the Spoke "FutureHPC & BigData" of the ICSC-Centro Nazionale di Ricerca in "High Performance Computing, Big Data and Quantum Computing", funded by the European Union - NextGenerationEU, and by the DYMAN project funded by the European Union - European Innovation Council under G.A. n. 101161930.

Disclosure of Interests. The authors have no competing interests to declare that are relevant to the content of this article.

References

1. Asadi, N., Davari, M., Mudur, S., Aljundi, R., Belilovsky, E.: Prototype-sample relation distillation: Towards replay-free continual learning. In: International Conference on Machine Learning, ICML 2023, 23-29 July 2023, Honolulu, Hawaii, USA. Proceedings of Machine Learning Research, vol. 202, pp. 1093–1106. PMLR (2023)
2. Bishop, C.: Pattern recognition and machine learning. Springer google scholar **2**, 531–537 (2006)
3. Cao, S., Li, M., Hays, J., Ramanan, D., Wang, Y., Gui, L.: Learning lightweight object detectors via multi-teacher progressive distillation. In: International Conference on Machine Learning, ICML 2023, 23-29 July 2023, Honolulu, Hawaii, USA. Proceedings of Machine Learning Research, vol. 202, pp. 3577–3598. PMLR (2023)
4. Cazenavette, G., Wang, T., Torralba, A., Efros, A.A., Zhu, J.: Generalizing dataset distillation via deep generative prior. In: IEEE/CVF Conference on Computer Vision and Pattern Recognition, CVPR 2023, Vancouver, BC, Canada, 17-24 June 2023. pp. 3739–3748. IEEE (2023)
5. Han, J., Feng, S., Zhou, M., Zhang, X., Ong, Y.S., Li, X.: Diffusion model in normal gathering latent space for time series anomaly detection. In: Bifet, A., Davis, J., Krilavičius, T., Kull, M., Ntoutsi, E., Žliobaitė, I. (eds.) Machine Learning and Knowledge Discovery in Databases. Research Track. ECML PKDD 2024. LNCS, vol. 14943. Springer, Cham (2024). https://doi.org/10.1007/978-3-031-70352-2_17
6. Heusel, M., Ramsauer, H., Unterthiner, T., Nessler, B., Hochreiter, S.: Gans trained by a two time-scale update rule converge to a local nash equilibrium. In: Guyon, I., et al (eds.) Advances in Neural Information Processing Systems 30: Annual Conference on Neural Information Processing Systems 2017, 4-9 December 2017, Long Beach, CA, USA, pp. 6626–6637 (2017)
7. Ho, J., Jain, A., Abbeel, P.: Denoising diffusion probabilistic models. Adv. Neural. Inf. Process. Syst. **33**, 6840–6851 (2020)
8. Ho, J., Saharia, C., Chan, W., Fleet, D.J., Norouzi, M., Salimans, T.: Cascaded diffusion models for high fidelity image generation. J. Mach. Learn. Res. **23**(1), 2249–2281 (2022)
9. Jabri, A., Fleet, D.J., Chen, T.: Scalable adaptive computation for iterative generation. In: International Conference on Machine Learning, ICML 2023, 23-29 July 2023, Honolulu, Hawaii, USA. Proceedings of Machine Learning Research, vol. 202, pp. 14569–14589. PMLR (2023)
10. Krizhevsky, A., Hinton, G., et al.: Learning multiple layers of features from tiny images (2009)
11. Li, Y., et al.: Snapfusion: text-to-image diffusion model on mobile devices within two seconds. arXiv preprint arXiv:2306.00980 (2023)
12. Liu, J., Yi, X., Wu, S., Yin, X., Zhang, T., Huang, X., Jin, S.: Continuous geometry-aware graph diffusion via hyperbolic neural PDE. In: ECML PKDD 2024, Vilnius, Lithuania, September 9-13, 2024, Proceedings, Part III. Springer (2024)
13. Liu, X., Liu, A., den Broeck, G.V., Liang, Y.: Understanding the distillation process from deep generative models to tractable probabilistic circuits. In: International Conference on Machine Learning, ICML 2023, 23-29 July 2023, Honolulu, Hawaii, USA. Proceedings of Machine Learning Research, vol. 202, pp. 21825–21838. PMLR (2023)
14. Liu, Z., Luo, P., Wang, X., Tang, X.: Deep learning face attributes in the wild. In: Proceedings of International Conference on Computer Vision (ICCV) (December 2015)

15. Meng, C., et al.: On distillation of guided diffusion models. In: Proceedings of the IEEE/CVF Conference on Computer Vision and Pattern Recognition, pp. 14297–14306 (2023)
16. Nagel, J.: https://github.com/joseph-nagel/diffusion-demo/blob/main/notebooks/swissroll.ipynb
17. Ninniri, M., Podda, M., Bacciu, D.: Classifier-free graph diffusion for molecular property targeting. In: ECML PKDD 2024, Vilnius, Lithuania, 9-13 September 2024, Proceedings, Part III. Springer (2024). https://doi.org/10.1007/978-3-031-70359-1_19
18. Ronneberger, O., Fischer, P., Brox, T.: U-Net: convolutional networks for biomedical image segmentation. In: Navab, N., Hornegger, J., Wells, W.M., Frangi, A.F. (eds.) MICCAI 2015. LNCS, vol. 9351, pp. 234–241. Springer, Cham (2015). https://doi.org/10.1007/978-3-319-24574-4_28
19. Salimans, T., Ho, J.: Progressive distillation for fast sampling of diffusion models. In: The Tenth International Conference on Learning Representations, ICLR 2022, Virtual Event, April 25-29, 2022. OpenReview.net (2022)
20. Sohl-Dickstein, J., Weiss, E., Maheswaranathan, N., Ganguli, S.: Deep unsupervised learning using nonequilibrium thermodynamics. In: International Conference on Machine Learning, pp. 2256–2265. PMLR (2015)
21. Song, J., Meng, C., Ermon, S.: Denoising diffusion implicit models. In: 9th International Conference on Learning Representations, ICLR 2021, Virtual Event, Austria, 3-7 May 2021. OpenReview.net (2021)
22. Song, Y., Dhariwal, P., Chen, M., Sutskever, I.: Consistency models. In: Krause, A., Brunskill, E., Cho, K., Engelhardt, B., Sabato, S., Scarlett, J. (eds.) International Conference on Machine Learning, ICML 2023, 23-29 July 2023, Honolulu, Hawaii, USA. PMLR (2023)
23. Song, Y., Sohl-Dickstein, J., Kingma, D.P., Kumar, A., Ermon, S., Poole, B.: Score-based generative modeling through stochastic differential equations. In: ICLR 2021 (2020)
24. Yu, F., Zhang, Y., Song, S., Seff, A., Xiao, J.: Lsun: Construction of a large-scale image dataset using deep learning with humans in the loop. arXiv preprint arXiv:1506.03365 (2015)
25. Zhao, Y., Xu, Y., Xiao, Z., Hou, T.: Mobilediffusion: Subsecond text-to-image generation on mobile devices. arXiv preprint arXiv:2311.16567 (2023)

Loss Functions in Diffusion Models: A Comparative Study

Dibyanshu Kumar[✉], Philipp Väth, and Magda Gregorová

Center for Artificial Intelligence and Robotics, Technical University of Applied Sciences Würzburg-Schweinfurt, Franz-Horn-Straße 2, Würzburg, Germany
{dibyanshu.kumar,philipp.vaeth,magda.gregorova}@thws.de

Abstract. Diffusion models have emerged as powerful generative models, inspiring extensive research into their underlying mechanisms. One of the key questions in this area is the loss functions these models shall train with. Multiple formulations have been introduced in the literature over the past several years [4,7,11,13] with some links and some critical differences stemming from various initial considerations. In this paper, we explore the different target objectives and corresponding loss functions in detail. We present a systematic overview of their relationships, unifying them under the framework of the variational lower bound objective. We complement this theoretical analysis with an empirical study providing insights into the conditions under which these objectives diverge in performance and the underlying factors contributing to such deviations. Additionally, we evaluate how the choice of objective impacts the model's ability to achieve specific goals, such as generating high-quality samples or accurately estimating likelihoods. This study offers a unified understanding of loss functions in diffusion models, contributing to more efficient and goal-oriented model designs in future research.

Keywords: Diffusion Model · Loss Functions · Generative Modeling

1 Introduction

Diffusion models [4] have become a cornerstone of generative modeling in recent years, demonstrating remarkable capabilities in generating high-quality data. Given a sample $\mathbf{x}_0 \sim q(\mathbf{x})$ from a data distribution, the forward process in diffusion models incrementally corrupts the data by adding small amounts of Gaussian noise over multiple steps T. This process is defined as $q(\mathbf{x}_t \mid \mathbf{x}_{t-1}) = \mathcal{N}(\mathbf{x}_t; \alpha \mathbf{x}_{t-1}, \sigma^2 \mathbf{I})$, where α controls the scaling of the data $\mathbf{x}_{t-1}$, and σ controls the magnitude of the added noise. The objective is then to learn the reverse process $q(\mathbf{x}_{t-1} \mid \mathbf{x}_t)$ which enables the generation of new samples by starting from pure Gaussian noise $\mathbf{x}_T \sim \mathcal{N}(\mathbf{0}, \mathbf{I})$ and iteratively denoising it to recover

---

Supplementary Information The online version contains supplementary material available at https://doi.org/10.1007/978-3-032-05981-9_12.

© The Author(s), under exclusive license to Springer Nature Switzerland AG 2026
R. P. Ribeiro et al. (Eds.): ECML PKDD 2025, LNAI 16014, pp. 190–205, 2026.
https://doi.org/10.1007/978-3-032-05981-9_12

realistic data. This framework of probabilistic modeling allows diffusion models to capture complex data distributions, making them highly effective for a wide range of generative tasks.

The class of diffusion models has seen several notable contributions, particularly in the development of training objectives. In score-based modeling [13], the reverse process is learned by minimizing a denoising score-matching objective. Ho et al. [4], in their work on DDPM, generated high quality images by adopting noise prediction ϵ as the primary objective. Variational Diffusion Models (VDM) [7] used the training objective, formulated in terms of the Signal-to-Noise Ratio (SNR), which achieved the best likelihood estimation. Additionally, the authors of Progressive Distillation [11] modeled the rate of change in data distribution over time, presenting a novel loss function that combines the data representation $\mathbf{x}$ and the noise component ϵ. This objective was instrumental in reducing the number of sampling steps required to generate high-quality samples. These advancements highlight the critical role of loss function design in improving the performance and efficiency of diffusion models.

Existing research has explored the theoretical equivalence of various training objectives used in diffusion models. For instance, [15] established connections between score matching and diffusion-based generative frameworks by leveraging stochastic differential equations to model the forward process, thereby aligning it with continuous distributions that evolve over time. Similarly, [7] introduced the Evidence Lower Bound (ELBO) objective for diffusion, inspired by Variational Autoencoders [8]. More recently, [6] demonstrated that diffusion model objectives are fundamentally equivalent and closely related to the ELBO framework. However, while these works highlight the theoretical equivalence of the loss functions, they lack a structured analysis of their formulations under a single framework. Furthermore, there is no empirical study investigating whether the mathematical equivalence between objectives persists when training diffusion models with deep neural networks. Therefore, there is only limited understanding of how these loss formulations differ in terms of performance. This gap highlights the need for a systematic exploration of outcomes of these theoretical connections.

In this study, we conduct a comprehensive comparison of different training objectives, specifically the weighted and the ELBO objectives, formulated for four different target predictions of the diffusion models: data $\mathbf{x}$, noise ϵ, rate of change in the data distribution $\mathbf{v}$ and score $\mathbf{s}$. We derive the negative ELBO loss in terms of these targets and establish mathematical relationships with the most commonly used diffusion loss functions. These relationships help us to design experiments that evaluate whether the theoretical equivalence between these objectives holds in practice when used for training over the same datasets. Our experiments highlight the differences and similarities in the theoretical foundations and practical behavior of these loss functions, particularly in terms of loss convergence during training and the quality of generated samples. We explore the loss behavior across different diffusion timesteps, providing insights into the mechanisms that drive their performance and functionality. Additionally, we compare the outcomes of these training objectives in terms of data density estimation and sample quality, offering a comprehensive understanding of their roles in optimizing diffusion models.

The paper is structured as follows: Sect. 2 provides the background on diffusion models. In Sect. 3 we introduce the various target predictions used in diffusion models, derive the loss functions under different framework, and show the relation between them. In Sect. 4 we describe the experiments we perform and give insights on the results obtained. Finally, we conclude by summarizing our findings and suggesting directions for future research. The code used in this study is available at: https://github.com/dibyanshu100/LFDM.

2 Model

In this section, we provide an overview of the forward and reverse processes used in diffusion models.

2.1 Forward Diffusion Process

The forward process in diffusion models is a Markov process, where the information in a given data $\mathbf{x}$ is progressively destroyed by adding noise in a series of timesteps, producing intermediate latent variables, denoted as $\mathbf{z}_t$, where $t \in [0, 1]$ represents the corresponding timestep. To achieve this, a schedule is used to define the amount of noise to be added and the signal to be removed at each timestep, regulated by parameters α_t and σ_t. The distribution of latent variables and the Markov transition distribution in the forward process is defined as follows:

$$q(\mathbf{z}_t \mid \mathbf{x}) = \mathcal{N}(\mathbf{z}_t; \alpha_t \mathbf{x}, \sigma_t^2 \mathbf{I})$$
$$q(\mathbf{z}_t \mid \mathbf{z}_s) = \mathcal{N}(\mathbf{z}_t; \alpha_{t|s} \mathbf{z}_s, \sigma_{t|s}^2 \mathbf{I}) \tag{1}$$

where $0 \leq s \leq t \leq 1$, $\alpha_{t|s} = \frac{\alpha_t}{\alpha_s}$ and $\sigma_{t|s}^2 = \sigma_t^2 - \alpha_{t|s}^2 \sigma_s^2$

The scheduling parameters, α_t and σ_t are strictly positive, smooth, monotonically decreasing and increasing functions of time respectively. Based on this we can define the Signal-to-Noise ratio SNR(t) as:

$$\text{SNR}(t) = \frac{\alpha_t^2}{\sigma_t^2} \tag{2}$$

As time t progresses, the SNR decreases. This implies that for $s < t$, we have $\text{SNR}(s) > \text{SNR}(t)$. At $t = 0$ the data is least noisy and at $t = 1$ there is no more signal left in the data, hence $q(\mathbf{z}_1 \mid \mathbf{x}) = \mathcal{N}(\mathbf{z}_1; 0, \mathbf{I})$.

The choice of schedule significantly impacts the performance of diffusion models, and there are several ways of noise scheduling. DDPM [4] employed a linear schedule to add noise over 1000 discrete timesteps. Nichol and Dhariwal [9], used cosine scheduling and found it to perform better due to its smooth transition between low and high levels of noise. In VDM [7], the authors learned the forward noise schedule, moreover they demonstrate that increasing the number of timesteps resulted in a decrease in loss, thereby achieving good results with a continuous-time model. The schedules used in the above mentioned works were variance preserving ($\alpha_t^2 = 1 - \sigma_t^2$), which ensures that the variance of the data remains constant throughout the forward process. Alternatively, in the case of variance-exploding schedules [14,15], $\alpha_t^2 = 1$. It was demonstrated by Kingma et al. [7] that the variance preserving and variance exploding formulations can be considered equivalent in continuous time.

2.2 Reverse Generative Process

The reverse diffusion process $q(\mathbf{z}_s \mid \mathbf{z}_t)$ is also a Markov chain with Gaussian transition probability and aims to recover the original data $\mathbf{x}$ from the noisy data $\mathbf{z}_t$. Since the true reverse process $q(\mathbf{z}_s \mid \mathbf{z}_t)$ is intractable, it is approximated with a learned distribution $p_\theta(\mathbf{z}_s \mid \mathbf{z}_t)$. This forms a hierarchical generative model that samples a sequence of latent variables $\mathbf{z}_t$, with time progressing from $t=1$ to $t=0$, gradually denoising the data over T steps to recover the original distribution. For discrete time case number of steps T is finite and is discretized into uniform timesteps of width $1/T$, with $s(i) = \frac{i-1}{T}$ and $t(i) = \frac{i}{T}$,

The overall reverse process is defined as,

$$p_\theta(\mathbf{x}) = \int_{\mathbf{z}} p(\mathbf{z}_1) p_\theta(\mathbf{x} \mid \mathbf{z}_0) \prod_{i=1}^{T} p_\theta(\mathbf{z}_{s(i)} \mid \mathbf{z}_{t(i)}) d\mathbf{z} \qquad (3)$$

To approximate the true data distribution we need to minimize the negative log likelihood. However, that is intractable and we minimize the tractable negative variational lower bound also called negative evidence lower bound (NELBO) instead, which is standard in latent variable models and is expressed as,

$$-\log p_\theta(\mathbf{x}) \leq \text{NELBO}(\mathbf{x}) = \underbrace{D_{\text{KL}}\left(q(\mathbf{z}_1 \mid \mathbf{x}) \,\|\, p(\mathbf{z}_1)\right)}_{\text{Prior Loss}} +$$

$$\underbrace{\mathbb{E}_{q(\mathbf{z}_0 \mid \mathbf{x})}\left[-\log p_\theta(\mathbf{x} \mid \mathbf{z}_0)\right]}_{\text{Reconstruction Loss}} + \qquad (4)$$

$$\underbrace{\sum_{i=1}^{T} \mathbb{E}_{q(\mathbf{z}_{t(i)} \mid \mathbf{x})} D_{\text{KL}}\left[q(\mathbf{z}_{s(i)} \mid \mathbf{z}_{t(i)}, \mathbf{x}) \,\|\, p_\theta(\mathbf{z}_{s(i)} \mid \mathbf{z}_{t(i)})\right]}_{\text{Diffusion Loss } (L_T(\mathbf{x}))}$$

Based on the assumptions of the forward process, $\mathbf{z}_0$ is nearly identical to $\mathbf{x}$ because only a small amount of noise is added, making the reconstruction loss in the equation (4) negligible and therefore can be dropped from the objective in practice. Moreover, as discussed in Sect. 2.1, $q(\mathbf{z}_1 \mid \mathbf{x})$ approaches a pure Gaussian distribution at the end of the forward process which matches our fixed prior $p(\mathbf{z}_1) = \mathcal{N}(\mathbf{z}_1; 0, \mathbf{I})$. As a result, the KL divergence $D_{\text{KL}}\left(q(\mathbf{z}_1 \mid \mathbf{x}) \,\|\, p(\mathbf{z}_1)\right)$ tends to zero, hence this term is also dropped. The remaining term is the diffusion loss $L_T(\mathbf{x})$ which depends on the number of timesteps T determining the depth of the generative model.

3 Loss Formulations

In the previous section, we defined the NELBO objective (4). For the denoising model there are several options for the target prediction in addition to the data **x**. For example, some approaches focus on predicting the noise ϵ added during the forward process [4,9,12]. Another approach predicts the rate of change in the data distribution over time, also known as **v**-prediction [11]. Some methods target the score function $\nabla_\mathbf{x} \log p(\mathbf{x})$ [13,15], which is the gradient of the log-probability density of the data.

For each of these targets, we can derive the NELBO loss formulation (L) from equation (4). In addition, other loss formulations are also proposed in the literature, typically designed to prioritize perceptual sample quality or computational efficiency. We call these weighted loss functions ($\mathcal{L}$) as they can all be shown as a weighted function of the NELBO where the weight $w(t)$ is a suitable chosen weighting function.

$$\mathcal{L} = w(t) L \tag{5}$$

In the following sections, we explore the various target predictions and corresponding loss formulations in detail. We present a systematic review of these relationships, unifying them under the framework of the NELBO objective. Specifically, we derive the NELBO in terms of these alternative targets and show that all the different objectives, whether predicting the original data **x**, noise ϵ, rate of change in the data distribution **v**, or score **s** can be expressed as weighted functions of the NELBO. For clarity, we refer to different target objectives as **x**-space, ϵ-space, **v**-space, and **s**-space throughout this paper.

3.1 x-Space

As shown in Sect. 2.2, the NELBO reduces to diffusion loss which is the last term of equation (4). This can be further simplified to the following form (a detailed derivation of these steps is provided in appendix B.1).

$$L_T(\mathbf{x}) = \frac{T}{2} \mathbb{E}_{\epsilon \sim \mathcal{N}(\mathbf{0},\mathbf{I}), i \sim \mathrm{U}\{1,T\}} \left[(\mathrm{SNR}(s(i)) - \mathrm{SNR}(t(i))) \, \|\mathbf{x} - \hat{\mathbf{x}}_\theta(\mathbf{z}_t; t)\|_2^2 \right] \tag{6}$$

where $\hat{\mathbf{x}}_\theta(\mathbf{z}_t; t)$ is the prediction of the original data **x** by our denoising model given the noisy data $\mathbf{z}_t = \alpha_t \mathbf{x} + \sigma_t \epsilon$ at timestep t.

For the continuous-time case, $T \to \infty$. Here, the timestep t is treated as a continuous variable, and the transition process is referred to as the continuous-time diffusion process [7]. In this setting, equation (6) transforms into the following form,

$$L(\mathbf{x}) = -\mathbb{E}_{t \sim \mathcal{U}(0,1), \epsilon \sim \mathcal{N}(\mathbf{0},\mathbf{I})} \left[\mathrm{SNR}'(t) \, \|\mathbf{x} - \hat{\mathbf{x}}_\theta(\mathbf{z}_t; t)\|_2^2 \right] \tag{7}$$

where we prove that for cosine noise schedule, $\text{SNR}'(t) = \frac{-\pi \alpha_t}{\sigma_t^3}$ (see appendix B.1). Note that we use $U\{1,T\}$ to denote sampling from a discrete uniform distribution, while $\mathcal{U}(0,1)$ denotes sampling from a continuous uniform distribution in the continuous-time setting.

Moreover we can define the weighted loss as,

$$\mathcal{L}(\mathbf{x}) = -\mathbb{E}_{t \sim \mathcal{U}(0,1), \epsilon \sim \mathcal{N}(\mathbf{0},\mathbf{I})} \left[w_{\mathbf{x}}(t) \, \text{SNR}'(t) \, \|\mathbf{x} - \hat{\mathbf{x}}_\theta(\mathbf{z}_t; t)\|_2^2 \right] \tag{8}$$

By choosing $w_{\mathbf{x}}(t) = -\frac{1}{\text{SNR}'(t)}$, this further simplifies as an expected value of the mean squared error between the original data and the predicted data,

$$\mathcal{L}(\mathbf{x}) = \mathbb{E}_{t \sim \mathcal{U}(0,1), \epsilon \sim \mathcal{N}(\mathbf{0},\mathbf{I})} \left[\|\mathbf{x} - \hat{\mathbf{x}}_\theta(\mathbf{z}_t; t)\|_2^2 \right] = w_{\mathbf{x}}(t) L(\mathbf{x}) \tag{9}$$

3.2 ϵ-space

The ϵ-space loss formulation is one of the most commonly used objective in diffusion models, as proposed in DDPM [4]. Instead of directly reconstructing the original data $\mathbf{x}$, we model the noise component ϵ that was added to the data in every time step during the forward diffusion process. The authors of the paper claimed that this approach simplifies the learning task, as the prediction of noise aligns with the stochastic nature of the diffusion process.

We derive the NELBO loss in ϵ-space, as detailed in the appendix B.2,

$$L(\epsilon) = -\mathbb{E}_{t,\epsilon} \left[\frac{\text{SNR}'(t)}{\text{SNR}(t)} \|\epsilon - \hat{\epsilon}_\theta(\mathbf{z}_t; t)\|_2^2 \right] \tag{10}$$

The loss proposed in DDPM is different from the NELBO loss. They used the weighted ϵ loss, which implies that the model learns to predict the noise sampled from the unit Gaussian and not the scaled noise which was added to the original data $\mathbf{x}$ at every timestep during the forward diffusion process. The weighted ϵ-loss is given as below and can be seen as a weighted function of (10) with weight $w_\epsilon(t) = -\frac{\text{SNR}(t)}{\text{SNR}'(t)}$:

$$\mathcal{L}(\epsilon) = \mathbb{E}_{t,\epsilon} \left[\|\epsilon - \hat{\epsilon}_\theta(\mathbf{z}_t; t)\|_2^2 \right] = w_\epsilon(t) L(\epsilon) \tag{11}$$

3.3 v-space

The v-space loss, introduced in [11], combines the data $\mathbf{x}$ and noise ϵ. This formulation is particularly beneficial for model distillation to reduce the number of sampling steps, as while sampling the standard noise objective becomes unstable when the SNR approaches zero. In such cases α_t tends to zero, leading to instability in reconstructing the data from the predicted noise as $\hat{\mathbf{x}}_\theta(\mathbf{z}_t) = \frac{1}{\alpha_t}(\mathbf{z}_t - \sigma_t \hat{\epsilon}_\theta(\mathbf{z}_t))$. The authors showed that this issue has less impact in conventional diffusion models, where clipping the reconstructed data in the desired range and using a large number of sampling steps can mitigate errors but becomes a key factor in distillation, where efficient sampling is essential in a limited number of steps.

This approach expresses the noisy data using an angular parameter ϕ_t, where $\mathbf{z}_{\phi_t} = \cos(\phi_t)\mathbf{x} + \sin(\phi_t)\boldsymbol{\epsilon}$, and $\phi_t = \arctan\left(\frac{\sigma_t}{\alpha_t}\right)$. The target $\mathbf{v}_{\phi_t}$ is then calculated as $\mathbf{v}_{\phi_t} = \frac{d\mathbf{z}_{\phi_t}}{d\phi_t} = \cos(\phi_t)\boldsymbol{\epsilon} - \sin(\phi_t)\mathbf{x}$, which represents the instantaneous direction and rate of change required to transform the noisy data $\mathbf{z}_{\phi_t}$ along a circular trajectory parameterized by the angle ϕ_t.

The NELBO loss in **v**-space as derived in appendix B.3 is given as,

$$L(\mathbf{v}) = -\mathbb{E}_{t,\epsilon}\left[\frac{\sigma_t^2}{\alpha_t^2 + \sigma_t^2}\text{SNR}'(t)\|\mathbf{v} - \hat{\mathbf{v}}_\theta(\mathbf{z}_t;t)\|_2^2\right] \quad (12)$$

The weighted **v** loss can be formulated as the weighted function of NELBO with weight $w_\mathbf{v}(t) = -\frac{(\alpha_t^2+\sigma_t^2)}{\sigma_t^2\text{SNR}'(t)}$

$$\mathcal{L}(\mathbf{v}) = \mathbb{E}_{t,\epsilon}\left[\|\mathbf{v} - \hat{\mathbf{v}}_\theta(\mathbf{z}_t;t)\|_2^2\right] = w_\mathbf{v}(t)L(\mathbf{v}) \quad (13)$$

3.4 s-Space

Score modeling, introduced by Song et al. [13] uses denoising score matching [17] to approximate the score function and then use a neural network to learn it. The idea behind score matching is to add a small amount of noise to the data, which makes the score calculation tractable, and therefore learn the score of perturbed distribution instead of the original distribution, which is expressed as $\nabla_{\mathbf{z}_t} \log q(\mathbf{z}_t \mid \mathbf{x})$. The authors demonstrate that minimizing the denoising score matching objective across multiple noise scales enables high quality sample generation. This theory is closely aligned with the diffusion process, as both approaches aim to refine the noisy data toward its original distribution.

In [15], the authors bridged the gap between score modeling and diffusion models by proposing score based modeling using stochastic differential equations (SDE). They showed that the forward diffusion process can be interpreted as a discretization of a continuous-time SDE, and the reverse process corresponds to solving the reverse-time SDE using the learned score function.

We demonstrate here that the NELBO loss can once again be formulated in s-space and can be expressed as below (see in appendix B.4),

$$L(\mathbf{s}) = -\mathbb{E}_{t,\epsilon}\left[\frac{\sigma_t^4}{\alpha_t^2}\text{SNR}'(t)\|\nabla_{\mathbf{z}_t}\log q(\mathbf{z}_t \mid \mathbf{x}) - \hat{\mathbf{s}}_\theta(\mathbf{z}_t;t)\|_2^2\right] \quad (14)$$

The weighted loss in s-space can be formulated as the weighted function of NELBO with weight $w_\mathbf{s}(t) = -\frac{\alpha_t^2}{\sigma_t^4\text{SNR}'(t)}$

$$\mathcal{L}(\mathbf{s}) = \mathbb{E}_{t,\epsilon}\left[\|\nabla_{\mathbf{z}_t}\log q(\mathbf{z}_t \mid \mathbf{x}) - \hat{\mathbf{s}}_\theta(\mathbf{z}_t;t)\|_2^2\right] = w_\mathbf{s}(t)L(\mathbf{s}) \quad (15)$$

Furthermore, for Gaussian noise perturbation the score simplifies to:

$$\mathbf{s} = \nabla_{\mathbf{z}_t}\log q(\mathbf{z}_t \mid \mathbf{x}) = -\frac{(\mathbf{z}_t - \alpha_t\mathbf{x})}{\sigma_t^2} \quad (16)$$

3.5 Equivalence of Loss Functions

All the NELBO loss formulations across different parameter spaces are derived from same equation (7), therefore, they are fundamentally equivalent. However, to derive the weighted loss from the NELBO loss, we need to apply different weights, which essentially removes the SNR scalings associated with the ℓ_2 difference between the target and the prediction. As a result, these weighted loss functions are not equivalent, even though they are all initially derived from the same NELBO formulation.

To establish a relationship between the weighted loss formulations, we rescale the weighted loss in $\boldsymbol{\epsilon}$, $\mathbf{v}$ and $\mathbf{s}$ space to make it equal to $\mathcal{L}(\mathbf{x})$. We call them rescaled loss $\widetilde{\mathcal{L}}$ that is equivalent across all targets and can be easily obtained using the weights derived in the previous sections,

$$\widetilde{\mathcal{L}}(\boldsymbol{\epsilon}) = \frac{\sigma_t^2}{\alpha_t^2}\mathcal{L}(\boldsymbol{\epsilon}) = \mathcal{L}(\mathbf{x}) \tag{17}$$

$$\widetilde{\mathcal{L}}(\mathbf{v}) = \frac{\sigma_t^2}{\alpha_t^2 + \sigma_t^2}\mathcal{L}(\mathbf{v}) = \mathcal{L}(\mathbf{x}) \tag{18}$$

$$\widetilde{\mathcal{L}}(\mathbf{s}) = \frac{\sigma_t^4}{\alpha_t^2}\mathcal{L}(\mathbf{s}) = \mathcal{L}(\mathbf{x}) \tag{19}$$

Table 1 summarizes all the loss formulations across different targets for the denoising model.

Table 1. Overview of all the loss formulations across different scenarios. While the NELBO and the rescaled loss are equivalent and comparable, the weighted losses are not equivalent and are expected to exhibit different empirical performance.

Target	NELBO loss (L)	Weighted loss $(\mathcal{L})$	Rescaled loss $(\widetilde{\mathcal{L}})$
$\mathbf{x}$	$-\mathbb{E}\big[\mathrm{SNR}'(t)\,\|\mathbf{x}-\hat{\mathbf{x}}_\theta\|_2^2\big]$	$\mathbb{E}\big[\|\mathbf{x}-\hat{\mathbf{x}}_\theta\|_2^2\big]$	$\mathbb{E}\big[\|\mathbf{x}-\hat{\mathbf{x}}_\theta\|_2^2\big]$
$\boldsymbol{\epsilon}$	$-\mathbb{E}\big[\frac{\mathrm{SNR}'(t)}{\mathrm{SNR}(t)}\|\boldsymbol{\epsilon}-\hat{\boldsymbol{\epsilon}}_\theta\|_2^2\big]$	$\mathbb{E}\big[\|\boldsymbol{\epsilon}-\hat{\boldsymbol{\epsilon}}_\theta\|_2^2\big]$	$\mathbb{E}\big[\frac{\sigma_t^2}{\alpha_t^2}\|\boldsymbol{\epsilon}-\hat{\boldsymbol{\epsilon}}_\theta\|_2^2\big]$
$\mathbf{v}$	$-\mathbb{E}\big[\frac{\sigma_t^2}{\alpha_t^2+\sigma_t^2}\mathrm{SNR}'(t)\|\mathbf{v}-\hat{\mathbf{v}}_\theta\|_2^2\big]$	$\mathbb{E}\big[\|\mathbf{v}-\hat{\mathbf{v}}_\theta\|_2^2\big]$	$\mathbb{E}\big[\frac{\sigma_t^2}{\alpha_t^2+\sigma_t^2}\|\mathbf{v}-\hat{\mathbf{v}}_\theta\|_2^2\big]$
$\mathbf{s}$	$-\mathbb{E}\big[\frac{\sigma_t^4}{\alpha_t^2}\mathrm{SNR}'(t)\|\mathbf{s}-\hat{\mathbf{s}}_\theta\|_2^2\big]$	$\mathbb{E}\big[\|\mathbf{s}-\hat{\mathbf{s}}_\theta\|_2^2\big]$	$\mathbb{E}\big[\frac{\sigma_t^4}{\alpha_t^2}\|\mathbf{s}-\hat{\mathbf{s}}_\theta\|_2^2\big]$

Although researchers have claimed that some training objectives outperform others in diffusion models, the reasons behind these differences remain unclear and are often attributed to empirical observations rather than theoretical foundations. For instance, while some works prefer more complex weights for loss functions [1,3,5], others [4,9] find that simpler objectives (e.g. ℓ_2 loss between target and prediction) perform just as well or even better in practice. This discrepancy raises questions about the fundamental role of loss formulations in training diffusion models and whether the observed performance gaps are due to the loss functions themselves or other factors such as model architecture, training dynamics, or noise schedules.

In our theoretical analysis, we formulated the NELBO loss for different denoising models. Specifically, we showed that different formulations of the learned model (i.e. predicting original data $\mathbf{x}$, noise ϵ, rate of change of data distribution $\mathbf{v}$ and score function $\mathbf{s}$) can be mapped to one another, and their corresponding NELBO objectives are mathematically interchangeable. We also formulated the relations between the weighted loss formulations.

In principle, the mathematical equivalence we established should hold when we train the various denoising models with equivalent loss formulations under similar conditions (e.g., dataset, model architecture etc.). In the next section, we outline the experiments conducted to validate this hypothesis and provide a detailed analysis of the results obtained.

4 Experiments

In this section, we outline the experimental setup used to conduct our tests and present the results obtained from these experiments. Additionally, we give a detailed analysis and insights into the findings.

4.1 Experimental Setup

To conduct our experiments, we first work with 2-dimensional synthetic datasets that we generated ourselves. These datasets are well-suited for detailed analysis as it is easy to plot numerous examples and visually analyze the complete data manifold. To ensure the generalizability of our findings, we select four distinct 2D datasets with 100K samples each. These datasets are: Cluster data, Ring data, Swiss roll data and Waves data, the scatter plots of these datasets can be seen in Fig. 1. In Fig. 2 we show the effect of gaussian noise added in the forward process for all these datasets.

We also perform experiments on a high-dimensional image dataset, CIFAR-10, which is a publicly available dataset that contains 32×32 color images across 10 classes. While we present results on an image dataset, our main focus is not on extensive image generation experiments but understanding the behavior of different loss formulations. However, this work sets the foundation for future research to explore their impact on image data more deeply.

We used a variance-preserving cosine schedule for the forward process, combined with a continuous-time reverse model $T \to \infty$. Hence, the noisy data at time $t \sim \mathcal{U}(0,1)$, is given as $\mathbf{z}_t = \cos(0.5\pi t)\mathbf{x} + \sin(0.5\pi t)\epsilon$. To ensure comparability across experiments, for the 2D datasets, we modeled the reverse process using a simple feedforward neural network architecture consisting of 7 fully connected layers followed by a ReLU activation. In addition, we maintained consistent training dynamics for all datasets. For the image dataset, we used an architecture inspired by diffusers UNet model [10].

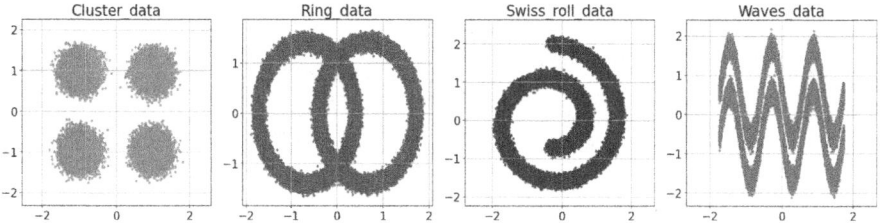

Fig. 1. Scatter plot for 2D datasets

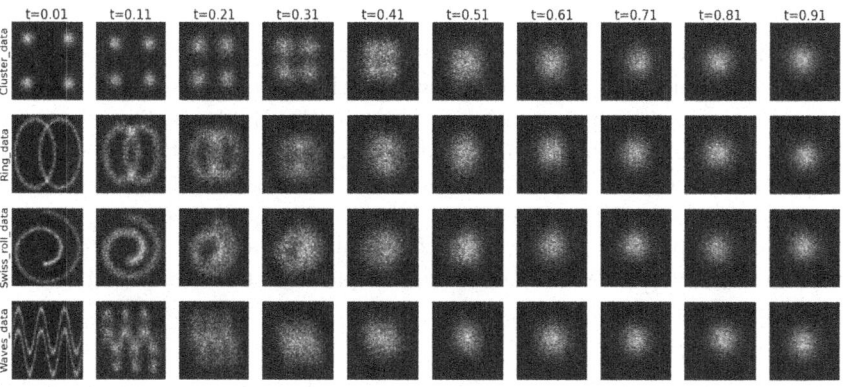

Fig. 2. Effects of adding cosine scheduled Gaussian noise in the forward process

4.2 Experimental Results and Discussion

In our analysis, we examine the performance of diffusion model trained with various loss formulations from three key perspectives: (i) loss convergence over epochs indicating the training and stability efficiency, (ii) the quality of generated samples that reveals how well the model produces realistic and high fidelity samples, and (iii) loss behavior at different timesteps t that give insights into how different loss formulations influence the reverse diffusion process over time. Due to space limitations, we present some results only for the ring data, while results for other datasets follow similar patterns and are provided in the appendix C for completeness.

Loss Convergence vs Epochs: We begin by training the denoising model using the NELBO loss formulations L for different target predictions. Given their theoretical equivalence as discussed in Sect. 3, we expect them to behave similarly in experiments. Figure 3 illustrates the NELBO test loss for different datasets. The loss curves for predictions in the v and ϵ space are close, and so is loss in x and s space. However, these two groups differ significantly for all scenarios indicating a discrepancy in their training dynamics.

We attribute these differences to the different SNR scaling of the targets within the NELBO formulation which is inversely proportional to the weight-

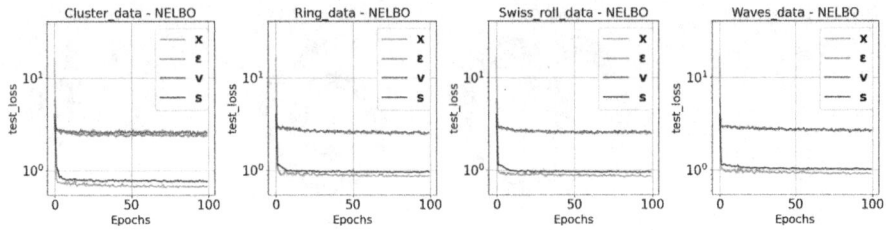

Fig. 3. NELBO test loss for different datasets

ing function and is given by $\frac{1}{w(t)}$. These scaling factors control how much each timestep contributes to the overall loss, and therefore have an impact on how the model learns during training. As shown in Fig. 4, the scaling for ϵ and $\mathbf{v}$ space are substantially higher in the early time steps, when the noise added to the data is minimal. While $\mathbf{x}$ space also exhibits large initial scaling, its decay is more gradual over time. In contrast, the $\mathbf{s}$ space has higher scaling at later timesteps. This pattern suggests that excessively high scaling at early timesteps, when noise levels are low, may negatively impact the model's overall likelihood performance.

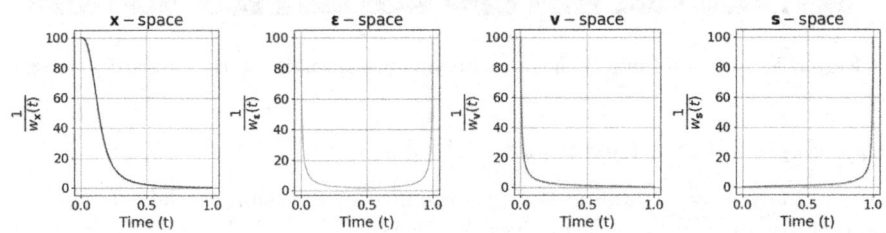

Fig. 4. SNR scalings ($\frac{1}{w(t)}$) with respect to timesteps for various NELBO formulations

Next, we train the model using the weighted loss formulations $\mathcal{L}$ for different datasets as shown in Fig. 5 (left). As outlined in Sect. 3.5, the weighted loss formulations are not equivalent and therefore not comparable. To address this, we rescale the weighted test loss as defined in equations (17), (18), and (19). This gives the rescaled loss, $\tilde{\mathcal{L}}$, which is mathematically equivalent to $\mathcal{L}(\mathbf{x})$. The rescaled loss is plotted in Fig. 5 (right), where we observe that, after rescaling, the loss curves are very close to each other. This confirms that the mathematical equivalency holds. Moreover, this indicates that the weighted loss formulation is more stable compared to the NELBO formulations, as there are no additional factors influencing the training dynamics.

Generated Samples: The quality of generated samples shows a different trend compared to loss convergence, indicating that better likelihood estimation does

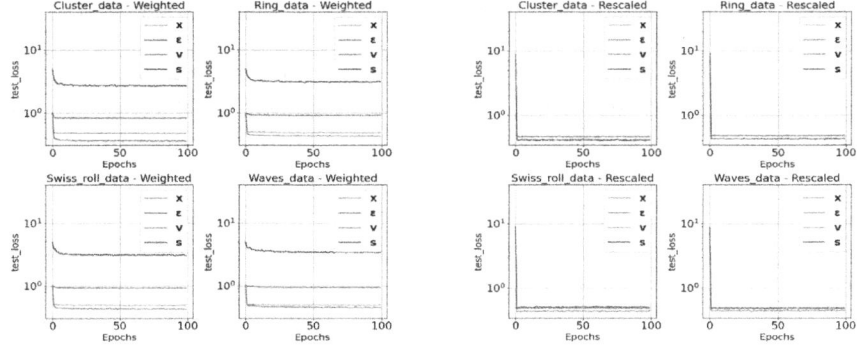

Fig. 5. The weighted test loss $\mathcal{L}$ (left), is not directly comparable across different target predictions. However, the rescaled test loss $\tilde{\mathcal{L}}$ (right), is comparable and demonstrates the mathematical equivalence discussed in Sect. 3.5.

not necessarily correlate with better sample generation, as also discussed in [16]. To analyze the discrepancy, we compare the sample quality using moment-based metrics. Specifically, we measure the mean distance (Euclidean distance between dataset means) and covariance distance (Frobenius norm of the difference between covariance matrices) between real and generated samples. The results are shown in Table 2. We see that although the NELBO is better for **x** and **s** space the sample quality is better for ϵ and **v** space. Moreover, the sample quality for weighted and NELBO loss are similar in most of the cases as also illustrated in Fig. 6 which shows 2K generated samples for the ring dataset using weighted and NELBO loss formulations, respectively. This suggests that while the scaling in the NELBO loss functions influences how the model converges, it has little effect on the quality of the generated samples.

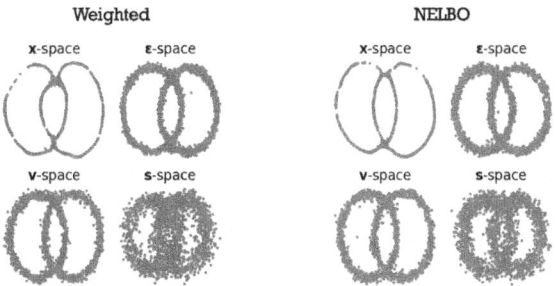

Fig. 6. Comparing 2K samples generated after 512 sampling steps from model trained using weighted loss formulation (left) and NELBO formulation (right)

Table 2. Comparison of NELBO and weighted loss formulations for 2D datasets

Data	Loss Form	NELBO Loss (L)			Weighted loss ($\mathcal{L}$)		
		Nelbo↓	Mean dist.↓	Covar dist.↓	Loss↓	Mean dist.↓	Covar dist.↓
Cluster data	x	0.6777	0.1754	0.5746	0.4754	0.4300	0.2715
	ϵ	2.3636	0.0364	0.0706	0.3522	0.0634	0.1430
	v	2.5396	0.0307	0.0409	0.8264	0.0389	0.0363
	s	0.7657	0.2279	0.1498	2.6934	0.2688	0.1633
Ring data	x	0.8785	0.2744	0.3807	0.4932	0.2807	0.3974
	ϵ	2.5700	0.0914	0.1107	0.4266	0.0983	0.0366
	v	2.5452	0.0459	0.0718	0.9227	0.0453	0.0088
	s	0.9577	0.2254	0.1563	3.0981	0.2220	0.1637
Swiss data	x	0.8640	0.1133	0.2645	0.4934	0.5256	0.6875
	ϵ	2.5324	0.0689	0.0941	0.4261	0.0857	0.0824
	v	2.4861	0.0418	0.0598	0.9171	0.0427	0.0269
	s	0.9493	0.1266	0.1972	3.0274	0.0893	0.1227
Waves data	x	0.9104	0.1593	0.5559	0.4939	0.1869	0.6911
	ϵ	2.6805	0.0405	0.0757	0.4500	0.0748	0.0778
	v	2.6873	0.0447	0.0738	0.9411	0.0131	0.0271
	s	1.0210	0.0353	0.1369	3.4165	0.0178	0.1676

Loss vs Timesteps: In Fig. 7, we illustrate the generation of samples using different numbers of sampling steps in the reverse process for the model trained with the weighted loss. The results are similar to those observed with the NELBO loss (see appendix C.1). It can be seen in the image that for the **x**-space, sample quality declines with more sampling steps but outperforms other objectives with fewer steps, effectively capturing data structure and scale. In contrast, the ϵ-space produces poorer samples with fewer steps, and the sample quality gradually increases. The **v**-space, captures the data structure well even with fewer sampling steps and the sample quality continues to improve with more steps. The quality of samples generated in the **s**-space is not good, however, it improves with the number of steps.

One of the reasons for this difference is the loss behavior of various target predictions across timesteps. We visualize the weighted train loss across timesteps for all target predictions on the ring dataset, as shown in Figure (8). Similar trends are observed for other datasets, with corresponding graphs provided in the appendix C.3. In the **x**-space, the model predicts the original data point at each timestep during the reverse diffusion. As noise increases in the forward process Fig. 2, the SNR drops significantly, making prediction harder and resulting in higher losses at later timesteps. In contrast, for ϵ-space, the task is to predict the noise that was added to the data at each timestep. As more noise is introduced, predicting it becomes progressively easier. The **v**-space formulation as shown in Sect. 3.3 interpolates between data **x** and noise ϵ, weighted by time

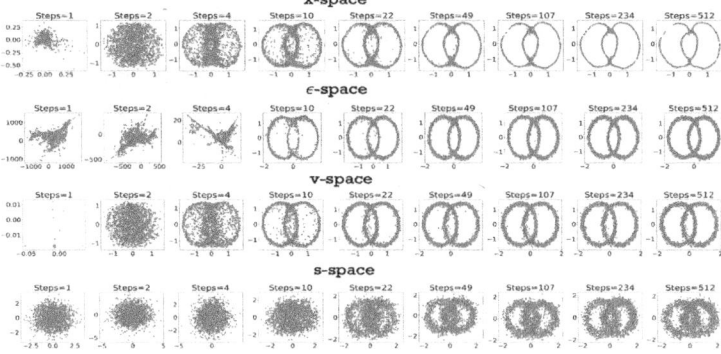

Fig. 7. Generated samples for ring data for different number of sampling steps from model trained on weighted loss $\mathcal{L}$

dependent functions, requiring the model to find a balance between the two. In s-space the loss is significantly higher in the starting timesteps due to the sensitivity of score matching to noise variance (σ_t), as seen in equation (16). At early timesteps, σ_t^2 becomes negligible and the score function becomes very large in magnitude as $\mathbf{s} \propto \frac{1}{\sigma^2}$, leading to a significant rise in the loss.

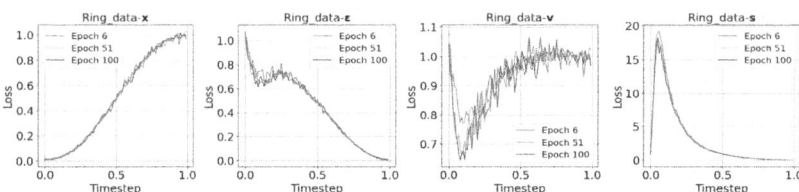

Fig. 8. Behavior of weighted train loss with respect to timesteps for ring data at different epochs

4.3 Results on Image Dataset

The results of different loss formulations in the image dataset are presented in Table 3. We do not include results for score-based metrics because accurately computing them for continuous-time diffusion models in high-dimensional image space requires modeling reverse and forward Stochastic Differential Equations (SDEs), which is beyond the scope of this study and left for future research.

To evaluate the models, we used the NELBO loss to measure how well the model approximates the data likelihood, and the Frechet Inception Distance (FID) to assess the quality of generated samples, which were produced using 500 reverse diffusion steps. We found that the NELBO formulation in **x**-space has the best performance both in sample quality and probability density estimation.

For ϵ and $\mathbf{v}$ space we found that the weighted loss formulation has better FID scores compared to NELBO. This again indicates that a more accurate likelihood estimation does not necessarily correspond to better sample quality. The images generated from these experiments are provided in the appendix D.

Table 3. Comparison of NELBO and weighted loss formulations for CIFAR10

Data	Loss Form	NELBO Loss (L)		Weighted loss ($\mathcal{L}$)	
		Nelbo↓	FID↓	Loss↓	FID↓
CIFAR10	x	0.0907	17.35	0.0544	19.08
	ϵ	0.8499	39.77	0.0605	20.03
	v	0.8576	36.84	0.1188	31.21

5 Conclusion

In this work, we explored both the theoretical foundations and empirical behavior of various target prediction in diffusion models, with a focus on their corresponding loss formulations under the NELBO and weighted loss frameworks. By systematically deriving and relating the loss functions for different target predictions, that is data $\mathbf{x}$, noise ϵ, rate of change of data distribution $\mathbf{v}$, and score $\mathbf{s}$, we established a unified understanding of how these objectives are connected at a theoretical level.

We designed experiments to evaluate whether the mathematical equivalence of these objectives translates into similar empirical performance. Our results show that, despite theoretical equivalence, practical performance can differ significantly in certain scenarios. In particular, we observed variation in loss convergence, likelihood estimation, and sample quality across loss formulations. Among the NELBO variants, the formulation in the $\mathbf{x}$-space yielded the best likelihood estimates. The quality of generated samples was found to be comparable across both NELBO and weighted loss formulations in most cases for 2D datasets. In contrast, for image data, the weighted loss showed improved performance in the ϵ and $\mathbf{v}$-spaces.

While our analysis is primarily conducted on 2D synthetic datasets, the insights gained offer a foundation for more extensive experiments on high dimensional image data. These findings highlight the importance of the choice of training objective in diffusion models and its impact on both model performance and sample quality. Overall, our study provides insights into the practical consequences of loss formulations and lays the groundwork for further research on optimizing training objectives in diffusion models.

Acknowledgments. This research is supported by the Center for Artificial Intelligence (CAIRO) at the Technical University of Applied Sciences Würzburg-Schweinfurt (THWS), Würzburg, Germany.

Disclosure of Interests. The authors have no competing interests to declare that are relevant to the content of this article.

References

1. Choi, J., Lee, J., Shin, C., Kim, S., Kim, H., Yoon, S.: Perception prioritized training of diffusion models. In: Proceedings of the IEEE/CVF Conference on CVPR (2022)
2. Efron, B.: Tweedie's formula and selection bias. J. Am. Statist. Associat. (2011)
3. Hang, T., et al.: Efficient diffusion training via min-snr weighting strategy. In: Proceedings of the IEEE/CVF International Conference on Computer Vision (2023)
4. Ho, J., Jain, A., Abbeel, P.: Denoising diffusion probabilistic models. Adv. Neural Inform. Process. Syst. (2020)
5. Karras, T., Aittala, M., Aila, T., Laine, S.: Elucidating the design space of diffusion-based generative models. Adv. Neural Inform. Process. Syst. (2022)
6. Kingma, D., Gao, R.: Understanding diffusion objectives as the elbo with simple data augmentation. Adv. Neural Inform. Process. Syst. (2024)
7. Kingma, D., Salimans, T., Poole, B., Ho, J.: Variational diffusion models. Adv. Neural Inform. Process. Syst. (2021)
8. Kingma, D.P., Welling, M., et al.: An introduction to variational autoencoders. Foundations Trends® Mach. Learn. (2019)
9. Nichol, A.Q., Dhariwal, P.: Improved denoising diffusion probabilistic models. In: International Conference on Machine Learning (2021)
10. Ronneberger, O., Fischer, P., Brox, T.: U-Net: convolutional networks for biomedical image segmentation. In: Navab, N., Hornegger, J., Wells, W.M., Frangi, A.F. (eds.) MICCAI 2015. LNCS, vol. 9351, pp. 234–241. Springer, Cham (2015). https://doi.org/10.1007/978-3-319-24574-4_28
11. Salimans, T., Ho, J.: Progressive distillation for fast sampling of diffusion models. arXiv preprint arXiv:2202.00512 (2022)
12. Song, J., Meng, C., Ermon, S.: Denoising diffusion implicit models. arXiv preprint arXiv:2010.02502 (2020)
13. Song, Y., Ermon, S.: Generative modeling by estimating gradients of the data distribution. Adv. Neural Inform. Process. Syst. (2019)
14. Song, Y., Ermon, S.: Improved techniques for training score-based generative models. Adv. Neural Inform. Process. Syst. (2020)
15. Song, Y., Sohl-Dickstein, J., Kingma, D.P., Kumar, A., Ermon, S., Poole, B.: Score-based generative modeling through stochastic differential equations. arXiv preprint arXiv:2011.13456 (2020)
16. Theis, L., Oord, A.v.d., Bethge, M.: A note on the evaluation of generative models. arXiv preprint arXiv:1511.01844 (2015)
17. Vincent, P.: A connection between score matching and denoising autoencoders. Neural Comput. (2011)

Diffusion Classifier Guidance for Non-robust Classifiers

Philipp Vaeth[1,2](✉)[iD], Dibyanshu Kumar[1][iD], Benjamin Paassen[2][iD], and Magda Gregorová[1][iD]

[1] Center for Artificial Intelligence and Robotics, Technical University of Applied Sciences Würzburg-Schweinfurt, Franz-Horn-Straße 2, Würzburg, Germany
{philipp.vaeth,magda.gregorova}@thws.de
[2] Bielefeld University, Universitätsstraße 25, Bielefeld, Germany
bpaassen@techfak.uni-bielefeld.de

Abstract. Classifier guidance is intended to steer a diffusion process such that a given classifier reliably recognizes the generated data point as a certain class. However, most classifier guidance approaches are restricted to robust classifiers, which were specifically trained on the noise of the diffusion forward process. We extend classifier guidance to work with general, non-robust, classifiers that were trained without noise. We analyze the sensitivity of both non-robust and robust classifiers to noise of the diffusion process on the standard CelebA data set, the specialized SportBalls data set and the high-dimensional real-world CelebA-HQ data set. Our findings reveal that non-robust classifiers exhibit significant accuracy degradation under noisy conditions, leading to unstable guidance gradients. To mitigate these issues, we propose a method that utilizes one-step denoised image predictions and implements stabilization techniques inspired by stochastic optimization methods, such as exponential moving averages. Experimental results demonstrate that our approach improves the stability of classifier guidance while maintaining sample diversity and visual quality. This work contributes to advancing conditional sampling techniques in generative models, enabling a broader range of classifiers to be used as guidance classifiers.

Keywords: DDPM · Diffusion Models · Conditional Sampling · Classifier Guidance · Gradient Guidance

1 Introduction

Denoising diffusion probabilistic models (DDPM) [9] are state of the art generative models, modelling an intractable data distribution $x_0 \sim p_{\text{data}}$ via a learned

Reproducibility: The code, the trained model weights and the supplementary material to reproduce the results is available at https://github.com/philippvaeth/nrCG.

Supplementary Information The online version contains supplementary material available at https://doi.org/10.1007/978-3-032-05981-9_13.

© The Author(s), under exclusive license to Springer Nature Switzerland AG 2026
R. P. Ribeiro et al. (Eds.): ECML PKDD 2025, LNAI 16014, pp. 206–221, 2026.
https://doi.org/10.1007/978-3-032-05981-9_13

latent variable model $p_\theta(\boldsymbol{x}_0) = \int p(\boldsymbol{x}_T) \prod_{t=1}^{T} p_\theta(\boldsymbol{x}_{t-1} \mid \boldsymbol{x}_t) d\boldsymbol{x}_{1:T}$. Through a Markov chain Gaussian forward process $(\boldsymbol{x}_0 \to \boldsymbol{x}_T)$ with noising transitions $q(\boldsymbol{x}_t \mid \boldsymbol{x}_{t-1}) := \mathcal{N}\left(\boldsymbol{x}_t; \sqrt{1-\beta_t}\boldsymbol{x}_{t-1}, \beta_t \mathbf{I}\right)$, the data $\boldsymbol{x}_0$ is progressively noised with a pre-defined variance schedule $\beta_1, \ldots, \beta_T$. The Gaussian Markov reverse process $(\boldsymbol{x}_T \to \boldsymbol{x}_0)$ with learned denoising steps $p_\theta(\boldsymbol{x}_{t-1} \mid \boldsymbol{x}_t)$ reverses the forward process from random noise $\boldsymbol{x}_T \sim \mathcal{N}(0, I)$ to produce samples following the data distribution $p_\theta \approx p_{\text{data}}$.

A special property of this type of generative model is the iterative sampling procedure where conditional information can be added without the need for training a specific conditional model through a procedure known as *classifier guidance* [4,18]. For an unconditionally trained DDPM $p_\theta(\boldsymbol{x}_{t-1} \mid \boldsymbol{x}_t) = \mathcal{N}(\boldsymbol{x}_{t-1}; \mu_\theta(\boldsymbol{x}_t), \Sigma_t(\boldsymbol{x}_t))$, the mean $\mu_\theta(\boldsymbol{x}_t)$ of the transitions can be shifted by the gradients of a classifier trained over the noisy data $\boldsymbol{x}_t$ as:

$$\mu_\theta(\boldsymbol{x}_t)' = \mu_\theta(\boldsymbol{x}_t) + s\, \Sigma_t(\boldsymbol{x}_t) \nabla_{\boldsymbol{x}_t} \log p_{\text{cl}}(y \mid \boldsymbol{x}_t) \ , \qquad (1)$$

where s is a gradient scaling factor controlling the strength of the classifier guidance, and $\mu_\theta(\boldsymbol{x}_t)'$ is the new mean of the reverse transition used for conditionally sampling the previous sample $\boldsymbol{x}_{t-1}$.

Classifier guidance is commonly used to add conditional information during the diffusion reverse process (e.g., in explainability [1], in protein design [7] and in molecular design [21]). The main limitation of classifier guidance is that the classifier needs to be robust to noise similar to that added during the diffusion forward process [4] so that the gradients $\nabla_{\boldsymbol{x}_t} \log p_{\text{cl}}(y \mid \boldsymbol{x}_t)$ in Eq. 1 are meaningful. This requires training a guidance classifier for each specific diffusion model and re-training it if the desired conditioning changes or if the diffusion forward process definition changes. Extending classifier guidance to classifiers not trained over the specific DDPM noise (non-robust classifiers) remains a challenge.

A previously proposed solution is to let the classifier decide on a one-step denoised image from the diffusion model instead of the noisy images directly, referred to as $\hat{\boldsymbol{x}}_0^{(\boldsymbol{x}_t)}$-prediction [1,2,20]. We introduce the $\hat{\boldsymbol{x}}_0^{(\boldsymbol{x}_t)}$-prediction in detail in Sect. 2.4 (Eq. 5), and show that it is not enough to solve the challenge of non-robust classifier guidance. Based on a detailed analysis of the classifier gradients including the $\hat{\boldsymbol{x}}_0^{(\boldsymbol{x}_t)}$-prediction, we propose in Sect. 2.5 to leverage methods from stochastic optimization to additionally stabilize the non-robust guidance gradients further, bridging the gap to the performance of robust classifier guidance. Finally, we transfer our proposed stabilization method to the diffusion reverse process in Sect. 3 and show that the stabilization enables the use of non-robust classifiers for guided sampling. In summary, we provide a detailed analysis of how non-robust and robust classifiers behave during the diffusion forward process, and propose a guidance stabilization technique that allows non-robust classifiers to be used effectively for guidance in the diffusion reverse process.

2 Diffusion Forward Process

We start our analysis by comparing the classifier accuracy over different levels of noisy data in Sect. 2.1. We then showcase how the logits (Sect. 2.2) and gradients (Sect. 2.3) of the classifier behave over time t for similar inputs. Finally in Sect. 2.5, we analyze how the $\hat{x}_0^{(x_t)}$-prediction (Eq. 5) influences the gradients of non-robust classifiers and, as a result, propose stabilization techniques to further improve non-robust classifier guidance. We conclude Sect. 2 by recommending a stabilization technique for non-robust classifier guidance and test this on the reverse diffusion process in Sect. 3.

For our analysis, we train two standard MobileNetV3 [11] classifiers on the CelebA [14] data set with an image size of 64×64 (details in Sect. 3) to detect the binary attribute *female*: (1) a **non-robust** classifier trained on the original non-noisy data and (2) a **robust classifier** trained on data augmented by the forward noising process of the diffusion model. In detail, for a standard training batch of n images, we draw n time steps from a discrete uniform distribution $t \sim \mathcal{U}\{0, T\}$ and run the diffusion forward process for each image as:

$$q\left(x_t \mid x_0\right) = \mathcal{N}\left(x_t; \sqrt{\bar{\alpha}_t} x_0, (1 - \bar{\alpha}_t)\mathbf{I}\right) , \qquad (2)$$

with $\bar{\alpha}_t := \prod_{s=1}^{t} \alpha_s$ and $\alpha_t := 1 - \beta_t$ [9]. An increasing β_t noise schedule therefore corresponds to progressively noisier samples x_t for a higher t.

For our diffusion model, we train a standard DDPM [9] with a linear noise schedule ($\beta_0 = 0.0001, \beta_T = 0.02$), $T = 400$ diffusion steps, a standard U-Net architecture [16] for the noise predictor, and the simplified MSE noise prediction training objective [9]. Our diffusion models are implemented using the open-source Diffusers toolbox [15] and trained for 1000 epochs (around 3 d on a single NVIDIA A80 GPU).

2.1 Accuracy of the Classifiers on Noisy Data

In Fig. 1, we compare the classification accuracy of the robust and the non-robust classifiers over the noisy validation data set (by applying Eq. 2) and see that the non-robust classifier accuracy (red) drops significantly with increasing noise levels added through increasing diffusion steps, up to the point of random guessing at less than 25% of the total diffusion steps T. This analysis of the classification performance is a simple way to understand classifier robustness over different noise levels. However, the classification performance analysis works over the validation set perturbed by different amount of random noise, disregarding previous time steps (Eq. 2). In the diffusion forward process, the dependency on the previous sample is critical for the model definition and the sampling procedure (Markov property).

2.2 Sensitivity of the Classifier Logits

To further investigate the implications of low classification accuracy in the presence of noisy data points, we propose to analyze the sensitivity of the classifier's output scores (logits) to small changes in input features over time. This approach allows us to measure how the quantity of noise in the data points affects the decision boundary and robustness of the classifier. Specifically, starting from

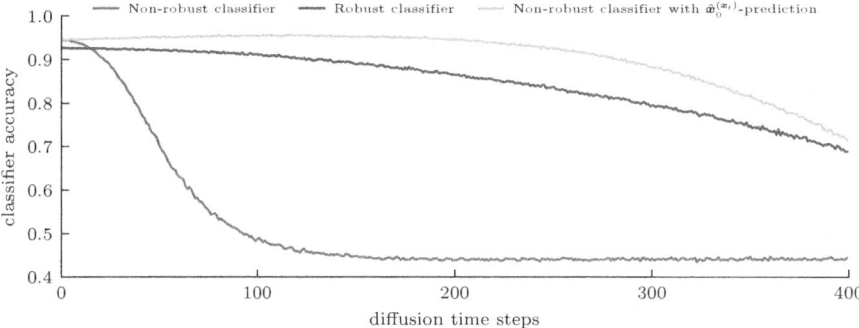

Fig. 1. Classification accuracy comparison of the robust, non-robust, and non-robust with $\hat{x}_0^{(x_t)}$-prediction (Eq. 5) classifiers on the CelebA binary attribute female. The metric is reported as the average over the validation data set.

the same image x_0, we do not sample two adjacent noisy versions x_t and x_{t-1} independently (Eq. 2), but instead use the same noise to produce both noisy images. This results in small changes by construction, where the same features are perturbed in x_t and x_{t-1} but at different scales based on the β schedule of the DDPM forward process. This is in line with the diffusion forward process definition in Sect. 1, in which x_t is a more noisy version of x_{t-1}. We consider a classification function $f : \mathcal{X} \to \mathcal{Y}^D$ which maps an RGB input image to a D-dimensional vector of class logits and define the metric S_l as:

$$S_l(x_t, x_{t-1}) = \frac{\| f(x_t) - f(x_{t-1}) \|_2}{\| x_t - x_{t-1} \|_2} . \qquad (3)$$

For two noisy data points x_t and x_{t-1} on the same diffusion trajectory (starting from the same x_0), small differences between these points should correspond to small differences in logits for a robust classifier. Note that the metric S_l is similar to the discrete approximation of derivatives. We compare the score S_l (Eq. 3) over the entire diffusion forward process for our classifiers in Fig. 2 to analyze the noise sensitivity of classifier logits over time. The results confirm that the non-robust classifier is indeed much more sensitive to small input changes than the robust classifier. This means that the non-robust classifier function is not smooth and reacts with different output logits for small input perturbations, hinting to possibly undesired behavior for the guidance of the diffusion reverse process based on classifier gradients.

2.3 Stability of the Classifier Gradients

Going a step further beyond logits, we can directly compute gradients just as they would be used in the sampling process of the diffusion model to confirm that unstable logits over time t indeed affect the gradients necessary in classifier guidance. We run the same experiment, but compare the sensitivity of gradients

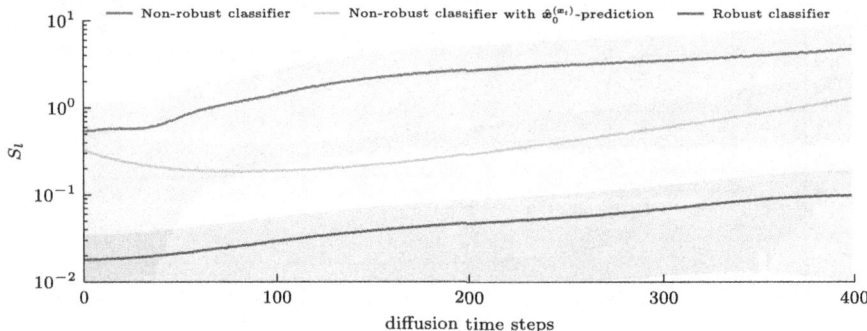

Fig. 2. Logit sensitivity S_l (log scale) as defined in Eq. 3 over time t for the robust, non-robust, and non-robust with $\hat{x}_0^{(x_t)}$-prediction (Eq. 5) classifiers on CelebA. The metric is reported as the average (and std) over the validation data set.

over time t instead of logits:

$$S_g(x_t, x_{t-1}) = \frac{\|\nabla_{x_t} f(x_t) - \nabla_{x_{t-1}} f(x_{t-1})\|_2}{\|x_t - x_{t-1}\|_2} . \tag{4}$$

An alternative interpretation of Eq. 4 is in terms of geometry. Equation 4 quantifies to what degree the guidance vectors point in similar directions for adjacent time steps t and $t-1$. We note that S_g is connected to the discrete approximation of second-order derivatives, that is the curvature of the classification function over time. In practice, a low S_g score would correspond to gradual introduction of features during conditional diffusion sampling instead of sudden feature changes. Based on this intuition, we can quantify through the metric S_g how informative classifier gradients are for conditional sampling.

In Fig. 3, we show the metric S_g over time for the same experimental setup as previously, confirming that the non-robust classifier with unstable logit outputs (as demonstrated in Fig. 2), indeed does not have informative gradients and is therefore not suitable for conditional guidance. On the contrary, the robust classifier (blue line in Fig. 3) shows low gradient sensitivity as measured by S_g, enabling the use of the robust classifier for classifier guidance.

2.4 Informative classifier gradients through $\hat{x}_0^{(x_t)}$-prediction

To summarize, we have shown that classifying noisy data points with a classifier not trained over the same noise results in a loss of accuracy and high sensitivity of the classifier outputs to such noise. We have also shown that this results in unstable and therefore non-informative gradients, which are not suitable for the use in classifier guidance. One approach to resolve this issue is to apply the classifier not on the noisy diffusion data x_t but on an approximation of the fully denoised image x_0 [1,2,20]. We can estimate the $\hat{x}_0^{(x_t)}$-prediction via:

$$\hat{x}_0^{(x_t)} = \frac{x_t}{\sqrt{\bar{\alpha}_t}} - \frac{\sqrt{1-\bar{\alpha}_t}}{\sqrt{\bar{\alpha}_t}} \epsilon_\theta(x_t, t) . \tag{5}$$

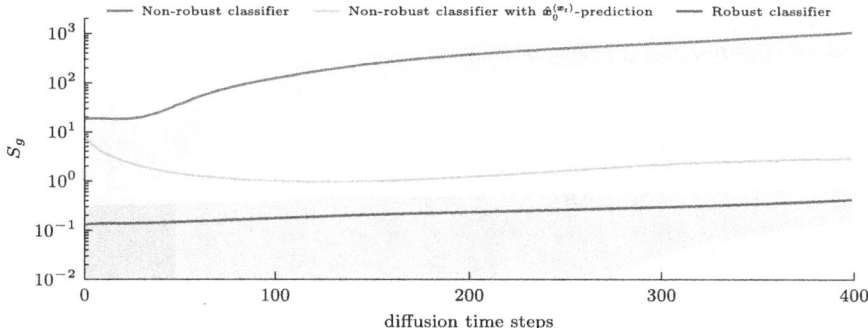

Fig. 3. Gradient sensitivity S_g (log scale) as defined in Eq. 4 over time t for the robust, non-robust, and non-robust with $\hat{x}_0^{(x_t)}$-prediction (Eq. 5) classifiers on CelebA. The metric is reported as the average (and std) over the validation set.

The $\hat{x}_0^{(x_t)}$-prediction seemingly resolves the issue of non-robust classifiers for classifier guidance, supported by the high classification accuracy over noisy data when applying the $\hat{x}_0^{(x_t)}$-prediction before the classification (orange line in Fig. 1). In addition to classification accuracy, however, we also consider the gradient sensitivity for $\hat{x}_0^{(x_t)}$-prediction:

$$\hat{S}_g(x_t, x_{t-1}) = \frac{\|\nabla_{x_t} f(\hat{x}_0^{(x_t)}) - \nabla_{x_{t-1}} f(\hat{x}_0^{(x_{t-1})})\|_2}{\|x_t - x_{t-1}\|_2} \ . \tag{6}$$

We show in Fig. 3, that the classifier with $\hat{x}_0^{(x_t)}$-prediction (orange line) substantially reduces gradient sensitivity (and hence improves gradient stability), but does not yet achieve the level of a robust classifier. Hence, we believe that further improvements, beyond the $\hat{x}_0^{(x_t)}$-prediction, are required. We note that $\hat{x}_0^{(x_t)}$-prediction dramatically increases memory cost because gradients need to be propagated not only through the classifier but also through the diffusion model at each denoising step.

2.5 Stable Classifier Gradients Through Moving Averages

We begin our improvements with the insight that the classifier guidance process in Eq. 1 effectively acts as a moving average because the mean of the reverse sampling process in every step is the sum of the mean of the previous step and the classifier guidance vector. However, the guidance vectors are computed independently in each step t, meaning that their directions can drastically change between time steps as discussed in Sect. 2.3 and shown in Figs. 2 and 3. Accordingly, it stands to reason to adjust classifier guidance to explicitly perform a moving average over the guidance vectors, thus enhancing the gradient stability. We explore two stabilization techniques inspired by the two most common stochastic optimization algorithms, SGD with momentum [17] and ADAM [13]. For a given guidance gradient $\boldsymbol{g}$, momentum strength β and $\epsilon > 0$, we define:

$$\nu_t^{\mathrm{ema}}(\boldsymbol{g}, \beta) = \beta \nu_{t-1}^{\mathrm{ema}} + (1-\beta)\boldsymbol{g} \,, \tag{7}$$

$$\nu_t^{\mathrm{adam}}(\boldsymbol{g}) = \frac{\nu_t^{\mathrm{ema}}(\boldsymbol{g}, \beta = 0.9)}{\sqrt{\nu_t^{\mathrm{ema}}(\boldsymbol{g}^2, \beta = 0.999)} + \epsilon} \,. \tag{8}$$

We do not include any de-biasing terms into Eqs. 7 and 8 to compensate for extremely noisy samples with barely any signal in the initial denoising steps ($\boldsymbol{x}_T, \boldsymbol{x}_{T-1}, \dots$), which results in unreliable gradients. We therefore omit these de-biasing terms deliberately to bias the guidance terms toward zero. In the reverse process, this will avoid adding unreliable conditioning information early in the sampling steps, which could potentially break the diffusion sampling process due to unlikely starting points.

We again experimentally validate on the forward process how these stabilization techniques change the gradient stability over time. For this, we apply both techniques (Eqs. 7 and 8) directly on the gradients in our gradient stability metric S_g (Eq. 6). We show the gradient stability over time t in Fig. 4, contrasting the robust classifier to the non-robust classifier with $\hat{\boldsymbol{x}}_0^{(\boldsymbol{x}_t)}$-prediction and with the stabilization techniques. For ADAM, the gradient stability deteriorates over increasing time t due to the rescaling of the gradients by the running estimate of the second moment (see Eq. 8), amplifying differences between time steps t and $t-1$ based on the variance of the gradient (denominator of Eq. 8). For exponential moving averaging, the differences between neighboring diffusion time steps

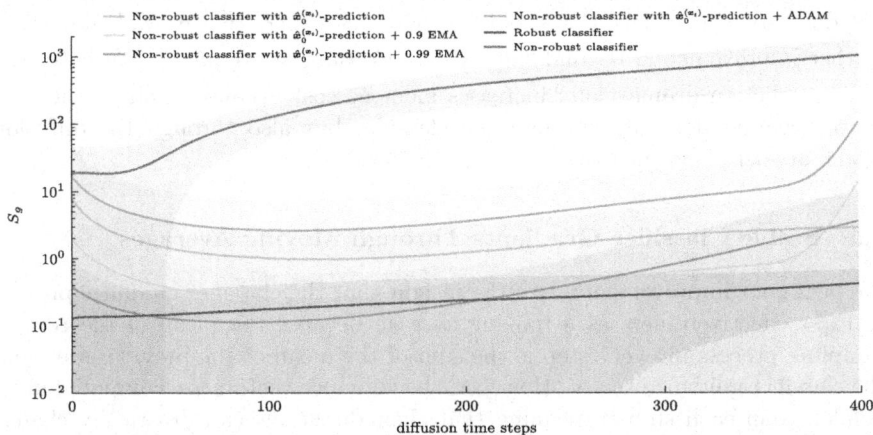

Fig. 4. Gradient sensitivity S_g (log scale) over time t for the robust, non-robust, and non-robust with $\hat{\boldsymbol{x}}_0^{(\boldsymbol{x}_t)}$-prediction (Eq. 5) classifiers, as well as multiple stabilization techniques (eq. 7,8). The metric is reported as the average (and std) over the CelebA validation data set.

become naturally smaller, with a larger window size ($\beta = 0.99$) contributing to even more stability over time. Interestingly, the EMA stabilization with the large window size reaches the gradient stability of the robust classifier, especially during the first half of the forward process ($t < 200$).

Our analysis demonstrates that gradient stability, measured by pairwise differences over time, is connected to the classifier accuracy. Additionally, we show that $\hat{x}_0^{(x_t)}$-prediction enhances gradient quality from this perspective. Furthermore, by explicitly enforcing stable feature changes over the diffusion time steps t through exponential moving averaging of classifier gradients, we can bridge the gap between the non-robust classifier and the robust classifier in terms of gradient stability. These observations have so far been on the diffusion forward process to observe the gradient behavior in isolation without interference of the diffusion reverse (sampling) process. In Sect. 3, we will translate these findings to the diffusion reverse process.

3 Diffusion Reverse Process

In the diffusion reverse process, we apply the techniques from Sect. 2 to diffusion sampling. In algorithm 1, we provide details about the implementation of our guided sampling setup. The only difference to the standard DDPM classifier guidance are lines 3 and 4, which is where we apply our stabilization techniques. We introduce the data sets in Sect. 3.1, define the metrics used to evaluate the generated samples in Sect. 3.2, and then use algorithm 1 in Sect. 3.3 to produce conditional samples for our non-robust classifiers.

Algorithm 1. Guided DDPM Sampling

1: $x_T \sim \mathcal{N}(0, I)$, classifier guidance scale s, unconditionally trained DDPM $\mu_\theta(x_t)$, DDPM forward process variance $\Sigma_t(x_t)$, guidance stabilization function ν
2: **for** $t = T, \ldots, 1$ **do**
3:     $g = \nabla_{x_t} \log p_{cl}\left(y \mid \hat{x}_0^{(x_t)}\right)$ if $\hat{x}_0^{(x_t)}$-prediction (eq.5), else $\nabla_{x_t} \log p_{cl}(y \mid x_t)$
4:     $g = \nu(g)$ if guidance-stabilization   ▷ See eq. 7 and eq. 8
5:     $x_{t-1} = \mathcal{N}(x_{t-1}; \mu_\theta(x_t), \Sigma_t(x_t))$ ▷ See diffusion reverse transition in sec. 1
6:     $x'_{t-1} = x_{t-1} + s\, \Sigma_t(x_t) \nabla_{x_t} g$ ▷ See eq. 1
7: **end for**
8: **return** x'_0

3.1 Data Sets

For the data sets used in conditional sampling, we chose CelebA [14] as a standard image generation benchmark data set, use the SportBalls data set [19] as a custom data set specifically created for conditional generations, and use Celeba-HQ [12] as the real-world high resolution data set with an off-the-shelf diffusion model. We train a standard MobileNetV3 [11] classifier on all data sets.

We train the non-robust classifier without data augmentation and the robust classifier with the training data corrupted by the same noise occurring in the diffusion forward process.

For the CelebA data set (64 × 64), we train the classifiers on the binary attribute *female* (58.3% of the total images). This class was chosen based on easily distinguishable features of the classes and the relatively clear classification boundary. The classifiers are trained on over more than 160k training images and evaluated over 20k validation images.

For a synthetic, more controllable, conditional sampling setup we use the SportBalls data set (64 × 64). The custom data set is created by randomly selecting one out of three sport balls (multi-class classification) and placing them at random coordinates on white background with random rotation and scaling. The data set is carefully created to have similar objects (i.e., scaling, shape, size, rotation and placement) but with clear semantic differences (i.e., colors and pattern). This data set is specifically constructed for conditional sampling due to clear class boundaries with balanced classes for the classifier and the white background for unambiguous generations without artifacts in the images. The goal for the conditional DDPM sampling is to generate *baseballs*. The classifiers are trained on 80k training images and evaluated on 20k validation images.

For the real-world use-case on CelebA-HQ-256 (256 × 256), we train the same simple classifier just as for the other data sets, but use the pre-trained DDPM model from [9]. We use the DDPM model without modification in our stabilized guided sampling setup to showcase how our contribution translates to third-party models and higher dimensional data. The class to generate is *female* (64.1% of the total images). The non-robust classifier is trained on 28k training images and evaluated on 2k validation images.

3.2 Metrics

To evaluate the resulting samples on the CelebA and SportBalls data sets, we compute all following metrics over 50176 conditionally generated samples for the different stabilization setups (3-7 h on a single NVIDIA A80 graphics card). For Celeba-HQ, we compute the metrics over 1024 samples (4 h on a single NVIDIA A80 graphics card) due to computational constraints.

To quantify if the guiding classifier successfully introduced class-conditional features, we apply the classifier on the final generated samples and compute the accuracy for the target class. Different stabilization setups and guidance scales will lead to higher accuracy at the expense of image quality and diversity.

A common metric to quantify the visual quality of generated images is the Fréchet inception distance (FID) [8], which compares statistics of extracted features from a pre-trained network between the training data and generated images. For this comparison, we randomly draw the same amount of generated samples from the training data as we generate. A low FID score indicates visual similarity of the generated samples to the training data. This metric also serves as a measure for diversity, as generated samples with only class-specific features are generally less close to the training set with a diverse set of features.

To complement the accuracy and the unconditional FID metric for visual quality, we compute a class-specific FID score which only operates on the data of the target class (cFID). In practice, this means we compare the statistics of the conditionally generated samples not to that of the entire data set but only to training images of the target class. A low cFID score ensures that the generated samples are visually close to the ground-truth images of the target class, ignoring potential features of other classes.

3.3 DDPM Sampling with Stabilized Non-robust Classifiers

We start our improved sampling experiments on the CelebA data set and conclude the section with experiments on the SportBalls and the CelebA-HQ data sets. The key hyperparameter in classifier guidance is the scale s (see algorithm 1 and Eq. 1), known to trade-off class conditioning and sample diversity [4]. We explore the robust classifier and the non-robust classifier with stabilization techniques, and present the accuracy over different guidance scales in Fig. 5, the unconditional FID in Fig. 6 and the conditional FID in Fig. 7.

We can observe that for a high enough guidance scale, all classifier setups except the non-robust classifier without stabilization techniques produce consistent class-conditional samples according to the classifier (Fig. 5). The non-robust classifier guidance fails without stabilization by offsetting the unconditional diffusion mean by so much that the diffusion reverse process can not recover, ultimately not producing any samples. We can see that the ADAM stabilization requires a much lower scaling than the other stabilization techniques as the rescaling of the gradients by the variance (Eq. 8) amplifies the guidance scale.

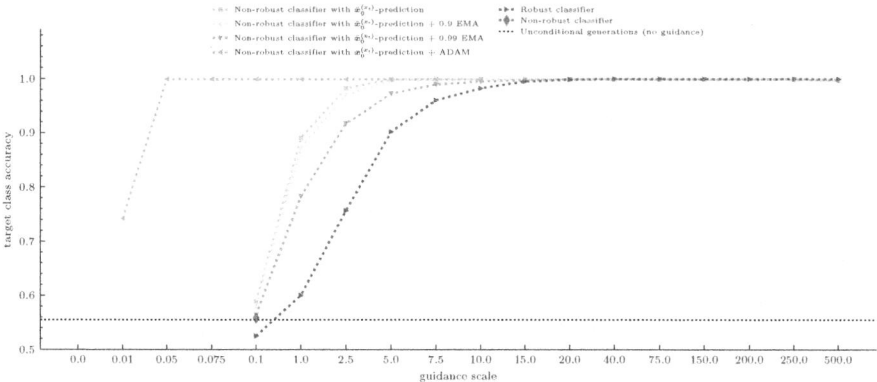

Fig. 5. Accuracy comparison for conditional sampling on CelebA with various stabilization setups (Eq. 7, 8). The accuracy is presented as the average over 50176 generated samples.

From the image quality as measured by the FID in Fig. 6, we can notice the FID of the robust classifier increases with a higher guidance scale. This is

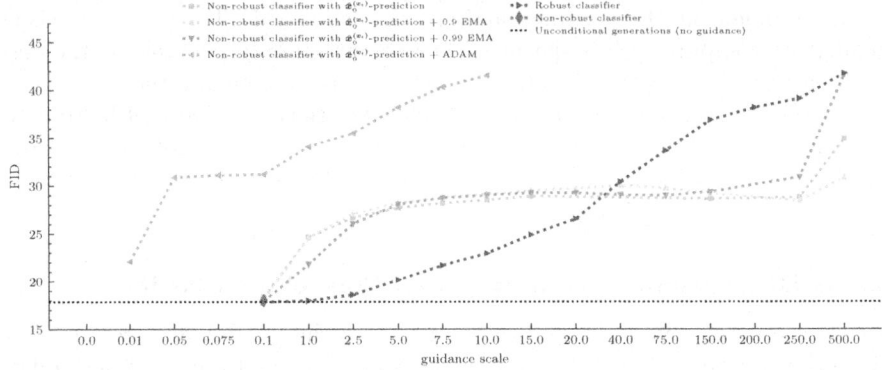

Fig. 6. Unconditional FID comparison for conditional sampling on CelebA with various stabilization setups (Eq. 7, 8). The unconditional FID is calculated over 50176 generated samples.

expected behavior, as the quality of the images measured by the closeness to the entire data set should decrease if the diffusion model is constrained to generate features of one class only and therefore loses diversity. The non-robust classifier with $\hat{x}_0^{(x_t)}$-prediction and ADAM stabilization exhibits a more rapid increase in FID as the guidance scale increases, compared to the robust classifier. The non-robust classifiers with $\hat{x}_0^{(x_t)}$-prediction and with $\hat{x}_0^{(x_t)}$-prediction + EMA stabilization all exhibit similar behavior with an increasing FID just as the target class accuracy increases. This levels off to a stable FID value even for very high guidance scales until too much guidance strength (>500 in this case) eventually increases the FID again. This indicates an optimal range just

Table 1. Metrics and first 10 samples for unconditional diffusion sampling (left) and conditional diffusion sampling (right) with the non-robust classifier, $\hat{x}_0^{(x_t)}$-prediction (Eq. 5), 0.99-EMA stabilization (Eq. 7) and guidance scale of 150.0 on CelebA. Metrics calculated over a batch of 50176 samples. More images are shown in the supplementary material.

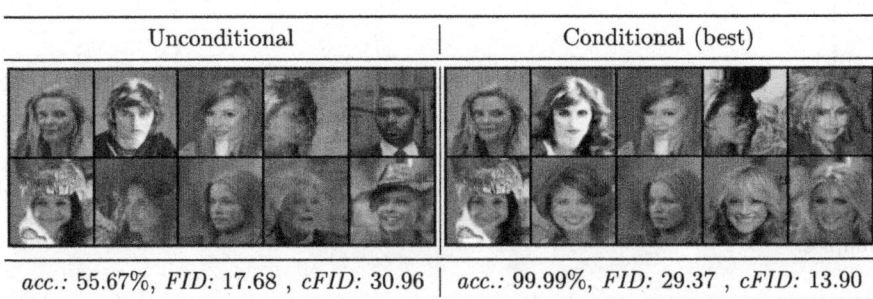

Unconditional	Conditional (best)
acc.: 55.67%, FID: 17.68 , cFID: 30.96	acc.: 99.99%, FID: 29.37 , cFID: 13.90

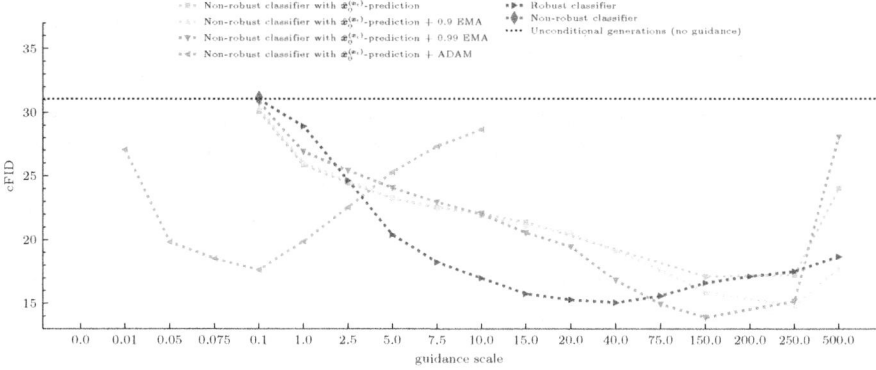

Fig. 7. Target class FID comparison for conditional sampling on CelebA with various stabilization setups (Eq. 7, 8). The class-conditional FID is calculated over 50176 generated samples.

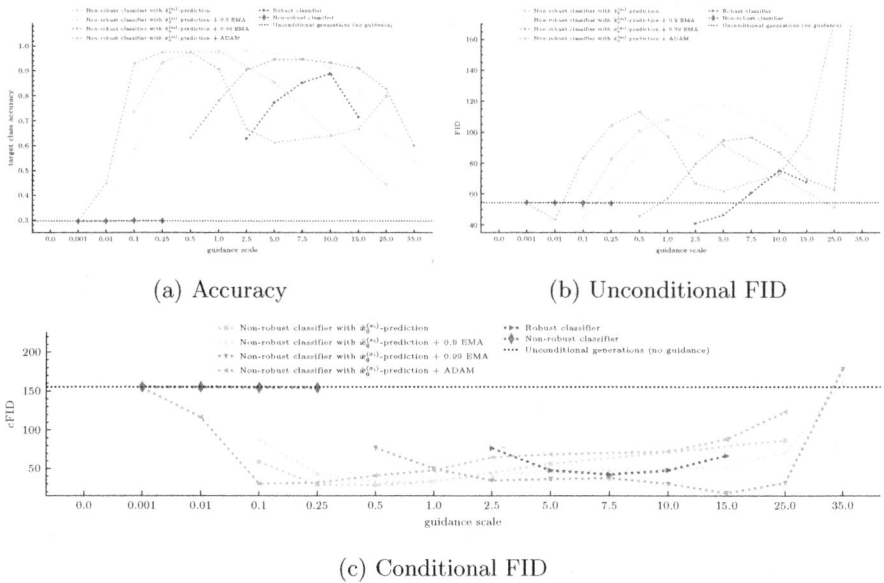

Fig. 8. Accuracy, FID and cFID metrics for conditional sampling on SportBalls with stabilization setups (Eq. 7, 8) calculated over 50176 generated samples.

before this increase, where substantial guidance strength can be applied without compromising sample quality or overwhelming the diffusion process.

For the class-conditional FID in Fig. 7, we observe a decrease in cFID score with more guidance strength for the robust classifier up to a turning point (here $s > 40$) when the cFID score increases again. This means for higher guidance strength the overall sample quality (FID) decreases due to lower diversity as compared to the complete mixed-class training set, but the class-conditional sample quality (cFID) increases. However, if the guidance strength is too high, the cFID reaches a turning point where the conditioning overpowers the diffusion process, generating samples not coherent with the underlying data distribution. A similar behavior is shown by all guidance setups, highlighting that the choice of guidance strength trades-off sample quality and class conditioning. Our proposed guidance setup, using $\hat{x}_0^{(x_t)}$-prediction and EMA stabilization with $\beta = 0.99$, achieves the best cFID score (13.9) while maintaining good overall image quality (FID of 29.37). This guidance setup outperforms even the unmodified robust classifier, demonstrating the potential of non-robust classifiers for conditional sampling when appropriately stabilized. This confirms our findings from the diffusion forward process analysis in Sect. 2. By introducing the $\hat{x}_0^{(x_t)}$-prediction into the classifier guidance, the classifier gradients of the non-robust classifier are more meaningful. Through exponential moving averaging of the classifier gradients, we can enforce stable feature changes over the guided reverse diffusion process. The combination of the $\hat{x}_0^{(x_t)}$-prediction and the exponential moving average of the gradients leads to successful classifier guidance even for the non-robust classifier. We show generations for our best guidance setup as well as without guidance in Table 1. More images are provided in the supplementary material.

We repeat the previous experiment on the more controlled multi-class Sport-Balls data set. We present the accuracy in Fig. 8a, the unconditional FID in Fig. 8b and the conditional FID in Fig. 8c for the different guidance setups and scaling strength. Sample images are shown in Fig. 2. The robust classifier generates class-conditional samples, trading off the overall image quality with the amount of conditioning added to the diffusion reverse process (Fig. 8c). All guidance setups improve the guidance mechanism for the non-robust classifier, with the 0.99-EMA stabilization reaching the lowest cFID score of 18.5 while maintaining good overall image quality with a FID of 69.6. The guidance by the non-robust classifier fails similarly as on the CelebA data without any stabilization techniques. The special setup of the data set with clear class boundaries and unambiguous class features is visible in the results, where the cFID decreases drastically when classifier guidance is successfully applied (Table 2).

For our real-world CelebA-HQ data set, we test our best guidance setup on an off-the-shelf DDPM. We evaluate the metrics on 1024 samples and show the first 10 generated samples as well as the corresponding metrics in Fig. 3. The stabilized classifier guidance for the non-robust classifier with $\hat{x}_0^{(x_t)}$-prediction and 0.99-EMA successfully generates class-conditional samples by achieving $> 99\%$ target class accuracy, reducing the cFID by 7.52 points and trading-off conditioning with overall sample quality (FID increased by 5.1 points). Visually, male faces are slightly altered towards what the classifier believes are female features.

Table 2. Metrics and first 10 samples for unconditional diffusion sampling (left) and conditional diffusion sampling (right) with the non-robust classifier, $\hat{x}_0^{(x_t)}$-prediction (Eq. 5), 0.99-EMA stabilization (Eq. 7) and guidance scale of 15.0 on the SportBalls data set. Metrics calculated over a batch of 50176 samples. More images are shown in the supplementary material.

Unconditional	Conditional (best)
acc.: 29.63%, *FID:* 54.37 , *cFID:* 155.19	*acc.:* 91.05%, *FID:* 69.64 , *cFID:* 18.52

Table 3. Metrics and samples for unconditional diffusion sampling (left) and conditional diffusion sampling (right) with $\hat{x}_0^{(x_t)}$-prediction (Eq. 5), 0.99-EMA stabilization (Eq. 7) and guidance scale of 10.0 on CelebA-HQ. Metrics calculated over a batch of 1024 samples. The top row shows the first 5 generations, the bottom row shows 5 hand-picked seeds for which the unconditional model produces the class male. More images are shown in the supplementary material.

Unconditional	Conditional

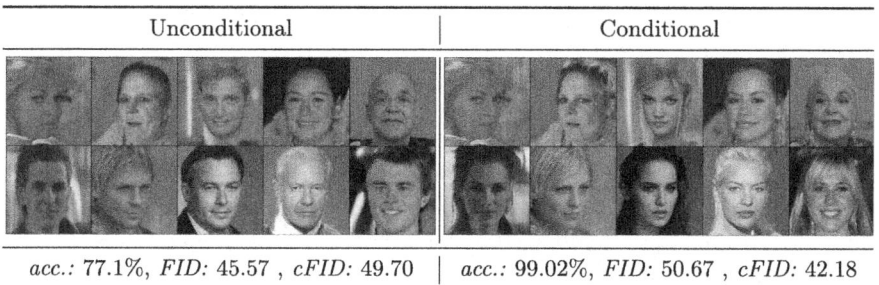

| *acc.:* 77.1%, *FID:* 45.57 , *cFID:* 49.70 | *acc.:* 99.02%, *FID:* 50.67 , *cFID:* 42.18 |

4 Related Work

Classifier guidance as proposed in [4] requires a classifier, which was trained on the same noise as introduced in the diffusion forward process. A one-step estimate of the denoised image from the diffusion model was proposed to apply classifier guidance to noise-unaware classifiers [2], which we refer to as $\hat{x}_0^{(x_t)}$-prediction in our paper. In combination with the $\hat{x}_0^{(x_t)}$-prediction, a robust classifier restricting the non-robust classifier gradients can be used in conjunction to enable guidance on arbitrary classifiers [1]. However, to the best of our knowledge, no paper has so far specifically addressed the challenge of non-robust classifiers for classifier guidance without training a specialized classifier or diffusion model. For classifier guidance with robust classifiers, multiple improvements have been suggested, for example [5,6].

Classifier-free guidance [10], as the predecessor of classifier guidance, subsumes the auxiliary classifier into a Bayesian implicit classifier in the form of a conditional diffusion model. Through training a conditional diffusion model, the unconditional and conditional denoising steps can be traded-off to achieve conditioning during sampling. We mention this parallel line of work for completeness, but note that classifier-free guidance always requires training a conditional diffusion model, which therefore does not allow adding arbitrary conditioning information in the diffusion reverse process without retraining.

5 Conclusion

In this study, we have extended classifier guidance techniques to non-robust classifiers within denoising diffusion probabilistic models (DDPMs). By addressing the inherent limitations of requiring specifically trained robust classifiers for classifier guidance, we built on top of previously proposed one-step denoised image predictions to stabilizes guidance gradients during the sampling process. Our findings demonstrate that incorporating stabilization techniques, particularly exponential moving averages, enhances gradient stability, bridging the performance gap between non-robust and robust classifiers. The experimental results on the CelebA data set indicate that our approach not only improves classification accuracy but also maintains sample diversity and visual quality in generated images. Future work will focus on refining these methods and exploring their applicability to other generative models and diffusion samplers. Especially other techniques from stochastic optimization and dynamic guidance schedules will be explored.

Limitations Classifier-guidance is sensitive to hyperparameter choices, especially the guidance scaling. We explored many hyperparameter choices in this study but did not specifically optimize for state-of-the-art FID scores. We only explored two stabilization techniques based on SGD with momentum and ADAM as the two most commonly used methods from stochastic optimization. This shows stabilization techniques are promising candidates to improve classifier guidance, other techniques not explored in this study may however improve gradient stability even further. We also use the FID metric as-is with the feature extractor pre-trained on ImageNet [3]. This results in higher FID values for CelebA and very high FID values for SportBalls, since the features in the data sets are different to features extracted on ImageNet. In our analysis, we used one representative classifier architecture (MobileNetV3). Other architectures may require different hyperparameter choices. The same applies for the diffusion process, where we only used the standard DDPM setup. Translating our findings to other diffusion reverse samplers is subject to future work.

Acknowledgments. This research is supported by the Center for Artificial Intelligence (CAIRO) at the Technical University of Applied Sciences Würzburg-Schweinfurt (THWS), Würzburg, Germany and the Bavarian Hightech Agenda.

Disclosure of Interests. The authors have no competing interests to declare that are relevant to the content of this article.

References

1. Augustin, M., Boreiko, V., Croce, F., Hein, M.: Diffusion visual counterfactual explanations. In: NeurIPS (2022)
2. Avrahami, O., Lischinski, D., Fried, O.: Blended diffusion for text-driven editing of natural images. In: CVPR (2022)
3. Deng, J., Dong, W., Socher, R., Li, L.J., Li, K., Fei-Fei, L.: Imagenet: A Large-scale Hierarchical Image Database. In: CVPR (2009)
4. Dhariwal, P., Nichol, A.: Diffusion models beat gans on image synthesis. In: NeurIPS (2021)
5. Dinh, A.D., Liu, D., Xu, C.: Pixelasparam: a gradient view on diffusion sampling with guidance. In: ICML (2023)
6. Dinh, A.D., Liu, D., Xu, C.: Rethinking conditional diffusion sampling with progressive guidance. In: NeurIPS (2024)
7. Gruver, N., et al.: Protein design with guided discrete diffusion. In: NeurIPS (2024)
8. Heusel, M., Ramsauer, H., Unterthiner, T., Nessler, B., Hochreiter, S.: Gans trained by a two time-scale update rule converge to a local nash equilibrium. In: NeurIPS (2017)
9. Ho, J., Jain, A., Abbeel, P.: Denoising diffusion probabilistic models. In: NeurIPS (2020)
10. Ho, J., Salimans, T.: Classifier-free diffusion guidance. In: NeurIPS Workshop on Deep Generative Models and Downstream Applications (2021)
11. Howard, A., Sandler, M., et al.: Searching for Mobilenetv3. In: ICCV (2019)
12. Karras, T., Aila, T., Laine, S., Lehtinen, J.: Progressive Growing of gans for improved quality, stability, and variation. In: ICLR (2018)
13. Kingma, D.P., Ba, J.: Adam: a method for stochastic optimization. In: ICLR (2015)
14. Liu, Z., Luo, P., Wang, X., Tang, X.: Deep learning face attributes in the wild. In: ICCV (2015)
15. von Platen, P., et al.: Diffusers: State-of-the-art Diffusion Models (2022). https://github.com/huggingface/diffusers
16. Ronneberger, O., Fischer, P., Brox, T.: U-Net: convolutional networks for biomedical image segmentation. In: Navab, N., Hornegger, J., Wells, W.M., Frangi, A.F. (eds.) MICCAI 2015. LNCS, vol. 9351, pp. 234–241. Springer, Cham (2015). https://doi.org/10.1007/978-3-319-24574-4_28
17. Rumelhart, D.E., Hinton, G.E., Williams, R.J.: Learning representations by back-propagating errors. Nature (1986)
18. Sohl-Dickstein, J., Weiss, E., Maheswaranathan, N., Ganguli, S.: Deep unsupervised learning using nonequilibrium thermodynamics. In: ICML (2015)
19. Vaeth, P., Fruehwald, A.M., Paassen, B., Gregorova, M.: Generative Example-based Explanations: Bridging the Gap Between Generative Modeling and Explainability. arXiv:2410.20890 (2024)
20. Vaeth, P., Fruehwald, A.M., Paassen, B., Gregorova, M.: Gradcheck: Analyzing Classifier Guidance Gradients for Conditional Diffusion Sampling. arXiv:2406.17399 (2024)
21. Weiss, T., Mayo Yanes, E., Chakraborty, S., Cosmo, L., Bronstein, A.M., Gershoni-Poranne, R.: Guided diffusion for inverse molecular design. Nat. Comput. Sci. (2023)

Improving Discriminator Guidance in Diffusion Models

Alexandre Verine[1]($\boxtimes$), Ahmed Mehdi Inane[2], Florian Le Bronnec[3], Benjamin Negrevergne[3], and Yann Chevaleyre[3]

[1] École Normale Supérieure Paris, PSL University, Paris, France
alexandre.verine@ens.fr
[2] Mila, Quebec AI Institute, Université de Montréal, Montreal, Canada
mehdi-inane.ahmed@mila.quebec
[3] LAMSADE, CNRS, Université Paris-Dauphine-PSL, Paris, France
{florian.le-bronnec,benjamin.negrevergne,yann.chevaleyre}@dauphine.psl.eu

Abstract. Discriminator Guidance has become a popular method for efficiently refining pre-trained Score-Matching Diffusion models. However, in this paper, we demonstrate that the standard implementation of this technique does not necessarily lead to a distribution closer to the real data distribution. Specifically, we show that training the discriminator using Cross-Entropy loss, as commonly done, can in fact increase the Kullback-Leibler divergence between the model and target distributions, particularly when the discriminator overfits. To address this, we propose a theoretically sound training objective for discriminator guidance that properly minimizes the KL divergence. We analyze its properties and demonstrate empirically across multiple datasets that our proposed method consistently improves over the conventional method by producing samples of higher quality. (Code: https://github.com/AlexVerine/BoostDM and Supplementary Materials https://arxiv.org/abs/2503.16117).

Keywords: Diffusion Models · Discriminator Guidance

1 Introduction

Diffusion based generative models have proven to be effective in numerous fields, including image and video generation [5,8,9,15], graphs [19], and audio synthesis [17], among others. Diffusion models are trained to iteratively denoise samples from a noise distribution to approximate the target data distribution. They have gained success in the generative modeling community for their ability to generate both high-quality samples, and to cover well the estimated distribution. However, this comes with a high computational cost both for sampling new data (which requires multiple denoising steps) and for training (which requires training the model multiple time for each level of denoising).

Supplementary Information The online version contains supplementary material available at https://doi.org/10.1007/978-3-032-05981-9_14.

Fig. 1. Illustration of generating samples by a reverse diffusion process to sample from the target distribution P using true score function $\nabla \log p_t$, from the learned distribution $\widehat{P}$ using the learned score function s_θ, from a poor approximation $\widetilde{P}_{\text{CE}}$ using a refined score $s_\theta + \nabla d_\phi$ with low cross-entropy $\mathcal{L}_{\text{CE}^d(\phi)}$ and, finally, from a good approximation $\widetilde{P}_{\text{MSE}}$ using a refined score $s_\theta + \nabla d_\phi$ with low loss $\mathcal{L}_{\text{MSE}^d(\phi)}$ introduced in Sect. 5.

Consequently, several approaches focus on post-training strategies to refine a pre-trained model's distribution at a lower computational cost [6,20,26,32]. Among these, Discriminator Guidance (DG) [14] has recently emerged as a promising refinement method, demonstrating strong empirical results [13,14,28]. This approach refines the generation process by training a discriminator to distinguish generated samples from real samples at different diffusion steps. The discriminator is then used to estimate the log density ratio between the real data distribution P and the learned distribution $\widehat{P}$, with the gradient of this estimate acting as a correction term during generation.

However, this introduces a fundamental discrepancy between training and inference: while the discriminator is trained to approximate the density ratio, inference relies on its gradient, which is **not necessarily a reliable estimate of the target gradient**. As a result, refining the pre-trained model in this way can degrade generation quality.

In this work, we make the following contributions:

- We formally demonstrate in Theorem 1 that training a discriminator to minimize Cross-Entropy and using it for refinement can lead to arbitrarily poor results in the final distribution.
- In Theorem 2, we show that overfitting the discriminator is a sufficient condition for the refined distribution to deteriorate in terms of KL divergence compared to the pre-trained model.
- We propose a reformulation of the DG objective, introducing a new optimization criterion that directly improves the refined distribution by leveraging the gradient of the log-likelihood ratio rather than its value (its benefits over standard Cross-Entropy minimization are illustrated on Fig. 1).
- Finally, we demonstrate that our method enhances sample quality in diffusion models across benchmark image generation datasets, including CIFAR-10, FFHQ, and AFHQ-v2.

By providing a theoretically grounded alternative to the standard DG objective, our approach improves both the understanding and effectiveness of discriminator-guided refinement in generative modeling.

Notations: We denote P, $\widehat{P}$ and $\widetilde{P}$ the target, the learned and the refined distributions defined on $\mathbb{R}^d$. Their densities are denoted p, $\widehat{p}$ and $\widetilde{p}$. We will denote with an indexed t the diffused distribution P_t, $\widehat{P}_t$ and $\widetilde{P}_t$ at time t and their densities p_t, $\widehat{p}_t$ and $\widetilde{p}_t$. We denote by $\mathcal{D}_{\text{KL}}$ the Kullback-Leibler divergence.

2 Related Works

In a trained diffusion model, the divergence between the learned distribution $\widehat{P}$ and the target distribution P arises from two primary sources of error: *sampling* errors, which stem from the discretization scheme used to solve the stochastic differential equation for sample generation, and *estimation* errors, which originate from the discrepancy between the model's final estimate of the score, $\nabla \log \widehat{p}_t$ and the target score $\nabla \log p_t$. This section reviews existing approaches that aim to mitigate this discrepancy by addressing one or both sources of error:

- **Sampling strategies:** A first line of work attempts to correct the sampling error due to the discretization of the backward SDE (Eq. (2)). Since solving this equation numerically is fundamental to sample generation in diffusion models, the choice of the discretization scheme significantly impacts sample quality. Traditional solvers, such as the Euler-Maruyama method [16], are widely used but can introduce bias or require a large number of function evaluations to achieve high fidelity. To address these limitations, researchers have explored improved numerical schemes specifically tailored to score-based generative modeling. For example, Jolicoeur-Martineau et al. [11] propose an adaptive step size strategy for the SDE solver, allowing for more efficient sample generation by dynamically adjusting the discretization step. This approach reduces numerical error and enables high-quality sample synthesis in fewer iterations compared to fixed-step solvers. Xu et al. [33] proposed the Restart sampling algorithm, which alternates between adding noise through additional forward steps and strictly following a backward ordinary differential equation (ODE). This approach balances discretization errors and the contraction property of stochasticity, resulting in accelerated sampling speeds while maintaining or enhancing sample quality.
- **Correcting the estimation:** Another line of work attempts to correct the estimated score function with additional information from auxiliary models. For instance, the classifier-guided approach refines score estimation by incorporating gradients from an external classifier trained to predict class probabilities. These gradients are used to adjust the predicted score of the diffusion model, steering the sampling process toward more semantically meaningful outputs [6]. Since the estimation error term is given by the gradient of the log density ratio between the target distribution P and model distribution $\widehat{P}$, Kim et al. [14] introduced *discriminator guidance*, a method leveraging a

traditional density estimation technique by training a discriminator d_ϕ. The gradient of the output of d_ϕ is then added to the score estimate during sampling, which provably reduces the discrepancy between P and $\hat{P}$. This method builds on a broad body of literature that leverages discriminators to estimate the log-density ratio for enhancing the generation process of Generative Adversarial Networks [2–4,29,30]. Recent works have proposed complementary algorithmic improvements to this approach: Kelvinius and Lindsten [13] propose a sequential Monte-Carlo based algorithm to correct the estimation errors of the discriminator for autoregressive diffusion models, and Tsonis et al. [28] propose a hybrid algorithm that merges discriminator guidance and a scaling factor to mitigate the exposure bias induced by the training process of diffusion models. Our work focuses on improving the training of the discriminator itself, and can be integrated with all the aforementioned methods to further improve sample quality and model performance.

3 Background on Score-Matching Diffusion Models

3.1 Diffusion Process

Let $\{x_t\}_{t \in [0,T]}$ be a diffusion process defined by an Îto SDE:

$$\mathrm{d}x_t = f(x_t, t)\mathrm{d}t + g(t)\mathrm{d}w, \tag{1}$$

where $f(.,t) \in \mathbb{R}^d \to \mathbb{R}^d$ is the drift, $g(t) : \mathbb{R} \to \mathbb{R}$ is the diffusion coefficient and $w \in \mathbb{R}^d$ is a standard Wiener process. It defines a sequence of distributions $\{P_t\}_{t \in [0,T]}$, with densities p_t. With this definition, the target distribution is $P = P_0$ and f, g and T are chosen such that P_T tends toward a tractable distribution Q with density q. In practice, Q is a normal distribution in $\mathbb{R}^d$. Using the time-reversed diffusion process [1] of Eq. (1) we can define a generation scheme to sample from the target distribution P. We have the reverse SDE:

$$\mathrm{d}x_t = \left[f(x_t, t) - g(t)^2 \nabla_{x_t} \log p_t(x_t)\right] \mathrm{d}t + g(t)\mathrm{d}\bar{w}, \tag{2}$$

where $\mathrm{d}\bar{w}$ denotes a different standard Wiener process.

3.2 Score-Based Generative Models

Taking advantage of the reverse SDE in Eq. (2), we can train generative models based on scores by training a neural network $s_\theta(x_t, t)$ to estimate the value of the score $\nabla_{x_t} \log p_t(x_t)$. To do so, we train U-Net Ronneberger et al. [23], a function $\mathbb{R}^d \times \mathbb{R} \to \mathbb{R}^d$, to minimize the *score matching loss* [10]:

$$\mathcal{L}_{\mathrm{SM}}^s(\theta) = \frac{1}{2} \int_0^T \lambda(t) \mathbb{E}_{P_t} \left[\|\nabla_{x_t} \log p_t(x_t) - s_\theta(x_t, t)\|_2^2\right] \mathrm{d}t. \tag{3}$$

Note that the weighting function $\lambda : [0,T] \to]0, +\infty[$ depends on the type of SDE. Although the score matching loss is not directly computable, there exist methods to estimate it using Sliced Score Matching [25]. Vincent [31] shows that the score matching loss is equivalent, up to a constant additive term independent of θ, to the *denoising score matching* loss:

$$\mathcal{L}_{\mathrm{MSE}}^s(\theta) = \int_0^T \lambda(t) \mathbb{E}_{P_0, P_{t|x_0}} \left[\|\nabla_{x_t} \log p_t(x_t|x_0) - s_\theta(x_t, t)\|_2^2 \right] \mathrm{d}t, \quad (4)$$

where $P_{t|x_0}$ is conditional distribution of x_t given x_0. This distribution is typically chosen to be a Gaussian distribution with a mean depending on x_0 and t and a variance depending on t. Therefore, this loss is based on the mean square error of the denoised reconstruction, which is widely used in practice as it is easier to compute and optimize [12]. The learned score function defines a new reverse diffusion process:

$$\mathrm{d}x_t = \left[f(x_t, t) - g(t)^2 s_\theta(x_t, t) \right] \mathrm{d}t + g(t) \mathrm{d}\bar{w}. \quad (5)$$

It defines learned distributions $\left\{ \widehat{P}_t \right\}_{t \in [0,T]}$ with densities $\widehat{p}_t$ such that:

$$\begin{cases} \widehat{p}_T(x_T) = q(x_T), \\ \nabla_{x_t} \log \widehat{p}_t(x_t, t) = s_\theta(x_t, t). \end{cases} \quad (6)$$

In general, the induced distribution $\widehat{P}_0 = \widehat{P}$ does not perfectly match the target distribution. Song et al. [24] shows that under the right assumptions (detailed in Appendix A.1), the Kullback-Leibler divergence is given by:

$$\mathcal{D}_{\mathrm{KL}}(P\|\widehat{P}) = \mathcal{D}_{\mathrm{KL}}(P_T\|Q) + \frac{1}{2} \int_0^T g^2(t) \mathbb{E}_{P_t} \left[\|\nabla_{x_t} \log p_t(x_t) - s_\theta(x_t, t)\|_2^2 \right] \mathrm{d}t. \quad (7)$$

In practice, the score function s_θ is learned using a U-Net architecture [23] trained to minimize $\mathcal{L}_{\mathrm{MSE}}^s$ and thus helps to reduce the dissimilarity between the learned distribution $\widehat{P}$ and the target distribution P.

3.3 Discriminator Guided Diffusion

To enhance the generative process and minimize the discrepancy between the generated distribution $\widehat{P}$ and the target distribution P, Kim et al. [14] propose leveraging the density ratio $p_t(x_t)/\widehat{p}_t(x_t)$. By incorporating this density ratio, the score estimation can be refined using the following identity:

$$\nabla_{x_t} \log p_t(x_t) = \nabla_{x_t} \log \widehat{p}(x_t) + \nabla_{x_t} \log p_t(x_t)/\widehat{p}_t(x_t). \quad (8)$$

However, the density ratio cannot be computed directly. To address this, the authors propose training a discriminator to approximate it. In practice, the discriminator is implemented as a neural network $d_\phi(x_t, t)$, which is trained to minimize the cross-entropy (CE) loss between real and generated data:

$$\mathcal{L}_{\text{CE}}^{d}(\phi) = \int_{0}^{T} \lambda(t) \Big[\mathbb{E}_{P_t} \left[-\log \sigma \left(d_\phi(\boldsymbol{x}_t, t) \right) \right] + \mathbb{E}_{\widehat{P}_t} \left[-\log \left(1 - \sigma \left(d_\phi(\boldsymbol{x}_t, t) \right) \right) \right] \Big] \mathrm{d}t, \tag{9}$$

where σ is the sigmoid function. If the discriminator $d_\phi(.,t)$ were capable of representing any measurable function from $\mathbb{R}^d$ to $\mathbb{R}$, then the optimal discriminator could be used to compute the density ratio [21,22,27]:

$$r^*(\boldsymbol{x}_t, t) = p_t(\boldsymbol{x}_t)/\widehat{p}_t(\boldsymbol{x}_t) = e^{d_{\phi^*}(\boldsymbol{x}_t, t)}. \tag{10}$$

However, in practice, the expressivity of the discriminator is limited, and thus the discriminator does not perfectly estimate the density ratio, and the estimated density ratio is defined as $r_\phi(\boldsymbol{x}_t, t) = \exp(d_\phi(\boldsymbol{x}_t, t))$. Using this estimation, the score refinement can be computed as $\nabla_{\boldsymbol{x}_t} \log r_\phi(\boldsymbol{x}_t, t) = \nabla_{\boldsymbol{x}_t} d_\phi(\boldsymbol{x}_t, t)$. The reverse diffusion process using the discriminator guidance defines a sequence of refined distributions $\{\widetilde{P}_t\}_{t \in [0,T]}$, with densities $\widetilde{p}_t$ such that:

$$\begin{cases} \widetilde{p}_T(\boldsymbol{x}_T) = \pi(\boldsymbol{x}_T), \\ \nabla_{\boldsymbol{x}_t} \log \widetilde{p}_t(\boldsymbol{x}_t, t) = s_\theta(\boldsymbol{x}_t, t) + \nabla_{\boldsymbol{x}_t} d_\phi(\boldsymbol{x}_t, t) :- \widetilde{s}_{\theta,\phi}(\boldsymbol{x}_t, t). \end{cases} \tag{11}$$

Similarly to the classical generative process, $\widetilde{P} = \widetilde{P}_0$ does not perfectly match the target distribution. The Kullback-Leibler divergence between the refined distribution and the target distribution can be computed as follows applying the same assumptions as Eq. (7).

$$\mathcal{D}_{\text{KL}}(P\|\widetilde{P}) = \mathcal{D}_{\text{KL}}(P_T\|Q) + \frac{1}{2} \int_0^T g(t)^2 \mathbb{E}_{P_t} \Big[\|\nabla_{\boldsymbol{x}_t} \log p_t(\boldsymbol{x}_t) - \widetilde{s}_{\theta,\phi}(\boldsymbol{x}_t, t)\|_2^2 \Big] \mathrm{d}t. \tag{12}$$

In Eq. (12), we note that the dissimilarity between the target distribution and the refined distribution depends on the MSE between the difference in scores and the discriminator *gradient*. However, the model is trained to minimize CE and there is no guaranty that the CE is the optimal loss for the refinement.

4 Misalignment Between the Cross-Entropy and the Kullback-Leibler Divergence

The DG framework [14] approximates the density ratio $p_t/\widehat{p}_t$ by training a discriminator with the CE and using its gradient for refinement. In this section, we formally show that minimizing cross-entropy does not necessarily improve the refined distribution. Furthermore, we establish that this issue is not limited to pathological cases but naturally arises in the common overfitting regime, where the refined distribution deteriorates.

Well-Trained Discriminator with Poorly Refined Distribution: Our first result, stated in Theorem 1, shows that it is possible to construct a discriminator with an arbitrarily low CE, while the refined distribution is arbitrarily far from the target:

Theorem 1. *Let $\{x(t)\}_{t \in [0,T]}$ be a diffusion process defined by Eq. (1). Assume that $\nabla \log \widehat{p}_t = s_\theta$ and $\nabla \log \widetilde{p}_t = s_\theta + \nabla d_\phi$ and that the induced distribution P, $\widehat{P}$, and $\widetilde{P}$ satisfies the assumptions detailed in Appendix A.1. Then, for every $\varepsilon > 0$ and for every $\delta > 0$, there exists a discriminator $d : \mathbb{R}^d \times \mathbb{R} \to \mathbb{R}$ trained to minimize the cross-entropy such that:*

$$\mathcal{L}_{\mathrm{CE}}^d(\phi) \leq \varepsilon \quad \text{and} \quad \mathcal{D}_{\mathrm{KL}}(P \| \widetilde{P}) \geq \delta, \tag{13}$$

where $\widetilde{P}$ is the distribution induced by discriminator guidance with d.

Sketch of Proof. The detailed proof of Theorem 1 is provided in Appendix A.2. The key insight is that the CE evaluates the discriminator's values $d_\phi(x, t)$ but not its gradient $\nabla_x d_\phi(x, t)$, which affects the generation process. The main argument is that a learned discriminator d_ϕ oscillating around the optimal discriminator d^* can still achieve a low CE (Fig. 2a). Specifically, the magnitude of these oscillations determines how low the CE is, while their frequency degrades the approximation of $\nabla_x d_\phi(x, t)$, leading to an increase in $\mathcal{D}_{\mathrm{KL}}(P \| \widetilde{P})$.

Theorem 1 establishes that minimizing cross-entropy does not necessarily yield a better-refined distribution. Theorem 2 further demonstrates that this issue is not limited to rare or pathological cases but naturally emerges in the overfitting regime, a common occurrence in practical settings. As the discriminator memorizes the training data, its learned function develops high-frequency oscillations:

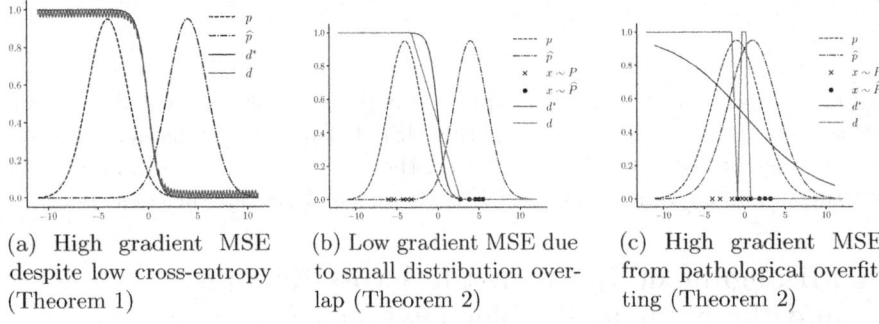

(a) High gradient MSE despite low cross-entropy (Theorem 1)

(b) Low gradient MSE due to small distribution overlap (Theorem 2)

(c) High gradient MSE from pathological overfitting (Theorem 2)

Fig. 2. Illustration of pathological cases from Theorem 1 and Theorem 2. (Left) The cross-entropy loss $\mathcal{L}_{\mathrm{CE}}^d(\phi)$ is low, yet the MSE loss $\mathcal{L}_{\mathrm{MSE}}^d(\phi)$ is high due to substantial gradient mismatch. (Middle) Low cross-entropy loss with low MSE, as distributions minimally overlap. (Right) Despite low cross-entropy loss, the MSE loss diverges due to significant overlap, highlighting pathological overfitting.

Theorem 2. *Let P and $\widehat{P}$ be distributions on $\mathbb{R}$ with intersecting supports, admitting L-Lipschitz densities p and $\hat{p}$. Let $x_1, \ldots, x_N \sim P^N$ and $x'_1, \ldots, x'_N \sim \widehat{P}^N$. Assume that there exists $\epsilon > 0$ such that the discriminator d_ϕ achieves logistic loss for each sample*

$$-\log \sigma(d_\phi(x_i)) \quad \text{and} \quad -\log(1 - \sigma(d_\phi(x'_i))) \leq \epsilon.$$

Then there exists a constant $c > 0$, depending asymptotically on $\log^2(\epsilon)$ as $\epsilon \to 0$, such that:

$$\lim_{N \to \infty} \frac{\mathbb{E}\left[\mathcal{L}_{\mathrm{MSE}}^d(\phi)\right]}{N} = c, \quad \text{with} \quad c \sim (1 - TV(P, \widehat{P}))^4 \log^2(\epsilon),$$

where $TV(P, \widehat{P})$ denotes the total variation distance between P and $\widehat{P}$. In other words, when $TV(P, \widehat{P}) > 0$, as the discriminator overfits the cross-entropy loss ($\epsilon \to 0$), the mean-squared error scales as $N \log^2(\epsilon)$ and becomes arbitrarily large.

Sketch of Proof. The proof of the theorem is provided in Appendix A.4. For clarity, we focus on the one-dimensional case, which explicitly illustrates the link between the similarity of P and $\widehat{P}$ and the discriminator's behavior. However, the argument extends to higher dimensions. Overfitting leads the discriminator to assign highly different values to real and generated samples. As P and $\widehat{P}$ get closer, generated samples increasingly appear near real ones, forcing the discriminator to separate them sharply. This induces high-frequency oscillations in d_ϕ, where small input changes cause large output variations, resulting in excessive gradients even where the true gradient should be smooth.

Interpretation. Theorem 2 highlights the behavior when the discriminator is *overly confident*, with logits approaching $\pm \infty$. Two distinct scenarios arise:

- When P and $\widehat{P}$ differ significantly ($TV(P, \widehat{P}) \approx 1$), the discriminator's confidence is well-founded, resulting in stable MSE (Fig. 2b).
- However, if the distributions P and $\widehat{P}$ overlap significantly ($TV(P, \widehat{P}) \ll 1$), forcing high discriminator confidence ($\epsilon \to 0$) constitutes overfitting. In this scenario, the constant c grows unbounded, causing the gradient MSE to diverge even though the training CE is minimized (Fig. 2c). The situation of overlapping P and $\widehat{P}$ is the common framework for refining diffusion models, as the pre-trained model ideally generates a distribution $\widehat{P}$ that closely aligns with P.

5 Improved Discriminator Guidance

In this section, we introduce a discriminator loss designed to explicitly approximate the gradient of the density ratio. We analyze its theoretical properties and practical implications.

5.1 Proposed Loss Function

To overcome the limitations we exposed in Sect. 4, we propose to add a term to the loss that explicitly accounts for the gradient of the density ratio. Ideally, if we wanted the gradient of the discriminator to approximate the gradient of the true density ratio, we could optimize the following loss:

$$\mathcal{L}_{\text{SM}}^d(\phi) = \int_0^T \lambda(t) \mathbb{E}_{P_0, P_t}\left[\|\nabla_{\boldsymbol{x}_t} \log p_t(\boldsymbol{x}_t)/\widehat{p}_t(\boldsymbol{x}_t) - \nabla_{\boldsymbol{x}_t} d_\phi(\boldsymbol{x}_t, t)\|_2^2\right] dt. \quad (14)$$

But, minimizing this loss suffers from the same obstacle as the score matching loss defined in Eq. (3): the gradient of the true log-likelihood $\nabla_{\boldsymbol{x}_t} \log p_t(\boldsymbol{x}_t)$ is unknown. Hopefully, we can use the same argument as Vincent [31] and instead use the denoising score matching loss Eq. 15. Proposition 1 shows that minimizing $\mathcal{L}_{\text{SM}}^d(\phi)$ is equivalent to minimize $\mathcal{L}_{\text{MSE}}^d(\phi)$.

$$\mathcal{L}_{\text{MSE}}^d(\phi) = \int_0^T \lambda(t) \mathbb{E}_{P_0, P_{t|x_0}}\left[\|\nabla_{\boldsymbol{x}_t} \log p_t(\boldsymbol{x}_t|\boldsymbol{x}_0) - \boldsymbol{s}_\theta(\boldsymbol{x}_t, t) - \nabla_{\boldsymbol{x}_t} d_\phi(\boldsymbol{x}_t, t)\|_2^2\right] dt. \quad (15)$$

Proposition 1. *Assume that P and $\widehat{P}$ satisfy the assumptions detailed in Appendix A.1. Then, the following holds:*

$$\operatorname*{argmin}_\phi \mathcal{L}_{\text{SM}}^d(\phi) = \operatorname*{argmin}_\phi \mathcal{L}_{\text{MSE}}^d(\phi). \quad (16)$$

Sketch of Proof. The proof of Proposition 1 is given in Appendix A.5. It follows from the fact that the losses differ only by an additive constant independent of ϕ.

Therefore, training a discriminator with $\mathcal{L}_{\text{MSE}}^d(\phi)$ will correctly make its gradient a reliable estimate of the log-likelihood ratio.

5.2 Practical Considerations

In practice, we combine our introduced loss term with the standard cross-entropy loss to facilitate learning, and optimize the loss Eq. 17.

$$\mathcal{L}_{\text{train}}^d(\phi) = \mathcal{L}_{\text{MSE}}^d(\phi) + \gamma \mathcal{L}_{\text{CE}}^d(\phi), \quad (17)$$

where γ is a hyperparameter that controls the importance of the cross-entropy loss. We detail the algorithmic implementation of our method in Algorithm 1.

Optimizing $\mathcal{L}_{\text{CE}}^d(\phi)$ and $\gamma \mathcal{L}_{\text{MSE}}^d(\phi)$. Optimizing both terms yields to different considerations:

Algorithm 1. Training Discriminator with $\mathcal{L}_{\mathrm{CE}}^d$ and $\mathcal{L}_{\mathrm{MSE}}^d$

1. Input: Pre-trained model s_θ, Set of real data $\mathcal{X}$, Set of generated samples $\hat{\mathcal{X}}$ weighting function $\lambda(t)$, Distribution of timesteps $\mathcal{T}$, batch size b
2. Initialize discriminator parameters ϕ
3. Repeat until convergence:
   (a) Sample a batch $\{x_i\}_{i=1}^b$ from the training data $\mathcal{X}$ and $\{t\}_{i=1}^b \sim \mathcal{T}$
   (b) Perturb the samples $\{x_i\}_{i=1}^b$ to timesteps t_i to $\{x_i^t\}_{i=1}^b$
   (c) **Cross-Entropy Optimization (Baseline Loss):**
       – Sample a batch $\{\hat{x}_i\}_{i=1}^b$ from $\hat{\mathcal{X}}$ and perturb to timesteps t_i: $\{\hat{x}_i^t\}_{i=1}^b$
       – Compute the CE loss:

$$\widehat{\mathcal{L}_{\mathrm{CE}}^d}(\phi) = \frac{1}{b}\sum_{i=1}^n \lambda(t_i)\left[-\log\left(\sigma\left(d_\phi(x_i^t, t)\right)\right) - \log\left(1 - \sigma\left(d_\phi(\hat{x}_i^t, t)\right)\right)\right].$$

   (d) **Gradient Matching Optimization (Proposed Loss):**
       – Compute target and pre-trained model's scores on the perturbed training batch $\{x_i^t\}_{i=1}^b$: $\nabla_{x_i^t} \log p_t(x_i^t|x_i)$ and $s_\theta(x_i^t, t)$
       – Compute discriminator gradient: $\nabla_{x_i^t} d_\phi(x_i^t, t)$ (e.g. autodifferentiation)
       – Compute gradient-matching loss:

$$\widehat{\mathcal{L}_{\mathrm{MSE}}^d}(\phi) = \frac{1}{b}\sum_{i=1}^b \lambda(t_i)\|\nabla_{x_i^t}\log p_t(x_i^t|x_i) - s_\theta(x_i^t, t) - \nabla_{x_i^t} d_\phi(x_i^t, t)\|^2$$

   (e) Update ϕ via gradient descent on $\widehat{\mathcal{L}_{\mathrm{train}}^d}(\phi) = \widehat{\mathcal{L}_{\mathrm{CE}}^d}(\phi) + \gamma \widehat{\mathcal{L}_{\mathrm{MSE}}^d}(\phi)$

– **Optimizing $\mathcal{L}_{\mathrm{CE}}^d(\phi)$.** In Kim et al. [14], the discriminator is trained on real and generated samples, drawn from the target distribution P and the refined distribution $\hat{P}$. Since generated samples are typically precomputed and stored, training with $\mathcal{L}_{\mathrm{CE}}^d(\phi)$ exposes the discriminator to a fixed dataset, increasing the risk of overfitting. However, cross-entropy loss is easier to optimize than MSE loss, as it does not require computing the target distribution gradient. This results in faster training and lower memory usage.
– **Optimizing $\mathcal{L}_{\mathrm{MSE}}^d(\phi)$.** Our proposed loss introduces dynamic perturbations to training samples, exposing the model to greater variability. While it correctly estimates the target gradient, this comes with computational overhead: each sample requires computing both $\nabla_{x_t}\log p_t(x_t|x_0)$ and $s_\theta(x_t, t)$. Additionally, backpropagation is more complex, as gradients must be propagated through $\nabla_{x_t} d_\phi(x_t, t)$ rather than directly through d_ϕ. These factors lead to increased computational time and memory requirements.

6 Experiments

In this section we compare our proposed method to the baseline from Kim et al. [14]. We demonstrate the benefits of our approach on both synthetic and real-world datasets. We will (1) observe the effect of overfitting on the quality of the refinement, (2) show the behavior of the training loss on the discriminator guidance, and (3) compare effectiveness of the proposed method for different training/generation settings and finally (4) compare the quality of the samples generated by the EDM, the EMD+DG and our method.

6.1 Visualizing the Discriminator Guidance in Low-Dimension

We consider two distinct Gaussian mixtures in $\mathbb{R}^2$, representing P and $\widehat{P}$. Using a subVP-SDE [26], we derive the closed-form expression of the score ratio $\nabla_x \log p(x)/\widehat{p}(x)$ and employ it to refine samples from $\widehat{P}$ towards P. We evaluate the performance of a discriminator trained with cross-entropy loss $\mathcal{L}_{\text{CE}}^d$ and mean squared error loss $\mathcal{L}_{\text{MSE}}^d$.

Training with $\mathcal{L}_{\text{MSE}}^d$ Gives a Better Gradient Approximation. We plot the resulting gradient norms in Fig. 3 (full vector fields are depicted in Fig. 2 in Appendix B). On this synthetic examples, we see that the discriminator trained with $\mathcal{L}_{\text{MSE}}^d$ achieves a much more precise gradient estimation, resulting in improved samples refinement than the discriminator trained with $\mathcal{L}_{\text{CE}}^d$. This is confirmed in Fig. 1, where we compare the estimated density of the refined distribution for both methods, demonstrating that the MSE loss yields superior refinement quality.

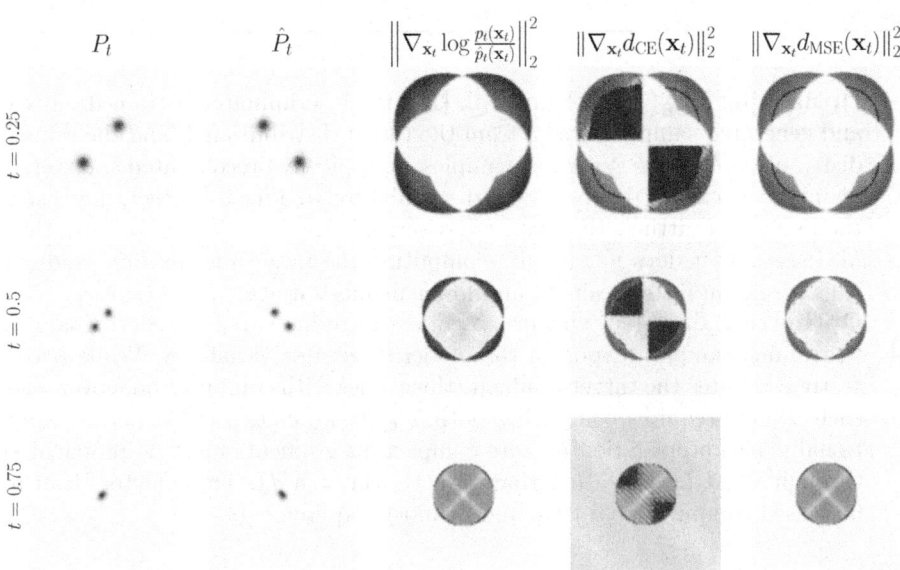

Fig. 3. Visualizing the estimation of $\nabla_{x_t} \log p_t(x_t)/\log \hat{p}_t(x_t)$ for the discriminator trained with low CE or low MSE loss. We plot the norms for better readability.

6.2 Testing Our Approach the Methods on Real-World Dataset

For high-dimensional image datasets, we implement our approach using the unconditional pre-trained EDM model [12] on CIFAR-10, FFHQ in resolution 64 × 64, and AFHQv2 in resolution 64 × 64. We apply the generation algorithm introduced by Kim et al. [14] to the EDM framework. To generate samples from the pre-trained model with a discriminator, they introduce a weight w to balance the contributions of the pre-trained model and the discriminator:

$$\widetilde{s}_\theta(x) = s_\theta(x) + w\nabla_x d_\phi(x). \tag{18}$$

As a baseline, we use a discriminator trained with cross-entropy loss $\mathcal{L}_{CE}^d$, denoted as (EDM+DG), and compare it with our method, which employs $\mathcal{L}_{train}^d$ introduced in Eq. (17). The generation processes are evaluated using the Fréchet Inception Distance (FID) [7], as well as Precision and Recall with $k = 3$ [18]. For FID computation, we use 50k samples for the CIFAR-10 and FFHQ datasets and 15k samples for the AFHQv2 dataset. For Precision and Recall, we set $k = 3$ and use 10k samples for each dataset.

Finally, the discriminators are parametrized following Kim et al. [14]: we adopt the ADM architecture, freezing the upper layers and training only the final layers. This results in training only 2.88M parameters, compared to the total of 50.6M, 68.3M, and 68.3M parameters for CIFAR-10, FFHQ, and AFHQv2, respectively. For comparison, the pre-trained EDM model consists of 55.7M, 61.8M, and 61.8M parameters for these datasets. Generation is conducted on 2×GPU-H100, while evaluation is performed on 2×GPU-V100. A complete list of hyperparameters is available at https://github.com/AlexVerine/BoostDM.

Observing Overfitting in the Discriminator. We analyze how the training loss of the discriminator evolves on CIFAR-10 by varying the number of training samples from 500 to 50,000. Figure 4 presents the key metrics. While Precision remains relatively stable regardless of dataset size, both Recall and the FID score change notably: Recall decreases as the number of training samples increases, while the FID score rises. This indicates that the discriminator overfits the training set, ultimately degrading the refinement quality. Additionally,

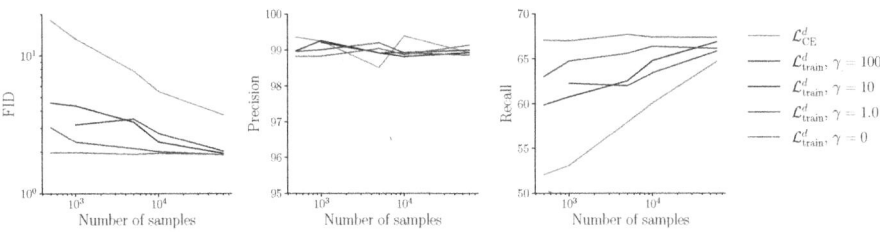

Fig. 4. Discriminator guidance using a different number of samples for the training set. Generation is performed on CIFAR-10 with $w = 1$ for all methods. FID (↓), Precision (↑), and Recall (↑) are reported.

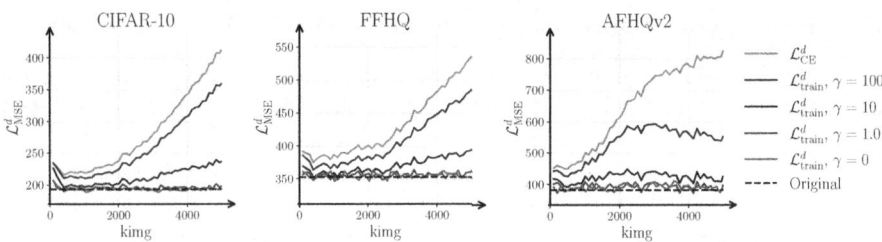

Fig. 5. Comparison of the proposed loss $\mathcal{L}_{\text{train}}^d$ and the standard loss $\mathcal{L}_{\text{CE}}^d$ for the discriminator guidance. We plot the evolution of the loss during training.

our proposed method shows greater robustness to dataset size. However, when the balance between MSE and CE losses increases (i.e., for higher γ values), sensitivity to the number of training samples also increases.

Observing the Effect of the Regularization Parameter γ. We compare how the estimated score behaves with the two different training losses. To assess how the discriminator captures the gradient of the log density ratio, we plot in Fig. 5 the evolution during of $\mathcal{L}_{\text{MSE}}^d$ introduced in Eq. (15). We observe that the lower γ is, the better the discriminator is at estimating the gradient of the log density ratio. This is consistent with the results of the previous section.

Comparing the Effect of the Weight w. Depending on the training loss, the gradient of the discriminator can have different ranges and for the refinement to be effective, the weight w must be adjusted. We evaluate the effect of w on the FID score for the EDM+DG and EDM+Ours methods on CIFAR-10, FFHQ, and AFHQv2. The results are shown in Fig. 6. We observe that the optimal w is different for each dataset but that the proposed method typically leads to lower effect of the discriminator and therefore a larger w is needed. For each method and dataset, we report the FID, Precision, and Recall scores for the parameters w and γ that yield the best FID score in Table 1.

Comparing EDM, EDM+DG and Our Method. In Table 1, we compare the FID, Precision, and Recall scores for the EDM, EDM+DG, and EDM+Ours

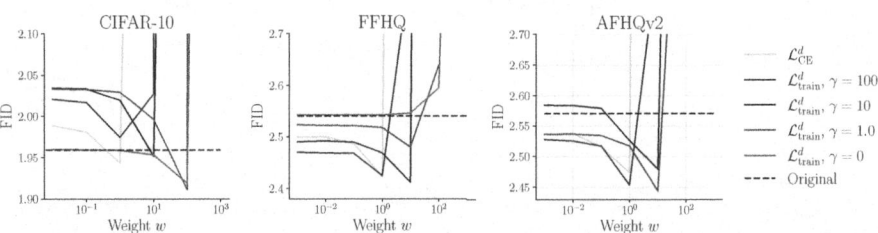

Fig. 6. FID score for different values of w on CIFAR-10, FFHQ, and AFHQv2.

Table 1. Comparison of the proposed method with optimal w on CIFAR-10, FFHQ and AFHQv2. We report the FID (↓), Precision (↑), and Recall (↑) scores and the number of GPUs used for training and generation, the time for training step in seconds per 1000 images, and the memory consumption in Gi.

Dataset	Method	FID	P	R	GPUs	Time	Mem. (Gi)
CIFAR-10	EDM	1.96	99.10	67.48	–	–	–
	EDM+DG	1.94	98.91	67.44	4xV100	1.18	2.24
	EDM+Ours	1.91	98.86	66.14	4xV100	4.00	9.18
FFHQ	EDM	2.54	99.69	69.69	–	–	–
	EDM+DG	2.42	99.60	69.16	4xH100	1.05	7.03
	EDM+Ours	2.41	99.56	69.09	4xH100	4.74	20.26
AFHQv2	EDM	2.57	99.99	75.64	–	–	–
	EDM+DG	2.47	99.83	74.41	4xH100	1.05	7.03
	EDM+Ours	2.44	99.96	74.58	4xH100	4.74	20.26

methods on CIFAR-10, FFHQ, and AFHQv2. We observe that our method consistently outperforms the EDM+DG method in terms of FID score. The Precision is not significantly affected by the method used, while the Recall can be slightly lower for our method. We can observe on Fig. 7 that the samples generated by our method are closer to the samples generated by the EDM model than the EDM+DG method. On this uncurated set of samples from the AFHQv2 dataset, we can see that the samples generated by the EDM+DG method often changes the class of the sample while our method does not. We plot more samples in Appendix B.

(a) EDM (b) EDM+DG (c) EDM+Ours

Fig. 7. Samples generated on the AFHQv2 dataset.

7 Conclusion and Discussion

In this paper, we have demonstrated that discriminator guidance can be significantly improved by refining the loss function used for training the discriminator. Our theoretical analysis reveals that minimizing cross-entropy can lead to unreliable refinement, particularly in the overfitting regime, where the discriminator learns to separate real and generated samples too aggressively. To mitigate this issue, we introduced an alternative training approach that minimizes the reconstruction error, resulting in more accurate gradient estimation and improved sample quality in EDM diffusion models across diverse datasets.

Our findings highlight a fundamental challenge: while a discriminator can estimate the density ratio, accurately capturing its gradient remains difficult in practice. This issue is exacerbated by overfitting, where the discriminator's learned function develops high-frequency oscillations that distort the refinement process. Although discriminator guidance is theoretically optimal with a perfect discriminator, real-world constraints—such as finite data, model capacity, and training instability—limit its practical effectiveness.

Acknowledgments. This work was granted access to the HPC resources of IDRIS under the allocations 2025-A0181016159, 2025-AD011014053R2 made by GENCI.

References

1. Anderson, B.D.O.: Reverse-time diffusion equation models. Stochastic Process. Appl. **12**(3), 313–326 (1982). ISSN 0304-4149, https://doi.org/10.1016/0304-4149(82)90051-5
2. Ansari, A.F., Ang, M.L., Soh, H.: Refining deep generative models via discriminator gradient flow (2021). http://arxiv.org/abs/2012.00780, arXiv:2012.00780 [cs, stat]
3. Azadi, S., Olsson, C., Darrell, T., Goodfellow, I., Odena, A.: Discriminator rejection sampling (2019). http://arxiv.org/abs/1810.06758, arXiv:1810.06758 [cs, stat]
4. Che, T., et al.: Your GAN is secretly an energy-based model and you should use discriminator driven latent sampling. In: Advances in Neural Information Processing Systems, vol. 33, pp. 12275–12287. Curran Associates, Inc. (2020). https://proceedings.neurips.cc/paper/2020/hash/90525e70b7842930586545c6f1c9310c-Abstract.html
5. Dhariwal, P., Nichol, A.: Diffusion models beat GANs on image synthesis (2021)
6. Dhariwal, P., Nichol, A.: Diffusion models beat GANs on image synthesis (2021). http://arxiv.org/abs/2105.05233, arXiv:2105.05233 [cs, stat]
7. Heusel, M., Ramsauer, H., Unterthiner, T., Nessler, B., Hochreiter, S.: GANs trained by a two time-scale update rule converge to a local Nash equilibrium. In: Advances in Neural Information Processing Systems, vol. 30, Curran Associates, Inc. (2017)
8. Ho, J., et al.: Imagen video: high definition video generation with diffusion models (2022)
9. Ho, J., Salimans, T., Gritsenko, A., Chan, W., Norouzi, M., Fleet, D.J.: Video diffusion models (2022)

10. Hyvarinen, A.: Estimation of non-normalized statistical models by score matching (2005)
11. Jolicoeur-Martineau, A., Li, K., Piché-Taillefer, R., Kachman, T., Mitliagkas, I.: Gotta go fast when generating data with score-based models (2021). http://arxiv.org/abs/2105.14080, arXiv:2105.14080 [cs, math, stat]
12. Karras, T., Aittala, M., Aila, T., Laine, S.: Elucidating the design space of diffusion-based generative models (2022). http://arxiv.org/abs/2206.00364, arXiv:2206.00364 [cs, stat]
13. Kelvinius, F.E., Lindsten, F.: Discriminator guidance for autoregressive diffusion models (2023)
14. Kim, D., Kim, Y., Kwon, S.J., Kang, W., Moon, I.C.: Refining generative process with discriminator guidance in score-based diffusion models. In: Proceedings of the 40 th International Conference on Machine Learning, Honolulu, Hawaii, USA, vol. 202, JMLR (2023). http://arxiv.org/abs/2211.17091, arXiv:2211.17091 [cs] version: 3
15. Kim, D., et al.: Consistency trajectory models: learning probability flow ode trajectory of diffusion (2024)
16. Kloeden, P.E., Platen, E., Kloeden, P.E., Platen, E.: Stochastic Differential Equations. Springer, Heidelberg (1992). https://doi.org/10.1007/978-3-662-02847-6
17. Kong, Z., Ping, W., Huang, J., Zhao, K., Catanzaro, B.: Diffwave: a versatile diffusion model for audio synthesis (2021)
18. Kynkäänniemi, T., Karras, T., Laine, S., Lehtinen, J., Aila, T.: Improved precision and recall metric for assessing generative models. In: 33rd Conference on Neural Information Processing Systems (NeurIPS 2019), Vancouver, Canada (2019). arXiv: 1904.06991
19. Liu, C., et al.: Generative diffusion models on graphs: methods and applications (2023)
20. Lu, H., Tunanyan, H., Wang, K., Navasardyan, S., Wang, Z., Shi, H.: Specialist diffusion: plug-and-play sample-efficient fine-tuning of text-to-image diffusion models to learn any unseen style. In: Proceedings of the IEEE/CVF Conference on Computer Vision and Pattern Recognition (CVPR), pp. 14267–14276 (2023)
21. Nguyen, X., Wainwright, M.J., Jordan, M.I.: On surrogate loss functions and f-divergences. Ann. Stat. **37**(2) (2009). ISSN 0090-5364, https://doi.org/10.1214/08-AOS595
22. Nowozin, S., Cseke, B., Tomioka, R.: f-GAN: training generative neural samplers using variational divergence minimization (2016). http://arxiv.org/abs/1606.00709
23. Ronneberger, O., Fischer, P., Brox, T.: U-Net: convolutional networks for biomedical image segmentation (2015). https://doi.org/10.48550/arXiv.1505.04597, http://arxiv.org/abs/1505.04597, arXiv:1505.04597 [cs]
24. Song, Y., Durkan, C., Murray, I., Ermon, S.: Maximum likelihood training of score-based diffusion models (2021). http://arxiv.org/abs/2101.09258, arXiv:2101.09258 [cs, stat]
25. Song, Y., Garg, S., Shi, J., Ermon, S.: Sliced score matching: a scalable approach to density and score estimation (2019). http://arxiv.org/abs/1905.07088, arXiv:1905.07088 [cs, stat]
26. Song, Y., Sohl-Dickstein, J., Kingma, D.P., Kumar, A., Ermon, S., Poole, B.: Score-based Generative Modeling Through Stochastic Differential Equations (2021)
27. Sugiyama, M., Suzuki, T., Kanamori, T.: Density ratio estimation: a comprehensive review (2010)
28. Tsonis, E., Tzouveli, P., Voulodimos, A.: Mitigating exposure bias in discriminator guided diffusion models (2023)

29. Verine, A., Negrevergne, B., Pydi, M.S., Chevaleyre, Y.: Precision-recall divergence optimization for generative modeling with GANs and normalizing flows. In: Advances in Neural Information Processing Systems, vol. 36, 32539–32573 (2023). https://proceedings.neurips.cc/paper_files/paper/2023/hash/67159f1c0cab15dd34c76a5dd830a389-Abstract-Conference.html
30. Verine, A., Pydi, M.S., Negrevergne, B., Chevaleyre, Y.: Optimal budgeted rejection sampling for generative models. In: Proceedings of The 27th International Conference on Artificial Intelligence and Statistics (2024). http://arxiv.org/abs/2311.00460, arXiv:2311.00460 [cs]
31. Vincent, P.: A connection between score matching and denoising autoencoders. Neural Comput. **23**(7), 1661–1674 (2011). ISSN 0899-7667, 1530-888X, https://doi.org/10.1162/NECO_a_00142
32. Xie, E., et al.: Difffit: unlocking transferability of large diffusion models via simple parameter-efficient fine-tuning (2023)
33. Xu, Y., Deng, M., Cheng, X., Tian, Y., Liu, Z., Jaakkola, T.: Restart sampling for improving generative processes (2023). http://arxiv.org/abs/2306.14878, arXiv:2306.14878 [cs, stat]

JKDM: A Joint Structural and Semantic Diffusion-Generated Knowledge Completion Model

Wendong Zhang[1], Haoqi Chen[1], and Song Yu[2(✉)]

[1] School of Software, Xinjiang University, Urumqi 830000, Xinjiang, China
wdzhang@xju.edu.cn, 107552304905@stu.xju.edu.cn
[2] School of Computer Science and Engineering, Central South University, Changsha 410083, Hunan, China
ys@csu.edu.cn

Abstract. Knowledge Graph Completion (KGC) aims to predict missing triples in a graph based on known relationships between entities. However, most KGC methods face the challenge of diversification representations among entities, making it difficult for models to link entities effectively. This article proposes a Joint Knowledge (Structure-Semantics) Diffusion Model (JKDM) to capture entity diversification relationships. By leveraging the probabilistic generative capabilities of diffusion models, JKDM generates diversification outputs that align with the distribution of target entities rather than producing a single deterministic result. Considering the insufficient structural information of sparse entities, which leads to their representations tending toward a smooth distribution, making it difficult for diffusion models to learn their probability distributions, we jointly enhance sparse entity representations using structural and semantic information. Structurally, a Dual-channel Graph Attention Network (DGAT) is introduced to capture structural embeddings of entities from different perspectives. Semantically, a contextual path strategy is applied to pre-trained language models (PLMs) to enrich entity semantics. Under the condition of joint embeddings, JKDM gradually denoises to generate the probability distribution of target entities. Experiments demonstrate that JKDM outperforms SOTA methods on the FB15k-237, WN18RR, and UMLS datasets, achieving improvements of 2.3%, 1.5%, and 0.43% in MRR scores, respectively.

Keywords: Diffusion Models · Knowledge Graph Completion · Attention Networks · Link Prediction

1 Introduction

Knowledge Graphs (KG) store real-world facts in triples, represented as (h, r, t). Although KGs play a crucial role in numerous applications, such as KG-enhanced

---

Supplementary Information The online version contains supplementary material available at https://doi.org/10.1007/978-3-032-05981-9_15.

LLMs and recommendation systems, they still face the issue of incompleteness. Knowledge Graph Embedding (KGE) is an effective approach for inferring missing triples, such as TransE [1], which map entities and relations into low-dimensional vector spaces and use scoring functions to calculate the plausibility of predicted triples. However, these methods struggle to handle the diverse representations among entities. To address this issue, most KGC methods focus on encoding tasks or aggregating more information structurally to enhance the diverse features of entities. For example, CompGCN [2] aggregate neighborhood information of entities to obtain diverse information. Alternatively, they aim to semantically understand the meaning behind entity texts, uncovering more hidden knowledge connections. For instance, KG-BERT [3] leverage PLMs to capture the contextual features of entities. However, in decoding tasks, using only KGE for deterministic result computation still struggles to handle the issue of diverse representations among entities. Diffusion models (DM), by combining randomness and multimodal modeling capabilities, can generate uncertain results, enabling them to produce multiple plausible outcomes from the same input. However, when faced with sparse distribution data, DM often struggles to generate ideal results due to insufficient precision in the denoising process. In KG, sparse entities tend to have sparse distributions due to insufficient structural information, making it difficult for diffusion models to learn their probability distributions, affecting the generated results.

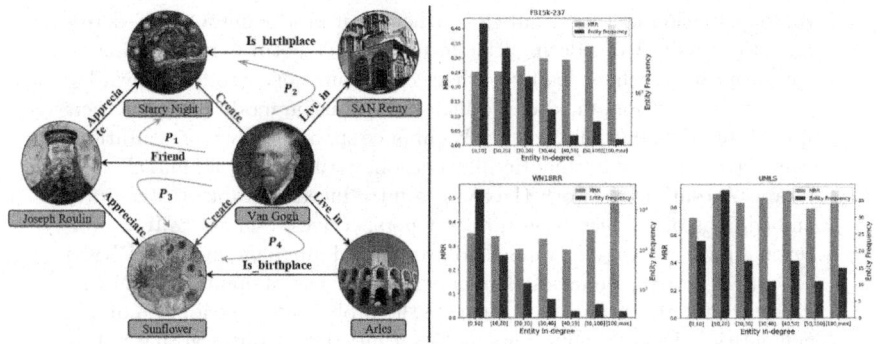

Fig. 1. The left side illustrates that the "Create" relationship carries multiple potential associations. The right side demonstrates the different contextual paths in which the triple exists. On the FB15k-237, WN18RR, and UMLS datasets, the results based on the RotatE [4] model for entities with different in-degrees and MRR reveal that sparse entities perform poorly in knowledge reasoning tasks.

Despite significant progress in KGC, limitations still exist. **Challenge 1:** Sparse entities in knowledge graphs suffer from insufficient structural information. We investigated several widely recognized KGs to explore the relationship between entity frequency and link prediction, as shown in Fig. 1. It was observed that there is a correlation between model performance and entity sparsity. To address sparsity, previous methods often introduce textual features for enhancement but lack a deep understanding of triple context. Some approaches map neighboring entities to different representation spaces to enrich structural embeddings, yet the neighborhood information of sparse entities remains unchanged, and the structural features provided are still limited. **Challenge 2:** The issue of diverse representations among entities. Due to relationships often encompassing different semantic levels, entity pairs can exhibit one-to-many, many-to-one, and other associations. For example, as shown in Fig. 1, the relationship *"Create"* carries multiple potential associations. Existing methods primarily rely on KGE models for deterministic entity prediction, which can only capture specific semantics of relationships but lack the ability to handle diverse relationships between entities.

We propose the Joint Knowledge Diffusion Model (JKDM) to address these issues. The diverse representations among entities lead to relationships in KGs that may be nonlinear and complex. As a probabilistic generative model, DM enables the generation of complex distributions. Therefore, we designed a Knowledge Diffusion Generation (KDG) module using DM for multi-relational semantic reasoning, gradually adding noise and learning the reverse process to generate complex probability distributions. However, sparse entities lack sufficient neighborhood information, causing their representations to tend toward sparse distributions, making it difficult for DM to learn their probability distributions. While densification techniques can supplement sparse structures, the introduced dense relationships may affect the original relational features. Therefore, we designed a Dual-channel Graph Attention Network (DGAT) module consisting of two independent GAT networks: RGAT and EGAT. RGAT operates on the non-densified graph, focusing on neighborhood relation aggregation and capturing interaction patterns between entities and specific relations. EGAT emphasizes aggregating neighboring entities in the densified graph, computing the intrinsic interactions between the central entity and its original neighboring entities and similar entities. Additionally, we designed a Contextual Path Enhancement for Semantics (CPES) module to uncover hidden connections behind knowledge. This module formulates questions about the target entity using question-answering templates and answers them using the reasoning paths of the target entity, thereby enriching the semantics of the target entity through contextual paths. For example, as shown in Fig. 1, the triple $(VanGogh, Create, Sunflower)$ is transformed into $(What\ did\ VanGogh\ create?\ Sunflower)$, and the semantic representation of the entity *"Sunflower"* is enriched through the path $(VanGogh, Friend, JosephRoulin, Admire, Sunflower)$. The main contributions are as follows:

- We propose a Joint Knowledge Diffusion Model (JKDM). The DGAT and CPES modules enhance the representations of sparse entities from structural and semantic perspectives, while the KDG module leverages structural and semantic features to diffusively generate representations of predicted entities.
- To address the issue of incomplete structural information, DGAT enhances the structural information of sparse entities by leveraging Dense Graph information in a dual-channel GAT manner. CPES employs a question-answering

template format and trains PLMs using a contextual path strategy to enhance entity semantics.
- To address the issue of diverse representations among entities, the Knowledge Diffusion Generation (KDG) module is designed. By leveraging diffusion models to gradually add noise and learn the reverse process, it enables the generation of complex probability distributions.
- The model JKDM is evaluated on three datasets. The experimental results demonstrate that JKDM achieves superior performance.

2 Related Work

2.1 Knowledge Completion

Structure-Based Methods: Early research applied CNNs to KGC, such as ConvE [5]. These methods focus on individual triples, overlooking the topological structure. Therefore, GNN-based KGC methods, such as CompGCN, have been proposed, which jointly embed entities and relations into the knowledge graph using composition operators. SACN [6] designs a weighted GCN by assigning different weights to different relation types.

Semantics-Based Methods: The sparsity of knowledge graphs makes it difficult for models to learn high-quality entity embeddings. Therefore, researchers have begun to introduce textual information to enhance entity embeddings. AATE [7] encodes text and combines it with topological structures to enhance entity embeddings, but this method lacks the utilization of contextual representations of triples. In contrast, KG-BERT treats triple text sequences as input to PLMs to obtain contextual semantic representations of entities.

Structure-Semantics-Based Methods: The model leverages structural and semantic information to enhance entity features. For instance, GS-InGAT [8] considers neighbourhood interactions and global semantics, while SEA-KGC [9] uses PLMs to learn unified representations from entity structures and text. However, existing methods lack deep contextual understanding and fail to address incomplete structural information for sparse entities. These methods rely on deterministic entity prediction, capturing only specific relationship semantics and struggling with diverse entity relationships. This article's JKDM enhances sparse entity neighbourhoods with densified graphs and enriches semantics via contextual paths. It also introduces diffusion models to generate complex probability distributions by adding noise and learning the reverse process.

2.2 Diffusion Model

The diffusion process of diffusion models is implemented through two Markov chains: the forward noising process gradually corrupts samples into Gaussian noise, while the reverse denoising process progressively restores the data. In the past, diffusion models have been primarily applied in computer vision, such as visual generation, multimodal generation, and image restoration.

In recent years, researchers have begun to introduce diffusion models for knowledge graph tasks. For example, FDM [10] utilizes diffusion models to directly learn the distribution of credible facts from known knowledge graphs. KGDM [11] transforms entity prediction tasks into conditional fact generation tasks using diffusion models. However, the methods above overlook the knowledge graph's topological structure and semantic information, insufficiently representing entity features. Therefore, we propose the Joint Knowledge Diffusion Model (JKDM), which enhances entity representations by combining structural and semantic features of the knowledge graph. Using the designed Joint Embedding Condition Denoising (JECD) module, JKDM learns the reverse diffusion process under the joint embedding conditions of entities and relations.

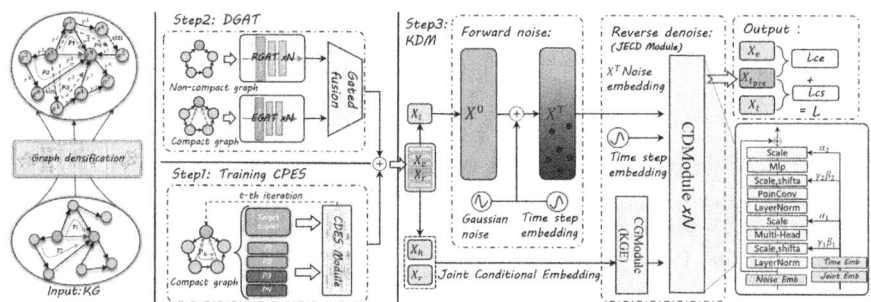

Fig. 2. Step 1: The CPES module aims to obtain contextual semantic; Step 2: The DGAT module aims to obtain structural; Step 3: The KDM module implements diffusion generation through a forward noising process and a reverse denoising process.

3 Methodology

We treat the KG as a set of triples $\mathcal{G} = \{(e^i, r^u, e^j)\}$, where e^i and e^j denote the head and tail entities, and r^u represents the relation. The architecture of the JKDM model is shown in Fig. 2. JKDM mainly consists of three modules:

3.1 Graph Densification

Dense Graph (DG): The sparsity of knowledge graphs leads to missing structural information. Malaviya et al. [12] introduced graph densification techniques to address this issue. The graph densification process is achieved solely through semantic similarity between entity texts, neglecting the contextual information of entities. Liu X et al. [13] indicate that extracting entity semantic embeddings without context or solely from the [CLS] token is suboptimal. Inspired by this, We calculate contextual semantic similarity to densify sparse entities. For example, the context of the head entity e^i in the triple (e^i, r^u, e^j) is defined as the set of triples containing e^i, i.e. $C_{e^i} = \{(e^i, r^u, e^j) | (e^i, r^u, e^j) \in G \cup (e^j, r^u, e^i) \in G\}$. To obtain the semantics of e^i in the context of C_{e^i}, e^i is replaced with $[S]e^i[/S]$, and markers are added at both ends of e^i to capture its textual semantic embeddings. Using Bert, all marker pairs $[S]e^i[/S]$ captured from the context of the target entity are aggregated through average pooling to obtain the full semantics of e^i in C_{e^i}.

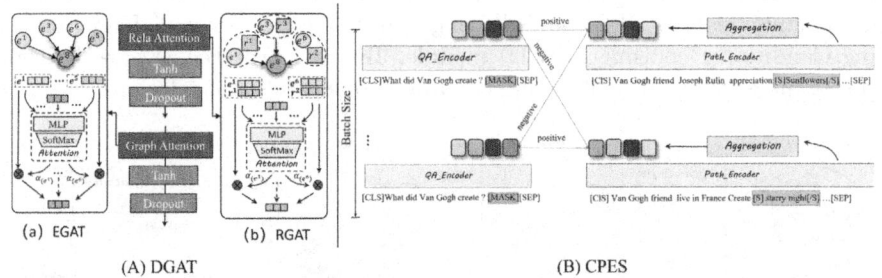

Fig. 3. A.(a) EGAT performs attention-based weighted aggregation of the DG from the entity perspective. (b) RGAT performs weighted aggregation on the KG from the entity-relation perspective. B. The CPES module encodes T_{QA} and T_{Path} using the QA_Encoder and Path_Encoder, respectively.

3.2 Context Path Enhance Semantics

Inspired by Pan Y et al. [14], we designed the CPES module to fine-tune PLMs using contextual paths for semantic enhancement. CPES employs a dual-encoder structure combining QA_Encoder and Path_Encoder. It formulates questions and answers in the form of questions-answers templates (QA) for the predicted entities, transforming the triple into question and answer sequences, denoted as T_{QA} and T_{Path}, respectively, as shown in Fig. 3(B).

QA_Encoder: Converts (e^i, r^u, e^j) into a question sequence T_{QA}. For example, $(VanGogh, Create, StarryNight)$ is transformed into $(What\ did\ VanGogh\ Create\ ?)$. Then, the target entity $(StarryNight)$ is masked, and the question and mask are concatenated to form the question sequence $(What\ did\ VanGogh\ Create?\ [MASK])$. The formula is as follows:

$$T_{QA} = Q_r(e^i) \oplus [MASK]_{e^j} \quad (1)$$

where $\oplus$ denotes the concatenation operation, $Q_r(e^i)$ denotes the transformation of triple into a question sequence, and $[MASK]_{e^j}$ masks the target entity.

Path_Encoder: Converts the set of contextual paths from entity e^i to entity e^j into an answer sequence T_{Path}. The set of contextual paths is searched using the Breadth-First Search (BFS) algorithm. However, the sparsity of the knowledge graph may make it difficult to find contextual paths within k hops for certain target triples. Therefore, this article conducts path searches on the DG. The formula for $\mathcal{T}_{Path}$ is as follows:

$$\mathcal{T}_{Path} = (e^i, r^u, e^j) \oplus \mathcal{P}_{e^i \to e^j}, \quad h_e = Pool\bigl([h_{e,1}, ..., h_{e,m}]\bigr) \quad (2)$$

where $\mathcal{P}_{e^i \to e^j}$ denote the paths from entity e^i to entity e^j. To obtain the representation of the answer entity e^j in different paths, visual marker pairs [S][\S] are added to the answer entity in the path set. For example, $(e^i, r^1, ..., e^j)$ is marked as $(e^i, r^1, ..., [S]e^j[\backslash S])$. The semantic representations of entity e^j in different contextual paths, denoted as $h_{e,1}, \ldots, h_{e,m}$, are aggregated using average pooling $Pool$ to obtain the comprehensive contextual path semantics of entity.

CPES utilizes PLM to encode the $\mathcal{T}_{QA}$ sequence and $\mathcal{T}_{Path}$ sequence separately. In a question-answering format, the masked semantics in $\mathcal{T}_{QA}$ are semantically aligned with the comprehensive contextual path semantics in $\mathcal{T}_{Path}$ for fine-tuning the PLM. The main idea is to leverage the intrinsic connection between questions and answers to enhance the semantic understanding capability of the PLM. A semantic alignment loss $\mathcal{L}_{aligned}$ is designed in CPES for contrastive learning between positive and negative samples. It calculates the distance between the embedding of $[MASK]_{e^j}$ and the contextual path embeddings in $\mathcal{T}_{Path}$, as well as the distance to negative sample embeddings as follows:

$$\mathcal{L}_{aligned} = \max\bigl(0, d(h_{[MASK]_e}, h_{\bar{e}}) - d(h_{[MASK]_e}, h_e) + \eta\bigr) \quad (3)$$

where d calculates the distance between the positive and negative samples and the masked embedding. $h_{[MASK]_e}$ represents the masked embedding in $\mathcal{T}_{QA}$, $h_{\bar{e}}$ denotes the comprehensive contextual path semantics, $h_{\bar{e}}$ represents the comprehensive contextual path semantics of negative samples, and η is the hyperparameter for the margin loss. After training, the entity text (e, r) is input into the trained CPES module, and the hidden state of the [CLS] token is used as the node semantic embedding, denoted as $h_e^S = ([cls]|e), h_r^S = ([cls]|r)$.

3.3 Dual-Channel GAT Module

DGAT consists of two independent GAT Networks: the RGAT Network and the EGAT Network. In the form of a dual-channel GAT, it captures entity structural features in different feature spaces and employs a gating network for feature fusion. The overall architecture of this part is shown in Fig. 3(A). The formula is as follows:

$$h_{e^i}^G = \left(gate * LR\left(W_{fuse}\left(h_{e^i}^{(R)}, h_{e^i}^{(E)}\right)\right) + (1 - gate)h_{e^i}^{(R)}\right) + h_{e^i}^{(R)} \quad (4)$$

$$gate = Sigmoid\left(W_{gate}\left(h_{e^i}^{(R)}, h_{e^i}^{(E)}\right)\right) \quad (5)$$

where $h_{e^i}^G$ represents the entity structural embedding, $h_{e^i}^{(R)}$ denotes the entity embedding of the RGAT layer, $h_{e^i}^{(E)}$ denotes the entity embedding of the EGAT layer, and *gate* represents the gating vector. LR represents the LeakyReLU activation function. $W_{gate} \in \mathbb{R}^{2 \times d}, W_{fuse} \in \mathbb{R}^{2 \times d}$ respectively represent the weight matrices of the gating vector generator and the feature fusion module.

RGAT Channel: The edges in KG are relationships with specific semantics. During the message-passing process, RGAT updates the features of the central entity by considering the features of neighboring entities and the specific relationship features. The formula is as follows:

$$h_{e^i}^{(R)(l)} = \delta \left(\sum_{(u,j) \in N_i} \alpha_{iuj} f(h_{e^j}, h_{r^u}) + W^l h_{e^i}^{(R)(l-1)} \right) \quad (6)$$

where δ denotes the Tanh activation function, α_{iuj} denotes the relational attention weight of the triple. $f\left(h_{e^j}^{(R)(l-1)}, h_{r^u}^{(R)(l-1)}\right)$ denotes the local topological context aggregation message of the triple, specifically denoting the fusion operation between $h_{e^j}^{(R)(l-1)}, h_{r^u}^{(R)(l-1)}$, such as $h_{e^j} - h_{r^u}$. α_{iuj} is used to distinguish the importance of different triples in the neighborhood. α_{iuj} defined as:

$$\alpha_{iuj} = Softmax\left(W_1^{(l)}\left(\delta\left(W_2^{(l)}\left(h_{e^i}^{(l-1)}, h_{r^u}^{(l-1)}, h_{e^j}^{(l-1)}\right)\right)\right)\right) \quad (7)$$

where δ represents the LeakyReLU activation function, $W_1^{(l)} \in \mathbb{R}^{1 \times d}$ and $W_2^{(l)} \in \mathbb{R}^{3 \times d}$ are learnable parameters in RGAT. $h_{e^i}^{(R)(l-1)}, h_{r^u}^{(R)(l-1)}$ and $h_{e^j}^{(R)(l-1)}$ denote the embedding of the head entity, relation, and tail entity at the l-1-th layer. Then, the attention score are normalized using $Softmax$. The relation representation is also transformed as follows:

$$h_{r^u}^G = h_{r^u}^{(l)(R)} = W_{rela}^{(l)} \cdot h_{r^u}^{(l-1)(R)} \quad (8)$$

where $h_{r^u}^G$ represents the structural embedding of the relation, and $W_{rela}^{(l)} \in \mathbb{R}^{1 \times d}$ is the trainable weight matrix for the relation embedding at layer l.

EGAT Channel: The EGA module operates on the DG, capturing the intrinsic interactions between the central node and its neighboring nodes, as well as similar nodes, without considering the relational features within the neighborhood. Specifically, it aggregates the dense neighborhood information of the central entity in the DG to enhance the structural features of sparse entities. The formula is as follows:

$$h_{e^i}^{(E)(l)} = \delta^1 \left(\sum_{e^j \in N_i} \alpha_{ij} \cdot h_{e^j}^{(E)(l-1)} + W^l h_{e^i}^{(E)(l-1)} \right) \quad (9)$$

$$\alpha_{ij} = Softmax\left(W_1^{(l)}\left(\delta^2\left(W_2^{(l)}\left(h_{e^i}^{(l-1)}, h_{e^j}^{(l-1)}\right)\right)\right)\right) \quad (10)$$

where δ^1 represents the Tanh activation function, δ^2 represents the LeakyReLU activation function, α_{ij} denotes the relational attention weight of the triple to distinguish their importance.

3.4 Knowledge Diffusion Generation

The diffusion model consists of the noise-adding process and the conditional denoising process, as shown in Fig. 2. Specifically, the noise-adding process disrupts the vector distribution of the target entity by adding noise. In contrast, the denoising process learns the reverse denoising process step by step, enabling it to understand the underlying distribution of the target entity.

Noise-Adding Process: The entity and relation features are defined as $X_e = Cat(h_e^G, h_e^S), X_r = Cat(h_r^G, h_r^S)$, where X_h, X_t, and X_r represent the head entity, tail entity, and relation, respectively. The noise-adding process gradually adds Gaussian noise to the tail entity X_t until the time step $T_p = T$, at which point X_t is corrupted by Gaussian noise and mapped to a pure noise embedding, denoted as $X_t^{T_p}$. The formula is as follows:

$$q\left(X_t^{T_p} | X_t^{T_p-1}\right) = \mathcal{N}\left(X_t^{T_p}; \sqrt{1-\beta^{T_p}} X_t^{T_p-1}, \beta^{T_p} I\right) \tag{11}$$

where T_p is the total number of time steps in the diffusion process, and β^{T_p} represents the variance in the diffusion process. After reparameterization, the output X_t^k at any time step $T_p = k$ takes the form:

$$X_t^k = \sqrt{\bar{\alpha}^k} X_t^0 + \sqrt{1-\bar{\alpha}^k} \varepsilon^k \tag{12}$$

where $\alpha^k = 1 - \beta^k, \bar{\alpha}^k = \prod_{z=1}^{k} \alpha^z$, and ε^k represents as Gaussian noise, $\varepsilon^k \sim \mathcal{N}(0, I)$.

Conditional Denoising Process: Conditioned on the known head entity embedding X_h, relation embedding X_r, and the time step T_p, it gradually denoises the pure noise embedding $X_t^{T_p}$ generated by the noise-adding process. Finally, the predicted entity X_t^{pre} is generated in the vector space. The formula is as follows:

$$p_\theta\left(X_t^{T_p-1} | X_t^{T_p}, T_p, X_h, X_r\right) = \mathcal{N}\left(X_t^{T_p}; \mu_\theta\left(X_t^{T_p}, T_p, X_h, X_r\right), \sigma_{T_p}^2 I\right) \tag{13}$$

where $\sigma_{T_p}^2$ is the constant variance, μ_θ represented as the computed mean of the normal distribution, θ represented as the reverse conditional denoising process parameters.

$$\mu_\theta\left(X_t^{T_p}, T_p, X_h, X_r\right) = \frac{1}{\sqrt{\alpha^{T_p}}} X_t - \frac{1-\alpha^{T_p}}{\sqrt{\alpha^{T_p}}\sqrt{1-\bar{\alpha}^{T_p}}} \varepsilon_\theta\left(X_t^{T_p}, T_p, X_h, X_r\right) \tag{14}$$

where β^{T_p} is the variance of the forward process, $\beta^{T_p} = 1-\alpha^{T_p}$, $\alpha^{T_p} = \prod_{s-1}^{T_p} \alpha^s$ is used to predict the additional noise ε_{pre}^k at any time step $T_p = k$. It consists of the Condition Generation Module (CGModule) and the Condition Denoising Module (CDModule), as shown in the following formula:

$$\varepsilon_\theta\left(X_t^{T_p}, T_p, X_h, X_r\right) = \text{CDModule}\left(X_t^{T_p}, T_p, \text{CGModule}(X_h, X_r)\right) \tag{15}$$

CGModule: To ensure that the entities generated during the denoising process align more closely with the actual knowledge graph, we employ Knowledge Graph Embedding (KGE) methods for deterministic conditional embedding generation (CGModule), such as TransE. This ensures that the generation process adheres to the structural constraints of the knowledge graph. For instance, at each step of the denoising process in the diffusion model, the embeddings of X_h and X_r are used to compute gradients to adjust the generation direction.

CDModule: It aims to combine noise, conditional embeddings, and time step embeddings to achieve the denoising process. To fully leverage conditional embeddings for guidance, parameters α, β, γ are set for scaling and shifting operations to adjust the vector distribution. Additionally, multi-head attention mechanisms and PoinConv extract and process features at different levels, helping the model better understand and utilize conditional embedding information. Finally, residual connections enhance the model's stability and performance.

3.5 Training and Reasoning

Supervised contrastive learning [15] aims to bring the generated embeddings of the same entity closer together and push the generated embeddings of different entities farther apart. At the same time, entity category labels guide the model in learning more discriminative feature representations. The loss is calculated as follows:

$$\mathcal{L}_{CL} = \sum_{t \in \mathcal{T}} \frac{-1}{|\mathcal{T}_t|} \sum_{X_t^{pro} \in \mathcal{T}_t} \log \frac{\exp(X_t^{pre} \cdot X_t/\tau)}{\sum_{k \in \mathcal{T}_t} \exp(X_k^{pre} \cdot X_t/\tau)} \quad (16)$$

where $\mathcal{T}$ represents the entity embeddings, $\mathcal{T}_t$ is the set of entity t, and t is a learnable parameter that controls the balance between uniformity and tolerance. X_t^{pre} represents the generated entity embedding from the reverse conditional denoising process and scores all candidate entities using the dot product. The cross-entropy loss is as follows:

$$\mathcal{L}_{CE} = -\frac{1}{|\mathcal{T}|} \sum_{(h,r) \in \mathcal{T}} \sum_{t \in E} y_{(h,r)}^t \cdot \log \hat{y}_{(h,r)}^t \quad (17)$$

where $\mathcal{T}$ represents the training triples in the batch, E denotes all entities present in the KG, $y_{(h,r)}^t$ represents the true label, $\hat{y}_{(h,r)}^t$ represents the plausibility score between the generated entity and the candidate entity set, and $X_e \in \mathcal{R}^{2 \times d \times |E|}$ represents the joint embedding representation of all entities. The final loss is optimized by combining the contrastive and cross-entropy losses.

We jointly optimize the two loss objectives $\mathcal{L} = \mathcal{L}_{CE} + \mathcal{L}_{CL}$, computing the similarity of diffusion-generated embeddings for the same entity and calculating the contrastive loss with embeddings of other entities. Simultaneously, we compute the similarity scores with the candidate entity set and calculate the cross-entropy loss. During the inference phase, the trained DGAT and CPES perform coarse-grained aggregation of entities. Then, KDG iteratively denoises random Gaussian noise conditioned on the entity feature (X_e, X_r) until $T_p = T$, generating the predicted entity X_t^{pre} in the vector space.

4 Experiment

4.1 Experimental Setup

Dataset: We considered three widely recognized datasets to evaluate the JKDM. FB15k-237 [16]: A subset of FB15k with inverse relations removed. WN18RR [5]: A subgroup of WN18, primarily featuring symmetric/antisymmetric and compositional relation patterns. UMLS [18]: A collection of medical vocabularies and standards. For detailed statistical data, please refer to Appendix A.1.

Evaluation Metrics: The JKDM is evaluated using link prediction task metrics, including Mean Reciprocal Rank (MRR) and Hits@N. MRR represents the average reciprocal rank of the correct predicted entity from the candidate entity set, while Hits@k indicates the proportion of correctly predicted entities within the top k ranks. This work sets k to (1, 3, 10).

Baselines: We evaluate JKDM against the latest knowledge completion models: GS-InGAT [8], SEA-KGC [9], FDM [10], KGDM [11], TDS [19], KRACL [20], DRR-GAT [21], MGTCA [22], LCA-KGC [23], SimKGC [24], CSProm-KG [25], FTL-LM [26], C-LMKE [27], BMKGC [28], HONARL [29], PEMLM-F [30], Relphormer [31].

Experimental Details: The model was trained using a single A40 GPU, with some hyperparameters set as follows: the time step was set to 40, and the dimension was set to 400. The url is https://github.com/Irreproachability/JKDM.

Table 1. The experimental results on FB15k-237, WN18RR, and UMLS are as follows. The best results are highlighted in bold, the second-best results are underlined, and "–" indicates no result.

Model	FB15K-237				WN18RR				UMLS			
	MRR	H@10	H@3	H@1	MRR	H@10	H@3	H@1	MRR	H@10	H@3	H@1
TDN	.358	.561	.403	.273	.499	.579	.523	.455	.938	.997	.983	.891
KRACL	.360	.548	.395	.266	.527	.613	.547	.482	–	–	–	–
DRR-GAT	.361	.549	.415	.268	.468	.579	.508	.421	–	1.00	–	–
MGTCA	.393	.583	.428	.291	.511	.593	.525	.475	–	–	–	–
LCA-KGC	.372	.554	.407	.276	.492	.585	.510	.456	–	–	–	–
SimKGC	.336	.511	.362	.249	.666	.800	.717	.587	–	–	–	–
CSProm-KG	.358	.538	.393	.269	.575	.678	.596	.522	–	–	–	–
C-LMKE	.306	.484	.331	.218	.619	.789	.671	.523	–	–	–	–
CP-KGC	.329	.503	.353	.243	.648	.773	.683	.580	.780	.951	.857	.678
BMKGC	.332	.514	.365	.247	.669	.807	.720	.590	–	–	–	–
SEA-KGC	.367	.553	.401	.275	.653	.795	.696	.577	–	–	–	–
GS-InGAT	.382	.567	.416	.283	.546	.625	.556	.491	–	–	–	–
HONARL	.367	.568	.406	.287	.513	.611	.541	.473	.907	.990	.951	.856
PEMLM-F	.355	.538	.389	.264	.556	.648	.573	.509	–	.997	–	–
Relphormer	.371	.481	–	.314	.401	.591	–	.448	–	.992	–	–
FDM	.485	.681	.529	.386	.506	.592	.518	.456	.922	.970	.944	.893
KGDM	.520	.708	.566	.423	.516	.593	.519	.457	.909	.973	.937	.872
Our (JKDM)	.532	.786	.639	.367	.679	.892	.770	.557	.942	.984	.967	.913

4.2 Performance Comparison

To demonstrate the effectiveness of JKDM, experiments were conducted on the WN18RR, FB15k-237, and UMLS datasets, and the performance was compared with existing models, as shown in Table 1.

Based on observations, JKDM outperforms other baseline models across the three datasets on most metrics. Specifically, on the FB15k-237, WN18RR, and UMLS datasets, the MRR scores improved by 1.2% (a 2.3% improvement relative to KGDM), 1% (a 1.5% improvement relative to BMKGC), and 0.4% (a 0.43% improvement relative to TDN), respectively, compared to the SOTA models.

Additionally, it is observed that JKDM significantly improves the performance on the Hits@10 and Hits@3 metrics, while the improvement on the Hits@1 metric is less pronounced. We analyze that JKDM, by leveraging structural and semantic enhancements to entity embeddings, captures more patterns and features of entities during the diffusion process. This enhanced generalization capability contributes to improved performance on Hits@3 and Hits@10. However, as the number of diffusion steps increases, noise may be introduced, or important information may be lost. This means that even if the initial embeddings contain rich information, this information may become blurred after multiple diffusion steps, affecting the final ranking accuracy (Hits@1).

Table 2. Ablation results on FB15k-237 and WN18RR. The best results are highlighted in bold, the second-best results are underlined.

Model	FB15K-237				WN18RR			
	MRR	H@10	H@3	H@1	MRR	H@10	H@3	H@1
JKDM w/o K	.298	.478	.327	.210	.457	.535	.470	.418
JKDM w/o D	.506	.764	.618	.352	.601	.824	.680	.481
JKDM w/o C	.497	.753	.616	.338	.628	.818	.699	.524
JKDM w/o C, D	.462	.687	.558	.325	.530	.706	.587	.438
JKDM w/o RGAT	.512	**.793**	**.651**	.346	.648	.868	.739	.525
JKDM w/o EGAT	.510	.770	.626	.357	.657	.880	.756	.547
JKDM w/o DG	<u>.519</u>	.779	.631	<u>.361</u>	<u>.662</u>	<u>.882</u>	<u>.762</u>	<u>.549</u>
JKDM w/o PE	.516	.780	.634	.358	.651	.860	.736	.537
JKDM	**.532**	<u>.786</u>	<u>.639</u>	**.367**	**.679**	**.892**	**.770**	**.557**

4.3 Ablation Experiment

Table 2 presents the ablation results of modules. "w/o C" and "w/o D" indicate the removal of the CPES and DGAT modules, respectively. It is observed that the MRR scores of "w/o C" and "w/o D" decreased by (4.9%, 6.8%) and (3.3%,10.8%), respectively. This demonstrates that the CPES and DGAT modules enhance entity features and improve model performance. By observing the decline ratios, it is noted that on the WN18RR dataset, the MRR metric of "w/o D" shows a more significant relative decline. In contrast, on the FB15k-237 dataset, the MRR metric of "w/o C" shows a more significant relative decline. We analyze that the WN18RR dataset is sparser (as shown in Table 1), making the structural feature enhancement by DGAT more significant for WN18RR. Therefore, the performance decline is more pronounced when the DGAT module is removed. We also removed CPES and DGAT ("w/o C, D"). It is observed that all metrics show a significant decline, with the MRR scores decreasing by 11.7% and 21.4%, respectively. This proves that combining structural and semantic features can effectively enhance entity embeddings. We conducted a case study to validate the effectiveness of the multi-model JKDM incorporating DGAT and CPES. For a detailed introduction, please refer to Appendix A.2.

Next, by removing the Knowledge Diffusion Generation (KDG) module ("w/o K"), it is observed that the MRR scores decrease by 43.0% and 32.2%, respectively. This indicates that using only KGE cannot effectively address the issue of diverse representations among entities. It demonstrates that diffusion models can effectively handle diverse entity representations and generate the distribution of target entities. Additionally, we conducted further ablation analysis. For details, please refer to Sect. 4.4.

4.4 Further Analysis of Ablation Experiment

Explore the Effectiveness of DGAT Module: "w/o RGAT" indicates the removal of the RGAT channel. In FB15k-237, the metrics H@10 and H@3 increase while H@1 decreases. We analyze that since FB15k-237 is denser than WN18RR and contains more relational information, removing RGAT weakens the model's ability to capture fine-grained relational features, leading to a decline in the accuracy of precise matching. "w/o EGAT" indicates the removal of the EGAT channel, and all metrics show a decline. After removing EGAT, we analyze that sparse entities lack densified neighborhoods, resulting in lower utilization of neighborhood information and insufficient intrinsic interaction information between entities. To validate this point, we conducted a densification ablation experiment ("w/o DG"), and the results show a decline in all metrics. This result proves that densified graph structures can effectively supplement the structural information of sparse entities, enhancing the model's ability to utilize neighborhood information and thereby improving overall performance.

Additionally, to avoid performance improvements solely due to the stacking of RGAT and EGAT layers, we conducted hyperparameter experiments on the number of GAT layers, as shown in Fig. 4. The experiments demonstrate that, with the same number of layers, the model using DGAT consistently outperforms the "w/o EGAT" and "w/o RGAT" models. This result validates the effectiveness of DGAT in better capturing complex relationships in knowledge graphs. DGAT not only enhances the ability to model relationships but also supplements the neighborhood information of sparse entities.

Explore the Effectiveness of CPES Module: "w/o PE" indicates replacing entity contextual enhancement semantics with entity text semantics. The results show a decline in all metrics, proving the effectiveness of contextual paths in enhancing entity semantics. Specifically, contextual paths contain structured relational information between entities, which helps the model better understand the semantics and associations of entities. In contrast, entity text semantics typically only include surface-level descriptions of entities and lack relational information between entities, resulting in weaker performance when modeling complex relationships. We conducted experiments on different PLM. For a detailed introduction, please refer to Appendix A.3.

Explore the Impact of Diffusion Parameters on KDG: experiments were conducted on different time step parameters and the number of CDModules. In Fig. 4(3), we tested the performance under different time step parameters and observed that the model performs best when the time step parameter $T = 40$. Increasing the time step may cause the model to overly rely on specific conditional feature details, reducing its robustness. In Fig. 4(4), we tested different numbers of CDModules and found that the performance is optimal when the number of layers is 3. Deeper networks may lead to overfitting, resulting in a decline in performance. We conducted experiments on different CGModules. For a detailed introduction, please refer to Appendix A.4.

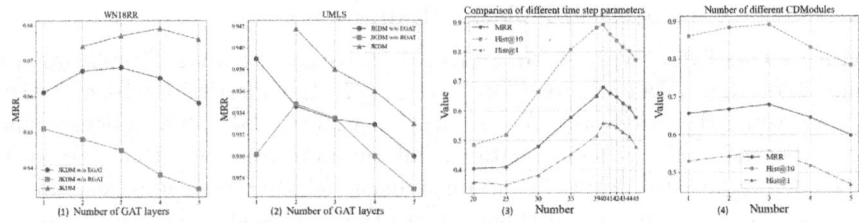

Fig. 4. (1) and (2) illustrate the performance comparison of different numbers of GAT layers in the channels of the DGAT. (3) and (4) represent the hyperparameter experiments conducted with varying time steps and numbers of CDModules.

4.5 Performance Evaluation By Relation Type

Next, we analyze the performance of JKDM in FB15k-237 by relation categories (Wang et al. 2014) [32]. Table 3 shows the MRR for different categories, and the results indicate that JKDM significantly improves performance when predicting N-1 tail entities and 1-N head entities. The experimental results suggest that the JKDM exhibits stronger robustness and generalization capabilities when handling complex relations, with its performance advantages being particularly pronounced when dealing with sparse entities. We conducted a case study to further demonstrate the JKDM's diverse generative capabilities. For a detailed introduction, please refer to Appendix A.5.

Table 3. MRR scores by relation type in FB15k-237, with the best results are highlighted in bold, the second-best results are underlined, and "–" indicates no result.

Model	Tail Pred				Head Pred			
	1-1	1-N	N-1	N-N	1-1	1-N	N-1	N-N
TransE	.476	.536	.060	.287	.484	.080	.329	.219
DisMult	.257	.575	.032	.184	.255	.038	.322	.131
ConvE	.366	.762	.069	.375	.374	.091	.444	.261
CompGCN	.453	.779	.076	.395	.457	.112	.471	.275
JKDM	**.522**	**.782**	**.424**	**.525**	**.523**	**.263**	**.623**	**.528**

4.6 Knowledge Sparsity Research

To further validate JKDM's sensitivity to sparse knowledge graphs, we randomly removed triples from the FB15k-237 training set at varying proportions (while maintaining the connectivity of the KG) and compared our experiments with TransE, RotatE, and w/o C, D, as shown in Fig. 5. As the entity degree increases, the performance of all models improves, with JKDM consistently outperforming the baseline models. This result demonstrates that the JKDM exhibits remarkable robustness when handling sparse entities, effectively addressing the challenges posed by incomplete information in the KG.

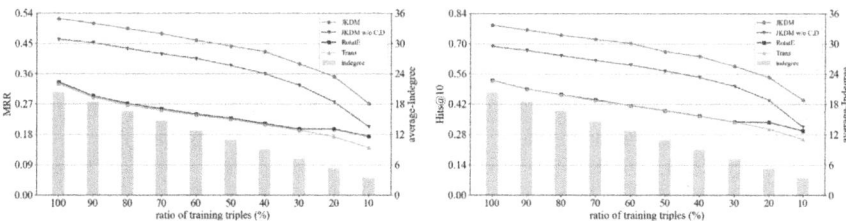

Fig. 5. Performance comparison between JKDM on sparse knowledge graphs and baseline models on the FB15k-237 dataset.

5 Conclusion

In this article, we propose the Joint Knowledge Diffusion Model (JKDM), which leverages diffusion models to capture diverse relationships between entities and generate the probability distribution of target entities. Additionally, we introduce a dual-channel GAT and a contextual path strategy to enhance the features of sparse entities, improving the generative capability of diffusion models for such entities. However, PLMs have limited understanding of entity contextual logic, while LLMs often increase the model's time cost. Therefore, in future work, we will explore knowledge distillation from LLMs to enhance PLMs' contextual logic comprehension while maintaining their time efficiency.

Acknowledgments. We thank Professor Song Yu and Professor Zhang Wendong for their valuable discussions and insights. We acknowledge the GPU equipment support provided by the Research Center of Xinjiang University. We also thank the anonymous reviewers for their constructive feedback, which has greatly improved this paper.

References

1. Bordes, A., Usunier, N., Garcia-Duran, A., Weston, J., Yakhnenko, O.: Translating embeddings for modeling multi-relational data. In: Advances in Neural Information Processing Systems, vol. 26. (2013)
2. Vashishth, S., Sanyal, S., Nitin, V., Talukdar, P.: Composition-based multi-relational graph convolutional networks. arXiv preprint arXiv:1911.03082 (2019)
3. Yao, L., Mao, C., Luo, Y.: KG-BERT: BERT for knowledge graph completion. arXiv preprint arXiv:1909.03193 (2019)
4. Sun, Z., Deng, Z. H., Nie, J. Y., et al.: RotatE: knowledge graph embedding by relational rotation in complex space. arXiv preprint arXiv:1902.10197 (2019)
5. Dettmers, T., Minervini, P., Stenetorp, P., Riedel, S.: Convolutional 2d knowledge graph embeddings. In: Proceedings of the AAAI Conference on Artificial Intelligence, vol. 32, no. 1 (2018)
6. Lin, Y., Liu, Z., Sun, M., Liu, Y., Zhu, X.: Learning entity and relation embeddings for knowledge graph completion. In: Proceedings of the AAAI Conference on Artificial Intelligence, vol. 29, no. 1 (2015)
7. Sun, Z., Deng, Z.-H., Nie, J.-Y., Tang, J.: Rotate: knowledge graph embedding by relational rotation in complex space. arXiv preprint arXiv:1902.10197 (2019)
8. Yin, H., Zhong, J., Wang, C., Li, R., Li, X.: GS-InGAT: an interaction graph attention network with global semantic for knowledge graph completion. Expert Syst. Appl. **228**, 120380 (2023)
9. Je, S.-H., Choi, W., Oh, K.: Unifying structure and language semantic for efficient contrastive knowledge graph completion with structured entity anchors. arXiv preprint arXiv:2311.04250 (2023)
10. Long, X., Zhuang, L., Li, A., et al.: Fact embedding through diffusion model for knowledge graph completion. In: Proceedings of the ACM Web Conference 2024, pp. 2020–2029 (2024)
11. Nguyen, T.-K., Fang, Y.: Diffusion-based negative sampling on graphs for link prediction. In: Proceedings of the ACM Web Conference 2024, pp. 948–958 (2024)
12. Cai, Y., et al.: Predicting the unpredictable: uncertainty-aware reasoning over temporal knowledge graphs via diffusion process. In: Findings of the Association for Computational Linguistics, ACL 2024, pp. 5766–5778 (2024)
13. Jiang, Y., Yang, Y., Xia, L., Huang, C.: Diffkg: knowledge graph diffusion model for recommendation. In: Proceedings of the 17th ACM International Conference on Web Search and Data Mining, pp. 313–321 (2024)
14. Pan, Y., Liu, J., Zhao, T., Zhang, L., Wang, Q.: Context-aware commonsense knowledge graph reasoning with path-guided explanations. IEEE Trans. Knowl. Data Eng. **36**(8), 3725–3738 (2024)

15. Gunel, B., Du, J., Conneau, A., Stoyanov, V.: Supervised contrastive learning for pre-trained language model fine-tuning. arXiv preprint arXiv:2011.01403 (2020)
16. Toutanova, K., Chen, D.: Observed versus latent features for knowledge base and text inference. In: Proceedings of the 3rd Workshop on Continuous Vector Space Models and Their Compositionality, pp. 57–66 (2015)
17. Dettmers, T., Minervini, P., Stenetorp, P., Riedel, S.: Convolutional 2d knowledge graph embeddings. In: Proceedings of the AAAI Conference on Artificial Intelligence, vol. 32, no. 1 (2018)
18. Kok, S., Domingos, P.: Statistical predicate invention. In: Proceedings of the 24th International Conference on Machine Learning, pp. 433–440 (2007)
19. Wang, J., Wang, B., Gao, J., Li, X., Hu, Y., Yin, B.: TDN: Triplet distributor network for knowledge graph completion. IEEE Trans. Knowl. Data Eng. **35**(12), 13002–13014 (2023)
20. Tan, Z., et al.: KRACL: contrastive learning with graph context modeling for sparse knowledge graph completion. In: Proceedings of the ACM Web Conference 2023, pp. 2548–2559 (2023)
21. Xin, Z., Zhang, C., Guo, J., Peng, C., Niu, Z., Wu, X.: Graph attention network with dynamic representation of relations for knowledge graph completion. Expert Syst. Appl. **219**, 129684 (2023)
22. Shang, B., Zhao, Y., Liu, J., Wang, D.: Mixed geometry message and trainable convolutional attention network for knowledge graph completion. In: Proceedings of the AAAI Conference on Artificial Intelligence, vol. 38, no. 8, pp. 8966–8974 (2024)
23. Shang, B., Zhao, Y., Liu, J.: Learnable convolutional attention network for knowledge graph completion. Knowl.-Based Syst. **285**, 111360 (2024)
24. Wang, L., Zhao, W., Wei, Z., Liu, J.: SimKGC: simple contrastive knowledge graph completion with pre-trained language models. arXiv preprint arXiv:2203.02167 (2022)
25. Chen, C., Wang, Y., Sun, A., Li, B., Lam, K.: Dipping PLMS sauce: bridging structure and text for effective knowledge graph completion via conditional soft prompting. arXiv preprint arXiv:2307.01709 (2023)
26. Lin, Q., Mao, R., Liu, J., Xu, F., Cambria, E.: Fusing topology contexts and logical rules in language models for knowledge graph completion. Inf. Fus. 253–264 (2023)
27. Wang, X., He, Q., Liang, J., Xiao, Y.: Language models as knowledge embeddings. arXiv preprint arXiv:2206.12617 (2022)
28. Kong, Y., Fan, C., Chen, Y., Zhang, S., Lv, Z., Tao, J.: Bilateral masking with prompt for knowledge graph completion. In: Findings of the Association for Computational Linguistics: NAACL 2024, pp. 240–249 (2024)
29. Yin, H., Zhong, J., Li, R., Shang, J., Wang, C., Li, X.: High-order neighbors aware representation learning for knowledge graph completion. IEEE Trans. Neural Networks Learn. Syst. 1234–1245 (2024)
30. Qiu, C., Qian, P., Wang, C., Yao, J., Liu, L., Wei, F., Eddie, E.: Joint pre-encoding representation and structure embedding for efficient and low-resource knowledge graph completion. In: Proceedings of the 2024 Conference on Empirical Methods in Natural Language Processing, pp. 15257–15269 (2024)
31. Bi, Z., Cheng, S., Chen, J., Liang, X., Xiong, F., Zhang, N.: Relphormer: relational graph transformer for knowledge graph representations. Neurocomputing **566**, 127044 (2024)
32. Wang, Z., et al.: Knowledge graph embedding by translating on hyperplanes. In: Proceedings of the AAAI Conference on Artificial Intelligence, vol. 28, no. 1, pp. 613–619 (2014)

Ensemble Learning

EM-SEC: Efficient Multi-head Set-Valued Evidential Classification

Grigor Bezirganyan[1(✉)], Sana Sellami[1], Laure Berti-Équille[2], and Sébastien Fournier[1]

[1] Aix-Marseille University, CNRS, LIS, Marseille, France
{grigor.bezirganyan,sana.sellami,sebasiten.fournier}@univ-amu.fr
[2] IRD, ESPACE-DEV, Montpellier, France
laure.berti@ird.fr

Abstract. In machine learning and deep learning, uncertainty quantification helps to accurately assess a model's confidence in its predictions, enabling the rejection of uncertain outcomes in safety-critical applications. However, in scenarios involving AI-assisted decision-making, proposing multiple plausible decisions can be more beneficial than either not making any decisions or risking incorrect ones. Set-valued classification is a relaxation of standard multiclass classification where, in cases of uncertainty, the classifier returns a set of potential labels instead of a single label. Current methods for set-valued classification often suffer from high computational complexity or fail to adequately quantify uncertainty. In this paper, we introduce a novel, computationally efficient approach to set-valued classification leveraging evidential deep learning and subjective logic, explicitly providing a measure of classification uncertainty. Our method employs a dual-head architecture: one head conducts multiclass evidential classification, while the other suggests candidate label sets when uncertainty is high. The proposed approach has linear worst-case computational complexity with respect to the number of classes. Extensive evaluation on several benchmark datasets demonstrates that our method showcases comparable performance to baseline set-valued methods, while being up to 23 times faster at inference on the benchmark datasets.

Keywords: set-valued classification · evidential deep learning · subjective logic · utility maximization · uncertainty quantification

1 Introduction

Artificial Intelligence (AI) has experienced a rapid surge in recent years, driven by advancements in deep learning, large-scale data availability, and increased computational power. From healthcare diagnostics to financial forecasting and autonomous systems, AI is increasingly used for both autonomous and assisted decision-making. Nevertheless, it has been shown that deep neural networks can produce incorrect output with high confidence [11], which can be catastrophic in safety-critical areas. To alleviate this issue, different uncertainty quantification (UQ) techniques have been suggested [1] to understand the true confidence of the models and reject the decision of the model in case of high uncertainty.

Most of the UQ techniques for classification tasks operate in *precise classification* setting[1], where the model can either make a single prediction, or refuse to make a prediction under high uncertainty. However, in many applications of deep learning models for assisted decision-making, where a human expert makes the final decision, it would be more beneficial to suggest a reduced set of decision options with lower uncertainty rather than completely rejecting uncertain predictions. *Set-valued* or *imprecise* classification [5] tries to address this issue by suggesting a set of possible outputs in uncertain situations. [7] has recently demonstrated through trials that set-valued predictions enhance human decision-making and increase accuracy compared to no assistance or top-k predictions (suggesting the most probable k options).

Recent work [15,24,29] concentrates on using Dempster-Shafer (DS) theory of belief functions [8,22] to model uncertainty and imprecision in deep learning models. DS theory is a mathematical framework for reasoning under uncertainty, generalizing probability theory by allowing belief assignment to sets of possibilities rather than single events. However, considering all possible subsets of the power set of the label space can be computationally expensive and infeasible for large label spaces [19]. [19] proposes efficient set-valued classification algorithm, with $K \log K$ time complexity, where K is the number of classes. However, the method takes conditional class probabilities as a measure of uncertainty, which may not be accurate in practice [11].

In this work, we propose a novel set-valued evidential classification method, EM-SEC, which uses a multi-head architecture to efficiently model set-valued predictions. The first multiclass head is used to perform evidential multiclass classification, where it uses subjective logic (SL) [14] to get beliefs for each class as well as the total uncertainty. The second head is used to suggest one set-valued candidate set, which is obtained by evidential multi-label classification. Finally, subjective logic is used to allocate some belief mass from the uncertainty mass of the first head to the candidate set. At inference time, the model takes the prediction with highest belief mass, which can be either a singleton class or a set of classes. Our contributions hence are the following:

– We propose EM-SEC (**E**fficient **M**ulti-head **S**et-valued **E**vidential **C**lassification), a novel set-valued classification approach that scales linearly with the number of classes, hence being up to 23 times faster in our experiments compared with baseline methods.
– EM-SEC provides the uncertainty of the decision for both: single class and set-valued predictions. The uncertainty value can be used to avoid making uncertain decisions in safety-critical areas.

---

[1] *Precise* classification refers to returning only one class, in contrast to imprecise classification, which returns multiple classes, often referred to as *set-valued or imprecise* classification.

- We show that EM-SEC achieves comparable results with the baseline models on CIFAR-10 and CIFAR-100 datasets [17].
- The code of EM-SEC is open and experiments are reproducible at https://github.com/bezirganyan/em_sec.

2 Related Work

Set-valued classification aims to minimize both the error rate and the expected size of the prediction set. A common approach is Top-K classification, which outputs a fixed number of labels per sample. However, choosing an optimal K is difficult, as different samples require different set sizes: high-confidence samples need fewer labels, while ambiguous ones benefit from larger sets.

Another approach is to use thresholding on the output probabilities of a multiclass classifier, where the classes with probabilities above a certain threshold are selected. However, a fixed threshold may not be optimal for all samples, and the set size can vary considerable by slight changes in the threshold [19]. Similar to EM-SEC, [10] propose a two-headed architecture, where the second (multi-label) head is trained on pseudo-labels derived from the softmax scores of the first head. These pseudo-positives are selected to maintain a batch-wise average set size of K. At test time, only the output of the multi-label head is used. However, this approach does not account for model uncertainty. In contrast, EM-SEC performs per-sample evidential fusion: if the Dirichlet evidence from the single-label head is sufficiently confident, it outputs a single class; otherwise, it defers to the evidential multi-label head's candidate set, while also providing a measure of uncertainty.

Conformal Prediction (CP) [23, 26] is another popular framework for set-valued classification. CP is a distribution-free framework that provides a prediction set (or region in the case of regression) that is guaranteed to contain the true label with a certain probability. The theoretical guarantees and the simplicity of the framework make it a popular choice for set-valued classification. However, while these guarantees hold on the error rate, the expected set size is not guaranteed to be minimized, and the set size can be quite large for some datasets [19, 27]. Conformal Prediction with strong coverage guarantees (full conformal prediction) can also be quite expensive and infeasible for big datasets, while optimized variants (e.g., split conformal prediction) have weaker coverage guarantees [4].

Another direction, to which this paper belongs to, stems from decision theory, and tries to combine the error-rate minimization and set-size minimization objectives into a single utility function. [19] proposed an efficient set-valued classification, that relies on the conditional class probabilities and tries to find the subset of classes that maximizes the expected utility. This method is computationally efficient, but assumes that the uncertainty is quantified by class-conditional probabilities. It was shown [11] that standard deep learning models can be overconfident and poorly calibrated, which also motivates our use of evidential neural networks in this work. The efficient set-valued classifier proposed by [19] also sorts the classes by their conditional probabilities at inference time, which, while can be negligible for small label spaces, can be computationally expensive for large label spaces.

Approaches based on Dempster-Shafer (DS) theory [8,22] offer an alternative framework for set-valued classification by directly addressing the inherent uncertainty in the data through belief assignments. In these methods, classifiers generate belief masses over subsets of the label space, following the principles laid out in DS theory. By assigning non-zero mass to composite hypotheses, DS-based methods enable the classifier to express uncertainty with a finer granularity than traditional probability estimates. [9] introduced an approach to neural network classification that integrates evidential reasoning. In this method, the similarity between an input pattern and a limited set of prototypes is evaluated, with each prototype contributing evidence about class membership in the form of belief functions. These individual pieces of evidence are then combined using Dempster's rule of combination to reach a final decision. Initially, the method could make only singleton predictions, or refuse to make a prediction under high uncertainty (classification with rejection). Later, [18] extended this approach to set-valued classification by allowing the classifier to output multiple classes. [24] integrated the set-valued classification framework for deep convolutional neural networks, showcasing their capabilities on complex data. Nevertheless, both [18,24] require computation of the extended utility matrices with shapes $(2^k - 1 \times k)$. Although this matrix can be precomputed, in our experiments we observed that for $k > 20$, the matrices already did not fit in the memory. Moreover, besides the memory limitation, the approach also requires $k(2^k - 1 - k)$ computations, which is infeasible for large label spaces. To solve that issue, [18] suggested to only consider 2-element sets, and the full set. This, however, limits the expressiveness of the model and still requires $\mathcal{O}(k^3)$ computations. In [24], the authors propose identifying, for each class, the two (or more) most similar classes and restricting the utility computation to these class pairs. While this approach can help reduce computational complexity, its performance heavily depends on the dataset's inherent structure (e.g. one class can have many similar classes), and it may still limit the overall expressiveness of the model.

[13] proposed an imprecise re-labeling procedure that revises the training data by replacing precise class labels with subsets of candidate classes for samples located in overlapping or isolated regions, and then uses DS theory for learning and reasoning. However, the reasoning step of this approach can still be computationally expensive for large label spaces. The re-labeling step also depends on prediction methods to provide reliable posterior probabilities; if these estimates are poor, the subsequent imprecise labels may not accurately capture the underlying uncertainty. The work of [15] is also notable for combining evidential neural networks with conformal prediction to provide set-valued predictions with guaranteed error rates.

In this paper, however, our work mostly falls in the domains of evidential set-valued classifiers [9,18,24], and utility function maximization [18,19,24]. In our approach, we reduce the exponential computational complexity required by evidential classifiers, by considering only one additional set, suggested by a second candidate proposal head. This allows us to scale linearly with the number of classes. The use of evidential neural network also enables us more accurate uncertainty quantification compared to standard deep learning models.

Similar to the work discussed in the previous paragraphs [9,18,24], we propose an evidential classification algorithm. However, instead of learning prototypes and fusing them using Dempster's rule, our architecture directly learns the parameters of the Dirichlet distribution, as introduced in [21]. The Dirichlet distribution models a distribution over class probabilities while also capturing the uncertainty in predictions. Following [21], we leverage subjective logic to reason about uncertainty. The next section provides a detailed discussion of subjective logic and evidential deep learning as used in this work.

3 Preliminaries

In this section, we provide background on Subjective Logic and precise evidential deep learning algorithms, as they form the foundation of our methodology.

3.1 Subjective Logic

Subjective Logic (SL) [14] is an extension of DS theory that provides an intuitive framework for modeling uncertain and imprecise information. SL defines the *domain* $\mathbb{X}$ as the set of all possible states (or classes), analogous to the frame of discernment in DS theory. Additionally, SL defines the *hyperdomain* $\mathscr{R}(\mathbb{X})$ as the reduced superset of $\mathbb{X}$, which is the set of all non-empty proper subsets of $\mathbb{X}$, excluding the full set $\mathbb{X}$ itself.

In SL, beliefs about states in domain $\mathbb{X}$ or hyperdomain $\mathscr{R}(\mathbb{X})$ are represented using *belief masses*. The belief mass distribution $\mathbf{b}_X$ assigns belief masses to the possible values of random variable X, where X can be a state in the domain or a set of states in the hyperdomain. The belief mass on the whole domain is denoted as the *uncertainty mass* u. The additivity property of belief masses is defined as $\sum_{X \in \mathscr{D}} b_X(X) + u_X = 1$, where $\mathscr{D} \in \{\mathbb{X}, \mathscr{R}(\mathbb{X})\}$.

A *subjective opinion* in SL is defined as a triplet $\omega_X = (\mathbf{b}_X, u_X, \mathbf{a}_X)$, where $\mathbf{b}_X$ is the belief mass vector, u_X is the uncertainty mass, and $\mathbf{a}_X$ is the vector of base rates. Base rates are the prior probabilities of the states in the domain $\mathbb{X}$ or hyperdomain $\mathscr{R}(\mathbb{X})$. The opinions are called *multinomial opinions* if $X \in \mathbb{X}$ and *hypernomial opinions* if $X \in \mathscr{R}(\mathbb{X})$. In other words, a multinomial opinion asigns belief masses to precise singleton states, while a hypernomial opinion assigns belief masses to sets of states. Belief mass assigned to a composite value represents vagueness and is referred as *vague belief mass*. A special case of multinomial opinion is when the opinion is about a binary state, which is called a *binomial opinion* and is represented as $\omega_X = (b_X, d_X, a_X, u_X)$, where b_X is the belief mass, d_X is the disbelief mass, a_X is the base rate, and u_X is the uncertainty mass.

Subjective logic also provides a convenient bijective mapping between multinomial opinions and Dirichlet distributions [14]. Dirichlet distribution with parameters $\boldsymbol{\alpha} = (\alpha_1, \ldots, \alpha_K)$ is a probability distribution over the K-simplex, and is defined as:

$$\text{Dir}(\mathbf{p} \mid \boldsymbol{\alpha}) = \begin{cases} \frac{1}{B(\boldsymbol{\alpha})} \prod_{k=1}^{K} p_k^{\alpha_k - 1}, & \text{for } \mathbf{p} \in \mathcal{S}_K \\ 0, & \text{otherwise} \end{cases} \quad (1)$$

where $B(\boldsymbol{\alpha})$ is the multivariate beta function, and $\mathcal{S}_K$ is the K-simplex. The Dirichlet distribution is convenient for modeling multinomial opinions, as the parameters $\boldsymbol{\alpha}$ can be interpreted as the number of observations of each class. The bijective mapping between multinomial opinions and Dirichlet distributions is given by:

$$b_k = \frac{e_k}{S} = \frac{\alpha_k - 1}{S}, u = \frac{K}{S}, \quad (2)$$

where $S = \sum_{k=1}^{K} \alpha_k$ is called the Dirichlet strength, and $e_k = \alpha_k - 1$ is the supporting evidence for class k. To be able to represent hypernomial opinions using Dirichlet distributions, [14] suggests to use the hyper-Dirichlet distribution, which is a generalization of the Dirichlet distribution to the hyperdomain. The hyper-Dirichlet distribution is defined similarly to the Dirichlet distribution, but with an additional artificial assumption that the states in hyperdomain are mutually exclusive (i.e. $\forall x, y \in \mathcal{R}(\mathbb{X}), x \cap y = \emptyset$).

3.2 Evidential Deep Learning Using Subjective Logic

Subjective logic has been used in deep learning to model uncertainty and imprecision in classification tasks. [21] proposed an evidential deep learning framework that uses subjective logic to model uncertainty in deep neural networks. In this framework, the output logits of the neural network are transformed into evidences with some monotonically increasing and non-negative activation function (e.g., softplus, exponent, ReLU, etc.). Then, the evidences are transformed into the parameters of a Dirichlet distribution, with $\alpha_k = e_k + 1$ for each class k. The network is trained using the adapted cross-entropy loss, which is defined as:

$$\begin{aligned} L_{ace}(\boldsymbol{\alpha}_n) &= \int \left[\sum_{k=1}^{K} -y_{nk} \log p_{nk} \right] \frac{\prod_{k=1}^{K} p_{nk}^{\alpha_{nk}-1}}{B(\boldsymbol{\alpha}_n)} d\mathbf{p}_n \\ &= \sum_{k=1}^{K} y_{nk} \left(\psi(S_n) - \psi(\alpha_{nk}) \right), \end{aligned} \quad (3)$$

where ψ is the digamma function, $S_n = \sum_{k=1}^{K} \alpha_{nk}$ is the Dirichlet strength, and y_{nk} is the one-hot encoded target label for sample n. An additional Kullback-Leibler divergence term is added between incorrect class probabilities and the uniform distribution to encourage the network to output high uncertainty for incorrect predictions. The KL divergence term is defined as:

$$L_{KL}(\boldsymbol{\alpha}_n) = KL\left[D\left(\boldsymbol{p}_n \mid \tilde{\boldsymbol{\alpha}}_n\right) \| D\left(\boldsymbol{p}_n \mid \mathbf{1}\right)\right]$$
$$= \log\left(\frac{\Gamma\left(\sum_{k=1}^{K} \tilde{\alpha}_{nk}\right)}{\Gamma(K)\prod_{k=1}^{K}\Gamma\left(\tilde{\alpha}_{nk}\right)}\right) + \sum_{k=1}^{K}(\tilde{\alpha}_{nk} - 1)\left[\psi\left(\tilde{\alpha}_{nk}\right) - \psi\sum_{k=1}^{K}\tilde{\alpha}_{nk}\right], \quad (4)$$

where $\tilde{\boldsymbol{\alpha}}_n = \mathbf{y}_n + (\mathbf{1} - \mathbf{y}_n) \odot \boldsymbol{\alpha}_n$ are the Dirichlet parameters after removing the misleading evidence, and the Γ is the gamma function. The total loss is defined as $L = L_{ace} + \sigma_t L_{KL}$, where $\sigma_t [0, 1]$ is an annealing coefficient.

4 Our Methodology

In this paper, we propose a novel approach for Evidential Set-Valued Classification based on Subjective Logic. As discussed in previous section, set-valued classification, especially the ones utilizing DS theory or utility functions often face the problem of handling the exponentially growing number of possible subsets of the frame of discernment. Similarly, in subjective logic, the cardinality of the hyperdomain grows exponentially with the number of states and is equal to $2^K - 2$. Modeling these sets with a neural network becomes infeasible quickly, especially for large K. To address this issue, we propose a novel approach, which suggests assigned belief masses on a reduced hyperset consisting of $K + 1$ elements. We propose to use a 2-head approach, where the first head, called the **multinomial head**, is responsible for providing precise multinomial evidences $e_1, e_2, \ldots, e_K$, and the second head, called the **candidate proposal head**, is responsible for proposing candidate sets of classes and providing the evidence $e_\mathcal{C}$ (Fig. 1). More formally, instead of modeling the evidence of the hyperset $e_H = \{e_1, e_2, \ldots, e_K, e_{K+1}, \ldots, e_{(2^K-2)}\}$, we model the evidence of $e_H = \{e_1, e_2, \ldots, e_K, e_\mathcal{C}\}$, where e_k, $k \in \{1, \ldots, K\}$ are the evidences for the singleton classes predicted from the multinomial head, and $e_\mathcal{C}$ is the evidence on a set of classes $\mathcal{C} \subset \mathcal{X}$ predicted from the candidate proposal head. Finally, the outputs of the two heads are combined using subjective logic to obtain the set-valued predictions together with the uncertainty estimates. The combination strategy ensures that the model provides set-valued predictions when the uncertainty is high, and singleton predictions when the uncertainty is low.

4.1 Multinomial Head

This head is a standard evidential multi-class classifier, which outputs a multinomial opinion for each class. The output of this head are evidences $e_1, e_2, \ldots, e_K$, which are obtained by applying an activation function with non-negative outputs, such as exponential function or softplus function, to the logits of the model. The evidences then can be converted either to multinomial opinions, or to the

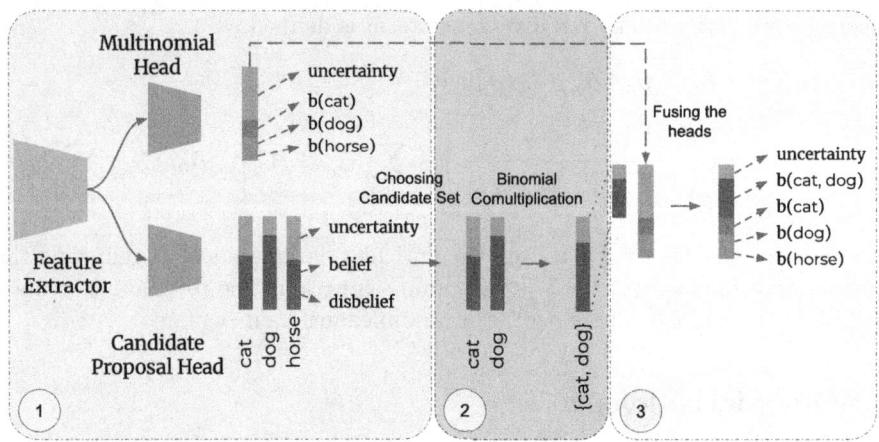

Fig. 1. Pipeline of the proposed approach. (1) Extracted features are fed into multinomial and candidate proposal heads. (2) The candidate proposal head's outputs determine the candidate set using belief and disbelief masses, followed by binomial co-multiplication to compute belief and uncertainty masses. The disbelief masses are merged with the uncertainty mass. (3) The final hypernomial output is obtained by scaling and fitting these masses into the multinomial head's uncertainty. In the figure b(·) represents the belief mass on the specific class.

parameters of Dirichlet distribution. For notation convenience, we note the subjective multinomial opinion representation as: $\omega_M(\mathbf{b}_M, \mathbf{a}_M, u_M)$, where

$$b_{Mk} = \frac{e_k}{\sum_{i=1}^{K} e_i + 1}; \quad a_{Mk} = \frac{1}{K}; \quad u_M = \frac{1}{\sum_{i=1}^{K} e_i + 1}. \tag{5}$$

As we can see, the multinomial head does not provide any set-valued predictions, but unlike standard softmax based classifiers, it provides the uncertainty in the form of uncertainty mass. Traditionally, the uncertainty mass is used to reject the prediction of the model in case of high uncertainty. However, instead of rejecting predictions due to high uncertainty, our approach proposes making multiple plausible predictions.

4.2 Candidate Proposal Head

The candidate proposal head is responsible for proposing candidate sets of classes. This task can be framed similarly to multi-label classification, where the model is trained to predict the likelihood of each class being associated with the input sample, allowing for the possibility of multiple classes being selected simultaneously. However, unlike multilabel classification, the ground truth includes only one positive label. Training with single positive and $k - 1$ negative classes penalizes the model for predicting any class other than the ground truth, restricting or preventing multiple predictions. To address this issue, we follow the approach proposed by [6], where the authors propose to reduce the penalty of false positives by down-weighting the terms in the loss function corresponding to the negative classes. To achieve this they propose the *weak assume negative (WAN)* loss defined as:

$$\mathcal{L}_{\text{WAN}}(\mathbf{p}_n, \mathbf{y}_n) = -\frac{1}{K}\sum_{k=1}^{K}\left[\mathbb{1}_{[y_{nk}=1]}\log(p_{nk})\right.\\ \left. +\mathbb{1}_{[y_{nk}\neq 1]}\gamma\log(1-p_{nk})\right], \quad (6)$$

where K is the number of classes, $\mathbf{p}_n$ are the conditional class probabilities of the probabilistic classifier, $\mathbf{y}_n$ is the ground truth, $\mathbb{1}_{[\cdot]}$ is the indicator function, and $\gamma = \frac{1}{K-1}$ is the down-weighting factor.

This approach, while suiting to our candidate proposing task, does not quantify the uncertainties in the candidate set, and will also not allow us to obtain a joint belief mass for the proposed set. To address this issue, we will make use of evidential multi-label classification [30], which is a generalization of evidential multi-class classification to multi-label setting. The evidential multi-label classifier puts a prior Beta $(\alpha_{nk}, \beta_{nk})$ on the presence of each class k in the candidate set. The parameters of the Beta distribution are obtained by a neural network predicting two evidence parameters e_{nk}^+ and e_{nk}^- for each class. The evidences are then converted to the parameters of the Beta distribution α_{nk} and β_{nk} by adding one to each evidence. The model is learned by optimizing the Beta loss defined as:

$$\mathcal{L}_n(\boldsymbol{\theta}) = \sum_{k=1}^{K}\int \text{BCE}(y_{nk}, p_{nk})\,\text{Beta}(p_{nk}; \alpha_{nk}, \beta_{nk})\,dp_{nk}\\ = \sum_{k=1}^{K}[y_{nk}(\psi(\alpha_{nk}+\beta_{nk})-\psi(\alpha_{nk}))\\ +(1-y_{nk})(\psi(\alpha_{nk}+\beta_{nk})-\psi(\beta_{nk}))], \quad (7)$$

where K is the number of classes, $\text{BCE}(\cdot)$ is the binary cross entropy loss, $\psi(\cdot)$ is the digamma function. The parameters α_{nk} and β_{nk} can also be converted to subjective binomial opinions $\omega(b_{nk}, d_{nk}, a_{nk}, u_{nk})$, which we will use later for joint belief mass calculation. We can integrate the weak assume negative loss and the Beta loss to obtain the *weak assume negative evidential (WANE)* loss:

$$\mathcal{L}_{n\text{WANE}}(\alpha_n, \beta_n, \mathbf{y}_n) = \sum_{k=1}^{K}[y_{nk}(\psi(\alpha_{nk}+\beta_{nk})-\psi(\alpha_{nk}))\\ +\gamma(1-y_{nk})(\psi(\alpha_{nk}+\beta_{nk})-\psi(\beta_{nk}))]. \quad (8)$$

To control how generous or strict the models shall be in terms of set-sizes, we propose two strategies. First, we introduce penalties prediction set-sizes, to directly control how big the prediction is allowed to be. Second, we employ learnable down-weighting factors that allow the model to infer class-specific preferences for set size strictness directly from the data.

4.3 Constraint-Based WANE Optimization

An important aspect of the candidate proposal head is that it should propose a set of classes, where the cardinality of the set is higher than one: $|\mathcal{C}| > 1$. To achieve this, we can define a penalty term in the loss function, which penalizes the model for $|\mathcal{C}| \leq 1$. The penalty term can be defined as:

$$\mathcal{L}_{p2}(\mathbf{p}) = \lambda \cdot \min\left(0, \sum_{k=1}^{K} \mathbb{1}_{[p_k > 0.5]} - 2\right), \tag{9}$$

where λ is the penalty coefficient. However, the indicator function is not a differentiable function, hence we perform a smooth relaxation of the penalty term by using an estimated soft cardinality. For predicted conditional probabilities $\mathbf{p} = [p_1, \ldots, p_L]$, we define the estimated (soft) cardinality s as:

$$s = \sum_{k=1}^{K} \sigma\left(\eta\left(p_k - 0.5\right)\right), \tag{10}$$

where $\sigma(\cdot)$ is the sigmoid function and η is the steepness parameter. Then, the relaxed penalty term will become:

$$\mathcal{L}_{p2}^{r}(\mathbf{p}) = \lambda \cdot \min\left((s-2), 0\right). \tag{11}$$

The resulting loss function in its current form constrains the candidate set's cardinality from below, but it does not regulate its average size. Following [6], the original formulation sets $\gamma = \frac{1}{K-1}$, which reduces the penalty on all negative classes in the loss. Although this allows the model to propose multiple classes, it inadvertently encourages high-cardinality outputs. Instead, our objective is to design a loss function that imposes higher penalties for false positives from classes not relevant to the input, while applying lower penalties for false negatives in the relevant classes. To address this issue, we propose a cardinality-based loss term that directly controls the average size of the candidate set. Our approach leverages a differentiable approximation of the set's cardinality from Eq. 10. We then augment the original loss (e.g. the WANE loss defined in Eq. 8) with a penalty term that directly discourages excessively large candidate sets:

$$\mathcal{L}_{\text{card}} = \gamma\, h(s), \tag{12}$$

where $\gamma > 0$ is a hyperparameter, and the penalty function $h(s)$ is chosen to be monotonically increasing in s. Inspired by decision-theoretic utility functions, a reasonable choice is

$$h(s) = 1 - \frac{1 + \beta^2}{s + \beta^2}, \tag{13}$$

with *beta* (distinct from parameters of the Beta distribution) controlling the tolerance for larger candidate sets. Lower β values enforce stricter cardinality control, while higher β values allow for larger sets.

In our proposed training regime, the overall loss is defined as

$$\mathcal{L}_{\text{const}} = \mathcal{L}_{\text{WANE}} + \mathcal{L}_{\text{p2}}^{r} + \mathcal{L}_{\text{card}}, \tag{14}$$

which ensures that the model is penalized not only for misclassifications but also for deviating from the desired candidate set size. We train the model with $\mathcal{L}_{\text{WANE}}$ and $\mathcal{L}_{\text{p2}}^{r}$ for a number of epochs to obtain reliable conditional class probabilities, and the cardinality penalty is introduced gradually (via an annealing coefficient $\tau \in [0,1]$) so that the loss function adapts smoothly to the new objective.

4.4 Alternative Learnable-Factor Based WANE Optimization

In the previous sub-section, we introduced two penalty terms to enforce a minimum cardinality for the predicted set and to penalize excessively large sets. However, this soft-thresholding approach introduces several challenges. First, the soft estimate of the set size, computed using sigmoid activations, is only an approximation of the true cardinality. When the predicted probabilities are close to the 0.5, the estimated size can deviate significantly from the actual number of selected elements. Second, using steep sigmoid functions to approximate hard thresholds can lead to optimization issues such as vanishing or unstable gradients. Third, the gradients induced by the WANE loss and the cardinality-based penalties may conflict, potentially pulling the model in opposing directions and hindering effective learning. Finally, the penalties are not class-dependent, meaning the model applies the same set-size constraints uniformly across all classes. This prevents the model from adapting its prediction behavior based on class-specific characteristics, such as semantic similarity or varying levels of ambiguity between classes. To address this issue we propose an alternative optimization idea based on learnable, class-specific down-weighting factors.

As discussed before, the down-weighting factor γ in Eq. 8 is controlling how strong the penalization for false positives shall be. While the authors [6] choose $\gamma = \frac{1}{K-1}$, it puts a uniform penalty for false positives on all classes. Nevertheless, based on the semantics of classes and the uncertainties, it may be more acceptable to have false positives for some classes than the others. For example, for an image of a dog, it is more acceptable to have the class wolf as a false positive, than the class car. To achieve this, we propose to have a matrix of down-weighting factors $\Gamma = [\gamma_{jk}] \in [0,1]^{K \times K}$, where each γ_{jk} represents the down-weighting factor for penalization of a sample belonging to class j with a false positive in class k. The WANE loss wit learnable factors then will be:

$$\mathcal{L}_{n\text{WANE-LF}}(\alpha_n, \beta_n, \mathbf{y}_n) = \sum_{k=1}^{K} [y_{nk}(\psi(\alpha_{nk} + \beta_{nk}) - \psi(\alpha_{nk})) \tag{15}$$
$$+ \gamma_{ji}(1 - y_{nk})(\psi(\alpha_{nk} + \beta_{nk}) - \psi(\beta_{nk}))],$$

where j is the index of the correct ground truth class, such that $y_{nj} = 1$.

To obtain the matrix $\Gamma = [\gamma_{jk}]$, we introduce a learnable real-valued parameter matrix $Z = [z_{jk}] \in \mathbb{R}^{K \times K}$. Each element γ_{jk} is then computed as

$\gamma_{jk} = \sigma(z_{jk})$, where $\sigma(\cdot)$ denotes the sigmoid function. This ensures that all down-weighting factors γ_{jk} lie in the range $[0,1]$, while allowing the model to learn them in a fully differentiable manner.

However, since the down-weighting parameters are now learnable, the optimal values for minimizing the WANE-LF loss could trivially become $\gamma_{jk} = 0$, effectively ignoring false positive penalties. To prevent Γ from collapsing to zero, we introduce a regularization term to the loss function:

$$\mathcal{L} = \frac{1}{N} \sum_{n=1}^{N} \mathcal{L}_{n\text{WANE-LF}} + \lambda e^{-\bar{z}}, \tag{16}$$

where $\bar{z} = \frac{1}{K^2} \sum_{i,j=1}^{K} z_{ij}$ is the average of the elements of the Z matrix, and $\lambda \geq 0$ is a hyperparameter that controls the strength of the regularization. By adjusting the value of λ, we can effectively control how tolerant the model is to larger predicted label sets. Lower values of λ encourage the model to assign lower down-weighting factors γ_{jk}, thereby reducing the penalty for false positives and promoting broader predictions. Conversely, higher values of λ result in stricter penalization, favoring more conservative and precise label sets.

In contrast to the optimization strategy proposed in the previous section, the learnable discounting factors introduce a quadratic number of parameters with respect to the number of classes. However, these factors are required only during training and are not used at inference time, which ensures that the inference complexity remains linear.

4.5 Combining the Heads

The outputs of the two heads are combined using subjective logic. The output of the multinomial head is a set of multinomial evidences, which can be converted to subjective multinomial opinions. The output of the candidate proposal head is a set of positive and negative evidences, which can be converted to subjective binomial opinions about each class. More formally, the output of the multinomial head can be represented as $\omega_M(\mathbf{b}, a, \mathbf{u})$, and the output of the candidate proposal head can be represented as the set $\{\omega_k\}, k \in \{1, \ldots, K\}$, where $\omega_k = \omega(b_k, d_k, a_k, u_k)$. We want to combine the evidences in such a way, that the model provides set-valued prediction only on very hard samples, where providing a precise prediction would have high risk of being incorrect. Conveniently, in most evidential deep learning approaches, the loss function is designed to assign higher uncertainty masses to incorrect classifications. This is achieved by decreasing the Kullback-Leibler (KL) divergence between the incorrect predictions and the uniform distribution [21]. Hence, the uncertainty value of the multinomial head is a good measure to assess the complexity of the sample. It then follows that to reduce the classification error, we want to make set-valued predictions when the uncertainty mass is high. To achieve this, we will move some of the uncertainty mass from the multinomial head as a belief mass to the candidate proposal head.

First, let us recall that in the candidate proposal head, we have belief, disbelief and uncertainty masses for each of the classes, but not for the selected candidate set. To obtain these masses for the candidate set, we will make use of the binomial co-multiplication operation from subjective logic.

Definition 1 (Subjective Binomial Co-multiplication [14]). *Let* $\mathbb{X} = \{x, \bar{x}\}$ *and* $\mathbb{Y} = \{y, \bar{y}\}$ *be two domains. Let* $\omega_x = \omega(b_x, d_x, a_x, u_x)$ *and* $\omega_y = \omega(b_y, d_y, a_y, u_y)$ *be two independent subjective binomial opinions on* x *and* y *respectively. The binomial co-multiplication* $\omega_x \sqcup \omega_y$ *provides the subjective binomial opinion on disjunction* $x \vee y = \{(xy), (x\bar{y}), (\bar{x}y)\}$ *and is defined as:*

$$\omega_{x \vee y} : \begin{cases} b_{x \vee y} = b_x + b_y - b_x b_y, \\ d_{x \vee y} = d_x d_y + \frac{a_x(1-a_y)d_x u_y + (1-a_x)a_y u_x d_y}{a_x + a_y - a_x a_y}, \\ u_{x \vee y} = u_x u_y + \frac{a_y d_x u_y + a_x u_x d_y}{a_x + a_y - a_x a_y}, \\ a_{x \vee y} = a_x + a_y - a_x a_y. \end{cases} \quad (17)$$

Since our candidate proposal head is designed similar to multi-label classification, we can follow the binary relevance approach [28] of assuming independence between the candidates, and apply the binomial co-multiplication operation to obtain the subjective binomial opinion on the candidate set. To achieve this, first we form the candidate set by selecting all the classes where the belief mass is greater than the disbelief mass: $\mathcal{C} = \{i | b_i > d_i\}$. Then we apply the binomial co-multiplication operation to obtain the joint belief mass $b_\mathcal{C}$ with:

$$b_\mathcal{C} = 1 - \prod_{i \in \mathcal{C}}(1 - b_i). \quad (18)$$

The proof of Eq. 18 can be found in the our GitHub repository. To simplify the computations we will join the disbelief mass and the uncertainty mass into a single uncertainty mass, which can be obtained with: $u_\mathcal{C} = 1 - b_\mathcal{C}$, due to the additivity property of belief masses. Having the subjective binomial opinion on the candidate set, we can now combine it with the subjective multinomial opinion from the multinomial head. To do that, we need to scale the belief and uncertainty masses of the candidate to fit into the uncertainty mass of the multinomial opinion. The scaled belief and uncertainty masses of the candidate set can be obtained with:

$$b'_\mathcal{C} = b_\mathcal{C} \cdot u_M \quad u'_\mathcal{C} = u_\mathcal{C} \cdot u_M \quad a_\mathcal{C} = \sum_{i \in \mathcal{C}} a_i, \quad (19)$$

where u_M is the uncertainty mass from the multinomial opinion. Finally, the combined hyper-opinion $\omega_H(\mathbf{b}_H, \mathbf{a}_H, u_H)$ can be formed, where:

$$\mathbf{b}_H = \{b_{M1}, b_{M2}, \ldots, b_{MK}, b'_\mathcal{C}\}, \quad \mathbf{a}_H = \{a_{M1}, a_{M2}, \ldots, a_{MK}, a_\mathcal{C}\}, \quad u_H = u'_\mathcal{C}. \quad (20)$$

During the decision making stage, a singleton class can be selected if the belief b_{Mi} is greater than the other belief masses, and the proposed candidate set can be selected if the belief $b'_\mathcal{C}$ is greater than the other belief masses.

All operations described here have worst case $\mathcal{O}(k)$ time complexity, which means our approach scales linearly with the number of classes.

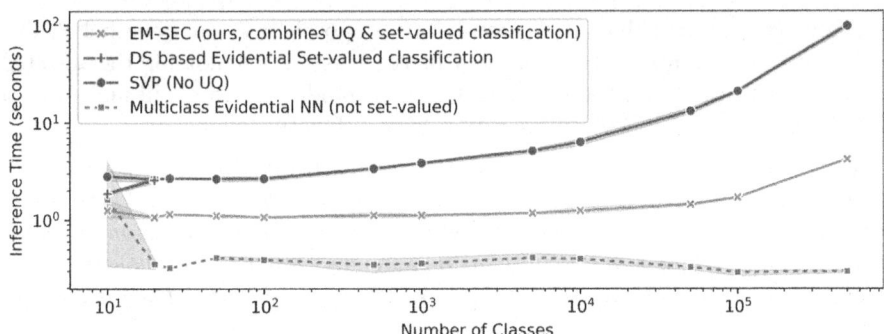

Fig. 2. Inference time (log-log scale) on 10,000 samples for varying class counts. DS is only reported for 10 and 20 classes due to scalability issues. EM-SEC is 2–23× faster than SVP and DS. Multiclass evidential runtime is shown for reference, but not as a baseline, since t does not perform set-valued classification.

5 Experiments

We conduct extensive experiments to evaluate the performance of our proposed method. As baselines, we use the evidential classifier by [24], referred to as DS (Dempster-Shafer-based Classifier), and the efficient set-valued classifier SVP by [19]. We denote with EM-SEC the model with WANE loss (Eq. 8), while EM-SEC-LF is the model with WANE-LF loss (Eq. 15). These baselines demonstrate that EM-SEC(-LF) is both faster than other evidential set-valued classifiers and competitive with the highly efficient SVP.

For evaluation, we use CIFAR-10 and CIFAR-100 [17] due to their widespread use in image classification benchmarks. Since the original DS implementation was in TensorFlow, we adapted it to PyTorch for compatibility. The SVP implementation was in C++, which posed an unfair advantage. To ensure a fair comparison, we used a Large Language Model (ChatGPT o3-mini-high) to translate it into Python and verified that key components fully utilized PyTorch vectorized operations. We used ResNet-18 [12] architecture as encoders for all baselines.

Scalability Analysis. First, we will try to understand how the proposed approach scales to classification tasks with higher number of classes. To have a controlled experimental setting, we will take random 32×32 images, and try to classify them into 10–500,000 classes, and log the inference time for 10000 samples. For the DS approach, the extended utility matrix did not fit in GPU memory for $K > 20$. Hence, we will not provide the results for DS for classes higher than 20. **As we can see in Figure 2, the proposed EM-SEC[2] approach is consistently faster (from 2 up to 23 times) than the other baseline set-valued classifiers. Specifically, for 500,000 classes the inference takes around 4 s for EM-SEC and 97 s for SVP.**

---

[2] EM-SEC and EM-SEC-LF have identical inference times due to shared architecture.

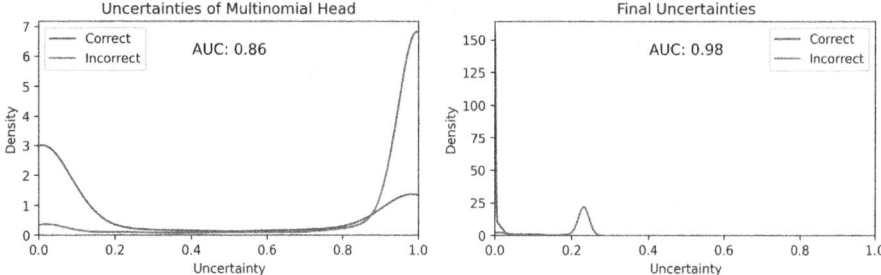

Fig. 3. Uncertainties of the multinomial head (left) and after fusing with candidate proposal head (right) on CIFAR-100 dataset. The AUC score of misclassification detection based on uncertainties is also provided. The average set size is 1.69. In the multinomial head incorrectly classified samples have very high uncertainty and correctly classified ones have low uncertainty. After fusing with candidate proposal head, most of the incorrect classification uncertainty mass is moved to correct classification.

Uncertainty Analysis. Here, we empirically motivate our approach by analyzing uncertainties before and after EM-SEC set-valued classification. As shown in Fig. 3, in standard evidential multiclass classification (multinomial head), incorrectly classified samples exhibit high uncertainty, with an area-under-the-curve (AUC) value of 0.86. With EM-SEC, we identify these high-uncertainty points and instead predict multiple possible labels. As illustrated in Fig. 3, EM-SEC redistributes most of the uncertainty mass from misclassified samples to correctly classified points with low uncertainty. We also observe a secondary spike in uncertainty after fusion, which can serve as a reject option, enabling the model to further reduce incorrect classifications. **Notably, with a misclassification detection AUC score of 0.98, our approach effectively eliminates the risk of incorrect predictions on this dataset while maintaining an average of just 1.69 predictions per set.**

Another important consideration is the type of uncertainty used to determine when to provide set-valued decisions. In the uncertainty quantification (UQ) literature, two main types of uncertainty are typically defined: epistemic and aleatoric [16]. Epistemic uncertainty arises from a lack of knowledge in the model, whereas aleatoric uncertainty reflects inherent noise in the data. In subjective logic, the uncertainty mass is more closely related to epistemic uncertainty. **Compared to the baseline methods, EM-SEC efficiently estimates the epistemic, and if needed aleatoric uncertainties.** Ideally, set-valued predictions are suited for high aleatoric uncertainty, while no decision shall be made under high epistemic uncertainty. However, as shown by [20], these two often correlate strongly. Our results in Fig. 4 confirm this, so we do not distinguish between them in our approach.

Utility-Based Comparison. In this section, we compare model performances using the F_β measure ($F_\beta(s) = \frac{1+\beta^2}{s+\beta^2}$). Higher β values are more tolerant to larger

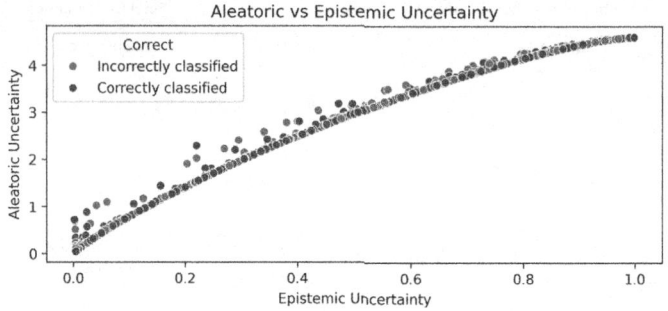

Fig. 4. Aleatoric vs Epistemic uncertainties of multinominal head on CIFAR-100 dataset. The disentanglement is performed following the formulas from [25].

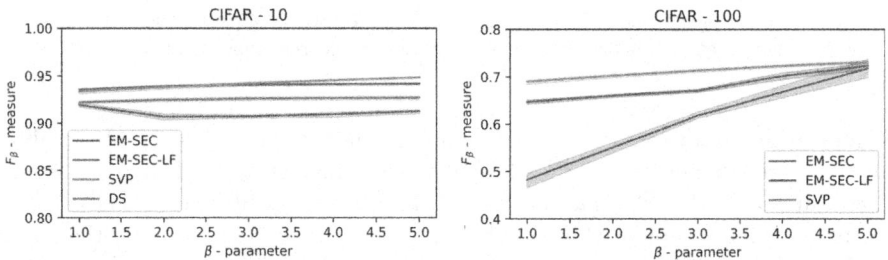

Fig. 5. F_β Utility for various beta values. EM-SEC represents the model with WANE loss (Eq. 8), while EM-SEC-LF is the model with WANE-LF loss (Eq. 15).

set sizes, whereas lower values impose stricter penalties. A high F_β score at low β values indicates accurate predictions with minimal expected set sizes. For SVP and EM-SEC, the β parameter was chosen corresponding to the evaluation F_β-score. For DS method, the γ parameter was chosen as 0.9, since it provided the best results in the paper. Finally, for EM-SEC-LF the λ parameter was tuned for each F_β measure (See the supplementary material in GitHub for more details).

As shown in Fig. 5, on the CIFAR-10 dataset, EM-SEC achieves utility values comparable to the DS method for $\beta = 1$, but the performance worsens with higher values of β. This suggests that EM-SEC provides better predictions with lower set-size budget. In contrast, EM-SEC-LF, which incorporates learnable down-weighting factors, reaches performance on par with SVP, indicating its effectiveness in adapting to class-specific uncertainties. On the more challenging CIFAR-100 dataset, EM-SEC underperforms for lower β values but shows improved results as β increases, gradually approaching the performance of SVP. EM-SEC-LF significantly narrows the performance gap with SVP across all β values, with a similar upward trend as β increases. We were unable to evaluate the DS on CIFAR-100 due to out-of-memory issues.

6 Conclusion

In this paper, we introduced the efficient evidential set-valued classification approach, EM-SEC, that leverages subjective logic and evidential deep learning to quantify prediction uncertainty and generate set-valued outputs when uncertainty is high. Our experiments demonstrate that EM-SEC scales efficiently to datasets with a large number of classes in terms of inference time and provides reliable uncertainty estimates that can filter out unreliable predictions.

Given the promising performance of EM-SEC in the unimodal case, we aim to extend it to a multimodal setting, where conflicting information across modalities introduces additional uncertainty and increased computational complexity. While [2] address modality conflict by reallocating conflict mass to uncertainty through evidential fusion, we propose an alternative approach: redirecting the conflict mass toward composite classes. We also plan to evaluate the effectiveness of this strategy using multimodal extensions of CIFAR, such as the LUMA dataset [3].

References

1. Abdar, M., Pourpanah, F., Hussain, S., Rezazadegan, D., Liu, L., Ghavamzadeh, M., Fieguth, P., et al.: A review of uncertainty quantification in deep learning: techniques, applications and challenges. Inf. Fus. **76**, 243–297 (2021)
2. Bezirganyan, G., Sellami, S., Berti-Equille, L., Fournier, S.: Multimodal learning with uncertainty quantification based on discounted belief fusion. In: Proceedings of The 28th International Conference on Artificial Intelligence and Statistics. Proceedings of Machine Learning Research, vol. 258, pp. 3142–3150. PMLR (2025)
3. Bezirganyan, G., Sellami, S., Berti-Équille, L., Fournier, S.: Luma: a benchmark dataset for learning from uncertain and multimodal data. In: Proceedings of the 48th International ACM SIGIR Conference on Research and Development in Information Retrieval (2025)
4. Cherubin, G., Chatzikokolakis, K., Jaggi, M.: Exact optimization of conformal predictors via incremental and decremental learning. In: International Conference on Machine Learning, pp. 1836–1845. PMLR (2021)
5. Chzhen, E., Denis, C., Hebiri, M., Lorieul, T.: Set-valued classification–overview via a unified framework. arXiv preprint arXiv:2102.12318 (2021)
6. Cole, E., Mac Aodha, O., Lorieul, T., Perona, P., Morris, D., Jojic, N.: Multi-label learning from single positive labels. In: Proceedings of the IEEE/CVF Conference on Computer Vision and Pattern Recognition, pp. 933–942 (2021)
7. Cresswell, J.C., Sui, Y., Kumar, B., Vouitsis, N.: Conformal prediction sets improve human decision making. In: International Conference on Machine Learning, pp. 9439–9457. PMLR (2024)
8. Dempster, A.P.: A generalization of bayesian inference. J. Roy. Stat. Soc.: Ser. B (Methodol.) **30**(2), 205–232 (1968)
9. Denoeux, T.: A neural network classifier based on dempster-shafer theory. IEEE Trans. Syst. Man, Cybern.-Part A: Syst. Hum. **30**(2), 131–150 (2000)

10. Garcin, C., Servajean, M., Joly, A., Salmon, J.: A two-head loss function for deep average-k classification. In: 2025 IEEE/CVF Winter Conference on Applications of Computer Vision (WACV), pp. 7358–7367. IEEE (2025)
11. Guo, C., Pleiss, G., Sun, Y., Weinberger, K.Q.: On calibration of modern neural networks. In: International Conference on Machine Learning, pp. 1321–1330. PMLR (2017)
12. He, K., Zhang, X., Ren, S., Sun, J.: Deep residual learning for image recognition. In: Proceedings of the IEEE Conference on Computer Vision and Pattern Recognition, pp. 770–778 (2016)
13. Imoussaten, A., Jacquin, L.: Cautious classification based on belief functions theory and imprecise relabelling. Int. J. Approximate Reasoning **142**, 130–146 (2022)
14. Jøsang, A.: Subjective Logic, vol. 3. Springer, Cham (2016). https://doi.org/10.1007/978-3-319-42337-1
15. Kempkes, M.C., Dunjko, V., van Nieuwenburg, E., Spiegelberg, J.: Reliable classifications with guaranteed confidence using the dempster-shafer theory of evidence. In: Joint European Conference on Machine Learning and Knowledge Discovery in Databases, pp. 89–105. Springer, Cham (2024). https://doi.org/10.1007/978-3-031-70344-7_6
16. Kiureghian, A.D., Ditlevsen, O.: Aleatory or epistemic? Does it matter? Struct. Saf. **31**(2), 105–112 (2009)
17. Krizhevsky, A., Hinton, G., et al.: Learning multiple layers of features from tiny images (2009)
18. Ma, L., Denoeux, T.: Partial classification in the belief function framework. Knowl.-Based Syst. **214**, 106742 (2021)
19. Mortier, T., Wydmuch, M., Dembczyński, K., Hüllermeier, E., Waegeman, W.: Set-valued prediction in multi-class classification. In: 31st Benelux conference on Artificial Intelligence (BNAIC 2019); 28th Belgian Dutch conference on Machine Learning (Benelearn 2019), vol. 2491. CEUR (2019)
20. Mucsányi, B., Kirchhof, M., Oh, S.J.: Benchmarking uncertainty disentanglement: specialized uncertainties for specialized tasks. Adv. Neural. Inf. Process. Syst. **37**, 50972–51038 (2024)
21. Sensoy, M., Kaplan, L., Kandemir, M.: Evidential deep learning to quantify classification uncertainty. In: Advances in Neural Information Processing Systems, vol. 31 (2018)
22. Shafer, G.: A Mathematical Theory of Evidence. Princeton University Press (1976)
23. Shafer, G., Vovk, V.: A tutorial on conformal prediction. J. Mach. Learn. Res. **9**(3) (2008)
24. Tong, Z., Xu, P., Denoeux, T.: An evidential classifier based on dempster-shafer theory and deep learning. Neurocomputing **450**, 275–293 (2021)
25. Ulmer, D., Hardmeier, C., Frellsen, J.: Prior and posterior networks: a survey on evidential deep learning methods for uncertainty estimation. Trans. Mach. Learn. Res. **2023** (2023)
26. Vovk, V., Gammerman, A., Shafer, G.: Algorithmic Learning in a Random World, vol. 29. Springer, Switzerland AG (2005). https://doi.org/10.1007/978-3-031-06649-8
27. Wang, Z., Qiao, X.: Set-valued classification with out-of-distribution detection for many classes. J. Mach. Learn. Res. **24**(375), 1–39 (2023)
28. Zhang, M.-L., Li, Y.-K., Liu, X.-Y., Geng, X.: Binary relevance for multi-label learning: an overview. Front. Comp. Sci. **12**(2), 191–202 (2018). https://doi.org/10.1007/s11704-017-7031-7

29. Zhang, Z., Liu, Z., Ning, L., Martin, A., Xiong, J.: Representation of imprecision in deep neural networks for image classification. IEEE Trans. Neural Networks Learn. Syst. (2023)
30. Zhao, C., Du, D., Hoogs, A., Funk, C.: Open set action recognition via multi-label evidential learning. In: Proceedings of the IEEE/CVF Conference on Computer Vision and Pattern Recognition, pp. 22982–22991 (2023)

A Complementarity-Enhanced Mixture of Human-AI Teams for Decision-Making

Hefei Liang[1], Jiaqi Liu[1(✉)], Bin Guo[1], and Zhiwen Yu[1,2]

[1] School of Computer Science, Northwestern Polytechnical University, Xi'an, China
craneflyliang@mail.nwpu.edu.cn
{jqliu,guob,zhiwenyu}@nwpu.edu.cn
[2] Harbin Engineering University, Harbin, China

Abstract. With the rapid development of deep learning, Artificial Intelligence (AI) has evolved from a mere tool to a collaborator in decision-making, sparking increasing attention to the human-AI cooperation. The Mixture of Experts (MoE) framework, originally proposed to capture domain-specific expertise and now widely adopted in large-scale models, naturally aligns with the requirements of human-AI teams. However, deploying MoE in human-AI cooperation involves two challenges: 1) While machine experts can be continuously optimized during training, human experts remain fixed, significantly reducing the effectiveness of traditional sparse activation strategies; 2) Some existing methods fuse all expert predictions during training phase but select only the highest weighted expert during testing phase, thereby introducing inconsistencies between the two phases. To overcome this, we propose the Complementarity-Enhanced Mixture of Human-AI Teams (CE-MoHAIT) framework. Our approach decomposes the gating network's output into two branches, i.e., a human expert branch and a classifier branch, thereby explicitly modeling the complementarity between human and AI capabilities. Moreover, we introduce a method called Adaptive and Complementary Construction (ACC) that directly optimizes the gating network by constructing weighted labels, enabling the classifier model to compensate for the deficiencies of human experts and ensuring consistent task allocation across training and testing. Experiments on CIFAR-100 and two real-world medical image datasets show that our approach surpasses the existing methods, improving test accuracy by up to 20%, especially with larger teams and weaker experts. Code is available in the repository at https://github.com/H-F-Liang/CE-MoHAIT.

Keywords: Human-AI Collaboration in Classification · Human-AI Teams · Human-in-the-Loop

1 Introduction

With the rapid development of advanced deep learning technologies [2,3], AI has already achieved or even surpassed human-level performance in many specific domains [1]. However, in some real-world scenarios, especially in high-risk domains such as healthcare [4,5], AI still exhibits inherent shortcomings such as limited generalization ability, noise immunity, and interpretability, which underscores the growing need for human-AI collaboration. In human-AI collaboration, how to leverage the complementary capabilities of humans and AI, and assign tasks to the appropriate human or machine based on task characteristics is important [6–8]. Mixture of Experts (MoE) [29] is a framework initially proposed and widely adopted in Large Language Model (LLM), characterized by its ability to perceive knowledge differences across domains or expertise among individuals. This makes MoE potentially well-suited for human-AI collaboration scenarios.

The MoE framework consists of multiple multilayer perceptrons with different knowledge, called machine experts, and a gating network that decides which machine expert to activate according to the task's characteristics. In the training phase, MoE adopts a sparse activation strategy due to the large scale of the model parameters [30], where only a few, or even just one, machine expert is activated during each forward pass. However, When applying MoE to human-AI collaboration scenarios, some machine experts are replaced by human experts and therefore the sparse activation strategy can lead to difficulties in convergence. This is because that the abilities of human experts are fixed, and thus they cannot learn the corresponding knowledge even if activated during training. Moreover, due to the lack of targeted optimization for the gating network, it is challenging for the gating network to leverage the complementary capabilities between humans and machines.

Hemmer et al. [13] proposed a solution that adopts a weighted aggregation of predictions from all experts during the training phase and selects only one expert during the testing phase. However, this weighted aggregation approach introduces inconsistency: during the training phase, multiple predictions are fused by their weights to compute loss, whereas during the testing phase, only the highest-weighted prediction is used, potentially degrading performance and limiting the generalizability of the method. To overcome this limitation, we propose a novel Adaptive and Complementary Construction (ACC) method. It directly optimizes the output of the gating network in MoE by constructing weighted labels, rather than aggregating expert predictions. Specifically, the method directly constructs labels corresponding to the gating network's output weights and allows the machine expert to complement the deficiencies of human experts, significantly enhancing the complementarity between humans and AI models in the MoE framework.

Based on the MoE framework, we propose a Complementarity-Enhanced Mixture of Human-AI Teams (CE-MoHAIT) framework for human-AI collaboration in classification tasks. CE-MoHAIT jointly trains a gating network and one classifier model, i.e., the machine expert, where the gating network determines the weight of each team member, and the task is ultimately assigned to the member with the highest weight. To explicitly consider the complementarity between humans and AI models, we decompose the output weights of the gating network into two branches: a human expert weight branch and a classifier weight branch. The classifier model is designed to complement the deficiencies of human experts. During the training phase, we use the ACC to encourage the gating network to assign tasks that human experts are less competent to the classifier model for learning, thereby maximizing team complementarity. Furthermore, since the task is always assigned to the member with the highest weight during both the training and testing phases, the behavioral consistency between training and testing enhances the performance of the team. Overall, our contributions are as follows:

- We propose a novel framework called Complementarity-Enhanced Mixture of Human-AI Teams (CE-MoHAIT), which explicitly considers the complementarity between humans and AI models by decomposing the output weights of the gating network into a human expert weight branch and a classifier weight branch.
- We introduce a new team loss function that utilizes Adaptive and Complementary Construction (ACC) to construct team weight labels, optimizing two weight branches. This approach enables the classifier to better learn from and complement for the weaknesses of human experts, explicitly maximizing human-AI complementarity and ensuring optimal team performance.
- We conduct comprehensive experiments on the classical CIFAR-100 dataset and two real-world medical image datasets [14,15], demonstrating the effectiveness and applicability of our method. Our method achieves up to a 20% performance improvement, especially in scenarios where human experts possess lower individual capabilities.

2 Related Work

Traditional deep learning methods mainly focus on optimizing AI systems in isolation, rather than considering human-AI collaboration. As a result, recent research [23–25] has proposed various approaches to coordinate humans and AI models, offering advantages in efficiency, interpretability, and ethical considerations.

Currently, most human-AI collaboration methods fall under the broader concept of Human-in-the-Loop (HITL) [32], which emphasizes continuous human participation and feedback throughout the operation of the system. The core idea of HITL is to integrate expert feedback with data-driven learning strategies to compensate for the limitations of traditional automation in data-scarce or noisy environments, while also providing additional prior knowledge during model optimization. For example, some researchers have embedded human preferences into the reward function [33], achieving significant improvements in policy optimization in deep reinforcement learning. Based on this, many other optimization methods based on human preferences have also been derived [34–37]. In high-risk domains such as finance and healthcare, the complete autonomous decision-making by AI models often lacks transparency and interpretability [39].

Selectively delegating decision-making power to humans can also enhance trust and the interpretability of human-AI collaboration [26–28].

One common approach in this domain is Learning to Defer, which assumes that humans are highly capable but costly decision-makers [9–12]. Its objective is to learn how to defer tasks that the AI model finds uncertain or challenging to human experts. For instance, some work [18] focuses on scenarios with cost constraints and limited expert workload. Other studies emphasize combining the predictions of AI models with those of human experts. For example, Steyvers et al. [19] introduced a Bayesian framework that attempts to integrate human and AI predictions to improve the overall performance of human-AI systems. Many existing Learning to Defer studies focus on single-expert settings, where difficult samples are deferred to one expert. However, this approach can impose a significant workload on the human expert and is impractical in real-world scenarios where a single expert cannot handle all tasks. Consequently, some work has explored deferring challenging samples to multiple experts. For example, Verma et al. [20] built on earlier research by Verma and Nalisnick [21] and refined the softmax surrogate loss introduced by Mozannar and Sontag [22] to propose consistent and calibrated surrogate losses for multi-expert settings. More recently, Zhang et al. [12] combined learning to complement with learning to defer, achieving superior performance in multi-expert settings with noisy labels compared to standalone human experts or AI models.

Another highly relevant yet often overlooked direction in this context is Mixture of Experts (MoE). Initially proposed for modularizing multilayer supervised networks, MoE can be seen as a system composed of multiple independent networks, where each network processes a subset of training data. A gating network is used to determine which model should learn from each data sample [29]. This process closely resembles task allocation in human-AI collaboration. Later, to enable the model to dynamically select a small number of machine experts for computation and reduce computational costs, introduced a sparse gating mechanism-based MoE structure has been proposed [30], which remains the most mainstream MoE architecture to date. However, dynamically selecting a small number of experts may result in the gating network frequently favoring the more capable experts. To mitigate this issue, another work proposed an auxiliary loss [31]. Inspired by MoE, Hemmer, P., et al. [13] was the first to propose Human-AI Teams, consisting of one classifier and multiple human experts. This approach leverages the classifier to learn tasks that humans struggle with, thereby improving team performance. However, the strategy of using weighted averaging during training while adopting the *argmax* function during testing is not entirely appropriate, as it creates a significant gap between training and testing, negatively impacting generalization.

3 Methodology

In this section, we first present the problem formulation, and then illustrate the proposed Complementarity-Enhanced Mixture of Human-AI Teams (CE-MoHAIT) framework.

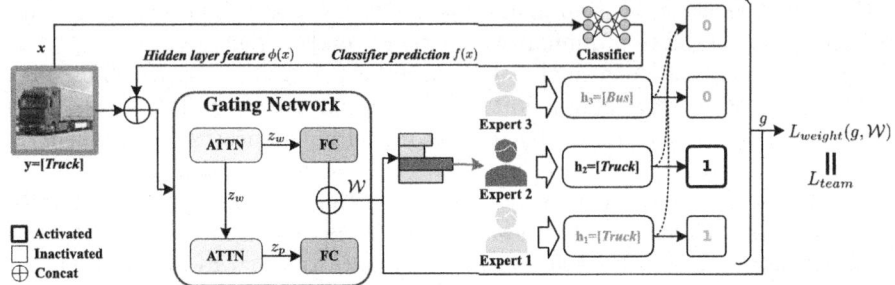

Fig. 1. The framework of the proposed CE-MoHAIT. The left part of the figure illustrates the structure of the gating network and how it generates the team weight $\mathcal{W}$. The right part of the figure demonstrates how we construct the weight label **g** to optimize the team weight $\mathcal{W}$.

3.1 Problem Formulation

A human-AI team for a k-class classification task consists of one classifier and m human experts. The classifier outputs a prediction denoted by $f(x) \in \mathbb{R}^k$, where $f(x)$ represents the predicted probability distribution over the k possible classes. Each human expert provides a prediction in the form of a k-dimensional one-hot vector $\mathbf{h} \in H$, indicating their chosen class. Given a training sample $x_i \in \mathcal{X}$ with ground truth label $y_i \in \mathcal{Y}$ and related human prediction $\mathbf{h}_i \in H$, the training dataset is presented as $D = \{(x_i, y_i, \mathbf{h}_i)\}_{i=1}^{n} \sim P$, where $n = |D|$ is the total number of samples and P is an unknown data distribution.

The final prediction is selected from these $m+1$ candidates through a gating network $g : \mathbb{R}^k \times \mathbb{R}^d \times \mathcal{X} \to \mathbb{R}^{m+1}$, Its input consists of three components: the prediction of classifier $f(x) \in \mathbb{R}^k$, the d-dimensional feature vector extracted by the classifier $\phi(x) \in \mathbb{R}^d$, and the original data sample $x \in \mathcal{X}$, formally expressed as $g(f(x), \phi(x), x)$. The network outputs a $(1+m)$-dimensional vector $\mathcal{W} = [p, \mathbf{w}]$, where $p \in \mathbb{R}$ denotes the confidence in the prediction of classifier, and $\mathbf{w} = [w_1, \ldots, w_m] \in \mathbb{R}^m$ are the scores assigned to the human experts.

The final team prediction $\hat{y}_{\text{team}}$ is determined by selecting the team member with the highest weight. Our goal is to minimize the team loss defined as

$$L_{\text{team}}(f, g, x, y, \mathbf{h}) = \mathbb{E}_{(x,y,\mathbf{h}) \sim P} \left[l\left(y, \hat{y}_{\text{team}}\right) \right]. \qquad (1)$$

To minimize team loss, it is essential to consider the differences in capabilities among human-AI teams members, especially the complementary characteristics between humans and AI.

3.2 Implementation

The overall framework of the proposed framework is shown in Fig. 1. The system can be considered as a collaborative decision-making team consisting of one classifier and m human experts. First, the sample x is input to the classifier, which outputs the extracted hidden layer features $\phi(x)$ and the predicted result $f(x)$. These outputs, along with the sample x, serve as inputs to the gating network. The function of the gating network is to coordinate task allocation. It outputs a weight vector for the team members $\mathcal{W}$, and based on $\mathcal{W}$, we select the most suitable member of the team to make the final decision.

In human-AI collaboration methods, expert predictions cannot directly compute loss for backpropagation. These methods typically obtained a weighted vector through fusion and calculated the loss between the weighted vector and the true labels for backpropagation. However, this approach often relies on predictions from multiple members, which can lead to dependency on certain members. Furthermore, during testing, if only the prediction from the member with the highest weight is selected, this results in an inconsistency between the training and testing phases. To address this issue, we propose an approach called Adaptive and Complementary Construction (ACC), which directly optimizes the member weights $\mathcal{W}$ and explicitly considers the complementarity between humans and AI, thereby improving the team performance.

Gating Network. As shown in Fig. 1, the gating network takes the feature vector as input and outputs the team member weights $\mathcal{W}$. Its primary function is to perceive the differences and complementarities between human and machines. To achieve this, we employ two attention layers to extract features from human experts and the classifier separately. We begin by extracting the topic features related to expert capability

$$z_w = \text{AttentionLayer}(x, f(x), \phi(x)), \quad z_w \in \mathbb{R}^{d_h}, \tag{2}$$

where d_h denotes the dimension of the hidden layer. Meanwhile, to explicitly leverage human-AI complementarity, we need to obtain a topic feature associated with human-AI complementarity

$$z_p = \text{AttentionLayer}(x, g(x), M(x), z_w), \quad z_p \in \mathbb{R}^{d_h}. \tag{3}$$

The topic feature z_p is used to represent the capability differences between the classifier and the human experts. In the attention layer, multi-dimensional features are mapped to Q, K, and V

$$Q = W_Q \cdot z, \quad K = W_K \cdot z, \quad V = W_V \cdot z, \tag{4}$$

where $Q, K, V \in \mathbb{R}^{h \times d_k}$, h is the number of attention heads, d_h is the hidden layer dimension, and $d_k = d_h/h$. Attention weights are then computed and used to obtain the weighted output

$$\mathbf{Z} = \text{Softmax}\left(\frac{QK^T}{\sqrt{d_k}}\right) V. \tag{5}$$

Finally, after passing through the linear layer, p and $\mathbf{w}$ are concatenated to obtain the output:

$$\mathbf{w} = \text{MLP}(z_w), \quad p = \text{MLP}(z_p),$$
$$\mathcal{W} = \text{Concat}(p, \mathbf{w}). \tag{6}$$

Team Loss. To leverage MoE for instance allocation in a human-AI collaboration team, the loss computation of MoE needs to be modified. In MoE, a sparse activation strategy is typically used, where only the selected networks are trained. However, in a human-AI collaboration team, the predictions provided by selected human experts are non-differentiable, indicating that the weights output by the gating network are difficult to optimize. Therefore, in [13], a weighted fusion strategy was adopted during training to obtain the final team prediction, ensuring that gradients propagate back to the gating network. Following this work, we have

$$\hat{y}_{team} = f(\mathbf{x}_i)w_1 + \sum_{i=2}^{1+m} w_i h_{i-1}. \tag{7}$$

However, this leads to a dependency of the prediction results of the team on multiple members. In real-world scenarios, due to considerations of collaboration efficiency and cost, we only select the best member to make the prediction. Thus, using the above strategy for training may affect the robustness and generalization of team predictions. In contrast, our method mitigates the inconsistency between training and testing behaviors and explicitly accounts for human-AI complementarity during the training phase by constructing weight labels.

First, in both training and testing phases, we select only the best-performing member. For each sample, we take the member with the highest weight, obtaining its predicted logits vector t_j where $j = \arg\max \mathcal{W}$, and compute the cross-entropy loss with the ground truth label y_i as follows

$$L_{CE} = -\sum_{i=1}^{N}\sum_{j=1}^{k} y_j^{(i)} \log\left(\frac{\exp(t_j^{(i)})}{\sum_{j=1}^{k} \exp(t_j^{(i)})}\right). \tag{8}$$

But it should be noted, that when the member represented by j is a human expert, the predicted label does not have a gradient; hence, the loss cannot be backpropagated. This loss works only when j corresponds to a classifier, meaning it is used exclusively for optimizing the classifier.

Next, we consider the team weight vector $\mathcal{W}$ output by the gating network. It consists of two branches, i.e., the human expert weighting branch $\mathbf{w}$ and the classifier weighting branch p, as in Equation (6). This addresses the issue that the predictions provided by human experts are *non-differentiable*, so we need a method to construct target labels for $\mathcal{W}$ during the training phase and this method is the Adaptive and Complementary Construction (ACC) that we mentioned earlier.

In the ACC method, for the human expert weight branch, during the training phase, we know the predictions of all experts, and therefore we can determine whether the prediction of human expert for the current sample is correct, denoted as

$$g_{ij} = \mathbb{1}\{h_{i,j} = y_i\}. \tag{9}$$

Then, for the classifier weight branch, we have illustrated two cases in Fig. 2 for an intuitive explanation. To enhance the complementarity between the classifier and human experts, it is essential to ensure that when all human experts

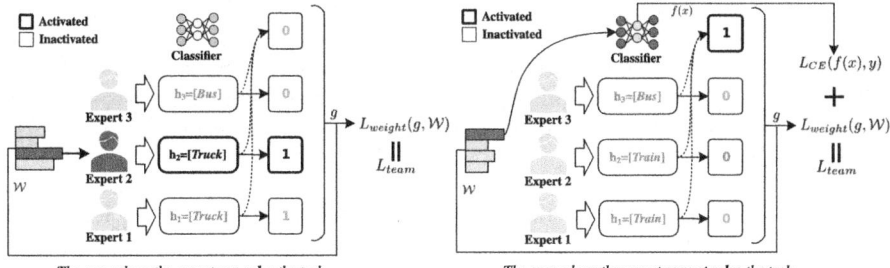

Fig. 2. An intuitive explanation of constructing weight labels. We illustrate two different cases: the left part of the figure presents the **case where experts can solve the task**, while the right part of the figure shows the **case where experts cannot solve the task**.

make incorrect predictions, the classifier should be selected and learn the current sample, denoted as

$$g_{i1} = \mathbf{1}\left\{\sum_{j=1}^{1+m} \delta_i(j) = 0\right\}, \tag{10}$$

where $\delta_i(j) = g_{ij} = \mathbf{1}\{h_{i,j} = y_i\}$. Thus, the target label vector constructed for the gating network using the ACC method is

$$\mathbf{g}_i = (g_{i1}, \ldots, g_{i(1+m)}) \in \{0,1\}^{1+m}. \tag{11}$$

Then, we use binary cross-entropy to calculate the weight loss for the gating

$$L_{\text{weight}} = -\frac{1}{N}\sum_{i=1}^{N}\sum_{j=1}^{1+m}\left(g_{ij}\log\sigma(\mathcal{W}_{ij}) + (1-g_{ij})\log(1-\sigma(\mathcal{W}_{ij}))\right), \tag{12}$$

where $\sigma(z) = \frac{1}{1+\exp(-z)}$.

Finally, the overall team loss in Equation (1) can be expressed as the sum of Equation (8) and Equation (12):

$$L_{\text{team}} = L_{\text{CE}} + L_{\text{weight}}. \tag{13}$$

4 Experiments

In this section, we evaluate our proposed approach on three datasets. First, we simulate the performance of our approach under different team member abilities and team sizes using the classic CIFAR-100 dataset, explaining how our approach optimizes team performance. Next, we further validate our approach on two real-world medical image datasets, NIH and Chaoyang. Particularly, the NIH dataset includes annotations from 22 radiologists, providing comprehensive human expert labeling.

4.1 Experimental Setup

Datasets. We evaluated our approach on three datasets. The first is the CIFAR-100 dataset, used for simulation experiments. The other two are real-world medical image datasets, NIH and Chaoyang, containing annotations from multiple human experts.

- CIFAR-100: This dataset consists of 60,000 32×32 color images across 100 classes, with 600 images per class. It is split into 50,000 training images and 10,000 testing images;
- NIH: This dataset, collected by the National Institutes of Health (NIH) Clinical Center, includes chest X-ray images with annotations from 22 radiologists. It contains 4,374 chest X-ray images with up to three possible symptoms per image, making it a multi-label classification dataset;
- Chaoyang: This dataset consists of 6,160 colon slide patches, each with a resolution of 512×512. Each patch includes three noisy labels provided by pathologists, and each image belongs to one of four categories.

Since the CIFAR-100 dataset does not contain annotations from multiple human experts, we simulated experts with different levels of expertise to generate corresponding expert labels. For a team of m human experts, we assume that each expert can perfectly classify a subset of categories. Specifically, we sample the capability value of each expert as $c_i \sim \mathcal{N}(c_{\text{mean}}, c_{\text{std}})$, where $i \in \{1, ..., m\}$, c_i denotes the number of categories that expert i specializes in, c_{mean} represents the average number of categories an expert is proficient in, and c_{std} is the standard deviation of expertise distribution. In our experiments, we set different values of m, c_{mean}, and c_{std} to simulate the performance of teams with varying sizes and levels of expertise.

The NIH and Chaoyang datasets contain human expert annotations, and thus we directly use them in our experiments. The Chaoyang dataset features comprehensive expert annotations, allowing us to form an expert team with two experts and train on the full dataset. However, in the NIH dataset, not every sample is annotated by all experts. To ensure reliability and consistency, we selected pairs of experts and retained samples with the most overlapping annotations.

Baselines. We compared the performance of our approach, CE-MoHAIT, with six baseline methods.

- One Classifier: Single classifier model;
- Classifier Team: A team consisting of m classifier models;
- Random Expert: A team consisting of m experts, where each instance is randomly assigned to one expert for prediction;
- Expert Team: A team consisting of m experts, where the expert with the highest weight selected by a gating network makes the prediction;
- JSF: A team consisting of one classifier and m experts, with separate loss calculations for the classifier and the expert team [38];

- HAIT: A team consisting of one classifier and m experts, with overall system loss computed through weighted fusion of all member predictions [13];

Table 1. Team accuracies of our approach and the baselines on the CIFAR-100 dataset. To evaluate the impact of different expert ability settings on method performance, we sample the number of categories each expert can classify from a normal distribution $\mathcal{N}(c_{mean}, c_{std})$, where c_{mean} represents the average number of categories an expert can classify, and c_{std} represents the variance of expert abilities.

Method	CIFAR-100		
	$\mathcal{N}(25,5)$	$\mathcal{N}(50,5)$	$\mathcal{N}(75,5)$
One Classifier	78.50(±0.20)	78.50(±0.20)	78.50(±0.20)
Classifier Team	77.06(±0.49)	77.06(±0.49)	77.06(±0.49)
Random Expert	27.13(±1.38)	51.80(±1.01)	76.81(±0.79)
Expert Team	40.02(±1.83)	65.94(±1.65)	87.80(±0.88)
JSF	63.39(±0.93)	54.25(±1.33)	78.75(±1.37)
HAIT	57.95(±1.60)	69.52(±2.12)	90.38(±0.71)
CE-MoHAIT(Ours)	**80.31(±0.46)**	**85.08(±0.67)**	**94.62(±0.46)**

Training Details. For all the experiments, we adopted ResNet-18 [16] pre-trained on ImageNet-1K [17] as the feature extraction network. The Adam optimizer and a cosine annealing scheduler were used, with the cosine annealing period set to one-fifth of the total training epochs. On CIFAR-100, we used 40,000 images for training, 10,000 for validation, and 10,000 for testing. The initial learning rate was set to 2×10^{-4}, the batch size was 512, and the model was trained for 50 epochs. On the NIH and Chaoyang datasets, due to their smaller scales, we employed 10-fold cross-validation with an initial learning rate of 2×10^{-4}, a batch size of 64, and 20 epochs per fold. All the reported experimental results were obtained by repeating training five times with fixed but different random seeds.

4.2 Experimental Results and Analysis

In Table 1, we present the results on the CIFAR-100 dataset. We fixed the number of experts in the team to 2 and reported the team performance when the expert capability c_{mean} was set to 25, 50, and 75. More detailed experimental results on the CIFAR-100 dataset are illustrated in Fig. 3. The three subfigures illustrate controlled experiments that investigate the effects of team size and individual human expert capability. Specifically, we vary the team size from 2 to 12 with a step of 2. The average human expert capability c_{mean} is set to 25, 50, and 75, with a fixed standard deviation c_{std} of 5. The results demonstrate that our approach consistently outperforms the current state-of-the-art Human-AI Teams

Table 2. Team accuracies of our approach and the baselines including standard errors on the NIH and Chaoyang datasets. In the NIH dataset, each radiologist participating in the annotation process has a unique ID. We select two experts to form an expert team, with four different pairs used for the experiment.

Method	Chaoyang	NIH			
		ID=(357,121)	ID=(249,124)	ID=(357,117)	ID=(249,296)
One Classifier	78.23(±0.28)	84.70(±0.13)	84.59(±0.12)	83.13(±0.21)	83.63(±0.08)
Classifier Team	76.88(±0.25)	85.09(±0.17)	84.83(±0.23)	83.44(±0.16)	83.69(±0.27)
Random Expert	83.88(±0.23)	88.04(±0.48)	88.30(±0.49)	89.15(±0.37)	84.58(±0.62)
Expert Team	90.57(±0.12)	90.98(±0.12)	88.54(±0.50)	95.34(±0.00)	91.34(±0.05)
JSF	86.30(±0.01)	90.90(±0.19)	88.26(±0.25)	94.94(±0.69)	90.52(±1.08)
HAIT	90.39(±0.05)	91.01(±0.16)	88.76(±0.50)	95.34(±0.00)	91.36(±0.06)
CE-MoHAIT(Ours)	**91.05(±0.29)**	**91.50(±0.75)**	**88.79(±0.41)**	**95.41(±0.13)**	**91.60(±0.43)**

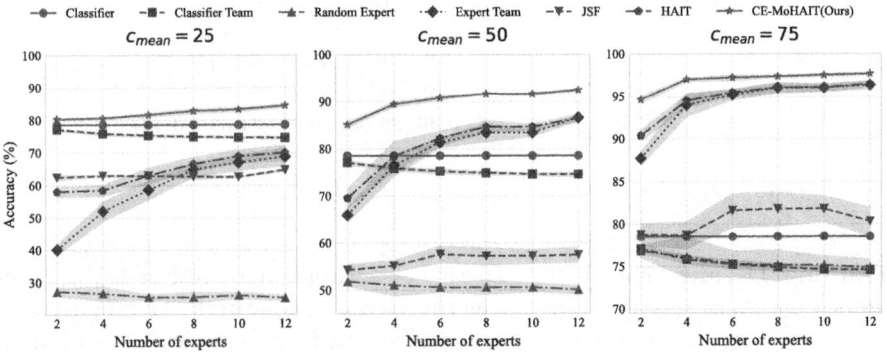

Fig. 3. Team test accuracy of our approach (CE-MoHAIT) in different expert ability(c_{mean}) with increasing team size on the CIFAR-100. Shaded regions display standard errors.

(HAIT) across different team sizes and human expert capabilities. Notably, when the average human expert capability is low ($c_{\mathrm{mean}} = 25$), our approach achieves an improvement of 15% to 18% over HAIT [13], depending on the team size. These results highlight the robustness of our approach across varying team sizes and expert capabilities. Additionally, we observe that the gating network retains significant potential for improvement in expert assignment when human experts have lower individual capabilities.

In Table 2, we further present the validation results on two real-world medical image datasets, NIH and Chaoyang. We focus on one class in the NIH dataset called *airspace opacity*, which accounts for 49.5% of the data. It is a common pulmonary manifestation indicating pneumonia or other fluid-related pathologies. We selected experts with a larger amount of data, forming four groups of paired experts, and annotated the ID of each expert. For the Chaoyang dataset, we construct teams using two out of three available experts, as the remain-

Table 3. The experimental results on CIFAR-100. We conducted experiments under the settings where the number of human experts (m) is 2 and 12, and the human expert capability (c_{mean}) is 25, 50, and 75, respectively, and analyzed the influences of removing the weight loss and varying the ratio between the classifier and human expert weight branches on team performance.

Method	m=2			m=12		
	$\mathcal{N}(25,5)$	$\mathcal{N}(50,5)$	$\mathcal{N}(75,5)$	$\mathcal{N}(25,5)$	$\mathcal{N}(50,5)$	$\mathcal{N}(75,5)$
CE-MoHAIT$_{9:1}$	80.00(±0.51)	83.76(±0.39)	93.80(±0.33)	81.95(±1.16)	92.18(±0.38)	97.66(±0.18)
CE-MoHAIT$_{7:3}$	80.29(±0.24)	84.81(±0.77)	94.55(±0.45)	83.92(±0.65)	92.35(±0.42)	97.49(±0.15)
CE-MoHAIT$_{3:7}$	80.41(±0.42)	85.04(±0.62)	94.59(±0.45)	84.26(±0.73)	92.34(±0.56)	**97.74(±0.17)**
CE-MoHAIT$_{1:9}$	**80.64(±0.25)**	84.91(±0.72)	**94.62(±0.42)**	84.15(±1.00)	**92.47(±0.42)**	97.62(±0.17)
CE-MoHAIT$_{w/o\ WL}$	79.65(±0.31)	76.79(±1.35)	91.07(±1.34)	58.72(±5.08)	74.08(±6.71)	87.99(±1.99)
CE-MoHAIT	80.31(±0.46)	**85.08(±0.67)**	**94.62(±0.46)**	**84.61(±0.69)**	91.87(±0.75)	97.30(±0.31)

ing expert serves as the ground truth standard of dataset. Compared to the synthetic dataset results, the performance gains on real-world datasets are relatively smaller. This observation aligns with the results shown in Fig. 3, where the performance gap diminishes as individual expert capabilities increase. However, in real-world scenarios, considerations such as expert workload and cost often lead to situations where experts specialize in a narrow range of tasks, resulting in lower average expert capabilities. This further underscores the advantage of our approach in practical applications.

In Table 3, we analyze the influence of two key factors on our method using the CIFAR-100 dataset: 1) the removal of the weight loss, defined in Equation (12) and computed from the weight labels constructed by the ACC method; and 2) the investigation of the effect of the ratio between the two weight branches—the classifier weight branch and the human expert weight branch—on team performance. When Equation (12) is removed, the method no longer explicitly accounts for the complementarity between humans and AI, resulting in a significant decline in team performance. Moreover, even with an increased number of human experts, tasks cannot be appropriately allocated to the suitable members, sometimes leading to even worse performance. Additionally, under team sizes of 2 and 12, we sequentially adjusted the ratio between the classifier weight branch and the human expert weight branch to 1:9, 3:7, 7:3, and 9:1. The results indicate that when the ratio is 1:9, that is, when the classifier weight constitutes a lower proportion—the team performance tends to be better. Intuitively, this is likely because, under the MoE framework, the gating network's task assignment is highly random during the early stages of training; if the classifier weight branch's proportion is too high, it may converge too rapidly and mistakenly learn tasks that are better suited for human experts, thereby undermining the intended human-AI complementarity.

Finally, to demonstrate the stability of our method, we further plotted the training curves in Fig. 4. We selected training processes with team sizes of 2 and 12 and expert capabilities of 25, 50, and 75, respectively. The experimen-

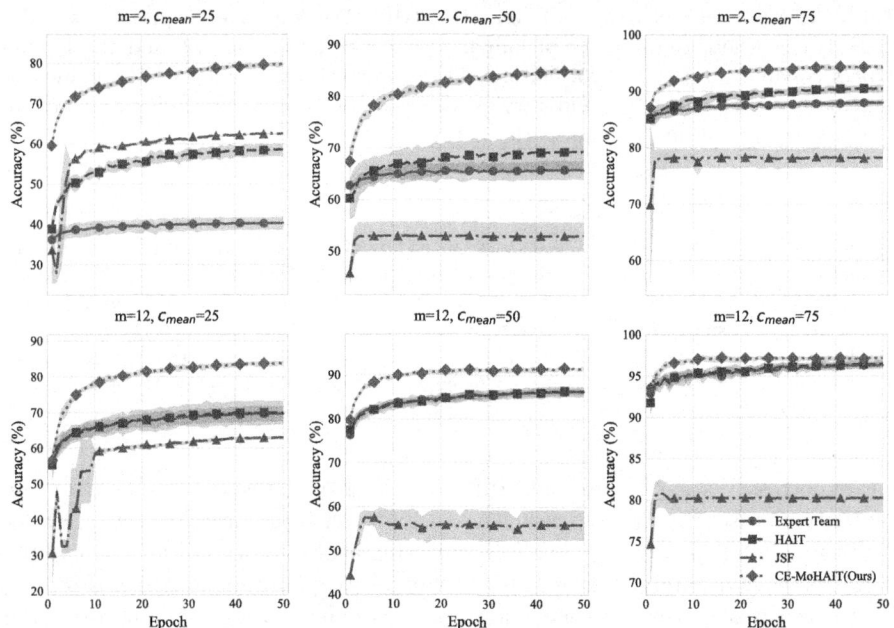

Fig. 4. Team test accuracy during training under setting where the number of human experts (m) is set to 2 and 12, and the expert ability (c_{mean}) is set to 25, 50, and 75, respectively. Shaded regions display standard errors.

tal results show that our method exhibits a significant advantage in both final performance and convergence speed, confirming its effectiveness and stability.

5 Conclusion

In this paper, we propose a framework called Complementarity-Enhanced Mixture of Human-AI Teams (CE-MoHAIT). Based on the MoE framework, CE-MoHAIT is applied to human-AI collaboration scenarios to construct a human-AI team consisting of one classifier model and m human experts. By splitting the output weights of the gating network into two branches—the classifier weight branch and the human expert weight branch—we enhance the complementarity between humans and AI within the team. Moreover, we adopt an Adaptive and Complementary Construction (ACC) method to specifically construct weight labels that directly optimize the gating network's output weights, thereby yielding a novel team loss function. Experimental results demonstrate that our method leads to a significant improvement in team performance.

However, the experimental results also reveal a potential shortcoming of CE-MoHAIT. As the team size increases, the overall performance improvement remains limited, indicating that a more fine-grained approach is still required to perceive the differences in capabilities among team members, enhance their complementarity, and thus better allocate tasks. In future work, we plan to introduce more effective methods to address this issue.

Acknowledgments. This work was supported in part by the National Key R&D Program of China (No.2021ZD0113305), the National Natural Science Foundation of China (No.62372381), and the National Science Fund for Distinguished Young Scholars (No.62025205).

References

1. He, K., Zhang, X., Ren, S., Sun, J.: delving deep into rectifiers: surpassing human-level performance on imagenet classification. In: Proceedings of the 2015 IEEE International Conference on Computer Vision, pp. 1026–1034. IEEE Computer Society, USA (2015). https://doi.org/10.1109/ICCV.2015.123
2. Brown, T., Mann, B., Ryder, N., et al.: Language models are few-shot learners. Adv. Neural. Inf. Process. Syst. **33**, 1877–1901 (2020)
3. Vaswani, A., Shazeer, N., Parmar, N., et al.: Attention is all you need. In: Proceedings of the 31st International Conference on Neural Information Processing Systems, pp. 6000–6010. Curran Associates Inc., USA (2017)
4. Summers, R.: Nih chest x-ray dataset of 14 common thorax disease categories. Bethesda, MD, USA, NIH Clinical Center (2019)
5. Bilic, P., Christ, P., Li, H.B., et al.: The liver tumor segmentation benchmark (LiTS). Med. Image Anal. **84**, 102680 (2023)
6. Strouse, D.J., McKee, K.R., Botvinick, M., et al.: Collaborating with humans without human data. In: Proceedings of the 35th International Conference on Neural Information Processing Systems (2021)
7. Hemmer, P., Schemmer, M., Kühl, N., et al.: Complementarity in human-AI collaboration: concept, sources, and evidence. arXiv preprint arXiv:2404.00029 (2024)
8. Zhao, X., et al.: HAIformer: Human-AI Collaboration Framework for Disease Diagnosis via Doctor-Enhanced Transformer. ECAI 2024. IOS Press, 1495–1502 (2024)
9. Mozannar, H., Sontag, D.: Consistent estimators for learning to defer to an expert. In: International conference on machine learning, pp. 7076–7087. PMLR (2020)
10. Raghu, M., Blumer, K., Corrado, G., et al.: The algorithmic automation problem: prediction, triage, and human effort. arXiv preprint arXiv:1903.12220 (2019)
11. Hemmer, P., Thede, L., Vössing, M., et al.: Learning to defer with limited expert predictions. In: Proceedings of the AAAI Conference on Artificial Intelligence **37**(5), 6002–6011 (2023)
12. Zhang, Z., Ai, W., Wells, K., et al.: Learning to complement and to defer to multiple users. In: European Conference on Computer Vision, pp. 144–162. Springer, Cham (2024). https://doi.org/10.1007/978-3-031-72992-8_9
13. Hemmer, P., Schellhammer, S., Vössing, M., et al.: Forming Effective Human-AI Teams: building machine learning models that complement the capabilities of multiple experts. In: International Joint Conference on Artificial Intelligence (2022)
14. Majkowska, A., Mittal, S., Steiner, D.F., et al.: Chest radiograph interpretation with deep learning models: assessment with radiologist-adjudicated reference standards and population-adjusted evaluation. Radiology **294**(2), 421–431 (2020)

15. Zhu, C., Chen, W., Peng, T., et al.: Hard sample aware noise robust learning for histopathology image classification. IEEE Trans. Med. Imaging **41**(4), 881–894 (2021)
16. He, K., Zhang, X., Ren, S., Sun, J.: Deep residual learning for image recognition. In: Proceedings of the IEEE Conference on Computer Vision and Pattern Recognition, pp. 770–778 (2016)
17. Deng, J., Dong, W., Socher, R., et al.: ImageNet: a large-scale hierarchical image database. In: 2009 IEEE Conference on Computer Vision and Pattern Recognition, pp. 248–255 (2009)
18. Alves, J.V., Leitão, D., Jesus, S., et al.: Cost-sensitive learning to defer to multiple experts with workload constraints. arXiv preprint arXiv:2403.06906 (2024)
19. Steyvers, M., Tejeda, H., Kerrigan, G., Smyth, P.: Bayesian modeling of human-AI complementarity. Proc. Natl. Acad. Sci. **119**(11), e2111547119 (2022)
20. Verma, R., Barrejón, D., Nalisnick, E.: Learning to defer to multiple experts: consistent surrogate losses, confidence calibration, and conformal ensembles. In: International Conference on Artificial Intelligence and Statistics, pp. 11415–11434 (2023)
21. Verma, R., Nalisnick, E.: Calibrated learning to defer with one-vs-all classifiers. In: International Conference on Machine Learning, pp. 22184–22202 (2022)
22. Mozannar, H., Sontag, D.: Consistent estimators for learning to defer to an expert. In: International Conference on Machine Learning, pp. 7076–7087 (2020)
23. Agarwal, N., Moehring, A., Rajpurkar, P., Salz, T.: Combining human expertise with artificial intelligence: experimental evidence from radiology. National Bureau of Economic Research (2023)
24. Pradier, M.F., Zazo, J., Parbhoo, S., et al.: Preferential mixture-of-experts: interpretable models that rely on human expertise as much as possible. AMIA Summits Transl. Sci. Proc. **2021**, 525 (2021)
25. Wilder, B., Horvitz, E., Kamar, E.: Learning to complement humans. In: Proceedings of the Twenty-Ninth International Joint Conference on Artificial Intelligence, pp. 1526–1533 (2020). https://doi.org/10.24963/ijcai.2020/212
26. Chiou, E.K., Lee, J.D.: Trusting automation: designing for responsivity and resilience. Hum. Factors **65**(1), 137–165 (2023)
27. Shin, D.: The effects of explainability and causability on perception, trust, and acceptance: implications for explainable AI. Int. J. Hum Comput Stud. **146**, 102551 (2021)
28. Lu, Z., Yin, M.: Human reliance on machine learning models when performance feedback is limited: heuristics and risks. In: Proceedings of the 2021 CHI Conference on Human Factors in Computing Systems, pp. 1–16 (2021)
29. Jacobs, R.A., Jordan, M.I., Nowlan, S.J., Hinton, G.E.: Adaptive mixtures of local experts. Neural Comput. **3**(1), 79–87 (1991)
30. Shazeer, N., Mirhoseini, A., Maziarz, K., et al.: Outrageously large neural networks: the sparsely-gated mixture-of-experts layer. In: International Conference on Learning Representations (2017)
31. Lepikhin, D., Lee, H., Xu, Y., et al.: GShard: scaling giant models with conditional computation and automatic sharding. In: International Conference on Learning Representations (2021)
32. Munro, R.: Human-in-the-Loop Machine Learning. Manning Publications (2021)
33. Knox, W.B., Stone, P.: Tamer: training an agent manually via evaluative reinforcement. In: 2008 7th IEEE International Conference on Development and Learning, pp. 292–297 (2008)

34. Rafailov, R., Sharma, A., Mitchell, E., et al.: Direct preference optimization: your language model is secretly a reward model. Adv. Neural. Inf. Process. Syst. **36**, 53728–53741 (2023)
35. Azar, M.G., Guo, Z.D., Piot, B., et al.: A general theoretical paradigm to understand learning from human preferences. In: International Conference on Artificial Intelligence and Statistics, pp. 4447–4455 (2024)
36. Ethayarajh, K., Xu, W., Muennighoff, N., et al.: KTO: Model alignment as prospect theoretic optimization. In: Proceedings of the 41st International Conference on Machine Learning (2024)
37. Xu, H., Sharaf, A., Chen, Y., et al.: Contrastive preference optimization: pushing the boundaries of LLM performance in machine translation. In: Forty-first International Conference on Machine Learning (2024)
38. Keswani, V., Lease, M., Kenthapadi, K.: Towards unbiased and accurate deferral to multiple experts. In: Proceedings of the 2021 AAAI/ACM Conference on AI, Ethics, and Society, pp. 154–165 (2021)
39. Kroll, J.A.: Why AI is Just Automation. Brookings Institution (2021)

MEAN: Multi-Expert Adaptive Network For Customer Lifetime Value Prediction

Kelin Liu[1,2], Yao Zhou[1(✉)], Bin Liu[2], Hanjing Su[1], and Shouzhi Chen[1]

[1] WeChat Pay Research and Development Department, Tencent, Shenzhen, China
{clingliu,yaozzhou,justinsu,easychen}@tencent.com, Cling798as@gmail.com
[2] Key Laboratory of Data Engineering and Visual Computing, Chongqing University of Posts and Telecommunications, Chongqing, China
liubin@cqupt.edu.cn

Abstract. Customer Lifetime Value (CLTV) is a crucial metric for evaluating the economic value that users bring to a business over their entire service cycle. Accurately predicting CLTV is essential for resource optimization, improving user retention, and maximizing return on investment (ROI). However, predicting CLTV remains challenging due to the inherent sparsity and long-tail distribution of customer spending behavior, particularly in payment scenarios where user decisions are highly dynamic and influenced by external factors. Existing methods attempt to alleviate these issues but struggle with embedding quality and distribution selection, limiting their effectiveness in capturing complex user behaviors. To address these challenges, we propose the Multi-Expert Adaptive Network (MEAN), a novel CLTV prediction framework that improves embedding representations and mitigates distribution-related errors. MEAN integrates a Multi-View Feature Express (MVFE) module to optimize multi-view representations through expert-driven feature extraction and a Distribution Adaptive Module (DAM) for soft distribution assignment, preventing error amplification from incorrect sub-distribution choice. Furthermore, we introduce an alignment mechanism to synergize MVFE and DAM via bi-directional probability alignment. Extensive offline experiments and real-world online A/B testing on the WeChat financial experimental platform demonstrate the effectiveness of MEAN.

Keywords: Customer Lifetime Value Prediction · Multi-View Features · Distribution Adaptation · Attention Joint Alignment

1 Introduction

The Customer Lifetime Value (CLTV) represents the total economic benefit that a single user brings to a product or application over their lifetime. As a core operational metric, assisting service providers in carrying out targeted marketing to improve customer retention and reduce churn rates [1,6,13,17]. Therefore, accurate CLTV predictions can effectively enhance resource utilization, such as advertising costs for user acquisition and personalized service costs. This enables the allocation of limited resources among different users to maximize the return on investment (ROI) [12].

Due to variations in individual behaviors and the inherent characteristics of customer activity over time, CLTV typically exhibits a long-tail distribution. Notably, the user attrition rate reaches approximately 90% after initial use, i.e., major users do not contribute any revenue after their registration (CLVT=0), while there are only about 10% of users transition to effective usage within one-month post-activation ((CLVT> 0)).

To handle the sparsity of non-zero samples in CLTV prediction, previous works adopt a two-stage cascading architecture to divide users into several groups and train different models for each group to predict purchase propensity and potential monetary value [4,15]. These methods typically employ ensemble machine learning models, such as random forests [15] and the XGBoost [4], which require substantial storage to maintain multiple models and struggle to capture high-level feature representations. In addtion, the two-stage cascading process can introduce error accumulation, further affecting prediction accuracy.

In recent years, end-to-end CLTV prediction models have seen significant advancements. Wang et al. [16] propose the ZILN loss function, which enables multi-objective optimization by combining purchase probability with log-normal distribution parameters. Li et al. [8] introduce a multi-expert strategy that decomposes the skewed distribution into sub-distributions, but this hard partitioning is susceptible to data noise. OptDist [18] adaptively learns optimal sub-distribution segments, but its hard distribution selection heavily depends on the accuracy of the sub-distribution assignment. MDAN [9] alleviates data sparsity through a channel weighting mechanism and a distance similarity loss to constrain the hidden-space distribution. While it employs soft distribution assignment to mitigate error propagation from sub-distribution selection, its predictions remain sensitive to scale transformations of CLTV values, particularly in scenarios with scarce positive samples. Therefore, existing methods can not properly handle the long-tail CLTV distribution.

Predicting CLTV in payment scenarios presents additional challenges due to the inherent complexity of user consumption behavior and the influence of external disturbances Consumption decisions are primarily driven by subjective awareness, characterized by high sparsity and dynamic instability [19]. For example, WeChat Credit Pay, a consumer credit product that allows users to make purchases utilizing their predetermined credit limits, has observed that users predominantly opt for this payment method in limited consumption scenarios. Moreover, exogenous variables such as promotional activities and scene adaptability interact non-linearly with users' implicit preferences, making it difficult to extract high-level features and accurately capture their latent representations.

To tackle these challenges, we propose the Multi-Expert Adaptive Network (MEAN), a novel framework for CLTV prediction. MEAN effectively mitigates the limitations of insufficient embedding representation caused by inadequate adaptation to payment scenarios. Additionally, it addresses the issues of error propagation in hard distribution selection and the high dependency on labels in soft distribution combinations, particularly under atypical long-tail distributions. The core of MEAN is a framework based on a multi-view expert network, where Multi-View Feature Express (MVFE) module jointly optimizes multi-view features and distributions to extract complementary and robust knowledge. Specifically, instead of using the same data samples for all distributions, we pre-set multiple experts to focus on and extract different prior features of the distributions. We notice that there is a clear ordinal relationship between the distributions. Therefore, we use linear attention [20] to amplify the distinctions between the distributions, to obtain high-quality embedding representations, thereby reducing the overall complexity of CLTV modeling. To mitigate bias in MVFE, we introduce a Distribution Adaptive Module (DAM). This differs from existing methods that use the hard distribution selection criteria, as DAM can approximate the output distribution to assist MVFE, thereby preventing error amplification caused by selecting the wrong distribution. However, due to the differences in the outputs of these two modules, integrating MVFE and DAM within this framework still presents challenges. Therefore, we propose a novel alignment mechanism to address this issue, which bi-directionally aligns the probabilities output of DAM with the attention scores from MVFE. It can incorporate the distributional knowledge from DAM into MVFE, achieving a soft combination of distributions without relying on the label scale transformation. We conduct offline and online experiments on a real CLTV dataset constructed based on real users from the WeChat Payment Center, and the empirical results demonstrate the effectiveness of the proposed MEAN. The main contributions are summarized as follows:

- We propose a novel end-to-end CLTV prediction framework, MEAN, which effectively addresses the complexity of CLTV prediction and enhances adaptability to payment scenarios by optimizing high-quality embeddings for multiple candidate probability distributions.
- We design two key modules: MVFE for efficient feature encoding and DAM for distribution approximation representation. To improve model synergy, we introduce a dual-module joint optimization strategy that incorporates an attention score alignment constraint within DAM.
- Extensive offline experiments demonstrate the effectiveness of our approach, while online A/B testing on the WeChat financial experimental platform further validates the utility of MEAN in real-world marketing activities.

2 Related Work

Customer Lifetime Value modeling estimates the future revenue that new customers are expected to generate based on information about existing customers. Segmenting customers based on their CLTV and employing different marketing strategies for each segment is the initial demand of CLTV estimation. Early CLTV prediction methods focus on building rule-based or probabilistic models based on customers' historical behavior. Pareto/NBD [14] models the future purchase frequency based on customer behaviors through random process modeling, and it is typically used in scenarios where customers can make purchases at any time. Fader and others, based on the hypothesis that users with recent purchases or relatively high purchase frequency are more likely to make future purchases, use the RFM framework [5] to group users according to the recency, frequency, and monetary value of their purchases, to estimate the CLTV of user segments. Pfeifer et at. [11] constructs a transition probability matrix using Markov chains and estimates CLTV by combining it with the initial value distribution. Machine learning methods have been widely used to directly estimate CLTV based on user features. Vanderveld et al. proposed a two-stage modeling approach [15], constructing two random forests based on user characteristics to separately predict the probability and amount of user consumption. User embedding representations are constructed using Word2Vec [3] to predict CLTV.

In recent years, end-to-end models have emerged. For example, Wang et al. designed a representative loss function, ZILN [16], based on the data distribution, assuming that the payment amounts follow a log-normal distribution. It uses a multi-task approach to simultaneously optimize purchase propensity, distribution mean, and distribution standard deviation. The final prediction of CLTV is the expected value from the log-normal distribution. Li et al. [8] focus on different lifecycle sequential dependencies and design the ODMN. They address distribution imbalance by designing the MDME module, which uses the divide-and-conquer approach to partition the imbalanced distribution into multiple relatively balanced sub-distributions. This module selects the appropriate expert to predict CLTV values within specific ranges. However, this approach heavily relies on the selection of sub-distributions, and modeling these sub-distributions remains challenging due to data noise, imbalance, and other factors. To address label imbalance and sparsity issues, MDAN [9] uses a channel learning controller and a multi-channel network to mitigate data imbalance through weighted adjustments, and designs a distance similarity loss to directly bring the hidden vectors closer to the CLTV value distribution. Unfortunately, it heavily relies on the scaling of CLTV values, which can easily lead to predicted values lacking clear distinction. OptDist [18] explores multiple candidate probability distributions and selects the optimal sub-distribution for each example, thereby addressing the complex and variable nature of customer lifetime value distributions. However, the use of hard selection during the inference process limits the model's adaptability.

3 Proposed Method

In this section, we introduce a novel CLTV prediction model, Multi-Expert Adaptive Network(MEAN). The overall framework of our model, as shown in Fig. 1. The model consists of a multi-view feature express network (MVFE) and a distribution approximation Module (DAM). The shared layer transforms the original features into dense vectors. MVFE comprises a multi-gate mixture of experts network (MMoE) [10] and an attention mechanism, to learn unique representations of specific distributions and amplify the differences between distributions, respectively. At the same time, our label's distribution division criterion is to set CLTV values within a certain range as a distribution, with the ranges being adjustable as needed. Zero values are considered a separate distribution. The DAM includes a distribution approximation network designed to capture the user's original distribution tendencies. Then, we describe the alignment mechanism between modules to optimize our model.

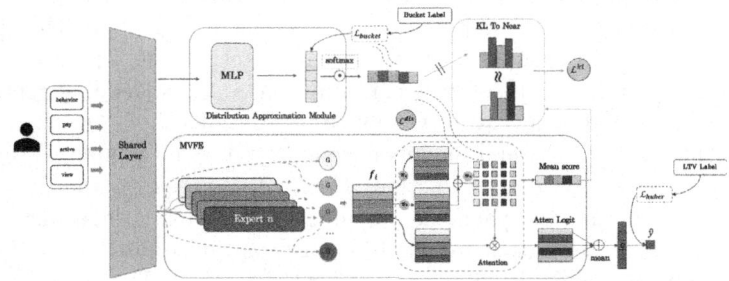

Fig. 1. The overall structure of our proposed MEAN

3.1 Problem Definition

Given a user group $\mathcal{U}$ and predict the total revenue that user u will bring to the product/service over some fixed lifecycle (e.g., 365 days). During this period the user's CLTV is marked as 0 if no consumption behaviour occurs, and CLTV is marked as the sum of multiple consumptions if multiple consumption behaviours occur. The training dataset $\mathcal{D} = \{(x_u, y_u) \mid u \in \mathcal{U}, y_u \in [0, +\infty)\}$ contains each sample input feature x_u and the CLTV label $y_u \geq 0$. In general, we train the model $F(\cdot)$ to predict CLTV, which can be expressed as follows:

$$\hat{y}_u = F(x_u \mid \mathcal{D}, \Theta) \tag{1}$$

where $\hat{y}_u$ is the predicted CLTV, Θ denotes the parameters of the model.

3.2 MEAN Framework

Multi-View Feature Express Module. Specifically, complex distribution of CLTV comprises several sub-distributions, and each user belongs to one of these sub-distributions. The diversity of input features is strongly correlated with the biased distribution of data. Noticing the varying importance of features across different CLTV distributions or segments, we observed that different users exhibit significantly different consumption behaviors based on CLTV segmentation. To address this issue, we designed a Multi-View Feature Expression network to learn and focus on the unique expressions of various distributions for different user groups. Currently, we employ M experts to represent multiple predefined distributions from different vector spaces, and use a gating network to simulate the varying focus on features for each distribution. Based on the input feature x_u, the Multi-View Feature Express Network generates multiple distribution outputs as shown in the following formula:

$$f_i = \sum_{j=1}^{M} G(x_u)_i E_j(x_u), i \in [1, 2, ..., n] \qquad (2)$$

$$G(x_u)_i = softmax(W_g x_u) \qquad (3)$$

where i is the distribution sequence number, n is the total number of CLTV distributions, M is the total number of view expert networks, f_i is the embedding of the corresponding distribution output, $G(x_u)_i$ is each gating network, $W_g \in \mathbb{R}^{N \times d}$ is a trainable matrix, d is the feature dimension, and $E_j(x_u)$ is each view expert network.

Then, we use an attention mechanism to generate richer feature representations. By discarding the hard selection method of distributions, attention-weighted aggregation can effectively improve the quality of representations, especially in scenarios with dispersed multi-distribution information. Using the attention mechanism, we allow the generation process to focus on different parts across distributions, rather than encoding the entire input into a fixed-length sequence. Importantly, we enable the model to learn to focus on what is relevant based on the existing distribution embeddings. In our setup, the input consists of the stacked representations of multiple distribution embeddings $H = concat[f_1, f_2, ..., f_n]^T$, where each distribution hidden state is denoted as h_t. There is a clear sequential order among the distributions, treating each distribution as a continuous token. We introduce an attention layer with an attention matrix $A \in \mathbb{R}^{n \times n}$, α_i is the i-th row of matrix A, where α_t is used to capture the distinctiveness of adjacent distributions. Our implementation of the attention mechanism is as follows:

$$g_t' = Tanh(W_q h_t + W_k h_t + b_{g'}) \qquad (4)$$

$$\alpha_t = softmax(g_t' W_a + b_a) \qquad (5)$$

where W_q and W_k represent the weight matrices for the hidden state h_t, W_a is the weight matrix for their corresponding nonlinear combination, and $b_{g'}$ and b_a are the bias terms.

Each distribution's attention-focused hidden representation is obtained by a weighted sum of the embeddings of other distributions and its current distribution's embedding similarity α_t. This is directly derived using matrix multiplication, where $A = concat[\alpha_1, \alpha_2, ..., \alpha_n]^T$. After obtaining all the distribution similarity embeddings, the final embedding e is achieved by averaging all the embeddings. This can be expressed as:

$$e = \frac{1}{n}\sum_{i=i}^{n} A_i h_i \tag{6}$$

After obtaining the final embedding of the multi-view feature representation, the CLTV prediction can be expressed as:

$$\hat{y} = FC(e) \tag{7}$$

where $\hat{y}$ is the CLTV prediction value, and FC is a fully connected layer without activation. As previously mentioned, the zero-inflated log-normal distribution [16] was proposed specifically for the CLTV distribution but is prone to extreme prediction values. However, the MSE loss is overly sensitive to these extreme values, causing the overall predictions to tend towards the mean. Therefore, we use Huber Loss to constrain $\hat{y}$ learning, enhancing discriminability between $\hat{y}$ and ensuring $\hat{y}$ remains within a controllable range. The loss function is expressed as:

$$\mathcal{L}^{cltv} = \begin{cases} \frac{1}{2}(y-\hat{y})^2, & \text{for } |y-\hat{y}| <= \delta \\ \delta\left(|y-\hat{y}| - \frac{1}{2}\delta\right), & \text{otherwise} \end{cases} \tag{8}$$

where δ is the value that controls the turning point between the two types of loss functions.

Distribution Approximate Module. Previously, we proposed a multi-view feature representation network, which aims to aggregate more influential final embeddings from the perspectives of feature and distribution debiasing. However, the specific distribution lacks clear supervisory signals. Therefore, we propose to use a bypass to construct a distribution approximation network. By using the output of such a network to constrain attention learning. The input feature x_u is projected to a high-dimensional feature vector via a simple shared layer, and then is used to produce a n dimensional feature k via MLP network:

$$k = MLP(ReLU(W_s x_u + b_s)) \tag{9}$$

where MLP is a network structure with the last layer outputting a dimension of n, W_s and b_s are the parameters of the shared layer. We normalize the n dimensional feature vector to $\hat{b}$, ensuring the sum of all its elements to be 1, and use a multi-class classification loss to guide the learning of $\hat{b}$. The formula is as follows:

$$\hat{b}_i = \frac{e^{k_i - max(k)}}{\sum_{i=1}^{n} e^{k_i - max(k)}} \tag{10}$$

$$\mathcal{L}_{buckect} = -\frac{1}{B} \sum_{(x_u,z) \in B} \sum_{i=1}^{n} z_i log \hat{b}_i \qquad (11)$$

where B is the number of samples in a batch, z is the n dimensional one-hot vector representing the true distribution bucket label, $\hat{b}_i$ is the probability value of belonging to the $i-th$ bucket.

Constrained Attention Joint Alignment Mechanism. Next, we introduce a constrained attention joint alignment mechanism in our method, Aiming to integrate the outputs of the two modules, incorporating distribution information into the MVFE module, in order to refine the final embeddings that contain distribution supervisory signals. We need to optimize the loss function with outputs from both modules. To effectively guide the direction of attention learning and prevent the attention from shifting away from focusing on effective inter-distribution information, we average the attention scores represented as $\hat{\vartheta}$. By minimizing the Kullback-Leibler (KL) divergence [2] between the normalized n dimensional feature $\hat{b}$ and $\hat{\vartheta}$, we aim to utilize the outputs of the DAM to guide the learning of attention, represented as follows:

$$\hat{\vartheta} = \frac{1}{n} \sum_{i=1}^{n} A_i \qquad (12)$$

$$\mathcal{L}^{kl} = \sum_{i=1}^{n} \hat{b}_i log \frac{\hat{b}_i}{\hat{\vartheta}_i} \qquad (13)$$

where A is the attention matrix.

However, we do not want the learning of attention to be entirely guided by the output of the DAM. We also aim to transfer the information from the attention module to the DAM. Here, we use a combination of soft and hard labels through high-temperature distillation. The higher the temperature, the smoother the output probability distribution of the softmax, facilitating the transfer of knowledge from our attention module to our distribution approximation network. This achieves the purpose of mutually constrained joint alignment. The formula is expressed as follows:

$$\mathcal{L}^{dis} = \beta * \mathcal{H}(z, \sigma(k; T=1)) + \gamma * \mathcal{H}\left(\sigma(\hat{\vartheta}; T=\tau), \sigma(k; T=\tau)\right) \qquad (14)$$

$$\mathcal{H}(p,q) = -\sum_{i}^{n} p_i log(q_i + \xi) \qquad (15)$$

$$\sigma(o; T) = \frac{e^{o_i/T}}{\sum_{i=1}^{n} e^{o_i/T}} \qquad (16)$$

where σ is the softmax function with the temperature parameter T, $\hat{\vartheta}$ is the output of the attention scores, β and γ are coefficients, ξ is a very small constant. It is worth noting that when $T = 1$, $\mathcal{H}(y, \sigma(k; T = 1))$ is equivalent to the distribution multi-classification loss $\mathcal{L}_{buckect}$. In summary, the overall loss of MEAN is defined as:

$$\mathcal{L}^{MEAN} = \mathcal{L}^{cltv} + \mathcal{L}^{kl} + \mathcal{L}^{dis} \tag{17}$$

4 Experiments

4.1 Experimental Setup

Dataset. The dataset for this experiment is derived from the user growth operations of WeChat Credit Pay. WeChat Credit Pay is a consumer credit product that allows users to make purchases using their allocated credit limits. Due to customers' autonomy in choosing payment methods and amounts, along with the significant influence of concurrent marketing activities on most users, the distribution of CLTV exhibits a high level of complexity. The features of the data set include user profile data, channel-related information, and transaction records prior to the activation of the service. In addition, periodic, seasonal, and social information is also incorporated as part of the features, resulting in a total of 720-dimensional features. We sample 22 million users as the experimental dataset. In the dataset, we randomly split them into 7:1:2 as the training, validation, and test sets, respectively. Labels are defined as the total consumption amount of new users within one month, one quarter, six months, and one year after activating the WeChat Credit Pay product. Based on consumption habits and user attributes before activation by new users, we need to simultaneously estimate $cltv_{30}, cltv_{90}, cltv_{180}$, and $cltv_{365}$.

Metrics. The Percentile MAPE is an evaluation metric based on Decile MAPE (DM) [16], used to evaluate the accuracy of CLTV prediction, but with finer granularity. The Gini coefficient [16] is a commonly used metric for evaluating CLTV model performance. This metric serves as a quantitative evaluation standard for the effectiveness of high-value user identification, and its value is strictly positively correlated with the model's discriminative ability: the larger the Gini coefficient, the more accurately the model distinguishes the value of top users. Spearman Correlation (SC) [16] quantitatively evaluates the ordinal consistency of the predicted values of the model, specifically representing the monotonic preservation ability of the predicted CLTV and the actual CLTV in the user value ranking. AUC is used to assess the recognition ability of high-value users. AUC focuses only on the order of relationships and can be used to evaluate the accuracy of rankings.

Baselines. We compared our method with several state-of-the-art CLTV prediction methods, which are summarized as follows:

- *DNN-ZILN* [16]: A method that unifies binary classification and regression based on the log-normal distribution.
- *MTL-ZILN*: Using a multi-task learning paradigm to evaluate different CLTV periods to assist in long-term prediction.
- *ODMN* [8]: A multi-distribution multi-expert method for CLTV prediction, which divides training samples into multiple sub-distributions and buckets, estimates deviations within buckets to obtain fine-grained CLTV values.
- *MDAN* [9]: A method for predicting CLTV using multi-channel learning, where the final embedding is obtained through weighted summation fusion.
- *OptDist* [18]: An end-to-end CLTV prediction framework adaptively selects the optimal sub-distribution for each example by exploring multiple candidate probability distributions. The framework includes two modules, DLM and DSM, designed for learning sub-distributions and making distribution choices, respectively. Combined with an alignment mechanism, it enables flexible selection.

Hyperparameter Settings. We use a two-layer MLP with ReLU activation functions as the shared layer. The size of the shared layer was set to [512,256], [256,128,64] for the MLP. In our main model, there is only one layer followed by a batch normalization operation. We use Adam [7] as the optimizer for our model, with a learning rate of 1e-3. The batch size is set to 1024 and the number of expert networks is set to 5. We employ an early stopping mechanism, and the model typically converges within 12 to 15 epochs. We scaled the labels and truncated them to the range [0, 20]. The parameter δ of Huber Loss and the soft label distillation coefficient γ are set to 1.0. The parameters τ of L^{dis} is set to 2.0. We also pre-divided the data into 5 distributions, with zero values being treated as a separate distribution. Our code is publicly available on an anonymous GitHub repository [1].

4.2 Performance Comparison

In Table 1, we present the evaluation results of each model on the test set. Firstly, *MTL-ZILN* outperforms *DNN-ZILN* overall because it can aggregate information from multiple periods through shared experts. Secondly, in the *ODMN* method, the error propagation caused by multiple distribution buckets can lead to significant errors in calculating the CLTV value due to misclassified distributions and buckets. In particular, We attempted to apply the multi-task prediction method from the baseline to the *MTL-MEAN*, outputting multiple periods simultaneously and summing the losses for joint optimization. Although this approach achieved some positive results, the numerous cascading losses caused the optimization direction to become unclear, resulting in performance that was not as good as single-task prediction.

---

[1] https://anonymous.4open.science/r/ltv-F54B.

Table 1. The overall performance of different models on all datasets, where the symbol ↑(↓) indicates that the higher (lower) the metric value, the better the performance.

Period	Method	Percentile Mape ↓	GINI ↑	Spearman ↑	AUC ↑
$cltv_{30}$	DNN-ZILN	0.7552	0.4861	0.3933	0.7295
	MTL-ZILN	0.7239	0.4960	0.4075	0.7397
	ODMN	0.6503	0.4449	0.4050	0.7395
	MDAN	0.1658	0.5080	0.4309	0.7428
	OptDist	0.3925	0.4918	0.4098	0.7418
	MTL-MEAN	0.1630	0.5112	0.4298	0.7518
	MEAN	**0.1258**	**0.5127**	**0.4358**	**0.7549**
$cltv_{90}$	DNN-ZILN	0.5755	0.5056	0.4206	0.7361
	MTL-ZILN	0.5269	0.5044	0.4233	0.7393
	ODMN	0.4855	0.4771	0.4215	0.7388
	MDAN	0.1332	0.5177	0.4566	0.7501
	OptDist	0.1918	0.5098	0.4322	0.7450
	MTL-MEAN	0.1033	0.5192	0.4596	0.7536
	MEAN	**0.0753**	**0.5275**	**0.4687**	**0.7571**
$cltv_{180}$	DNN-ZILN	0.5262	0.5081	0.4231	0.7300
	MTL-ZILN	0.4551	0.5085	0.4292	0.7359
	ODMN	0.3591	0.5068	0.4382	0.7417
	MDAN	0.1034	0.5239	**0.4846**	0.7487
	OptDist	0.1222	0.5118	0.4562	0.7469
	MTL-MEAN	0.1129	0.5244	0.4669	0.7588
	MEAN	**0.0927**	**0.5298**	0.4805	**0.7615**
$cltv_{365}$	DNN-ZILN	0.3821	0.4968	0.4272	0.7249
	MTL-ZILN	0.2890	0.5069	0.4376	0.7313
	ODMN	0.1779	0.4988	0.4257	0.7247
	MDAN	0.1206	0.5232	0.4829	0.7587
	OptDist	0.1063	0.5072	0.4804	0.7529
	MTL-MEAN	0.0972	0.5194	0.4920	0.7597
	MEAN	**0.0871**	**0.5292**	**0.4987**	**0.7649**

The performance of our proposed MEAN model surpasses all baselines in the key metric, Percentile Mape. Moreover, it also demonstrates superior performance in both GINI and AUC metrics. This indicates that our method effectively handles imbalanced data, highlighting the robustness of our model. In addition, observing the Spearman metric, our method shows greater generalization ability in maintaining the monotonic relationship between predicted and actual values. At the same time, MDAN outperforms other methods in the Spearman metric for the prediction of $cltv_{180}$, indicating that the scaled values of this period label can be more easily fitted through the RankSim loss. However, this does not imply generalization capability. This further validates the effectiveness and generality of our carefully designed model in predicting CLTV.

4.3 Ablation Study

In this section, we conduct ablation experiments to evaluate the effectiveness of each innovative module of *MEAN*. We compare the differences in Percentile Mape and AUC for the four periods of the overall sample across different modules of *MEAN*. Percentile Mape and AUC are the primary reference metrics for distinguishing the capabilities of our model. They represent the accuracy of the model in predicting CLTV and the precision in identifying top users, respectively. Main content: (1) Without $\mathcal{L}^{kl}$: Remove the KL divergence loss term from the alignment mechanism; (2) Without the soft label distillation term $\mathcal{L}_2^{dis}$: Remove the soft label distillation term from the alignment mechanism; (3) Without DAM and $\mathcal{L}^{dis}$ and $\mathcal{L}^{kl}$: Remove the entire alignment mechanism, only using the Multi-View Feature Express Network module.

Table 2. Percentile Mape results of MEAN and its variants for different prediction periods.

Method	$cltv_{30}$	$cltv_{90}$	$cltv_{180}$	$cltv_{365}$
MEAN	**0.1258**	**0.0753**	**0.0927**	**0.0871**
$Without - \mathcal{L}^{kl}$	0.1918	0.1706	0.1162	0.0953
$Without - \mathcal{L}_2^{dis}$	0.1727	0.1001	0.1228	0.1121
MVFE	0.2317	0.1571	0.1129	0.1279

Table 3. AUC of MEAN and its derivative methods for different prediction periods on the dataset.

Method	$cltv_{30}$	$cltv_{90}$	$cltv_{180}$	$cltv_{365}$
MEAN	**0.7549**	**0.7571**	**0.7615**	**0.7649**
$Without - \mathcal{L}^{kl}$	0.7514	0.7532	0.7521	0.7588
$Without - \mathcal{L}_2^{dis}$	0.7523	0.7516	0.7500	0.7558
MVFE	0.7539	0.7531	0.7508	0.7551

Then we summary the results of the ablation experiments in Table 2 and Table 3. It demonstrates that our alignment mechanism can effectively improve the accuracy and stability of CLTV prediction. When the soft label distillation term and KL divergence loss term are not used, the overall performance of CLTV prediction decreases, indicating that the model's spontaneous attention focus cannot be controlled. We further investigated the impact of the two constraint terms within the alignment mechanism. When only one constraint term is used, the short-term prediction performance without the KL divergence loss is better than that without the soft label distillation term, while the long-term prediction performance shows the opposite trend. This indicates that the two constraint terms focus on different aspects, potentially leading to excessive guidance in attention learning. This validates our design of the constrained attention joint alignment mechanism. Specifically, *MVFE* enables us to obtain better embedded representations of features, though it has certain instability. By employing the constrained attention joint alignment mechanism, the overall performance of the model is improved, resulting in highly accurate CLTV predictions over both long and short periods.

4.4 Online A/B Test

To further validate the effectiveness of MEAN on real-world applications, we perform an A/B test on the financial experiment platform of WeChat Pay. Our experiment divided users into two groups, those who have activated the feature and those who have not, to ensure homogeneity among users. We assigned 50% of the traffic to the control group and 50% to the experimental group. The model was employed to estimate users' $cltv_{365}$, and marketing efforts were directed towards users with high $cltv_{365}$. To facilitate the observation of experimental results, the modeling label in the $cltv_{365}$ estimation was set as the user's total loan amount one year later. The experimental group's strategy was to target the top 10% as predicted by the model, while the control group's strategy was to randomly target 10%. For each marketing campaign, we separately observed the online effects after 7 days, 14 days, and 30 days. We then calculated the activation rate (only for users who had not activated), the loan rate, and the average daily loan amount during the experiment period.

Table 4. The improvement of various metrics in A/B testing

Method	Activation Rate	Loan Rate	Average Daily Loan Amounts
Not Activated UPLIFT - 7	1.51%	0.08%	2.20%
Not Activated UPLIFT - 14	2.47%	0.11%	4.31%
Not Activated UPLIFT - 30	4.24%	0.18%	7.01%
Activated UPLIFT - 7	-	0.03%	1.98%
Activated UPLIFT - 14	-	0.06%	2.77%
Activated UPLIFT - 30	-	0.11%	5.56%

To ensure company privacy, Table 4 only presents the improvement values of our method relative to the control group. Our method demonstrates superior performance, and due to the large base of traffic, the increase in revenue is also highly significant. This further validates the effectiveness of our proposed model and the accuracy in identifying high-value users.

4.5 Hyperparameter Analysis

In this section, we investigate the impact of two key hyperparameters on our method: the parameter δ of Huber Loss and the number of sub-distributions n. We primarily focus on the evaluation of Percentile MAPE for the overall sample in practical business scenarios, as this metric reflects the model's prediction accuracy. Additionally, we will use the predictions to guide the allocation of marketing resources. Therefore, we will discuss the impact of different parameters on the performance of *MEAN* with respect to this metric. The parameter δ controls the transition of the CLTV loss. Figure 2 shows the performance of the framework under different values of δ. As δ decreases, L^{cltv} increases, resulting in a smaller alignment mechanism loss initially, which weakens the constraints. Furthermore, We change the number of sub-distributions in the set $\{2, 3, 4, 5, 6, 7\}$. Figure 3 shows the model performance under different numbers of sub-distributions. Similarly, as the number of sub-distributions is increasing, the overall loss of the alignment mechanism is increasing, shifting the focus of the overall optimization of the framework, leading to a decrease in prediction accuracy. In real-world scenarios, we recommend practitioners search these hyperparameters according to the key metrics in the corresponding applications.

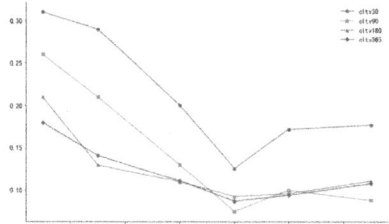

Fig. 2. The impact of parameter δ on model performance under different prediction periods.

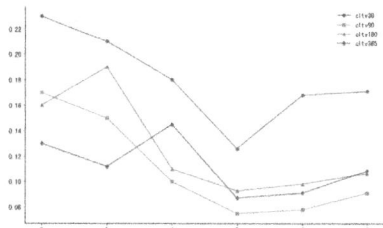

Fig. 3. The impact of the number of sub-distributions on model performance under different prediction periods.

5 Conclusion

In this paper, we propose a new framework for customer lifetime value prediction called MEAN. MEAN obtains feature perspective expressions through multiple expert networks for different CLTV distributions and uses an attention mechanism to amplify the differences between distributions. The aggregated user embeddings contain feature diversity and distributional distinctiveness. Additionally, we propose a joint alignment mechanism that uses DAM to approximate the distribution of the original features, constraining the direction of attention. At the same time, the attention scores guide the output of DAM, achieving mutual constraints, thereby making the optimization more effective. In this way, MEAN pays more attention to the differences between different features and different distributions, making the CLTV prediction capability more intuitive. Finally, our method has achieved considerable gains in both offline experiments and online applications on real-world industrial datasets, with consistent results demonstrating the effectiveness of MEAN.

Acknowledgements. This work was supported by the National Natural Science Foundation of China (62302074) and the Science and Technology Research Program of Chongqing Municipal Education Commission (KJQN202300631).

References

1. Berger, P.D., Nasr, N.I.: Customer lifetime value: marketing models and applications. J. Interact. Mark. **12**(1), 17–30 (1998)
2. Bishop, C.M., Nasrabadi, N.M.: Pattern Recognition and Machine Learning, vol. 4. Springer, Cham (2006)
3. Chen, P.P., Guitart, A., del Río, A.F., Periánez, A.: Customer lifetime value in video games using deep learning and parametric models. In: 2018 IEEE International Conference on Big Data (Big Data), pp. 2134–2140. IEEE (2018)
4. Drachen, A., et al.: To be or not to be... social: incorporating simple social features in mobile game customer lifetime value predictions. In: Proceedings of the Australasian Computer Science Week Multiconference, pp. 1–10 (2018)
5. Fader, P.S., Hardie, B.G.S., Lee, K.L.: RFM and CLV: using ISO-value curves for customer base analysis. J. Mark. Res. **42**(4), 415–430 (2005)
6. He, B., et al.: Rankability-enhanced revenue uplift modeling framework for online marketing. In: Proceedings of the 30th ACM SIGKDD Conference on Knowledge Discovery and Data Mining, pp. 5093–5104 (2024)
7. Kingma, D.P., Ba, J.: Adam: a method for stochastic optimization. arXiv preprint arXiv:1412.6980 (2014)
8. Li, K., Shao, G., Yang, N., Fang, X., Song, Y.: Billion-user customer lifetime value prediction: an industrial-scale solution from kuaishou. In: Proceedings of the 31st ACM International Conference on Information & Knowledge Management, pp. 3243–3251 (2022)
9. Liu, W., Xu, G., Ye, B., Luo, X., He, Y., Yin, C.: MDAN: multi-distribution adaptive networks for LTV prediction. In: Pacific-Asia Conference on Knowledge Discovery and Data Mining, pp. 409–420. Springer, Cham (2024)
10. Ma, J., Zhao, Z., Yi, X., Chen, J., Hong, L., Chi, E.H.: Modeling task relationships in multi-task learning with multi-gate mixture-of-experts. In: Proceedings of the 24th ACM SIGKDD International Conference on Knowledge Discovery & Data Mining, pp. 1930–1939 (2018)
11. Pfeifer, P.E., Carraway, R.L.: Modeling customer relationships as Markov chains. J. Interact. Mark. **14**(2), 43–55 (2000)
12. Phillips, P.P.: Return on investment (ROI) basics. Association for Talent Development (2023)
13. Pollak, Z.: Predicting customer lifetime values–ecommerce use case. arXiv preprint arXiv:2102.05771 (2021)
14. Schmittlein, D.C., Morrison, D.G., Colombo, R.: Counting your customers: who are they and what will they do next? Manage. Sci. **33**(1), 1–24 (1987)

15. Vanderveld, A., Pandey, A., Han, A., Parekh, R.: An engagement-based customer lifetime value system for e-commerce. In: Proceedings of the 22nd ACM SIGKDD International Conference on Knowledge Discovery and Data Mining, pp. 293–302 (2016)
16. Wang, X., Liu, T., Miao, J.: A deep probabilistic model for customer lifetime value prediction. arXiv preprint arXiv:1912.07753 (2019)
17. Weng, Y., Tang, X., Chen, L., Liu, D., He, X.: Expected transaction value optimization for precise marketing in fintech platforms. arXiv preprint arXiv:2401.01525 (2024)
18. Weng, Y., et al.: Optdist: learning optimal distribution for customer lifetime value prediction. In: Proceedings of the 33rd ACM International Conference on Information and Knowledge Management, pp. 2523–2533 (2024)
19. Xing, M., et al.: Learning reliable user representations from volatile and sparse data to accurately predict customer lifetime value. In: Proceedings of the 27th ACM SIGKDD Conference on Knowledge Discovery & Data Mining, pp. 3806–3816 (2021)
20. Zheng, G., Mukherjee, S., Dong, X.L., Li, F.: Opentag: open attribute value extraction from product profiles. In: Proceedings of the 24th ACM SIGKDD International Conference on Knowledge Discovery & Data Mining, pp. 1049–1058 (2018)

Enabling ControlNet to follow Localized Descriptions Using Cross-Attention Control

Denis Lukovnikov[✉] and Asja Fischer

Ruhr University Bochum, Bochum, Germany
{denis.lukovnikov,asja.fischer}@rub.de

Abstract. ControlNet enables fine-grained control over image layout in prominent generators like Stable Diffusion. However, it lacks the ability to take into account localized textual descriptions that indicate which image region is described by which phrase in the prompt. In this work, we enable ControlNet to use localized descriptions using a training-free approach that modifies the cross-attention scores during generation. For doing so, we adapt and investigate several existing cross-attention control methods and identify shortcomings that cause failure or image degradation under some conditions. To address these shortcomings, we develop a novel cross-attention manipulation method. Qualitative and quantitative experimental studies demonstrate the effectiveness of the proposed augmented ControlNet.

Keywords: localized descriptions · layout-to-image · diffusion models

1 Introduction

Diffusion-based text-to-image models like Stable Diffusion [23] can generate high-quality images of various types of subjects from textual description. However, they lack fine-grained control over the composition of the generated image, which would increase their usefulness in various applications. The default training method does not address generation scenario's where additional control inputs can be used to describe the desired composition of the image (e.g., using line art or segmentation maps). Recent work has explored fine-tuning adapters (e.g. ControlNet [34], GLIGEN [15], T2I-Adapters [20]) to the diffusion model's U-Net that enable precise control over the layout of the generated images. Arguably the most popular and effective among these is ControlNet. However, it lacks the ability to use localized descriptions that specify which objects should be generated in the different parts of the image.

Therefore, in this work, we extend the pre-trained segmentation-based ControlNet for controlling image layout with cross-attention control as a means to

---

Supplementary Information The online version contains supplementary material available at https://doi.org/10.1007/978-3-032-05981-9_19.

© The Author(s), under exclusive license to Springer Nature Switzerland AG 2026
R. P. Ribeiro et al. (Eds.): ECML PKDD 2025, LNAI 16014, pp. 310–327, 2026.
https://doi.org/10.1007/978-3-032-05981-9_19

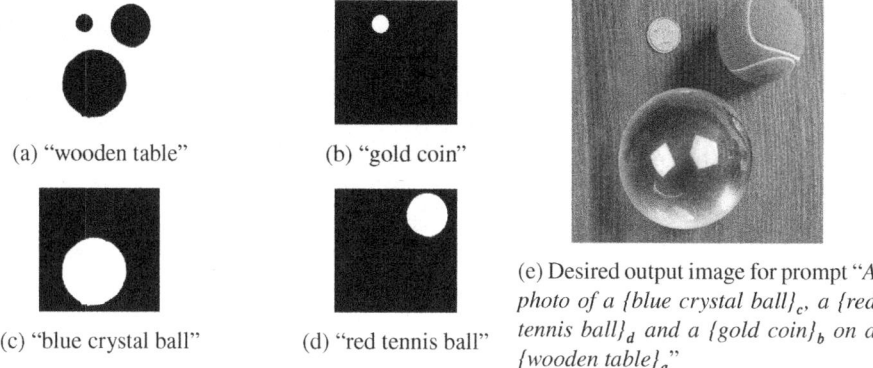

Fig. 1. An example of the task. The input consists of masks (a)-(d) and the annotated prompt in the caption of (e). The desired output is shown in (e). See Sect. 2.

improve the assignment of objects and reduce missing or misplaced objects and concept bleeding that frequently occur when ControlNet is used for more complicated scenes with multiple similar objects. Cross-attention control methods have the advantages that they neither require significant computational overhead nor additional training and that they can be easily plugged into existing models. Specifically, the contributions of this work are three-fold. Firstly, we investigate several training-free attention-based extensions of ControlNet to improve its grounding with a given localized textual description and identify important characteristics of such methods. To the best of our knowledge, this investigation presents the first in-depth comparison of this family of methods in the context of ControlNet. Secondly, we develop a novel cross-attention (CA) control method that facilitates better object alignment between the text prompt and the generated image, while minimizing image quality degradation. Lastly, we conduct an extensive empirical study using the newly developed SIMPLESCENES dataset as well as COCO2017 [17]. Qualitative and quantitative experiments demonstrate the effectiveness of CA control in conjunction with ControlNet, as well as improvements compared to other CA control methods and other baselines that do not rely on ControlNet.

2 Task: Layout-to-Image with Localized Descriptions

The focus of this work lies in improving the faithfulness of a generated image of height H and width W to a localized description. The input for this task consists of (1) a prompt X consisting of N tokens, (2) a collection of R region masks $\{\mathbf{B}_r\}_{r=0,...,R}$, where $\mathbf{B}_r \in \{0,1\}^{H \times W}$[1], and (3) region-token alignments

---

[1] The region mask $\mathbf{B}_r$ contains the value 1 for pixels where the object should be present.

$f_{RT} : [1..N] \rightarrow [0..R]^2$ that specify which region each token in the text prompt belongs to. As an example, consider the prompt "*A photo of a {blue crystal ball}$_1$, a {red tennis ball}$_2$, and a {gold coin}$_3$ on a {wooden table}$_4$*", where each colored sub-sequence is associated with the corresponding mask shown in Figs. 1a to 1d.

The goal is to generate an image where (1) object boundaries follow mask boundaries and (2) where the objects described by the region-specific parts of the prompts (i.e., the region descriptions) are generated in the parts of the output image associated with their region description. The desired output for our example is given in Fig. 1e.

3 Background

In this section, we briefly review the diffusion-based text-to-image generation process, ControlNet, and some existing cross-attention control methods designed for using localized descriptions with diffusion models (DMs).

3.1 Text-to-Image with Denoising Diffusion

In text-to-image DMs, first, a textual description X of N input tokens is encoded by the text encoder, producing the text embeddings $\mathbf{X} = \{x_n\}_{n=0..N}$, where each $x_n \in \mathbb{R}^{d_x}$. Here, d_x is the dimensionality of the embedding. Stable Diffusion uses CLIP [22] as encoder, which is a transformer pre-trained on a text-image similarity task.

Then, a denoising model is used to iteratively denoise an initial $z_T \sim \mathcal{N}(0, I)$ into an image z_0 using some solver, such as DDIM [27]. At every iteration, the solver computes $z_{t-\delta} = s(u(z_t, t, \mathbf{X}), t, \delta)$, where t is the denoising step, $u(\cdot)$ is the denoising model, $s(\cdot)$ is the solver algorithm, and δ is the step size. The denoising model can be implemented as a U-Net [24], which is conditioned on both the input text X, and the noisy image z_t.

Conditioning on the text can be accomplished by using a cross-attention mechanism between the token embeddings $\mathbf{X} \in \mathbb{R}^{N \times d_x}$ and pixel-wise features $\mathbf{H} \in \mathbb{R}^{H \times W \times d_h}$:

$$\mathbf{A} = \text{softmax}\left(\frac{\mathbf{Q}\mathbf{K}^T}{\sqrt{d}}\right) \quad \text{and} \quad \mathbf{C} = \mathbf{A}\mathbf{V} \ . \tag{1}$$

Here, $\mathbf{Q} = f_Q(\mathbf{H}) \in \mathbb{R}^{(H \cdot W) \times d}$ are the query vectors computed by projecting the pixel-wise feature maps $\mathbf{H}$. $\mathbf{K} = f_K(\mathbf{X}) \in \mathbb{R}^{N \times d}$ and $\mathbf{V} = f_V(\mathbf{X}) \in \mathbb{R}^{N \times d}$ are the key and value projections of the token embeddings. $\mathbf{A} \in \mathbb{R}^{(H \cdot W) \times N}$ are the cross-attention scores. Note that we omit layer and head indexes for clarity and that the dimensions H and W as well as the size of feature vectors d and d_h vary depending on the layer.

---

[2] Region 0 is the entire image, so a token assigned to region 0 is relevant everywhere in image.

3.2 ControlNet

ControlNet [34] was recently proposed to improve control over the image composition. In addition to the prompt X, ControlNet expects an image c_{img} as part of the input for the generation process. In order to incorporate conditioning based on c_{img}, first a control model is defined that copies the down-sampling and middle blocks of the latent diffusion model's U-Net. The control model also contains an additional block of convolutional layers that encodes the control signal c_{img} and is trained from scratch. The features computed by the control model are added to the features computed by its sibling in the main U-Net before feeding them into the up-sampling blocks of the main U-Net. We refer the reader to Supplement C and to the original work [34] for a more detailed explanation. ControlNet supports different types of conditioning input, such as segmentation maps, depth maps or human pose. Each type requires the training of a separate control model dedicated to that type of conditioning. Combining several control signals [35] is an active research area.

Note that while ControlNet allows us to control the image layout using segmentation maps, it lacks a mechanism to precisely control what object is generated inside each region. As a consequence, when faced with ambiguous layouts or improbable region assignments, plain ControlNet can not correctly process the prompt, as illustrated in our qualitative study in Sect. 5.1.

3.3 Cross-Attention Control

Modifying cross-attention [2] scores in the transformer [29] blocks of the U-Net can provide a degree of spatial control and attribute assignment. Here we give a brief introduction to previously proposed methods aimed at implementing the ability to follow localized descriptions via cross-attention control. In addition to the token embeddings x_n, these methods expect the region masks $\mathbf{B}_r$, as well as the region-token alignments f_{RT} as inputs. In general, CA control mechanisms stimulate cross-attention from the specified region to the corresponding set of tokens and/or prevent from attending to the descriptions of other regions.

eDiff-I (Community Edition). The first cross-attention control method we consider is a re-implementation [26] of the approach proposed by Balaji et al. [3]. It takes the region-annotated prompt and the region masks, and forces cross-attention to attend to certain words from the corresponding regions by modifying the cross-attention scores to[3]

$$\mathbf{A} = \text{softmax}\left(\mathbf{W} + \frac{\mathbf{Q}\mathbf{K}^T}{\sqrt{d}}\right) \text{ , with} \qquad (2)$$

$$\mathbf{W} = W' \cdot \log(1 + \sigma^2) \cdot \text{std}(\mathbf{Q}\mathbf{K}^T) \cdot \mathbf{B}_{f_{\text{RT}}} \text{ .} \qquad (3)$$

---

[3] Note that this formulation by the community slightly differs from the one proposed by [3]. We use this formulation since in our early experiments, we found it to perform slightly better.

Here, $\mathbf{W}$ is scheduled to decrease as the denoising process progresses, due to the dependence on σ, which is a scalar specifying the current noise level. W' is a hyper-parameter controlling the overall degree of attention change and $\mathbf{B}_{f_{\text{RT}}} \in \{0,1\}^{(H \cdot W) \times N}$ are the masks $\mathbf{B}_r$ stacked according to f_{RT}.

CAC. Instead of boosting cross-attention scores between regions and their descriptions in the prompt, CAC [9] applies a binary mask that eliminates attention between regions and non-matching region descriptions. The binary mask is applied *after* softmax normalization, that is[4]

$$\mathbf{A} = \text{softmax}\left(\frac{\mathbf{Q}\mathbf{K}^T}{\sqrt{d}}\right) \odot \max(1 - \mathbf{B}_R, \mathbf{B}_{f_{\text{RT}}}) , \qquad (4)$$

and thus attention weights are no longer normalized after applying the mask. $\mathbf{B}_R \in \{0,1\}^{(H \cdot W) \times N}$ is a mask that is set to one for all tokens that belong to *any* region description.

DenseDiffusion. In this variant of cross-attention control [12], attention scores for the tokens describing a region are increased while attention scores to other tokens are decreased. In addition, the method also proposes to scale the degree of change by the region size fraction S and uses a schedule that decreases polynomially. Cross-attention scores are modified by redefining $\mathbf{W}$ from Eq. 2 as follows

$$\mathbf{W} = W' \cdot \left(\frac{t}{T}\right)^5 \cdot (1 - S) \cdot (\mathbf{B}_{f_{\text{RT}}} \odot \mathbf{M}_+ - (1 - \mathbf{B}_{f_{\text{RT}}}) \odot \mathbf{M}_-) , \qquad (5)$$

where $\mathbf{M}_+$ and $\mathbf{M}_-$ specify the maximum increase and decrease for every token, i.e.

$$\mathbf{M}_+ = \max(\mathbf{Q}\mathbf{K}^T) - \mathbf{Q}\mathbf{K}^T \quad \text{and} \quad \mathbf{M}_- = \mathbf{Q}\mathbf{K}^T - \min(\mathbf{Q}\mathbf{K}^T) . \qquad (6)$$

In addition to cross-attention control, DenseDiffusion [12] also includes self-attention control using a similar method.

4 Approach

In this work, we use the segmentation-based ControlNet on top of Stable Diffusion as it already provides us with a means to control image layout with high precision by specifying segmentation maps. Note that even though the image layout is controlled, it still leaves the model with freedom how to assign the objects mentioned in the text prompt to the regions. In this work we focus on investigating cross-attention control methods in conjunction with ControlNet to enable it to solve the task described in Sect. 2.

---
[4] Since the source code for [9] has not been made available at the time of this writing, we had to rely on the descriptions given in the paper for our implementation.

4.1 Cross-Attention Control in ControlNet

In a first attempt to enable ControlNet to solve the task defined in Sect. 2, we adapt and integrate several representative cross-attention control methods into ControlNet. More precisely, we implement the methods described in Sect. 3.3, and apply cross-attention control in both the control network as well as the main diffusion U-Net. Note that different layers of the U-Net work at different resolutions as the network consists of a stack of down-scaling layers, followed by up-scaling layers. Therefore, we down-scale the mask $\mathbf{B}_r$ as necessary.

4.2 Cross-Attention Control Design Considerations

The previously discussed cross-attention control methods have certain shortcomings. Firstly, most methods are sensitive to the selection of the time steps during which attention manipulation is performed and to what degree it is performed. Most methods studied here rely on the assumption that the image layout is determined in the initial denoising steps and do not modify attention in later generation stages. Such methods (e.g., DenseDiffusion and eDiff-I) therefore place a high degree of control in the initial stages of decoding and quickly drop it to near-zero values by roughly $t = 750$ (if generation starts with $t = T = 1000$). However, this procedure can still lead to concept bleeding in highly ambiguous cases, for example when generating objects of similar shapes and color. After the initial heavily controlled stage, the model becomes uncontrolled and fine details such as object texture can no longer be clearly assigned when multiple similar objects are present. Thus, it is desirable to have an attention control method that remains active throughout the denoising process while still minimizing image quality degradation.

A second consideration is that at different heads of different layers and at different generation stages, the attention weights behave differently and indiscriminate boosting of attention can lead to a decrease in image quality and a higher sensitivity to the attention control schedule. The exception is CAC, since it only disables attention to the descriptions of irrelevant regions throughout the entire generation process.

Thirdly, when simply disabling attention to irrelevant tokens, like CAC, the attention "mass" is either mostly transfered to the most probable tokens or is lost. This can be problematic when the initial random image x_T leads the model to mostly attend to the wrong region descriptions, in this case, attention to the wrong regions is dropped but the attention weights to the correct region remain at their initial (possibly low) values. In addition, in CAC-style control, the attention weights no longer sum to one.

4.3 Attention Redistribution

To address these shortcomings, we propose a cross-attention manipulation method that we refer to as **cross-attention redistribution (CA-Redist)**

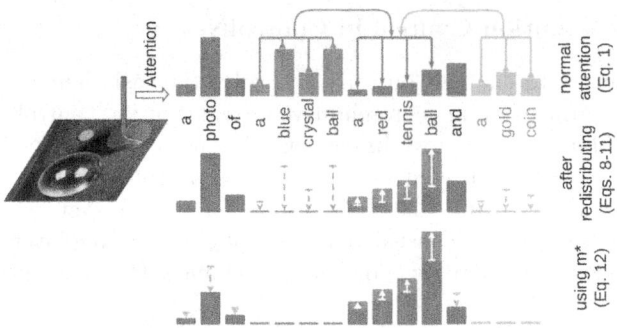

Fig. 2. A diagram illustrating attention redistribution and attention boosting.

and that redistributes attention from irrelevant region descriptions to the relevant one. Concretely, this is accomplished by (1) computing the total amount of region-specific attention m, which can vary across heads and layers, (2) separately normalizing region-specific and region-agnostic attention weights to obtain $\mathbf{A}_{\text{local}}$ and $\mathbf{A}_{\text{global}}$, respectively, and (3) mixing the two resulting attention distributions using $m \in [0,1]^{H \cdot W}$. Note that this is done separately for every pixel, and that it is assumed that every pixel in the image is assigned to exactly one region description. Figure 2 provides an illustration of CA-Redist. This method is defined as follows:

$$\mathbf{A} = m \odot \mathbf{A}_{\text{local}} + (1 - m) \odot \mathbf{A}_{\text{global}} \ , \quad \text{with} \tag{7}$$

$$\mathbf{A}_{\text{local}} = \text{softmax}\left(\log(\mathbf{B}_{f_{\text{RT}}}) + \frac{\mathbf{Q}\mathbf{K}^T}{\sqrt{d}} \right) \ , \tag{8}$$

$$\mathbf{A}_{\text{global}} = \text{softmax}\left(\log(1 - \mathbf{B}_R) + \frac{\mathbf{Q}\mathbf{K}^T}{\sqrt{d}} \right) \quad \text{and} \tag{9}$$

$$m = \sum_{n=0}^{N} \mathbf{A}[\cdot, n] \cdot \mathbf{B}_R[\cdot, n] \ , \tag{10}$$

where $\mathbf{A}$ is defined as in Eq. 1, $\mathbf{A}[\cdot, n]$ is its n-th column, and $\mathbf{B}_R$ and $\mathbf{B}_{f_{\text{RT}}}$ are as defined earlier in Sect. 3.3. Thus, $\mathbf{A}_{\text{global}}$ computes an attention distribution over all tokens except those in any region description and $\mathbf{A}_{\text{local}}$ is zero everywhere except the correct region description. The mixture between the two makes sure to retain the same attention weights for the non-region tokens (in other words, keeping $\mathbf{A}_{\text{global}} \approx \mathbf{A}$ for tokens where $\mathbf{B}_R$ is zero).

The attention to relevant region-specific parts of the prompt can further be increased by replacing m with m^* as defined below, where m can be modified in two ways, using hyper-parameters $W_m \geq 0$ and $W_a \geq 0$ that boost the attention to relevant parts of the prompt multiplicatively or additively, respectively.

$$m^* = \min\left(1, \max\left(0, m \cdot (1 + W_m \cdot W'') + W_a \cdot W'' \cdot (1 - S)\right)\right) \ , \tag{11}$$

where S is the fraction of the surface area that a region occupies in the image (same as defined for DenseDiffusion) and W'' specifies the schedule of attention boost in CA-Redist and depends on the current denoising step t:

$$W'' = \begin{cases} 1 & \text{if } t \geq T_s \\ \frac{1}{2} + \frac{1}{2}\sin(\pi \cdot \frac{t-T_{\text{thr}}}{T_s - T_e}) & \text{if } T_s > t > T_e \\ 0 & \text{if } T_e \geq t \end{cases} \quad (12)$$

with $T_s = T_{\text{thr}} + RT/2$ and $T_e = T_{\text{thr}} - RT/2$. (13)

This schedule is controlled by the threshold step $T_{\text{thr}} \in [1..T]$ and the threshold softness $R \in [0, 1]$. Unless otherwise specified, in our experiments, we set $T_{\text{thr}} = T$. This simplifies the schedule to the following:

$$W'' = \begin{cases} \frac{1}{2} + \frac{1}{2}\sin(\pi \cdot \frac{t-T}{R \cdot T}) & \text{if } t > T \cdot (1 - R/2) \\ 0 & \text{otherwise} \end{cases} \quad (14)$$

In Eq. 12, t starts from T so attention boost is active more in the initial stages of denoising with a value between zero and one and gradually decays to zero as denoising progresses. This schedule for $R = 0.4$ is illustrated in Fig. 3.

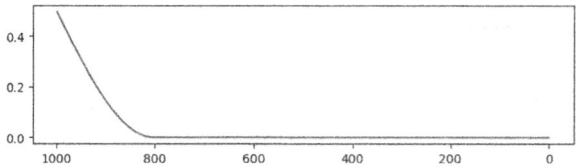

Fig. 3. CA-Redist schedule W'' if $T_{\text{thr}} = T$ and $R = 0.4$.

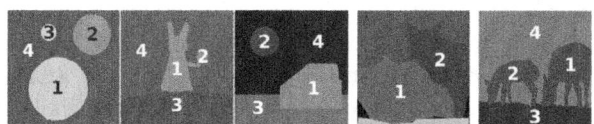

Fig. 4. Layouts used for qualitative comparison throughout this paper (Fig. 5 and Fig. 6).

Multiplicative manipulation using W_m is stronger for heads with higher attention weights to region descriptions and remains low for those that attended to tokens outside of any region description. Additive manipulation using W_a forces attention to increase to region-specific tokens in all heads. Note that the computational overhead this attention manipulation introduces is similar to other attention control methods, and is negligible compared to the computational requirements of running the diffusion model.

5 Experiments

We compare the following methods of cross-attention control on top of the (lightly fine-tuned) ControlNet: (1) eDiff-I, (2) CAC, (3) DenseDiffusion (DD), and (4) CA-Redist. We also compare against the original implementations of GLIGEN[5] and DenseDiffusion[6] as points of reference of related work that does not rely on ControlNet. Note that we used the main variant of GLIGEN that takes as input bounding boxes and localized descriptions.[7] Comparison with SceneComposer [33] and SpaText [1] was not possible because the code and data have not been publicly released at the time of this writing. It must also be noted that both these approaches have been extensively trained, whereas our proposed method also works training-free with segmentation- and scribble-based ControlNet. In our experiments, we did minimal fine-tuning of a small part of ControlNet on a readily available dataset to align color schemes since we found it slightly improved image quality in our early experiments. To adapt to the task, we fine-tuned the segmentation ControlNet on panoptic segmentation data from COCO2017 [17] using randomized colors. More details on the experimental setup can be found in Supplement A.2 . Our code is available at https://github.com/lukovnikov/ca-redist.

5.1 Qualitative Study

A qualitative comparison of the different attention control methods is presented in Fig. 5. The layouts used are specified by the first three images in Fig. 4, where the numbers correspond to the numbered phrases in the prompts in Fig. 5. For a qualitative comparison using ControlNet trained for sketch conditioning (scribbles), please see Supplement D .

Comparison of Baselines: The baselines that don't rely on ControlNet appear to fail at the task with challenging inputs. Note that **GLIGEN** [15] only allows to use bounding boxes for conditioning in image generation with localized descriptions, so the exact layout is not expected to match. But despite enabling its adapter throughout the entire generation process ($\tau = 1$), GLIGEN mostly failed to assign the right textures and colors to objects for the challenging prompts involving multiple round objects. This can be speculated to be attributable to the fact that during training, GLIGEN is insufficiently exposed to such challenging examples and doesn't learn to take into account localized descriptions in later generation steps.

In comparison, the original implementation of **DenseDiffusion** [12] is better at assigning objects to regions. However, we see it fail in examples where the shape and colors in the early generation stages are ambiguous, as illustrated in

---

[5] As provided in the Huggingface Diffusers library.
[6] https://github.com/naver-ai/densediffusion.
[7] GLIGEN also provides a variant that takes a segmentation map as conditioning but it does not use localized textual descriptions so it is unfit for comparison.

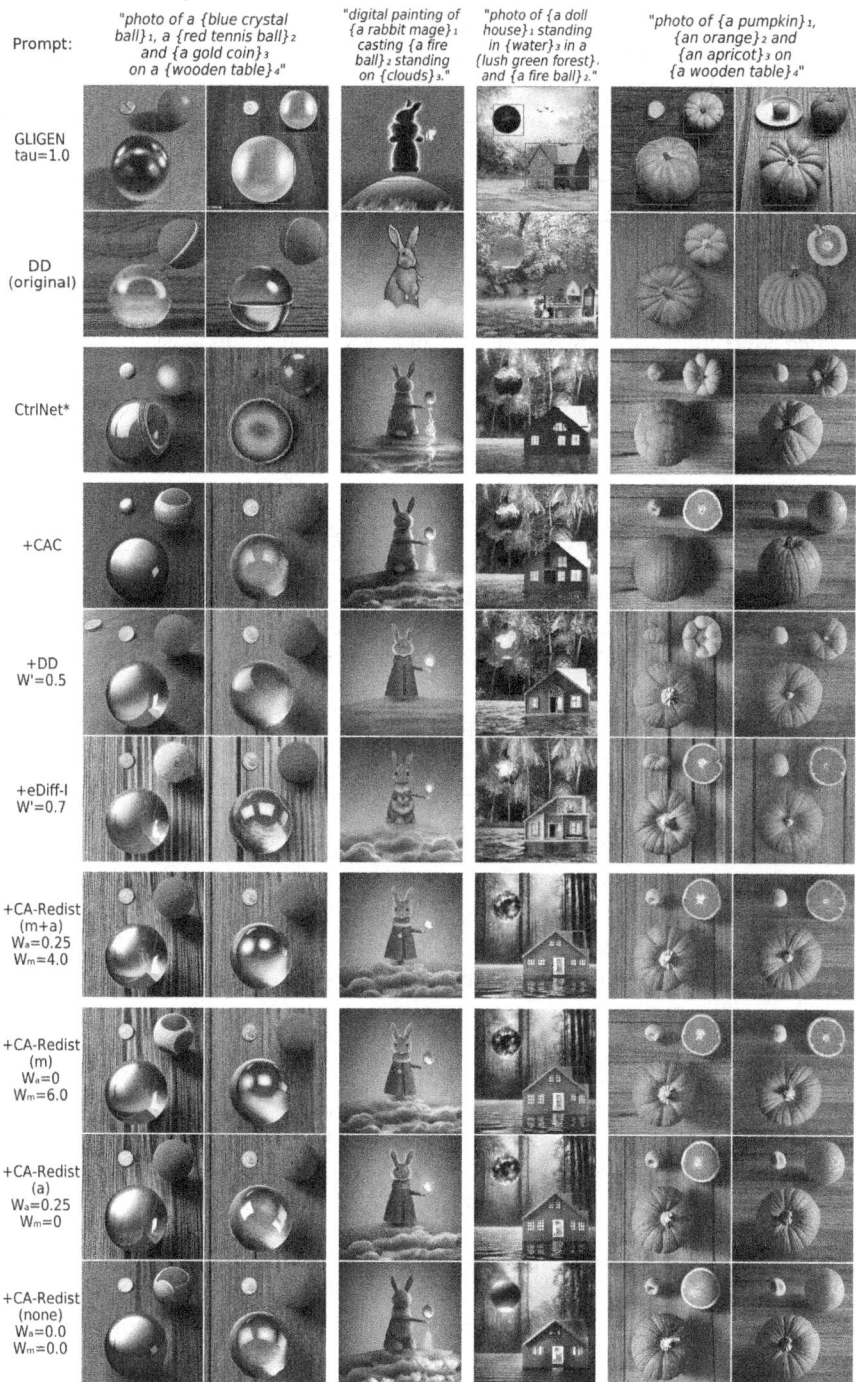

Fig. 5. A qualitative comparison of different cross-attention control methods in ControlNet-extended Stable Diffusion 1.5. See Fig. 4 for layout specification.

the last two columns of Fig. 5. Also, it seems to ignore smaller object masks and does not adhere to mask boundaries as precisely as ControlNet (however, it must be noted that DenseDiffusion is completely training-free).

Finally, **plain ControlNet**, pre-trained with semantic segmentation labels, and fine-tuned on COCO2017 data for panoptic segmentation with randomized colors (referred to as ControlNet* in the figures and tables), can already assign the correct description to the correct region if the mask shapes are distinctive enough. This is illustrated in the fifth column, where all shapes can be unambiguously matched with a region description (e.g. "fire ball" is a circular shape, "doll house" is a trapezoid shape). However, when faced with ambiguity in layout specification (e.g. three circles), plain ControlNet randomly assigns objects and colors and suffers from concept bleeding (for example, assigning "*gold*" to a ball whereas we described a gold coin). Additionally, it can struggle when faced with improbable descriptions, such as a rabbit mage standing on clouds.

Comparison of Attention Control Methods: For **CAC**-style control, we observe that it does help resolve ambiguity and improve grounding behavior, but not very consistently across different seeds. In the first column, for example, the assignment completely failed. We also see that it does not resolve the issue of improbable assignments, leaving the images largely the same as plain ControlNet for the rabbit example. We also observed that small objects are sometimes not generated.

The other methods appear to provide satisfactory degree of control over object assignment in most cases. However, as we can see in the last two columns of Fig. 5, for the prompt "*an apricot, a pumpkin, and an orange*", **DenseDiffusion** and **eDiff-I** suffer from the aforementioned control scheduling problems, where objects of similar color and shape are not assigned correctly. Both generate two or three pumpkins, ignoring other described objects. We observed similar behavior with other test cases.

In contrast, CA-Redist adheres to localized descriptions better than DenseDiffusion and eDiff-I in more challenging control scenarios (objects of similar shape and color) while maintaining image quality.

Ablation: The bottom three rows of Fig. 5 show an ablation of CA-Redist, which shows it is still effective when only W_m is non-zero (CA-Redist (m)) or only W_a is non-zero (CA-Redist (a)). When both are zero (CA-Redist (none)), the images don't always satisfy all region descriptions. This shows that some form of attention boosting is still necessary.

Qualitative Analysis with Objects from COCO-2017: A comparison of different methods using object shapes from COCO-2017 examples is shown in Fig. 6. Note that baselines (+CAC, +DD, +eDiff-I) fail to always assign the correct descriptions to the right locations and properly separate features. For example, for cats and dogs, +DD generates two cats and eDiff-I, while largely performing quite well still assigns a mixture of cat- and dog-like features to the region annotated as a "grey dog".

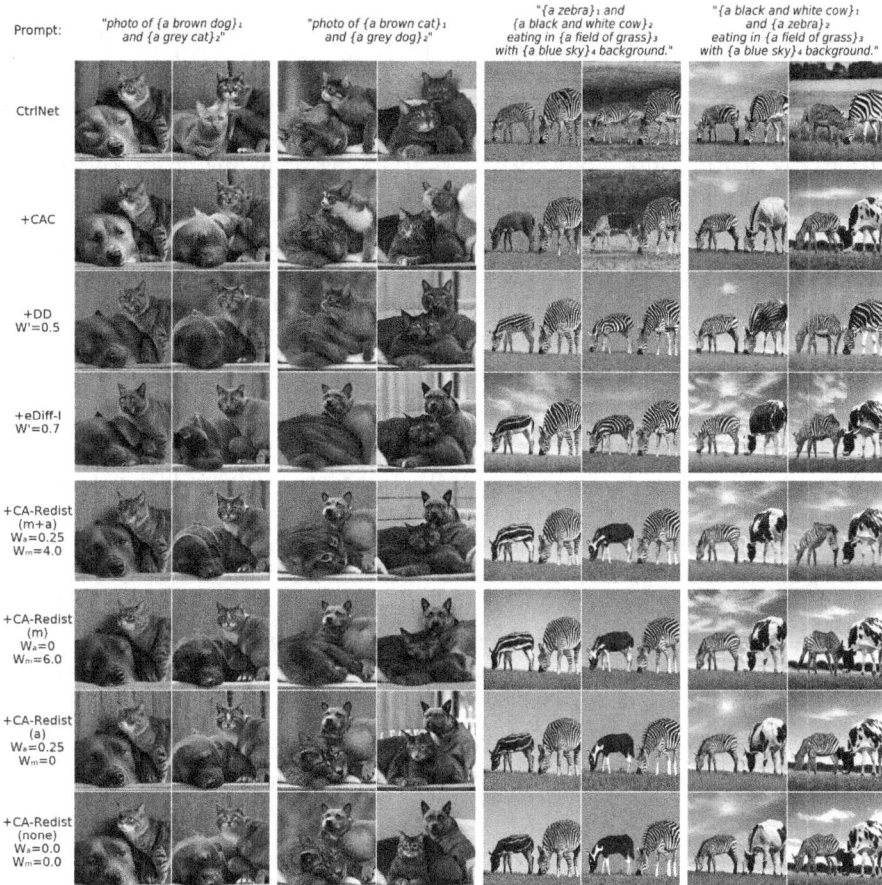

Fig. 6. A qualitative comparison with complex shapes. In the example for cats and dogs, region 1 corresponds to the bottom left region and region 2 to the region on the right. In the example for cows and zebras, region 1 corresponds to the animal shape on the right and region 2 to the animal shape on the left. For exact layout specifications, see Fig. 4. We can observe some concept bleeding for different methods, especially evident in the cows and zebras examples, even for CA-Redist. Concept bleeding is more severe for the DenseDiffusion and eDiff-I baselines while the CAC baseline generated a brown animal instead of a black and white cow.

5.2 Quantitative Study

Automatic evaluation for this task is challenging because of the inherent difficulty of evaluating image quality and faithfulness to a localized description. Moreover, there is a lack of standardized open-sourced datasets and evaluation methodology. Nevertheless, to be able to perform a quantitative analysis, we constructed a challenging dataset of simple scenes with multiple objects (SIMPLESCENES) that allows to estimate image faithfulness of localized descriptions as well as image quality, and additionally investigate image quality on COCO2017.

SIMPLESCENES. Our goals are two-fold: measuring (1) image quality to detect image degradation and (2) faithfulness to localized descriptions.[8] Since COCO images frequently contain objects with overlapping bounding boxes, these could pollute metrics for measuring conformity to localized descriptions.

Dataset: For this reason, and to focus on more challenging cases, we create the SIMPLESCENES dataset. The dataset consists of 124 examples, each containing 3–4 objects and randomized descriptions, which proved to be challenging for the tested methods. The dataset is described in more detail in Supplement A.1.

Metrics: We use the following evaluation methodology for this dataset. For measuring general image quality, we use reference-free (since we don't have reference images) image quality assessment methods, such as BRISQUE [19] and MANIQA [32], as well as the LAION Aesthetics Score predictor [25]. For measuring conformity to localized description, we use the localized CLIP (LocalCLIP) Logits and Probabilities, which are computed as follows: For every object mask, we crop the image to contain only the masked region of the generated image, and use CLIP to compute text-image similarities between all the localized phrases (e.g. "blue crystal ball") and all the cropped object images. The reported CLIP Logits correlate linearly with the similarities while the reported CLIP Probabilities result from normalizing the logits over all objects in the image.

Results: The numbers reported in Table 1 demonstrate that CA-Redist does not suffer from image quality loss, with all image quality metrics being on par with

Table 1. Image quality and localized prompt faithfullness using our SIMPLESCENES dataset. Arrows indicate if higher (↑) or lower (↓) is better. The format is MEAN$^{\pm\text{STD}}$(BEST), over five seeds.

	BRISQUE ↓	LAION Aest ↑	LocalCLIP Logits ↑	LocalCLIP Prob. ↑
GLIGEN ($\tau = 1$)	30.56 $^{\pm 1.78}$ (10.23)	5.51 $^{\pm 0.04}$ (6.08)	21.60 $^{\pm 0.17}$ (23.19)	0.33 $^{\pm 0.01}$ (0.50)
DD (original)	32.69 $^{\pm 1.14}$ (12.96)	5.76 $^{\pm 0.03}$ (6.33)	21.52 $^{\pm 0.06}$ (22.83)	0.45 $^{\pm 0.01}$ (0.58)
ControlNet*	25.23 $^{\pm 1.46}$ (7.65)	5.70 $^{\pm 0.02}$ (6.25)	20.99 $^{\pm 0.12}$ (22.60)	0.25 $^{\pm 0.01}$ (0.41)
+CAC	26.97 $^{\pm 1.02}$ (8.99)	5.71 $^{\pm 0.05}$ (6.29)	22.28 $^{\pm 0.23}$ (23.84)	0.44 $^{\pm 0.02}$ (0.61)
+DD (w=0.5)	24.50 $^{\pm 1.94}$ (8.39)	5.74 $^{\pm 0.05}$ (6.21)	22.93 $^{\pm 0.11}$ (24.18)	0.48 $^{\pm 0.02}$ (0.59)
+eDiff-I (w=0.5)	23.75 $^{\pm 1.15}$ (10.86)	5.73 $^{\pm 0.02}$ (6.22)	23.36 $^{\pm 0.13}$ (24.43)	0.58 $^{\pm 0.02}$ (0.68)
+CA-Redist (m+a)	25.40 $^{\pm 2.29}$ (10.10)	5.74 $^{\pm 0.02}$ (6.22)	23.77 $^{\pm 0.11}$ (24.89)	0.62 $^{\pm 0.01}$ (0.73)
+CA-Redist (m)	27.37 $^{\pm 2.00}$ (10.54)	5.68 $^{\pm 0.05}$ (6.18)	23.70 $^{\pm 0.13}$ (24.80)	0.62 $^{\pm 0.01}$ (0.72)
+CA-Redist (a)	24.86 $^{\pm 1.33}$ (8.41)	5.69 $^{\pm 0.01}$ (6.20)	23.52 $^{\pm 0.07}$ (24.74)	0.58 $^{\pm 0.01}$ (0.70)
+CA-Redist (none)	25.13 $^{\pm 1.54}$ (8.14)	5.65 $^{\pm 0.04}$ (6.20)	23.26 $^{\pm 0.04}$ (24.60)	0.56 $^{\pm 0.01}$ (0.70)

---

[8] ControlNet follows segmentation map conditioning very well so we do not evaluate this.

Table 2. FID and KID w.r.t. COCO2017 validation images.

	FID ↓	KID ($\times 10^3$) ↓
GLIGEN ($\tau = 1.0$)	23.84	4.289
DD (original)	37.68	7.923
ControlNet*	28.84	5.150
+CAC	27.42	4.916
+DD (w=0.5)	28.30	5.422
+eDiff-I (w=0.5)	28.72	6.074
+CA-Redist (m+a)	27.11	5.276
+CA-Redist (m)	27.78	5.547
+CA-Redist (a)	26.15	4.618

plain ControlNet. BRISQUE values are significantly lower than that for GLIGEN and DenseDiffusion. Regarding MANIQA numbers, all tested methods achieved MANIQA scores of 0.665 ± 0.015, thus not showing any measurable image quality differences among the tested methods. We did not report these numbers in Table 1 because of space constraints. On the other hand, the LocalCLIP metrics indicate that CA-Redist is superior when it comes to conformity to localized descriptions: while plain ControlNet achieves lower values than GLIGEN and DenseDiffusion, ControlNet with CA-Redist leads to a significant improvement in LocalCLIP scores.

Ablation: From the three ablation settings (CA-Redist variants (a), (m) and (none)), it appears that moderately boosting attention does not result in measurable image quality decrease. However, no attention boost (CA-Redist (none)) results in slightly lower faithfulness to the localized prompt (as indicated by the localized CLIP metrics), which confirms our qualitative observations.

COCO2017 To further investigate image quality, we report FID [10] and KID [5] scores between 5000 samples generated using the segmentation maps from the COCO2017 validation set and the corresponding 5000 real images in Table 2. Even though ControlNet has worse FID and KID than GLIGEN, the addition of CA control does not result in quality loss measurable by these metrics. Note that GLIGEN and DenseDiffusion don't always adhere to the masks as closely as ControlNet since GLIGEN only uses bounding boxes instead of segmentation maps as input, and DenseDiffusion uses self-attention control. Thus, both don't follow the input segmentation maps as closely as ControlNet.

5.3 Image Quality vs Control Strength

In Fig. 8 are shown some images generated using eDiff-I-based and Dens Diffusion-based attention control. We can observe that at lower attention control strengths (controlled by the inference hyper-parameter W'), eDiff-I does

Fig. 7. A qualitative comparison between sketch-based ControlNet with and without CA-Redist. See Supplement D for a full comparison.

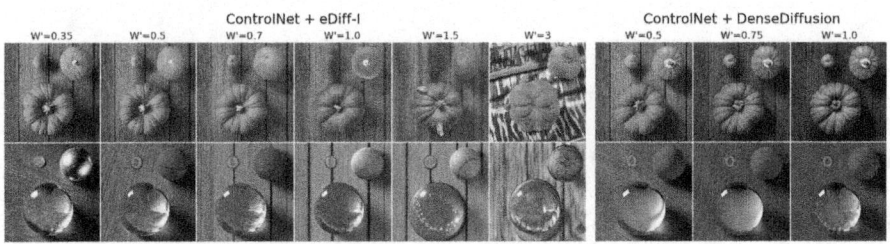

Fig. 8. Image quality with increasing control strength for eDiff-I and DenseDiffusion cross-attention control with ControlNet.

not correctly follow localized descriptions. Fidelity increases with increasing W', however, it comes at a cost to image quality, which is particularly noticeably for higher values. For DenseDiffusion, increasing W' to its maximum value of 1.0 does not improve fidelity to localized descriptions but also introduces more subtle image quality changes.

5.4 CA-Redist for Sketch-Based Control

We performed additional analysis into using sketch (scribble) conditioning instead of segmentation maps, as well as using more complex shapes. In Fig. 7, we show that CA-Redist also performs well with ControlNet trained for sketch conditioning (scribbles). A full qualitative comparison is provided in Supplement D.

6 Related Work

Since the early works on controllable image synthesis [7,11], the emergence of neural-network based generative models opened new frontiers for this task, especially with methods like ControlNet [34] and GLIGEN [15]. Several works have addressed tasks similar to ours with GANs [16,28,39]. However, these works either do not use descriptions or are limited to a restricted set of object classes.

More recently, several works have proposed methods [1,3,4,6,8,9,12,18,21, 31,33,36] for image synthesis with localized descriptions and regions specified by masks or bounding boxes. Several works [1,14,30,33,38] modify and train the diffusion model or adapters to condition on localized prompts (and localized reference images). Several training-free methods for this task have also been proposed [3,4,6,8,9,12,18,21,31], many of which rely on manipulating cross-attention (and self-attention) in some way.

7 Conclusion

The analysis performed in this work indicates that ControlNet is able to interpret region descriptions when mask shapes are un-ambiguous. However, when faced with similarly shaped masks, it no longer has sufficient information to correctly interpret the prompt. In such cases, additional input from the user can be used to specify which objects should be generated where. However, ControlNet is not able to process such inputs. As we demonstrate, this can be solved by integrating cross-attention control. We found, however, that some design choices are crucial in more ambiguous conditions, such as when generating multiple different objects of similar shape and color. To cover these cases better, it is important to prevent cross-attention from attending to tokens from irrelevant region descriptions throughout the *entire* generation process. Taking these considerations into account, we develop a novel cross-attention control method that shows superior generation results in our qualitative and quantitative analysis. For the latter we created a small but challenging data set, which can serve as a testbed for future work.

An interesting avenue for future work would be looking into hierarchical regions with localized descriptions that specify the objects as well as their parts (e.g. specifying where a tiger should be drawn and where its eye). It is not clear how well the current attention control methods support overlapping regions. In addition, the segmentation-based ControlNet we used for most of our study does not support overlapping regions and tries to strictly follow the region outlines.

Acknowledgments. We would like to thank all the anonymous reviewers for their feedback, which helped improve this work. This work was funded by the Ministry of Culture and Science of Northrhine-Westphalia as part of the Lamarr Fellow Network.

References

1. Avrahami, O., et al.: Spatext: spatio-textual representation for controllable image generation. In: Proceedings of the IEEE/CVF Conference on Computer Vision and Pattern Recognition, pp. 18370–18380 (2023)

2. Bahdanau, D., Cho, K., Bengio, Y.: Neural machine translation by jointly learning to align and translate. CoRR **abs/1409.0473** (2014). https://api.semanticscholar.org/CorpusID:11212020
3. Balaji, Y., et al.: ediff-i: text-to-image diffusion models with an ensemble of expert denoisers. arXiv preprint arXiv:2211.01324 (2022)
4. Bar-Tal, O., Yariv, L., Lipman, Y., Dekel, T.: Multidiffusion: fusing diffusion paths for controlled image generation (2023)
5. Bińkowski, M., Sutherland, D.J., Arbel, M., Gretton, A.: Demystifying mmd gans. arXiv preprint arXiv:1801.01401 (2018)
6. Chen, M., Laina, I., Vedaldi, A.: Training-free layout control with cross-attention guidance. arXiv preprint arXiv:2304.03373 (2023)
7. Chen, T., Cheng, M.M., Tan, P., Shamir, A., Hu, S.M.: Sketch2photo: internet image montage. ACM Trans. Graph. (TOG) **28**(5), 1–10 (2009)
8. Couairon, G., Careil, M., Cord, M., Lathuilière, S., Verbeek, J.: Zero-shot spatial layout conditioning for text-to-image diffusion models. In: Proceedings of the IEEE/CVF International Conference on Computer Vision, pp. 2174–2183 (2023)
9. He, Y., Salakhutdinov, R., Kolter, J.Z.: Localized text-to-image generation for free via cross attention control. arXiv preprint arXiv:2306.14636 (2023)
10. Heusel, M., Ramsauer, H., Unterthiner, T., Nessler, B., Hochreiter, S.: Gans trained by a two time-scale update rule converge to a local Nash equilibrium. In: Advances in Neural Information Processing Systems, vol. 30 (2017)
11. Johnson, M., Brostow, G.J., Shotton, J., Arandjelovic, O., Kwatra, V., Cipolla, R.: Semantic photo synthesis. In: Computer Graphics Forum, vol. 25, pp. 407–413. Wiley Online Library (2006)
12. Kim, Y., Lee, J., Kim, J.H., Ha, J.W., Zhu, J.Y.: Dense text-to-image generation with attention modulation. In: Proceedings of the IEEE/CVF International Conference on Computer Vision, pp. 7701–7711 (2023)
13. Kingma, D.P., Ba, J.: Adam: a method for stochastic optimization. arXiv preprint arXiv:1412.6980 (2014)
14. Li, L., et al.: Omnibooth: learning latent control for image synthesis with multimodal instruction. arXiv preprint arXiv:2410.04932 (2024)
15. Li, Y., et al.: Gligen: open-set grounded text-to-image generation. In: Proceedings of the IEEE/CVF Conference on Computer Vision and Pattern Recognition, pp. 22511–22521 (2023)
16. Li, Z., Wu, J., Koh, I., Tang, Y., Sun, L.: Image synthesis from layout with locality-aware mask adaption. In: Proceedings of the IEEE/CVF International Conference on Computer Vision, pp. 13819–13828 (2021)
17. Lin, T.-Y., et al.: Microsoft COCO: common objects in context. In: Fleet, D., Pajdla, T., Schiele, B., Tuytelaars, T. (eds.) ECCV 2014. LNCS, vol. 8693, pp. 740–755. Springer, Cham (2014). https://doi.org/10.1007/978-3-319-10602-1_48
18. Mao, J., Wang, X.: Training-free location-aware text-to-image synthesis. arXiv preprint arXiv:2304.13427 (2023)
19. Mittal, A., Moorthy, A.K., Bovik, A.C.: No-reference image quality assessment in the spatial domain. IEEE Trans. Image Process. **21**(12), 4695–4708 (2012)
20. Mou, C., et al.: T2i-adapter: learning adapters to dig out more controllable ability for text-to-image diffusion models. arXiv preprint arXiv:2302.08453 (2023)
21. Phung, Q., Ge, S., Huang, J.B.: Grounded text-to-image synthesis with attention refocusing. arXiv preprint arXiv:2306.05427 (2023)
22. Radford, A., et al.: Learning transferable visual models from natural language supervision. In: International Conference on Machine Learning (ICLR) (2021)

23. Rombach, R., Blattmann, A., Lorenz, D., Esser, P., Ommer, B.: High-resolution image synthesis with latent diffusion models. In: IEEE / CVF Computer Vision and Pattern Recognition Conference (CVPR) (2022)
24. Ronneberger, O., Fischer, P., Brox, T.: U-Net: convolutional networks for biomedical image segmentation. In: Navab, N., Hornegger, J., Wells, W.M., Frangi, A.F. (eds.) MICCAI 2015. LNCS, vol. 9351, pp. 234–241. Springer, Cham (2015). https://doi.org/10.1007/978-3-319-24574-4_28
25. Schuhmann, C., et al.: LAION-5B: an open large-scale dataset for training next generation image-text models. In: Conference on Neural Information Processing Systems (NeurIPS) (2022)
26. Simo, R.: Paint-with-words, implemented with stable diffusion (2023). https://github.com/cloneofsimo/paint-with-words-sd
27. Song, J., Meng, C., Ermon, S.: Denoising diffusion implicit models. In: International Conference on Learning Representations (ICLR) (2022)
28. Sushko, V., Schönfeld, E., Zhang, D., Gall, J., Schiele, B., Khoreva, A.: You only need adversarial supervision for semantic image synthesis. arXiv preprint arXiv:2012.04781 (2020)
29. Vaswani, A., et al.: Attention is all you need. In: Advances in Neural Information Processing Systems, vol. 30 (2017)
30. Wang, X., Darrell, T., Rambhatla, S.S., Girdhar, R., Misra, I.: Instancediffusion: instance-level control for image generation. In: Proceedings of the IEEE/CVF Conference on Computer Vision and Pattern Recognition, pp. 6232–6242 (2024)
31. Xiao, J., Li, L., Lv, H., Wang, S., Huang, Q.: R&b: region and boundary aware zero-shot grounded text-to-image generation. arXiv preprint arXiv:2310.08872 (2023)
32. Yang, S., et al.: Maniqa: multi-dimension attention network for no-reference image quality assessment. In: Proceedings of the IEEE/CVF Conference on Computer Vision and Pattern Recognition, pp. 1191–1200 (2022)
33. Zeng, Y., et al.: Scenecomposer: any-level semantic image synthesis. In: Proceedings of the IEEE/CVF Conference on Computer Vision and Pattern Recognition, pp. 22468–22478 (2023)
34. Zhang, L., Rao, A., Agrawala, M.: Adding conditional control to text-to-image diffusion models. In: Proceedings of the IEEE/CVF International Conference on Computer Vision, pp. 3836–3847 (2023)
35. Zhao, S., et al.: Uni-controlnet: all-in-one control to text-to-image diffusion models. arXiv preprint arXiv:2305.16322 (2023)
36. Zheng, G., Zhou, X., Li, X., Qi, Z., Shan, Y., Li, X.: Layoutdiffusion: controllable diffusion model for layout-to-image generation. In: Proceedings of the IEEE/CVF Conference on Computer Vision and Pattern Recognition, pp. 22490–22499 (2023)
37. Zhou, B., et al.: Semantic understanding of scenes through the ade20k dataset. Int. J. Comput. Vis. **127**(3), 302–321 (2019)
38. Zhou, D., Li, Y., Ma, F., Yang, Z., Yang, Y.: Migc++: advanced multi-instance generation controller for image synthesis. IEEE Trans. Pattern Anal. Mach. Intell. (2024)
39. Zhu, P., Abdal, R., Qin, Y., Wonka, P.: Sean: image synthesis with semantic region-adaptive normalization. In: Proceedings of the IEEE/CVF Conference on Computer Vision and Pattern Recognition, pp. 5104–5113 (2020)

Federated Learning

FedCluLearn: Federated Continual Learning Using Stream Micro-cluster Indexing Scheme

Milena Angelova[1(✉)], Veselka Boeva[1], Shahrooz Abghari[1], Selim Ickin[2], and Xiaoyu Lan[2]

[1] Blekinge Institute of Technology, Karlskrona, Sweden
{milena.angelova,veselka.boeva,shahrooz.abghari}@bth.se
[2] Ericsson AB, Stockholm, Sweden
{selim.ickin,xiaoyu.lan}@ericsson.com

Abstract. Artificial Neural Networks (NNs) are unable to learn tasks continually using a single model, which leads to forgetting old knowledge, known as *catastrophic forgetting*. This is one of the shortcomings that usually plague intelligent systems based on NN models. Federated Learning (FL) is a decentralized approach to training machine learning models on multiple local clients without exchanging raw data. A paradigm that handles model learning in both settings, federated and continual, is known as Federated Continual Learning (FCL). In this work, we propose a novel FCL algorithm, called FedCluLearn, which uses a stream micro-cluster indexing scheme to deal with catastrophic forgetting. FedCluLearn interprets the federated training process as a stream clustering scenario. It stores statistics, similar to micro-clusters in stream clustering algorithms, about the learned concepts at the server and updates them at each training round to reflect the current local updates of the clients. FedCluLearn uses only active concepts in each training round to build the global model, meaning it temporarily forgets the knowledge that is not relevant to the current situation. In addition, the proposed algorithm is flexible in that it can consider the age of local updates to reflect the greater importance of more recent data. The proposed FCL approach has been benchmarked against three baseline algorithms by evaluating its performance in several control and real-world data experiments. The implementation of FedCluLearn and the experimental results are available at https://github.com/milenaangeloval/FedCluLearn.

Keywords: Federated continual learning · Catastrophic forgetting · Concept drift · Data stream clustering · Time series data

---

This research was funded partly by the Knowledge Foundation, Sweden, through the Human-Centered Intelligent Realities (HINTS) Profile Project (contract 20220068).

1 Introduction

Federated Continual Learning (FCL) is built upon various decentralized devices, such as the Internet of Things (IoT) or smartphones, that constantly produce data to train models. Concept drift is a challenge for these models, as it leads to unpredictable changes in the statistical characteristics of the data over time. These changes can occur due to factors such as shifting user behavior or external circumstances. As a result, models can quickly become outdated when the data evolves. Therefore, it is crucial to implement methods for detecting and adapting to these changes. Artificial Neural Network (NN) models can suffer from a problem called *catastrophic forgetting*. This problem occurs when the model forgets information that it has learned in the past. This issue arises when the model is updated to work with data that has a different distribution than before. To tackle this problem, the concept of continual learning is introduced. Continual Learning (CL) aims to create models that can learn new information while keeping important insights from earlier data. It uses techniques such as memory replay mechanisms [25,27,31] to remind the model of past data and regularization techniques [4,18] to penalize changes that could harm previous learning. In [23], modular deep learning is considered as a promising solution to the challenges associated with developing models that specialize in multiple tasks.

In this study, we propose a novel FCL approach, called FedCluLearn, inspired by stream clustering algorithms such as CluStream [2] and ClusTree [15], to address the challenges of concept drift and catastrophic forgetting. These algorithms divide the clustering process into an *online* component that uses a micro-clustering approach to periodically store detailed summary statistics and an *offline* component that uses these summary statistics. In the context of FCL, the online component stores summary statistics about the locally learned concepts at each training round, while the offline component uses the stored information at the server to build the global model for that round. As discussed in [2], the efficient storage and use of statistical data for processing evolving data streams is a challenging problem. The authors introduce the concept of a pyramidal time frame combined with a micro-clustering approach. The pyramidal time frame helps determine the optimal moments for storing snapshots of statistical information. The micro-clusters maintain statistical information about the data locality, which defines a temporal extension of the cluster feature vector. FedCluLearn algorithm incorporates the micro-cluster indexing scheme, allowing for the storage of snapshots of the statistical information about local model updates during each global training round. In this study, the proposed FedCluLearn and its variation based on FedProx [17] optimization, called FedCluLearn-Prox, are studied and evaluated on real-world data. In addition, several control experiments are simulated to explore the algorithms' ability to deal with catastrophic forgetting and concept drift. The performance of FedCluLearn and FedCluLearn-Prox is compared to that of FedAvg [20], FedAtt [6], and FedProx [17].

2 Related Work

The main concepts in the CL paradigm include continuously acquiring, updating, accumulating, and exploiting knowledge [5,28]. CL algorithms have to deal with several challenges, such as catastrophic forgetting, data distribution shift, and issues related to imbalanced data and scarcity of labeled data. Catastrophic forgetting [7] refers to model performance degradation due to changes in data distribution cornering, e.g., the appearance of a new concept, which can lead to a downgrade in the model performance over previously learned concepts. Overall, catastrophic forgetting poses a significant challenge in the context of CL, which inherently involves learning incrementally from data. Additionally, there are other important challenges to consider, such as data distribution shifts, also known as concept drift. CL models must effectively handle such phenomena to prevent catastrophic forgetting [16]. The recent survey by Wang et al. [28] grouped CL methods into five major categories 1) regularization- 2) replay-, 3) optimization-, 4) representation-, and 5) architecture-based approaches.

Federated Learning (FL) is a distributed ML approach to train models on multiple local clients without exchanging raw data from client devices to a central server [20]. However, most existing solutions ignore the CL of incremental tasks from streaming data environments. An emerging paradigm that addresses model learning in both federated and continual learning environments is Federated Continual Learning (FCL). FCL combines the strengths of both FL and CL to establish a robust foundation for Edge-AI in dynamic and distributed environments [29]. The study [29] surveys FCL methods considering three federated task characteristics, namely class CL, domain CL, and task CL. While class CL aims to recognize new classes over time, it struggles with task identification, especially when combined with FL. Domain CL addresses the issue of dataset distribution across clients, with each client managing its private dataset as a separate domain. Concerning task CL, local clients learn various tasks and share their knowledge to develop a global model, which helps update and distribute knowledge about diverse tasks among them.

A recent survey on FCL presented in [30] discusses the integration between FL and CL, in particular via knowledge fusion. The study describes that local knowledge can be extracted from three main parts: data, models, and outcomes. Overall, existing knowledge fusion methods are divided into seven classes, where rehearsal and clustering belong to the data category, all gradients/parameters, parameter/layer isolation, and dynamic architecture belong to the models, and prototype and knowledge distillation concern output. The proposed classification considers FedAvg [20], under all gradients/parameters category, and FedProx [17] and FedAtt [6] to dynamic architecture. FedAvg [20] aggregates local model updates using a simple weighted averaging for building the global model. FedProx [17] is a generalization and re-parametrization of FedAvg with the capability to tackle heterogeneity in federated networks belonging to a dynamic architecture. FedAtt [6] builds a personalized FL method by incorporating attention-based grouping to facilitate collaborations among similar clients.

To improve the FL model performance, previous studies such as [10,11, 21], leverage clustering to group similar clients. While [10,21] use clustering approaches, they assume a fixed number of client groups throughout the training with no change in clients' data distribution. The study presented in [11] proposes grouping clients into clusters in a one-shot manner by measuring the similarity degrees among clients based on local models' weights. However, none of these works are suitable for the CL framework. The study [13] applies clustering to group the client models with similar concepts while running concept-matching algorithms that collaboratively train and update each model with data relevant to its concept.

According to the classification introduced in [29], the proposed FedCluLearn can be considered mostly related to the federated *domain* CL category, while it fits into the *model* class according to the classification in [30]. Compared with the solutions reviewed above, FedCluLearn proposes a new efficient way to deal with concept drift and catastrophic forgetting by storing and managing statistics about previously learned local models at the server. This allows FedCluLearn to make smart use of the stored information by aggregating into the global model only local updates currently relevant to the situation, and by choosing whether to use more recent or older clients' updates.

Researchers have extensively studied concept drift in data stream mining, proposing various detection and adaptation strategies. According to [9], there are two types of concept drift *virtual* and *real*. While virtual concept drift affects the input data distribution due to, e.g., imbalanced data, real concept drift is caused by, e.g., the appearance of new classes, concepts, or tasks, which can mainly be detected due to the model performance degradation. Agrahari et al. [3] classify drift detection methods into categories such as statistical significance, window-based, and model-dependent techniques. Similarly, Iwashita et al. [12] review approaches based on sliding windows, instance weighting, and classifier ensembles. Early works by Gama et al. [8] and Wadewale et al. [26] also define core types of concept drifts as *sudden, gradual, incremental, recurring*, and *blip or noise* where each of them affecting learning systems differently.

In the context of our FCL setting, we define concept drift at *local* and *global* levels. For example, sudden drift can affect one or more clients and potentially cause the global model's performance to deteriorate during global rounds. Gradual and incremental drifts can lead to inconsistencies among clients and cause the model to converge globally more slowly. Recurring drifts highlight the need for memory-aware strategies at local and global levels, as well as a model that can adapt to changes. Blips and noise require robust aggregation to prevent global degradation. Although the proposed FedCluLearn primarily addresses real concept drift, both virtual and real drifts [9] pose challenges for local and global models during the distributed training process.

3 FedCluLearn Algorithm

The main idea of the proposed FCL algorithm, FedCluLearn, is to interpret the FL training process as a stream clustering scenario. The FedCluLearn consists of two main phases: *Initialization* and *Iteration*. The different steps of these phases are described below. In addition, their pseudo codes are presented in Algorithm 1.

I. *FedCluLearn Initialization Phase* (see Algorithm 1):

I.1. Build the first global NN model by randomly initializing its weights.

I.2. Send the global model to the clients to be trained locally and return the local models' weights to the server.

I.3. Cluster the local models' weights into k clusters (initially learned concepts).

I.4. Compute the statistics of each cluster i, which initially has two feature vectors. One represents the first training round, and the other holds the overall cluster statistics up to the current training round. Note that a new feature vector will be created to store the statistics of each next round. The two types of feature vectors, CF_{ir} ($r = 1, 2, \ldots$) and $\boldsymbol{CF_{iT}}$, for cluster i are presented in (1). More details about them are given below.

$$\begin{array}{l} CF_{ir} = [\ n_{ir}\ \ LS_{ir}\ \ SS_{ir}\ \ F_{ir}] \\ \boldsymbol{CF_{iT}} = [\ \boldsymbol{n_{iT}}\ \ \boldsymbol{LS_{iT}}\ \ \boldsymbol{SS_{iT}}\ \ \boldsymbol{F_{iT}}] \end{array} \quad (1)$$

- *The feature vector CF_{ir}* created at training round r ($r = 1, 2, \ldots$) for cluster i contains the following information: (i) number of clients n_{ir}; (ii) linear sum of clients' local models' parameters LS_{ir}; (iii) squared sum of clients' local models' parameters SS_{ir}; (iv) an n dimensional binary vector F_{ir} showing which clients are assigned to this cluster at this training round, where n is the total number of clients.
- *The overall cluster feature vector $\boldsymbol{CF_{iT}}$* for cluster i can be obtained by $\sum_{r=1} CF_{ir}$. Note that here $\boldsymbol{F_{iT}}$ is an n-dimensional frequency vector showing clients' frequency of being assigned to this cluster.

In addition to the feature vectors, a cluster that receives new items during the current training round is flagged as the one representing an active concept.

I.5. The clusters (learned concepts) are organized in a list of pairs. The pair of cluster i, for $i \in \{1, 2, \ldots, k\}$, at the initialization phase contains two identical cluster feature vectors CF_{i1} and $\boldsymbol{CF_{iT}}$. In general, the first component of the pair stores the training rounds' feature vectors, while the second component contains only the total feature vector.

I.6. The global model G_r for the current round r is computed by averaging the recent linear sums of the active clusters $\left\{ \{LS_{it}\}_{t \in \mathcal{T}} \right\}_{i \in \mathcal{K}}$, where $\mathcal{K}$ is the set of clusters marked as active in this training round and $\mathcal{T}$ is the set of rounds considered in the global model aggregation. Note that $\mathcal{T}$ can include all training rounds or a percentage of the total training rounds. The expression used to calculate the global model G_r is given in (2).

$$G_r = \sum_{i \in \mathcal{K}} \sum_{t \in \mathcal{T}} LS_{it} / n_{it}. \quad (2)$$

Note that the formula in (2) can be replaced by another FL aggregation scheme. This way, as we show in our experiments, the used micro-cluster indexing scheme can be combined with other FL algorithms.

II. FedCluLearn Iteration Phase (see Algorithm 1):

II.1. At each training round r, for $r = 2, \ldots$, the global model G_{r-1} built at the previous round is sent to the clients to be trained locally, and after that, the local models' weights are returned to the server.

II.2. For each client's weights, the closest cluster is initially found. The Euclidean distance, or any other suitable distance measure, can be used to estimate the similarity between the client's weights and the mean vector of each cluster. The mean vector is calculated by using the cluster's overall feature vector.

II.3. When the nearest cluster is identified, two scenarios are evaluated: either the cluster is a suitable candidate to incorporate the client's updates, or the updates are too distant from this cluster, resulting in the formation of a new singleton cluster. There are different ways to figure out if the client belongs to the cluster, see Sect. 3.1 for more information.

II.4. The last step is to build the global model by applying (2). Then FedCluLearn returns to step *II.1*. Note that in this step, only active clusters are considered, meaning that FedCluLearn temporarily forgets the knowledge that is not relevant to the current situation.

Algorithm 1. FedCluLearn algorithm

1: **Input:** R: number of global rounds
2: Initialize w_0
3: **for** each round $r \in R$ **do**
4:    Send w_0 for local training
5:    **if** $r == 0$ **then**   ◁ **Initialization Phase**
6:       *clients* ← Send the clients' updates to the global server
7:       $C = \{C_1, C_2, ...C_i\}$ ← Group the *clients* in k clusters then
8:       **for** each $c \in C$ **do**
9:          *cStats* ← Calculate the LS, SS for cluster c
10:      *listOfPairs* ← Represent each $c \in cStats$ as pair $\langle CF_{cr}, CF_T \rangle$ **Eq. (1)**
11:      **end for**
12:   **else**
13:      **for** each $c \in listOfPairs$ **do**   ◁ **Iteration Phase**
14:         $maxSI$ ← Find the SI score between each *client* and the current c
15:         **if** $maxSI \geq threshold$ **then**
16:            *listOfPairs* ← Update the cluster's statistics for that cluster c
17:         **else**
18:            Create a new cluster c_{i+1} and append it to the *listOfPairs*
19:         **end if**
20:      **end for**
21:   **end if**
22:   Update the CF_T for each cluster $c \in listOfPairs$
23:   Build the G_r based on clusters' statistics from *listOfPairs*   **Eq. (2)**
24:   Send the G_r to all clients for the next training
25: **end for**

3.1 FedCluLearn Design Choices

In this section, we discuss the design choices of our FedCluLearn algorithm, first with respect to what information to store in the cluster feature (CF) vectors and when. Second, and related to this, is how to decide whether a client's model update belongs to its nearest micro-cluster centroid.

FedCluLearn stores a list of CF vectors, one at each training round, and updates the statistics of the overall CF vector, see (1). The overall CF vector contains information about: (i) the total number of clients assigned to the cluster; (ii) the linear sum of clients' model updates; (iii) the squared sum of clients' model updates; and (iv) the frequency with which the clients are assigned to that cluster. Information from (i) to (iv) is also stored in each CF vector kept at each training round and used to update the respective parts of the overall CF vector. Note that (i) and (ii) of the overall CF vector are used to compute the cluster centroid, which is needed to identify the closest cluster for each client's model updates at each training round. In addition, (i) and (ii) of the list of CF vectors stored at the training rounds of active clusters are used to compute the global model, see (2). Note that (iii) of the overall CF vector can be used, similar to the solution in [2], to define the maximum boundary of the cluster and determine whether a client update belongs to it. Finally, (iv) can be used to monitor and analyze clients' behavior during the federated training process, e.g., this can reveal clients with unstable behavior frequently changing their concepts.

In the current study, in step *I.3* k-means [19] is used for the initial grouping of the local models. Other clustering algorithms can also be applied, e.g., affinity propagation and Markov clustering [1]. In addition, in step *II.3* of FedCluLearn, we have used the Silhouette Index (SI) [24] to decide whether to assign a client model update to one of the existing clusters or to create a new cluster. The SI values vary between -1 and 1. FedCluLearn utilizes a predefined threshold to assess when the client's local model updates are similar enough, allowing them to be included in the statistics of an existing cluster. The threshold can be defined empirically before the start of the FL training or dynamically at each round.

4 Experimental Setup

4.1 Data and Implementation

We have used two real-world datasets, **5G network dataset** and **Air Quality dataset**, in our experiments.

The first is a **5G network dataset** [22] collected from three distinct urban locations in Barcelona, Spain, representing tourist (El Born), entertainment (Les Corts), and residential (Poble Sec) zones. These sites serve as individual FL nodes. The datasets preserve user anonymity and contain detailed traces of network usage aggregated over two-minute intervals. The data spans the following periods:

- **ElBorn**: 5,421 samples, from 2018-03-28 15:56:00 to 2018-04-04 22:36:00
- **LesCorts**: 8,615 samples, from 2019-01-12 17:12:00 to 2019-01-24 16:20:00

- **PobleSec**: 19,909 samples, from 2018-02-05 23:40:00 to 2018-03-05 15:16:00

Each record contains 11 aggregated features and five target variables, including uplink and downlink traffic volumes (Up, Down), RNTI (Radio Network Temporary Identifier) count, and the number of downlink and uplink resource blocks (RB Down, RB Up). Following the setup in [22], we treat the three nodes as Non-IID (Non-Independent and Identically Distributed) FL clients due to the varying sample sizes and distributional differences across sites. In contrast to previous work [22], which predicted multiple traffic-related features, we focus on the RNTI count as the target variable. The data distributions are depicted in Fig. 1.

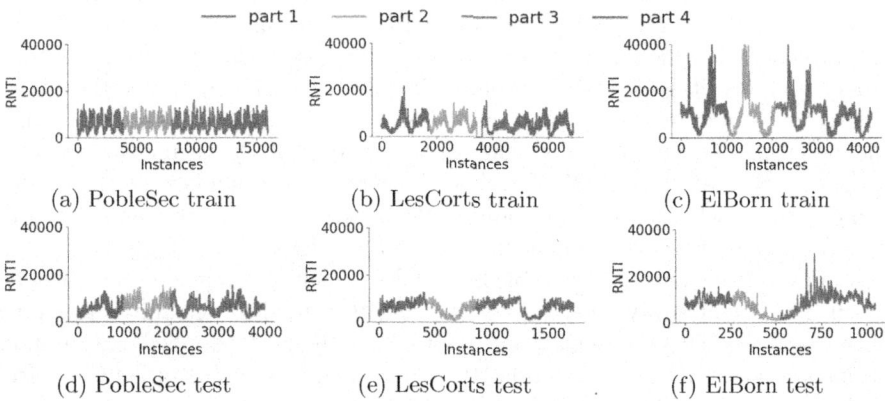

Fig. 1. 5G data distributions of train and test datasets divided into four equal partitions in experiment $B.1$.

The second dataset is the **Air Quality dataset** [32], which contains hourly measurements of PM2.5 concentrations collected from 12 monitoring stations across Beijing, China, between March 2013 and February 2017. The data originates from the Beijing Municipal Environmental Monitoring Center and is complemented with meteorological information from 15 weather stations operated by the China Meteorological Administration. The meteorological variables include air temperature, wind speed and direction, atmospheric pressure, relative humidity, and precipitation, with measurements provided at six-hour intervals. These additional variables are used better to capture the influence of weather conditions on PM2.5 levels and to enable spatial-temporal adjustments of pollution estimates. In total, each monitoring site provides approximately 35,000 hourly records over the four years. The full dataset contains 18 features, which combine air quality indicators and weather-related attributes. The target variable in this case is PM2.5 concentration, a key indicator of air pollution. Similar to the 5G dataset, we treat the 12 nodes as Non-IID FL clients due to the varying sample sizes and distributional differences.

In our implementation, FedCluLearn initializes an NN with input sizes of 10 (5G network) and 9 (Air Quality), two hidden layers (128 and 64 neurons), leaky ReLU activations, and a scalar output. Only numerical features are used, with missing values in the Air Quality dataset imputed with zero. Models are trained locally for three epochs using a batch size of 128 and a learning rate of 0.0001. Initial client clustering is performed using k-means, with the number of clusters and client assignments guided by the SI. A fixed SI threshold of 0.5, chosen empirically, is used throughout. Both datasets are split 80/20 for training and testing and exhibit non-stationary distributions, making them suitable for evaluating FL robustness under concept drift. Information about pre-processing details and data distributions is available in our public repository.

4.2 Baseline Algorithms

Three baseline FL algorithms are used as benchmarks in our experiments. These are **FedAvg**, **FedProx**, and **FedAtt**.

Federated Averaging (FedAvg) [20] is a distributed learning algorithm where multiple clients train local models on their own data without sharing it. A global model is then created by averaging these local models. However, FedAvg struggles with catastrophic forgetting as new updates overwrite past knowledge. Furthermore, it cannot detect and adapt to concept drift, which can lead to a decline in performance over time.

To improve training stability, **Federated Optimization (FedProx)** [17] extends FedAvg by incorporating a proximal term that limits local model updates, ensuring they remain close to the global model. While this helps when clients have heterogeneous data, FedProx still does not explicitly address concept drift, making it vulnerable to performance degradation and catastrophic forgetting as data distributions change.

To tackle concept drift more effectively, **Federated Attention (FedAtt)** [6] enhances FedAvg by incorporating a mechanism to retain past information effectively while adapting to sudden changes in data patterns, thereby minimizing forgetting of older knowledge over time.

The used baselines are representative of widely used FL approaches. Despite their advancements, none of these methods are explicitly designed for continual learning or concept drift scenarios. We include them in our evaluation to demonstrate how models lacking explicit mechanisms for long-term memory and adaptation can struggle under evolving data distributions. We do not intend to position FedCluLearn as a direct replacement, but rather to emphasize the importance of incorporating continual learning principles into federated setups.

4.3 Experiments

In this study, we investigate the effectiveness of our FedCluLearn model in mitigating catastrophic forgetting and dealing with concept drift in an FCL setting. The aim is to establish whether the model can retain previously acquired information while adapting to newly emerging concepts and to further analyze its performance in managing data trends over time. We have conducted a series of control experiments alongside experiments using real-world data. The control experiments are designed to explore the impact of concept drift and catastrophic forgetting on the behavior of FedCluLearn under small control scenarios. The experiments with real-world data can provide insight into the performance of the model in a real-world context.

Control experiments are grouped into three categories, representing different learning and concept drift scenarios. We have simulated parallel and continual learning of new concepts, leading to different concept drift scenarios. In the three experimental setups conducted, see Fig. 2, three clients participated in over 200 global rounds. The data represents three distinct concepts. Every 50 rounds, the concepts are rotated among the clients.

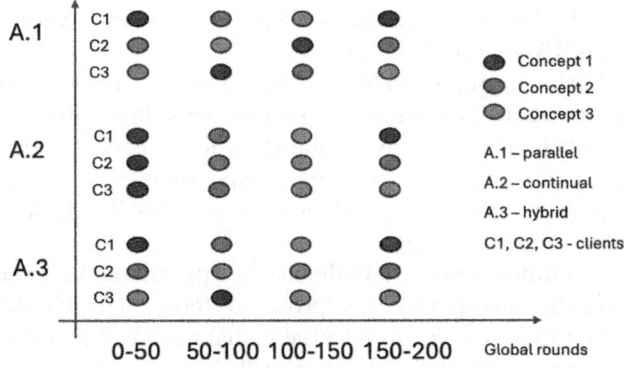

Fig. 2. Illustration of the control experiments conducted. They simulate three different learning and concept drift scenarios: parallel, continual, and hybrid.

The three control experiments are described in detail below:

- *Experiment A.1* simulates parallel learning of the three concepts represented in the clients' data. Concept drift occurs at the client level, where the same concept is distributed to all clients during the same training period. The setup evaluates the model's ability to handle local concept drift, where each client receives different data distributions that periodically change over time. This allows us to analyze the model's ability to adapt to local variations while retaining knowledge from previously learned concepts.
- *Experiment A.2* simulates continual learning of the three concepts, the drift occurs while the global model is being built. All clients receive the same concept during each interval. Every 50 global rounds, the concept shifts for all clients, leading to concept drift at the global level. In the last 50 global rounds, each client receives a different concept. The goal is to evaluate the model's ability to handle global concept drift, where all clients experience identical data distribution changes at the same time.

– *Experiment A.3* is a hybrid setup simulating local and global concept drifts. In the first two shifts (rounds 0 to 49 and 50 to 99), clients receive different concepts, experiencing local drift. In rounds 100 to 149, all clients learn the same concept, introducing global drift. A mix of learned local and global concepts is then introduced in the final phase. The goal is to assess the model's ability to simultaneously adapt to both drift types.

Experiments with real-world data are performed on two datasets, 5G network and Air Quality, as described below:

– *Experiment B.1* simulates an evolving streaming scenario and is carried out on 5G data. In this scenario, the three clients learn three different concepts, i.e., ElBorn, LesCorts, and PobleSec, each with a different size. These concepts are divided into four equal partitions, see Fig. 1. Each client receives different data every 50 rounds.
– *Experiment B.2* is similar to experiment *B*.1 and simulates a scenario with Air Quality data. Eleven clients each receive a distinct dataset with an equal number of instances representing different concepts. As in *B*.1, the datasets are divided into five equal partitions, and clients train on a new partition every 50 rounds.

In both types of experiments, we studied two different versions of our algorithm, called FedCluLearn and FedCluLearn-Prox, which use two distinct schemes to build the global model. The first version uses the aggregation formula (2) to construct the global model at each training round, while the second employs the optimization proposed in FedProx to address data heterogeneity.

From a convergence perspective, FedCluLearn may struggle in heterogeneous settings due to client drift. FedCluLearn-Prox addresses this issue by incorporating FedProx, which stabilizes training by penalizing deviation from the global model via a proximal term. This has been shown to improve convergence under Non-IID conditions by mitigating local overfitting [17]. Moreover, the proximal term retains the local updates near the global optimization trajectory, which reduces client divergence and accelerates convergence in environments with Non-IID data distributions. Experimental evidence across multiple FL benchmarks supports the effectiveness of this modification, particularly in scenarios with high statistical heterogeneity [14,17]. These results suggest that the incorporation of FedProx into FedCluLearn leads to more reliable and faster convergence in real-world Non-IID environments.

In addition, we conducted an ablation study in which we evaluated different aging schemes, e.g., from using all local modal updates to building the global model only from the updates of the last training round. The former reflects the scenario in which the aging component is omitted, while the latter explores the removal of the component using previously learned concepts. We have used **Mean Squared Error (MSE)** and **R-squared** (R^2) to evaluate the performance of the studied algorithms.

5 Experimental Results and Discussion

5.1 Control Experiments

In the three control experiments ($A.1$, $A.2$, and $A.3$), we examine the two versions of our algorithm mentioned above, FedCluLearn and FedCluLearn-Prox. In addition, three different data aging schemes of the two versions are evaluated in the three experiments.

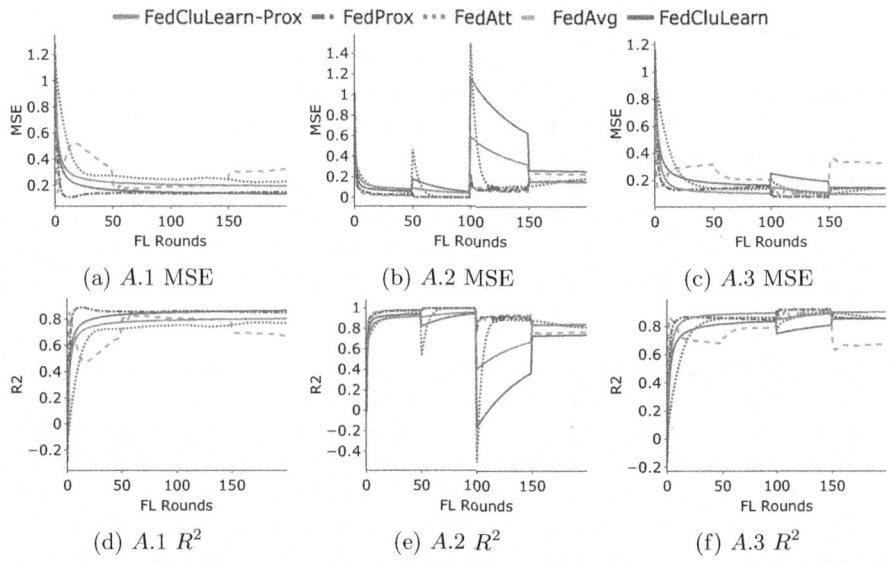

Fig. 3. Results of the evaluation of the global models built by FedAvg, FedAtt, FedProx, FedCluLearn, and FedCluLearn-Prox, in the three experiments $A.1$, $A.2$, and $A.3$. FedCluLearn and FedCluLearn-Prox aggregate all local model updates of the active concepts when building the global model in each training round.

Figure 3 shows the performance, evaluated in terms of MSE and R^2, of FedCluLearn and FedCluLearn-Prox, which aggregate all local model updates of the active concepts when building the global model. Their performance is compared to that of the three baseline algorithms. Note that this is an ablation study scenario in which the aging component is omitted. As we can see in *Experiment $A.1$*, FedCluLearn and FedCluLearn-Prox show better robustness to concept drifts that occur at the local level than FedAvg and FedAtt. Furthermore, the performance of FedCluLearn is comparable to that of FedProx, while the latter algorithm outperforms FedCluLearn-Prox. In *Experiment $A.2$*, FedCluLearn and FedCluLearn-Prox are observed to be much more affected by global concept drifts than FedAvg and FedProx, but as can be seen in the last shift, FedCluLearn-Prox remembers the already learned concepts better than the baseline algorithms. Our observations in *Experiment $A.3$* confirm those of the other two experiments. To understand whether the behavior of FedCluLearn and FedCluLearn-Prox in *Experiment A.2* is due to the SI threshold used (0.5), we also ran this experiment with threshold values of 0.7, 0.8, and 0.9, see Fig. 4. The two versions of our algorithm show different performance patterns with respect to different threshold values. In addition, both algorithms show significantly better performance at a value of 0.9. This is not surprising and is due to the construction of more clusters, i.e., a high discrimination between different local model updates.

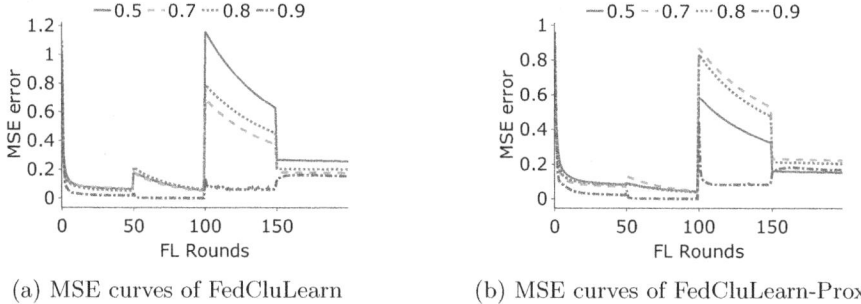

(a) MSE curves of FedCluLearn

(b) MSE curves of FedCluLearn-Prox

Fig. 4. Results of the evaluation of the global models built by FedCluLearn and FedCluLearn-Prox in the experiment $A.2$ with different SI threshold values.

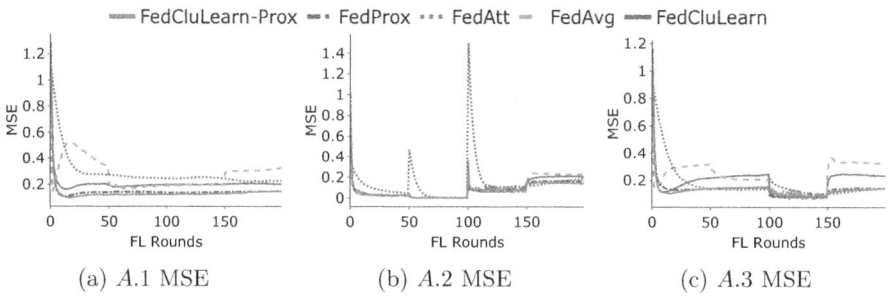

(a) $A.1$ MSE

(b) $A.2$ MSE

(c) $A.3$ MSE

Fig. 5. Results of the evaluation of the global models built by FedAvg, FedAtt, FedProx, FedCluLearn, and FedCluLearn-Prox, in the three experiments $A.1$, $A.2$, and $A.3$. FedCluLearn and FedCluLearn-Prox use only recent (from the last training round) local model updates of the active concepts when building the global model in each training round.

In Fig. 5, we study the FedCluLearn and FedCluLearn-Prox in the three control setups that utilize local model updates only from the last training round of the active concepts when building the global model. This is an ablation study scenario in which the component that uses previously learned concepts has been excluded. In this setting, FedCluLearn-Prox is shown to best handle local and global concept drift and forgetting in all three setups compared to the other evaluated algorithms. FedCluLearn also shows significantly better performance in the case of *Experiment A.2* and the third shift of *Experiment A.3*. This is because, in the case of global concept drift, more recent clients' model updates are more beneficial for the global model aggregation to capture the feature of a newly appeared concept. Furthermore, FedCluLearn-Prox outperforms all other algorithms in *Experiment A.1*, while FedCluLearn is better than FedAvg and FedAtt in the same setup. This is most likely due to the fact that the performance of the global models is not negatively affected by the earlier learned immature client updates. Note that the evaluation with respect to R^2 shows similar results and can be seen in our public repository.

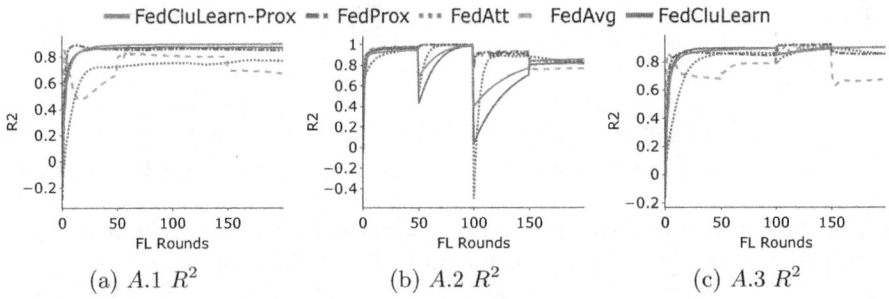

Fig. 6. Results of the evaluation of the global models built by FedAvg, FedAtt, FedProx, FedCluLearn, and FedCluLearn-Prox, in the three experiments *A.1*, *A.2*, and *A.3*. FedCluLearn and FedCluLearn-Prox aggregate only half of the last (most recent) local model updates of the active concepts when building the global model in each training round.

Figure 6 examines the FedCluLearn and FedCluLearn-Prox that aggregate only half of the local model updates of the active concepts when building the global model. Interestingly, this leads to an improved performance of FedCluLearn. Namely, in the current setting, both FedCluLearn and FedCluLearn-Prox outperform the baseline algorithms in *Experiment A.1*. In *Experiment A.2*, we observe the same performance patterns as in the case where all local model updates are used to build the global model, see Fig. 3. However, the performance of FedCluLearn is significantly improved in *Experiment A.3* compared to the two setups, whose results are shown in Fig. 3 and Fig. 5. We believe this is because only the most recent, mature local modal updates are used to build the global models. The evaluation results with respect to MSE are similar and can be seen in our public repository.

Our main finding from the control experiments is that the performance of both versions of our algorithm, FedCluLearn and FedCluLearn-Prox, is affected by the aging scheme used. In other words, they have shown better performance when the aging scheme included an appropriate number of previously learned concepts. Therefore, both components explored by our ablation study are important for the performance of the algorithms. The effect of the aging scheme on the performance of the algorithms is examined further in our experiments with real-world data. In addition to the above findings, FedCluLearn and FedCluLearn-Prox have shown superior robustness to local concept drift (Experiment $A.1$), while FedCluLearn-Prox has clearly demonstrated better memory retention in global drift scenarios (Experiment $A.2$). The hybrid experiment ($A.3$) has confirmed these results, reinforcing the effectiveness of FedCluLearn-Prox in dealing with both types of drift.

5.2 Experiments with Real-World Data

We report and discuss the results of two experiments conducted on real-world data below.

In Fig. 7, we compare the performance of FedCluLearn and FedCluLearn-Prox with that of the three baseline algorithms on 5G network data in *Experiment B.1*. We also examine how the performance of our algorithms is affected by the percentage of recent local model updates used to build the global model. In Fig. 7(b), we evaluate the performance of five versions of FedCluLearn, called FedCluLearn-total, FedCluLearn-recent, FedCluLearn-75%, FedCluLearn-50%, and FedCluLearn-25% in terms of MSE. FedCluLearn-total denotes the version that aggregates all local model updates of the active concepts when building the global model in each training round. FedCluLearn-recent, FedCluLearn-75%, FedCluLearn-50%, and FedCluLearn-25% refer to versions that only aggregate local model updates from the last training round and the respective percentage (75%, 50%, and 25%) of local model updates of the active concepts when building the global model. The same comparisons, but for the respective five versions of FedCluLearn-Prox, are shown in Fig. 7(c). Figure 7(a) then compares the best performing versions of FedCluLearn and FedCluLearn-Prox with the three baseline algorithms. These are FedCluLearn-50% and FedCluLearn-Prox-50%. As we can observe, FedCluLearn-Prox-50% significantly outperforms FedAvg and FedAtt, as well as its relative algorithm, FedProx. FedCluLearn-50% also shows significantly better performance compared to FedAvg, it also outperforms FedAtt and is very close to the performance of FedProx. It is interesting to note that the performance signatures of FedCluLearn-recent (see Fig. 7(b)) and FedAvg (see Fig. 7(a)) have very similar shapes, but the former algorithm shows better performance. We believe that this is due to the fact that FedCluLearn uses only local model updates from the currently active concepts to build the global model. A similar trend is observed for FedCluLearn-Prox-recent and FedProx (see Fig. 7(c) and Fig. 7(a)).

In Fig. 8, we compare the performance of FedCluLearn and FedCluLearn-Prox with the three baseline algorithms on the Air Quality data in *Experiment B.2*. Similar to *Experiment B.1*, we examine the five different versions of each of the two algorithms. In this experiment, the best performing versions of FedCluLearn and FedCluLearn-Prox are FedCluLearn-25% and FedCluLearn-Prox-25%. In Fig. 8(a), FedCluLearn-25% and FedCluLearn-Prox-25% have very

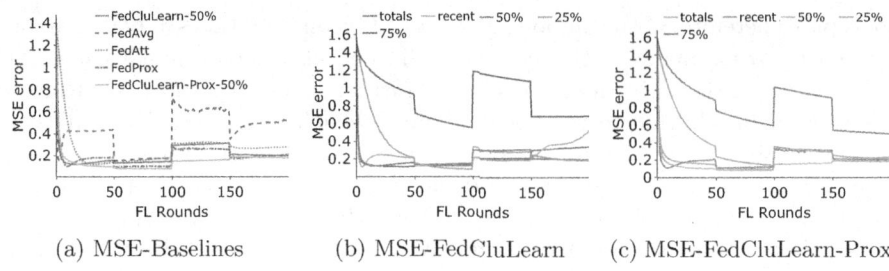

(a) MSE-Baselines   (b) MSE-FedCluLearn   (c) MSE-FedCluLearn-Prox

Fig. 7. Results of experiment $B.1$ with 5G network data simulating an evolving streaming scenario. The middle plot compares the performance of the three versions of FedCluLearn. The same comparison is shown in the right plot, but for FedCluLEarn-Prox. In the left plot, the best performing versions of FedCluLearn and FedCluLearn-Prox are compared to the three baseline algorithms.

similar performance that is better than that of FedAvg and FedAtt and comparable to that of FedProx in most data batches. In addition, both versions of our algorithm handle data drift in the last batch better than the three baselines.

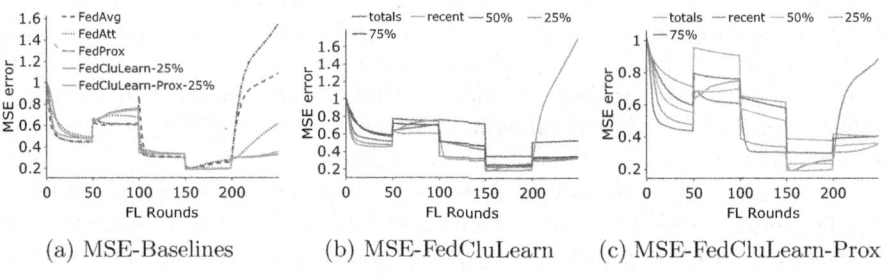

(a) MSE-Baselines   (b) MSE-FedCluLearn   (c) MSE-FedCluLearn-Prox

Fig. 8. Results of experiment $B.2$ with Air Quality data simulating an evolving streaming scenario. The middle plot compares the performance of the five versions of FedCluLearn. The same comparisons are shown in the right plot, but for FedCluLearn-Prox. In the left plot, the best performing versions of FedCluLearn and FedCluLearn-Prox are compared to the three baseline algorithms.

In summary, FedCluLearn has consistently shown better performance than FedAvg and FedAtt, while FedCluLearn-Prox has outperformed the three baselines and FedCluLearn in most experiments. However, both models are sensitive to aging schemes, with suboptimal strategies that compromise global drift adaptation. FedCluLearn-Prox-percentage-50% has shown the best overall performance, significantly outperforming FedAvg, FedAtt, and FedProx. Meanwhile, FedCluLearn-25% and FedCluLearn-Prox-25% have emerged as the best performing variants, confirming that the optimal aging scheme is data dependent.

The five versions of FedCluLearn and FedCluLearn-Prox are also evaluated with respect to R^2 in *Experiments* $B.1$ and $B.2$. The results are similar to those reported under MSE and can be seen in our public repository.

6 Conclusion and Future Work

In this study, we have proposed a novel Federated Continual Learning (FCL) algorithm, called FedCluLearn, which interprets the federated training process as a stream clustering scenario. It uses the stream micro-cluster indexing scheme to store statistics about local model updates to deal with catastrophic forgetting and concept drift. Additionally, FedCluLearn considers the recency of stored local model updates to determine how many to use in building the global model during each training round.

Two versions of the proposed FCL approach, FedCluLearn and FedCluLearn-Prox, have been evaluated in several control and real-world data experiments, studying various ablation scenarios using different aging schemes and comparing their performance with three baselines, FedAvg, FedProx, and FedAtt. The experimental results have shown that a balanced use of older local model updates can lead to robust handling of concept drift and catastrophic forgetting by both models. FedCluLearn has consistently shown better performance than FedAvg and FedAtt, while FedCluLearn-Prox has outperformed all three baselines, and FedCluLearn in most cases studied.

Future research will focus on dynamic aging schemes that adapt to evolving data distributions to enhance performance in global drift scenarios. To improve algorithm efficiency, we plan to organize cluster statistics on the server using a tree structure like B-trees or R-trees. Additionally, we aim to extend this work to larger, real-world federated environments with more heterogeneous clients to gain insights into FedCluLearn's scalability and applicability. We acknowledge that the current evaluation of the proposed FedCluLearn is primarily based on empirical evidence. Incorporating statistically significant tests is a crucial next step in strengthening the validity of our findings. We also intend to compare FedCluLearn with continual learning methods adapted for FL, in order to provide a more contextualized view of its performance in lifelong learning settings.

References

1. Aggarwal, C.C., Reddy, C.K.: Data Clustering: Algorithms and Applications, 1st edn. Chapman & Hall/CRC (2013)
2. Aggarwal, C.C., et al.: A framework for clustering evolving data streams. In: Freytag, J.C., et al. (eds.) Proceedings VLDB Conference, pp. 81–92. Morgan Kaufmann (2003)
3. Agrahari, S., Singh, A.K.: Concept drift detection in data stream mining: a literature review. J. King Saud Uni.-Comput. Inf. Sci. **34**(10), 9523–9540 (2022)
4. Benzing, F.: Unifying importance based regularisation methods for continual learning. In: International Conference on AI and Statistics, pp. 2372–2396. PMLR (2022)
5. De Lange, M., et al.: A continual learning survey: defying forgetting in classification tasks. IEEE Trans. Pattern Anal. Mach. Intell. **44**(7), 3366–3385 (2021)
6. Estiri, A.H., Maheswaran, M.: Attentive federated learning for concept drift in distributed 5G edge networks. arXiv abs/2111.07457 (2021)

7. French, R.M.: Catastrophic forgetting in connectionist networks. Trends Cogn. Sci. **3**(4), 128–135 (1999)
8. Gama, J., Žliobaitundefined, I., Bifet, A., Pechenizkiy, M., Bouchachia, A.: A survey on concept drift adaptation. ACM Comput. Surv. **46**(4) (2014)
9. Gepperth, A., Hammer, B.: Incremental learning algorithms and applications. In: European Symposium on Artificial Neural Networks (ESANN) (2016)
10. Ghosh, A., et al.: An efficient framework for clustered federated learning. In: Advances in Neural Information Processing Systems, vol. 33, pp. 19586–19597 (2020)
11. Islam, M.S., et al.: Fedclust: tackling data heterogeneity in federated learning through weight-driven client clustering. In: Proceedings of ICPP 2024, pp. 474–483 (2024)
12. Iwashita, A.S., Papa, J.P.: An overview on concept drift learning. IEEE Access **7**, 1532–1547 (2018)
13. Jiang, X., Borcea, C.: Concept matching: clustering-based federated continual learning. arXiv preprint arXiv:2311.06921 (2023)
14. Karimireddy, S., Kale, et al.: SCAFFOLD: stochastic controlled averaging for federated learning. In: Proceedings of the 37th International Conference on Machine Learning, vol. 119, pp. 5132–5143 (2020)
15. Kranen, P., et al.: The clustree: indexing micro-clusters for anytime stream mining. Knowl. Inf. Syst. **29**, 249–272 (2011)
16. Lesort, T., et al.: Continual learning for robotics: definition, framework, learning strategies, opportunities and challenges. Inf. Fusion **58**, 52–68 (2020)
17. Li, T., et al.: Federated optimization in heterogeneous networks. Proc. Mach. Learn. Syst. **2**, 429–450 (2020)
18. Lin, G., Chu, H., Lai, H.: Towards better plasticity-stability trade-off in incremental learning: a simple linear connector. In: Proceedings of the IEEE/CVF Conference on Computer Vision and Pattern Recognition, pp. 89–98 (2022)
19. MacQueen, J.: Some methods for classification and analysis of multivariate observations. In: Proceedings of the Fifth Berkeley Symposium on Mathematical Statistics and Probability, Volume 1: Statistics, vol. 5, pp. 281–298 (1967)
20. McMahan, B., et al.: Communication-efficient learning of deep networks from decentralized data. In: Proceedings of the 20th AISTATS (2017)
21. Ouyang, X., et al.: Clusterfl: a clustering-based federated learning system for human activity recognition. ACM Trans. Sens. Netw. **19**(1), 1–32 (2022)
22. Perifanis, V., et al.: Towards energy-aware federated traffic prediction for cellular networks. In: 2023 8th International Conference on FMEC, pp. 93–100 (2023)
23. Pfeiffer, J., et al.: Modular deep learning. arXiv abs/2302.11529 (2023)
24. Rousseeuw, P.J.: Silhouettes: a graphical aid to the interpretation and validation of cluster analysis. J. Comput. Appl. Math. **20**, 53–65 (1987)
25. Shin, H., Lee, J.K., Kim, J., Kim, J.: Continual learning with deep generative replay. In: Advances in Neural Information Processing Systems, vol. 30 (2017)
26. Wadewale, K., Desai, S.: Survey on method of drift detection and classification for time varying data set (2015)
27. Wang, L., et al.: Memory replay with data compression for continual learning. arXiv preprint arXiv:2202.06592 (2022)
28. Wang, L., et al.: A comprehensive survey of continual learning: theory, method and application. IEEE Trans. Pattern Anal. Mach. Intell. (2024)
29. Wang, Z., et al.: Federated continual learning for edge-AI: a comprehensive survey. arXiv preprint arXiv:2411.13740 (2024)

30. Yang, X., et al.: Federated continual learning via knowledge fusion: a survey. IEEE Trans. Knowl. Data Eng. **36**(8), 3832–3850 (2024)
31. Yoon, J., Madaan, D., Yang, E., Hwang, S.J.: Online coreset selection for rehearsal-based continual learning. arXiv preprint arXiv:2106.01085 (2021)
32. Zhang, S., et al.: Cautionary tales on air-quality improvement in Beijing. Proc. R. Soc. A: Math. Phys. Eng. Sci. **473** (2017)

FedRNL: Federated Rationalization with Soft Parameter Sharing

Lingxiao Kong, Jiahui Jiang, Haozhao Wang, Lei Wu[✉], and Ruixuan Li

School of Computer Science and Technology, Huazhong University of Science and Technology, Wuhan, China
leiwu@hust.edu.cn

Abstract. Interpretability is crucial in natural language processing to enhance transparency and trust. Rationalization models achieve this by extracting key input fragments, i.e., rationales, to explain decisions while preserving predictive performance. On the other side, Federated Learning (FL) is recently emerging as a key paradigm for training machine learning models because it can leverage training data from multiple clients without the requirement of uploading their original data. Considering this, we firstly propose training Rationalization models in a FL manner. However, we find that simply combining them suffers from serious performance degradation due to the data heterogeneity among clients, where there exists inconsistent rationale generation. To solve this issue, we propose FedRNL which introduces a soft-sharing mechanism to align generator and predictor encoders, ensuring shallow-consistency and deep-generalization. An encoder loss minimizes feature discrepancies, and a layer-wise aggregation strategy separately updates the generator and predictor at the server, enhancing model stability. Extensive experiments show that FedRNL significantly improves the performance as compared to existing general heterogeneity mitigation methods.

Keywords: Federated learning · Rationalization · Non-IID

1 Introduction

Interpretability is crucial in natural language processing (NLP) as it enhances model transparency, fosters user trust, and supports decision-making [19,26,31]. However, deep learning models are often black-box systems, making their reasoning processes challenging to understand, thus necessitating better interpretability in NLP models. Rationalization models address this need by extracting key input fragments (i.e., rationales) that explain model decisions while preserving predictive performance [5,15,24]. They consist of a generator and a predictor: the generator selects the most informative text subset as rationales, which is

---

Supplementary Information The online version contains supplementary material available at https://doi.org/10.1007/978-3-032-05981-9_21.

© The Author(s), under exclusive license to Springer Nature Switzerland AG 2026
R. P. Ribeiro et al. (Eds.): ECML PKDD 2025, LNAI 16014, pp. 350–366, 2026.
https://doi.org/10.1007/978-3-032-05981-9_21

then passed to the predictor for final classification or decision-making. However, existing research focuses on centralized implementations of these models, leaving their adaptation to distributed learning scenarios largely unexplored. As concerns about data privacy and security continue to rise, extending rationalization models to distributed environments such as Federated Learning (FL) has become a crucial direction. However, the challenge posed by non-independent and identically distributed (non-IID) data complicates this transition.

In FL, data heterogeneity arises as different clients collect data from distinct sources, leading to significant distribution shifts. This non-IID nature results in inconsistent learning directions across clients, degrading the overall model performance and causing potential model drift. This issue is particularly pronounced for Rationalization models, as variations in textual styles, feature distributions, or annotation standards across clients. This inconsistency makes it challenging for the model to generate stable and coherent rationales, weakening its interpretability and generalization ability.

Many approaches have been proposed to address the non-IID issue, including parameter regularization [2,17], personalized FL [33,40], and local model alignment [10,29]. While these approaches alleviate non-IID issues to some extent, optimizing federated learning performance for rationalization models while preserving their interpretability remains an open problem. Luo [21] found that the classifier has the lowest feature similarity between local models and suggested that bias in FL can be mitigated solely by rectifying the deep-networks (the classifier) of the deep network after federated training. On the other hand, Liu [20] found that maintaining shallow-networks consistency between the generator and predictor enables the model to learn more informative rationales. This contradiction raises an important question: *is deep-networks classifier calibration more critical, or does shallow-networks generator-predictor consistency play a bigger role in addressing non-IID challenges? More importantly, can we reduce classifier bias while preserving interpretability to further enhance Rationalization models in federated learning?*

To answer this question, we propose FedRNL, the first work to study training rationalization models through FL. Our goal is to mitigate the accuracy performance degradation of rationalization models in FL which is caused by non-IID. Specifically, FedRNL shares the encoder layers between the generator and predictor in a soft manner, and introduces an encoder loss to minimize the parameter inconsistency between encoders while allowing the deep network to adapt to the non-IID data distribution. Each client optimizes its local model independently while following the soft-sharing constraint to align generator and predictor representations. At the server, we adopt a layer-wise aggregation strategy, separately updating the generator and predictor parameters to enhance the stability of the global model further. The main contributions of this paper are:

- To the best of our knowledge, this is the first work to study training the rationalization models in a FL manner.
- We propose a soft-sharing mechanism between the generator and predictor. This mechanism ensures an adaptable consistency in the shallow network and

allows the deep network to adapt to the non-IID data distribution, enhancing the model's generalizability and interpretability in FL.
- We provide a theoretical analysis that guarantees the convergence of the proposed method. Besides, the experimental results demonstrate that existing FL methods are unsuitable for rationalization tasks, while FedRNL significantly improves accuracy while preserving the interpretability under various non-IID settings.

2 Related Work

Rationalization Models. Rationalization models aim to enhance interpretability in NLP by selecting key input fragments (rationales) that justify model predictions while maintaining predictive performance [15,24]. These models typically consist of a generator that extracts the most informative text subset and a predictor that makes the final decision based on the selected rationales. As research on rationalization models advances, they can be further categorized into abstract and extractive approaches. Extractive rationalization models identify and extract keywords or sentences from the input text, capturing the most salient features to explain predictions [5,6]. Some works study extractive methods using an encoder-decoder framework [3,15]. The encoder assigns each word in the input sequence a binary tag to indicate whether it is part of the rationale. The decoder then processes only the highlighted rationale words and maps them to target categories [35]. Other works use attention mechanisms to extract rationales [34,39]. Abstractive rationalization models generate rationales by constructing explanations using new words and restructured sentences from the input text [30]. Some works study text-to-text methods, which utilize sequence-to-sequence translation models, incorporating both the label and explanation simultaneously [12,27]. Others use generative methods, which generate a free-form explanation and then make a prediction based on the produced abstractive rationale [4]. Despite significant progress, most rationalization models are designed for centralized training, assuming access to a single dataset. The challenge of adapting them to FL remains largely unexplored.

Non-IID in Federated Learning. Many existing studies have proposed solutions to mitigate client drift caused by non-IID data [25,29,36]. Some approaches rely on personalization techniques to tailor model optimization to each client's unique data distribution [28,40]. For instance, FedROD [7] integrates a globally shared general model with personalized client models through a joint training mechanism. FedProto [33] leverages prototypes—central representations of classes—to facilitate personalized model training for each client. There are also some works on improving the generalization ability of the global model, such as parameter regularization [1,17] and local model alignment methods [28,41]. For example, FedProx [18] introduces a proximal term to the local subproblem, adjusting local updates to account for the discrepancy between the global and local models. FedPer [2] combines each client with globally shared model parameters. FedNH [10] mitigates the impact of data heterogeneity on federated learning by incorporating class prototypes into the global model. However, these methods are not applicable to Rationalization models.

3 Preliminary

Rationalization. We use rationalization models, denoted as $R(x)$, which consists of two components: the generator and the predictor. The generator generates an extractive rationale $z = gen(x)$ for an input paragraph x. Then, the generated rationale z is employed in the class prediction of x. The prediction process can be formulated as $\hat{y} = pre(x, z)$. The whole process, i.e., class prediction with the rationale, can be integrated as one model and denoted as $R(x) = pre(gen(x)))$. FR [20] divides the structure of $gen(\cdot)$ and $pre(\cdot)$ into encoder layers $encoder_g(\cdot)$ and linear layers $linear_g(\cdot)$. The generator and predictor share the same $encoder_g(\cdot)$, ensuring shallow network consistency.

Federated Learning. We consider there are N clients, and each client i ($i \in [1, N]$) has a local dataset $D_i = \{(x_{ij}, y_{ij})\}_{j=1}^{m_i}$ where m_i is the data number of dataset D_i. The non-IID of FL represents that the distribution of D_i differs among clients. We denote $G(\cdot; \delta)$ represent global model and $L_i(\cdot; \theta, \phi)$ represent local model of client i. The local loss function is denoted by $\mathcal{L}$, which is used to optimize the local model on the local dataset D_i. After each communication round t ($t \in [1, T]$), the server aggregates the updates from each client by weighted averaging to update the global model. The standard FL process typically follows the FedAvg [23]. Each client i trains its local model on its own dataset D_i and computes the local model update, the local update process of local model is:

$$\theta_i^{t+1} = \theta_i^t - \eta \nabla_{\theta_i} \mathcal{L}(\theta_i^t, D_i), \quad \phi_i^{t+1} = \phi_i^t - \eta \nabla_{\phi_i} \mathcal{L}(\phi_i^t, D_i) \quad (1)$$

where η is the learning rate. The server aggregates the local model updates from all clients with weighted averaging, where m_i is the dataset size of i:

$$\delta^{t+1} = \sum_{i=1}^{m} \frac{m_i}{m} \delta_i^t \quad (2)$$

where $m = \sum_{i=1}^{N} m_i$ is the total number of samples across all clients.

4 Methodology

In this section, we propose a simple yet effective method named FedRNL to mitigate the model drift. Specifically, the core idea is to adopt a soft-sharing mechanism between the generator and predictor, ensuring consistency in the shallow network while allowing the deep network to adapt to the non-IID data distribution (i.e. shallow-consistency and deep-generalization). This approach enables the Rationalization model to maintain its interpretability while improving classification performance in non-IID scenarios, thereby achieving better generalization ability. An overview of the proposed framework is shown in Fig. 1. The algorithm workflow is presented in Algorithm 1.

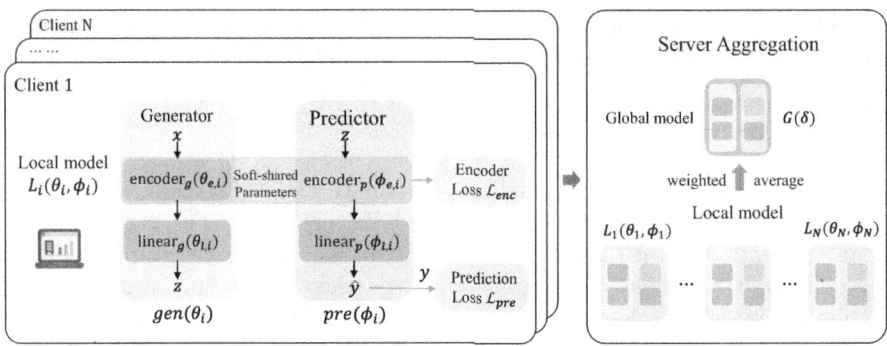

Fig. 1. The overall architecture of FedRNL.

4.1 Motivation

In FL, non-IID increases the difficulty of model training, particularly in Rationalization models that consist of a Generator and a Predictor. Existing FR methods [20] aim to enhance the interpretability of rationalization models by enabling the Generator and Predictor to share the same Encoder, thereby improving their consistency in shallow networks. However, the effectiveness of this approach in a FL setting remains unclear. To evaluate FR's performance in FL, we use the Gold Rationale F1 (GR) to measure the model's interpretability, Test Accuracy(ACC) to measure the model's prediction performance, and Centered Kernel Alignment (CKA) [14] similarity to assess the representation similarity between the Generator and Predictor across different clients' local models. As shown in Fig. 2, FR successfully reduces the similarity between generators while increasing the similarity between predictors, improving consistency in shallow networks. However, it does not effectively mitigate the non-IID issue—ACC even drops by 0.93% compared to FedAvg, and the improvement in interpretability is minimal. The core idea of the FR is to enhance model interpretability through shallow network consistency. **However, experimental results indicate that forcibly sharing the shallow network alone does not significantly improve interpretability. Moreover, it may restrict the expressiveness of the deep network, making it difficult for the model to adapt to the non-IID data distribution in the FL.**

Thus, we propose a key question: can we design a method that ensures consistency in the shallow network to maintain the interpretability of rationalization models while allowing the deep network to adapt flexibly to non-IID data distributions? In FL, the non-IID problem requires models to achieve strong generalization across different data distributions. If the generator and predictor share an identical shallow network, they may lack the necessary flexibility to adapt to diverse local data distributions, ultimately affecting overall performance. Therefore, a new strategy is needed—one that ensures shallow network consistency to enhance interpretability, while enabling the deep network to achieve greater generalization, allowing it to adapt effectively to non-IID data distributions.

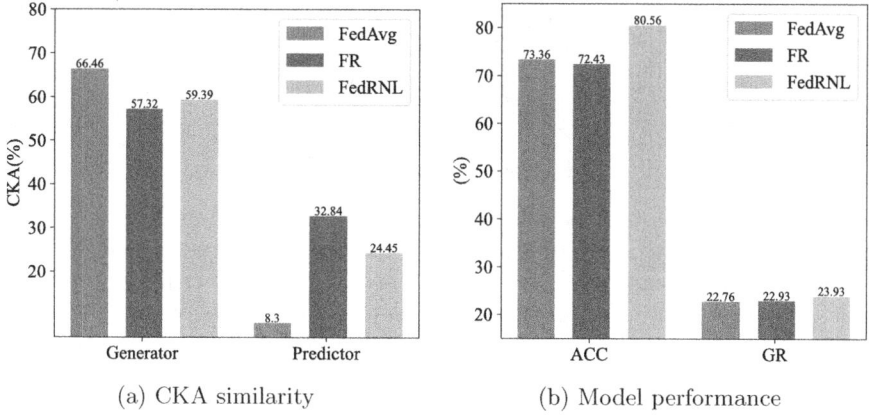

Fig. 2. Impact of non-IID over different methods.

4.2 Local Model Update

In the FedRNL framework, each client i trains its local model L_i using the dataset D_i it has access to, while maintaining privacy and avoiding direct sharing of raw data. For simplicity, we will omit the i marker in the subsequent sections of this section. The local model L consists of two components: the generator $gen(\cdot; \theta)$ and the predictor $pre(\cdot; \phi)$. We further decompose these two components into encoder layers and linear layers. Specifically, the generator $gen(\cdot; \theta_e, \theta_l)$ includes the $encoder_g(\cdot; \theta_e)$ and $linear_g(\cdot; \theta_l)$, while the predictor $pre(\cdot; \phi_e, \phi_l)$ consists of the $encoder_p(\cdot; \phi_e)$ and $linear_p(\cdot; \phi_l)$.

The generator is responsible for producing a rationale $z = gen(x; \theta_e, \theta_l)$ from the input data x, where z represents a subset or transformation of the input that is deemed most relevant for the prediction. First, the generator's encoder layer extracts the semantic features from the input text x and generates a feature representation $r_g = encoder_g(x; \theta_e)$ for each token of x. r_g are then passed to the generator's linear layer and generate a mask $z = linear_g(r_g; \theta_l)$ to select the most important parts of the text for the classification task. Through this process, the generator creates the rationale z, providing the necessary information for subsequent prediction. Then z is passed into the encoder layer of the predictor, which is responsible for extracting the feature representation $r_p = encoder_p(z; \phi_e)$ of z. r_p are then processed through the linear layer of the predictor, followed by the classification layer, which performs the classification task and outputs the final prediction $\hat{y} = linear_p(r_p; \phi_l)$. This process enables the predictor to make accurate predictions based on the rationale provided by the generator.

The whole process, i.e., class prediction with the rationale, can be integrated as one model and defined as $L(x) = pre(gen(x; \theta_e, \theta_l), \phi_e, \phi_l)$. To train the performance of the rationalization model, we calculate the cross-entropy loss between the predictions $\hat{y}$ outputted by the predictor and the ground-truth labels y. This loss is referred to as prediction loss $\mathcal{L}_{pre}$. The optimization constraint used in the training process is defined as follows:

$$\mathcal{L}_{pre} = \sum_{(x,y)\in \mathbb{D}_i} \mathcal{L}(L(x;\theta_e,\theta_l,\phi_e,\phi_l),y) \qquad (3)$$

where the $\mathcal{L}$ represents the cross-entropy loss of the rationalization model.

Encoder Loss. To enforce feature alignment between the generator and predictor, we introduce a soft-sharing mechanism that aligns the encoder layer learned by the generator and the predictor across clients. Specifically, we design an encoder loss $\mathcal{L}_{enc}$ to control the parameter similarity between the encoder layers $encoder_g$ and $encoder_p$, aimed at optimizing the parameters of these two encoders, ensuring that their feature representations remain consistent. The optimization constraint is defined as follows:

$$\mathcal{L}_{enc} = \|\theta_e - \phi_e\|_2 \qquad (4)$$

where $\|\cdot\|_2$ denotes the squared L2 norm, which calculates the Euclidean distance between the two parameters. By minimizing this loss, the parameters of $encoder_g$ and $encoder_p$ are guided to optimize towards more similar directions, improving the coordination between the generator and the predictor and, ultimately, enhancing the performance of the model facing non-iid problem.

Joint Loss. The total loss for each client is the sum of the prediction loss and the encoder loss:

$$\mathcal{L} = \mathcal{L}_{pre} + \lambda \mathcal{L}_{enc} \qquad (5)$$

where λ is a hyperparameter that controls the balance between the prediction loss and the encoder loss.

4.3 Global Model Aggregation

In aggregating the global model, we use the FedAvg algorithm to aggregate the local model parameters from all clients. At round t, the server receives local model parameters from each client and updates the global model parameters. Specially, the parameters of the generator and predictor are aggregated separately to update the global model. The global aggregation is formulated as:

$$\sigma_g^{(t+1)} = \sum_{i=1}^{N} \frac{m_i}{m}\theta_i^{(t)}, \quad \sigma_p^{(t+1)} = \sum_{i=1}^{N} \frac{m_i}{m}\phi_i^{(t)} \qquad (6)$$

where $\sigma_g^{(t+1)}$ and $\sigma_p^{(t+1)}$ represent the global model parameters of the generator and predictor. $\theta_i^{(t)}$ represent the local model parameters of generator, which consist of encoder layer parameters $\theta_{e,i}^{(t)}$ and linear layer parameters $\theta_{l,i}^{(t)}$. $\phi_i^{(t)}$ represent the local model parameters of predictor, which consist of encoder layer parameters $\phi_{e,i}^{(t)}$ and linear layer parameters $\phi_{l,i}^{(t)}$.

Algorithm 1. Training Process of FedRNL

Input: clients N, local dataset $\mathbb{D}_i, i = 1, \ldots, N$, communication rounds T, local epoch M, learning rate η, encoder weight λ

Global server does:
1: Initialize global model $G(.; \delta)$
2: **for** $t = 1$ to T **do**
3:     Select N_t participated clients
4:     **for** each client $i \in [N_t]$ **in parallel do**
5:         $L_i(.; \theta_i, \phi_i) \leftarrow$ LocalUpdate$(i, G(\delta))$
6:     **end for**
7:     Aggregate global model $G(.; \delta)$ by Eq. (6)
8: **end for**

LocalUpdate$(i, G(\delta))$:
1: **for** $m = 1$ to M **do**
2:     **for** batch $(x_{ij}, y_{ij} \in \mathbb{D}_i)$ **do**
3:         Compute loss using λ by Eq. (5)
4:         Update local model $L_i(.; \theta_i, \phi_i)$ according to the loss
5:     **end for**
6: **end for**
7: **return** $L_i(.; \theta_i, \phi_i)$

5 Theoretical Analysis

We make the following assumptions for these objectives, which are widely adopted in FL [32,36].

Assumption 1 (*L-smoothness*). The objective function $\mathcal{L}_i$ is L-smooth with Lipschitz constant $L > 0$, i.e., $\|\nabla \mathcal{L}_i(\theta, \phi) - \nabla \mathcal{L}_i(\theta', \phi')\|_2 \leq \mathcal{L}_i(\|\theta - \theta'\| + \|\phi - \phi'\|)_2$ for all $\theta, \phi, \theta', \phi'$.

Assumption 2 (*Bounded Variance*). For all parameters θ, ϕ, the variance of the local stochastic gradient in each client is bounded by σ^2, i.e., $\mathbb{E}\|\nabla \mathcal{L}_i(\theta, \varphi) - \nabla \mathcal{L}(\theta, \varphi)\|^2 \leq \sigma^2$.

Assumption 3 (*Bounded diversity*). Under non-IID data distribution, the variance of local gradients to global gradient is bounded by ζ^2, i.e., $\|\nabla \mathcal{L}_i(\theta_i, \varphi_i) - \nabla \mathcal{L}_g(\sigma_g, \sigma_p)\|^2 \leq \zeta^2$.

Based on Assumption 1, we have

$$\mathcal{L}_g(\sigma_g^{t+1}, \sigma_p^{t+1}) \leq \mathcal{L}_g(\sigma_g^t, \sigma_p^t) + \langle \nabla \mathcal{L}_g(\sigma_g^t, \sigma_p^t), (\sigma_g^{t+1} - \sigma_g^t, \sigma_p^{t+1} - \sigma_p^t) \rangle \\ + \frac{L}{2} \|(\sigma_g^{t+1} - \sigma_g^t, \sigma_p^{t+1} - \sigma_p^t)\|^2 \quad (7)$$

Based on Assumption 2 and 3, we have

$$\mathbb{E}\mathcal{L}_g(\sigma_g^{t+1}, \sigma_p^{t+1}) \leq \mathbb{E}\mathcal{L}_g(\sigma_g^t, \sigma_p^t) - \eta \|\nabla \mathcal{L}_g(\sigma_g^t, \sigma_p^t)\|^2 + \frac{L\eta^2}{2}(\sigma^2 + \zeta^2). \quad (8)$$

Based on the above, we have the following theory for the convergence of the proposed algorithm.

Theorem 1. *If the learning rate η diminishes with $O\left(\frac{1}{\sqrt{T}}\right)$, then the global model achieves asymptotic convergence, i.e.,*

$$\mathbb{E}\mathcal{L}_g(\sigma_g^T, \sigma_p^T) - \mathcal{L}_g^* \leq \frac{1}{\sqrt{T}}\left(\mathcal{L}_g(\sigma_g^0, \sigma_p^0) - \mathcal{L}_g^*\right) + \frac{L}{2\sqrt{T}}(\sigma^2 + \zeta^2). \tag{9}$$

The details of the proof can be found in Appendix A.

6 Experiments

Datasets. Following [20], we implemented the performance on two widely used rationalization dataset: **Beer Reviews** [22] and **Hotel Reviews** [37], which is a token-level multi-aspect sentiment analysis dataset for beer. Our experiments employ four aspects: Appearance, Palate, Taste, and Aroma. The training set, development set, and test set consist of 33782, 8731, and 936 available examples. The federated learning system comprises five clients for non-IID settings, each exclusively owning data sampled from one of five distinct datasets.

Evaluation Metrics. For task performance evaluation, we employ *classification accuracy (ACC)* and *Gold Rationale F1 (GR)*. ACC is used to assess classification performance by comparing the predicted class label with the actual label. GR[8], defined as the F1 score between the predicted and human-annotated rationale, is used to evaluate the quality of rationale generation. A higher GR score signifies a more substantial alignment between the model-generated and Gold rationale, indicating better interpretability of the model.

Configurations. We emplóy the GRU-base models [9] to encode text, which has been adopted by most previous works [11,20,38]. We use Adam optimizer[13] for model training. The max sequence length, the network dropout rate, the sparsity trade-off, and the continuity trade-off are set to 256, 0.2, 10, and 10, respectively. The learning rate η, the communication round T, the batch size, and the hidden dims are set to 1×10^{-5}, 500, 512, and 200, respectively. Unless otherwise mentioned, each client's local epoch M is set to 5, and encoder weight λ is set to 2. Our models are trained with NVIDIA GeForce RTX 3090 (Ubuntu 22.04 LTS PyTorch).

Baselines. We compare FedRNL with several popular and state-of-the-art FL methods: FedAvg [23], FedProx [18], FedBABU [28], FedDyn [1], and Moon [16].

6.1 Performance Evaluation

To evaluate the effectiveness of FedRNL, we conduct experiments on the Beer dataset, which concludes 4 aspects: Appearance, Palate, Taste, and Aroma, and the Hotel dataset, which concludes 3 aspects: Cleanliness, Location, and Service.

Table 1. Best test accuracy(%) and GR(%) over Beer datasets. **Bold** fonts highlight the best accuracy.

Methods	Appearance		Palate		Taste		Aroma		Average	
	GR	ACC	GR	ACC	GR	ACC	GR	ACC	GR	ACC
FedAvg	22.77	72.73	22.76	73.92	22.76	73.02	22.76	73.75	22.76	73.36
FedProx	22.43	72.51	22.45	72.51	22.44	73.21	22.44	72.96	22.44	72.80
FedBABU	22.93	66.54	22.94	68.01	22.94	67.33	22.94	67.25	22.94	67.28
FedDyn	22.28	75.8	22.25	75.89	22.28	75.97	22.32	76.2	22.28	75.97
Moon	22.83	77.57	22.84	77.52	22.84	77.6	22.84	77.55	22.84	77.56
FedRNL	**23.92**	**80.56**	**23.93**	**80.67**	**23.95**	**80.42**	**23.94**	**80.59**	**23.93**	**80.56**

Table 2. Best test accuracy(%) and GR(%) over Hotel datasets. **Bold** fonts highlight the best accuracy.

Methods	Cleanliness		Location		Service		Average	
	GR	ACC	GR	ACC	GR	ACC	GR	ACC
FedAvg	14.72	87.97	14.70	86.95	14.75	87.29	14.72	87.40
FedProx	14.98	87.63	15.01	87.80	14.97	86.95	14.99	87.46
FedBABU	15.09	87.12	15.11	87.12	15.06	87.97	15.09	87.40
FedDyn	15.02	83.05	14.97	82.54	14.98	82.71	14.99	82.77
Moon	14.35	85.08	14.36	84.75	14.38	84.92	14.36	84.92
FedRNL	**15.52**	**89.66**	**15.78**	**90.68**	**15.50**	**89.15**	**15.60**	**89.83**

We assess model performance on the validation sets of these aspects independently. Additionally, to measure the model's generalization ability across different aspects, we construct a mixed validation set by randomly sampling 50% of the data from each validation set and reporting the average performance. Table 1 and Table 2 demonstrate the superior performance of FedRNL compared to traditional federated learning methods across the Beer and Hotel datasets. In Table 1 (Beer dataset), FedRNL achieves the highest ACC of 80.56% and the best GR of 23.93% at the highest non-IID level, significantly outperforming other methods such as second-best method Moon (77.56% ACC, 22.84% GR) and FedAvg (73.36% ACC, 22.76% GR). Similarly, in Table 2 (Hotel dataset), FedRNL again achieves the best performance with an ACC of 89.83% and GR of 15.60% at the highest non-IID level, surpassing the second-best method, FedProx (87.46% ACC, 14.99% GR). These results indicate that FedRNL not only improves model accuracy but also enhances generalization across different datasets, effectively mitigating the significant challenges posed by non-IID data in federated learning and improving the model's interpretability.

Furthermore, the results on the mixed validation set confirm that FedRNL maintains strong generalization capabilities when handling data from multiple aspects. Unlike FedBABU, which exhibits weak performance in specific categories such as Appearance and Taste (66.54% and 67.33%, respectively), FedRNL achieves a more balanced and consistent improvement across different aspects. This suggests that the soft-sharing strategy between the generator and predictor ensures consistency in the shallow network while allowing the deep network to adapt to the non-IID data distribution. The substantial performance gap between FedRNL and other methods further highlights its robustness in heterogeneous federated learning scenarios.

6.2 Ablation Study

To further verify the contributions of our proposed method, we conduct ablation studies in different settings. The learning rate of the model training and other settings remains consistent.

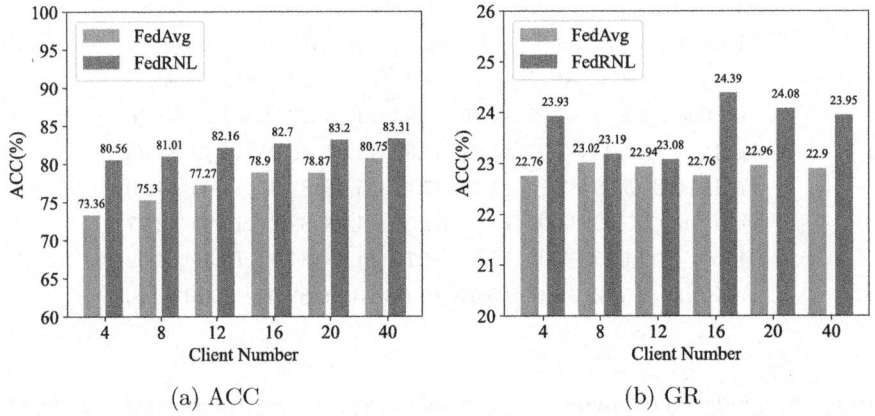

Fig. 3. Model performance comparison under different non-IID levels.

Impact of Different Non-IID Level. To evaluate the performance of FedRNL under different non-IID levels (i.e., different numbers of clients), we compared the ACC and GR of FedRNL with FedAvg across varying numbers of clients on Beer dataset. We partitioned each aspect data into 10 subsets, resulting in a total of 40 subsets while ensuring that each subset maintains the same label distribution. Each client randomly selects one subset for training. Clients originating from the same dataset are categorized as IID clients, whereas those from different datasets are considered non-IID clients. As the number of clients decreases, the degree of non-IID increases, leading to more pronounced data heterogeneity. Figure 3a presents the ACC across different client settings, demonstrating that FedRNL consistently outperforms FedAvg, with the performance gap becoming more pronounced in highly non-IID scenarios. Specifically, when the number of clients is 4 (highest non-IID level), FedRNL achieves 80.56% accuracy, significantly surpassing FedAvg (73.36%), indicating its superior ability to mitigate performance

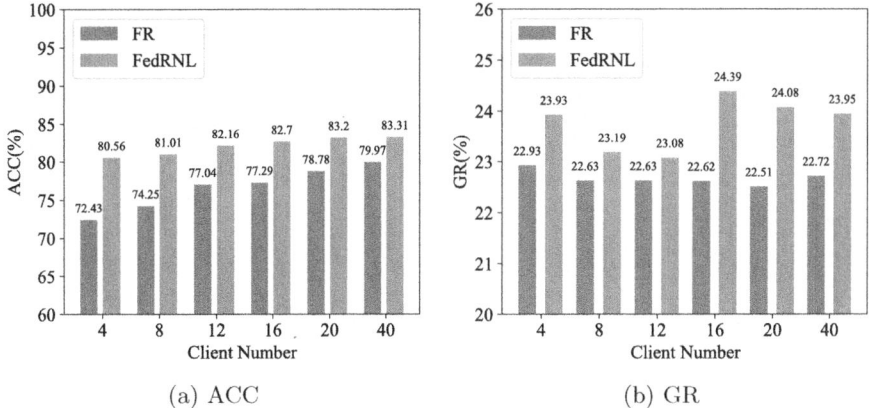

Fig. 4. Model performance comparison under different sharing ways.

degradation caused by data heterogeneity. As the number of clients increases, the non-IID effect weakens, and the accuracy of both methods improves, but FedRNL maintains a consistent advantage. Figure 3b shows that FedRNL consistently achieves higher GR scores than FedAvg, with a peak GR of 23.93% at 4 clients, compared to 22.76% for FedAvg. This suggests that FedRNL not only improves accuracy but also enhances interpretability by generating rationales that better align with human annotations.

Impact of Different Sharing Ways. To analyze FedRNL's effectiveness compared to FR, we evaluate performance under different non-IID levels on the Beer dataset. FR uses a hard-sharing experimental setup that uses an identical encoder, meaning that the encoder parameters of both the generator and the predictor are completely the same. Figure 4a shows that FedRNL consistently outperforms FR in ACC, demonstrating the advantages of soft-sharing encoder parameters instead of enforcing full parameter sharing. When the number of clients is 4 (highest non-IID level), FedRNL achieves 80.56% accuracy, significantly outperforming FR's 72.43%, indicating that FR sharing limits the model's adaptability to non-IID data, whereas FedRNL's soft-sharing approach enables better feature extraction and generalization across different client distributions. Figure 4b indicates that FedRNL consistently achieves higher GR scores than FR across all client settings. The gap is most prominent at 4 clients (highest non-IID level), where FedRNL attains 23.93% compared to FR's 22.93%, demonstrating that soft-sharing encoders improve rationale alignment in highly non-IID level.

Impact of Different Local Epoch. We evaluate the impact of varying the number of local epochs on ACC and GR on the Beer dataset. Figure 5 shows that FedRNL consistently outperforms FedAvg, demonstrating superior model performance. However, as the number of local epochs increases from 2 to 7, both FedRNL and FedAvg exhibit a slight decline in ACC and GR, which may be attributed to local overfitting caused by excessive local updates in a highly

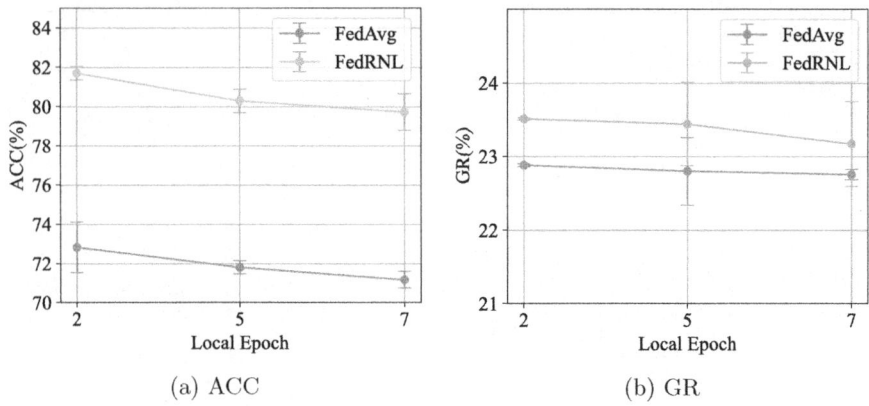

Fig. 5. Model performance comparison under different local epoch.

Table 3. Best test accuracy(%) and GR(%) using different encoder loss over Beer dataset. **Bold** fonts highlight the best accuracy.

Loss	4		8		12		16		20		40	
	GR	ACC	GR	ACC	GR	ACC	GR	ACC	GR	ACC	GR	ACC
FedAvg	22.76	73.36	23.02	75.30	22.94	77.27	22.76	78.90	22.46	78.87	22.90	80.75
Cos	22.43	75.13	22.68	76.65	22.71	77.88	22.80	78.81	22.59	80.28	22.86	81.15
L1	20.27	78.76	22.52	79.74	21.13	64.86	24.30	80.30	20.03	70.26	**24.54**	80.92
L2	21.23	76.14	22.46	77.32	21.67	80.25	21.78	81.37	21.80	82.72	21.62	82.95
Frobenius	**23.93**	**80.56**	**23.19**	**81.01**	**23.08**	**82.16**	**24.39**	**82.70**	**24.08**	**83.20**	23.95	**83.31**

non-IID setting. Despite this decline, FedRNL maintains a significant accuracy and interpretability advantage over FedAvg across all settings, highlighting its robustness in FL scenarios.

Impact of Different Encoder Loss. To evaluate the effect of different encoder loss functions on model performance, we compare FedAvg under different non-IID levels with four loss functions: Cosine Similarity (Cos), L1 loss, L2 loss, and Frobenius norm loss. Table 3 shows that across different non-IID levels, the Frobenius norm loss consistently achieves the highest accuracy, outperforming other loss functions, including FedAvg. For instance, with 40 clients, the Frobenius loss reaches 83.31%, which is the best among all configurations. And the L1 loss also performs relatively well. The GR values show a similar trend, where Frobenius loss achieves the highest GR across different non-IID levels, only 0.59% below the L1 function at 40 clients. Experimental results demonstrate the ability of our proposed encoder loss to guarantee model interpretability and alleviate non-IID problems. And Frobenius loss is the most effective encoder loss function, as it provides the best balance between accuracy and generalization.

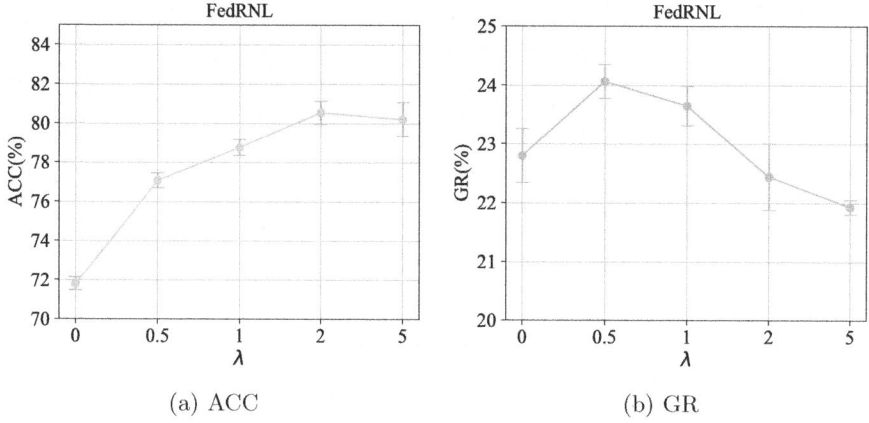

Fig. 6. Model performance comparison under different encoder weight.

Impact of Different Encoder Weight. To evaluate the impact of the encoder weight on FedRNL's performance, we conduct experiments with varying values of λ over Beer dataset. Figure 6a shows that ACC improves consistently as λ increases, reaching a peak at approximately 80%. This suggests that incorporating encoder alignment enhances model consistency and improves performance. However, further increasing λ to 5 results in a slight decline in ACC, indicating that over-constrained representations may restrict the model's learning flexibility and hinder adaptation to diverse client distributions. Figure 6b reveals a non-monotonic trend in GR. The generalization ratio initially increases, peaking at $\lambda = 0.5$ with a value above 24%, demonstrating that moderate encoder alignment improves the quality of rationales. However, GR starts to decline as λ further increases beyond 1, suggesting that excessive alignment may lead to over-constrained representations, reducing rationale diversity and quality.

7 Conclusion

In this work, we introduce FedRNL, the first method to adapt rationalization models to federated learning (FL) while addressing the challenges of non-IID data. By incorporating soft-sharing between generator and predictor encoders, we ensure consistency in the shallow network while allowing the deep network to adapt to the non-IID data distribution. Additionally, the encoder loss function ensures feature alignment, while our layer-wise aggregation strategy improves robustness in global model updates. Our theoretical results guarantee the convergence of FedRNL. Experimental results on benchmark datasets demonstrate that FedRNL significantly improves both classification accuracy and rationale quality, effectively bridging the gap between interpretability and FL robustness.

Acknowledgments. This work is supported by the National Key Research and Development Program of China under grant 2024YFC3307900; the National Natural Science

Foundation of China under grants 62376103, 62302184, 62436003 and 62206102; Major Science and Technology Project of Hubei Province under grant 2024BAA008; Hubei Science and Technology Talent Service Project under grant 2024DJC078; and Ant Group through CCF-Ant Research Fund.

Disclosure of Interests. The authors have no competing interests to declare that are relevant to the content of this article.

References

1. Acar, D.A.E., Zhao, Y., Navarro, R.M., Mattina, M., Whatmough, P.N., Saligrama, V.: Federated learning based on dynamic regularization. In: 9th International Conference on Learning Representations, ICLR 2021, Virtual Event, Austria, 3–7 May 2021. OpenReview.net (2021)
2. Arivazhagan, M.G., Aggarwal, V., Singh, A.K., Choudhary, S.: Federated learning with personalization layers. arXiv preprint arXiv:1912.00818 (2019)
3. Arous, I., Dolamic, L., Yang, J., Bhardwaj, A., Cuccu, G., Cudré-Mauroux, P.: Marta: leveraging human rationales for explainable text classification. In: AAAI, vol. 35, pp. 5868–5876 (2021)
4. Atanasova, P.: Generating fact checking explanations. In: Accountable and Explainable Methods for Complex Reasoning over Text, pp. 83–103. Springer, Cham (2024)
5. Bastings, J., Aziz, W., Titov, I.: Interpretable neural predictions with differentiable binary variables. In: Proceedings of the 57th AMACL, pp. 2963–2977. ACL Anthology (2019)
6. Chan, A., et al.: Unirex: a unified learning framework for language model rationale extraction. In: International Conference on Machine Learning, pp. 2867–2889. PMLR (2022)
7. Chen, H., Chao, W.: On bridging generic and personalized federated learning for image classification. In: The Tenth International Conference on Learning Representations, ICLR 2022, Virtual Event, 25–29 April 2022. OpenReview.net (2022)
8. Chen, H., He, J., Narasimhan, K., Chen, D.: Can rationalization improve robustness? In: 2022 Conference of the North American Chapter of the Association for Computational Linguistics: Human Language Technologies, NAACL 2022, pp. 3792–3805. Association for Computational Linguistics (ACL) (2022)
9. Cho, K., et al.: Learning phrase representations using RNN encoder-decoder for statistical machine translation. arXiv preprint arXiv:1406.1078 (2014)
10. Dai, Y., Chen, Z., Li, J., Heinecke, S., Sun, L., Xu, R.: Tackling data heterogeneity in federated learning with class prototypes. In: Proceedings of the AAAI Conference on Artificial Intelligence, vol. 37, pp. 7314–7322 (2023)
11. Huang, Y., Chen, Y., Du, Y., Yang, Z.: Distribution matching for rationalization. In: Proceedings of the AAAI Conference on Artificial Intelligence, vol. 35, pp. 13090–13097 (2021)
12. Jang, M., Lukasiewicz, T.: Are training resources insufficient? Predict first then explain! arXiv preprint arXiv:2110.02056 (2021)
13. Kingma, D.P., Ba, J.: Adam: a method for stochastic optimization. In: Bengio, Y., LeCun, Y. (eds.) 3rd International Conference on Learning Representations, ICLR 2015, San Diego, CA, USA, 7–9 May 2015, Conference Track Proceedings (2015)

14. Kornblith, S., Norouzi, M., Lee, H., Hinton, G.: Similarity of neural network representations revisited. In: International Conference on Machine Learning, pp. 3519–3529. PMLR (2019)
15. Lei, T., Barzilay, R., Jaakkola, T.: Rationalizing neural predictions. In: Proceedings of the 2016 Conference on Empirical Methods in Natural Language Processing, pp. 107–117 (2016)
16. Li, Q., He, B., Song, D.: Model-contrastive federated learning. In: Proceedings of the IEEE/CVF Conference on Computer Vision and Pattern Recognition, pp. 10713–10722 (2021)
17. Li, T., Hu, S., Beirami, A., Smith, V.: Ditto: fair and robust federated learning through personalization. In: International Conference on Machine Learning, pp. 6357–6368. PMLR (2021)
18. Li, T., Sahu, A.K., Zaheer, M., Sanjabi, M., Talwalkar, A., Smith, V.: Federated optimization in heterogeneous networks. Proc. Mach. Learn. Syst. **2**, 429–450 (2020)
19. Lipton, Z.C.: The mythos of model interpretability: in machine learning, the concept of interpretability is both important and slippery. Queue **16**(3), 31–57 (2018)
20. Liu, W., Wang, H., Wang, J., Li, R., Yue, C., Zhang, Y.: FR: folded rationalization with a unified encoder. In: Advances in Neural Information Processing Systems, vol. 35, pp. 6954–6966 (2022)
21. Luo, M., Chen, F., Hu, D., Zhang, Y., Liang, J., Feng, J.: No fear of heterogeneity: classifier calibration for federated learning with non-IID data. In: Advances in Neural Information Processing Systems, vol. 34, pp. 5972–5984 (2021)
22. McAuley, J.J., Leskovec, J., Jurafsky, D.: Learning attitudes and attributes from multi-aspect reviews. In: ICDM 2012, pp. 1020–1025. IEEE Computer Society (2012)
23. McMahan, B., Moore, E., Ramage, D., Hampson, S., Arcas, B.A.: Communication-efficient learning of deep networks from decentralized data. In: Artificial Intelligence and Statistics, pp. 1273–1282. PMLR (2017)
24. Mendez Guzman, E., Schlegel, V., Batista-Navarro, R.: From outputs to insights: a survey of rationalization approaches for explainable text classification. Front. Artif. Intell. **7**, 1363531 (2024)
25. Meng, L., et al.: Improving global generalization and local personalization for federated learning. IEEE Trans. Neural Netw. Learn. Syst. (2024)
26. Mosbach, M., Gautam, V., Vergara-Browne, T., Klakow, D., Geva, M.: From insights to actions: the impact of interpretability and analysis research on NLP. arXiv preprint arXiv:2406.12618 (2024)
27. Narang, S., Raffel, C., Lee, K., Roberts, A., Fiedel, N., Malkan, K.: Wt5?! training text-to-text models to explain their predictions. arXiv preprint arXiv:2004.14546 (2020)
28. Oh, J., Kim, S., Yun, S.Y.: Fedbabu: towards enhanced representation for federated image classification. arXiv preprint arXiv:2106.06042 (2021)
29. Qi, Z., Meng, L., Chen, Z., Hu, H., Lin, H., Meng, X.: Cross-silo prototypical calibration for federated learning with non-IID data. In: Proceedings of the 31st ACM International Conference on Multimedia, pp. 3099–3107 (2023)
30. Rajani, N.F., McCann, B., Xiong, C., Socher, R.: Explain yourself! leveraging language models for commonsense reasoning. In: ACL 2019 Volume 1: Long Papers, pp. 4932–4942 (2019)
31. Sun, X., et al.: Interpreting deep learning models in natural language processing: a review. arXiv preprint arXiv:2110.10470 (2021)

32. T. Dinh, C., Tran, N., Nguyen, J.: Personalized federated learning with Moreau envelopes. In: Advances in Neural Information Processing Systems, vol. 33, pp. 21394–21405 (2020)
33. Tan, Y., et al.: Fedproto: federated prototype learning across heterogeneous clients. In: Proceedings of the AAAI Conference on Artificial Intelligence, vol. 36, pp. 8432–8440 (2022)
34. Vashishth, S., Upadhyay, S., Tomar, G.S., Faruqui, M.: Attention interpretability across NLP tasks. arXiv preprint arXiv:1909.11218 (2019)
35. Wang, H., Dou, Y.: Recent development on extractive rationale for model interpretability: a survey. In: 2022 International Conference on Cloud Computing, Big Data and Internet of Things (3CBIT), pp. 354–358. IEEE (2022)
36. Wang, H., Zheng, P., Han, X., Xu, W., Li, R., Zhang, T.: FedNLR: federated learning with neuron-wise learning rates. In: Proceedings of the 30th ACM SIGKDD Conference on Knowledge Discovery and Data Mining, pp. 3069–3080 (2024)
37. Wang, H., Lu, Y., Zhai, C.: Latent aspect rating analysis on review text data: a rating regression approach. In: Rao, B., Krishnapuram, B., Tomkins, A., Yang, Q. (eds.) Proceedings of the 16th ACM SIGKDD, pp. 783–792. ACM (2010)
38. Yu, M., Zhang, Y., Chang, S., Jaakkola, T.: Understanding interlocking dynamics of cooperative rationalization. In: Advances in Neural Information Processing Systems, vol. 34, pp. 12822–12835 (2021)
39. Zhang, D., Sen, C., Thadajarassiri, J., Hartvigsen, T., Kong, X., Rundensteiner, E.: Human-like explanation for text classification with limited attention supervision. In: 2021 IEEE International Conference on Big Data, pp. 957–967. IEEE (2021)
40. Zhang, L., et al.: Towards few-label vertical federated learning. ACM TKDD (2024)
41. Zhu, Z., Hong, J., Zhou, J.: Data-free knowledge distillation for heterogeneous federated learning. In: International Conference on Machine Learning, pp. 12878–12889. PMLR (2021)

Bkd-FedGNN: A Benchmark for Classification Backdoor Attacks on Federated Graph Neural Network

Fan Liu[1], Siqi Lai[1], Yansong Ning[1], and Hao Liu[1,2](✉)

[1] AI Thrust, The Hong Kong University of Science and Technology (Guangzhou), Guangzhou, China
{fliu236,slai125,yansongning}@connect.hkust-gz.edu.cn
[2] CSE, The Hong Kong University of Science and Technology, Hong Kong, China
liuh@ust.hk

Abstract. Federated Graph Neural Network (FedGNN) has recently emerged as a rapidly growing research topic, as it integrates the strengths of graph neural networks and federated learning to enable advanced machine learning applications without direct access to sensitive data. Despite its advantages, the distributed nature of FedGNN introduces additional vulnerabilities, particularly backdoor attacks stemming from malicious participants. Although graph backdoor attacks have been explored, the compounded complexity introduced by the combination of GNNs and federated learning has hindered a comprehensive understanding of these attacks, as existing research lacks extensive benchmark coverage and in-depth analysis of critical factors. To address these limitations, we propose Bkd-FedGNN, a benchmark for backdoor attacks on FedGNN. Specifically, Bkd-FedGNN decomposes the graph backdoor attack into trigger generation and injection steps, and extends the attack to the node-level federated setting, resulting in a unified framework that covers both node-level and graph-level classification tasks. Moreover, we thoroughly investigate the impact of multiple critical factors in backdoor attacks on FedGNN. These factors are categorized into global-level and local-level factors, including data distribution, the number of malicious attackers, attack time, overlapping rate, trigger size, trigger type, trigger position, and poisoning rate. Finally, we conduct comprehensive evaluations on 13 benchmark datasets and 13 critical factors, comprising 1,725 experimental configurations for node-level and graph-level tasks from six domains. These experiments encompass over 8,000 individual tests, allowing us to provide a thorough evaluation and insightful observations that advance our understanding of backdoor attacks on FedGNN. Our code is available at https://github.com/usail-hkust/BkdFedGCN.

Keywords: Federated graph learning · Backdoor attack · Graph learning

Supplementary Information The online version contains supplementary material available at https://doi.org/10.1007/978-3-032-05981-9_22.

1 Introduction

The Federated Graph Neural Network (FedGNN) has emerged as a fast-evolving research area that combines the capabilities of graph neural networks and federated learning. Such integration allows for advanced machine learning applications without requiring direct access to sensitive data [15–17,25,26]. However, despite its numerous advantages, the distributed nature of FedGNN introduces additional vulnerabilities, particularly related to backdoor attacks originating from malicious participants. In particular, these adversaries have the ability to inject graph backdoor triggers into their training data, thereby undermining the overall trustworthiness of the system [21,24,29,42].

Although considerable research efforts have explored graph backdoor attacks on FedGNN [5,12,44,46], a comprehensive understanding of these attacks is hindered by the compounded complexity introduced by the combination of Graph Neural Networks (GNNs) and Federated Learning (FL). Existing studies suffer from a lack of extensive benchmark coverage and in-depth analysis of critical factors. **(1) Lack of Extensive Benchmark Coverage.** Specifically, the lack of extensive benchmark coverage poses challenges in fairly and comprehensively comparing graph backdoor attacks on FedGNN across different settings. These settings can be categorized into two levels: the graph backdoor attack level and the FedGNN task level. At the graph backdoor attack level, trigger generation and injection steps are involved. Additionally, the classification tasks in FedGNN encompass both node and graph classification tasks. However, there is still a dearth of comprehensive exploration of graph backdoor attacks on FedGNN under these various settings. **(2) Insufficient Exploration of Multiple Factors.** Furthermore, there has been the insufficient exploration of multiple factors that impact FedGNN. The combination of GNN with FL introduces various factors that affect backdoor attacks, such as trigger type, trigger size, and data distribution. The insufficient exploration and analysis of these multiple factors make it difficult to understand the influence of key factors on the behavior of FedGNN.

To address these limitations, we propose a benchmark for graph backdoor attacks on FedGNN, called Bkd-FedGNN. As far as we are aware, our work is the first comprehensive investigation of graph backdoor attacks on FedGNN. Our contributions can be summarized as follows. (1) **Unified Framework**: We propose a unified framework for classification backdoor attacks on FedGNN. Bkd-FedGNN decomposes the graph backdoor attack into trigger generation and injection steps and extends the attack to the node-level federated setting, resulting in a unified framework that covers both node-level and graph-level classification tasks. (2) **Exploration of Multiple Critical Factors**: We thoroughly investigate the impact of multiple critical factors on graph backdoor attacks in FedGNN. We systematically categorize these factors into two levels: global level and local level. At the global level, factors such as data distribution, the number of malicious attackers, the start time of backdoor attacks, and the overlapping rate play significant roles. In addition, the local level factors involve factors such as trigger size, trigger type, trigger position, and poisoning rate.

(3) **Comprehensive Experiments and Analysis**: We conduct comprehensive experiments on both benchmark experiments and critical factor analysis. For the benchmark experiments, we consider combinations of trigger types, trigger positions, datasets, and models, resulting in 315 configurations for the node level and 270 configurations for the graph-level tasks. Regarding the critical factors, we consider combinations of factors, datasets, and models, resulting in 672 configurations for the node-level tasks and 468 configurations for the graph-level tasks. Each configuration is tested five times, resulting in approximately 8,000 individual experiments in total. Based on these experiments, we thoroughly evaluate the presented comprehensive analysis and provide insightful observations that advance the field.

2 Federated Graph Neural Network

In this section, we provide an introduction to the preliminary aspects of FedGNN. Currently, FedGNN primarily focuses on exploring common classification tasks, which involve both node-level and graph-level classification. The FedGNN consists of two levels: client-level local training and server-level federated optimization. We will begin by providing an overview of the notations used, followed by a detailed explanation of the client-level local training, which encompasses message passing and readout techniques. Lastly, we will introduce server-level federated optimization.

2.1 Notations

Assume that there exist K clients denoted as $\mathcal{C} = \{c_k\}_{k=1}^{K}$. Each client, c_i, possesses a private dataset denoted as $\mathcal{D}^i = \{(\mathcal{G}_j^i, \mathbf{Y}_j^i)\}_{j=1}^{N_i}$, wherein $\mathcal{G}_j^i = (\mathcal{V}_j^i, \mathcal{E}_j^i)$ is the graph, where $\mathcal{V}^i = \{v_t\}_{t=1}^{n_i}$ (n_i denotes the number of nodes) is the set of nodes, and $\mathcal{E}^i = \{e_{tk}\}_{t,k}$ is the set of edges (for simplicity, we exclude the subscript j that indicates the index of the j-th dataset in the dataset $\mathcal{D}^i$). $N_i = |\mathcal{D}^i|$ denotes the total number of data samples in the private dataset of client c_i. We employ the notation $\mathbf{A}_j^i$ to denote the adjacency matrix of graph $\mathcal{G}_j^i$ belonging to client c_i within the set of clients $\mathcal{C}$. $\mathbf{X}_j^i$ represents the node feature set , and $\mathbf{Y}_j^i$ corresponds to the label sets.

2.2 Client-Level Local Training

To ensure versatility and inclusiveness, we employ the message passing neural network (MPNN) framework [9,14,32], which encompasses a diverse range of spectral-based GNNs, such as GCN [19], as well as spatial-based GNNs including GAT [37] and GraphSage [13], *etc.*. Each client possesses a GNN model that collaboratively trains a global model. The local graph learning process can be divided into two stages: message passing and readout.

Message Passing. For each client c_i, the l-th layer in MPNN can be formulated as follows,

$$\mathbf{h}_j^{l,i} = \sigma(w^{l,i} \cdot (\mathbf{h}_j^{l-1,i}, Agg(\{\mathbf{h}_k^{l-1,i}|v_k \in \mathcal{N}(v_j)\}))), \tag{1}$$

where $\mathbf{h}_j^{l,i}$ ($l = 0, \cdots, L-1$) represents the hidden feature of node v_j in client c_i and $\mathbf{h}_j^{0,i} = \mathbf{x}_j$ denotes the node v_j's raw feature. The σ represents the activation function (e.g., ReLU, sigmoid). The parameter $w^{l,i}$ corresponds to the l-th learnable parameter. The aggregation operation Agg (e.g., mean pooling) combines the hidden features $\mathbf{h}_k^{l-1,i}$ of neighboring nodes $v_k \in \mathcal{N}(v_j)$ for node v_j, where $\mathcal{N}(v_j)$ represents the set of neighbors of node v_j. Assume that the $\mathbf{w}^i = \{w^{l,i}\}_{l=0}^{L-1}$ is the set of learn able parameters for client c_i.

Readout. Following the propagation of information through L layers of MPNN, the final hidden feature is computed using a readout function for subsequent tasks.

$$\hat{y}_I^i = R_{\theta^i}(\{\mathbf{h}_j^{L,i}|v_j \in \mathcal{V}_I^i\}), \tag{2}$$

where $\hat{y}_I^i$ represents the prediction for a node or graph. Specifically, I serves as an indicator, where $I = v_j$ denotes the prediction for node v_j, and $I = \mathcal{G}^i$ denotes the prediction for the graph $\mathcal{G}^i$. The readout function $R_{\theta^i}(\cdot)$ encompasses methods such as mean pooling or sum pooling *etc..*, where θ^i is the parameter for readout function.

2.3 Server-Level Federated Optimization

Let us consider that $\mathbf{w}^i = \{w^{l,i}\}_{l=0}^{L-1}$ represents the set of trainable parameters within the MPNN framework associated with client c_i. Consequently, we define the overall model parameters as $\mathbf{W}^i = \{\mathbf{w}^i, \theta^i\}$ for each client $c_i \in \mathcal{C}$. The GNNs, which constitute a part of this framework, can be represented as $f_i(\mathbf{X}_j^i, \mathbf{A}_j^i; \mathbf{W}^i)$. The objective of FL is to optimize the global objective function while preserving the privacy of local data on each individual local model. The overall objective function can be formulated as follows,

$$\min_{\{\mathbf{W}^i\}} \sum_{i \in \mathcal{C}} \frac{N_i}{N} F_i(\mathbf{W}^i), \quad F_i(\mathbf{W}^i) = \frac{1}{N_i} \sum_{j \in \mathcal{D}^i} \mathcal{L}((f_i(\mathbf{X}_j^i, \mathbf{A}_j^i; \mathbf{W}^i), \mathbf{Y}_j^i), \tag{3}$$

where $F_i(\cdot)$ denotes the local objective function, and $\mathcal{L}(\cdot)$ denote the loss function (*e.g.*, cross-entropy *etc..*), and $N = \sum_{i=1}^{K} N_i$ represent the total number of data samples encompassing all clients.

We illustrate the process of federated optimization, aimed at achieving a generalized model while ensuring privacy preservation, by utilizing a representative federated algorithm, FedAvg [28]. Specifically, in each round denoted by t, the central server transmits the global model parameter $\mathbf{W}_t$ to a subset of clients that have been selected for local training. Subsequently, each chosen client c_i refines the received parameter $\mathbf{W}_t$ using an optimizer operating on its private

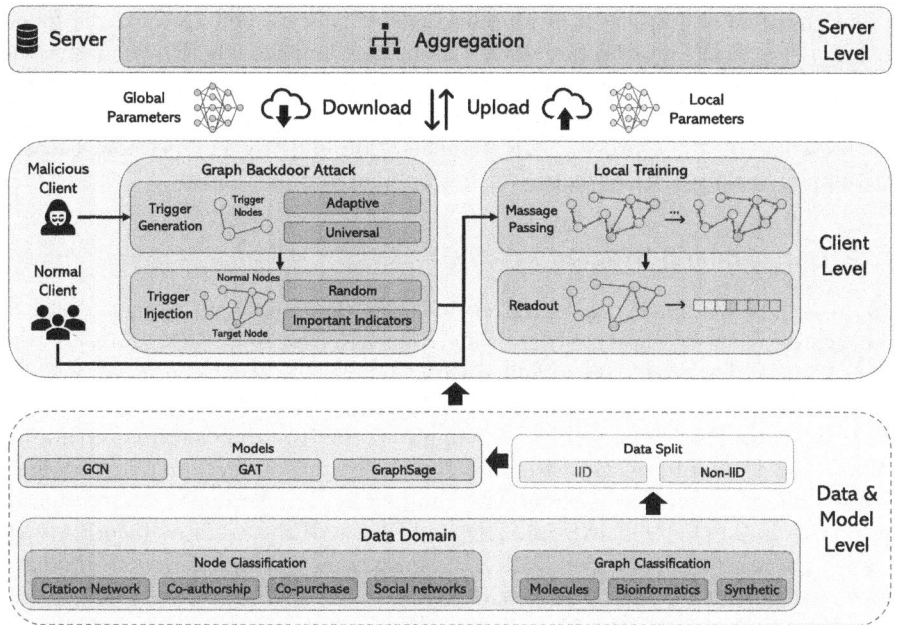

Fig. 1. A unified framework for classification backdoor attack on FedGNN.

dataset $\mathcal{D}^i$. Following this, the selected clients upload the updated model parameter $\mathbf{W}_t^i$, and the central server aggregates the local model parameters to obtain the enhanced global model parameter $\mathbf{W}_{t+1}$.

In FedGNN setting, there exist diverse scenarios involving distributed graphs that are motivated by real-world applications. In these scenarios, classification tasks can be classified into two distinct settings based on how graphs are distributed across clients. **Node-level FedGNN**. Each client is equipped with a subgraph, and the prevalent tasks involve node classification. Real-world applications, such as social networks, demonstrate situations where relationships between nodes can span across different clients, and each node possesses a unique label. **Graph-level FedGNN**. Each client possesses a set of graphs, and the primary focus lies on graph classification tasks. Real-world applications, such as protein discovery, exemplify instances where each institution holds a limited graph along with associated labels (Fig. 1).

3 A Unified Framework for Classification Backdoor Attack on FedGNN

This section presents a unified framework for classification backdoor attacks on federated GNNs. Our primary focus is on graph-based backdoor attacks, where malicious entities strategically insert triggers into graphs or subgraphs to compromise the trustworthiness of FedGNN. A comprehensive illustration of our unified framework for classification backdoor attacks on FedGNN can be found in Fig. 1. In detail, we first introduce the dataset and models and then give the evaluation metric, then introduce the threat model. Next, we introduce the federated graph backdoor attack, which involves the formulation of the attack goal and a two-step attack process: trigger generation and trigger injection. Finally, we explore various critical factors at both global and local levels.

3.1 Datasets and Models

In this study, we have considered six distinct domains comprising a total of thirteen datasets, along with three widely used GNNs. *Node-level Datasets:* For node-level analysis, we have included three extensively studied citation graphs, such as Cora, CiteSeer, and PubMed. Additionally, we have incorporated the Co-authorship graphs (CS and Physics), along with the Amazon Co-purchase graphs (Photo and Computers). *Graph-level Datasets:* For graph-level analysis, we have utilized molecular graphs such as AIDS and NCI1. Furthermore, bioinformatics graphs, including PROTEINS-full, DD, and ENZYMES, have been incorporated. Lastly, a synthetic graph, COLORS-3, has also been employed. *Models:* We have employed three widely adopted GNNs: GCN, GAT, and GraphSage, which have been demonstrated effective in various graph-based tasks. For detailed statistical information about the graphs used, please refer to Appendix.

3.2 Evaluation Metrics

To assess the effectiveness of the graph backdoor attack on FedGNN, three metrics are employed: the average clean accuracy (ACC) across all clients, the average attack success rate (ASR) on malicious clients, and the transferred attack success rate (TAST) on normal clients. The ACC metric evaluates the performance of federated GNNs when exposed to clean examples from all clients. The ASR metric measures the performance of the graph backdoor attack specifically on the malicious clients. Lastly, the TAST metric gauges the vulnerability of normal clients to the graph backdoor attack. For the detailed equations corresponding to these metrics, please refer to Appendix.

3.3 Threat Model

Attack Objective. Assuming there are a total of K clients, with M ($M \leq K$) of them being malicious, each malicious attacker independently conducts the backdoor attack on their own models. The primary goal of a backdoor attack is to manipulate the model in such a way that it misclassifies specific pre-defined labels (known as target labels) only within the poisoned data samples. It is important to ensure that the model's accuracy remains unaffected when processing clean data. **Attack Knowledge.** In this setting, we assume that the malicious attacker has complete knowledge of their own training data. They have the capability to generate triggers. It should be noted that this scenario is quite practical since the clients have full control over their own data. **Attacker Capability.** The malicious client has the ability to inject triggers into the training datasets, but this capability is limited within predetermined constraints such as trigger size and poisoned data rate. The intention is to contaminate the training datasets. However, the malicious client lacks the ability to manipulate the server-side aggregation process or interfere with other clients' training processes and models.

3.4 Federated Graph Backdoor Attack

Mathematically, the formal attack objective for each malicious client c_i during round t can be defined as follows,

$$\mathbf{W}_t^{i*} = \arg\min_{\mathbf{W}_t^i} \frac{1}{N_i} \left[\sum_{j \in \mathcal{D}_p^i} \mathcal{L}((f_i(\mathbf{X}_j^i, g_\tau \circ \mathbf{A}_j^i; \mathbf{W}_{t-1}^i), \tau) + \sum_{j \in \mathcal{D}_c^i} \mathcal{L}((f_i(\mathbf{X}_j^i, \mathbf{A}_j^i; \mathbf{W}_{t-1}^i), \mathbf{Y}_j^i) \right], \quad (4)$$

$$\forall j \in \mathcal{D}_p^i, N_\tau = |g_\tau| \leq \triangle_g \quad \text{and} \quad \rho = \frac{|\mathcal{D}_p^i|}{|\mathcal{D}^i|} \leq \triangle_p,$$

where $\mathcal{D}_p^i$ refers to the set of poisoned data and $\mathcal{D}_c^i$ corresponds to the clean dataset. Noted that $\mathcal{D}_p^i \sqcup \mathcal{D}_c^i = \mathcal{D}^i$ and $\mathcal{D}_p^i \sqcap \mathcal{D}_c^i = \phi$, indicating the union and intersection of the poisoned and clean data sets, respectively. $g_\tau \circ \mathbf{A}_j^i$ represents the poisoned graph resulting from an attack. g_τ represents the trigger generated by the attacker, which is then embedded into the clean graph, thereby contaminating the datasets. Additionally, τ denotes the target label. $N_\tau = |g_\tau|$ denotes the trigger size and $\triangle_g$ represents the constrain to ensures that the trigger size remains within the specified limit. $\rho = \frac{|\mathcal{D}p^i|}{|\mathcal{D}^i|}$ represents the poisoned rate, and $\triangle p$ denotes the budget allocated for poisoned data.

In the federated graph backdoor attack, to generate the trigger and poisoned data sets, the graph backdoor attack can be divided into two steps: trigger generation and trigger injection. The term "trigger" (a specific pattern) has been formally defined as a subgraph in the work by Zhang et al. (2021), providing a clear and established framework for its characterization [50].

Trigger Generation. The process of trigger generation can be defined as the function $\varphi(\mathbf{X}_j^i, \mathbf{A}_j^i)$, which yields the generated trigger g_τ through $\varphi(\mathbf{X}_j^i, \mathbf{A}_j^i) = g_\tau$.

Trigger Injection. The process of trigger injection can be defined as the function $a(g_\tau, \mathbf{A}_j^i)$, which generates the final poisoned graph $g_\tau \circ \mathbf{A}_j^i$ by incorporating the trigger g_τ into the pristine graph $\mathbf{A}_j^i$.

3.5 Factors in Federated Graph Backdoor

The graph backdoor attack framework in FedGNN encompasses various critical factors that warrant exploration. These factors can be categorized into two levels: the global level and the local level. At the global level, factors such as data distribution, the number of malicious attackers, the start time of backdoor attacks, and overlapping rate play significant roles. On the other hand, the local level involves parameters like trigger size, trigger type, trigger position, and poisoning rate. Notably, the overlapping rate holds particular importance in node-level FedGNN, as it involves cross-nodes across multiple clients.

Global Level Factors: **Data Distribution.** The data distribution encompasses two distinct types: independent and identically distributed (IID) and non-independent and identically distributed (Non-IID). In detail, IID refers to data distribution among clients remaining constant, while Non-IID (L-Non-IID [39,49], PD-Non-IID [7], N-Non-IID [22]) refers that the data distribution among clients exhibiting variations. **Number of Malicious Attackers.** The concept of the number of malicious attackers, denoted as M, can be defined in the following manner. Let us assume that the set of malicious clients is denoted as $\mathcal{C}_m$, and the set of normal clients is denoted as $\mathcal{C}_n$. It can be inferred that $\mathcal{C}_m \sqcup \mathcal{C}_n = \mathcal{C}$ and $\mathcal{C}_m \sqcap \mathcal{C}_c = \phi$. **Attack Time.** In the context of FL, the attack time denotes the precise moment when a malicious attack is launched. The attack time can be denoted by t^*. **Overlapping Rate (specific to Node-level FedGNN).** The overlapping rate, represented by the variable α, pertains to the proportion of additional samples of overlapping data that across clients. This phenomenon arises in node-level FedGNN, 6where cross-client nodes exist, resulting in the sharing of common data samples between different clients.

Local Level Factors: **Trigger Size.** The size of the trigger can be quantified by counting the number of nodes within the corresponding graph. The trigger size is denoted by N_τ. **Trigger Type.** Based on the methods used to generate triggers(*e.g.*, Renyi [50], WS [40], BA [1], RR [35], GTA [41], and UGBA [6] *etc..*), the categorization of trigger types can be refined into two categories: universal triggers and adaptive triggers. Universal triggers are pre-generated through graph generation techniques, such as the Erdős-Rényi (ER) model [8], which are agnostic to the underlying graph datasets. On the other hand, adaptive triggers are specifically designed for individual graphs using optimization methods. **Trigger Position.** The trigger position refers to the specific location within a graph or sub-graph where the trigger is injected. Typically, the trigger position can be categorized into two types: random position and important indicator position. In the case of the random position, the trigger is injected into the graph in a random manner without any specific consideration. Conversely, the important indicator position entails injecting the trigger based on certain crucial centrality values, such as the degree or cluster-based scores, that indicate the significance of specific nodes within the graph. **Poisoning Rate.** The concept of poisoning rate, denoted as ρ, can be defined as the ratio of the cardinality of the set of poisoned data samples, $\mathcal{C}_p^i$, to the total number of data samples, denoted as $\mathcal{D}^i$. Mathematically, this can be expressed as $\rho = \frac{|\mathcal{D}_p^i|}{|\mathcal{D}^i|}$, where $\forall c_i \in \mathcal{C}$ signifies that the cardinality calculations are performed for every client c_i belonging to the set $\mathcal{C}$.

Table 1. Critical factors in federated graph backdoor.

	Factors	Symbol	Node Level	Graph Level
Global Level	Data Distribution	-	{IID*, L-Non-IID}	{IID*, PD-Non-IID, N-Non-IID }
	# of Malicious Attackers	M	{1*, 2, 3, 4, 5}	
	Attack Time	t^*	$T * \{0.0^*, 0.1, 0.2, 0.3, 0.4, 0.5\}$	
	Overlapping Rate	α	{0.1*, 0.2, 0.3, 0.4, 0.5}	-
Local Level	Trigger Size	N_τ	{3*, 4, 5, 6, 7, 8, 9, 10}	$N_d * \{0.1^*, 0.2, 0.3, 0.4, 0.5\}$
	Trigger Type	g_τ	{Renyi*, WS, BA, GTA, UGBA }	{ Renyi*, WS, BA, RR, GTA }
	Trigger Position	-	{Random*, Degree, Cluster }	
	Poisoning Rate	ρ	{0.1*, 0.2, 0.3, 0.4, 0.5}	

4 Experimental Studies

In this section, we present the experimental studies conducted to investigate classification backdoor attacks on FedGNN. Our main objective is to evaluate the impact of graph backdoor attacks on FedGNN covering both the node and graph level tasks. Additionally, we aim to explore the critical factors that influence the effectiveness of graph backdoor attacks on FedGNN, considering aspects from both the global and local levels.

4.1 Experimental Settings

Factors Settings. We present the detailed factors setup considered in our study. It is important to note that the first value presented represents the default setting. To assess the individual impact of each factor, we keep the remaining factors fixed while systematically varying the corresponding values in our experiments. The factors range is shown in Table 1. For the detailed setting for factor, please refer to Appendix.

Federated Graph Backdoor Attack. The federated graph backdoor attack can be characterized by the combination of trigger generation techniques (Renyi [50], WS [40], BA [1], RR [35], GTA [41], and UGBA [6]) and trigger position strategies (Random, Degree, and Cluster). For instance, the attack method Renyi-Random refers to the utilization of the ER model to generate the trigger, which is then randomly injected into the graph.

Implementation Details. Our implementation of the backdoor attack on FedGNN is based on the PyTorch framework. The experiments were carried out on two server configurations: three Linux Centos Servers, each with 4 RTX 3090 GPUs, and two Linux Ubuntu Servers, each with 2 V100 GPUs. In both node-level and graph-level tasks, we adopt the inductive learning settings as outlined in [6,44]. For each dataset, we ensure consistent experimental conditions by employing the same training and attack settings. We set the total number of clients to 5, and all clients participate in the training process at each round. Each experiment is repeated five times. For a detailed description of the training and attack settings, please refer to Appendix.

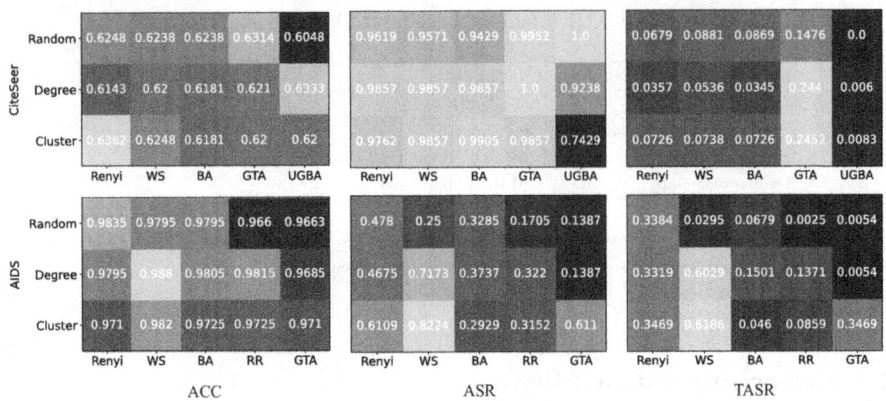

Fig. 2. Graph backdoor attack on both node and graph level tasks for GCN. (Color intensity corresponds to value magnitude)

4.2 Benchmark Results of Graph Backdoor Attack on FedGNN

The results of the benchmark for the graph backdoor attack on FedGNN are presented in Fig. 2. The observations are summarized as follows. (1) The node-level task exhibits higher vulnerability to attacks compared to the graph-level task at a relatively small trigger size. Specifically, a significant majority of graph backdoor attacks achieve an ASR (Attack Success Rate) exceeding 90%, while the highest ASR recorded at the graph level is 82.24%. (2) Despite not being intentionally poisoned by malicious attackers, the normal clients are still susceptible to graph backdoor attacks. For instance, in the node-level task, there is a TASR (Transfered Attack Success Rate) of 24.52%, while the graph-level task exhibits even higher vulnerability with a TASR of 61.86%. This observation suggests that the weights uploaded by the malicious clients can inadvertently influence the normal clients when they download the global model's weights. 3). The combination of trigger size and trigger position significantly influences the attack performance on the graph-level task compared to the node-level task. For instance, the attack WS-Cluster achieves an ASR of approximately 82.24%, while the GTA-Random achieves only about 13.87%. Due to the page limit, the benchmark results on other datasets and models please refer to Appendix.

4.3 Factors in Federated GNN

The overall results of factors can be shown in Figs. 3 and 4. *Global Level Factors:* **Data Distribution (DD).** For node-level tasks, there models trained on IID data are more vulnerable than models trained on Non-IID data. For graph-level tasks, the GCN trained on IID data are more vulnerable than models trained on Non-IID data (PD-Non-IID and N-Non-IID), while GAT and GraphSagr trained on Non-IID data are more vulnerable than models trained on IID data. **Number of Malicious Attackers (NMA).** For node-level tasks, an increase in NMA

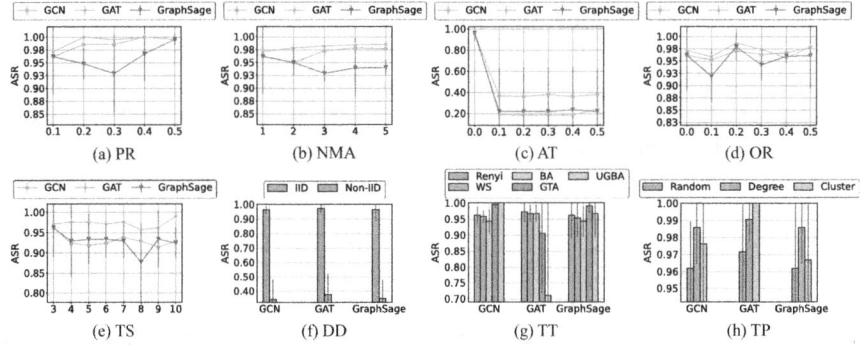

Fig. 3. Node-level task factors.

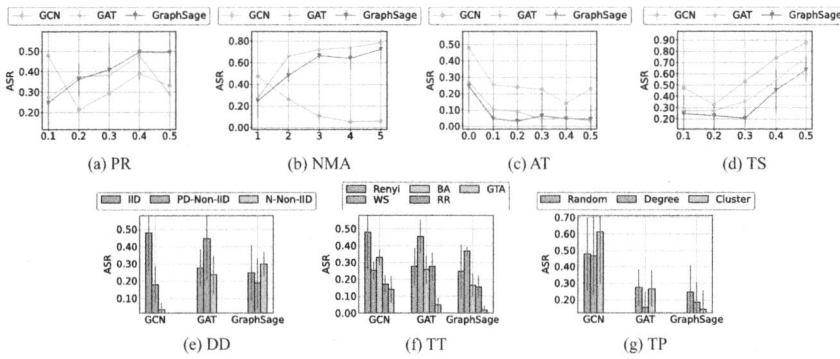

Fig. 4. Graph-level task factors.

leads to an increase in ASR for both GCN and GAT models. Conversely, an increase in NMA results in a decrease in ASR for both GraphSage. Concerning graph-level tasks, the ASR demonstrates an increase with the increase of NMA in the case of GAT and GraphSage. However, in the scenario of GCN, the ASR shows a decrease with the increase of NMA. **Attack Time (AT).** For both node-level and graph-level tasks, an increase in AT results in a decrease in ASR for three models. **Overlapping Rate (OR).** The ASR demonstrates an upward trend as the overlapping rate increases. This correlation can be attributed to the possibility that overlapping nodes facilitate the backdooring of normal clients, primarily through the presence of cross-edges.

Local Level Factors: **Trigger Size (TS).** For node-level tasks, an increase in TS leads to an increase in ASR for GCN. However, in the case of GAT and GraphSage, the ASR demonstrates a decrease with the increase of TS. Concerning the graph-level task, the ASR shows an increase with the increase of TS across all three GNNs. **Trigger Types (TT).** In the node-level task, the adaptive trigger demonstrates a higher ASR on most models. Conversely, in the graph-level task, the universal trigger exhibits higher ASR. **Trigger Position (TP).** In node-level tasks, we observed a significantly large ASR when using importance-based positions (Degree and Cluster) compared to random positions. However, for the graph-level task, while importance-based positions showed higher ASR for GCN, random positions yielded higher ASR for GAT and GraphSage. **Poisoning Rate (PR).** On node classification, an increase in PR results in a slight decrease in ASR. However, graph classification exhibits an upward trend in ASR. Due to the page limit, the results on other datasets and metrics, please refer to the Appendix.

4.4 Defense Methods Against Federated Graph Backdoor Attack

To comprehensively evaluate the impact of the graph backdoor attack on FedGNN, considering both adaptive optimizer settings and defense strategies, we conduct additional experiments utilizing state-of-the-art federated algorithms and defense techniques. This involves advanced federated algorithms (FedOpt [30], FedProx [23], and Scaffold [18]) the discarding aggregation methods (e.g., Krum [2], Multi-Krum [2], Bulyan) and non-discarding aggregations (e.g., Median, Trimmed-mean). The results of the federated defense experiments conducted under the backdoor attack "renyi-random" are illustrated in Fig. 5. Overall, the results reveal that even advanced federated methods and defense approaches have limitations in effectively mitigating the graph backdoor attack.

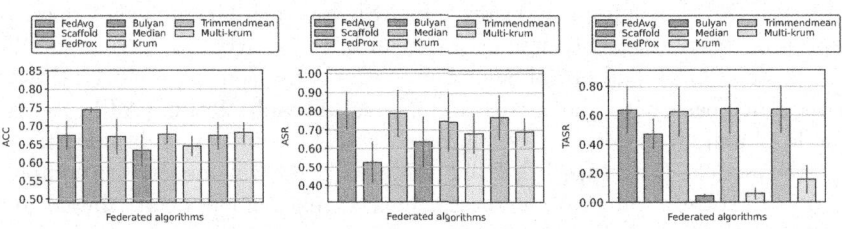

Fig. 5. Advanced federated algorithms Defense methods against backdoor attack.

> **Takeaways:**
>
> (1) Non-IID distribution is more susceptible to malicious activities.
> (2) More malicious clients corresponds to higher attack performance.
> (3) Malicious clients possess the capacity to initiate attacks during any phase of federated training rounds.
> (4) The inclusion of cross-client edges enhances the attack process by facilitating the transfer of malicious trigger knowledge across client, thereby amplifying the trigger signal.
> (5) A larger trigger size does not necessarily equate to higher attack capability.
> (6) The adaptive trigger is tailored to individual graphs, resulting in a higher attack success rate.
> (7) The placement of the trigger in a significant position leads to enhanced attack performance.
> (8) A higher poisoning rate corresponds to an elevated attack success rate.

5 Related Works

FedGNN. FedGNN present a distributed machine learning paradigm that facilitates collaborative training of GNNs among multiple parties, ensuring the privacy of their sensitive data. In recent years, extensive research has been conducted on FedGNN, with a particular focus on addressing security concerns [10–12,44,46]. Among these concerns, poisoning attacks have garnered significant attention, encompassing both data poisoning attacks and model poisoning attacks. Data poisoning attacks occur when an adversary employs tainted data to train the local model, while model poisoning attacks involve manipulation of either the training process or the local model itself. Currently, the majority of attacks on FedGNN primarily concentrate on data poisoning attacks. Chen et al. [5] proposed adversarial attacks on vertical federated learning, utilizing adversarial perturbations on global node embeddings based on gradient leakage from pairwise nodes. Additionally, Xu et al. [44] investigated centralized and distributed backdoor attacks on FedGNN.

Graph Backdoor Attacks. Backdoor attacks on GNNs have received significant attention in recent years [6,41,43,45,47,50,51]. Regarding graph backdoor attacks, they can be classified into two types based on the employed trigger: universal graph backdoor attacks and adaptive backdoor attacks. In universal graph backdoor attacks, Zhang et al. [50] generated sub-graphs using the Erdős-Rényi (ER) model as triggers and injected them into the training data. Additionally, Xu et al. [41] observed that the position of the trigger injection into the graph can also affect the attack's performance. As for adaptive trigger backdoor attacks, Xi et al. [41] developed an adaptive trigger generator that optimizes the attack's effectiveness for both transductive and inductive tasks. In our benchmark, we focus primarily on data poisoning attacks. While model poisoning attacks can be effective, data poisoning attacks may be more convenient because they do not require tampering with the model learning process, and they allow non-expert actors to participate [36].

6 Conclusions and Open Problems

Conclusions. In this paper, we proposed a unified framework for classification backdoor attacks on FedGNN. We then introduced the critical factors involved in graph backdoor attacks on FedGNN, including both global and local level factors. Along this line, we performed approximately 8,000 experiments on the graph backdoor attacks benchmark and conducted critical factor experiments to provide a comprehensive analysis.

Open Problems. (1) Enhancing the success rate of transferred attacks: Our findings reveal that malicious attackers can also backdoor normal clients through the FL mechanism. However, there is a need to explore methods that can identify and exploit the worst vulnerabilities under these circumstances. (2) Evaluating the defense method under backdoor attack: We demonstrate that FedGNN can be compromised by malicious attackers. However, assessing the effectiveness of defense mechanisms against such attacks still requires further exploration. (3) Cooperative malicious attackers: Currently, the majority of malicious attackers operate independently during the attack process, neglecting the potential benefits of collaboration. An intriguing research direction lies in investigating the utilization of collaboration to enhance attack performance.

Acknowledgement. This work was supported by the National Key R&D Program of China (Grant No. 2023YFF0725004), National Natural Science Foundation of China (Grant No. 92370204), the Guangzhou Basic and Applied Basic Research Program under Grant No. 2024A04J3279, Education Bureau of Guangzhou Municipality.

References

1. Barabási, A.L., Albert, R.: Emergence of scaling in random networks. Science **286**(5439), 509–512 (1999)
2. Blanchard, P., El Mhamdi, E.M., Guerraoui, R., Stainer, J.: Machine learning with adversaries: byzantine tolerant gradient descent. In: Advances in Neural Information Processing Systems, vol. 30 (2017)
3. Borgwardt, K.M., Ong, C.S., Schönauer, S., Vishwanathan, S.V.N., Smola, A.J., Kriegel, H.: Protein function prediction via graph kernels. In: Proceedings Thirteenth International Conference on Intelligent Systems for Molecular Biology 2005, Detroit, MI, USA, 25–29 June 2005, pp. 47–56 (2005)
4. Cheibub, J.A., Gandhi, J., Vreeland, J.R.: Democracy and dictatorship revisited. Public Choice, pp. 67–101 (2010)

5. Chen, J., Huang, G., Zheng, H., Yu, S., Jiang, W., Cui, C.: Graph-fraudster: adversarial attacks on graph neural network-based vertical federated learning. IEEE Trans. Comput. Soc. Syst. (2022)
6. Dai, E., Lin, M., Zhang, X., Wang, S.: Unnoticeable backdoor attacks on graph neural networks. In: WWW 2023, Proceedings of the ACM Web Conference 2023, pp. 2263–2273. New York, NY, USA (2023)
7. Fang, M., Cao, X., Jia, J., Gong, N.Z.: Local model poisoning attacks to byzantine-robust federated learning. In: 29th USENIX Security Symposium, USENIX Security 2020, August 12–14, 2020, pp. 1605–1622. USENIX Association (2020)
8. Gilbert, E.N.: Random graphs. Ann. Math. Stat. **30**(4), 1141–1144 (1959)
9. Gilmer, J., Schoenholz, S.S., Riley, P.F., Vinyals, O., Dahl, G.E.: Neural message passing for quantum chemistry. In: Proceedings of the 34th International Conference on Machine Learning, ICML 2017, Sydney, NSW, Australia, 6–11 August 2017. Proceedings of Machine Learning Research, vol. 70, pp. 1263–1272. PMLR (2017)
10. Guo, Z., Han, R., Liu, H.: Against multifaceted graph heterogeneity via asymmetric federated prompt learning. arXiv:2411.02003 (2024)
11. Guo, Z., Yao, D., Yang, Q., Liu, H.: Hifgl: a hierarchical framework for cross-silo cross-device federated graph learning. In: KDD 2024, Proceedings of the 30th ACM SIGKDD Conference on Knowledge Discovery and Data Mining, pp. 968–979. Association for Computing Machinery, New York, NY, USA (2024). https://doi.org/10.1145/3637528.3671660
12. Halimi, A., Kadhe, S., Rawat, A., Baracaldo, N.: Federated unlearning: how to efficiently erase a client in FL? CoRR arXiv:2207.05521 (2022)
13. Hamilton, W.L., Ying, Z., Leskovec, J.: Inductive representation learning on large graphs. In: Advances in Neural Information Processing Systems 30: Annual Conference on Neural Information Processing Systems 2017, December 4–9, 2017, Long Beach, CA, USA, pp. 1024–1034 (2017)
14. Han, J., Liu, H., Xiong, H., Yang, J.: Semi-supervised air quality forecasting via self-supervised hierarchical graph neural network. IEEE Trans. Knowl. Data Eng. **35**(5), 5230–5243 (2022)
15. Han, J., Zhang, W., Liu, H., Tao, T., Tan, N., Xiong, H.: Bigst: linear complexity spatio-temporal graph neural network for traffic forecasting on large-scale road networks. Proc. VLDB Endow. **17**(5), 1081–1090 (2024). https://doi.org/10.14778/3641204.3641217
16. He, C., Ceyani, E., Balasubramanian, K., Annavaram, M., Avestimehr, S.: Spread-GNN: decentralized multi-task federated learning for graph neural networks on molecular data (2021)
17. Huang, X., et al.: Dgraph: a large-scale financial dataset for graph anomaly detection. In: NeurIPS (2022)
18. Karimireddy, S.P., Kale, S., Mohri, M., Reddi, S.J., Stich, S.U., Suresh, A.T.: Scaffold: stochastic controlled averaging for on-device federated learning. arXiv preprint arXiv:1910.06378 (2019)
19. Kipf, T.N., Welling, M.: Semi-supervised classification with graph convolutional networks. In: 5th International Conference on Learning Representations, ICLR 2017, Toulon, France, April 24–26, 2017, Conference Track Proceedings. OpenReview.net (2017). https://openreview.net/forum?id=SJU4ayYgl
20. Knyazev, B., Taylor, G.W., Amer, M.: Understanding attention and generalization in graph neural networks. In: Advances in Neural Information Processing Systems, vol. 32 (2019)

21. Li, H., Wu, C., Zhu, S., Zheng, Z.: Learning to backdoor federated learning. arXiv preprint arXiv:2303.03320 (2023)
22. Li, Q., Diao, Y., Chen, Q., He, B.: Federated learning on non-iid data silos: an experimental study. In: 2022 IEEE 38th International Conference on Data Engineering (ICDE), pp. 965–978. IEEE (2022)
23. Li, T., Sahu, A.K., Zaheer, M., Sanjabi, M., Talwalkar, A., Smith, V.: Federated optimization in heterogeneous networks. Proc. Mach. learn. syst. **2**, 429–450 (2020)
24. Liu, F., et al.: Jailjudge: a comprehensive jailbreak judge benchmark with multi-agent enhanced explanation evaluation framework. arXiv:2410.12855 (2024)
25. Liu, F., Liu, H.: Subgraph federated unlearning. In: WWW 2025, Proceedings of the ACM on Web Conference 2025, pp. 1205–1215. Association for Computing Machinery, New York, NY, USA (2025). https://doi.org/10.1145/3696410.3714821
26. Maekawa, S., Noda, K., Sasaki, Y., Onizuka, M.: Beyond real-world benchmark datasets: An empirical study of node classification with GNNs. In: NeurIPS (2022)
27. McAuley, J., Targett, C., Shi, Q., van den Hengel, A.: Image-based recommendations on styles and substitutes. In: SIGIR 2015, Proceedings of the 38th International ACM SIGIR Conference on Research and Development in Information Retrieval, pp. 43–52. Association for Computing Machinery (2015)
28. McMahan, B., Moore, E., Ramage, D., Hampson, S., y Arcas, B.A.: Communication-efficient learning of deep networks from decentralized data. In: Proceedings of the 20th International Conference on Artificial Intelligence and Statistics, AISTATS 2017, 20–22 April 2017, Fort Lauderdale, FL, USA. Proceedings of Machine Learning Research, vol. 54, pp. 1273–1282. PMLR (2017)
29. Özdayi, M.S., Kantarcioglu, M., Gel, Y.R.: Defending against backdoors in federated learning with robust learning rate. In: Thirty-Fifth AAAI Conference on Artificial Intelligence, AAAI 2021, pp. 9268–9276. AAAI Press (2021)
30. Reddi, S., et al.: Adaptive federated optimization. arXiv preprint arXiv:2003.00295 (2020)
31. Riesen, K., Bunke, H.: IAM graph database repository for graph based pattern recognition and machine learning. In: Structural, Syntactic, and Statistical Pattern Recognition, Joint IAPR International Workshop, SSPR & SPR 2008, Orlando, USA, December 4–6, 2008. Proceedings. Lecture Notes in Computer Science, vol. 5342, pp. 287–297. Springer (2008)
32. Rong, Y., et al.: Deep graph learning: foundations, advances and applications. In: KDD 2020: The 26th ACM SIGKDD Conference on Knowledge Discovery and Data Mining, Virtual Event, CA, USA, August 23–27, 2020, pp. 3555–3556. ACM (2020)
33. Rossi, R., Ahmed, N.: The network data repository with interactive graph analytics and visualization. In: Proceedings of the AAAI Conference on Artificial Intelligence, vol. 29, no. 1 (2015)
34. Shchur, O., Mumme, M., Bojchevski, A., Günnemann, S.: Pitfalls of graph neural network evaluation. In: Relational Representation Learning Workshop, NeurIPS 2018 (2018)
35. Steger, A., Wormald, N.C.: Generating random regular graphs quickly. Comb. Probab. Comput. **8**(4), 377–396 (1999)
36. Tolpegin, V., Truex, S., Gursoy, M.E., Liu, L.: Data poisoning attacks against federated learning systems. In: Chen, L., Li, N., Liang, K., Schneider, S. (eds.) ESORICS 2020. LNCS, vol. 12308, pp. 480–501. Springer, Cham (2020). https://doi.org/10.1007/978-3-030-58951-6_24

37. Velickovic, P., Cucurull, G., Casanova, A., Romero, A., Liò, P., Bengio, Y.: Graph attention networks. In: 6th International Conference on Learning Representations, ICLR 2018, Vancouver, BC, Canada, April 30 – May 3, 2018, Conference Track Proceedings (2018). https://openreview.net/forum?id=rJXMpikCZ
38. Wale, N., Karypis, G.: Comparison of descriptor spaces for chemical compound retrieval and classification. In: Sixth International Conference on Data Mining (ICDM 2006), pp. 678–689 (2006). https://doi.org/10.1109/ICDM.2006.39
39. Wang, Z., et al.: Federatedscope-GNN: towards a unified, comprehensive and efficient package for federated graph learning. In: KDD 2022, Proceedings of the 28th ACM SIGKDD Conference on Knowledge Discovery and Data Mining, pp. 4110–4120. New York, NY, USA (2022). https://doi.org/10.1145/3534678.3539112
40. Watts, D.J., Strogatz, S.H.: Collective dynamics of 'small-world' networks. Nature **393**(6684), 440–442 (1998)
41. Xi, Z., Pang, R., Ji, S., Wang, T.: Graph backdoor. In: USENIX Security Symposium, pp. 1523–1540 (2021)
42. Xie, C., Chen, M., Chen, P., Li, B.: CRFL: certifiably robust federated learning against backdoor attacks. In: Proceedings of the 38th International Conference on Machine Learning, ICML 2021, 18–24 July 2021, Virtual Event. Proceedings of Machine Learning Research, vol. 139, pp. 11372–11382. PMLR (2021)
43. Xu, J., Abad, G., Picek, S.: Rethinking the trigger-injecting position in graph backdoor attack. arXiv preprint arXiv:2304.02277 (2023)
44. Xu, J., Wang, R., Koffas, S., Liang, K., Picek, S.: More is better (mostly): on the backdoor attacks in federated graph neural networks. In: Proceedings of the 38th Annual Computer Security Applications Conference, pp. 684–698 (2022)
45. Xu, J., Xue, M., Picek, S.: Explainability-based backdoor attacks against graph neural networks. In: Proceedings of the 3rd ACM Workshop on Wireless Security and Machine Learning, pp. 31–36 (2021)
46. Xu, R., Baracaldo, N., Zhou, Y., Anwar, A., Kadhe, S., Ludwig, H.: Detrust-FL: privacy-preserving federated learning in decentralized trust setting. In: IEEE 15th International Conference on Cloud Computing, CLOUD 2022, Barcelona, Spain, July 10–16, 2022. pp. 417–426. IEEE (2022)
47. Yang, S., et al.: Transferable graph backdoor attack. In: Proceedings of the 25th International Symposium on Research in Attacks, Intrusions and Defenses, pp. 321–332 (2022)
48. Yang, Z., Cohen, W.W., Salakhutdinov, R.: Revisiting semi-supervised learning with graph embeddings. In: Proceedings of the 33nd International Conference on Machine Learning, ICML 2016, New York City, NY, USA, June 19–24, 2016. JMLR Workshop and Conference Proceedings, vol. 48, pp. 40–48. JMLR.org (2016)
49. Zhang, K., Yang, C., Li, X., Sun, L., Yiu, S.M.: Subgraph federated learning with missing neighbor generation. In: Advances in Neural Information Processing Systems, vol. 34, pp. 6671–6682 (2021)
50. Zhang, Z., Jia, J., Wang, B., Gong, N.Z.: Backdoor attacks to graph neural networks. In: Proceedings of the 26th ACM Symposium on Access Control Models and Technologies, pp. 15–26 (2021)
51. Zheng, H., Xiong, H., Chen, J., Ma, H., Huang, G.: Motif-backdoor: rethinking the backdoor attack on graph neural networks via motifs. IEEE Trans. Comput. Soc. Syst. (2023)

Federated Time Series Generation on Feature and Temporally Misaligned Data

Zhi Wen Soi[1], Chenrui Fan[1], Aditya Shankar[2], Abel Malan[3], and Lydia Y. Chen[2,3](✉)

[1] University of Bern, Bern, Switzerland
{zhi.soi,chenrui.fan}@students.unibe.ch
[2] TU Delft, Delft, The Netherlands
a.shankar@tudelft.nl, lydiachen@ieee.org
[3] University of Neuchâtel, Neuchâtel, Switzerland
abele.malan@unine.ch

Abstract. Distributed time series data presents a challenge for federated learning, as clients often possess different feature sets and have misaligned time steps. Existing federated time series models are limited by the assumption of perfect temporal or feature alignment across clients. In this paper, we propose FedTDD, a novel federated time series diffusion model that jointly learns a synthesizer across clients. At the core of FedTDD is a novel data distillation and aggregation framework that reconciles the differences between clients by imputing the misaligned timesteps and features. In contrast to traditional federated learning, FedTDD learns the correlation across clients' time series through the exchange of local synthetic outputs instead of model parameters. A coordinator iteratively improves a global distiller network by leveraging shared knowledge from clients through the exchange of synthetic data. As the distiller becomes more refined over time, it subsequently enhances the quality of the clients' local feature estimates, allowing each client to then improve its local imputations for missing data using the latest, more accurate distiller. Experimental results on five datasets demonstrate FedTDD's effectiveness compared to centralized training, and the effectiveness of sharing synthetic outputs to transfer knowledge of local time series. Notably, FedTDD achieves 79.4% and 62.8% improvement over local training in Context-FID and Correlational scores. Our code is available at: https://github.com/soizhiwen/FedTDD.

Keywords: Federated Learning · Generative Models · Time Series

---

C. Fan and A. Shankar—Equal contribution.

Supplementary Information The online version contains supplementary material available at https://doi.org/10.1007/978-3-032-05981-9_23.

© The Author(s), under exclusive license to Springer Nature Switzerland AG 2026
R. P. Ribeiro et al. (Eds.): ECML PKDD 2025, LNAI 16014, pp. 384–399, 2026.
https://doi.org/10.1007/978-3-032-05981-9_23

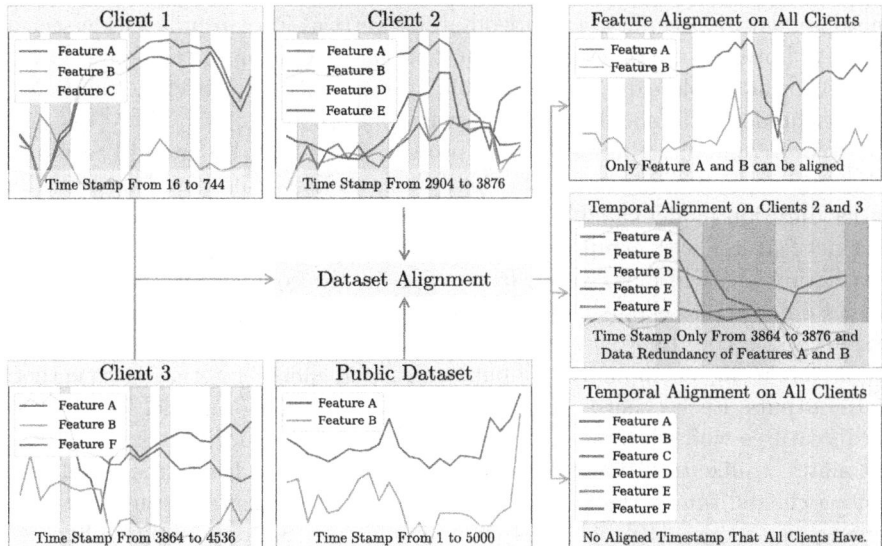

Fig. 1. Feature and temporally misaligned time series. The grey masking indicates missing data. (Color figure online)

1 Introduction

Multivariate time series data are pivotal in many domains, such as healthcare, finance, manufacturing, and sales [16]. Consider a collaboration between multiple clients, shown in Fig. 1. In a healthcare setting, these clients could be hospitals, each collecting patient data locally for a downstream task, such as predicting patient outcomes. The data gathered, such as vital signs like heart rate and blood pressure, is inherently *temporal*, i.e., time series data. Aggregating data from all the sources could improve model performance due to increased sampled diversity when training downstream predictive models. However, privacy regulations such as the General Data Protection Regulation (GDPR) and confidentiality agreements between hospitals prevent sharing of raw data [1,20,32].

Federated learning (FL) [19] takes a step towards tackling this privacy challenge by enabling clients to train a global model by sharing locally trained model parameters rather than raw data. However, this environment faces the challenge of *feature and temporal misalignment* [18], as hospitals may possess different feature sets with varying time intervals for data collection.

In *horizontal* FL [14], different clients have data for the same features but for different samples or timesteps. Hence, it can tackle situations involving temporal misalignment but not feature misalignment. On the other hand, in *vertical* FL [17], different clients possess different feature sets for the same samples or timesteps. While this can handle feature misalignment, it cannot tackle temporal misalignment. Hence, neither horizontal nor vertical FL can fully tackle scenarios with both feature and temporal misalignment. On top of this, data may be missing or incomplete due to unavailability or inconsistent collection frequencies, further hindering a model's ability to learn patterns [23].

To overcome these limitations, we propose **FedTDD** (Federated Learning in Multivariate Time Series via Data Distillation), a first-of-its-kind federated time series diffusion model capable of learning a time series synthesizer from clients' distinct features with temporal misalignment. FedTDD introduces a novel data distillation [27] and aggregation framework for the common feature set, whose values differ across clients and can be obtained from the public domain. In this framework, a coordinator maintains a global model called the *distiller*, trained iteratively using a combination of public data and clients' intermediate synthetic data outputs. Each client keeps a local time series diffusion model for imputing local features which leverages the latest distiller to improve the quality of local estimates. Unlike traditional federated learning, FedTDD learns the correlations among clients' time series through the exchange of synthetic outputs instead of aggregating models [19], effectively handling feature and temporal misalignment without sharing raw data.

Given the recent advancements of diffusion models over mainstream generative models like *Generative Adversarial Networks* (GANs) [7], we utilize a time series *Denoising Diffusion Probabilistic Model* (DDPM) [9], adapted to handle temporal dependencies through temporal embeddings and sequential conditioning. Specifically, we select **Diffusion-TS** [35] since it leverages both time and frequency domain information, effectively capturing trends and seasonality, which leads to a more accurate imputation of missing data. By imputing data from unaligned time steps, clients can obtain temporally aligned data without needing alignment on the features or sharing raw data.

In summary, our major contributions are as follows: (i) We propose a novel federated generative learning framework that effectively handles temporal and feature-level misalignment and data missing problems in time series data. (ii) We develop a data distillation and aggregation framework that learns correlations among clients' time series by exchanging synthetic data instead of model parameters, enabling clients to improve their local models without direct data sharing and effectively handling data discrepancies. (iii) We conduct extensive experiments on five benchmark datasets, showing up to 79.4% and 62.8% improvement over local training in Context-FID and Correlational scores under extreme feature and temporal misalignment cases and achieving performance comparable to centralized training.

2 Related Work

Time Series Generation. Generative models for time series data aim to capture temporal dependencies and sequential patterns inherent in such datasets. TimeGAN [34] combines *generative adversarial networks* (GANs) [7] with

Table 1. Overview of the related work.

Method	Model Type	Time Series	FL Type	Handles Temporal Misalignment	Handles Feature Misalignment
GTV [38]	GAN	×	Vertical	×	✓
DPGDAN [33]	GAN	×	Vertical	×	✓
SiloFuse [28]	DDPM	×	Vertical	×	✓
VFLGAN-TS [36]	GAN	✓	Vertical	×	✓
FedGAN [25]	GAN	✓	Horizontal	✓	×
T2TGAN [3]	GAN	✓	Horizontal	✓	×
FedTDD (Ours)	DDPM	✓	Hybrid	✓	✓

recurrent neural networks [22] to produce realistic multivariate time series. TimeVAE [5] utilizes variational autoencoders (VAEs) [11] tailored for time series to capture trends and seasonality. Recently, diffusion-based models like TimeGrad [26], CSDI [30], SSSD [2], TSDiff [13], and Diffusion-TS [35] have further advanced time series generation by producing high-fidelity sequences, outperforming the mainstream GANs and VAE-based techniques. Despite their effectiveness, these models operate in centralized settings and assume fully aligned data with consistent features and timestamps. They are not equipped to handle feature and temporal misalignments common in real-world distributed scenarios, making them unsuitable for federated environments with heterogeneous data distributions [21,24].

Federated Learning with Generative Models. Federated learning [37] has primarily been applied to image generation, such as FedCycleGAN [29] leverages CycleGAN [39] in federated settings to generate synthetic images while preserving data privacy. For tabular data, methods like GTV [38], DPGDAN [33], and SiloFuse [28] employ GANs and diffusion models within vertical federated learning frameworks to synthesize tabular datasets. However, these approaches focus on vertically partitioned data, where all clients have features corresponding to the same sample ID, and do not address data redundancy or misalignment issues. Federated learning with generative models for time series data remains under-explored. Existing works such as FedGAN [25], VFLGAN-TS [36], and T2TGAN [3] extend GANs to federated time series generation. VFLGAN-TS operates in a vertical federated learning context, tackling feature misalignment, but does not handle temporal misalignment. In contrast, T2TGAN tackles horizontal federated learning settings but introduces data redundancy due to overlapping data among clients and cannot handle feature mismatches between clients. As summarized in Table 1, these methods encounter issues as shown in Fig. 1, making them less effective for federated time series generation where both feature and temporal misalignments are prevalent.

Preliminary on Generative Modeling with DDPMs. For the generative backbone, we adopt the Diffusion-TS architecture [35], which extends DDPMs [9] to capture temporal patterns using a generative modeling process. DDPMs are models trained using a *forward noising* and *backward denoising* process. The forward phase progressively adds random Gaussian noise to the data s_0 at diffusion step t, where the transition is parameterized by $q(\mathbf{s}_t \mid \mathbf{s}_{t-1}) = \mathcal{N}(\mathbf{s}_t; \sqrt{1-\beta_t}\mathbf{s}_{t-1}, \beta_t \mathbf{I})$ with $\beta_t \in (0,1)$, eventually transforming it into pure noise $\mathbf{s}_T \sim \mathcal{N}(0, \mathbf{I})$. The backward phase is where the model learns to reverse this noising process. Starting from random noise $\mathbf{s}_T \sim \mathcal{N}(0, \mathbf{I})$, it iteratively removes the added noise step by step via $p_\theta(\mathbf{s}_{t-1} \mid \mathbf{s}_t) = \mathcal{N}(\mathbf{s}_{t-1}; \boldsymbol{\mu}_\theta(\mathbf{s}_t, t), \Sigma_\theta(\mathbf{s}_t, t))$, to reconstruct a new data sample resembling the original input distribution. The functions $\boldsymbol{\mu}_\theta$ and Σ_θ are generally estimated using a model.

Diffusion-TS extends standard DDPMs by incorporating mechanisms specifically designed for time series characteristics such as trends and seasonality [12]. Instead of treating data points independently, it utilizes an encoder-decoder transformer architecture [31] that processes entire sequences, effectively modeling temporal relationships. To handle trends, Diffusion-TS decomposes the time series into components that represent slow-varying behaviors over time. For capturing seasonality and periodic patterns, it employs frequency domain analysis using the Fast Fourier Transform (FFT) [8]. By integrating FFT, the model can analyze and reconstruct cyclical patterns [4] within the data, allowing it to learn both time and frequency domain representations [6]. This combination enables Diffusion-TS to generate more accurate and realistic time series data by effectively modeling complex temporal dynamics. Besides, Diffusion-TS supports both *unconditional* and *conditional* generation. In the unconditional generation, the model produces new samples solely based on the learned data distribution, starting from random noise and applying the learned denoising process. In the conditional generation, Diffusion-TS utilizes gradient-based guidance during sampling to incorporate the observed data $\mathbf{y}$. At each diffusion step, the model refines its estimated time series $\hat{\mathbf{s}}_0$ by adjusting it with a gradient term that enforces consistency with the observed data. The refinement can be computed via $\tilde{\mathbf{s}}_0(\mathbf{s}_t, t; \theta) = \hat{\mathbf{s}}_0(\mathbf{s}_t, t; \theta) + \eta \nabla_{\mathbf{s}_t}(\|\mathbf{y} - \hat{\mathbf{s}}_0(\mathbf{s}_t, t; \theta)\|^2 + \gamma \log p(\mathbf{s}_{t-1} \mid \mathbf{s}_t))$, where η is a hyperparameter that controls the strength of the gradient guidance, and γ balances the trade-off between fitting the observed data and maintaining the generative model's prior distribution $p(\mathbf{s}_{t-1} \mid \mathbf{s}_t)$. This iterative refinement ensures that the generated time series aligns with the provided observations and preserves the temporal patterns learned during training. Further details of Diffusion-TS are shown in Appendix B.2.

3 FedTDD

In this work, we address the problem of collaborative time series imputation in the presence of temporal and feature misalignments, without requiring the sharing of raw data. In a federated learning setting, clients may possess different subsets of features. We categorize features into two types: *common features* and *exclusive features*. Common features are those present in all clients and also available in a public dataset, while exclusive features are unique to each client and not shared. For example, market indices might be common features in financial data, while individual portfolio holdings are exclusive. Our proposed framework, FedTDD, as shown in Fig. 2, tackles this problem using two models. A global

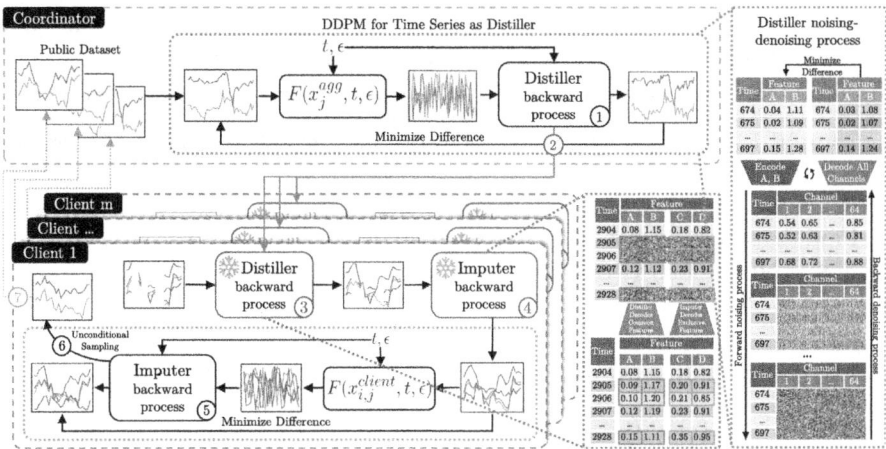

Fig. 2. FedTDD Structure. First, the Distiller is pre-trained on a public dataset. Then, each client uses the distiller and imputer to impute common and exclusive features, respectively. Finally, synthetic data is sent back to the coordinator to expand the public dataset for the next round. The order of execution(1-7) is labeled in the figure. Here the common features are A and B, and the exclusive features are C and D.

distiller first imputes missing common features across clients. Local imputer models then use the imputed common features to predict the missing exclusive features for each client, addressing both temporal and feature misalignments. Furthermore, clients protect their privacy by sharing only synthetic versions of the common features while collaboratively improving the global distiller. This cycle of iterative imputation and model refinement ultimately converges to yield good quality imputations, while ensuring that no raw data is shared.

3.1 Problem Definition

We consider a federated learning setup involving N clients and a coordinator. Each client i possesses a time series dataset, denoted as $\mathbf{X}^i = \left[X^i_{j,k}\right]_{\{j=1...T^i, k=1...C^i\}}$, where T^i is the number of time steps, and C^i is the number of channels. These datasets can be split into two components, one for the common features and one for the exclusive features, i.e., $\mathbf{X}^i = \mathbf{X}^i_{\text{comm}} \cup \mathbf{X}^i_{\text{ex}}$. The coordinator holds a public dataset $\mathbf{X}^{\text{pub}} = \left[X^{\text{pub}}_{j,k}\right]_{\forall j; k \in \mathcal{F}_{\text{comm}}}$, which contains data for the common features $\mathcal{F}_{\text{comm}}$ but without any missing values. This public dataset is time-indexed differently from the clients' data and provides a reliable reference for the common features. Each client's time series data comes from a distinct time interval, meaning that each client's time indices j are unique. The feature set for each client i, $\mathcal{F}^i$, consists of common features $\mathcal{F}_{\text{comm}}$, which are shared across all clients, and exclusive features $\mathcal{F}^i_{\text{ex}}$, which are specific to each client. Thus, the overall feature set for client i is represented as

$\mathcal{F}^i = \mathcal{F}_{\text{comm}} \cup \mathcal{F}^i_{\text{ex}}$. Conversely, clients may have missing values in both the common and exclusive features. These missing values are indicated by a binary mask matrix $\mathbf{M}^i = \left[M^i_{j,k} \right]_{\forall j,k}$, where $M^i_{j,k} = 1$ if the value $X^i_{j,k}$ is observed while 0 indicates it is missing. The mask can be split into two parts: $\mathbf{M}^i_{\text{comm}}$, which corresponds to missing data in the common features, and $\mathbf{M}^i_{\text{ex}}$, which corresponds to missing data in the exclusive features. The goal is to design a collaborative method that enables clients to leverage shared knowledge and the public dataset to input the missing data locally without sharing raw data. Appendix A summarizes the mathematical notations used.

3.2 Hybrid Federated Learning for Imputation Under Misalignment

Algorithm 1 presents the overview of FedTDD. The framework consists of two key components: the global distiller model $\mathcal{D}$ and the local imputer models $\mathcal{U}^i$. The global distiller $\mathcal{D}$ imputes missing common features shared across all clients, while each client trains a local imputer $\mathcal{U}^i$ to infer missing exclusive features specific to their data. These components work together to address temporal and feature misalignment by iteratively improving the imputation process over several rounds r ranging from 1 to R.

Algorithm 1: FedTDD

Input: Public dataset $\mathbf{X}^{\text{pub}}$, clients' datasets $\mathbf{X}^i$
Result: Global distiller model $\mathcal{D}$, local imputer models $\mathcal{U}^i$

1 **Initialize:** Train $\mathcal{D}$ on $\mathbf{X}^{\text{pub}}$
2 **for** $r = 1$ *to* R **do**
3   **for** *each client* i **do**
4   **Receive** global distiller $\mathcal{D}$
5       $\hat{\mathbf{X}}^i_{\text{comm}} \leftarrow \mathcal{D}\left(\mathbf{X}^i_{\text{comm}}, \mathbf{M}^i_{\text{comm}}\right)$;   ▷ Impute common features
6       $\hat{\mathbf{X}}^i_{\text{ex}} \leftarrow \mathcal{U}\left(\mathbf{X}^i_{\text{ex}}, \mathbf{M}^i_{\text{ex}}\right)$;   ▷ Impute exclusive features
7       $\mathbf{X}^i_{\text{train}} \leftarrow \hat{\mathbf{X}}^i_{\text{comm}} \cup \hat{\mathbf{X}}^i_{\text{ex}}$;   ▷ Combine with exclusive features
8   **Train** $\mathcal{U}^i$ on $\mathbf{X}^i_{\text{train}}$;   ▷ Train local imputer
9       $\hat{\mathbf{X}}^i \leftarrow \mathcal{U}^i(\mathbf{z}), \mathbf{z} \sim \mathcal{N}(0, \mathbf{I})$;   ▷ Generate synthetic data
10   **Send** $\hat{\mathbf{X}}^i_{\text{comm}}$ from $\hat{\mathbf{X}}^i$ to coordinator
11   **end**
12   **for** *each client* i **do**
13   Select $n_r = \dfrac{r}{R} \alpha \cdot L$ sequences from $\hat{\mathbf{X}}^i_{\text{comm}}$
14       $\mathbf{X}^{\text{pub}} \leftarrow \mathbf{X}^{\text{pub}} \cup \hat{\mathbf{X}}^i_{\text{comm}}[1:n_r]$;   ▷ Expand public dataset
15   **end**
16   **Finetune** $\mathcal{D}$ on updated $\mathbf{X}^{\text{pub}}$
17 **end**

The process begins with the coordinator training a global distiller model $\mathcal{D}$ using the public dataset $\mathbf{X}^{\text{pub}}$. $\mathcal{D}$ leverages a temporal DDPM backbone to apply a forward diffusion process by gradually adding noise to the data and learns to reverse this process. During training, $\mathcal{D}$ conducts *unconditional generation* by starting from Gaussian noise ϵ and learning to approximate the data distribution through the time and frequency domain components [35]. Formally, we have

$$\mathcal{L}_{\text{time}} = \mathbb{E}_{(j,k,t) \mid \mathbf{M}^{\text{pub}}_{j,k}=1} \left[\left\| \mathbf{X}^{\text{pub}}_{j,k} - \tilde{\mathbf{X}}^{\text{pub}}_{j,k}(\mathbf{X}^{\text{pub}}_{j,k,t}, t, \epsilon; \theta) \right\|^2 \right] \quad \text{and} \quad (1)$$

$$\mathcal{L}_{\text{freq}} = \mathbb{E}_{(j,k,t) \mid \mathbf{M}^{\text{pub}}_{j,k}=1} \left[\left\| \text{FFT}(\mathbf{X}^{\text{pub}}_{j,k}) - \text{FFT}\left(\tilde{\mathbf{X}}^{\text{pub}}_{j,k}(\mathbf{X}^{\text{pub}}_{j,k,t}, t, \epsilon; \theta)\right) \right\|^2 \right], \quad (2)$$

where $\epsilon \sim \mathcal{N}(0, \mathbf{I})$, $\mathbf{X}^{\text{pub}}_{j,k}$ is the (j,k)-th entry of $\mathbf{X}^{\text{pub}}$, $\tilde{\mathbf{X}}^{\text{pub}}_{j,k}$ is the denoised estimate from $\mathcal{D}$, and FFT denotes the Fast Fourier Transform [8], which is a mathematical operation that converts a finite-length time domain signal to its frequency domain representation. We take the following objective

$$\mathcal{L}_{\text{distiller}(\mathcal{D}^i)} = \mathbb{E}_{(j,k,t) \mid \mathbf{M}^{\text{pub}}_{j,k}=1} \left[w_t \left(\lambda_1 \mathcal{L}_{\text{time}} + \lambda_2 \mathcal{L}_{\text{freq}} \right) \right], \quad w_t = \frac{\lambda \gamma_t (1 - \bar{\gamma}_t)}{\delta_t^2}, \tag{3}$$

where λ_1 and λ_2 control the balance between time and frequency losses while w_t emphasizes learning at larger diffusion steps, with λ being a small constant. The parameter $\delta_t \in (0,1)$ determines the amount of noise added at each forward diffusion step, where t is a diffusion time step uniformly sampled from 1 to T during training. The cumulative product $\bar{\gamma}_t = \prod_{v=1}^{t} \gamma_v$, with $\gamma_t = 1 - \delta_t$, track how the original signal diminishes over time due to the added noise. By weighting the loss at different steps, w_t helps the model focus on reconstructing the signal under high-noise conditions.

After this initial training, the coordinator distributes the trained global distiller model $\mathcal{D}$ to all participating clients. Each client i then utilizes $\mathcal{D}$ to impute their missing common features. Since clients may have missing values in $\mathbf{X}^i_{\text{comm}}$, they input their data along with the corresponding mask $\mathbf{M}^i_{\text{comm}}$ to the distiller model, which will perform *conditional generation* to iteratively refine the imputed data by sampling from the conditional distribution guided by the observed data, shown in Eq. 17 in Appendix B.2. The imputation process follows $\hat{\mathbf{X}}^i_{\text{comm}} = \mathcal{D}(\mathbf{X}^i_{\text{comm}}, \mathbf{M}^i_{\text{comm}})$, where $\mathcal{D}$ reconstructs only the missing values, indicated by $\mathbf{M}^i_{\text{comm}} = 0$. Similarly, the local imputer imputes missing values in $\mathbf{X}^i_{\text{ex}}$ by inputting their data along with the corresponding mask $\mathbf{M}^i_{\text{ex}}$ to the imputer model via $\hat{\mathbf{X}}^i_{\text{ex}} = \mathcal{U}(\mathbf{X}^i_{\text{ex}}, \mathbf{M}^i_{\text{ex}})$. The imputed common features $\hat{\mathbf{X}}^i_{\text{comm}}$ are then combined with the available exclusive features $\hat{\mathbf{X}}^i_{\text{ex}}$ to form the training data $\mathbf{X}^i_{\text{train}} = \hat{\mathbf{X}}^i_{\text{comm}} \cup \hat{\mathbf{X}}^i_{\text{ex}}$ for the local imputer. Meanwhile, each client trains their local imputer model $\mathcal{U}^i$ using $\mathbf{X}^i_{\text{train}}$ as the ground truth. Since the imputed common features $\hat{\mathbf{X}}^i_{\text{comm}}$ are fully known (as they are outputs from the pre-trained and fine-tuned $\mathcal{D}$), they are entirely used as ground truth for training $\mathcal{U}^i$, regardless of the original mask $\mathbf{M}^i_{\text{comm}}$. For the exclusive features, only the observed entries indicated by the mask $\mathbf{M}^i_{\text{ex}}$ are used as ground truth since the quality of the imputer's generated data during training is not sufficient to be used as ground truth. We define the loss mask as $\mathbf{M}^i_{\text{loss}} = \mathbf{1}^i_{\text{comm}} \cup \mathbf{M}^i_{\text{ex}}$, where

$\mathbf{1}^i_{\text{comm}}$ is a matrix of ones corresponding to the common features of client i. This loss mask ensures that the reconstruction loss is computed over all entries of the imputed common features and the observed entries of the exclusive features. The training loss for the imputer $\mathcal{U}^i$ can be defined as follows:

$$\mathcal{L}_{\text{imputer}(\mathcal{U}^i)} = \mathbb{E}_{(j,k,t) \mid \mathbf{M}^i_{\text{loss}_{j,k}} = 1} \left[w_t \left(\lambda_1 \mathcal{L}^i_{\text{time}} + \lambda_2 \mathcal{L}^i_{\text{freq}} \right) \right], \qquad (4)$$

where $\mathcal{L}^i_{\text{time}} = \mathbb{E}_{(j,k,t) \mid \mathbf{M}^i_{\text{loss}_{j,k}} = 1} \left[\left\| \mathbf{X}^i_{\text{train}_{j,k}} - \tilde{\mathbf{X}}^i_{\text{train}_{j,k}} (\mathbf{X}^i_{\text{train}_{j,k,t}}, t; \theta) \right\|^2 \right]$

and $\mathcal{L}^i_{\text{freq}} = \mathbb{E}_{(j,k,t) \mid \mathbf{M}^i_{\text{loss}_{j,k}} = 1} \left[\left\| \text{FFT}(\mathbf{X}^i_{\text{train}_{j,k}}) - \text{FFT}\left(\tilde{\mathbf{X}}^i_{\text{train}_{j,k}} (\mathbf{X}^i_{\text{train}_{j,k,t}}, t; \theta) \right) \right\|^2 \right]$,

where $\mathbf{X}^i_{\text{train}_{j,k}}$ is the (j, k)-th entry of $\mathbf{X}^i_{\text{train}}$, $\tilde{\mathbf{X}}^i_{\text{train}_{j,k}}$ is the denoised estimate from $\mathcal{U}$. After training, each client uses the trained imputer $\mathcal{U}^i$ to generate a synthetic dataset through *unconditional synthesis*, which includes both the common features $\hat{\mathbf{X}}^i_{\text{comm}}$ and the exclusive features $\hat{\mathbf{X}}^i_{\text{ex}}$. Starting from Gaussian noise, the imputer generates samples $\hat{\mathbf{X}}^i = \mathcal{U}^i(\mathbf{z}), \mathbf{z} \sim \mathcal{N}(0, \mathbf{I})$, that capture the distribution of both common and exclusive features.

To protect privacy, only the common features from the synthetic dataset, $\hat{\mathbf{X}}^i_{\text{comm}}$, are shared with the coordinator. This ensures that no raw or exclusive client data is exposed during the collaborative learning. The coordinator uses the synthetic common feature data from the clients to expand its public dataset. Rather than simply absorbing all the synthetic data, the coordinator carefully controls the growth of the dataset by accepting a fraction of the sequences from each client. Specifically, the coordinator adds $\frac{r}{R}\alpha * L$, where L represents the length of the synthetic datasets $\hat{\mathbf{X}}^i_{\text{comm}}; \forall i \in \{1, 2, \ldots, N\}$, α is a hyperparameter between 0 and 1, and the ratio of r and R yields a number that linearly increases up to 1, allowing for a gradual expansion as the rounds increase. The coordinator retrains the global distiller $\mathcal{D}$ using this expanded dataset. The addition of synthetic data enhances the distiller's ability to learn the patterns necessary for imputing missing common features.

The overall process creates an iterative cycle of improvement. As clients' generative models, specifically their local imputers, become more accurate with each round, the quality of the synthetic data they generate also improves. This higher-quality synthetic data, in turn, improves the distiller model at the coordinator, which benefits all clients when it is redistributed. Over several training rounds, this mutual reinforcement drives both the global distiller and the local imputers to improve continuously. Ultimately, the process converges, yielding robust imputation models without requiring clients to share their raw data.

4 Experiments

We assess FedTDD's performance by showing its advantages and disadvantages when applied to multiple benchmark datasets. We leave the analysis of different training configurations in the Appendix C, where we examine the impact of limited public data, abundant sequences with missing data, imbalanced data distributions and different aggregation strategies on model performance.

Datasets. To assess the quality of synthetic data, we consider four real-world datasets and one simulated dataset with different properties, such as the number of features, correlation, periodicity, and noise levels. Each dataset is preprocessed using a sliding window technique [34] to segment the data into sequences of length 24 to capture meaningful temporal dependencies while keeping the computational cost manageable. **Stocks** is the daily historical Google stock data from 2004 to 2019 with highly correlated features. **ETTh** recorded the electricity transformers hourly between July 2016 and July 2018, including load and oil temperature data that consists of 7 features. **Energy** from UCI appliances energy prediction dataset with 10-minute intervals for about 4.5 months. **fMRI** is a realistic simulation of brain activity time series with 50 features. **MuJoCo** is a physics-based simulation time series containing 14 features. We show the statistics of all datasets in Appendix D.2.

Baselines. We compare FedTDD against approaches show in Fig. 3, 3b, 3c and 3d. For the **Centralized*** training, we aggregate all data from individual clients, including public data, into a single location, where a global model is trained using the combined dataset, and this will be trained with all available features in the dataset and without missing values. While **Centralized** uses the same training procedure as Centralized*, it is, however, trained on a combined dataset with missing values and corresponding features available from each client plus the public data. To deal with differing features across clients, we create the combined dataset consisting of the total number of features in the particular benchmark dataset and zero-fill any remaining features to ensure uniformity. On the other hand, **Local** training involves training a separate model for each client using only their local data, without any communication or data aggregation. This approach has to be done to verify that FedTDD can perform relatively better than train locally. Finally, the **Pre-trained** approach leverages a model trained on a public dataset and uses it to impute the common features in local data from each client. Again, there is no data aggregation for this approach. In comparison, FedTDD integrates the Pre-trained approach and applies data aggregation to it. We utilized a SOTA diffusion-based multivariate time series generative model, Diffusion-TS [35], as the backbone for these baselines and FedTDD. Alternatively, any other time series generative model can be adopted in these approaches in a plug-and-play manner.

Evaluation Metrics. We quantitatively assess the quality of the generated synthetic data using four key metrics (see Appendix D.3 for more details). **Context-Fréchet Inception Distance (Context-FID) score** [10] evaluates the similarity between the distribution of real and synthetic time series data by computing the Fréchet distance. **Correlational score** [15] measures the correlation between the features of multivariate time series in the synthetic data compared to its real data. **Discriminative score** [34] measures the realism of the synthetic data by training a binary classifier to distinguish between real and synthetic data. **Predictive score** [34] evaluates the utility of the synthetic data by training a sequence-to-sequence model on the synthetic data and measuring

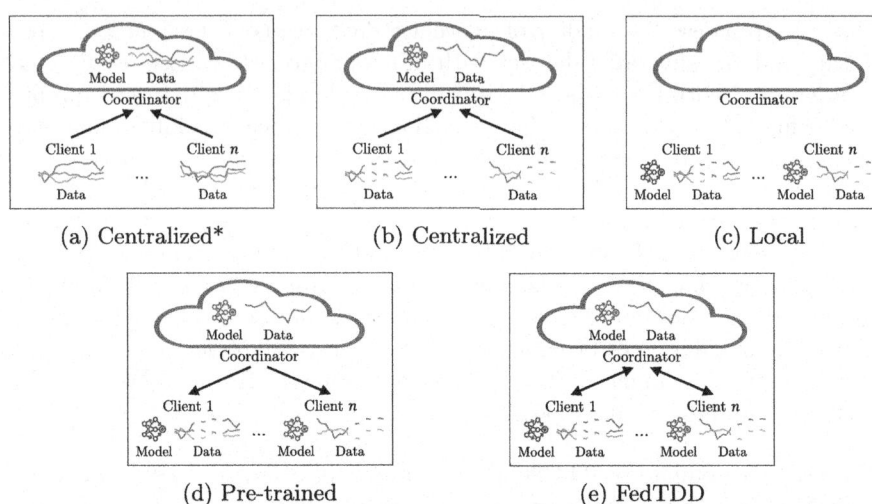

Fig. 3. Illustrations of different baselines compared to FedTDD. The data in the coordinator, also called public data, in Fig. 3b, 3d and 3e consists only common features time series. Dashes indicate temporal missing values.

Table 2. Results on multiple time series datasets. **Bold** indicates best performance.

Metric	Method	Stocks	ETTh	MuJoCo	Energy	fMRI
Context-FID	Centralized*	0.682 ± 0.106	0.281 ± 0.040	0.782 ± 0.138	0.533 ± 0.082	1.737 ± 0.125
	Centralized	3.548 ± 0.990	8.870 ± 2.295	10.00 ± 2.814	9.343 ± 2.808	13.56 ± 3.357
	Local	1.648 ± 0.229	1.313 ± 0.188	0.751 ± 0.121	1.179 ± 0.179	1.694 ± 0.153
	Pre-trained	1.047 ± 0.169	0.326 ± 0.040	0.617 ± 0.090	0.412 ± 0.054	**1.411 ± 0.102**
	FedTDD	**0.675 ± 0.087**	**0.271 ± 0.038**	**0.529 ± 0.068**	**0.376 ± 0.056**	1.459 ± 0.099
Correlational	Centralized*	0.061 ± 0.043	0.253 ± 0.094	1.989 ± 0.247	5.231 ± 1.294	7.900 ± 0.384
	Centralized	0.769 ± 0.336	0.340 ± 0.097	2.230 ± 0.518	5.681 ± 0.634	18.07 ± 2.311
	Local	0.156 ± 0.120	0.239 ± 0.079	1.298 ± 0.260	3.447 ± 0.838	**5.992 ± 0.383**
	Pre-trained	0.077 ± 0.052	0.165 ± 0.074	1.323 ± 0.171	2.821 ± 0.651	6.049 ± 0.349
	FedTDD	**0.058 ± 0.050**	**0.161 ± 0.064**	**1.296 ± 0.215**	**2.800 ± 0.686**	6.017 ± 0.364
Discriminative	Centralized*	0.136 ± 0.091	0.199 ± 0.061	0.297 ± 0.108	0.230 ± 0.080	0.422 ± 0.074
	Centralized	0.476 ± 0.042	0.475 ± 0.017	0.474 ± 0.024	0.496 ± 0.006	0.477 ± 0.030
	Local	0.340 ± 0.153	0.298 ± 0.060	0.200 ± 0.092	0.329 ± 0.087	**0.397 ± 0.061**
	Pre-trained	**0.175 ± 0.117**	0.115 ± 0.060	0.208 ± 0.068	**0.141 ± 0.068**	0.419 ± 0.051
	FedTDD	0.185 ± 0.105	**0.106 ± 0.061**	**0.153 ± 0.120**	0.153 ± 0.072	0.414 ± 0.051
Predictive	Centralized*	0.040 ± 0.000	0.127 ± 0.003	0.112 ± 0.015	0.292 ± 0.009	0.137 ± 0.004
	Centralized	0.047 ± 0.012	0.223 ± 0.020	0.165 ± 0.060	0.427 ± 0.053	0.233 ± 0.051
	Local	0.043 ± 0.003	0.118 ± 0.011	0.048 ± 0.006	0.204 ± 0.012	0.135 ± 0.006
	Pre-trained	0.046 ± 0.001	0.104 ± 0.004	0.052 ± 0.004	0.177 ± 0.005	0.133 ± 0.006
	FedTDD	**0.041 ± 0.001**	**0.101 ± 0.004**	**0.048 ± 0.004**	**0.175 ± 0.006**	**0.133 ± 0.004**

its performance on real data. All evaluation metrics are computed based on the respective features of the individual clients and then averaged over five trials, followed by calculating the overall average across the number of clients. The quality of synthetic data is considered the "best" when all metrics approach 0, meaning lower values indicate better quality.

Training Configurations. We run FedTDD and the baselines mentioned above with ten clients, five global rounds, 7500 local epochs for the first round, and 5000 for the rest. Besides, the coordinator trains on the public data consisting of common features, and each client contributes a set of features, which is the combination of common and exclusive features. The number of common features is around 50other hand, we use public ratio (PR) to manipulate the proportion of the public data that has to be reserved from the entire dataset before partitioning the dataset to all clients. Split ratio (SR) divides all sequences into two groups. In the first group, a mask is applied to just the common features, while in the second group, the mask is applied to all features. Moreover, missing ratio (MR) is the missing rate to mask on a sequence of multivariate time series, and we consider the missing scenario as shown in Appendix D.4. In the main experiments, we set PR, SR, and MR to 0.5. All the hyperparameters are listed in Appendix D.5.

4.1 Time Series Generation

In Table 2, we quantitatively analyze the quality of unconditionally generated 24-length time series for diverse time series datasets. FedTDD shows a strong performance comparable to the Centralized* approach. The proposed aggregation mechanism during fine-tuning proved essential to prevent the degradation of the coordinator model's performance and, in turn, the client models. By doing this, we achieved strong results across most datasets. We also present the generated synthetic samples of one representative client for ETTh and fMRI datasets in Fig. 4.

Challenges on fMRI Dataset. We observe that the fMRI dataset's imputation quality was lower than other datasets, as the mean square error between the imputed and real data is greater. Consequently, client models degraded due to training on low-quality imputed data. This suggests that the imputation strategy may need further refinement for such datasets, where the data distribution and complexity present greater challenges for accurate synthetic data generation and imputation. Besides, the Local approach achieves the best Correlational and Discriminative scores for the fMRI dataset. However, we cannot conclude that training locally is the best overall approach for fMRI. As we mentioned, the low performance of FedTDD and Pre-trained is primarily due to the poor quality of the imputed data, which affects training. This shows the advantage of Local training not relying on imputed data, making it seem better suited for the fMRI dataset compared to FedTDD and Pre-trained.

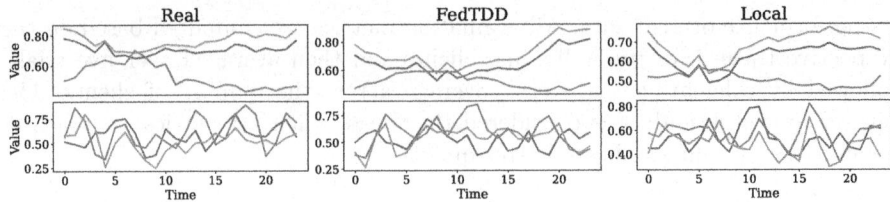

Fig. 4. Real samples and synthetic samples generated unconditionally from FedTDD and Local. The first and second rows of samples are from ETTh and fMRI datasets, respectively.

Table 3. Ablation study for a relatively small number of common features. **Bold** indicates best performance.

Metric	Method	Stocks	ETTh	MuJoCo	Energy	fMRI
Context-FID	Centralized*	0.682 ± 0.106	0.281 ± 0.040	0.782 ± 0.138	0.533 ± 0.082	1.737 ± 0.125
	Centralized	3.733 ± 0.959	11.54 ± 3.894	14.68 ± 4.263	13.17 ± 3.035	15.34 ± 4.789
	Local	1.982 ± 0.234	0.824 ± 0.105	0.660 ± 0.100	0.844 ± 0.127	1.220 ± 0.098
	Pre-trained	0.738 ± 0.142	0.316 ± 0.032	0.547 ± 0.099	0.381 ± 0.066	**1.178 ± 0.104**
	FedTDD	**0.680±0.123**	**0.267±0.036**	**0.510±0.072**	**0.331±0.051**	1.196 ± 0.098
Correlational	Centralized*	0.061 ± 0.043	0.253 ± 0.094	1.989 ± 0.247	5.231 ± 1.294	7.900 ± 0.384
	Centralized	0.697 ± 0.168	0.523 ± 0.095	2.317 ± 0.597	5.781 ± 0.924	31.35 ± 4.923
	Local	0.091 ± 0.052	0.167 ± 0.057	1.079 ± 0.196	1.984 ± 0.594	**4.929±0.395**
	Pre-trained	0.028 ± 0.027	**0.132±0.054**	1.115 ± 0.233	1.795 ± 0.577	5.033 ± 0.323
	FedTDD	**0.025±0.022**	0.137 ± 0.064	**1.060±0.209**	**1.737±0.282**	5.005 ± 0.317
Discriminative	Centralized*	0.136 ± 0.091	0.199 ± 0.061	0.297 ± 0.108	0.230 ± 0.080	0.422 ± 0.074
	Centralized	0.475 ± 0.041	0.469 ± 0.020	0.479 ± 0.026	0.494 ± 0.010	0.484 ± 0.023
	Local	0.300 ± 0.116	0.208 ± 0.070	0.190 ± 0.088	0.241 ± 0.071	**0.398±0.058**
	Pre-trained	0.119 ± 0.088	0.116 ± 0.067	0.163 ± 0.088	0.130 ± 0.058	0.418 ± 0.050
	FedTDD	**0.112±0.097**	**0.107±0.078**	**0.157±0.104**	**0.120±0.067**	0.412 ± 0.057
Predictive	Centralized*	0.040 ± 0.000	0.127 ± 0.003	0.112 ± 0.015	0.292 ± 0.009	0.137 ± 0.004
	Centralized	0.168 ± 0.025	0.196 ± 0.027	0.198 ± 0.049	0.314 ± 0.052	0.223 ± 0.029
	Local	0.084 ± 0.038	0.114 ± 0.009	0.069 ± 0.010	0.199 ± 0.007	**0.130±0.005**
	Pre-trained	0.028 ± 0.007	0.108 ± 0.004	0.063 ± 0.007	0.190 ± 0.005	0.132 ± 0.005
	FedTDD	**0.028 ± 0.005**	**0.107 ± 0.005**	**0.062 ± 0.006**	**0.186 ± 0.004**	0.130 ± 0.005

Comparison Between Centralized and Local Training. Both Centralized and Local approaches are trained on datasets with missing values, but their performance differs significantly. This could be due to the different model architectures used in each approach. As aforementioned, the Centralized model is trained on a combined dataset where the additional features are filled with zeros, which results in the worst performance. This shows the advantage of having an individual model trained locally for each client.

4.2 Ablation Study

In Table 3, we show the result of reducing the number of common features in FedTDD. We set the number of common features to around 25% of the total number of features in the corresponding dataset. As a result, we can observe the robustness of FedTDD when dealing with a relatively small number of common features across most datasets. However, FedTDD does not perform as expected on the fMRI dataset because of the poor quality of imputed data, as mentioned in Sect. 4.1. On the other hand, the performance of Centralized training slightly decreased due to more zeros filling out the combined dataset, especially in the public data.

5 Conclusion

While federated learning is increasingly applied for different regression tasks for time series (TS), it is still limited in handling generative tasks, especially when time series features are vertically partitioned and temporarily misaligned. We propose a novel federated TS generation framework, FedTDD, which trains TS diffusion model by leveraging the self-imputing capability of the diffusion model and globally aggregating from clients' knowledge through data distillation and clients' synthetic data. The central component of FedTDD is a distiller at the coordinator that first is pre-trained on the public datasets and then periodically fine-tuned by the aggregated intermediate synthetic data from the clients. Clients keep their personalized TS diffusion models and train them with local data and synthetic data of the latest distiller periodically. Our extensive evaluation across five datasets shows that FedTDD effectively overcomes the hurdle of feature partition and temporal misalignment, achieving improvements of up to 79.4% and 62.8% over local training on Context-FID and Correlational scores, while delivering performance comparable to centralized baselines.

Acknowledgments. This research is part of the Priv-GSyn, 200021E_229204, of Swiss National Science Foundation and the DEPMAT project, P20-22/N21022, of the research programme Perspectief which is partly financed by the Dutch Research Council (NWO).

Disclosure of Interests. The authors have no competing interests to declare that are relevant to the content of this article.

References

1. Alaa, A., Chan, A.J., van der Schaar, M.: Generative time-series modeling with fourier flows. In: International Conference on Learning Representations (2021)
2. Alcaraz, J.M.L., Strodthoff, N.: Diffusion-based time series imputation and forecasting with structured state space models. arXiv preprint arXiv:2208.09399 (2022)
3. Brophy, E., De Vos, M., Boylan, G., Ward, T.: Estimation of continuous blood pressure from PPG via a federated learning approach. Sensors **21**(18), 6311 (2021)
4. Ceneda, D., Gschwandtner, T., Miksch, S., Tominski, C.: Guided visual exploration of cyclical patterns in time-series. In: Proceedings of the IEEE Symposium on Visualization in Data Science (VDS). IEEE Computer Society (2018)

5. Desai, A., Freeman, C., Wang, Z., Beaver, I.: Timevae: a variational auto-encoder for multivariate time series generation. arXiv preprint arXiv:2111.08095 (2021)
6. Fons, E., Sztrajman, A., El-Laham, Y., Iosifidis, A., Vyetrenko, S.: Hypertime: implicit neural representation for time series. arXiv preprint arXiv:2208.05836 (2022)
7. Goodfellow, I., et al.: Generative adversarial networks. Commun. ACM **63**(11), 139–144 (2020)
8. Heckbert, P.: Fourier transforms and the fast fourier transform (FFT) algorithm. Comput. Graph. **2**(1995), 15–463 (1995)
9. Ho, J., Jain, A., Abbeel, P.: Denoising diffusion probabilistic models. In: Advances in Neural Information Processing Systems, vol. 33, pp. 6840–6851 (2020)
10. Jeha, P., et al.: PSA-GAN: progressive self attention GANs for synthetic time series. In: The Tenth International Conference on Learning Representations (2022)
11. Kingma, D.P.: Auto-encoding variational bayes. arXiv preprint arXiv:1312.6114 (2013)
12. Kitagawa, G., Gersch, W.: A smoothness priors-state space modeling of time series with trend and seasonality. J. Am. Stat. Assoc. **79**(386), 378–389 (1984)
13. Kollovieh, M., Ansari, A.F., Bohlke-Schneider, M., Zschiegner, J., Wang, H., Wang, Y.B.: Predict, refine, synthesize: self-guiding diffusion models for probabilistic time series forecasting. In: Advances in Neural Information Processing Systems, vol. 36 (2024)
14. Li, T., Sahu, A.K., Zaheer, M., Sanjabi, M., Talwalkar, A., Smith, V.: Federated optimization in heterogeneous networks. Proc. Mach. Learn. Syst. **2**, 429–450 (2020)
15. Liao, S., Ni, H., Szpruch, L., Wiese, M., Sabate-Vidales, M., Xiao, B.: Conditional sig-Wasserstein GANs for time series generation. arXiv preprint arXiv:2006.05421 (2020)
16. Lim, B., Zohren, S.: Time-series forecasting with deep learning: a survey. Phil. Trans. R. Soc. A **379**(2194), 20200209 (2021)
17. Liu, Y., et al.: Vertical federated learning: concepts, advances, and challenges. IEEE Trans. Knowl. Data Eng. (2024)
18. Luu, K., Khashabi, D., Gururangan, S., Mandyam, K., Smith, N.A.: Time waits for no one! analysis and challenges of temporal misalignment. arXiv preprint arXiv:2111.07408 (2021)
19. McMahan, B., Moore, E., Ramage, D., Hampson, S., y Arcas, B.A.: Communication-efficient learning of deep networks from decentralized data. In: Artificial Intelligence and Statistics, pp. 1273–1282. PMLR (2017)
20. Meijer, C., Huang, J., Sharma, S., Lazovik, E., Chen, L.Y.: Ts-inverse: a gradient inversion attack tailored for federated time series forecasting models. In: 2025 IEEE Conference on Secure and Trustworthy Machine Learning (SaTML), pp. 110–124. IEEE (2025)
21. Mendieta, M., Yang, T., Wang, P., Lee, M., Ding, Z., Chen, C.: Local learning matters: rethinking data heterogeneity in federated learning. In: Proceedings of the IEEE/CVF Conference on Computer Vision and Pattern Recognition, pp. 8397–8406 (2022)
22. Mogren, O.: C-RNN-GAN: continuous recurrent neural networks with adversarial training. arXiv preprint arXiv:1611.09904 (2016)
23. Pratama, I., Permanasari, A.E., Ardiyanto, I., Indrayani, R.: A review of missing values handling methods on time-series data. In: 2016 International Conference on Information Technology Systems and Innovation (ICITSI), pp. 1–6. IEEE (2016)

24. Qu, L., et al.: Rethinking architecture design for tackling data heterogeneity in federated learning. In: Proceedings of the IEEE/CVF Conference on Computer Vision and Pattern Recognition, pp. 10061–10071 (2022)
25. Rasouli, M., Sun, T., Rajagopal, R.: FedGAN: federated generative adversarial networks for distributed data. arXiv preprint arXiv:2006.07228 (2020)
26. Rasul, K., Seward, C., Schuster, I., Vollgraf, R.: Autoregressive denoising diffusion models for multivariate probabilistic time series forecasting. In: International Conference on Machine Learning, pp. 8857–8868. PMLR (2021)
27. Sachdeva, N., McAuley, J.: Data distillation: a survey. arXiv preprint arXiv:2301.04272 (2023)
28. Shankar, A., Brouwer, H., Hai, R., Chen, L.: Silofuse: cross-silo synthetic data generation with latent tabular diffusion models (2024)
29. Song, J., Ye, J.C.: Federated cycleGAN for privacy-preserving image-to-image translation. arXiv preprint arXiv:2106.09246 (2021)
30. Tashiro, Y., Song, J., Song, Y., Ermon, S.: CSDI: conditional score-based diffusion models for probabilistic time series imputation. In: Advances in Neural Information Processing Systems, vol. 34, pp. 24804–24816 (2021)
31. Vaswani, A.: Attention is all you need. In: Advances in Neural Information Processing Systems (2017)
32. Voigt, P., Von dem Bussche, A.: The EU general data protection regulation (GDPR). A Practical Guide, 1st ed., pp. 10–5555. Springer International Publishing, Cham (2017)
33. Wang, Z., Cheng, X., Su, S., Wang, G.: Differentially private generative decomposed adversarial network for vertically partitioned data sharing. Inf. Sci. **619**, 722–744 (2023)
34. Yoon, J., Jarrett, D., Van der Schaar, M.: Time-series generative adversarial networks. In: Advances in Neural Information Processing Systems, vol. 32 (2019)
35. Yuan, X., Qiao, Y.: Diffusion-TS: interpretable diffusion for general time series generation. arXiv preprint arXiv:2403.01742 (2024)
36. Yuan, X., Zhao, Z., Gope, P., Sikdar, B.: VFLGAN-TS: vertical federated learning-based generative adversarial networks for publication of vertically partitioned time-series data. arXiv preprint arXiv:2409.03612 (2024)
37. Zhang, C., Xie, Y., Bai, H., Yu, B., Li, W., Gao, Y.: A survey on federated learning. Knowl.-Based Syst. **216**, 106775 (2021)
38. Zhao, Z., Wu, H., Van Moorsel, A., Chen, L.Y.: GTV: generating tabular data via vertical federated learning. arXiv preprint arXiv:2302.01706 (2023)
39. Zhu, J.Y., Park, T., Isola, P., Efros, A.A.: Unpaired image-to-image translation using cycle-consistent adversarial networks. In: Proceedings of the IEEE International Conference on Computer Vision, pp. 2223–2232 (2017)

Graph Neural Networks

Distribution Matching for Graph Quantification Under Structural Covariate Shift

Clemens Damke[1]($\boxtimes$) and Eyke Hüllermeier[1,2,3]

[1] Institute of Informatics, LMU Munich, Munich, Germany
{clemens.damke,eyke}@ifi.lmu.de
[2] Munich Center for Machine Learning (MCML), Munich, Germany
[3] German Centre for Artificial Intelligence (DFKI, DSA), Bremen, Germany

Abstract. Graphs are commonly used in machine learning to model relationships between instances. Consider the task of predicting the political preferences of users in a social network; to solve this task one should consider, both, the features of each individual user *and* the relationships between them. However, oftentimes one is not interested in the label of a single instance but rather in the distribution of labels over a set of instances; e.g., when predicting the political preferences of users, the overall prevalence of a given opinion might be of higher interest than the opinion of a specific person. This label prevalence estimation task is commonly referred to as *quantification learning* (QL). Current QL methods for tabular data are typically based on the so-called *prior probability shift* (PPS) assumption which states that the label-conditional instance distributions should remain equal across the training and test data. In the graph setting, PPS generally does not hold if the shift between training and test data is structural, i.e., if the training data comes from a different region of the graph than the test data. To address such structural shifts, an importance sampling variant of the popular adjusted count quantification approach has previously been proposed. In this work, we extend the idea of structural importance sampling to the state-of-the-art KDEy quantification approach. We show that our proposed method adapts to structural shifts and outperforms standard quantification approaches.

Keywords: Quantification Learning · Graph Quantification · Covariate Shift

1 Introduction

Quantification learning (QL) refers to the task of estimating the distribution of labels $\mathcal{Y}$ over a set of instances $\mathcal{X}$ [8–10]. More specifically, one is given a set of labeled training instances $\mathcal{D}_L \subseteq \mathcal{X} \times \mathcal{Y}$ drawn from a distribution P and a set of unlabeled test instances $\mathcal{X}_U \subseteq \mathcal{X}$ drawn from a distribution Q for which the label distribution $Q(Y)$ is to be estimated. For example, the problem of predicting the prevalence of different opinions in a given population of people can be seen as a QL task. Here, the training data consists of a sample of people with known opinions, while the test data consists of a second sample of people with unknown opinions for which the opinion prevalences should be estimated.

A naïve way to solve a quantification problem is to use a standard classification model to label all test instances $\mathcal{X}_U$. The relative frequencies of the predicted labels could then be used as an estimate of $Q(Y)$. Given a perfect classifier, this so-called *Classify & Count* (CC) strategy would indeed yield a perfect estimate of the test label distribution. This is, however, an unrealistic assumption, leading to the question of whether an imperfect classifier can still provide good quantification results. Forman [8] showed that the simple CC approach can lead to poor quantification results if the classifier is biased. To understand why, note that the goal of a classifier is to minimize the number of classification errors, i.e., the sum of false positive and false negative predictions (FP + FN) in the binary case. In contrast, the goal of a quantifier is to minimize |FP − FN|; if FP = FN, the missing positive predictions are perfectly compensated for by the missing negative predictions, leading to a perfect quantification result. This implies that even a poor classifier (in terms of misclassifications) can provide good quantification results and vice versa. Therefore, quantification should be treated as a distinct task from classification [5].

Suppose the training and test data are drawn from the same distribution ($P = Q$). In that case, the quantification task is trivially solved using the label distribution of the sampled training data $\mathcal{D}_L$ as an unbiased estimate of the label distribution of the test data. The QL problem gets more challenging when the training and test data are drawn from different distributions, i.e., in the presence of so-called *distribution shift*. In this case, the distribution of training labels $P(Y)$ is not necessarily a good estimate of the test label distribution $Q(Y)$. In the extreme case, if the two sampling distributions are entirely unrelated and the training data thus is uninformative about the test data, the quantification task becomes intractable without other prior assumptions.

Therefore, one typically assumes at least some kind of relation between the training and test data. The most commonly assumed type of shift is called *prior probability shift* (PPS) [14,23], which states that the class-conditional instance distributions remain unchanged between P and Q. This assumption is made, among others, by the well-known *Adjusted Classify & Count* (ACC) quantification method [8] and by *distribution matching* (DM) methods, such as the *Mixture Models* (MM) approach [8], HDy [15], DyS [19] or KDEy [25].

While PPS is a reasonable assumption in many domains, there are problems where it does not hold. If the training and test data are drawn from different regions of the instance space, the PPS assumption may not be satisfied. In this case, P and Q may instead be related by *covariate shift* [23], which states that the distributions of the instances can differ, while the instance-conditional label distributions remain unchanged. González et al. [14] and Tasche [33] show, both empirically and theoretically, that the standard ACC and DM approaches are not robust to covariate shift.

One domain where covariate shift arises naturally is *node label quantification* in graph data. Here, instances are nodes in a graph which are connected by edges indicating some notion of relatedness. Consider the opinion quantification problem mentioned earlier, where people can be naturally represented as nodes in a social network with edges indicating social relations (coworkers, friendships, or familial relations). The structural information contained in such graph representations has been used with great success by *graph neural network* models to solve node classification tasks [16]. However, there has been little work on *graph quantification learning (GQL)*. Milli et al. [22] and Tang et al. [31] have proposed simple GQL methods based on community detection algorithms which do not make use of current predictive graph models. Recently, Damke and Hüllermeier [4] proposed the first classifier-based quantification method for graph data. They extend ACC to account for structural covariate shift by introducing the kernel-based *structural importance sampling* (SIS) method. ACC with SIS is shown to give unbiased estimates of $Q(Y)$ under covariate shift. However, state-of-the-art DM methods, such as KDEy, generally tend to outperform ACC methods under PPS [25]. Translating the practical advantages of DM to the covariate shift setting via SIS is therefore desirable.

In this work, we extend SIS to the DM framework and adapt KDEy to structural covariate shift and show that this combination outperforms previously proposed quantification approaches. To this end, we begin with a brief introduction to QL in general and DM methods in particular (Sect. 2). Section 3 then describes the SIS method and how it can be used in the DM framework. In Sect. 4, we evaluate the proposed method on a set of benchmark datasets under different types of distribution shift and compare it to other quantification approaches. Finally, we conclude with a brief outlook in Sect. 5.

2 An Overview of Quantification Learning

In the literature on QL, one typically distinguishes between *aggregative* and *non-aggregative* approaches [5]. Aggregative methods are based on a standard classification model that is trained on labeled training instances. The predictions of this model on the test data are aggregated to estimate the test label distribution. Non-aggregative methods, in contrast, are directly trained to predict label prevalences given a set of instances. Here, we focus on aggregative methods; the extension of non-aggregative quantification methods to covariate shift is left for future work. First, we fix some notation and formally define the quantification learning setting.

2.1 Notation and Problem Setting

As described in the introduction, let $\mathcal{X}$ denote the instance space and $\mathcal{Y} = \{1, \ldots, K\}$ the (finite) label space. Let P and Q be probability measures on $\mathcal{X} \times \mathcal{Y}$ representing the training and test data distributions, respectively. Let X and Y denote *random variables* that project the joint instance-label space to

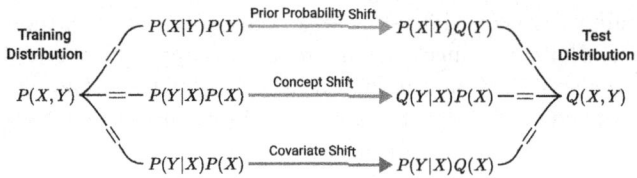

Fig. 1. Overview of the three typically considered types of distribution shift.

the instance and label spaces, respectively. In QL, we are given a labeled sample $\mathcal{D}_L \subseteq \mathcal{X} \times \mathcal{Y}$ drawn from P and an unlabeled sample $\mathcal{X}_U \subseteq \mathcal{X}$ drawn from $Q(X) = Q \circ X^{-1}$. The goal of QL is to estimate $Q(Y)$ from $\mathcal{D}_L$ and $\mathcal{X}_U$. The two measures P and Q are assumed to be related by some kind of distribution shift [23]:

(i) In *prior probability shift* (PPS), $P(Y)$ and $Q(Y)$ might differ but the label-conditional instance distributions remain equal, i.e., $P(X \mid Y) = Q(X \mid Y)$.
(ii) In *covariate shift*, the distributions of the instances $P(X)$ and $Q(X)$ differ, while the conditional label distributions remain unchanged, i.e., $P(Y \mid X) = Q(Y \mid X)$.
(iii) In *concept shift*, it is the conditional label distributions $P(Y \mid X)$ and $Q(Y \mid X)$ that change while the marginal instance distributions $P(X)$ and $Q(X)$ remain equal.

See Fig. 1 for an overview. Depending on the problem domain, different types of distribution shift can occur [23]. For example, PPS might arise in the context of epidemiological studies where the task is to estimate the prevalence of a disease in a population. Here, the training data might be collected via a case-control study where the percentage of healthy and infected people is fixed by design, while the test data is collected from a random sample of the population. In contrast, the opinion estimation problem mentioned earlier might be subject to covariate shift if the training data is collected in a different region of the population than the test data. Last, concept shift occurs if the meaning of labels change between training and test data, e.g., whether a newspaper article is about a local or world news depends on the location of the reader/newspaper.

Assuming PPS, the training and test distributions are related by $P(X \mid Y) = Q(X \mid Y)$. Consequently, for any measurable mapping $\phi : \mathcal{X} \to \mathcal{Z}$, we have $P(Z \mid Y) = Q(Z \mid Y)$ where $Z = \phi(X)$ [18]. This allows us to factorize $Q(Z)$ as follows:

$$Q(Z) = \sum_{i=1}^{K} Q(Z \mid Y = i) Q(Y = i) = \sum_{i=1}^{K} P(Z \mid Y = i) Q(Y = i) \qquad (1)$$

Given $\mathcal{D}_L$ and $\mathcal{X}_U$, both, $Q(Z)$ and $P(Z \mid Y)$ can (in principle) be estimated, resulting in a system of equations which can be solved for the desired test label distribution $Q(Y)$. This idea forms the basis for many QL methods, including ACC [2,8,10] and the family of DM methods [3,7,25]. The main difference between those methods lies in how the mapping ϕ is chosen and how the system of equations is solved. One common approach is to define ϕ in terms of a hard classifier $h : \mathcal{X} \to \mathcal{Y}$ or a probabilistic classifier $h_s : \mathcal{X} \to \Delta_K$, where Δ_K is the unit $(K-1)$-simplex. Let $\hat{Y} = h(X)$ denote the predicted label and $\hat{S}_i = h_s(X)_i$ be the predicted probability of label i.

For $\phi = h$, Eq. (1) turns into ACC, where $P(\hat{Y} \mid Y)$ is simply the confusion matrix of h. Tasche [32] shows that this results in an unbiased estimate of $Q(Y)$ under PPS. Similarly, using a confusion matrix derived from h_s leads to the *Probabilistic Adjusted Classify & Count* (PACC) approach [1], while the unadjusted pendant of CC is referred to as *Probabilistic Classify & Count* (PCC). Next, we will describe the distribution matching framework.

2.2 Histogram-Based DM Approaches

The first DM quantification method, simply refered to as *Mixture Models* (MM), was proposed by Forman [8]. MM is designed for binary quantification problems, i.e., $\mathcal{Y} = \{\oplus, \ominus\}$, and uses $\phi = h_s$, where $h_s : \mathcal{X} \to [0,1]$ is a soft binary classifier. Equation (1) then becomes

$$Q(\hat{S}) = \underbrace{P(\hat{S} \mid Y = \oplus)}_{P_\oplus} \underbrace{Q(Y = \oplus)}_{\alpha} + \underbrace{P(\hat{S} \mid Y = \ominus)}_{P_\ominus} \underbrace{Q(Y = \ominus)}_{1-\alpha} .$$

Here, the distribution of predicted probabilities $Q(\hat{S})$ is modeled as a mixture of the class-conditional predicted probability distributions $P_\oplus, P_\ominus$. Forman estimates those distributions via discrete *cumulative distribution functions* (CDFs) $\hat{p}_\oplus, \hat{p}_\ominus$ predicted by h_s on $\mathcal{D}_L$. Analogously, an estimate $\hat{q}$ of $Q(\hat{S})$ is obtained by computing the discrete CDF using $\mathcal{X}_U$. The mixture weight α is then determined by solving the following optimization problem:

$$\alpha^* = \arg\min_{\alpha \in [0,1]} \ell\left(\alpha \cdot \hat{p}_\oplus + (1-\alpha) \cdot \hat{p}_\ominus, \hat{q}\right) , \qquad (2)$$

where ℓ is a loss function measuring the discrepancy between the mixture CDF and $\hat{q}$. Forman proposes two different loss functions: PP-Area, which is equivalent to minimizing the L1-norm between the two CDFs [7], and the Kolmogorov-Smirnov statistic. González-Castro et al. [15] extend MM by proposing a variant that estimates the *probability density functions* (PDFs) of $P_\oplus$, $P_\ominus$ and $Q(\hat{S})$ via normalized histograms $\hat{p}_\oplus, \hat{p}_\ominus, \hat{q} \in \mathbb{R}^b$ instead of discrete CDFs estimates; here, $b \in \mathbb{N}_0$ is the number of bins. Additionally, they suggest using the *Hellinger distance* (HD) as a loss function ℓ between PDFs:

$$\mathrm{HD}(p, q) := \frac{1}{\sqrt{2}} \|\sqrt{p} - \sqrt{q}\|_2 \qquad (3)$$

This variant of MM is referred to as HDy. Note that, both, MM and HDy can only be applied to binary quantification problems. Extensions of HDy to the multi-class regime have been proposed by Firat [7] and Bunse [3]. If $K > 2$, one can compute a class-conditional histogram $\hat{p}_{j,i} \in \mathbb{R}^b$ of $P(\hat{S}_j \mid Y = i)$ for each pair of classes j, i and one histogram $\hat{q}_j$ of $Q(\hat{S}_j)$ for each $i \in \mathcal{Y}$. To obtain a representation of $P(\hat{S} \mid Y = i)$, one can then combine the class-conditional histograms by concatenating and renormalizing them to obtain a single histogram $\hat{p}_i = \frac{1}{K}(\hat{p}_{1,i}, \ldots, \hat{p}_{K,i}) \in \mathbb{R}^{bK}$ [7], or by directly averaging them, i.e., $\hat{p}_i = \frac{1}{K}\sum_{j=1}^{K}\hat{p}_{j,i}$ [3]. Moreo et al. [25] show that both of these histogram aggregation variants are theoretically flawed, since neither of them produces a proper estimate of the divergence between PDFs. The problem of those multi-class extensions of HDy is that the per-class histograms $\hat{p}_{j,i}$ and $\hat{q}_j$ are unable to capture inter-class information.

2.3 Kernel Density Estimation-Based DM

To address the shortcomings of histogram-based DM methods, Moreo et al. [25] propose the KDEy quantification approach. Unlike MM and HDy, KDEy does not represent $Q(\hat{S})$ and $P(\hat{S} \mid Y)$ by decomposing them into class-wise histograms but instead uses *kernel density estimation* (KDE) to model the PDFs of the predicted probabilities as *Gaussian mixture models* (GMMs). More specifically, let $q(\hat{s})$ be the PDF of $Q(\hat{S})$ and $p(\hat{s} \mid i)$ be the PDF of $P(\hat{S} \mid Y = i)$, with $s = (s_1, \ldots, s_K) \in \Delta_K$ being a vector of predicted label probabilities. Using KDE, we can estimate those PDFs as follows:

$$\hat{q}(\hat{s}) = \frac{1}{|\mathcal{X}_U|}\sum_{x \in \mathcal{X}_U} k(\hat{s}, h_s(x)) \quad \text{and} \quad \hat{p}(\hat{s} \mid i) = \frac{1}{|\mathcal{D}_L^i|}\sum_{(x,y) \in \mathcal{D}_L^i} k(\hat{s}, h_s(x)), \quad (4)$$

where $k : \Delta_K \times \Delta_K \to \mathbb{R}_{\geq 0}$ is a kernel function and $\mathcal{D}_L^i := \{(x, y) \in \mathcal{D}_L \mid y = i\}$. In KDEy, the kernel k is chosen to be a Gaussian kernel with bandwidth σ:

$$k(\hat{s}, \hat{s}') := \frac{1}{\sqrt{(2\pi)^K}\sigma^K} \exp\left(-\frac{1}{2\sigma^2}\|\hat{s} - \hat{s}'\|_2^2\right). \quad (5)$$

The bandwidth σ is treated as a model hyperparameter. Using the linearity of the Radon-Nikodym derivative[1] we can plug our PDF estimates into Eq. (1) to obtain the following equation:

$$\hat{q}(\hat{s}) = \sum_{i=1}^{K} \hat{p}(\hat{s} \mid i) q(i), \quad (6)$$

where both sides of the equation are GMMs and $q \in \Delta_K$ is the vector of label prevalences in the test distribution which we are looking for. Analogous to the histogram-based DM approaches, we can now solve for q by minimizing a divergence ℓ between the left-hand side and the right-hand side of Eq. (6):

$$\hat{q} = \arg\min_{q \in \Delta_K} \ell\left(\hat{q}(\hat{s}), \sum_{i=1}^{K} q_i \cdot \hat{p}(\hat{s} \mid i)\right). \quad (7)$$

---
[1] Note that $q(\hat{s}) = \frac{dQ(\hat{S})}{d\mu}$ and $p(\hat{s} \mid i) = \frac{dP(\hat{S}\mid Y=i)}{d\mu}$, with the Lebesgue measure μ.

Different choices of ℓ are possible here, e.g., HD (see Eq. (3)), L2, Cauchy-Schwarz, Jensen-Shannon or *Kullback-Leibler divergence* (KLD). Since ℓ has to be computed for continuous distributions which, depending on the divergence, can be computationally intractable, Moreo et al. [25] suggest a number of divergence-dependent optimization strategies. For the Cauchy-Schwarz divergence, they derive a closed-form solution to Eq. (7). For the HD, Jensen-Shannon and L2 divergences, they propose a Monte Carlo approximation approach. For the KLD, they show that Eq. (7) reduces to

$$\hat{q} = \arg\min_{q \in \Delta_K} - \sum_{x \in \mathcal{X}_U} \log \sum_{i=1}^{K} q_i \cdot \hat{p}(h_s(x) \mid i) \,, \tag{8}$$

which can be solved using standard (gradient-based) constrained optimization techniques. In their experiments, the different variants of KDEy generally outperform the histogram-based DM methods, with the HD- and KLD-based variants performing particularly strongly.

3 DM Under Structural Covariate Shift

The DM approaches for quantification described in the previous section are all based on the PPS assumption. However, as discussed before, this assumption is not always justified in practice. When dealing with graph data, covariate shifts are of particular interest. If the training data is collected from a different region of the graph than the test data, there is so-called *structural covariate shift* between P and Q. Damke and Hüllermeier [4] propose an extension of ACC to account for such structural covariate shifts via so-called *structural importance sampling* (SIS). We will now show how this idea can be extended to the DM framework.

To motivate our approach, consider the following example: Fig. 2 shows a simple graph consisting of three vertex clusters, each corresponding to one label $\mathcal{Y} = \{\mathsf{A}, \mathsf{B}, \mathsf{C}\}$. Most vertices in each cluster have the matching label; there are, however, a few outliers incident to the edges between clusters. Assume that the training data $\mathcal{D}_L$ is sampled uniformly at random from all three clusters and that the test data $\mathcal{X}_U$ comes only from the topmost cluster A (indicated by the large nodes), i.e., there is covariate shift between both samples. A probabilistic classifier h_s has high confidence on inlier vertices and low confidence for outliers. The simplex plots on the left of Fig. 2 show the PDFs of $P(\hat{S} \mid Y)$ for all three labels $\mathcal{Y}$. The standard KDEy method described in Sect. 2.3 tries to find an optimal mixture of those PDFs to match the target PDF $Q(\hat{S})$ of the test data (shown in black) by minimizing a divergence ℓ between the mixture PDF and $Q(\hat{S})$. Since outliers are rare for each class, the PDFs $P(\hat{S} \mid Y)$ are concentrated around the high confidence regions of each class. $\mathcal{X}_U$, on the other hand, contains many outliers, causing the test PDF $Q(\hat{S})$ to be less concentrated. In this case, the optimal mixture found by KDEy will put all weight on $P(\hat{S} \mid Y = \mathsf{A})$, resulting in a heavily biased estimate of $Q(Y)$.

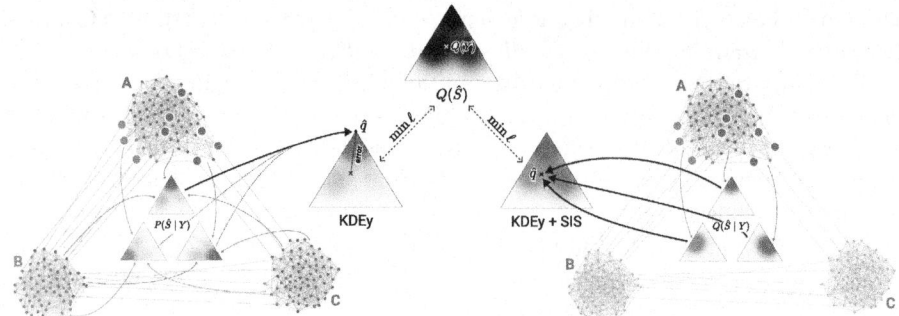

Fig. 2. Illustration of the advantage of SIS in the DM framework under structural covariate shift.

The problem is that the global PDFs $P(\hat{S} \mid Y)$ are not representative of the local (shifted) PDFs $Q(\hat{S} \mid Y)$. Instances with label **B** and **C** within cluster **A** will receive low confidence scores, as shown in the simplex plots on the right side of Fig. 2. By combining these estimates of $Q(\hat{S} \mid Y)$, as opposed to $P(\hat{S} \mid Y)$, one can find a PDF mixture that better matches $Q(\hat{Y})$ resulting in a better predicted label distribution. The core idea behind SIS is to use the graph structure to obtain such estimates. We will now describe SIS more formally and then adapt it to the DM framework.

3.1 Structural Importance Sampling for ACC

As described in Sect. 2.1, both, ACC and DM methods are based on the factorization in Eq. (1). Under covariate shift, this factorization does not hold, since $Q(Z \mid Y)$ is unknown. If $\phi = h$, i.e., $Z = \hat{Y} = h(X)$, we can rewrite $Q(\hat{Y} \mid Y)$ via importance sampling [4]:

$$Q(\hat{Y} = j \mid Y = i) = \int_{x \in \mathcal{X}} \mathbb{1}[h(x) = j] dQ(X = x \mid Y = i)$$

$$= \int_{x \in \mathcal{X}} \mathbb{1}[h(x) = j] \underbrace{\frac{q_{X\mid Y}(x \mid i)}{p_{X\mid Y}(x \mid i)}}_{=\rho_{X\mid Y}(x\mid i)} dP(X = x \mid Y = i) \quad (9)$$

Here, $q_{X\mid Y}$ and $p_{X\mid Y}$ denote the conditional PDFs of Q and P, and $\rho_{X\mid Y}$ denotes the ratio between those densities. Under (structural) covariate shift, we know that $p_{Y\mid X} = q_{Y\mid X}$, which allows us to rewrite $\rho_{X\mid Y}$:

$$\rho_{X\mid Y}(x \mid y) = \frac{q_{X\mid Y}(x \mid y)}{p_{X\mid Y}(x \mid y)} = \frac{q_{Y\mid X}(y \mid x) q_X(x) p_Y(y)}{p_{Y\mid X}(y \mid x) p_X(x) q_Y(y)} = \rho_X(x) \cdot \rho_Y(y)^{-1} \quad (10)$$

Plugging this into Eq. (9) gives us

$$Q(\hat{Y} = j \mid Y = i) = \frac{\rho_Y(i)^{-1} \int_{\mathcal{X}} \mathbb{1}[h(x) = j]\rho_X(x)dP(X = x \mid Y = i)}{\rho_Y(i)^{-1} \int_{\mathcal{X}} \rho_X(x)dP(X = x \mid Y = i)}$$
$$= \frac{\mathbb{E}_{P(X\mid Y=i)}[\mathbb{1}[\hat{Y} = j]\rho_X(X)]}{\mathbb{E}_{P(X\mid Y=i)}[\rho_X(X)]}. \quad (11)$$

To compute $\rho_X = \frac{q_X}{p_X}$, Damke and Hüllermeier [4] propose to use kernel density estimation. Since we are given samples $\mathcal{D}_L$ from P and samples $\mathcal{X}_U$ from $Q(X)$, q_X and p_X can be estimated as follows:

$$\hat{q}_X(x) = \frac{1}{|\mathcal{X}_U|} \sum_{x' \in \mathcal{X}_U} \kappa(x, x') \quad \text{and} \quad \hat{p}_X(x) = \frac{1}{|\mathcal{D}_L|} \sum_{(x', y') \in \mathcal{D}_L} \kappa(x, x'), \quad (12)$$

where $\kappa : \mathcal{X} \times \mathcal{X} \to \mathbb{R}_{\geq 0}$ is a suitable instance kernel function. Without any domain assumptions, choosing κ appropriately is difficult.

However, in the context of graph data where instances x are vertices, assuming structural covariate shift, the probability of sampling a vertex x from P or Q should depend on how close x is to the training or test vertices, respectively. Damke and Hüllermeier suggest that the appropriate notion of "closeness" in a graph depends on the nature of the covariate shift. For example, if the data is sampled via random walks, a *personalized page-rank* (PPR) kernel [27] is appropriate:

$$\kappa_{\mathrm{PPR}}(x_i, x_j) = \Pi_{i,j}, \quad \text{where} \quad \Pi = \left(\alpha \mathbf{I} + (1-\alpha)\bar{\mathbf{A}}\right)^L. \quad (13)$$

Here, $\bar{\mathbf{A}} = \mathbf{A}\mathbf{D}^{-1}$ is the normalized adjacency matrix of the graph, $\alpha \in (0,1)$ is a teleportation parameter and L is the number of steps in the random walk. If the vertex sampling process is based on the shortest path lengths between vertices, a *shortest path* (SP) kernel can be used, e.g.,

$$\kappa_{\mathrm{SP}}(x_i, x_j) = \exp\left(-\lambda \cdot d_{\mathrm{SP}}(x_i, x_j)\right), \quad (14)$$

where $d_{\mathrm{SP}}(x_i, x_j)$ is the length of the shortest path between x_i and x_j and λ is a scaling parameter. To summarize, k should be chosen based on available knowledge about the quantification problem at hand to reflect the nature of the shift as closely as possible.

3.2 SIS in the DM Framework

In ACC, the instance mapping ϕ reduces an instance X to a single label prediction $\hat{Y}$, discarding much, potentially valuable, information. As discussed in Sect. 2, DM methods instead consider the distribution of predicted probability vectors $\hat{S} = h_s(X)$. To apply SIS in the DM framework, we can rewrite $q(\hat{s} \mid y)$:

$$q(\hat{s} \mid y) = \int_{x \in \mathcal{X}} q(\hat{s} \mid x) dQ(X = x \mid Y = y)$$
$$= \int_{x \in \mathcal{X}} p(\hat{s} \mid x) \underbrace{\frac{q_{X \mid Y}(x \mid y)}{p_{X \mid Y}(x \mid y)}}_{= \rho_{X \mid Y}(x \mid y)} dP(X = x \mid Y = y) \quad (15)$$

Analogous to SIS for ACC, we can use Eq. (10) for the following replacement:

$$q(\hat{s} \mid Y = i) = \frac{\mathbb{E}_{P(X \mid Y = y)}[p(\hat{s} \mid X) \rho_X(X)]}{\mathbb{E}_{P(X \mid Y = y)}[\rho_X(X)]} . \quad (16)$$

Given $\mathcal{D}_L$ and $\mathcal{X}_U$ we can compute an estimate $\hat{\rho}_X(x)$ via Eq. (12). Additionally, $q(\hat{s} \mid Y = i)$ can be estimated via

$$\hat{q}(\hat{s} \mid y) = \frac{1}{\sum_{(x,y) \in \mathcal{D}_L^i} \hat{\rho}_X(x)} \sum_{(x,y) \in \mathcal{D}_L^i} p(\hat{s} \mid x) \cdot \hat{\rho}_X(x) \quad (17)$$

Since $p(\hat{s} \mid x) = \delta[\hat{s} = h_s(x)]$ is a Dirac delta, i.e., the density is zero everywhere except at $\hat{s} = h_s(x)$, this estimate is not particularly useful given a finite sample $\mathcal{D}_L$. To account for this, we replace the Dirac delta with a Gaussian kernel $k : \Delta_K \times \Delta_K \to \mathbb{R}_{\geq 0}$ and obtain

$$\hat{q}(\hat{s} \mid y) = \frac{1}{\sum_{(x,y) \in \mathcal{D}_L^i} \hat{\rho}_X(x)} \sum_{(x,y) \in \mathcal{D}_L^i} k(\hat{s}, h_s(x)) \cdot \hat{\rho}_X(x) . \quad (18)$$

The result is a weighted version of KDEy (cf. Eq. (4)), where the instance weights $\hat{\rho}_X(x)$ are themselves estimated via KDE using a vertex kernel κ. By reweighting the labeled samples $\mathcal{D}_L$ via SIS, KDEy can be applied to quantification problems with structural covariate shift.

4 Evaluation

We evaluate the proposed combination of SIS and KDEy on a set of benchmark datasets under different types of distribution shift using multiple node classifiers and quantification metrics. We compare our approach against PCC, PACC, PACC with SIS and standard KDEy without SIS. We use the QuaPy Python library [24] and torch-geometric [6] to implement our experiments[2]. For efficient GPU-based sampling of *breadth-first search* (BFS)-based test sets and the computation of the SP kernels, we use Nvidia's cuGraph library. All experiments were conducted using an AMD Ryzen 9 7950X CPU, 64GB RAM and an Nvidia RTX 4090 GPU.

---
[2] Code available at https://github.com/Cortys/graph-quantification.

4.1 Experimental Setup

Quantification Metrics. To compare the quality of a label distribution estimate $\hat{q}$ against the ground-truth label distribution q, we use the following two common quantification metrics: *Absolute error* (AE) and *relative absolute error* (RAE):

$$\text{AE}(q, \hat{q}) = \frac{1}{K} \sum_{i=1}^{K} |q_i - \hat{q}_i| \qquad \text{RAE}(q, \hat{q}) = \frac{1}{K} \sum_{i=1}^{K} \frac{|q_i - \hat{q}_i|}{q_i} \qquad (19)$$

While AE penalized all errors equally, RAE [15] penalizes errors on rare labels more heavily.

Datasets. We generate quantification tasks from the following five node classification datasets: 1. CoraML, 2. CiteSeer, 3. PubMed, 4. Amazon Photos and 5. Amazon Computers [12,13,20,21,26,29,30]. The first three datasets are citation networks, where the nodes are documents and the edges represent citations between them. The two Amazon datasets are product co-purchasing graphs, where the nodes are products and the edges represent that are often bought together. All nodes are labeled with the topic or product category they belong to. All datasets were split randomly 10 times into three partitions classifier train, quantifier train and quantifer test with sizes 5%/15%/80%. Using those splits, we train each classifier 10 times on each of the 10 classifier train sets and use each of the resulting 100 classifiers per dataset with each type of quantifier.

Distribution Shift. To evaluate the behavior of the quantifiers under distribution shift, we synthetically introduce shifts to the test partitions of the datasets, while the training data is sampled uniformly at random from the training split. We consider the following types of distribution shift:

1. PPS: We sample $10 \cdot K$ sets of 100 nodes such that each set has a prescribed label distribution $q \in \Delta_K$ which is sampled from a Zipf distribution over the labels [28].
2. Structural covariate shift via *random walks* (RWs): For each label, we select 10 corresponding vertices and for each of those vertices we sample 100 nodes via random walks of length 10 with teleportation parameter $\alpha = 0.1$.
3. Structural covariate shift via BFS: Analogous to the PPR setting, we also evaluate structural covariate shift by sampling 100 nodes via breadth-first search instead of random walks.

Classifiers. We use four types of vertex classifiers: 1. A standard *Multilayer Perceptron* (MLP) which does not use any graph information, 2. *Graph Convolutional Network* [17], 3. *Graph Attention Network* [34] and 4. *Approximate personalized propagation of neural predictions* (APPNP) [11]. All models consist of two hidden fully connected layers and two convolutional layers (where applicable) with widths of 64 and ReLU activations.

Quantifiers. We compare PACC and KDEy with and without SIS. Additionally, we include PCC, as it should, in principle, be able to account for covariate shift to some extent [14,33]. For KDEy, we use the KLD as the divergence, referred to as KDEy-ML by Moreo et al. [25], as this variant generally produces good quantification results while also being computationally tractable. For SIS, we use an interpolated version of the PPR kernel from Eq. (13) for the KDE estimate of q_X:

$$\kappa_\lambda(x, x') = \lambda \kappa_{\text{PPR}}(x, x') + (1 - \lambda) ,$$

where $\lambda \in [0, 1]$ is a hyperparameter that controls the minimum weight that should be assigned to each vertex. For the KDE estimate of p_X, we use a constant kernel $\kappa_1(x, x') = 1$ since the training data is not subject to synthetic distribution shift in our setup. This implies that $p_X \approx q_X$, simplifying the SIS estimation. Additionally, we evaluate SIS with the SP kernel from Eq. (14) with $\lambda = \frac{1}{2}$ in the BFS-based covariate shift setting to check whether the distance-based BFS sampling is better matched by this kernel.

4.2 Experimental Results

Table 1 shows the mean quantification performance for all combinations of quantifiers, classifiers, distributions shifts and datasets. Additionally, the last block of columns shows the average rank of each quantifier across all datasets for all combinations of classifiers and distribution shifts. **Bold numbers** indicate that there is no statistically significant difference between the reported mean and the best mean within a given block, determined by the 95th percentile of a one-sided t-test. The PPR quantifiers use SIS with the interpolated PPR kernel κ_λ for different values of λ.

Overall, looking at the average ranks, we find that KDEy with SIS outperforms KDEy without SIS and, both PCC and PACC. The results are consistent across all three types of distribution shift, all model types and, both the AE and RAE metrics. Under PPS, where SIS is not necessary, SIS generally does not significantly improve the quantification performance; nonetheless, we note that KDEy with SIS has a better average rank than KDEy without SIS.

Influence of the Classifier. Unsurprisingly, the choice of classifier has a significant impact on the quantification performance. Even though, a good classifier h is not required by QL to obtain an unbiased estimate of the label prevalences, the quality of this estimate is still correlated with the classifier's accuracy. Overall, the structure-unaware MLP classifier thus performs worst while APPNP performs best.

Influence of the Type of Covariate Shift. The κ_λ used in our experiments is based on the assumption that the distribution shift is induced by sampling localized random walks. In the RW covariate setting, this assumption is satisfied, while in the BFS setting, the PPR kernel is, at least in theory, not appropriate. Since the

Table 1. Quantification results (absolute error and relative absolute error).

Model & Shift	Quantifier	CoraML AE	CoraML RAE	CiteSeer AE	CiteSeer RAE	A. Photos AE	A. Photos RAE	A. Comp. AE	A. Comp. RAE	PubMed AE	PubMed RAE	Avg. AE	Rank RAE
MLP PPS	PCC	.0827	.8565	.0361	.2782	.0497	1.105	.0533	.6342	.0470	.1870	6.8	7.0
	PACC	**.0481**	**.4186**	.0336	**.2271**	.0191	.3036	.0334	**.3690**	**.0181**	**.0649**	3.6	4.0
	PACC PPR 0.5	.0482	.4199	**.0335**	.2263	.0190	.3034	.0334	.3688	**.0181**	.0646	3.0	3.2
	KDEy	.0469	.4076	.0345	.2289	.0178	.2642	.0389	.4072	.0178	.0623	3.0	3.6
	KDEy PPR 0.5	**.0468**	**.4065**	.0343	**.2282**	.0178	**.2639**	.0389	.4070	.0178	**.0622**	**2.4**	**2.4**
	KDEy PPR 0.9	.0471	.4095	.0339	.2266	**.0180**	**.2633**	**.0388**	**.4055**	.0178	**.0622**	3.0	**2.2**
	KDEy PPR 1.0	.0526	.4774	.0420	.2743	.0223	.3017	.0433	.4537	.0263	.0963	6.2	5.6
GAT PPS	PCC	.0479	.5323	.0219	.1573	.0314	.9570	.0398	.4674	.0463	.1911	6.8	7.0
	PACC	.0297	.2660	.0192	.1262	.0147	.2776	**.0217**	**.2326**	.0176	.0635	5.0	5.0
	PACC PPR 0.5	**.0295**	**.2647**	.0190	**.1251**	.0147	**.2785**	**.0217**	**.2321**	.0174	.0630	3.8	4.4
	KDEy	.0254	.2296	.0185	.1208	**.0132**	**.2055**	**.0217**	**.2311**	.0166	.0593	3.2	2.6
	KDEy PPR 0.5	**.0252**	**.2287**	.0183	.1200	**.0131**	**.2056**	**.0217**	**.2310**	**.0165**	**.0591**	**2.0**	**2.0**
	KDEy PPR 0.9	**.0246**	**.2267**	**.0178**	**.1168**	**.0132**	**.2078**	**.0216**	**.2302**	**.0164**	**.0585**	**1.4**	**1.4**
	KDEy PPR 1.0	.0277	.2700	.0220	.1427	.0165	.2773	.0243	.2612	.0321	.1192	5.8	5.6
GCN PPS	PCC	.0438	.4697	.0221	.1574	.0315	.8508	.0391	.4667	.0405	.1665	7.0	7.0
	PACC	.0246	.2216	.0190	.1259	.0122	.2056	**.0228**	**.2411**	.0161	.0591	5.2	5.0
	PACC PPR 0.5	.0243	.2204	.0188	.1248	.0122	.2065	**.0227**	**.2405**	.0160	.0584	4.2	4.4
	KDEy	.0212	.1971	.0181	.1197	.0102	.1430	**.0223**	**.2325**	.0152	.0553	2.8	2.6
	KDEy PPR 0.5	**.0211**	**.1970**	.0180	.1189	.0102	.1430	**.0223**	**.2324**	.0152	**.0551**	**1.8**	**1.6**
	KDEy PPR 0.9	**.0210**	**.1984**	**.0174**	**.1159**	**.0103**	**.1435**	**.0222**	**.2323**	**.0149**	**.0545**	**1.4**	**1.8**
	KDEy PPR 1.0	.0241	.2381	.0218	.1420	.0145	.1973	.0269	.2755	.0263	.0998	5.6	5.6
APPNP PPS	PCC	.0374	.4124	.0214	.1509	.0318	.9795	.0390	.4657	.0398	.1664	6.6	7.0
	PACC	.0217	.1986	.0184	.1211	.0124	.2442	**.0256**	**.2638**	.0165	.0597	4.4	4.2
	PACC PPR 0.5	**.0215**	**.1975**	.0182	**.1201**	.0124	**.2454**	**.0256**	**.2632**	.0163	**.0589**	3.4	3.6
	KDEy	**.0193**	**.1783**	.0181	.1194	.0102	.1535	.0299	.3088	.0154	.0550	2.4	2.4
	KDEy PPR 0.5	**.0193**	**.1784**	.0180	.1184	.0102	.1540	.0299	.3088	**.0153**	**.0549**	**2.2**	**2.2**
	KDEy PPR 0.9	**.0194**	**.1812**	**.0173**	**.1145**	**.0105**	**.1612**	.0300	.3089	**.0153**	**.0548**	2.6	2.6
	KDEy PPR 1.0	.0225	.2239	.0218	.1413	.0204	.3371	.0412	.4178	.0277	.1054	6.4	6.0
MLP BFS	PCC	.1243	7.212	.1588	14.84	.0668	4.028	.0662	3.635	.0800	10.44	7.6	7.8
	PACC	.0645	3.508	.1158	10.63	.0237	.9928	.0392	1.608	.0816	**7.663**	6.4	5.6
	PACC PPR 0.5	**.0637**	**3.458**	**.1155**	**10.61**	.0235	.9909	.0388	1.609	.0808	**7.661**	5.2	5.0
	KDEy	**.0547**	**2.883**	**.1015**	**9.315**	**.0191**	**.6689**	.0394	**1.069**	.0772	**7.218**	3.8	2.8
	KDEy PPR 0.5	**.0545**	**2.864**	**.0993**	**9.105**	**.0189**	**.6578**	.0391	**1.059**	.0768	**7.218**	2.6	**1.6**
	KDEy PPR 0.9	**.0552**	**2.972**	.1039	9.621	**.0187**	**.6592**	.0374	**1.023**	.0743	**7.146**	**2.4**	2.0
	KDEy PPR 1.0	.0685	4.145	.1494	14.01	.0218	1.041	**.0300**	**1.080**	**.0680**	10.55	4.2	6.6
	KDEy SP 0.5	.0613	3.550	.1478	13.81	.0209	.9092	.0379	1.142	**.0707**	**7.193**	3.8	4.6
GAT BFS	PCC	.0741	4.840	.0820	7.349	.0291	1.757	.0455	2.415	**.0650**	9.922	6.2	7.6
	PACC	.0561	2.533	.0656	5.347	.0243	.7255	.0331	.9463	**.0930**	6.906	6.8	6.0
	PACC PPR 0.5	.0545	2.460	.0646	5.261	.0240	.7220	.0327	.9424	**.0922**	6.898	5.8	5.0
	KDEy	.0449	**1.735**	.0520	4.118	**.0212**	**.6491**	.0305	**.8432**	.0855	**5.659**	4.2	2.6
	KDEy PPR 0.5	**.0430**	**1.608**	**.0483**	**3.797**	**.0208**	**.6266**	.0303	**.8296**	.0857	**5.858**	3.2	2.2
	KDEy PPR 0.9	**.0405**	**1.568**	**.0465**	**3.665**	**.0200**	**.6183**	.0295	**.8084**	.0850	**6.669**	**2.0**	**1.6**
	KDEy PPR 1.0	.0443	2.420	.1021	9.175	**.0187**	.8031	**.0259**	.9357	**.0680**	7.678	3.0	6.2
	KDEy SP 0.5	.0454	2.058	.0980	8.808	.0216	.7892	.0304	.9411	.0785	**5.707**	4.8	4.8
GCN BFS	PCC	.0539	3.489	.0783	7.060	.0256	1.513	.0418	2.255	**.0573**	9.553	6.2	7.4
	PACC	.0488	2.093	.0637	5.267	.0241	.5966	.0401	.9320	.0888	6.713	6.8	5.8
	PACC PPR 0.5	.0475	2.037	.0631	5.212	.0239	.5933	.0397	.9295	.0881	6.706	5.8	4.8
	KDEy	.0355	**1.340**	.0555	**4.533**	**.0174**	**.5114**	.0326	**.7999**	.0716	**4.876**	4.0	2.2
	KDEy PPR 0.5	**.0347**	**1.300**	**.0517**	**4.209**	**.0170**	**.4811**	.0325	**.8007**	.0714	**4.941**	2.8	**1.8**
	KDEy PPR 0.9	**.0340**	**1.376**	**.0513**	**4.211**	**.0167**	**.4799**	.0315	**.7807**	.0716	**5.732**	2.0	2.0
	KDEy PPR 1.0	.0400	2.408	.1084	10.08	.0184	.7908	**.0280**	**.8680**	**.0687**	9.987	4.0	6.8
	KDEy SP 0.5	.0394	1.991	.0989	9.203	.0188	.7241	.0319	.8874	**.0701**	5.927	4.4	5.2
APPNP BFS	PCC	.0469	3.074	.0737	6.609	.0271	1.492	.0468	2.339	**.0569**	9.867	6.0	7.6
	PACC	.0457	1.881	.0603	4.944	.0225	.5731	.0430	.9227	.0927	7.449	6.6	5.6
	PACC PPR 0.5	.0444	1.835	.0594	4.866	.0222	.5687	.0425	.9179	.0919	7.438	5.6	4.6
	KDEy	.0334	**1.143**	.0506	4.023	**.0168**	**.4527**	.0362	**.7739**	.0735	**5.278**	3.4	2.2
	KDEy PPR 0.5	**.0321**	**1.073**	**.0473**	**3.741**	**.0166**	**.4415**	.0362	**.7828**	.0736	**5.410**	2.8	**2.0**
	KDEy PPR 0.9	**.0304**	**1.071**	**.0457**	**3.671**	**.0176**	**.4705**	.0351	**.7556**	.0746	**6.468**	2.6	**2.0**
	KDEy PPR 1.0	.0368	2.154	.1096	10.05	.0295	.9202	**.0328**	.9331	**.0632**	7.743	4.6	7.2
	KDEy SP 0.5	.0372	1.803	.0989	9.044	.0186	.7283	.0351	.8860	**.0709**	**6.000**	4.4	4.8
MLP RW	PCC	.1263	5.275	.1494	13.84	.0727	3.820	.0718	3.224	.0913	1.376	7.0	7.0
	PACC	.0733	2.347	.0869	7.425	.0332	1.251	.0471	1.837	.0882	**.7452**	5.2	4.8
	PACC PPR 0.5	**.0728**	**2.327**	**.0870**	**7.448**	.0330	1.250	.0468	1.842	.0876	**.7474**	4.6	5.0
	KDEy	**.0639**	**1.667**	**.0799**	**6.857**	**.0261**	**.7495**	.0457	**1.235**	.0863	**.6486**	2.8	2.4
	KDEy PPR 0.5	**.0629**	**1.604**	**.0775**	**6.665**	**.0257**	**.7254**	.0453	**1.222**	.0860	**.6503**	**1.8**	**1.8**
	KDEy PPR 0.9	**.0653**	**1.713**	**.0824**	**7.225**	**.0245**	**.6922**	.0438	**1.171**	.0845	**.6638**	2.0	2.2
	KDEy PPR 1.0	.0825	2.968	.1397	12.92	.0265	1.038	**.0377**	**1.206**	.0892	.9004	4.6	4.8
GAT RW	PCC	.0799	3.555	.0766	6.693	.0340	1.689	.0500	2.195	**.0691**	**.7488**	5.6	6.8
	PACC	.0610	1.648	.0594	4.563	.0293	.7767	.0382	.9639	.0952	.6084	5.4	5.6
	PACC PPR 0.5	.0590	1.580	.0583	4.466	.0290	.7726	.0378	.9604	.0946	**.6062**	4.4	4.2
	KDEy	.0490	**.8774**	.0475	3.353	**.0239**	**.6194**	.0330	**.7808**	.1035	**.6065**	4.4	3.2
	KDEy PPR 0.5	**.0472**	**.8092**	**.0439**	**3.028**	**.0235**	**.5966**	.0328	**.7801**	.1030	**.6049**	3.2	2.0
	KDEy PPR 0.9	**.0443**	**.7559**	**.0425**	**2.938**	**.0226**	**.5964**	.0321	**.7815**	.0999	**.5951**	**2.2**	**1.4**
	KDEy PPR 1.0	.0479	1.445	.1008	8.699	**.0219**	**.8045**	**.0296**	**.9615**	.0864	**.6009**	2.8	4.8
GCN RW	PCC	.0539	2.085	.0694	5.990	.0276	1.247	.0451	1.961	**.0566**	**.4972**	4.8	5.8
	PACC	.0571	1.267	.0554	4.204	.0298	.6101	.0428	.8952	.0956	.5915	6.4	5.6
	PACC PPR 0.5	.0556	1.216	.0546	4.134	.0296	.6071	.0424	.8910	.0952	.5897	5.4	4.6
	KDEy	.0412	.6563	.0489	3.550	**.0190**	**.4836**	.0325	**.7496**	.0904	**.5459**	3.6	3.4
	KDEy PPR 0.5	**.0400**	**.6125**	**.0456**	**3.262**	**.0187**	**.4551**	.0323	**.7445**	.0899	**.5432**	2.6	2.4
	KDEy PPR 0.9	**.0373**	**.5533**	**.0432**	**3.092**	**.0182**	**.4516**	.0314	**.7375**	.0870	**.5252**	**1.6**	**1.4**
	KDEy PPR 1.0	.0430	1.324	.0984	8.784	.0196	.7839	**.0282**	**.8437**	.0761	**.4474**	3.6	4.8
APPNP RW	PCC	.0465	1.750	.0659	5.638	.0293	1.197	.0504	2.016	**.0546**	**.4160**	5.2	5.6
	PACC	.0527	1.121	.0541	4.060	.0282	.5726	.0452	.8693	.0979	.5958	6.2	5.4
	PACC PPR 0.5	.0513	1.074	.0530	3.962	.0280	.5685	.0449	.8662	.0974	.5941	5.2	4.4
	KDEy	.0388	.5171	.0468	3.225	**.0197**	**.4548**	.0378	**.7761**	.0941	**.5520**	3.6	3.2
	KDEy PPR 0.5	**.0373**	**.4688**	**.0434**	**2.928**	**.0194**	**.4332**	.0375	**.7773**	.0935	**.5495**	2.6	2.4
	KDEy PPR 0.9	**.0340**	**.4052**	**.0418**	**2.879**	**.0193**	**.4339**	.0362	**.7676**	.0902	**.5327**	**1.6**	**1.6**
	KDEy PPR 1.0	**.0400**	1.218	.1031	8.877	.0243	.7835	**.0322**	.9118	.0754	.4704	3.6	5.4

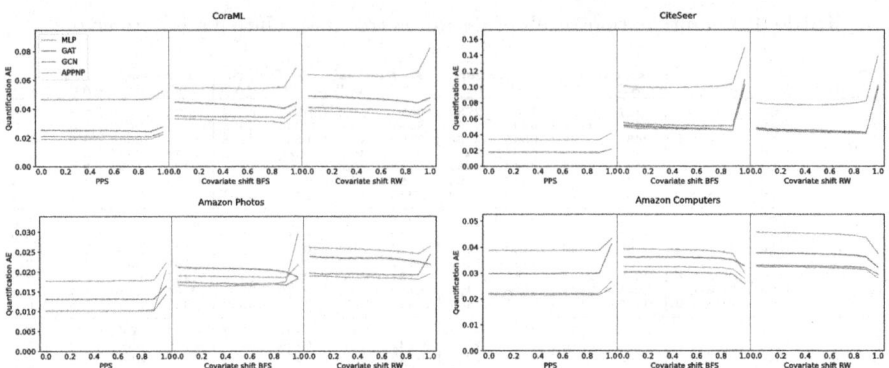

Fig. 3. Quantification performance of KDEy with SIS, using the PPR kernel κ_λ for different values of λ.

test vertices are selected by BFS based on their distance to some start vertex, a SP-based kernel, as in Eq. (14), seems plausible here. However, our results show that a perfect match between the SIS kernel and the underlying distribution shift is not necessary. In fact, the PPR kernel performs well even in the BFS setting, clearly outperforming all other quantifiers, while the SP kernel performs comparatively poorly.

Influence of κ on SIS. Note that the performance of SIS strongly depends on the choice of the kernel κ. For $\lambda = 1$, the PPR kernel performs poorly on all datasets except Amazon Computers. Figure 3 shows that decreasing λ slightly to 0.9 already improves the performance significantly, further decreasing λ then has little to no effect. This illustrates an important tradeoff to consider when using SIS: By making κ more aggressive, in the sense that little to no weight is assigned to distant vertices, one can in-principle improve the performance of SIS by reducing the influence of irrelevant or misleading vertices from different regions of the graph. However, if too many vertices are excluded, the effective sample size for the estimate $\hat{q}(\hat{s} \mid y)$ is reduced, making it more noisy.

The dataset-dependent optimal λ value differences can be explained by different connectivity patterns in the datasets. For example, while the CiteSeer dataset consists of multiple disconnected components, the Amazon Computers dataset mostly consists of a single large connected component (excluding a few disconnected outlier vertices). If all vertices in a structurally shifted test set are sampled from a single (small) connected component, the PPR kernel with $\lambda = 1$ will assign zero weight to all training vertices that are not in the same component, resulting in noisy estimates based on only a few vertices. For less connected datasets, where sampling a test set from a small component is more likely, it is therefore often beneficial to assign at least some weight even to disconnected vertices, which is achieved by using a $\lambda < 1$. For a well-connected dataset, such as Amazon Computers, this is not necessary.

To summarize, we have seen that KDEy combined with SIS and the PPR kernel perform very well across different datasets and shift types, corroborating that SIS is able to effectively account for (structural) covariate shift given an appropriate kernel.

5 Conclusion

We proposed a novel approach to quantification under structural covariate shift extending SIS from ACC to the KDEy quantification method. We showed the effectiveness of this approach on a set of benchmark datasets with different types of distribution shift. For future work, it would be interesting to investigate whether SIS can also be applied outside of the graph domain, e.g., in the context of timeseries data or geospatial data, where covariate shifts might occur in time or space. Second, a more thorough analysis of the influence of the choice of the kernel κ on the quantification performance is needed, especially since the choice of κ is crucial for the performance of SIS. Third, in this work we focused on the combination of SIS and KDEy, since KDEy is a state-of-the-art quantification method within the DM framework. Making other QL methods that assume PPS applicable to covariate shifts would be another avenue for future work. More specifically, investigating the combination of non-aggregative quantification approaches [28] would be interesting.

Disclosure of Interests. The authors have no competing interests to declare that are relevant to the content of this article.

References

1. Bella, A., Ferri, C., Hernández-Orallo, J., Ramírez-Quintana, M.J.: Quantification via Probability Estimators. In: 2010 IEEE International Conference on Data Mining, pp. 737–742 (2010). ISSN 2374-8486, https://doi.org/10.1109/ICDM.2010.75
2. Bunse, M.: On multi-class extensions of adjusted classify and count. In: Proceedings of the 2nd International Workshop on Learning to Quantify (LQ 2022), pp. 43–50 (2022)
3. Bunse, M.: Unification of Algorithms for Quantification and Unfolding. In: INFORMATIK 2022, Lecture Notes in Informatics (LNI) - Proceedings, Gesellschaft für Informatik, Bonn (2022)
4. Damke, C., Hüllermeier, E.: Adjusted Count Quantification Learning on Graphs (2025). https://doi.org/10.48550/arXiv.2503.09395
5. Esuli, A., Fabris, A., Moreo, A., Sebastiani, F.: Learning to Quantify, The Information Retrieval Series, vol. 1. Springer, Cham (2023), ISBN 978-3-031-20467-8
6. Fey, M., Lenssen, J.E.: Fast Graph Representation Learning with PyTorch Geometric (2019). https://doi.org/10.48550/arXiv.1903.02428
7. Firat, A.: Unified Framework for Quantification (2016). https://doi.org/10.48550/arXiv.1606.00868
8. Forman, G.: Counting positives accurately despite inaccurate classification. In: Proceedings of the 16th European Conference on Machine Learning, ECML 2005, pp. 564–575. Springer, Heidelberg (2005), ISBN 978-3-540-29243-2, https://doi.org/10.1007/11564096_55

9. Forman, G.: Quantifying trends accurately despite classifier error and class imbalance. In: Proceedings of the 12th ACM SIGKDD International Conference on Knowledge Discovery and Data Mining, KDD '06, pp. 157–166. Association for Computing Machinery, New York (2006), ISBN 978-1-59593-339-3, https://doi.org/10.1145/1150402.1150423
10. Forman, G.: Quantifying counts and costs via classification. Data Mining Knowl. Discovery **17**(2), 164–206 (2008). ISSN 1573-756X, https://doi.org/10.1007/s10618-008-0097-y
11. Gasteiger, J., Bojchevski, A., Günnemann, S.: Predict then propagate: graph neural networks meet personalized PageRank. In: International Conference on Learning Representations (2018)
12. Getoor, L.: Link-based classification. In: Bandyopadhyay, S., Maulik, U., Holder, L.B., Cook, D.J. (eds.) Advanced Methods for Knowledge Discovery from Complex Data, pp. 189–207, Advanced Information and Knowledge Processing, Springer, London (2005), ISBN 978-1-84628-284-3, https://doi.org/10.1007/1-84628-284-5_7
13. Giles, C.L., Bollacker, K.D., Lawrence, S.: CiteSeer: an automatic citation indexing system. In: Proceedings of the Third ACM Conference on Digital Libraries, DL '98, pp. 89–98. Association for Computing Machinery, New York (1998), ISBN 978-0-89791-965-4, https://doi.org/10.1145/276675.276685
14. González, P., Moreo, A., Sebastiani, F.: Binary quantification and dataset shift: an experimental investigation. Data Mining and Knowledge Discovery **38**(4), 1670–1712 (2024), ISSN 1573-756X, https://doi.org/10.1007/s10618-024-01014-1
15. González-Castro, V., Alaiz-Rodríguez, R., Alegre, E.: Class distribution estimation based on the Hellinger distance. Inf. Sci. **218**, 146–164 (2013), ISSN 0020-0255, https://doi.org/10.1016/j.ins.2012.05.028
16. Khemani, B., Patil, S., Kotecha, K., Tanwar, S.: A review of graph neural networks: Concepts, architectures, techniques, challenges, datasets, applications, and future directions. J. Big Data **11**(1), 18 (2024). ISSN 2196-1115, https://doi.org/10.1186/s40537-023-00876-4
17. Kipf, T.N., Welling, M.: Semi-supervised classification with graph convolutional networks. In: International Conference on Learning Representations (2017)
18. Lipton, Z., Wang, Y.X., Smola, A.: Detecting and correcting for label shift with black box predictors. In: Proceedings of the 35th International Conference on Machine Learning, pp. 3122–3130, PMLR (2018). ISSN 2640-3498
19. Maletzke, A., dos Reis, D., Cherman, E., Batista, G.: DyS: a framework for mixture models in quantification. In: Proceedings of the AAAI Conference on Artificial Intelligence 33(01), pp. 4552–4560 (2019). ISSN 2374-3468, https://doi.org/10.1609/aaai.v33i01.33014552
20. McAuley, J., Targett, C., Shi, Q., van den Hengel, A.: Image-based recommendations on styles and substitutes. In: Proceedings of the 38th International ACM SIGIR Conference on Research and Development in Information Retrieval, pp. 43–52, SIGIR '15. Association for Computing Machinery, New York (2015), ISBN 978-1-4503-3621-5, https://doi.org/10.1145/2766462.2767755
21. McCallum, A.K., Nigam, K., Rennie, J., Seymore, K.: Automating the construction of internet portals with machine learning. Inf. Retrieval **3**(2), 127–163 (2000). ISSN 1573-7659, https://doi.org/10.1023/A:1009953814988
22. Milli, L., Monreale, A., Rossetti, G., Pedreschi, D., Giannotti, F., Sebastiani, F.: Quantification in social networks. In: 2015 IEEE International Conference on Data Science and Advanced Analytics (DSAA), pp. 1–10 (2015). https://doi.org/10.1109/DSAA.2015.7344845

23. Moreno-Torres, J.G., Raeder, T., Alaiz-Rodríguez, R., Chawla, N.V., Herrera, F.: A unifying view on dataset shift in classification. Pattern Recogn. **45**(1), 521–530 (2012). ISSN 0031-3203, https://doi.org/10.1016/j.patcog.2011.06.019
24. Moreo, A., Esuli, A., Sebastiani, F.: QuaPy: a python-based framework for quantification. In: Proceedings of the 30th ACM International Conference on Information & Knowledge Management, CIKM 2021, pp. 4534–4543. Association for Computing Machinery, New York (2021), ISBN 978-1-4503-8446-9, https://doi.org/10.1145/3459637.3482015
25. Moreo, A., González, P., del Coz, J.J.: Kernel density estimation for multiclass quantification. Mach. Learn. **114**(4), 1–38 (2025). ISSN 1573-0565, https://doi.org/10.1007/s10994-024-06726-5
26. Namata, G., London, B., Getoor, L., Huang, B.: Query-driven active surveying for collective classification. In: Proceedings of the Workshop on Mining and Learning with Graphs (MLG-2012), Edinburgh, Scotland, UK (2012)
27. Page, L., Brin, S., Motwani, R., Winograd, T.: The PageRank Citation ranking: bringing order to the web. In: The Web Conference (1999)
28. Qi, L., Khaleel, M., Tavanapong, W., Sukul, A., Peterson, D.: A framework for deep quantification learning. In: Machine Learning and Knowledge Discovery in Databases: European Conference, ECML PKDD 2020, Ghent, Belgium, September 14–18, 2020, Proceedings, Part I, pp. 232–248, Springer, Heidelberg (2020). ISBN 978-3-030-67657-5, https://doi.org/10.1007/978-3-030-67658-2_14
29. Sen, P., Namata, G., Bilgic, M., Getoor, L., Galligher, B., Eliassi-Rad, T.: Collective classification in network data. AI Magaz. **29**(3), 93–93 (2008). ISSN 2371-9621, https://doi.org/10.1609/aimag.v29i3.2157
30. Shchur, O., Mumme, M., Bojchevski, A., Günnemann, S.: Pitfalls of graph neural network evaluation (2019). https://doi.org/10.48550/arXiv.1811.05868
31. Tang, L., Gao, H., Liu, H.: Network quantification despite biased labels. In: Proceedings of the Eighth Workshop on Mining and Learning with Graphs, MLG 2010, pp. 147–154. Association for Computing Machinery, New York (2010). ISBN 978-1-4503-0214-2, https://doi.org/10.1145/1830252.1830271
32. Tasche, D.: Fisher consistency for prior probability shift. J. Mach. Learn. Res. **18**(1), 3338–3369 (2017), ISSN 1532-4435
33. Tasche, D.: Class Prior Estimation under Covariate Shift: No Problem? (2022). https://doi.org/10.48550/arXiv.2206.02449
34. Veličković, P., Cucurull, G., Casanova, A., Romero, A., Liò, P., Bengio, Y.: Graph attention networks. In: International Conference on Learning Representations (2018)

Understanding and Improving Laplacian Positional Encodings for Temporal GNNs

Yaniv Galron[1(✉)], Fabrizio Frasca[1], Haggai Maron[1,4], Eran Treister[2], and Moshe Eliasof[3]

[1] Technion – Israel Institute of Technology, Haifa, Israel
yaniv.galron@campus.technion.ac.il
[2] Ben-Gurion University of the Negev, Beersheba, Israel
[3] University of Cambridge, Cambridge, UK
[4] NVIDIA, Santa Clara, USA

Abstract. Temporal graph learning has applications in recommendation systems, traffic forecasting, and social network analysis. Although multiple architectures have been introduced, progress in positional encoding for temporal graphs remains limited. Extending static Laplacian eigenvector approaches to temporal graphs through the supra-Laplacian has shown promise, but also poses key challenges: high eigendecomposition costs, limited theoretical understanding, and ambiguity about when and how to apply these encodings. In this paper, we address these issues by (1) offering a theoretical framework that connects supra-Laplacian encodings to per-time-slice encodings, highlighting the benefits of leveraging additional temporal connectivity, (2) introducing novel methods to reduce the computational overhead, achieving up to 56x faster runtimes while scaling to graphs with 50,000 active nodes, and (3) conducting an extensive experimental study to identify which models, tasks, and datasets benefit most from these encodings. Our findings reveal that while positional encodings can significantly boost performance in certain scenarios, their effectiveness varies across different models. The supplementary materials and code are available at https://github.com/YanivDorGalron/SLPE.

Keywords: Temporal Graphs · Positional Encodings · Graph Laplacian

1 Introduction

Temporal Graph Neural Networks (TGNNs) have emerged as a state-of-the-art paradigm for learning on dynamic graphs [3,10,16,27,28,32,34,36]. By simultaneously capturing evolving temporal dynamics and underlying graph structure, TGNNs have achieved remarkable performance across applications like temporal link prediction [7,25,43], node classification [33], edge classification [23] or temporal clustering [21].

Supplementary Information The online version contains supplementary material available at https://doi.org/10.1007/978-3-032-05981-9_25.

Positional Encoding (PE) techniques, fundamental to the success of Transformer architectures [4,9,35], enhance representational capacity by embedding crucial positional information within sequential and temporal data. In static graph contexts, positional encodings—particularly the Laplacian Positional Encoding (LPE) [2,5] derived from the spectral decomposition of the graph Laplacian—have demonstrated significant benefits in injecting structural information and in consistently elevating overall performance across node classification, link prediction and other graph learning tasks [5,6,19].

Despite their potential benefits, positional encodings for temporal graphs remain largely underexplored. A recent advancement has been the adaptation of LPEs for TGNNs through the novel application of supra-Laplacian eigenvectors [13]. The supra-Laplacian [8,17,20,31,41] extends traditional graph Laplacian frameworks by incorporating temporal connectivity between time steps, thereby elegantly capturing both intra-layer structural and inter-layer temporal dynamics. This approach enriches positional encodings with temporal information and has empirically demonstrated improved downstream performance.

However, the adoption of supra-Laplacian based PEs (SLPEs) presents several substantial challenges that warrant a thorough study. First, the theoretical underpinnings and properties of these novel encodings—and their specific relevance to temporal graph learning—remain insufficiently characterized, hampering our understanding of their effectiveness. Second, computing the eigendecomposition of the supra-Laplacian introduces considerable computational overhead due to the increased dimensionality from temporal connections. Third, while initial research [13] demonstrated promising results with specific transformer-based TGNN architecture and datasets, the generalizability of SLPEs across diverse architectural frameworks and learning tasks remains an open question.

Main Contributions. This paper systematically addresses the three aforementioned gaps to advance both the theoretical and practical understanding of Laplacian-based PEs for TGNNs:

1. We develop a theoretical analysis of supra-Laplacian PEs (SLPEs) as compared to single-layer Laplacian PEs (LPEs), and discuss the increased expressive power given by the supra-graph representation.
2. We introduce a computationally efficient framework for calculating SLPEs through approximate eigenvector computation, shown in Fig. 1.
3. We present extensive empirical evaluations across multiple Laplacian-based PEs, feature initializations, and architectural paradigms (message-passing- and transformer-based TGNNs), culminating in actionable practical guidelines.

2 Related Work

We now provide an overview of relevant topics to our work, namely TGNNs and the use of Laplacian Positional Encodings in graph learning.

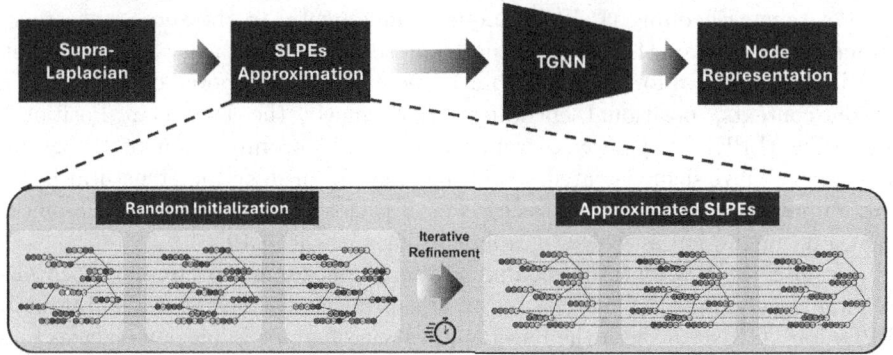

Fig. 1. An overview of our proposed fast SLPEs computation procedure. The SLPEs are generated via iterative solvers applied on the supra-Laplacian. Those start with random initialization and apply iterative refinement toward smooth PEs that act as the node representations.

Temporal Graph Neural Networks. TGNNs operate on both Continuous-Time Dynamic Graphs (CTDGs) [10,16,27,32] and Discrete-Time Dynamic Graphs (DTDGs) [30,39], with efforts to bridge the two domains [11,32]. For DTDGs, early methods like EGCN [24] use a Recurrent Neural Networks approach to apply a Graph Convolutional Network (GCN) over time. HTGN [40] leverages hyperbolic geometry to model complex, hierarchical structures in evolving networks. For CTDGs, pioneering methods like DyRep [34] and JODIE [16] process timestamped edge streams, while TGAT [38] focuses on inductive representation learning. Temporal Graph Networks (TGNs) [27] generalize these approaches, encompassing DyRep, JODIE, and TGAT as special cases. In the context of PEs, [32] incorporated relative PEs into CTDGs by counting node appearances on temporal walks and [37] constructed PEs for CTDGs by leveraging the Poisson point process to efficiently estimate personalized interaction intensity.

Laplacian-Based Positional Encodings. Graph Laplacian eigenvectors [2] have gained widespread adoption as effective graph embedding tools. In static graph neural networks, these embeddings encode crucial structural information that demonstrably enhances GNN expressive power [5,22,26]. The recent work in [6] revealed that approximate eigenvectors—as well as their computation trajectories—can match or surpass the performance of exact eigenvectors. Meanwhile, [19] developed novel neural architectures invariant to inherent eigenvector symmetries, specifically sign flips and more general basis transformations. Important theoretical challenges were addressed by [12], which investigated the non-uniqueness and instability issues where minor perturbations to the Laplacian can produce substantially different eigenspaces. Building on these advances, [13] recently extended Laplacian PEs to the temporal graphs for TGNNs, by incorporating the supra-Laplacian into an innovative transformer-based architecture. A theoretical analysis of the supra-Laplacian for applications to graph learning is, however, still missing, as well as their practical effectiveness on other known message-passing-based TGNNs.

3 Supra-Laplacian PEs in Temporal Graphs

In this section, we first introduce the notation used in the paper, and then define the supra-Laplacian and SLPEs that were proposed in the recent work [13] to extend Graph Transformers to DTDGs. We consider SLPEs for MPNNs as well.

Notations and Definitions. We follow the setup of [14] where temporal graphs are represented as a sequence of snapshots $\mathbb{G} = \{G_1, ..., G_T\}$. Each snapshot $G_t = (\mathcal{V}_t, \mathcal{E}_t)$ contains nodes $\mathcal{V}_t$ and edges $\mathcal{E}_t$ at time step t. Nodes $v_t \in \mathcal{V}_t$ possess feature vectors $\mathbf{h}_{v_t} \in \mathbb{R}^d$, while edges $(u_t, v_t) \in \mathcal{E}_t$ may have associated features $\mathbf{w}_e \in \mathbb{R}^{d_c}$. Collectively, input node features are denoted as $\mathbf{H}_t \in \mathbb{R}^{|\mathcal{V}_t| \times d}$. In addition, we denote by $\mathbf{P}_t \in \mathbb{R}^{|\mathcal{V}_t| \times c}$ the PEs at time t. As is standard [5,6], the PEs are combined with input node features to form an initial representation $\tilde{\mathbf{H}}_t = [\mathbf{H}_t \| \mathbf{P}_t] \in \mathbb{R}^{|\mathcal{V}_t| \times (d+c)}$, where $\|$ denotes channel-wise concatenation.

Supra-Laplacian and -Adjacency. The supra-Laplacian [8,17,20,31,41] leverages the multi-layer structure of temporal graphs by constructing a block matrix representation of the graph sequence. For a temporal graph $\mathbb{G}$, the supra-Laplacian matrix $\mathbf{L}_{\text{supra}} \in \mathbb{R}^{T|\mathcal{V}| \times T|\mathcal{V}|}$ is defined as:

$$\mathbf{L}_{\text{supra}} = \mathbf{D}_{\text{supra}} - \mathbf{A}_{\text{supra}}, \qquad (1)$$

where $\mathbf{A}_{\text{supra}}$ is the supra-adjacency matrix, $\mathbf{D}_{\text{supra}}$ is the corresponding degree matrix, and $|\mathcal{V}| = \max_{t=1,...,T} |\mathcal{V}_t|$. The supra-adjacency matrix is constructed by placing the adjacency matrices $\mathbf{A}_t$ of each snapshot G_t along the diagonal and adding inter-layer edges to model temporal dependencies, defined as:

$$\mathbf{A}_{\text{supra}} = \begin{bmatrix} \mathbf{A}_1 & \mathbf{B}_{12} & \cdots & \mathbf{B}_{1T} \\ \mathbf{B}_{21} & \mathbf{A}_2 & \cdots & \mathbf{B}_{2T} \\ \vdots & \vdots & \ddots & \vdots \\ \mathbf{B}_{T1} & \mathbf{B}_{T2} & \cdots & \mathbf{A}_T \end{bmatrix}, \qquad (2)$$

where $\mathbf{A}_t \in \mathbb{R}^{|\mathcal{V}| \times |\mathcal{V}|}$ is the adjacency matrix of snapshot G_t, and $\mathbf{B}_{ij} \in \mathbb{R}^{|\mathcal{V}| \times |\mathcal{V}|}$ represents the inter-layer edges modeling temporal dependencies between snapshots G_i and G_j. Here, we set $\mathbf{B}_{ij}$ to be the identity matrix $\mathbf{I}$ when $|i - j| = 1$, i.e., the snapshots are connected to their immediate previous and next layers. This choice restricts interactions to the same node across adjacent time steps. We note that it limits the model's ability to capture complex temporal patterns– such as seasonal cycles or delayed cross-node effects (e.g., a traffic jam at one node influencing another later). Future work could explore richer $\mathbf{B}_{ij}$ matrices to better model such dynamics.

To work with evolving graphs, one can use a subset of the most recent snapshots of $\mathbb{G}$ where the window size represents the number of consecutive time steps or graph snapshots. For simplicity, we consider the window to be of size T.

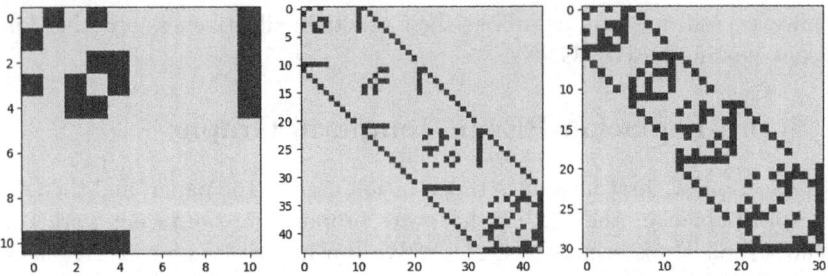

Fig. 2. Examples of adjacency matrices. Left: an adjacency matrix of a single snapshot with a global node connected only to the active nodes. Middle: the Supra-Adjacency matrix of shape $|\mathcal{V}|T \times |\mathcal{V}|T$ (middle). Right: the reduced Supra-Adjacency that contains only active nodes per snapshot.

Supra-Laplacian PEs (SLPEs). These PEs were firstly introduced in [13] where, for a node v at time t, they are derived from the eigenvectors of $\mathbf{L}_{\text{supra}}$ corresponding to the smallest eigenvalues. Let $\mathbf{X} \in \mathbb{R}^{T|\mathcal{V}| \times k}$ be the matrix of eigenvectors corresponding to the k smallest eigenvalues of $\mathbf{L}_{\text{supra}}$. The SLPEs $\mathbf{P}_t(v)$ for node v at time t is given by:

$$\mathbf{P}_t(v) = \mathbf{X}_{(t-1)|\mathcal{V}|+v,:k}, \tag{3}$$

where $\mathbf{X}_{(t-1)|\mathcal{V}|+v,:k}$ extracts the k-dimensional embedding corresponding to node v at time t. This encoding captures both the structural and temporal properties of the graph by leveraging the spectral properties of the supra-Laplacian. Furthermore, alongside these eigenvectors, the corresponding smallest eigenvalues of $\mathbf{L}_{\text{supra}}$ can also be concatenated to add further spectral information about the dynamic graph.

To enhance SLPEs, the work in [13] proposed two key modifications: (1) Global Node Integration: Each layer is augmented with a global node connected to all active nodes within that layer to better capture layer-wide activity and context (these nodes are considered part of $|\mathcal{V}|$); (2) Isolated Node Removal: Unconnected nodes are removed from the supra-adjacency matrix to eliminate the noise possibly introduced by considering uninformative eigenvectors.

4 Theoretical Understanding of Supra-Laplacian PEs

In this section, we enhance the theoretical understanding of SLPEs. First, we show how SLPEs inherently balance intra-layer structure preservation with inter-layer consistency through their smoothness. Second, we analyze the expressiveness advantages of the supra-adjacency matrix over layer-wise methods.

4.1 Time and Space Smoothness with SLPEs

We now show that computing the d lowest supra-Laplacian eigenvectors is equivalent to minimizing an objective function that balances the preservation of layer-

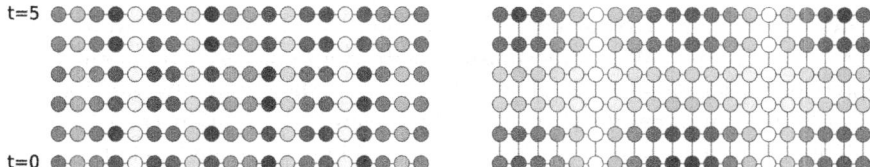

Fig. 3. Comparison of eigenvector smoothness in multilayer single path graphs. Left: Eigenvectors computed independently per layer, showing inconsistent sign assignments. Right: Eigenvector computed via the supra-Laplacian yield temporally smooth transitions. Graphs are single-path chains over time, highlighting the benefits of temporal regularization introduced by inter-layer edges.

specific structure while promoting smooth transitions across layers via a penalty term. The proof of the proposition below appears in Appendix C.1.

Proposition 1. *(Supra-Laplacian PEs Smoothness).* Let $\mathbb{G} = \{G_1, G_2, \ldots, G_T\}$ be a multilayer graph with T layers, where each layer G_t is represented by its adjacency matrix $\mathbf{A}_t$, the degree matrix $\mathbf{D}_t$, and the Laplacian matrix $\mathbf{L}_t$. In addition, $\mu > 0$ is a parameter that controls the weight of inter-layer connections. Then the eigenvectors of the supra-Laplacian matrix associated with $\mathbb{G}$ are the vectors $\mathbf{X}^{(t)} \in \mathbb{R}^{|\mathcal{V}| \times k}$ that minimize the following objective function:

$$\min_{\mathbf{X}^{(t)}} \sum_{t=1}^{T} tr\left(\mathbf{X}^{(t)T} \mathbf{L}_t \mathbf{X}^{(t)}\right) + \mu \sum_{t=2}^{T} \left\|\mathbf{X}^{(t)} - \mathbf{X}^{(t-1)}\right\|_F^2, \qquad (4)$$

subject to $\mathbf{X}^T \mathbf{X} = \mathbf{I}$, where $\mathbf{X}$ is the concatenation of all matrices $\mathbf{X}^{(t)}$ and $\|\|_F$ is the Frobenius norm.

The minimization in Eq. (4) shows that by using the supra-Laplacian eigenvectors, we achieve a balance between two key terms:

1. *Intra-layer smoothness*: The local connectivity structure of each layer G_t is preserved through the Laplacian quadratic form: $tr\left(\mathbf{X}^{(t)T} \mathbf{L}_t \mathbf{X}^{(t)}\right)$. Minimizing it makes the eigenvectors smooth according to the Laplacian $\mathbf{L}_t$.
2. *Inter-layer consistency*: The penalty terms $\mu \left\|\mathbf{X}^{(t)} - \mathbf{X}^{(t-1)}\right\|_F^2$, in contrast, enforces smooth transitions between eigenvectors of adjacent layers.

The inter-layer consistency promoted by the smoothness term not only ensures the smoothness of inter-layer transitions but also encourages consistent sign assignments for eigenvectors, as can be seen in Fig. 3. This is in contrast to independently computed eigenvectors for each layer, where consecutive eigendecompositions can lead to sign differences in each realization.

4.2 The Expressiveness Benefits of Using the Supra-Adjacency

Here, we shed light on the usefulness of considering the (multi-layer) supra-adjacency matrix rather than a single layer-wise approach. A key tool in our analysis is the Supra-Weisfeiler-Lehman (Supra-WL) test, which we define to extend the classical WL isomorphism test to snapshot-based temporal graphs represented as supra-graphs. Supra-WL operates by iteratively refining node colors in the supra-graph: (i) it starts by assigning a constant color $\bar{c}$ to each node in the supra-graph $\mathbb{G}(\tau)$, or one which uniquely encodes node features, if available; (ii) it refines these colors by injectively hashing the current color, the colors of its temporal neighbors, as well as the multiset of colors of its spatial neighbors within the same layer $G(t)$:

$$C_{v,t}^{(l+1)} = \text{HASH}\left(C_{v,t}^{(l)}, C_{v,t-1}^{(l)}, C_{v,t+1}^{(l)}, \{\!\!\{(C_{u,t}^{(l)}, e_{u,v,t}, t) | (u,v,t) \in G(t)\}\!\!\}\right) \quad (5)$$

where, for $t = 0$ and $t = \tau$ we have $C_{v,t-1}^{(l)} = C_{v,t+1}^{(l)} = \bar{\bar{c}}$. The test is applied in parallel to two temporal graphs; it terminates when the multisets of node colors for the two supra-graphs diverge, indicating non-isomorphism. If the colors stabilize without divergence, the test is inconclusive.

To understand the importance of the information contained in the supra-adjacency, we compare the Supra-WL to Layer-WL, a simple extension of WL to snapshot-based temporal graphs. Layer-WL runs 1-WL color refinement steps independently on each graph snapshot $G(t)$, comparing the overall multisets of node colors thereon. We now present a critical distinction between the two algorithms, shedding light on the enhanced capabilities of the Supra-WL test and, by extension, models considering supra-adjacency information.

Proposition 2. *(Supra-WL $\sqsubset$ Layer-WL). Supra-WL is strictly more powerful than Layer-WL in distinguishing non-isomorphic DTDGs.*

The proof of this proposition is deferred to Appendix C.2, and involves exhibiting a pair on non-isomorphic DTDGs that are distinguished by Supra-WL but not by Layer-WL, reported in Fig. 4. This example emphasizes how treating layers as interconnected rather than independent is essential for capturing structural differences in temporal or multi-layer graphs that would otherwise go unnoticed.

5 Efficient Computation of Supra-Laplacian PEs

Focusing on enhancing the efficiency of eigendecompositions for the scalable computation of (S)LPEs, we propose and evaluate several strategies centered around iterative eigendecomposition and trajectory-based analysis. The overview of the proposed procedure is illustrated in Fig. 1.

First, we propose exploring the use of the Lanczos method [18], an iterative algorithm designed for large, sparse, symmetric matrices like graph Laplacians. It constructs a Krylov subspace and diagonalizes a smaller tridiagonal matrix, achieving exact solutions with sufficient iterations. Second, questioning the necessity of exact eigendecomposition, we propose to utilize solutions derived from the Locally Optimal Block Preconditioned Conjugate Gradient (LOBPCG)

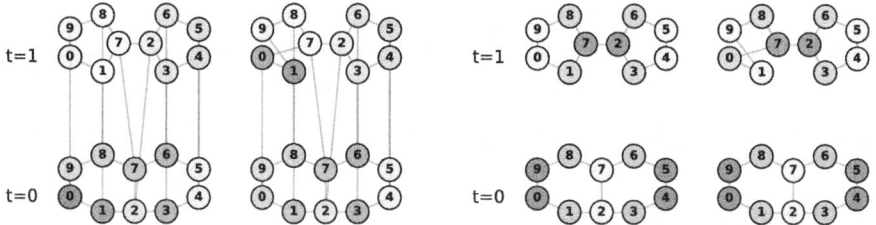

Fig. 4. Left: The Supra-WL test distinguishes two non-isomorphic temporal graphs by leveraging inter-layer edges, shown as vertical connections between time steps. Right: Layer-WL fails to distinguish the graphs as it considers only intra-layer structures.

method [15]. LOBPCG is another iterative algorithm specifically engineered to efficiently compute a limited number of extreme eigenvalues and eigenvectors. LOBPCG offers memory efficiency, particularly when only a subset of eigenvectors is required.

Furthermore, to leverage the information computed during iterative eigendecomposition solvers, we introduce a trajectory-based approach. Inspired by the work of [6] on static graphs, we extend this technique to temporal graphs. This approach recognizes that intermediate results from iterative solvers can be valuable and proposes to concatenate these intermediate results rather than solely relying on the achieved approximated solution. To address the inherent sign ambiguity of eigenvectors, for each eigenvector, we randomly choose a sign (+1 or -1) as was done in [5] and consistently apply this sign across all iterations of its trajectory. Specifically, at each iteration k of the eigendecomposition algorithm, let $\mathbf{U}^{(k)} \in \mathbb{R}^{n \times k}$ be the matrix of eigenvectors and $\mathbf{\Lambda}^{(k)}$ be the corresponding eigenvalues. Our trajectory-based approach constructs concatenated representations as follows: $\mathbf{U}_{\text{traj}} = \left[\mathbf{U}^{(1)}, \mathbf{U}^{(2)}, \ldots, \mathbf{U}^{(K)}\right], \mathbf{\Lambda}_{\text{traj}} = \left[\mathbf{\Lambda}^{(1)}, \mathbf{\Lambda}^{(2)}, \ldots, \mathbf{\Lambda}^{(K)}\right]$. Here, K represents the total number of iterations, determined by either convergence criteria or a predefined early stopping point. This concatenated form aims to capture the evolution of eigenvectors and eigenvalues across iterations, potentially providing a richer representation of the temporal graph dynamics.

6 Experiments

In this section, we present a detailed evaluation of Laplacian-based PE variants for temporal graphs with various architectures. Our experiments aim to assess the impact of these approaches on downstream performance across diverse real-world datasets and feature configurations. In particular, our focus is on comparing standard graph representations, such as single snapshot-based graphs, with supra-graph representations, which combine multiple snapshots into a single supra-graph. Additionally, we investigate the effects of using iterative and approximate solvers for eigendecomposition in these models. We aim to address the following questions:

1. Do Laplacian-based PEs enhance the performance of TGNNs, in general?

2. Which Laplacian-based PE scheme is best suited for TGNNs?
3. How do node features impact the performance of the Laplacian-based PEs?
4. What are the computational benefits of *approximate* Laplacian-based PEs?

Full details on experiments and additional results are provided in Appendix D.

6.1 Experimental Setup

We evaluate four temporal graph models: EGCN [24], GRUGCN [29], HTGN [40], and SLATE [13]. Further details about these models are provided in Appendix B. In our implementation of SLATE, we separated the SLPE component from the architecture, which allowed us to investigate various alternative PEs. Additionally, we performed a detailed time analysis comparing the full eigendecomposition, the Lanczos method (which we ran until convergence), and the LOBPCG method for computing the first 8 eigenvectors on both synthetic and real-world datasets. An overview of the proposed procedure is illustrated in Fig. 1.

Node Features. We process the datasets under various feature configurations. We start with one-hot encodings, a widely used approach in the literature [14,24], that assigns a unique identifier to each node in the observed snapshot. However, we argue that this method may not be realistic for dynamic graphs where the number of nodes can grow unpredictably over time. Additionally, one-hot encodings may be suboptimal in the presence of nodes with few interactions, as the parameters associated with such nodes could remain undertrained and lead to poorer generalization performance. Accordingly, we explore two additional feature encodings and their interplay with PEs. First, we experiment with uninformative, constant (zero) features, simulating the absence of node-specific information. Second, we study the impact of random node features. Although lacking any temporal and structural inductive bias, random features can, in principle, allow the model to identify nodes throughout its computations [1].

Laplacian-Based PE Variants. As a baseline, we report results without PEs (No PEs). In other cases, we compare several variants involving different PEs: SLPE and LPE, and different types of approximation: Exact eigenvalue computation *(E)*, Inexact computation *(I)*, and using the computation trajectory *(T)*, as explained in Sect. 5. We use the widely adopted Lanczos method for (E), appropriately run until convergence. LOBPCG is employed for (I). As for (T), we employ the full intermediate trajectory generated by the latter. We note that the modification to the graph mentioned in Sect. 3 and illustrated in Fig. 2 are also done to the standard Laplacian prior to PE computation.

Datasets, Task, and Performance Metric. The mentioned models are tested on the real-world datasets: CanParl, as733, dblp, and enron10 [40,42]. Each represents dynamic graphs derived from snapshot-based observations (see Appendix A for more details). The task is (dynamic) link prediction in all cases. Performance

Table 1. AUC performances of models across datasets and configurations for one-hot features. The top three models are highlighted by First, **Second**, Third.

Dataset	Variant	EGCN	GRUGCN	HTGN	SLATE
CanParl	No PEs	85.56±0.27	67.10±1.54	87.59±0.69	56.22±1.31
	SLPE-E	83.53±1.59	**72.92±1.90**	**89.47±0.29**	**59.32±0.63**
	LPE-E	85.41±1.44	74.92±0.74	89.62±0.16	59.99±1.07
	SLPE-I	83.45±1.59	**72.71±1.41**	89.26±0.55	57.42±0.97
	LPE-I	84.18±1.06	71.53±0.73	**89.61±0.19**	56.96±0.69
	SLPE-T	82.46±1.12	65.54±1.81	88.90±0.77	**58.71±1.44**
	LPE-T	81.72±0.89	67.11±1.79	88.98±0.31	55.04±1.28
as733	No PEs	92.47±0.04	94.96±0.35	98.75±0.03	99.85±0.01
	SLPE-E	93.54±0.87	95.46±1.59	98.28±0.33	99.81±0.02
	LPE-E	94.00±0.88	96.93±0.13	98.10±0.19	99.84±0.01
	SLPE-I	93.99±1.37	95.07±0.69	97.81±0.21	99.84±0.01
	LPE-I	93.52±0.65	96.13±1.11	97.61±0.34	99.80±0.01
	SLPE-T	93.19±0.89	**96.75±0.11**	91.62±0.75	99.81±0.02
	LPE-T	92.03±0.20	96.79±0.40	86.92±1.43	99.81±0.01
dblp	No PEs	83.88±0.53	84.60±0.92	89.26±0.17	89.43±0.42
	SLPE-E	87.10±0.23	**86.93±0.96**	88.67±0.55	89.68±0.56
	LPE-E	82.57±0.60	86.89±0.70	**88.74±0.15**	89.25±0.28
	SLPE-I	**86.66±0.34**	**86.93±0.46**	**88.77±0.12**	89.38±0.42
	LPE-I	83.90±0.48	87.04±0.98	88.52±0.36	89.40±0.19
	SLPE-T	**85.57±0.38**	86.29±0.78	88.59±0.31	**89.51±0.30**
	LPE-T	80.67±0.60	86.70±0.62	88.08±0.37	**89.46±0.34**
enron10	No PEs	90.12±0.69	92.47±0.36	94.17±0.17	95.66±0.45
	SLPE-E	91.54±0.69	**93.51±0.27**	94.49±0.08	**95.60±0.27**
	LPE-E	90.48±0.64	93.34±0.83	**94.37±0.24**	**95.49±0.33**
	SLPE-I	**91.40±0.75**	93.63±0.13	**94.45±0.54**	**95.49±0.31**
	LPE-I	89.89±0.31	**93.45±0.48**	**94.37±0.20**	**95.49±0.16**
	SLPE-T	89.89±1.27	92.62±1.01	92.99±0.52	95.41±0.30
	LPE-T	88.13±0.97	92.90±0.59	93.36±0.30	95.43±0.16

is measured using the Area Under the Curve (AUC) metric, reported as the mean and standard deviation over five runs. The top three performing configurations for each model-dataset pair are highlighted as First, **Second**, and Third, respectively, based on the mean test AUC score.

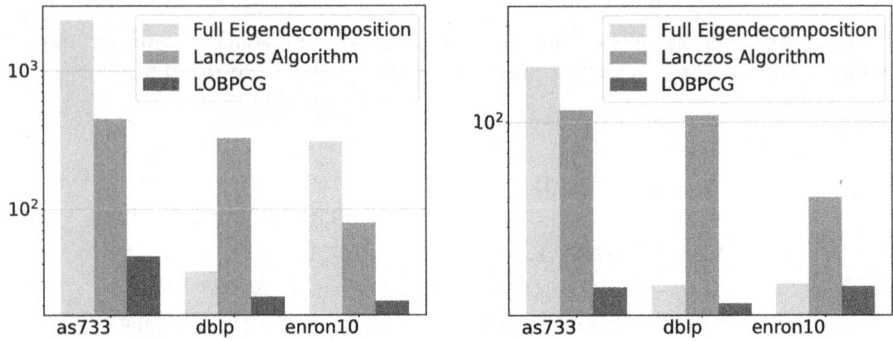

Fig. 5. Time (ms) performance comparison of Full Eigendecomposition, Lanczos, and LOBPCG methods on a real-world dataset presented by a Supra-Graph (left) and a single-layer-graph (right).

6.2 Results and Discussion

In this section we will presents the performance evaluation of various TGNN architectures across different datasets and PE schemes, focusing on the impact of Laplacian-based PEs and node feature configurations. We compare the effectiveness of one-hot, constant-zero, and random node features, with detailed results reported in Table 1, and additional results in Table 3 and Table 4 in Appendix D.2. Additionally, summarized performance metrics and comparisons across architectures and PE variants are provided in Table 2 and Table 3. We now address key questions regarding the efficacy of Laplacian-based PEs, the best-suited PE variants, the role of node features, and the computational efficiency.

Laplacian-Based PEs & TGNNs (Q1). From Table 1, Table 3 and Table 4 we observe that in $\approx 70.8\%$ of the overall number of cases, using Laplacian-based PEs led to the top-scoring results (First), and that in $\approx 64.5\%$ of the experiments, all the top-three ranking models employ Laplacian-based PEs. Quantitatively, Table 5 in Appendix D.2 reports statistics on the absolute performance improvements induced by Laplacian-based PEs for each architecture. In all cases, except for HTGN, we observe positive median performance improvements, with the largest impact attained on SLATE (16.63%) and EGCN (8.20%). Importantly, we also observe how PEs are most useful when employing constant-zero node features, where they scored First in $13/16$ cases, as shown in Table 3. As for the other feature configurations, they ranked First in $11/16$ cases (one-hot) and $8/16$ cases (random). From Table 6 in Appendix D.2, we note, more specifically, positive median AUC improvements are more pronounced in the case of constant features, where even HTGN seems to generally benefit from PEs. Quantitative improvements are also recorded, on average, for EGCN and GRUGCN across all feature variants, as well as SLATE when not using one-hot features. We conclude that Laplacian-based PEs are generally useful in improving generalization

Table 2. Average AUC (%) performance per feature and model when *Laplacian-based PEs are used* along with the difference between the max and min performance of different features for each model (Δ).

Feature	EGCN	GRUGCN	HTGN	SLATE	Avg
one-hot	87.87	86.75	91.73	85.66	88.00
random	81.72	80.89	88.59	77.63	82.21
constant	87.16	84.74	89.48	80.55	85.48
Δ	6.15	5.86	3.14	8.03	5.79

Table 3. Average AUC (%) performances across Laplacian-based PEs and feature inits.

Variant	one-hot	random	constant
No PEs	87.63	78.00	68.75
LPE-E	88.75	83.46	86.43
LPE-I	88.21	80.96	85.0
LPE-T	86.45	78.79	84.16
SLPE-E	**88.74**	**83.57**	**86.83**
SLPE-I	88.52	85.14	87.23
SLPE-T	87.37	81.33	83.24

performance, and they are more consistent when the model is not provided with node-identifying information.

Best Suited Laplacian-Based PE Variant for TGNNs (Q2). First, we compare SLPE variants to LPE variants. We found SLPE to perform better in 64.6% of considered cases, with an aggregated average improvement of 1.09% across models and datasets, as shown in Table 4. The improvement is more consistent, in particular in EGCN and SLATE, where the average absolute improvements are, resp., 3.91% and 0.66%. Notably, GRUGCN shows a small preference toward LPEs with an average performance difference of 0.30%. Next, we compare Exact variants with their Inexact counterparts. Overall, the former ones outperform the latter in 62.5% of cases, but the improvement is less pronounced in this case. As can be observed in Table 4, the distribution of performance differences is more dispersed, with median values close to zero in the case of HTGN and SLATE and only slightly in favor of Exact variants for EGCN and GRUGCN. These findings indicate that the faster Inexact variants have strong potential to be used in the development of more efficient processing pipelines. Finally, we compare variants overall, commenting on aggregated per-variant average performances as reported in Table 5. Across settings, SLPE-I leads with an average AUC of 86.96%, followed by SLPE-E with 86.38%, further confirming the suitability of approximate, iterative eigensolvers. Additional results separating different models, variants, and features can be seen in Table 6.

Impact of Features When Coupled with Laplacian-Based PEs (Q3). Refer to Table 2 for detailed per-model averages. When PEs are used, one-hot features outperform others with an aggregated average AUC of 88.00%. They excel across models (e.g., 91.73% for HTGN) and rank as the top performers in 18–23 cases per model. We argue that while one-hot encodings yield higher-performing models, those may be less practical for real-world scenarios where the number of

Table 4. AUC (%) Average and median performance differences between E and I variants per model and between SLPE and LPE variants.

Model	E - I		SLPE - LPE	
Diffs	Avg	Med [Q1, Q3]	Avg	Med [Q1, Q3]
EGCN	0.36	0.17 [−0.68, 0.57]	3.91	2.27 [0.70, 4.86]
GRUGCN	1.25	0.15 [−0.11, 1.43]	−0.30	−0.01 [−1.16, 0.69]
HTGN	0.003	0.02 [−0.08, 0.43]	0.08	0.04 [−0.21, 0.23]
SLATE	0.21	0.08 [−0.32, 0.36]	0.66	0.46 [−0.02, 3.77]
Mean Diff	0.46	0.04	1.09	0.69

Table 5. Average AUC (%) per variant across all models, datasets and features.

Variant	Average AUC
SLPE-I	**86.96**
SLPE-E	**86.38**
LPE-E	**86.21**
LPE-I	84.72
SLPE-T	83.98
LPE-T	83.13
No PEs	78.13

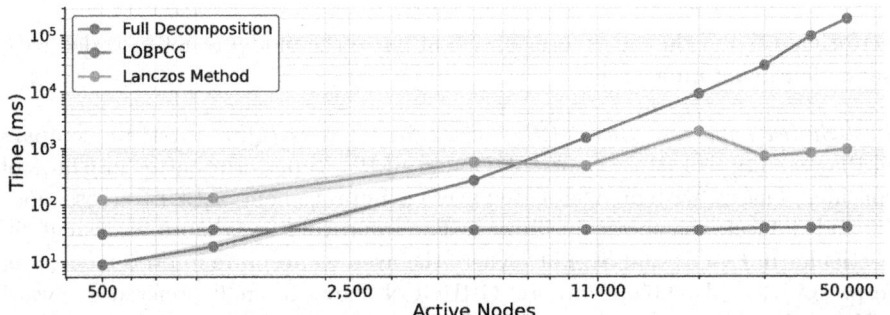

Fig. 6. Comparison of runtime (ms, log scale) for computing the first 8 eigenvectors of Barabási–Albert graphs using Full Eigendecomposition, Lanczos, and LOBPCG. LOBPCG and Lanczos scale substantially better than Full Decomposition, with LOBPCG exhibiting the most consistent performance across increasing numbers of active nodes.

nodes is unknown. Other features trail behind in both performance and frequency, with an average AUC of 85.48% for constant (zero) features and 82.21% for random features. A complementary angle to this discussion is offered by Table 3, where we report the average performance across models and datasets for each PE variant and feature choice. In agreement with our discussion in regards to Q1, we observe that PEs are most beneficial when using constant features. In addition to this, we note how the choice of PE variant is less impactful for one-hot features, while it leads to more result variability in the case of constant and random features. This effect is particularly pronounced in the latter case. In both settings, SLPEs achieve the best performance on average.

Computational Benefits of Approximate Laplacian-Based PEs (Q4). Our time measurements, depicted in Fig. 5, show that LOBPCG is the fastest method for calculating the approximate Laplacian, consistently outperforming both Lanczos and Full Eigendecomposition in in experiments on regular and Supra-graphs. In an effort to extend our time comparisons to even larger graphs, we synthesized random Barabási–Albert graphs with up to 50,000 active nodes, and timed the different methods thereon—see Fig. 6 for results. We observe that LOBPCG achieves a maximum speed-up of 56 times over Lanczos, with its efficiency advantage growing significantly as the effective size of the graph increases.

Table 6. Average AUC (%) performance across datasets. The top two scores for each model and feature combination are highlighted by First and **Second**.

Model	Variant	one-hot	randn	zeros	Model	Variant	one-hot	randn	zeros
EGCN	No PEs	88.01	81.43	50.0	HTGN	No PEs	92.44	91.08	85.37
	LPE-E	88.12	80.59	85.36		LPE-E	92.71	89.39	89.55
	LPE-I	87.87	73.74	85.2		LPE-I	92.53	89.2	88.99
	LPE-T	85.64	80.05	86.1		LPE-T	89.34	87.52	89.82
	SLPE-E	88.93	83.27	**88.79**		SLPE-E	92.73	88.94	89.28
	SLPE-I	**88.88**	87.62	89.55		SLPE-I	92.57	**89.52**	**89.76**
	SLPE-T	87.78	**85.08**	87.92		SLPE-T	90.52	86.99	89.44
GRUGCN	No PEs	84.78	79.68	84.14	SLATE	No PEs	85.29	59.81	55.49
	LPE-E	88.02	83.68	**88.96**		LPE-E	86.14	80.2	81.83
	LPE-I	87.04	80.4	84.56		LPE-I	85.41	80.49	81.23
	LPE-T	85.88	79.14	80.83		LPE-T	84.94	68.44	79.87
	SLPE-E	**87.2**	80.64	85.4		SLPE-E	**86.1**	81.44	**83.86**
	SLPE-I	87.08	**81.17**	**86.16**		SLPE-I	85.53	**82.25**	**83.43**
	SLPE-T	85.3	80.31	82.54		SLPE-T	85.86	72.96	73.05

Results Summary. In summary, our experiments demonstrate that integrating both LPEs and SLPEs into TGNNs generally enhances performance, especially when node features provide less discriminative information. When the node set is known in advance, one-hot features lead to the best performance, while constant features remain a solid alternative when coupled with Laplacian-based PEs, especially SLPEs. Specifically, regarding the choice of PEs: the SLPEs variants generally outperform LPEs except in the case of HTGN. Most notably, the SLPE-I variant emerges as a robust default, balancing high accuracy (86.96% average) with computational efficiency. Finally, our evaluation of eigenvector solvers reveals that approximate methods such as LOBPCG offer significant speed-ups, making them more suitable for large-scale graphs.

7 Conclusions

In this paper, we have thoroughly reviewed Laplacian-based PEs within the framework of TGNNs, providing a comprehensive understanding of their role and limitations. Our theoretical analysis of SLPEs reveals significant insights into their expressive power and connection to single-layer Laplacian PEs. In addition, we have demonstrated the practical implications of various PEs, providing actionable guidelines for practitioners seeking to optimize TGNN performance. Our findings highlight the benefits of incorporating Laplacian-based PEs and their interplay with node feature initialization schemes, underscoring how faster, approximate eigendecompositions can maintain a compelling tradeoff between run-time and model performance. We believe this work opens up interesting future research directions. These include exploring the study of further, more efficient eigensolvers for large graphs and the use of SLPEs in CTDGs.

Acknowledgments. F.F. conducted this work supported by an Andrew and Erna Finci Viterbi Fellowship and, partly, by an Aly Kaufman Post-Doctoral Fellowship. F.F. partly performed this work while visiting the Machine Learning Research Unit at TU Wien, led by Prof. Thomas Gärtner. H.M. is the Robert J. Shillman Fellow, and is supported by the Israel Science Foundation through a personal grant (ISF 264/23) and an equipment grant (ISF 532/23). M.E. is funded by the Blavatnik-Cambridge fellowship, the Cambridge Accelerate Programme for Scientific Discovery, and the Maths4DL EPSRC Programme. E.T. was partially supported by the Israeli Council for Higher Education (CHE) via Data Science Research Center, Ben-Gurion University of the Negev, Israel.

Disclosure of Interests. The author declares no competing interests relevant to the content of this article.

References

1. Abboud, R., Ceylan, İ.İ., Grohe, M., Lukasiewicz, T.: The surprising power of graph neural networks with random node initialization. In: Proceedings of the Thirtieth International Joint Conference on Artifical Intelligence (IJCAI) (2021)
2. Belkin, M., Niyogi, P.: Laplacian eigenmaps for dimensionality reduction and data representation. Neural Comput. **15**(6), 1373–1396 (2003)
3. Cong, W., Zhang, S., Kang, J., Yuan, B., Wu, H., Zhou, X., Tong, H., Mahdavi, M.: Do we really need complicated model architectures for temporal networks? In: The Eleventh International Conference on Learning Representations (2023), https://openreview.net/forum?id=ayPPc0SyLv1
4. Dosovitskiy, A., Beyer, L., Kolesnikov, A., Weissenborn, D., Zhai, X., Unterthiner, T., Dehghani, M., Minderer, M., Heigold, G., Gelly, S., Uszkoreit, J., Houlsby, N.: An image is worth 16 × 16 words: Transformers for image recognition at scale. In: International Conference on Learning Representations (2021), https://openreview.net/forum?id=YicbFdNTTy
5. Dwivedi, V.P., Joshi, C.K., Luu, A.T., Laurent, T., Bengio, Y., Bresson, X.: Benchmarking graph neural networks. J. Mach. Learn. Res. **24**(43), 1–48 (2023)

6. Eliasof, M., Frasca, F., Bevilacqua, B., Treister, E., Chechik, G., Maron, H.: Graph positional encoding via random feature propagation. In: International Conference on Machine Learning. pp. 9202–9223. PMLR (2023)
7. Fard, S.H., Ghassemi, M.: Temporal Link Prediction Using Graph Embedding Dynamics . In: 2023 IEEE Ninth Multimedia Big Data (BigMM). pp. 48–55. IEEE Computer Society, Los Alamitos, CA, USA (Dec 2023). https://doi.org/10.1109/BigMM59094.2023.00014, https://doi.ieeecomputersociety.org/10.1109/BigMM59094.2023.00014
8. Gómez, S., Díaz-Guilera, A., Gómez-Gardeñes, J., Pérez-Vicente, C.J., Moreno, Y., Arenas, A.: Diffusion dynamics on multiplex networks. Phys. Rev. Lett. **110**(2), 028701 (2013)
9. Heo, B., Park, S., Han, D., Yun, S.: Rotary position embedding for vision transformer. In: European Conference on Computer Vision. pp. 289–305. Springer (2024)
10. Huang, S., Poursafaei, F., Danovitch, J., Fey, M., Hu, W., Rossi, E., Leskovec, J., Bronstein, M., Rabusseau, G., Rabbany, R.: Temporal graph benchmark for machine learning on temporal graphs. Adv. Neural. Inf. Process. Syst. **36**, 2056–2073 (2023)
11. Huang, S., Poursafaei, F., Rabbany, R., Rabusseau, G., Rossi, E.: UTG: Towards a unified view of snapshot and event based models for temporal graphs. In: The Third Learning on Graphs Conference (2024), https://openreview.net/forum?id=ZKHV6Cpsxg
12. Huang, Y., Lu, W., Robinson, J., Yang, Y., Zhang, M., Jegelka, S., Li, P.: On the stability of expressive positional encodings for graphs. In: The Twelfth International Conference on Learning Representations (2024), https://openreview.net/forum?id=xAqcJ9XoTf
13. Karmim, Y., Lafon, M., Fournier-S'niehotta, R., THOME, N.: Supra-laplacian encoding for transformer on dynamic graphs. In: The Thirty-eighth Annual Conference on Neural Information Processing Systems (2024), https://openreview.net/forum?id=vP9qAzr2Gw
14. Kazemi, S.M., Goel, R., Jain, K., Kobyzev, I., Sethi, A., Forsyth, P., Poupart, P.: Representation learning for dynamic graphs: a survey. J. Mach. Learn. Res. **21**(1) (Jan 2020)
15. Knyazev, A.: Recent implementations, applications, and extensions of the locally optimal block preconditioned conjugate gradient method (lobpcg) (2017), https://arxiv.org/abs/1708.08354
16. Kumar, S., Zhang, X., Leskovec, J.: Predicting dynamic embedding trajectory in temporal interaction networks. KDD **2019**, 1269–1278 (2019)
17. Kuncheva, Z., Kounchev, O.: Spectral properties of the laplacian of temporal networks following a constant block jacobi model. Phys. Rev. E **109**, 064309 (Jun2024) https://doi.org/10.1103/PhysRevE.109.064309, https://link.aps.org/doi/10.1103/PhysRevE.109.064309
18. Lanczos, C.: An iteration method for the solution of the eigenvalue problem of linear differential and integral operators. J. Res. Natl. Bur. Stand. B **45**, 255–282 (1950). https://doi.org/10.6028/jres.045.026
19. Lim, D., Robinson, J.D., Zhao, L., Smidt, T., Sra, S., Maron, H., Jegelka, S.: Sign and basis invariant networks for spectral graph representation learning. In: The Eleventh International Conference on Learning Representations (2023), https://openreview.net/forum?id=Q-UHqMorzil
20. Lin, W., Zhou, S., Li, M., Chen, G.: Dismantling interdependent networks based on supra-laplacian energy. In: Science of Cyber Security, pp. 205–213. Lecture notes in computer science, Springer International Publishing, Cham (2021)

21. Liu, M., Liu, Y., Liang, K., Tu, W., Wang, S., Zhou, S., Liu, X.: Deep temporal graph clustering. arXiv [cs.LG] (May 2023)
22. Maskey, S., Parviz, A., Thiessen, M., Stärk, H., Sadikaj, Y., Maron, H.: Generalized laplacian positional encoding for graph representation learning. In: NeurIPS 2022 Workshop on Symmetry and Geometry in Neural Representations (2022), https://openreview.net/forum?id=BNhhZwAlVNC
23. Ozmen, M., Markovich, T.: Recent link classification on temporal graphs using graph profiler. Transactions on Machine Learning Research (2024), https://openreview.net/forum?id=BTgHh0gSSc
24. Pareja, A., Domeniconi, G., Chen, J., Ma, T., Suzumura, T., Kanezashi, H., Kaler, T., Schardl, T., Leiserson, C.: Evolvegcn: Evolving graph convolutional networks for dynamic graphs. In: Proceedings of the AAAI conference on artificial intelligence. vol. 34, pp. 5363–5370 (2020)
25. Qin, M., Yeung, D.Y.: Temporal link prediction: A unified framework, taxonomy, and review. ACM Comput. Surv. **56**(4) (Nov 2023). https://doi.org/10.1145/3625820, https://doi.org/10.1145/3625820
26. Rampášek, L., Galkin, M., Dwivedi, V.P., Luu, A.T., Wolf, G., Beaini, D.: Recipe for a General, Powerful, Scalable Graph Transformer. Advances in Neural Information Processing Systems **35** (2022)
27. Rossi, E., Chamberlain, B., Frasca, F., Eynard, D., Monti, F., Bronstein, M.: Temporal graph networks for deep learning on dynamic graphs. In: ICML 2020 Workshop on Graph Representation Learning (2020)
28. Sato, K., Oka, M., Barrat, A., Cattuto, C.: DyANE: Dynamics-aware node embedding for temporal networks. arXiv [physics.soc-ph] (Sep 2019)
29. Seo, Y., Defferrard, M., Vandergheynst, P., Bresson, X.: Structured sequence modeling with graph convolutional recurrent networks (2017), https://openreview.net/forum?id=S19eAF9ee
30. Skarding, J., Gabrys, B., Musial, K.: Foundations and modeling of dynamic networks using dynamic graph neural networks: A survey. IEEE Access **9**, 79143–79168 (2021). https://doi.org/10.1109/ACCESS.2021.3082932
31. Solé-Ribalta, A., De Domenico, M., Kouvaris, N.E., Díaz-Guilera, A., Gómez, S., Arenas, A.: Spectral properties of the laplacian of multiplex networks. Phys. Rev. E **88**, 032807 (Sep2013) https://doi.org/10.1103/PhysRevE.88.032807, https://link.aps.org/doi/10.1103/PhysRevE.88.032807
32. Souza, A.H., Mesquita, D., Kaski, S., Garg, V.K.: Provably expressive temporal graph networks. In: Oh, A.H., Agarwal, A., Belgrave, D., Cho, K. (eds.) Advances in Neural Information Processing Systems (2022), https://openreview.net/forum?id=MwSXgQSxL5s
33. Sun, J., Gu, M., Yeh, C.C.M., Fan, Y., Chowdhary, G., Zhang, W.: Dynamic graph node classification via time augmentation. In: 2022 IEEE International Conference on Big Data (Big Data). pp. 800–805. IEEE (2022)
34. Trivedi, R., Farajtabar, M., Biswal, P., Zha, H.: Dyrep: Learning representations over dynamic graphs. In: International Conference on Learning Representations (2019), https://openreview.net/forum?id=HyePrhR5KX
35. Vaswani, A., Shazeer, N., Parmar, N., Uszkoreit, J., Jones, L., Gomez, A.N., Kaiser, Ł., Polosukhin, I.: Attention is all you need. Advances in neural information processing systems **30** (2017)
36. Wang, Y., Chang, Y.Y., Liu, Y., Leskovec, J., Li, P.: Inductive representation learning in temporal networks via causal anonymous walks. In: International Conference on Learning Representations (2021), https://openreview.net/forum?id=KYPz4YsCPj

37. Wang, Z., Zhou, S., Chen, J., Zhang, Z., Hu, B., Feng, Y., Chen, C., Wang, C.: Dynamic graph transformer with correlated spatial-temporal positional encoding. In: Proceedings of the Eighteenth ACM International Conference on Web Search and Data Mining (2025)
38. da Xu, chuanwei ruan, evren korpeoglu, sushant kumar, kannan achan: Inductive representation learning on temporal graphs. In: International Conference on Learning Representations (ICLR) (2020)
39. Yang, L., Chatelain, C., Adam, S.: Dynamic graph representation learning with neural networks: A survey. IEEE Access **12**, 43460–43484 (2024)
40. Yang, M., Zhou, M., Kalander, M., Huang, Z., King, I.: Discrete-time temporal network embedding via implicit hierarchical learning in hyperbolic space. In: Proceedings of the 27th ACM SIGKDD Conference on Knowledge Discovery & Data Mining. pp. 1975–1985 (2021)
41. Yang, Y., Tu, L., Guo, T., Chen, J.: Spectral properties of supra-laplacian for partially interdependent networks. Appl. Math. Comput. **365**(124740), 124740 (2020)
42. Yu, L., Sun, L., Du, B., Lv, W.: Towards better dynamic graph learning: New architecture and unified library. Adv. Neural. Inf. Process. Syst. **36**, 67686–67700 (2023)
43. Zhang, X., Wang, Y., Wang, X., Zhang, M.: Efficient neural common neighbor for temporal graph link prediction (2024), https://arxiv.org/abs/2406.07926

ReDeLEx: A Framework for Relational Deep Learning Exploration

Jakub Peleška[✉] and Gustav Šír

Czech Technical University in Prague, Karlovo náměstí 13, Prague 121 35, Czechia
jakub.peleska@fel.cvut.cz, gustav.sir@cvut.cz

Abstract. Relational databases (RDBs) are widely regarded as the gold standard for storing structured information. Consequently, predictive tasks leveraging this data format hold significant application promise. Recently, Relational Deep Learning (RDL) has emerged as a novel paradigm wherein RDBs are conceptualized as graph structures, enabling the application of various graph neural architectures to effectively address these tasks. However, given its novelty, there is a lack of analysis into the relationships between the performance of various RDL models and the characteristics of the underlying RDBs.

In this study, we present ReDeLEx—a comprehensive exploration framework for evaluating RDL models of varying complexity on the most diverse collection of over 70 RDBs, which we make available to the community. Benchmarked alongside key representatives of classic methods, we confirm the generally superior performance of RDL while providing insights into the main factors shaping performance, including model complexity, database sizes and their structural properties.

Keywords: Relational Deep Learning · Relational Databases · Graph Neural Networks

1 Introduction

From their establishment [9], Relational Databases (RDBs) played a pivotal role in transforming our society into the current information age. Data stored as interconnected tables, safeguarded by integrity constraints, have proven to be an effective method for managing domain information. Consequently, RDBs still prevail today as a backbone of critical systems in a number of important domains ranging from healthcare [41] to government [28].

Although ubiquitous in modern application stacks, the data format of RDBs is deeply incompatible with classic Machine Learning (ML) workflows, which assume data in the standard form of fixed-size i.i.d. feature vectors, forming the common "tabular" learning format. Nevertheless, this assumption is clearly violated with the relationships between the differently-sized RDB tables. To address the discrepancy, the historically prevailing approach has been to turn the relational into the tabular format by means of *"propositionalization"* [25],

© The Author(s), under exclusive license to Springer Nature Switzerland AG 2026
R. P. Ribeiro et al. (Eds.): ECML PKDD 2025, LNAI 16014, pp. 438–456, 2026.
https://doi.org/10.1007/978-3-032-05981-9_26

which is essentially a feature extraction routine where relational substructures get aggregated from the relations into the attributes (features) of the tabular format, upon which classical ML methods may then operate. Nevertheless, this comes at the cost of information loss during this preprocessing step.

Recently, building on advances in graph representation learning [19], deep learning models directly exploiting the relational structure of RDBs have started to gain traction [13,32,43,44], establishing the field of *Relational Deep Learning* (RDL) [15]. Following the "message-passing" principles of *Graph Neural Networks* (GNN; [42]), RDL models treat the structure of an RDB as a heterogeneous (temporal) graph, where individual table rows correspond to nodes, and edges are formed through integrity constraints set by the primary and foreign keys. Utilizing the graph representation then allows for the application of various GNNs, and their various extensions, with adapted message-passing schemes.

The generality and spread of RDBs allow for a broad spectrum of domain information to be stored, upon which a variety of predictive tasks can be formulated, each with unique aspects and qualities. This presents a challenge for establishing a broad enough benchmark to appropriately assess the general performance of RDL. Currently, the most prominent effort in this area is the recently proposed RELBENCH [33], which introduced the evaluation of RDL, albeit with a very limited scope of simple models and just five accessible datasets. However, the overarching domain of *relational learning* [14], currently ignored by the RDL community, has a rich history of working with the relational data format [12,30], including benchmarking of the propositionalization techniques [25]. Notably, this includes the CTU Relational Learning Repository [29] that historically collected more than 70 diverse RDBs.

Our aim in this paper is to provide a bridge between the communities of traditional (logic-based) relational learning [14] and the contemporary RDL [33] towards a more comprehensive evaluation of the diverse existing methods. To that aim, we introduce ReDeLEx—an experimental framework for developing and benchmarking diverse RDL architectures against classic methods over the most comprehensive collection of tasks and datasets to date. The implementation of the framework is readily available on GitHub.[1]

2 Background

In this paper, we experimentally explore learning from RDBs (Sect. 2.1) with GNN-based models (Sect. 2.2) resulting in the RDL methodology (Sect. 2.3).

2.1 Relational Databases

Principles of RDBs are formally based on the *relational model* [10], which is grounded in relational logic [16]. This abstraction enables the definition of any database, regardless of specific software implementation, as a collection of n-ary

---
[1] https://github.com/jakubpeleska/ReDeLEx.

relations, which are defined over the domains of their respective attributes, managed by the Relational Database Management System (RDBMS) to ensure data consistency with the integrity constraints of the database schema. The key concepts to be used in this paper are as follows.

Relational Database. A Relational Database (RDB) $\mathcal{R}$ is defined as a finite set of relations $R_1, R_2, \ldots, R_n$. An instance of an RDB $\mathcal{R}$ is implemented through a RDBMS, enabling to perform Structured Query Language (SQL; [5]) operations, rooted in relational algebra.

Relation (Table). Formally, an n-ary relation $R_{/n}$ is a subset of the Cartesian product defined over the domains D_i of its n *attributes* A_i as $R_{/n} \subseteq D_1 \times D_2 \times \cdots \times D_n$, where $D_i = \mathsf{dom}(A_i)$. Each relation R consists of a heading (signature) $R_{/n}$, formed by the set of its attributes, and a body, formed by the values of the respective attributes, commonly represented as a *table* T_R of the relation R.

Attribute (Column). *Attributes* $\mathcal{A}_R = \{A_1, \ldots, A_n\}$ define the terms of a relation $R_{/n}$, corresponding to the *columns* of the respective table T_R. Each attribute is a pair of the attribute's name and a *type*, constraining the domain of each attribute as $\mathsf{dom}(A_i) \subseteq \mathsf{type}(D_i)$. An attribute *value* a_i is then a specific valid value from the respective domain of the attribute A_i.

Tuple (Row). An n–*tuple* in a relation $R_{/n}$ is a tuple of attribute values $t_i = (a_1, a_2, \ldots, a_n)$, where a_j represents the value of the attribute A_j in R. The relation can thus be defined extensionally by the *unordered* set of its tuples: $R = \{t_1, t_2, \ldots, t_m\}$, corresponding to the *rows* of the table T_R.

Integrity Constraints. In addition to the domain constraints $\mathsf{dom}(A_i)$, the most important integrity constraints are the primary and foreign keys. A *primary* key PK of a relation R is a minimal subset of its attributes $R[PK] \subseteq \mathcal{A}_\mathcal{R}$ that uniquely identifies each tuple: $\forall t_1, t_2 \in R : (t_1[PK] = t_2[PK]) \Rightarrow (t_1 = t_2)$. A *foreign* key FK_{R_2} in relation R_1 then refers to the primary key PK of another relation R_2 as $\forall t \in R_1 : t[FK] \in \{t'[PK] \mid t' \in R_2\}$. This constitutes the inter-relations in the database, with the RDBMS handling the *referential integrity* of $T_{R_1}[FK] \subseteq T_{R_2}[PK]$.

2.2 Graph Neural Networks

Graph Neural Networks constitute a comprehensive class of neural models designed to process graph-structured data through the concept of (differentiable) *message-passing* [42]. Given an input graph $G = (\mathcal{V}, \mathcal{E})$, with a set of nodes $\mathcal{V}$ and edges $\mathcal{E}$, let $h_v^{(l)} \in \mathbb{R}^{d^{(l)}}$ be the vector representation (embedding) of node v at layer l. The general concept of GNNs can then be defined through the following sequence of three functions:

(i) *Message* function $M^{(l)} : \mathbb{R}^{d^{(l)}} \times \mathbb{R}^{d^{(l)}} \to \mathbb{R}^{d_m^{(l)}}$ computes messages for each edge $(u,v) \in E$ as $m_{u \to v}^{(l)} = M^{(l)}(h_u^{(l)}, h_v^{(l)})$.

(ii) *Aggregation* function $A^{(l)} : \{\mathbb{R}^{d_m^{(l)}}\} \to \mathbb{R}^{d_m^{(l)}}$ aggregates the messages for each $v \in V$ as $M_v^{(l)} = A^{(l)}\left(\{m_{u \to v}^{(l)} \mid (u,v) \in E\}\right)$.

(iii) *Update* function $U^{(l)} : \mathbb{R}^{d^{(l)}} \times \mathbb{R}^{d_m^{(l)}} \to \mathbb{R}^{d^{(l+1)}}$ updates representation of each $v \in V$ as $h_v^{(l+1)} = U^{(l)}(h_v^{(l)}, M_v^{(l)})$.

The specific choice of message, aggregation, and update functions varies across specific GNN models, which are typically structured with a predefined number L of such layers, enabling the message-passing to propagate information across L-neighborhoods within the graph(s).

2.3 Relational Deep Learning

In this paper, we adopt the concept of RDL as extending mainstream deep learning models, particularly the GNNs (Sect. 2.2), for application to RDBs (Sect. 2.1). For completeness, in the relational learning community [12], a number of similar approaches combining relational (logic-based) and deep learning methods arose under a similar name of "deep relational learning" [35]. Nevertheless, for compatibility with the recently introduced frameworks [15], we hereby continue with the contemporary RDL view, where RDBs are first transformed into a graph-based representation suitable for the GNN-based learning.

Database Representation. The fundamental characteristic of RDL [15] is to represent an RDB as a heterogeneous graph.[2] The graph representation can be defined as $G = (\mathcal{V}, \mathcal{E}, \mathcal{T}^v, \mathcal{T}^e)$, where $\mathcal{V}$ is the set of nodes, $\mathcal{E}$ is the set of edges, $\mathcal{T}^v$ is a set of node types with a mapping $\phi : \mathcal{V} \to \mathcal{T}^v$, and $\mathcal{T}^e$ is a set of edge types with a mapping $\psi : \mathcal{E} \to \mathcal{T}^e$. The node types and edge types collectively form the graph *schema* $(\mathcal{T}^v, \mathcal{T}^e)$.

Given an RDB schema $\mathcal{R}$, the node types $T \in \mathcal{T}^v$ correspond to the relations (tables) T within the database $\mathcal{T}^v \overset{1:1}{\to} \mathcal{R}$, while the edge types $\mathcal{T}^e$ represent the undirected inter-relations between the tables, as defined by the primary-foreign key pairs: $\mathcal{T}^e = \{(R_i, R_j) \mid R_i[FK_{R_j}] \subseteq R_j[PK] \vee R_j[FK_{R_i}] \subseteq R_i[PK]\}$. For a specific *instance* of an RDB $\mathcal{R}$, the set of nodes $\mathcal{V}$ is then defined as the union of all tuples (rows) t_i from each relation $\mathcal{V} = \{v_{i,j} \mid R_i \in \mathcal{R}, t_j \in R_i\}$, and the set of edges $\mathcal{E}$ is defined as $\mathcal{E} = \{(v_{i,k}, v_{j,l}) \mid t_k \in R_i, t_l \in R_j, (R_i, R_j) \in \mathcal{T}^e\}$.

The graph representation is further enriched by *node embedding matrices*, *attribute schema*, and optionally a *time mapping*. Node embedding matrix $h_v^{(l)} \in \mathbb{R}^{d \times d_{\phi(v)}}$ contains the embedding representation of a node $v \in \mathcal{V}$ in a given layer l. With an attribute schema $\mathcal{A}_T$ that provides information about the types of attributes $A_1, \ldots, A_n$ associated with the nodes v of a specific node type $T \in \mathcal{T}^v$, the initial embedding tensors $h_v^{(0)} \in \mathbb{R}^{d^{(0)} \times n}$ are computed from the

---

[2] sometimes referred to as the "relational entity graph".

raw database attribute tuples $t_i = (a_1, a_2, \ldots, a_n)$ through multi-modal attribute encoders [15]. Finally, the *time mapping* is a function τ that assigns a timestamp t_v to each node $\tau : v \mapsto t_v$, effectively creating a dynamically growing graph in time, enabling the use of temporal graph sampling [34].

Predictive Tasks. In RDL, predictive tasks are implemented through the creation of dedicated training tables T_t that extend the existing relational schema of $\mathcal{R}$. As introduced in [15], a training table T_t contains two essential components: foreign keys $T_t[FK]$ that identify the entities of interest and target labels $y \in \mathcal{A}_{T_t} \setminus T_t[FK]$. Additionally, timestamps $t_v \in \mathcal{A}_{T_t}$ that define temporal boundaries for the prediction of y can also be included.

The training table methodology supports a diverse range of predictive tasks, including node-level predictions (e.g., customer churn, product sales), link predictions between entities (e.g., user-product interactions), and, crucially, both temporal and static predictions. In the case of temporal predictions, a timestamp attribute t_v in the training table T_t specifies when the prediction is to be made, restricting the model to only consider information available up to the point t_v in time.

Neural Architecture Space. Building upon the heterogeneous graph representation G, RDL models generally consist of the following four major stages.

1. **Table-level attribute encoder** creates the initial node embedding matrices $h_v^{(0)} \in \mathbb{R}^{d^{(0)} \times n}$, i.e. sequences of n embedding vectors $\mathbb{R}^{d_{\phi(v)}^{(0)}}$ for each attribute $A_1, \ldots, A_n$ of $\phi(v)$ based on its respective semantic data type.
2. **Table-level tabular model** allows to employ existing tabular learning models [6,21] to yield more sophisticated node embeddings $h_v^{(l)}$. Notably, in this stage, an RDL model *may* reduce the dimensionality of the node attribute matrix embedding $h_v^{(l)} \in \mathbb{R}^{d^{(l)} \times n}$ to a vector embedding $h_v^{(l)} \in \mathbb{R}^{d_{\phi(v)}^{(l)}}$.
3. **Graph neural model** then depends on the chosen embedding dimensionality of $h_v^{(l)}$. If there is a single embedding vector $h_v^{(l)} \in \mathbb{R}^{d_{\phi(v)}^{(l)}}$ per each node, the model can employ standard GNN (Sect. 2.2) heterogeneous message-passing [4,38], otherwise a custom message-passing scheme [32] is required.
4. **Task-specific model head** finally provides transformation of the resulting node embeddings into prediction, usually involving simple MLP layers.

3 The ReDeLEx Framework

The Relational Deep Learning Exploration (ReDeLEx) framework, which we introduce in this paper, offers a comprehensive environment for evaluating various RDL architectures over diverse RDB datasets.

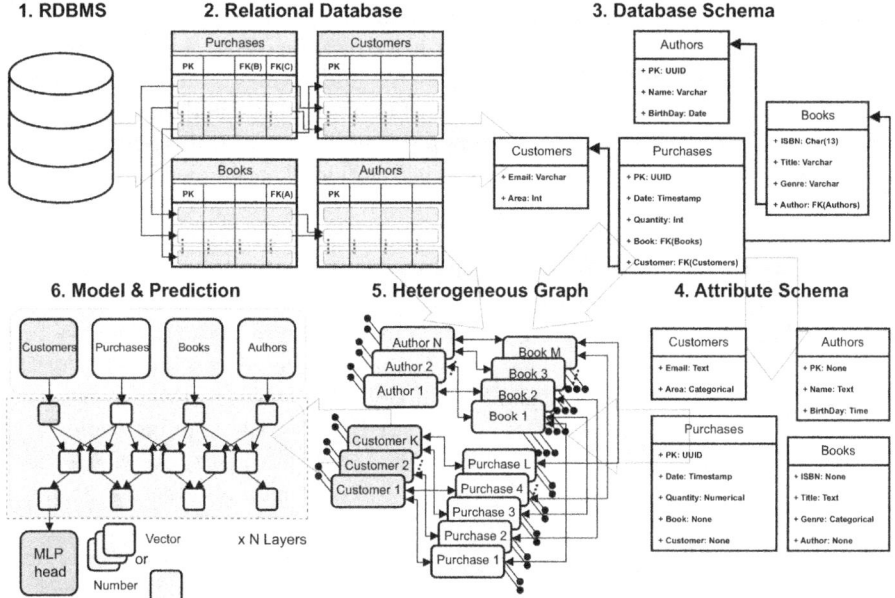

Fig. 1. REDELEX end-to-end workflow for RDL.

3.1 Workflow Components

The ReDeLEx workflow, depicted in Fig. 1, consists of modular blocks that enable systematic exploration of the neural architecture and database configuration space, significantly extending the current scope [33] of RDL experimentation.

Database Connectivity. In contrast to [33], the framework provides a standardized interface for connecting *directly* to an RDB [2], supporting various dialects of RDBMS. Notably, this enables a truly end-to-end deep learning pipeline, connecting to a possibly *remote* RDBMS, hosting the target RDB.

Attribute Schema. Attribute schema creation, which is a crucial yet overlooked step in RDL, mediates information regarding the attribute types A_T within the specific node type $T \in \mathcal{T}^v$ based on the original table attributes $A \in \mathcal{A}_T$. REDELEX automatically generates the attribute schema based on the SQL types and data from the RDBMS. Note that assessing a semantic type $\mathsf{dom}(A_i)$ is not straightforward since, e.g., a SQL `VARCHAR` attribute A_i often stores categorical, textual, as well as temporal values a_i. To disambiguate such cases, we employ in-built heuristics utilizing the SQL types, names of the attributes, ratio of unique values, and patterns in the data to facilitate proper attribute embedding.

Predictive Tasks. The existing benchmark [33] provides support solely for tasks with a training table T_t generated from historical data through an SQL query. While useful, without any changes to the underlying database, this setting renders many RDB prediction tasks infeasible. REDELEX addresses this problem by adding support for tasks that require more substantial modifications of the original database. Tasks leveraging this functionality then not only generate a new table T_t but a whole modified instance $\mathcal{R}'$ of the original database $\mathcal{R}$.

For example, assume the most common case where the database $\mathcal{R}$ already contains the target attribute A_T, used for some node-level prediction task. In such a case the table T_t containing the target needs to be split into two tables T_{t_1}, T_{t_2} where T_{t_1} contains all original data except the target attribute A_T and is part of the newly modified database $\mathcal{R}'$, and T_{t2} contains a duplicate of the primary key $T_t[PK]$, now used as a foreign key to the original table T_t, and the target attribute A_T. This table T_{t2} is then used as the new training table T'_t.

Importantly, this scheme can be applied to generate tasks for *unsupervised pretraining*. Pretraining tasks can be created by choosing any table $T \in \mathcal{R}$ in the database and duplicating it as T'. The unchanged duplicate T' can then be used as a training table T_t, while the values of cells in the original table T are randomly removed (masked out). The task is then to reconstruct any missing values in the classical tabular learning fashion [1], opening possibilities for sophisticated pretraining methods [36].

3.2 RDL-Suitable Databases and Tasks

Due to the generality of the relational model, RDBs often contain data with vastly diverse structural characteristics that, in some cases, do not properly exploit the relational model (Sect. 2.1). Likewise, not all of the 70+ available RDBs [29] are actually suitable for the relational learning models. In this section, we examine RDB characteristics in the context of RDL to identify suitable databases to be used in the experiments (Sect. 4).

Database Characteristics. To assess their overall characteristics, REDELEX associates each database task with various features pertinent to different parts if the training workflow (Fig. 1), which can be split into the below categories.

1. **Database features** provide high-level view of the data, including a domain (e.g. medicine, government, sport), whether the database is artificial or not, number of tables inside the database, number of foreign keys, number of factual (non-key) columns, number of columns with a specific variable type (e.g. numerical, categorical, time), total number of rows and total number of primary-foreign key pairs.
2. **Schema features** describe high-level structural aspects of the data. This includes the multiplicity of the relationships between the tables (one-to-one, one-to-many, many-to-many), features of the undirected graph induced by the primary-foreign key pairs (e.g. graph diameter,[3] or cycle detection).

---
[3] Graph diameter is the maximum length of all the shortest paths between the nodes.

3. **Task features** provide a similar type of information as the database features that are specific to the task and its target entity tables. This includes whether the task is temporal or static, number of training samples, multiplicity of relationships of the target entity table, etc.
4. **Graph features** inform about the properties of the transformed heterogeneous graph including, e.g., average eccentricity[4] of nodes or graph density.

Tabular Data. A salient feature of RDBs are the inter-relations between the tables (Sect. 2.1). As such, it is obvious that RDBs that contain a single table, or multiple tables without any primary-foreign key pairs, will not benefit from the use of RDL. Furthermore, databases consisting of multiple tables linked solely by one-to-one relationships fall under the same category, as they allow for a complete *join* of the whole RDB into a single table. Importantly, as all values of foreign keys are unique (with the exception of missing values), all the resulting rows remain independent of each other, turning the RDL setting into standard tabular learning (see Appendix Table 4 for a list of such databases).

Graph Data. On the other hand, RDBs are also characterized by building on the tabular representation, where an arbitrary number of attributes can be connected by a single relation. This is in contrast to the graph data which correspond to *binary* relational structures. Consequently, natively graph-structured data, such as molecules or family trees, although possible to be stored in an RDB, also do not fully exploit the relational model. In such cases, the RDL paradigm reduces to the simpler GNN setting [19], introducing an unnecessary complexity otherwise. More generally, RDL models for tasks on RDBs with a low number of non-key attributes (see Section 4.3) may suffer from information sparsity (see Appendix Table 5 for databases with the stated characteristics.)

4 Experiments

The aim of the experiments presented in this section is to demonstrate REDELEX in exploring the following selected RDL research questions:

Q1: How do RDL methods perform in comparison to the traditional methods over diverse benchmarking tasks (Sect. 4.1)?
Q2: Is it possible to apply tabular learning to a non-trivial RDB task while achieving results comparable to the RDL methods (Sect. 4.2)?
Q3: What are some of the essential RDB characteristics that contribute to a successful application of a given learning model (Sect. 4.3)?

Databases. To establish a comprehensive yet manageable list from the overall 70+ available RDBs [29] for the RDL experimentation, we separated databases that exhibit the tabular (Sect. 3.2) or graph-like (Sect. 3.2) characteristics, or are artificially[5] created (see Appendix Table 6 for the most suitable databases).

---

[4] The eccentricity of a node is the maximum distance from the node to all other nodes.
[5] with a single exception of the tpcd database.

RDL Models. REDELEX is designed to accommodate development of highly diverse RDL architectures. For comprehensibility of the experiments, we present three models of gradually increasing complexity, selected from recent works. All the models fit into the outlined neural architecture space (Sect. 2.3), while utilizing the same attribute encoders for the numerical, categorical, multi-categorical, textual, and temporal values.

1. **GraphSAGE with Linear Transformation** is the simplest of the RDL models, applying a linear transformation on top of a concatenation of the attribute $a_1, \ldots, a_n$ embeddings $h_v^{(0)} \in \mathbb{R}^{n \cdot d^{(0)}}$ to yield a single embedding vector $h_v^{(1)} = W h_v^{(0)}$ for each node v. The projected node embeddings $h^{(1)} \in \mathbb{R}^{d_{\phi(v)}}$ then form input into the GraphSAGE [18] model, forming the GNN stage. Finally, a task specific model head is applied.
2. **GraphSAGE with Tabular ResNet** is similar to the previous, with the tabular-level stage reducing the node embedding dimensionality, however, the operation is performed through a more sophisticated tabular ResNet model [17]. Notably, this model was previously used in [33], allowing to directly align results between the RELBENCH and REDELEX benchmarks.
3. **DBFormer** is an implementation of the Transformer-based RDL model from [32]. In constrast to the previous,[6] the model retains the original node embedding dimensionality $h_v^{(l)} \in \mathbb{R}^{n \times d^{(l)}}$ while exploiting the attention mechanism [37] for learning interactions between both the attributes and tuples through a custom message-passing scheme.

Classical Models. In addition to the selected RDL models, we include key representatives from related ML domains, including Gradient Boosted Decision Trees (GBDT; [31]), Deep Tabular Learning (DTL; [3]) and Propositionalization (Prop.; [24]). Particularly, we compare against the LightGBM [22]—representative of GBDT; the getML's [11] FastProp feature generator combined with XGBoost [8]—representative of propositionalization; and the standalone tabular ResNet [17]—representative of deep tabular learning. Importantly, the LightGBM and the ResNet have access only to data from the task's target table, as these models fall into the tabular learning category. In contrast, the propositionalization method of FastProp with XGBoost exploits the full RDB structure.

4.1 Benchmarking Tasks

We present comprehensive results over two types of node-level tasks—binary classification and multiclass classification. The tasks can be further differentiated by the origin of the target labels and usage of temporal values. Tasks performed on datasets from the RELBENCH collection use generated target table

---

[6] The key difference can be viewed analogously to the "fusion" and "cooperation" in multi-modal learning [20,27], considering the attributes as modalities. While the first two models *fuse* the representations of the discrete attributes at the beginning, the DBFORMER allows for *cooperation* of the attributes through the GNN stage.

Table 1. Overall results from the classification tasks, presenting AUC ROC values for the binary classification, and macro f1 score for the multiclass classification, respectively (higher is better). Static (non-temporal) tasks are tagged as "orig."

		GBDT		Prop.		Tab. DL		RDL					
	Model	LightGBM		GetML		Tabular		Linear		ResNet		DBFormer	
				XGBoost		ResNet		SAGE		SAGE			
Database	Task	val	test	val	test	val	test	val	test	val	test	val	test
					Binary Classification								
ergastf1	orig.	.579	.605	.086	.081	.543	.590	.910	.904	.913	.907	**.914**	**.910**
expend.	orig.	.852	.856	.295	.294	.846	.847	**.920**	**.918**	.918	.915	.894	.892
geneea	orig.	.994	.993	.317	.258	.990	.983	.985	.976	.986	.981	**.996**	**.995**
	temp.	.997	.990	.438	.455	.989	.982	.984	.971	.989	.973	**.998**	**.991**
hepatitis	orig.	.666	.626	.044	.055	.716	.634	**1.0**	.997	**1.0**	**1.0**	**1.0**	.996
imdb	orig.	.986	.986	.451	.454	.985	.985	**.993**	**.993**	**.993**	**.993**	**.993**	**.993**
mondial	orig.	.500	.500	NaN	NaN	.500	.542	.987	**.988**	**1.0**	.921	.987	.932
movielens	orig.	.583	.611	.223	.211	.563	.609	.790	.798	**.801**	.809	.778	**.813**
musk L	orig.	.500	.500	.381	.240	.643	.700	.905	.587	.937	.547	**.984**	**.720**
musk S	orig.	.500	.500	.200	.222	.625	.583	.867	.889	**.933**	**.889**	.800	.759
mutagen.	orig.	.917	.821	.095	.024	.917	**.940**	.952	.806	**.964**	.798	.960	.762
ncaa	orig.	.687	.426	.335	.212	.692	.559	.848	.759	**.897**	**.801**	.826	.720
stud.loan	orig.	.500	.500	.272	.247	.506	.532	**1.0**	**1.0**	**1.0**	**1.0**	**1.0**	**1.0**
amazon	ichurn	.738	.740	NaN	NaN	.653	.654	**.823**	.826	**.823**	**.827**	.818	.821
	uchurn	.579	.579	NaN	NaN	.526	.531	**.707**	**.707**	**.707**	**.707**	.703	.704
avito	clicks	.565	.539	NaN	NaN	.540	.541	.653	.635	**.654**	**.672**	**.654**	.649
	visits	.536	.528	NaN	NaN	.520	.516	**.702**	.662	**.702**	**.665**	.699	.660
f1	dnf	.684	.685	.324	.230	.683	.708	.723	.757	**.744**	.740	.733	**.759**
	top3	.729	.728	.300	.158	.661	.733	**.792**	**.844**	.714	.832	.766	.835
stack	badge	.785	.761	.083	.097	.689	.676	**.901**	.890	**.901**	**.891**	.897	.885
	engm.	.842	.832	.070	.071	.788	.782	.902	.906	**.903**	**.907**	.902	.903
trial	sout	**.676**	**.711**	.032	.034	.624	.664	.662	.702	.655	.692	.645	.675
					Multiclass Classification								
accidents	orig.	.379	.370	.506	.505	.363	.359	**1.0**	**1.0**	**1.0**	**1.0**	**1.0**	**1.0**
	temp.	.186	.170	.325	.336	.204	.187	.819	.583	.805	.566	**.825**	**.727**
craftbeer	orig.	.411	.266	.003	.017	.505	.231	.381	.255	.488	.329	**.513**	**.356**
dallas	orig.	.594	**.581**	NaN	NaN	.585	.572	.547	.499	.561	.473	**.688**	.511
	temp.	.570	.584	.288	.512	**.680**	.247	.589	.393	.615	.424	.580	.513
diabetes	orig.	.190	.190	.402	.383	.190	.190	.878	.870	**.892**	**.883**	.890	.875
financial	orig.	.461	.458	**.899**	.658	.698	.470	.586	.490	.738	**.729**	.644	.539
	temp.	.495	.492	**.636**	**.632**	.456	.449	.495	.492	.538	.340	.553	.256
genes	orig.	.060	.060	.066	.100	.060	.060	**1.0**	.898	**1.0**	**1.0**	**1.0**	.927
hockey	orig.	.707	.721	.395	.404	.707	.703	**.714**	.728	**.714**	.724	.713	**.740**
legalacts	orig.	**.933**	**.924**	.320	.316	.837	.824	.834	.822	.837	.825	.831	.821
	temp.	**.870**	**.851**	.226	.220	.788	.688	.791	.721	.786	.698	.784	.703
premiere-	orig.	.380	.411	.641	**.601**	.589	.362	**.659**	.400	.593	.332	.571	.352
league	temp.	.317	.222	.647	**.639**	.615	.370	**.650**	.384	.619	.390	.556	.407
tpcd	orig.	.191	.182	NaN	NaN	.191	.185	**.733**	**.732**	.546	.545	.722	.728
webkp	orig.	.139	.130	.350	**.366**	.139	.130	.315	.193	.295	.212	**.355**	.282
Avg. Rank		3.88		4.91		4.38		2.67		2.51		**2.47**	
		2.43		3.28		2.8				1.36			

attributes, while tasks on datasets from the CTU Relational use existing target table attributes. Additionally, tasks from the CTU Relational can be both static and temporal, while tasks from the RELBENCH collection are always temporal. Static and temporal tasks differentiate based on the constrains forced upon the sampling algorithm while generating a sub-subgraph used for training the model, and by the method of splitting the dataset between the training, validation and test data. Static tasks use neighborhood sampling [18] constrained only by the maximum number of neighbors, and data splitting is carried out at random w.r.t. a given ratio (e.g. 70:15:15). In contrast, temporal tasks extend the neighborhood sampling by incorporating temporal constraints, assuming only directed edges from nodes with an older timestamp and, similarly, the splits are carried out w.r.t. the timestamps where all training entities must precede validation and testing data, respectively (see Appendix A for the full experimental setup).

The results on classification tasks shown in Table 1 demonstrate a strong performance of the RDL models (Sect. 4) over the classical models (Sect. 4) on majority of the datasets. Specifically, the ResNet SAGE performs very well on binary classification tasks, especially on tasks with a training table generated from historical data. The higher complexity of the DBFORMER somewhat surprisingly seems to lead to higher robustness as the model slightly outperforms the ResNet SAGE in the average rank. Nevertheless, in a couple of cases, the simplest Linear SAGE model matches or even outperforms the score of both the models. Notably, on the `hepatits`, `mondial`, `student loan`, `accidents`, and `genes` datasets, all the RDL models present near-perfect predictions while the classical models show an order of magnitude worse score, highlighting the contribution of the RDL representation.

4.2 Tabular Learning

In this scenario, we compare results of the Tabular Learning (TL) models from the previous section to ones trained on new tables formed by join operations over the RDBs (Sect. 3.2). Particularly, we evaluate the TL models on tables generated by joins over *both* one-to-one and many-to-one relationships of the target table.[7] Additionally, we include evaluation of RDL models with exactly 2 layers in the graph neural stage, which is conceptually equivalent to the join operation. Finally, we include the overall best RDL models to put the results into context. Note that the previous Table 1 demonstrated that the TL methods perform significantly worse on an absolute majority of tasks. In this experiment, we aim to assess whether a simple RDB transformation could actually change the situation in some cases. Particularly, we select a subset of tasks from Table 1 where both the TL models showed at least 0.1 worse score than the best RDL model. The results in Table 2 show that, indeed, on a number of datasets the TL models register a significant improvement with results sometimes comparable to the best of RDL. Notably, on the `ncaa`, `premierleague` and `tpcd` they even set new best results. This experiment demonstrates existing weak spots in the new

---

[7] This is similar to a recent RelGNN method [7], albeit limited to the target table.

Table 2. Classification tasks over a subset of datasets formed by joining the target table, showing AUC ROC values for binary classification, and macro f1 score for multi-class classification, respectively (higher is better). Significant improvements (more than 0.05 score) are shown in bold, while new best results are underlined.

		LightGBM				ResNet Tabular				RDL			
	Model	Base		Joined		Base		Joined		2 layers		Best	
Database	Task	val	test	val	test	val	test	val	test	val	test	val	test
		Binary Classification											
ergastf1	orig.	.579	.605	**.919**	.904	.543	.590	**.899**	.892	.909	.905	.910	.904
hepatitis	orig.	.666	.626	**.940**	**.913**	.716	.634	.718	.632	1.0	1.0	1.0	1.0
mondial	orig.	.500	.500	**1.0**	.815	.500	.542	**1.0**	.898	.988	.944	.988	.944
movielens	orig.	.583	.611	.574	.622	.563	.609	.563	.609	.688	.691	.784	.796
ncaa	orig.	.687	.426	**.797**	<u>**.776**</u>	.692	.559	**.819**	**.741**	.801	.728	.861	.764
studentloan	orig.	.500	.500	**1.0**	**1.0**	.506	.532	**1.0**	**1.0**	1.0	1.0	1.0	1.0
amazon	uchurn	.579	.579	.577	.577	.526	.531	.526	.531	.705	.705	.706	.707
avito	clicks	.565	.539	.564	.556	.540	.541	.540	.541	.647	.658	.653	.649
	visits	.536	.528	.536	.532	.520	.516	.520	.516	.690	.656	.702	.664
stack	badge	.785	.761	.783	.759	.689	.676	.689	.676	.898	.887	.901	.891
		Multiclass Classification											
accidents	orig.	.379	.370	.377	.372	.363	.359	.366	.365	1.0	1.0	1.0	1.0
	temp.	.186	.170	.177	.163	.204	.187	.198	.178	.790	.579	.798	.582
craftbeer	orig.	.411	.266	**.488**	.245	.505	.231	.505	.231	.442	.301	.444	.311
diabetes	orig.	.190	.190	.190	.190	.190	.190	.190	.190	.885	.876	.885	.876
genes	orig.	.060	.060	.060	.060	.060	.060	.060	.060	.989	.922	1.0	.896
premiere-	orig.	.380	.411	**.470**	.416	.589	.362	.584	.325	.603	.371	.603	.371
league	temp.	.317	.222	**.527**	<u>**.485**</u>	.615	.370	.598	.399	.616	.431	.616	.431
tpcd	orig.	.191	.182	<u>**.846**</u>	<u>**.841**</u>	.191	.185	**.676**	**.666**	.579	.582	.579	.582
webkp	orig.	.139	.130	.139	.130	.139	.130	.139	.130	.265	.185	.308	.221

RDL approach [15], suggesting that caution and thorough analysis are still in order before deploying RDL on an RDB task.

4.3 Essential Characteristics

The overarching aim of REDELEX is to assess common characteristics of RDBs and tasks in the context of a used learning approach. While a fully comprehensive assessment is out of scope of this short paper, in Table 3 we summarize characteristics of the databases against the respective performances of the various model types. Following the analysis, RDL models generally tend to perform well on datasets with a large number of training samples and links. Proposition-

Table 3. Characteristics of databases and their tasks selected based on the best performing model. Features are sorted into the categories described in Section 3.2.

Feature	Base	RDL			Propositional			Tabular Learning		
	Med.	Q1	Median	Q3	Q1	Median	Q3	Q1	Median	Q3
#Tab.	6	3	7	8	3	4	8	3	4	13.5
#FK	6	2.25	6	12	2.5	5	8	3	4	14
#Factual	35	14	24	45	17	47	110	27	40	119
#Cat.	11	2.25	11	16	6	17	44	9	14	59
#Num.	6	2	4.5	13	4	6	12	2.5	3	9
#Text	6	2	6	10	1	2	3.5	3	14	20
#Time	2	0	2	7	0.5	3	5	1.5	3	5
#Rows	472k	96k	1.36M	5.59M	16.6k	81.8k	1.6M	32.1k	804k	2.54M
#Links	752k	182k	2.22M	7.98M	32.5k	82.6k	1.58M	45.6	851k	3.49M
Diameter	3	2	2.5	3	2	2	3	2	3	4.5
1-to-1	0	0	0	2	0	0	4	0	2	3
1-to-M	5	2	4.5	11	2.5	5	5	2.5	4	12.5
#Train	12k	2.22k	27.1k	1.15M	305	546	21.8k	1.96k	18.5k	348k
#T.Factual	5	1	3	6	2.5	5	5	4	10	15
#T.Cat	2	0	0	2	0.5	1	4	2	4	10
#T.Num	0	0	0	1	0	0	2	0	1	2
#T.Text	1	0	1	3	0	0	1.5	0	1	5.5
#T.Time	1	0	0	1	0	1	1	1	1	2
Eccentric.	10.6	7.13	15.3	19.5	3.3	9.7	15.8	3.39	10.6	17.4
Density	0.025	0.001	0.018	0.079	0.004	0.028	0.102	0.003	0.059	0.118

alization achieves best results mostly on smaller datasets with a low number of one-to-many relationships, yet with a large number of factual (non-key) columns. This is in line with some previous studies [26], despite the remaining prevalence of propositionalization methods in practice [11]. The TL methods then tend to perform best when there is a higher number of factual columns in the target table, which aligns with natural intuition. Moreover, these allow capturing more diverse attribute types where, e.g., both LightGBM and deep TL models are capable of utilizing textual attributes.

Related Work. As outlined in the Introduction, the REDELEX framework builds upon the CTU relational dataset collection [29] which it integrates with the RELBENCH [33] interface to facilitate a wider scope of RDL [15] experimentation. As such, it is naturally related to recent works introducing new RDL models, which include [7,32,43]. Besides RDL, related work includes other dataset and benchmarking frameworks that address some facets of learning from relational data, including [39,40]. The most salient feature of REDELEX, within the context of related work, is the provided bridge between the traditional relational learning methods [14] and the contemporary RDL [15].

5 Conclusion

In this study, we introduced REDELEX—a framework for exploring and evaluating Relational Deep Learning (RDL) models across diverse relational database contexts. The framework enables benchmarking on more than 70 databases, facilitating new insights into the relationships between the RDL neural architecture choices, traditional learning methods, and the underlying database characteristics. Our results demonstrated that RDL approaches mostly outperform the traditional methods. Nevertheless, a closer inspection revealed important cases in which the performance of the competing tabular learning methods could be easily improved to match or even surpass RDL, highlighting the interim immaturity of the field, and the need for further RDL exploration. Our general exploration in this paper demonstrated that RDL performs well on databases with complex relationships and large numbers of samples, while the traditional methods may still remain a sensible choice for smaller and flatter datasets.

Acknowledgments. This work has received funding from the European Union's Horizon Europe Research and Innovation program under the grant agreement TUPLES No. 101070149; and Czech Science Foundation grant No. 24-11664S.

Ethical Considerations. The performance of RDL models demonstrated in our research could enable more sophisticated inference of personal information from interconnected data sources. The framework's flexibility could facilitate deployment in domains with significant ethical implications, such as financial services, healthcare, and government operations. We encourage researchers using REDELEX to carefully assess privacy implications and implement appropriate anonymization techniques.

Disclosure of Interests. The authors have no competing interests to declare that are relevant to the content of this article.

A Experimental Setup

All deep learning models (including RDL) were trained for a minimum of 10 epochs with a total minimum of 1000 steps of Adam [23] optimizer with a learning rate of 0.001. Experiments on the RDL models were conducted with fixed hyperparameters with two exceptions—the number of layers of the graph neural model and the neighborhood graph sampling rate, which were searched for in a grid hyperparameter optimization. The hyperparameters include batch size—set to 512, message-passing aggregation function—set to summation, embedding vectors dimension, which is the same for both row and attribute embedding vectors—set to 64, neighborhood sampling rate—iterated over the values of 16, 32 and 64, and number of message-passing layers—a value in range of 1 to 4.

B Additional Tables

Here we provide additional tables with descriptive information about the databases available through ReDeLEx.

Table 4. Tabular-like databases available through ReDeLEx.

Database	Domain	#Tables	#FK	#Factual	one-to-one	many-to-one
atherosclerosis	Med.	4	3	191	2	1
bupa	Med.	9	8	16	7	1
cde	Gov.	3	2	87	2	0
pima	Med.	9	8	9	8	0
satellite	Indstr.	34	34	67	34	0
voc	Retail	8	7	89	6	1

Table 5. Graph-like databases available through ReDeLEx.

Database	Domain	#Tables	#FK	#Factual	one-to-one	many-to-one
carcinogenesis	Med.	6	13	4	2	11
cora	Edu.	3	3	2	0	3
mesh	Industry	29	33	37	24	9
pima	Med.	9	8	9	8	0
toxicology	Med.	4	5	3	0	5

Table 6. List of databases available for benchmarking in REDELEX.

Database	Dom.	#Tab.	#FK	#Fact.	Diam.	Cycle	1:1	1:N
CTU Relational Databases								
accidents	Gov.	3	3	38	1	✓	0	3
basketballmen	Sport	9	9	187	5	✓	2	8
biodegradability	Med.	5	5	6	3	✓	0	5
countries	Geo.	3	2	63	2	✗	0	2
craftbeer	Entmt.	2	1	8	1	✗	0	1
dallas	Gov.	3	2	24	2	✗	0	2
diabetes	Edu.	3	2	4	2	✗	0	2
ergastf1	Sport	13	19	82	3	✓	0	19
expenditures	Retail	3	2	19	2	✗	0	2
financial	Fin.	8	8	39	3	✓	6	5
fnhk	Med.	3	2	21	2	✗	0	2
geneea	Gov.	19	20	99	7	✓	8	16
genes	Med.	3	3	11	2	✓	0	3
grants	Edu.	12	11	30	4	✗	2	10
hepatitis	Med.	7	6	16	4	✗	6	3
hockey	Sport	19	27	273	4	✓	8	23
imdb	Entmt.	7	6	12	5	✗	0	6
lahman	Sport	25	31	319	6	✓	6	28
legalacts	Gov.	4	4	24	3	✓	0	4
mondial	Geo.	33	62	125	5	✓	12	55
movielens	Entmt.	7	6	14	4	✗	0	6
musklarge	Med.	2	1	167	1	✗	0	1
musksmall	Med.	2	1	167	1	✗	0	1
mutagenesis	Med.	3	3	9	2	✓	0	3
ncaa	Sport	8	15	99	3	✓	0	15
premiereleague	Sport	4	5	209	2	✓	0	5
restbase	Retail	3	3	10	1	✓	2	2
seznam	Retail	4	3	10	2	✗	0	3
sfscores	Gov.	3	2	22	2	✗	0	2
stats	Edu.	8	13	50	3	✓	2	12
studentloan	Fin.	10	9	15	3	✗	12	3
tpcd	Retail	8	8	48	4	✓	1	7
triazine	Med.	2	1	13	1	✗	0	1
walmart	Retail	4	3	27	3	✗	0	3
webkp	Edu.	3	3	5	2	✓	0	3
RELBENCH Databases								
amazon	Retail	3	2	10	2	✗	0	2
avito	Retail	8	11	23	2	✓	0	11
f1	Sport	9	13	45	3	✓	0	13
stack	Edu.	7	12	33	3	✓	2	11
trial	Med.	15	15	110	4	✓	4	13

References

1. Arik, S.Ö., Pfister, T.: Tabnet: attentive interpretable tabular learning. In: Proceedings of the AAAI Conference on Artificial Intelligence, pp. 6679–6687 (2021)
2. Bayer, M.: Sqlalchemy. In: The Architecture of Open Source Applications Volume II: Structure, Scale, and a Few More Fearless Hacks. aosabook.org (2012)
3. Borisov, V., Leemann, T., Seßler, K., Haug, J., Pawelczyk, M., Kasneci, G.: Deep neural networks and tabular data: a survey. IEEE Trans. Neural Netw. Learn. Syst. (2022)
4. Brody, S., Alon, U., Yahav, E.: How attentive are graph attention networks? In: International Conference on Learning Representations (2022)
5. Chamberlin, D.D., Boyce, R.F.: SEQUEL: a structured english query language. In: Proceedings of the 1974 ACM SIGFIDET (now SIGMOD) Workshop on Data Description, Access and Control, SIGFIDET '74, pp. 249–264. Association for Computing Machinery, New York (1974)
6. Chen, K.Y., Chiang, P.H., Chou, H.R., Chen, T.W., Chang, T.H.: Trompt: towards a better deep neural network for tabular data (2023)
7. Chen, T., Kanatsoulis, C., Leskovec, J.: RelGNN: composite message passing for relational deep learning. arXiv preprint arXiv:2502.06784 (2025)
8. Chen, T., Guestrin, C.: Xgboost: a scalable tree boosting system. In: Proceedings of the 22nd ACM SIGKDD International Conference on Knowledge Discovery and Data Mining, pp. 785–794 (2016)
9. Codd, E.F.: A relational model of data for large shared data banks. Commun. ACM **13**(6), 377–387 (1970)
10. Codd, E.F.: The relational model for database management: version 2. Addison-Wesley Longman Publishing Co., Inc. (1990)
11. Code17 GmbH: getml. https://getml.com
12. Cropper, A., Dumančić, S., Muggleton, S.H.: Turning 30: new ideas in inductive logic programming. In: Bessiere, C. (ed.) Proceedings of the Twenty-Ninth International Joint Conference on Artificial Intelligence, IJCAI-20, pp. 4833–4839 (2020)
13. Cvitkovic, M.: Supervised learning on relational databases with graph neural networks (2020)
14. De Raedt, L.: Logical and Relational Learning. Springer, Heidelberg (2008)
15. Fey, M., et al.: Position: Relational deep learning - graph representation learning on relational databases. In: Forty-First International Conference on Machine Learning (2024)
16. Gallier, J.H.: Logic for computer science: foundations of automatic theorem proving. Courier Dover Publications (2015)
17. Gorishniy, Y., Rubachev, I., Khrulkov, V., Babenko, A.: Revisiting deep learning models for tabular data. In: Proceedings of the 35th International Conference on Neural Information Processing Systems, NIPS '21, pp. 18932–18943. Curran Associates Inc., Red Hook (2021)
18. Hamilton, W., Ying, Z., Leskovec, J.: Inductive representation learning on large graphs. In: Advances in Neural Information Processing Systems, pp. 1024–1034 (2017)
19. Hamilton, W.L.: Graph Representation Learning. Morgan & Claypool Publishers (2020)
20. Hu, R., Singh, A.: Unit: Multimodal multitask learning with a unified transformer. In: Proceedings of the IEEE/CVF International Conference on Computer Vision, pp. 1439–1449 (2021)

21. Hu, X., Tang, W., Hsieh, C.K., Shi, S.: Tabtransformer: tabular data modeling using contextual embeddings. arXiv preprint arXiv:2012.06678 (2020)
22. Ke, G., et al.: LightGBM: a highly efficient gradient boosting decision tree. In: Proceedings of the 31st International Conference on Neural Information Processing Systems, NIPS'17, pp. 3149–3157. Curran Associates Inc., Red Hook (2017)
23. Kingma, D.P., Ba, J.: Adam: a method for stochastic optimization. arXiv preprint arXiv:1412.6980 (2014)
24. Kramer, S., Lavrač, N., Flach, P.: Propositionalization approaches to relational data mining. In: Relational Data Mining, pp. 262–291 (2001)
25. Krogel, M.A., Rawles, S., Železný, F., Flach, P.A., Lavrač, N., Wrobel, S.: Comparative Evaluation of Approaches to Propositionalization. Springer, Heidelberg (2003)
26. Lavrač, N., Podpečan, V., Robnik-Šikonja, M.: Machine learning background. In: Representation Learning, pp. 17–53. Springer, Cham (2021). https://doi.org/10.1007/978-3-030-68817-2_2
27. Liang, P.P., Zadeh, A., Morency, L.P.: Foundations & trends in multimodal machine learning: principles, challenges, and open questions. ACM Comput. Surv. **56**(10), 1–42 (2024)
28. Maali, F., Cyganiak, R., Peristeras, V.: Enabling interoperability of government data catalogues. In: Wimmer, M.A., Chappelet, J.-L., Janssen, M., Scholl, H.J. (eds.) EGOV 2010. LNCS, vol. 6228, pp. 339–350. Springer, Heidelberg (2010). https://doi.org/10.1007/978-3-642-14799-9_29
29. Motl, J., Schulte, O.: The ctu prague relational learning repository. arXiv preprint arXiv:1511.03086 (2015)
30. Muggleton, S., De Raedt, L.: Inductive logic programming: theory and methods. J. Logic Program. **19** (1994)
31. Natekin, A., Knoll, A.: Gradient boosting machines, a tutorial. Front. Neurorobot. **7**, 21 (2013)
32. Peleška, J., Šír, G.: Transformers meet relational databases. arXiv preprint arXiv:2412.05218 (2024)
33. Robinson, J., et al.: Relbench: a benchmark for deep learning on relational databases. In: The Thirty-Eight Conference on Neural Information Processing Systems Datasets and Benchmarks Track (2024)
34. Rossi, E., Chamberlain, B., Frasca, F., Eynard, D., Monti, F., Bronstein, M.: Temporal graph networks for deep learning on dynamic graphs. arXiv preprint arXiv:2006.10637 (2020)
35. Šír, G.: Deep Learning with Relational Logic Representations. Czech Technical University (2021)
36. Somepalli, G., Goldblum, M., Schwarzschild, A., Bruss, C.B., Goldstein, T.: Saint: improved neural networks for tabular data via row attention and contrastive pre-training (2021)
37. Vaswani, A., et al.: Attention is all you need. Adv. Neural Inf. Process. Syst. (2017)
38. Veličković, P., Cucurull, G., Casanova, A., Romero, A., Liò, P., Bengio, Y.: Graph attention networks. In: International Conference on Learning Representations (2018)
39. Vogel, L., Bodensohn, J.M., Binnig, C.: WikiDBs: a large-scale corpus of relational databases from wikidata. In: Globerson, A., et al. (eds.) Advances in Neural Information Processing Systems, vol. 37, pp. 41186–41201. Curran Associates, Inc. (2024)
40. Wang, M., et al.: 4dbinfer: a 4d benchmarking toolbox for graph-centric predictive modeling on rdbs. Adv. Neural. Inf. Process. Syst. **37**, 27236–27273 (2024)

41. White, J.: PubMed 2.0. Med. Ref. Serv. Q. **39**(4), 382–387 (2020)
42. Wu, Z., Pan, S., Chen, F., Long, G., Zhang, C., Philip, S.Y.: A comprehensive survey on graph neural networks. IEEE Trans. Neural Netw. Learn. Syst. (2020)
43. Zahradník, L., Neumann, J., Šír, G.: A deep learning blueprint for relational databases. In: NeurIPS 2023 Second Table Representation Learning Workshop (2023)
44. Zhang, H., Gan, Q., Wipf, D., Zhang, W.: Gfs: graph-based feature synthesis for prediction over relational databases. arXiv preprint arXiv:2312.02037 (2023)

Localized Heat Kernel for Graph Neural Networks

Taoyang Qin[1], Ke-Jia Chen[1,2(✉)], and Zheng Liu[1,2(✉)]

[1] School of Computer Science, Nanjing University of Posts and Telecommunications, Nanjing, China
{b21120725,chenkejia,zliu}@njupt.edu.cn
[2] Jiangsu Key Laboratory of Big Data Security and Intelligent Processing, Nanjing, China

Abstract. Graph Neural Networks (GNNs) with heat kernel effectively capture the smoothness of labels and features across nodes, preventing oscillations during propagation, and denoising the graph. However, existing models typically employ a global heat kernel, where the diffusion process depends on a single, uniform diffusion time, inevitably resulting in over-smoothing. Additionally, the global heat kernel struggles to handle heterophilic graphs, where nodes exhibit varying neighbor label distributions. To address the above issues, we extend the global heat kernel by a localized scale (i.e., node-level) and integrate it with graph convolution, yielding the Localized Heat Kernel for GNN (LHK-GNN). By adaptively adjusting the diffusion time for each node, our approach enables heat diffusion to accommodate local complexity on graph. Experiments demonstrate the effectiveness of LHK-GNN in mitigating over-smoothing and handling heterophilic graphs.

Keywords: graph convolution · heat kernel · over-smoothing · heterophily

1 Introduction

Recently, diffusion processes are introduced into Graph Neural Networks (GNNs), achieving superior performance [7,8,27]. Graph heat diffusion is a well-known diffusion process for graph data, which models the information flow across nodes to capture the graph's structural properties. The graph heat kernel [4] is a solution to the heat equation on graphs, which not only encapsulates the temporal evolution of the diffusion process but also serves as a powerful spectral tool. Specifically, many works [27,28] leverage the heat kernel to explore the propagating neighborhood in a continuous manner by tuning the heat diffusion time. Meanwhile, the exponential decay property of the heat kernel suppresses high-frequency signals, thereby enhancing the low-pass filtering effect [8].

However, existing graph heat kernels often employ a single, uniform diffusion time in the diffusion process, which has two major issues. (1) They face the over-smoothing problem, which means they fail to be *deep enough*: as the number of layers increases, the performance of the GNN degrades significantly [12,14]. From a dynamics perspective, the global heat diffusion process is inherently one where energy gradually dissipates as the diffusion time increases and ultimately converges to a stable thermal equilibrium state [11]. (2) They assume that graphs are homophilic. When handling heterophilic graphs, their performance deteriorates [18,30]. The labels of neighboring nodes vary significantly in heterophilic graphs, resulting in complex local patterns. The global heat kernel relies on a single overall diffusion time, making it ineffective in handling diverse local patterns.

To address the above issues, inspired by the concept of the generalized transfer operator in graph signal processing (GSP) [24] and the design of node-oriented spectral filters [29], we propose the Localized Heat Kernel for Graph Neural Network (LHK-GNN). Specifically, we design an independent and controllable heat diffusion process for each node, allowing the nodes to adaptively adjust the diffusion time. It can prevent excessive information diffusion and control the aggregation scope for relevant node features. Therefore, our method can help mitigate the over-smoothing problem and handle heterophilic graphs. We evaluate LHK-GNN on ten benchmark datasets, and the experimental results validate the effectiveness of our method.

Our contributions are summarized as follows:

- We extend the heat kernel function to the node-level one and integrate it into the spectral graph convolution, resulting in constructing a more fine-grained heat diffusion process.
- We propose a tensor-based method for efficient heat kernel approximation across all nodes. The approach reduces computational demands and demonstrates the successful extension of the heat kernel to the local scale.
- We theoretically prove that the over-smoothing issue observed in existing heat kernel-based GNNs is a consequence of the properties of the heat kernel, explicitly defining the connection.
- Existing experimental results validate the superiority of our method over other diffusion-based GNNs, particularly in mitigating the over-smoothing problem and handling heterophilic graphs. The code is available online[1].

2 Related Work

2.1 Diffusion Process on Graphs

Graph diffusion process is fundamental in graph learning and is typically formulated using partial differential equations (PDEs) to analyze how information diffuses across a graph [8,16,25]. One specific branch of graph diffusion is the heat diffusion model, which characterizes the spread of information in a way similar to heat flowing through connected nodes over time [4,27]. The second

---

[1] https://github.com/ridethelights/LHKGNN.

branch of graph diffusion is the random walk [7,25], which can be viewed as a discrete version of PDE-based diffusion. In a random walk, the state of nodes gradually converges to a stable distribution as time progresses. This process is analogous to the reaching of thermal equilibrium during heat diffusion [3]. The third branch of graph diffusion is anisotropic diffusion, which captures directional information flow by allowing different propagation rates in different regions of the graph [6,20].

2.2 GNNs with Heat Kernel

Xu et al. [27] first combine heat kernel with graph convolution and design a graph convolutional neural network based on heat kernel. Their method effectively captures the smoothness of labels and features across nodes influenced by the graph structure. Gasteiger et al. [8] construct a generalized diffusion matrix that incorporates heat kernel coefficients, and combine it with graph convolution networks, effectively smoothing the neighborhood over the graph and denoising the graph. Zhao et al. [28] combine the heat kernel with Simplifying Graph Convolutional Networks (SGC) [26], which can effectively prevent oscillations. Overall, previous works have guided feature propagation in GNNs from a global heat diffusion perspective. Unlike these methods, our approach assigns an independent heat kernel to each node. Each node can adaptively adjust the heat diffusion range, making the diffusion process more refined.

3 Preliminary

3.1 Notation

Let $\mathcal{G} = (V, E)$ be an undirected graph, where V is the set of nodes with n nodes, and E is the set of edges. Adjacency matrix $\mathbf{A}$ gives the connectivity of $\mathcal{G}$, with $\mathbf{A}_{ij} = \mathbf{A}_{ji}$ denoting the connection between nodes i and j. The normalized graph Laplacian matrix is defined as $\mathbf{L} = \mathbf{I} - \mathbf{D}^{-1/2}\mathbf{A}\mathbf{D}^{-1/2}$, where $\mathbf{I}$ is the identity matrix, and $\mathbf{D}$ is a diagonal matrix with $\mathbf{D}_{ii} = \sum_j \mathbf{A}_{ij}$. Since $\mathbf{L}$ is real and symmetric, it has orthonormal eigenvectors $\mathbf{U} = (u_1, u_2, \ldots, u_n)$ with non-negative eigenvalues $\{\lambda_i\}_{i=1}^n$. We assume $\lambda_1 \leq \lambda_2 \leq \cdots \leq \lambda_n$. Thus, $\mathbf{L} = \mathbf{U}\mathbf{\Lambda}\mathbf{U}^\mathbf{T}$, where $\mathbf{\Lambda} = \mathrm{diag}(\{\lambda_i\})$.

3.2 Spectral Graph Convolution

Regarding the eigenvectors of the normalized Laplacian matrix as a set of bases $\mathbf{U}$, the Fourier transform of a graph signal $x \in \mathbb{R}^n$ is defined as $\hat{x} = \mathbf{U}^\top x$, and its inverse is $x = \mathbf{U}\hat{x}$ [24]. Based on the graph Fourier transform, the spectral graph convolution operator $*_\mathcal{G}$ can be defined as:

$$x *_\mathcal{G} \mathbf{g} = \mathbf{U}\left((\mathbf{U}^\top \mathbf{g}) \odot (\mathbf{U}^\top x)\right) = \mathbf{U}\hat{\mathbf{g}}\mathbf{U}x, \quad (1)$$

where $\mathbf{g} \in \mathbb{R}^n$ denotes the kernel in spatial domain, $\hat{\mathbf{g}} = \mathbf{U}^\top \mathbf{g}$ denotes the spectral kernel, and $\odot$ represents Hadamard multiplication.

Early studies typically perform an eigendecomposition on the normalized Laplacian matrix $\mathbf{L}$ to derive the Fourier basis $\mathbf{U}$ and treat the spectral kernel $\hat{\mathbf{g}}$ as the trainable parameters. However, the high computational cost of eigenvalue decomposition severely limits the practical use of these methods. To bypass the eigendecomposition, current works [2,5] usually use the K-order polynomial to approximate different spectral kernels, which can be represented as:

$$\hat{\mathbf{g}} = \hat{g}(\mathbf{\Lambda}) = \sum_{k=0}^{K} \alpha_k \mathbf{\Lambda}^k, \tag{2}$$

where $\mathbf{\Lambda}$ denotes the eigenvalue matrix, $\hat{g}(\cdot)$ denotes the spectral filtering function, and α_k is the learnable coefficient for the k-th order. Inserting into Equation (1), the graph convolution can be represented as:

$$x *_\mathcal{G} \mathbf{g} = \mathbf{U} \sum_{k=0}^{K} \alpha_k \mathbf{\Lambda}^k \mathbf{U}^\top x = \sum_{k=0}^{K} \alpha_k \mathbf{L}^k x. \tag{3}$$

3.3 Heat Kernel for Spectral Graph Convolution

The heat kernel is defined as $\mathbf{h}(\lambda_i) = e^{-t\lambda_i}$, where t denotes the diffusion time. According to Xu et al. [27], the convolution based on heat kernel can be represented as:

$$x *_\mathcal{G} \mathbf{g} = \mathbf{U} \sum_{k=0}^{K} \alpha_k \mathbf{\Lambda}_t^k \mathbf{U}^\top x, \tag{4}$$

where $\mathbf{\Lambda}_t = \operatorname{diag}(\{\mathbf{h}(\lambda_i)\}_{i=1}^n)$. In other words, Eq. (3) can be represented as: $(\alpha_0 \mathbf{I} + \alpha_1 e^{-t\mathbf{L}} + \cdots + \alpha_K e^{-Kt\mathbf{L}})x$. Due to the high computational complexity, K is set to 1, thus $\hat{\mathbf{g}} = \hat{g}(\mathbf{\Lambda}) = \operatorname{diag}(\{\alpha_0 + \alpha_1 \mathbf{h}(\lambda_i)\}_{i=1}^n)$. When t is small, the computation of $e^{-t\mathbf{L}}$ can be approximated using the Taylor expansion, specifically: $e^{-t\mathbf{L}} \approx \sum_{k=0}^{\infty} \frac{(-t)^k}{k!} \mathbf{L}^k$. A more common approach to approximate $e^{-t\mathbf{L}}$ is using Chebyshev polynomials [10].

4 Methodology

Inspired by the generalized transition operator in graph signal processing [24] and the design of node-oriented spectral filters [29], we design the Localized Heat Kernel for GNN (LHK-GNN) that effectively overcomes the issues of oversmoothing and heterophily.

4.1 Spectral Graph Convolution with Localized Heat Kernel

We first adapt the spectral graph convolution to operate on individual nodes. Then we extend the graph heat kernel to the node level, creating a localized heat kernel. The localized kernel is then integrated with node-oriented spectral graph convolution. The design of our approach is based on the generalized transition operator [24], defined as follows:

Definition 1. *For any spatial kernel* $\mathbf{g} \in \mathbb{R}^n$ *on a given graph* $\mathcal{G}$*, and any* $i \in \{1, \ldots n\}$*, the generalized transition operator* $\mathbf{T}_i : \mathbb{R}^n \to \mathbb{R}^n$ *is expressed via generalized convolution with the Kronecker delta function* δ_i *centered at node* i:

$$\mathbf{T}_i(\mathbf{g}) := \sqrt{N}(\mathbf{g} * \delta_i) = \sqrt{N} \sum_{l=1}^{n} u_l u_l^T(i) \hat{g}(\lambda_l).$$

For node-oriented filtering [29], $\mathbf{g}$ is first aligned at node i using the operator $\mathbf{T}_i$, then spectrally convolved with x. This operation can be written as:

$$x *_{\mathcal{G}} \mathbf{T}_i(\mathbf{g}) = \sqrt{N} \sum_{l=1}^{n} u_l \hat{x}(\lambda_l) u_l^T(i) \hat{g}(\lambda_l). \tag{5}$$

Defining $\hat{g}_i(\lambda_l)$ as: $\hat{g}_i(\lambda_l) = \sqrt{N} u_l^T(i) \hat{g}(\lambda_l)$, which leads to the following expression for the convolution:

$$x *_{\mathcal{G}} \mathbf{T}_i(\mathbf{g}) = \sum_{l=1}^{n} \hat{g}_i(\lambda_l) u_l u_l^T x = \mathbf{U} \hat{\mathbf{g}}_i \mathbf{U}^T x. \tag{6}$$

Here, $\hat{g}_i(\lambda_l)$ represents the value of the signal at node i after the spectral filtering operation, where $u_l^T(i)$ is the i-th element of the l-th eigenvector u_l, and $\hat{g}(\lambda_l)$ is the spectral filter evaluated at eigenvalue λ_l. Considering the $\hat{g}(\cdot)$ in Sect. 3.3, the $\hat{g}_i(\lambda_l)$ can be represented as:

$$\begin{aligned}\hat{g}_i(\lambda_l) &= \sqrt{N} u_l^T(i) \left(\alpha_0 + \alpha_1 e^{-t\lambda_l}\right) \\ &= \sqrt{N} u_l^T(i) \alpha_0 + \sqrt{N} u_l^T(i) \alpha_1 e^{-t\lambda_l}.\end{aligned} \tag{7}$$

Now, we extend the heat kernel in Sect. 3.3 to the node level by using a localized scale: $\mathbf{h}_i(\lambda_l) = e^{-t_i \lambda_l}$, which serves as the heat kernel for node i. Due to the learnability of α_0 and α_1, we can approximate $\sqrt{N} u_l^T(i) \alpha_0$ and $\sqrt{N} u_l^T(i) \alpha_1 e^{-t\lambda_l}$ as γ_{i0} and $\gamma_{i1} \mathbf{h}_i(\lambda_l)$, respectively. Based on this, we have the following:

$$\begin{aligned}\hat{g}_i(\lambda_l) &\approx \gamma_{i0} + \gamma_{i1} \mathbf{h}_i(\lambda_l), \\ \hat{\mathbf{g}}_i &= \mathrm{diag}\left(\{\gamma_{i0} + \gamma_{i1} \mathbf{h}_i(\lambda_l)\}_{l=1}^{n}\right).\end{aligned} \tag{8}$$

Thus, the convolution with localized (i.e., node-level) heat kernel can be represented as follows:

$$\begin{aligned}x *_{\mathcal{G}} \mathbf{T}_i(\mathbf{g}) &= \delta_i \left(\mathbf{U} \left(\gamma_{i0} \mathbf{I} + \gamma_{i1} e^{-t_i \mathbf{\Lambda}}\right) \mathbf{U}^\top x\right) \\ &= \delta_i (\gamma_{i0} \mathbf{I} + \gamma_{i1} e^{-t_i \mathbf{L}}) x,\end{aligned} \tag{9}$$

where $\delta_i = [0, 0, \ldots, 1, \ldots, 0]$ denotes a row vector with the i-th element being 1 and the remaining elements being zeros.

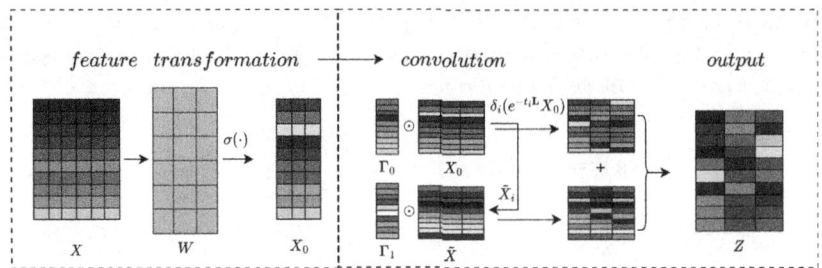

Fig. 1. The workflow. The feature matrix X is first transformed by an MLP to obtain X_0. $A \odot B$ denotes the Hadamard product, which applies broadcasting to A if necessary. After undergoing localized heat kernel convolution, we obtain $\tilde{X}$, where $\tilde{X}_i = \delta_i(e^{-t_i \mathbf{L}} X_0)$. Finally, the output Z is a weighted combination of X_0 and $\tilde{X}$.

4.2 The Implementation of LHK-GNN

This section describes the implementation of LHK-GNN, including its overall architecture and the method used to approximate the localized heat kernel. Figure 1 presents the overall workflow.

Architecture. To reduce the dimensionality of features and enhance the model's performance, we firstly employ an MLP to non-linearly transform [9] the raw feature matrix $X \in \mathbb{R}^{n \times f}$, yielding $X_0 = \mathrm{MLP}(X; \Theta)$. Thus the feature propagation rule of LHK-GNN can be represented as:

$$Y_i = \delta_i(\gamma_{i0}\mathbf{I} + \gamma_{i1}e^{-t_i \mathbf{L}})X_0. \tag{10}$$

We treat t_i as a learnable parameter, enabling each node to adaptively adjust the diffusion time. For the node classification task, we adopt the negative log-likelihood (NLL) loss. Thus we need to apply the softmax function [1] on Y_i to obtain the predication $Z_i = softmax(Y_i)$.

Approximation for Localized Heat Kernel. We use the Chebyshev polynomial to approximate $e^{-t_i \mathbf{L}}$. Specifically,

$$e^{-t_i \mathbf{L}} \approx \sum_{k=0}^{K-1} c_k(t_i) T_k(\tilde{\mathbf{L}}),$$

where $\tilde{\mathbf{L}} = \mathbf{L} - \mathbf{I}$ and $T_k(\tilde{\mathbf{L}})$ denotes the k-th Chebyshev polynomial. The coefficients $c_k(t_i)$ depend on the diffusion time t_i and can be computed as follows:

$$c_k(t_i) = \frac{\beta}{\pi} \int_{-1}^{1} T_k(x) e^{-t_i(1+x)} \, dx = \beta(-1)^k e^{-t_i} I_k(t_i), \tag{11}$$

Algorithm 1: LHK-GNN

Input: Feature matrix X, scaled Laplacian $\tilde{L}$, number of expansions K
Parameters: Learnable vector $\mathcal{T}$, parameters Γ_0, Γ_1, MLP parameters Θ
Note: $I_k(\mathcal{T})$ denotes the modified Bessel function of the first kind; $A \odot B$ denotes the Hadamard product, which applies broadcasting to A if necessary.

1 **Feature Transformation:**
2 $X_0 \leftarrow \text{MLP}(X; \Theta)$;
3 **Chebyshev Expansion:**
4 **for** $k \leftarrow 0$ **to** $K - 1$ **do**
5   **if** $k = 0$ **then**
6       $c_0 \leftarrow \exp(-\mathcal{T}) \odot I_0(\mathcal{T})$;
7   **else**
8       $c_k \leftarrow 2\exp(-\mathcal{T}) \odot (-1)^k I_k(\mathcal{T})$;
9   **end**
10 **end**
11 **Chebyshev Polynomials:**
12 $T_0 \leftarrow X$;
13 $T_1 \leftarrow \tilde{\mathbf{L}} X$;
14 **for** $k \leftarrow 2$ **to** $K - 1$ **do**
15    $T_k \leftarrow 2\tilde{\mathbf{L}} T_{k-1} - T_{k-2}$;
16 **end**
17 $\tilde{X} \leftarrow \sum_{k=0}^{K}(c_k \odot T_k)$;
18 **Output:**
19 $Z \leftarrow \Gamma_0 \odot X_0 + \Gamma_1 \odot \tilde{X}$;

---

where $\beta = 1$ for $k = 0$ and $\beta = 2$ for $k \geq 1$, and $I_k(t_i)$ is the modified Bessel function of the first kind. By combining the revised coefficients, we obtain the following approximation for $e^{-t_i L}$:

$$e^{-t_i \mathbf{L}} \approx e^{-t_i} I_0(t_i) T_0(\tilde{\mathbf{L}}) + 2 \sum_{k=1}^{K-1} (-1)^k e^{-t_i} I_k(t_i) T_k(\tilde{\mathbf{L}}). \qquad (12)$$

In practice, implementing LHK-GNN by iteratively approximating each node's heat kernel would require an enormous amount of computational resources. Therefore, a more efficient approach is to approximate the heat kernels for all nodes simultaneously using a tensor-based method (as shown in Algorithm 1), which avoids the overhead associated with iterative traversal.

4.3 Analysis for LHK-GNN: Tackling Over-Smoothing and Heterophily

Compared to other GNNs with heat kernel, the most significant distinction of our model is its ability to adaptively adjust the heat diffusion time for each node, which helps address the issues of over-smoothing and heterophily.

Tackling Over-Smoothing. Over-smoothing refers to the phenomenon in GNNs where node representations become indistinguishable from each other as the number of layers increases. Consequently, the performance of GNNs gradually deteriorates with deeper architectures. Based on Chien et al. [2], we formally define the over-smoothing problem as follows:

Definition 2. *Given a propagation matrix $\mathcal{A}$ and a graph feature matrix X, the k-step feature propagation can be expressed as $X^{(k)} = \mathcal{A}^k X^{(0)}$. If $\lim_{k \to \infty} X^{(k)} = X^{(\infty)}$, the phenomenon is referred to as over-smoothing.*

According to Definition 2, the over-smoothing problem can be equivalently described as $\lim_{k \to \infty} \mathcal{A}^k = \mathcal{A}^\infty$, meaning that as the power k increases, $\mathcal{A}$ converges to a steady-state matrix. Based on the above discussion, we theoretically analyze that traditional heat kernel-based GNNs may exhibit the over-smoothing phenomenon. Specifically, we have the following:

Proposition 1. *Let $\mathcal{A} = \alpha_0 \mathbf{I} + \alpha_1 e^{-t\mathbf{L}}$, where $\mathbf{L}$ is the normalized Laplacian, $\alpha_0 + \alpha_1 = 1$, and $0 < \alpha_1 < 2$. Then, for any $t > 0$, the sequence of matrix powers converges, i.e., $\lim_{k \to \infty} \mathcal{A}^k = \mathcal{A}^\infty$, where $\mathcal{A}^\infty$ is a projection matrix onto the invariant subspace corresponding to the eigenvalue 1.*

Proof. Since $\mathbf{L}$ is the normalized Laplacian, it is symmetric and diagonalizable. Let $\{\lambda_i\}$ be its eigenvalues (with $\lambda_i \geq 0$), and denote by $\mathbf{U}$ an orthogonal matrix that diagonalizes $\mathbf{L}$.

Then, the heat kernel can be written as $e^{-t\mathbf{L}} = \mathbf{U} e^{-t\mathbf{\Lambda}} \mathbf{U}^T$, where $\mathbf{\Lambda}$ is the diagonal matrix of eigenvalues. Consequently, $e^{-t\mathbf{L}}$ is also symmetric and diagonalizable with eigenvalues $e^{-t\lambda_i}$. Thus, the eigenvalues of $\mathcal{A} = \alpha_0 \mathbf{I} + \alpha_1 e^{-t\mathbf{L}}$ are given by $\mu_i = \alpha_0 + \alpha_1 e^{-t\lambda_i}$. In particular, when $\lambda_i = 0$, we have

$$\mu_i = \alpha_0 + \alpha_1 = 1. \tag{13}$$

For $\lambda_i > 0$, note that

$$\mu_i = 1 - \alpha_1 \left(1 - e^{-t\lambda_i}\right). \tag{14}$$

Since $0 < e^{-t\lambda_i} < 1$ for $t > 0$ and $\lambda_i > 0$, and given $0 < \alpha_1 < 2$, it follows that $|\mu_i| < 1$. Because $\mathcal{A}$ is diagonalizable (and hence all eigenvalues are semisimple), taking powers of $\mathcal{A}$ yields $\mathcal{A}^k = \mathbf{U}(\theta_0 \mathbf{I} + \theta_1 e^{-t\mathbf{\Lambda}})^k \mathbf{U}^T$. As $k \to \infty$, all components corresponding to eigenvalues with $|\mu_i| < 1$ decay to zero, while the components corresponding to $\mu_i = 1$ remain unchanged. Thus,

$$\lim_{k \to \infty} \mathcal{A}^k = \mathcal{A}^\infty, \tag{15}$$

where $\mathcal{A}^\infty$ is the projection onto the invariant subspace associated with the eigenvalue 1.

This completes the proof.

The above analysis of over-smoothing in heat kernels is based on feature iteration. From a diffusion perspective, we can similarly conclude that heat kernels induce over-smoothing. Considering the heat kernel e^{-tL}, as $t \to \infty$, it converges to a steady-state matrix. This indicates that when the heat diffusion time is too long, the graph approaches a *thermal equilibrium* state, where node *energy* no longer changes with increasing diffusion time. Therefore, reducing t can alleviate the over-smoothing issue.

However, an excessively small t may compromise the properties of the heat kernel, preventing sufficient smoothing of graph labels. Thus, adaptively adjusting the heat diffusion time t for each node provides a more flexible way to control the diffusion process. According to [13], nodes with high degrees tend to converge to their stable states earlier than low-degree nodes, as evident. Based on this, for nodes with high degrees and similar or identical neighbor labels, a smaller t is required to prevent rapid convergence to a *thermal equilibrium* state. Conversely, for nodes with diverse or highly dissimilar neighbor labels, a larger t is needed. This allows for identifying similar nodes by adjusting the diffusion range while preventing the incorporation of misleading information due to an overly restricted scope.

Tackling Heterophily. Heterophily refers to the tendency of connected nodes to have different labels or features. According to [19], the node-level homophily ratio is a metric for measuring node homophily, defined as follows:

Definition 3. *Let $G = (V, E)$ be a labeled graph where each node v has a label $y(v)$. The node-level homophily of a node v is defined as:*

$$\mathcal{H}(v) = \frac{1}{|\mathcal{N}(v)|} \sum_{u \in \mathcal{N}(v)} \mathbf{1}\big[y(u) = y(v)\big],$$

where $\mathcal{N}(v)$ denotes the set of neighbors of v, and $\mathbf{1}[\cdot]$ is an indicator function that returns 1 if the condition is true, and 0 otherwise.

Traditional models rely on a global heat diffusion time to process graph data, which performs well on homophilic graphs but often proves ineffective on heterophilic graphs. The reason is that these methods are fundamentally based on the homophily assumption, which posits that connected nodes tend to have the same label or similar features. From the perspective of heat diffusion, since the diffusion time t defines the range of neighbors [27], traditional methods assign the same neighbor range to each node, which does not guarantee the effective exclusion of nodes with different labels for every node. In contrast, the node-specific LHK-GNN defines an independent neighbor range for each node (as shown in Fig. 2), which theoretically allows for the effective exclusion of nodes with different labels for each node.

Balancing Over-Smoothing and Heterophily. A special case arises when high-degree nodes exhibit low homophily. If a small diffusion time is applied, it may fail to effectively aggregate features from similar nodes, leading to performance degradation. To address this, one solution is to categorize nodes into

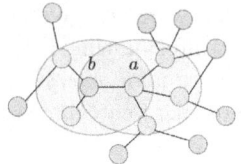 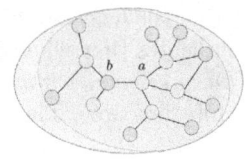 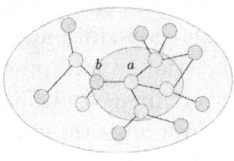

(a) The optimal diffusion range of node a

(b) The optimal diffusion range of node b

(c) The diffusion range of LHK-GNN

Fig. 2. Illustration of different diffusion ranges. (a): We restrict diffusion to integer-order neighbors. Since most of node a's first-order neighbors share its label, its optimal range is first-order (light blue). However, in this setting, node b aggregates features only from its first-order neighbors, whose labels differ from b, preventing it from effectively capturing useful information. (b): Node b's optimal range is third-order (light pink). In this setting, node a fails to learn effective features. (c): Traditional methods enforce a uniform range like (a) and (b), preventing optimal diffusion. LHK-GNN instead enables each node to diffuse within its optimal range. (Color figure online)

different intervals based on their homophily levels, measured by homophily ratio in Definition 3, and assign each interval an upper bound ϵ_i and a lower bound η_i for diffusion time. The diffusion time for each node is then learned within these threshold constraints. The upper bound in high-degree intervals is set lower than that in low-degree intervals, though the difference remains moderate to ensure that high-degree nodes can still adaptively adjust their diffusion range according to the downstream task's loss function. This approach prevents excessively small diffusion times from failing to aggregate meaningful features while avoiding overly large diffusion times that lead to over-smoothing, thereby achieving a balance between over-smoothing and heterophily.

5 Experiments

In this section, we evaluate the performance of LHK-GNN on node classification tasks across 10 benchmark datasets. Section 5.1 provides details on the datasets, baselines, and hyperparameter settings used in the experiments. Section 5.2 presents the experimental results, including the performance on both homophilic and heterophilic graphs. Section 5.3 provides an analysis of the influence of diffusion time. Section 5.4 provides the parameter study.

5.1 Experimental Setup

Datasets. We evaluate our model on ten commonly used real-world datasets. Among them, five are homophilic datasets: Cora, CiteSeer, and PubMed [22], Computers, and Photo [23], and the other are heterophilic datasets: Chameleon and Squirrel [21], Actor, Texas, and Cornell [19]. Besides, we follow [2] to adopt two data splitting strategies: the sparse splitting 2.5%/2.5%/95% for training, validation, and testing, respectively, and the dense

Table 1. Statistics of the datasets

Datasets	Homophilic datasets					Heterophilic datasets				
	Cora	Cite.	PubMed	Comp.	Photo	Cham.	Squi.	Actor	Texas	Corn
Nodes	2,708	3,327	19,717	13,752	7,650	2,277	5,201	7,600	183	183
Edges	5,278	4,552	44,324	245,861	119,081	31,371	198,353	26,659	279	277
Features	1,433	3,703	500	767	745	2,325	2,089	932	1,703	1,703
Classes	7	6	3	10	8	5	5	5	5	5
$\mathcal{H}_\mathcal{G}$	0.81	0.70	0.79	0.80	0.83	0.24	0.22	0.21	0.05	0.30

splitting 60%/20%/20%. For experiments, we perform 100 runs with different random splits. The dataset statistics are provided in Table 1. Note that $H_\mathcal{G}$ is used to measure the proportion of homophily in the graph, defined as: $\mathcal{H}_\mathcal{G} = \frac{|\{(u,v)\in E | y_u = y_v\}|}{|E|}$.

Baselines. We select commonly used diffusion-based GNNs as baselines, including GCN [15], GraphHeat [27], APPNP [7], GDC [8], HKGCN [28], GPRGNN [2], and HiD-Net [17]. Among them, GCN, GraphHeat, and HKGCN can be regarded as heat kernel-based GNNs (with GCN considered as a first-order heat diffusion GNN). APPNP and GPRGNN are random walk-based GNNs, where their iterative node feature updates can still be viewed as an information diffusion process. GDC defines a generalized diffusion matrix that supports multiple diffusion modes, including heat diffusion. HiD-Net constructs a generalized neural diffusion framework on Graphs.

Hyper-Parameters. For the baselines, we use the best combination of hyperparameters provided in the original paper to report the results for each dataset. For our proposed LHK-GNN, we use a 2-layer MLP for feature transformation. For each dataset, we search for the optimal hyperparameters within {1e–3, 5e–3, 1e–2, 5e–2} for learning rate, within {0.3, 0.5, 0.7, 0.8, 0.9} for dropout, within {16, 32, 64} for hidden channels, and within {0, 1e–5, 5e–5, 1e–4, 5e–4} for weight decay to achieve the best performance. In all experiments, we use the Adam optimizer and apply standard early stopping after 200 epochs.

5.2 Experimental Results

We use sparse splitting for homophilic graphs and dense splitting for heterophilic graphs according to [2]. The results are presented in Table 2 and Table 3, respectively. The results show that LHK-GNN achieves the best performance on 7 datasets and the second-best performance on 3 datasets. Compared to the baselines, LHK-GNN has superior performance on heterophilic graph datasets, especially on Chameleon and Squirrel, LHK-GNN outperforming the baselines by an average of 5.64% and 10.35%, respectively. Apart from that, compared to heat

Table 2. Results on real-world homophilic datasets in the sparse splitting (2.5%/2.5%/95%): Mean accuracy across runs (%) ± 95% confidence interval. Boldface denotes the best results, and underlining denotes the second-best.

Method	Cora	CiteSeer	PubMed	Computers	Photo
GCN	76.43 ±0.87	66.71 ±0.73	84.35 ±0.90	82.46 ±0.75	90.61 ±1.08
GraphHeat	77.67 ±1.04	66.84 ±0.96	83.62 ±1.12	82.78 ±0.63	90.68 ±0.89
APPNP	78.74 ±1.06	67.34 ±1.02	84.46 ±0.83	82.13 ±0.67	90.43 ±1.15
GDC	77.79 ±0.78	67.16 ±0.55	84.62 ±0.68	82.78 ±0.72	91.19 ±1.10
GPRGNN	79.34 ±0.81	67.73 ±0.72	84.27 ±1.14	82.97 ±0.90	91.72 ±0.95
HKGCN	78.52 ±0.92	67.05 ±0.91	83.89 ±0.88	82.34 ±0.59	90.75 ±0.97
HiD-Net	79.53 ±1.03	66.87 ±0.99	84.32 ±0.74	**84.14** ±0.60	91.45 ±0.91
LHK-GNN	**80.02** ±1.13	**67.92** ±0.87	**84.81** ±0.56	83.36 ±0.75	**92.3** ±1.25

Table 3. Results on real-world heterophilic datasets in the dense splitting (60%/20%/20%): Mean accuracy across runs (%) ± 95% confidence interval. Boldface denotes the best results, and underlining denotes the second-best.

Method	Chameleon	Squirrel	Actor	Texas	Cornell
GCN	61.21 ±0.95	44.92 ±0.87	32.14 ±0.94	76.45 ±1.20	68.31 ±0.88
GraphHeat	64.68 ±0.79	45.61 ±0.66	34.51 ±1.02	80.82 ±1.08	72.92 ±1.15
APPNP	62.16 ±0.91	40.66 ±0.75	39.44 ±1.11	91.24 ±0.87	91.26 ±1.00
GDC	67.53 ±0.92	44.83 ±0.81	39.32 ±1.02	91.66 ±1.05	91.43 ±0.98
GPRGNN	67.78 ±0.82	50.27 ±0.65	39.65 ±0.85	91.83 ±0.91	92.17 ±0.88
HKGCN	63.44 ±0.88	46.76 ±0.93	34.73 ±1.06	78.63 ±0.82	74.66 ±1.04
HiD-Net	68.41 ±0.81	48.86 ±0.79	**40.07** ±0.93	92.54 ±0.95	**92.37** ±1.10
LHK-GNN	**70.67** ±0.92	**56.34** ±0.87	39.88 ±0.95	**93.47** ±1.08	92.24 ±1.20

kernel-based GNNs such as GraphHeat and HKGCN, LHK-GNN achieves significant performance gains on every dataset–including an average improvement of about 12% on heterophilic graphs. These comparisons demonstrate that LHK-GNN is more effective than existing diffusion-based GNNs in handling both homophilic and heterophilic graphs.

5.3 The Influence of Diffusion Time

Each node has an independent heat diffusion time, resulting in a complex heat diffusion pattern. To better understand how this heat diffusion pattern helps mitigate over-smoothing and handle heterophilic graph datasets, we study the relationship between each node's diffusion time and its degree, and separately, between its diffusion time and its heterophily ratio.

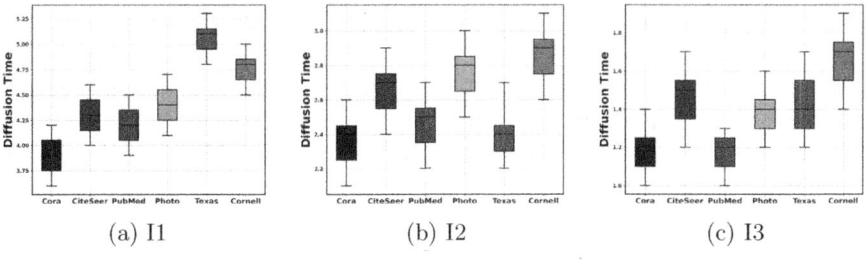

Fig. 3. Boxplots of diffusion times for each dataset across three intervals.

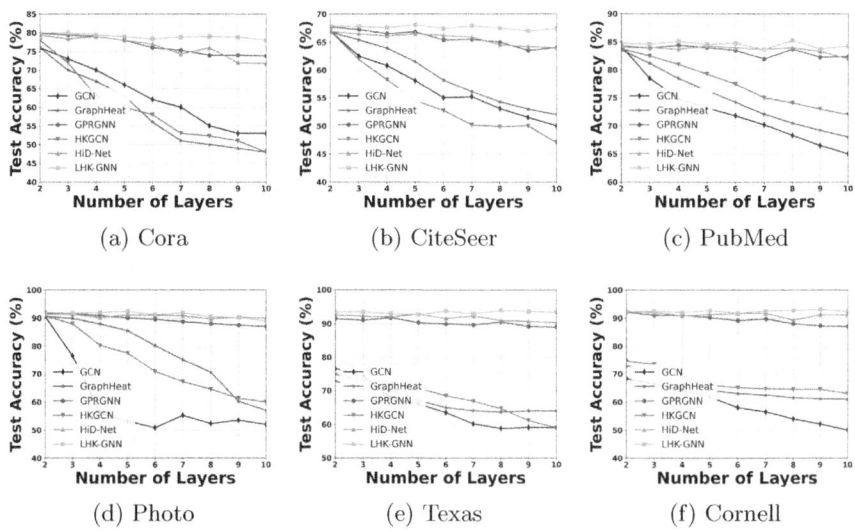

Fig. 4. Test accuracy with increasing number of propagation steps.

Over-Smoothing. The key to mitigating over-smoothing is to adjust the diffusion time for different local patterns. According to Sect. 4.3, different local patterns can be distinguished based on the degree of the nodes. Taking 6 datasets as examples, we divide the diffusion time into five intervals based on the degree and train the diffusion time in each interval I_i, constraining it with different thresholds ϵ_i and η_i. The results, as shown in Fig. 3. Under the settings specified in Fig. 3 for LHK-GNN, we compare LHK-GNN with other graph diffusion models while varying the propagation step k from 2 to 10. The baselines include two models that are effective in handling over-smoothing–GPRGNN and HiD-Net–as well as other models, such as GCN, GraphHeat, and HKGCN. The results are shown in Fig. 4. From the results, we can observe that with the increase of k, LHK-GNN consistently performs better than other baselines.

Heterophily. According to Section 4.3, the key to handling heterophilic datasets is adaptively adjusting the heat diffusion time for each node based on the level of homophily ratio. To verify whether our model can adjust the heat diffusion range based on nodes with different homophily ratios, we relate the heat diffusion times learned by LHK-GNN and GraphHeat to the homophily ratio of each node. Using Chameleon, Squirrel and Texas as examples, the results are shown in Fig. 5. The results show that LHK-GNN increases diffusion time in low-homophily regions and decreases it in high-homophily regions, while GraphHeat keeps the diffusion time unchanged. This validates that our method can adaptively adjust diffusion time based on the homophily of nodes, thereby enabling flexible and effective handling of heterophilic graphs.

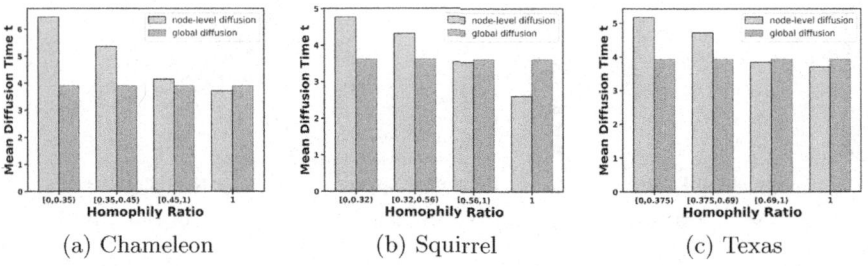

Fig. 5. LHK-GNN and GraphHeat diffusion time comparison.

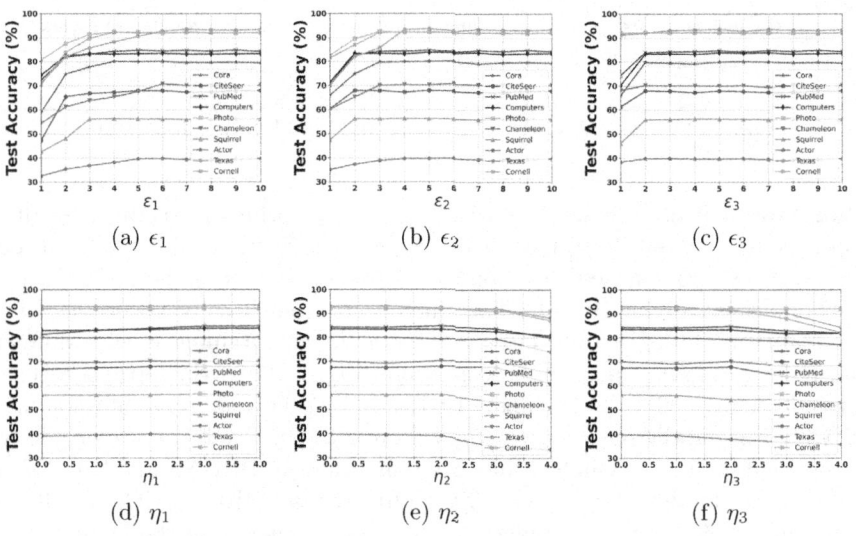

Fig. 6. Parameter influence on performance.

5.4 Parameter Study

In this section, we investigate the sensitivity of parameters on all datasets. There are two types of parameters: each interval has an upper bound ϵ_i and a lower bound η_i.

From the results (as shown in Fig. 6), we have following observations: (1) as ϵ_i increases, the model's performance on all datasets improves and converges to a stable state. This implies that when ϵ_i is sufficiently large, the model can learn the optimal diffusion time in each interval and is not affected by further increases in ϵ_i. (2) Increasing η_1 has no impact on performance, indicating that low-degree nodes (interval I_1) require a longer diffusion time for effective feature aggregation. In contrast, rising η_2 and η_3 gradually degrade performance, suggesting that nodes in intervals I_2 and I_3 (with higher degrees) need a moderate diffusion time to avoid aggregating too many harmful features.

6 Conclusion

In this paper, we extend the heat kernel to the node level and integrate it with graph convolution to propose the Localized Heat Kernel for GNN (LHK-GNN). Our method allows each node to adaptively adjust the diffusion time, enabling different diffusion ranges based on node degree and the similarity of neighboring labels. This approach theoretically alleviates over-smoothing and effectively handles heterophilic graphs. Experimental results demonstrate the effectiveness of our method in mitigating over-smoothing and handling heterophilic graphs.

Acknowledgments. We would like to thank reviewers for their constructive comments.

Disclosure of Interests. The authors have no competing interests to declare that are relevant to the content of this article.

References

1. Bridle, J.S.: Probabilistic interpretation of feedforward classification network outputs, with relationships to statistical pattern recognition. In: NATO Neurocomputing (1989). https://api.semanticscholar.org/CorpusID:59636530
2. Chien, E., Peng, J., Li, P., Milenkovic, O.: Adaptive universal generalized pagerank graph neural network. arXiv preprint arXiv:2006.07988 (2020)
3. Chung, F.: The heat kernel as the pagerank of a graph. Proc. Natl. Acad. Sci. **104**(50), 19735–19740 (2007)
4. Chung, F.R.: Spectral Graph Theory, vol. 92. American Mathematical Soc. (1997)
5. Defferrard, M., Bresson, X., Vandergheynst, P.: Convolutional neural networks on graphs with fast localized spectral filtering. Adv. Neural Inf. Process. Syst. **29** (2016)
6. Fu, G., Zhao, P., Bian, Y.: p p -laplacian based graph neural networks. In: International Conference on Machine Learning, pp. 6878–6917. PMLR (2022)

7. Gasteiger, J., Bojchevski, A., Günnemann, S.: Predict then propagate: graph neural networks meet personalized pagerank. arXiv preprint arXiv:1810.05997 (2018)
8. Gasteiger, J., Weißenberger, S., Günnemann, S.: Diffusion improves graph learning. Adv. Neural Inf. Process. Syst. **32** (2019)
9. Glorot, X., Bordes, A., Bengio, Y.: Deep sparse rectifier neural networks. In: Proceedings of the Fourteenth International Conference on Artificial Intelligence and Statistics, pp. 315–323. JMLR Workshop and Conference Proceedings (2011)
10. Hammond, D.K., Vandergheynst, P., Gribonval, R.: Wavelets on graphs via spectral graph theory. Appl. Comput. Harmon. Anal. **30**(2), 129–150 (2011)
11. Han, A., Shi, D., Lin, L., Gao, J.: From continuous dynamics to graph neural networks: neural diffusion and beyond. arXiv preprint arXiv:2310.10121 (2023)
12. Hossain, T., Saifuddin, K.M., Islam, M.I.K., Tanvir, F., Akbas, E.: Tackling oversmoothing in gnn via graph sparsification: a truss-based approach. arXiv preprint arXiv:2407.11928 (2024)
13. Huang, R., Li, P.: Hub-hub connections matter: improving edge dropout to relieve over-smoothing in graph neural networks. Knowl.-Based Syst. **270**, 110556 (2023)
14. Keriven, N.: Not too little, not too much: a theoretical analysis of graph (over)smoothing. Adv. Neural. Inf. Process. Syst. **35**, 2268–2281 (2022)
15. Kipf, T.N., Welling, M.: Semi-supervised classification with graph convolutional networks. arXiv preprint arXiv:1609.02907 (2016)
16. Kondor, R.I., Lafferty, J.: Diffusion kernels on graphs and other discrete structures. In: Proceedings of the 19th International Conference on Machine Learning, vol. 2002, pp. 315–322 (2002)
17. Li, Y., Wang, X., Liu, H., Shi, C.: A generalized neural diffusion framework on graphs. In: Proceedings of the AAAI Conference on Artificial Intelligence, vol. 38, pp. 8707–8715 (2024)
18. Luan, S., et al.: Is heterophily a real nightmare for graph neural networks to do node classification? arXiv preprint arXiv:2109.05641 (2021)
19. Pei, H., Wei, B., Chang, K.C.C., Lei, Y., Yang, B.: Geom-gcn: geometric graph convolutional networks. arXiv preprint arXiv:2002.05287 (2020)
20. Poli, M., Massaroli, S., Park, J., Yamashita, A., Asama, H., Park, J.: Graph neural ordinary differential equations. arXiv preprint arXiv:1911.07532 (2019)
21. Rozemberczki, B., Allen, C., Sarkar, R.: Multi-scale attributed node embedding. J. Complex Netw. **9**(2), cnab014 (2021)
22. Sen, P., Namata, G., Bilgic, M., Getoor, L., Galligher, B., Eliassi-Rad, T.: Collective classification in network data. AI Mag. **29**(3), 93–93 (2008)
23. Shchur, O., Mumme, M., Bojchevski, A., Günnemann, S.: Pitfalls of graph neural network evaluation. arXiv preprint arXiv:1811.05868 (2018)
24. Shuman, D.I., Narang, S.K., Frossard, P., Ortega, A., Vandergheynst, P.: The emerging field of signal processing on graphs: extending high-dimensional data analysis to networks and other irregular domains. IEEE Signal Process. Mag. **30**(3), 83–98 (2013)
25. Tsiatas, A.: Pagerank and diffusion on large graphs. UCSD Res. Exam **14** (2009)
26. Wu, F., Souza, A., Zhang, T., Fifty, C., Yu, T., Weinberger, K.: Simplifying graph convolutional networks. In: International Conference on Machine Learning, pp. 6861–6871. PMLR (2019)
27. Xu, B., Shen, H., Cao, Q., Cen, K., Cheng, X.: Graph convolutional networks using heat kernel for semi-supervised learning. arXiv preprint arXiv:2007.16002 (2020)
28. Zhao, J., Dong, Y., Tang, J., Ding, M., Wang, K.: Generalizing graph convolutional networks via heat kernel (2021)

29. Zheng, S., Zhu, Z., Liu, Z., Li, Y., Zhao, Y.: Node-oriented spectral filtering for graph neural networks. IEEE Trans. Pattern Anal. Mach. Intell. **46**(1), 388–402 (2023)
30. Zheng, X., et al.: Graph neural networks for graphs with heterophily: a survey. arXiv preprint arXiv:2202.07082 (2022)

Graph Neural Network Leveraging Higher-Order Class Label Connectivity for Heterophilous Graphs

Takuto Takahashi(✉), Itsuki Nakayama, Takahiro Mitani, Ryosuke Kikuchi, Yuya Sasaki, and Makoto Onizuka

The University of Osaka, 1-5 Yamadaoka, Suita, Osaka, Japan
{takahashi.takuto,nakayama.itsuki,mitani.takashiro,
kikuchi.ryosuke,sasaki,onizuka}@ist.osaka-u.ac.jp

Abstract. Node classification in graph neural networks (GNNs) has been widely applied in various fields of graph analysis. GNNs achieve high-accuracy node classification in homophilous graphs, where nodes with the same class label tend to be connected. However, their performance remains limited in heterophilous graphs, where nodes with different class labels are more likely to be connected. In particular, current GNNs derived from graph convolutional networks cannot capture higher-order class label connectivity, which is frequently observed in real-world heterophilous graphs. To address this issue, we propose a novel classifier, Label Context Classifier (LCC), designed to capture higher-order class label connectivity in directed graphs. LCC estimates the class label of a target node by leveraging *label context* embeddings that are generated through four distinct types of walks. In addition, our approach allows the integration of LCC and any GNN by adaptively learning their importance. Experimental results demonstrate that GNNs integrated with LCC outperform SOTA methods and the label context embeddings improve the node classification performance in heterophilous directed graphs.

Keywords: Graph neural networks · Node classification · Heterophilous graphs

1 Introduction

Node classification in graphs is one of the important tasks in graph analysis, aiming to predict the class labels of nodes. This task has a wide range of applications, including the analysis of social networks and biological networks, such as genes and proteins [3,16,17,25]. A representative approach for node classification is Graph Neural Networks (GNNs) [1,4,6,7,9,11,18,21–23,28]. Traditional GNNs such as Graph Convolutional Network (GCN) [7] are designed for homophilous graphs, where nodes with the same class labels/features are more likely to be connected. However, their effectiveness is limited for heterophilous graphs, where nodes with different class labels/features tend to be connected [26,27]. To improve the performance in heterophilous graphs,

---

Supplementary Information The online version contains supplementary material available at https://doi.org/10.1007/978-3-032-05981-9_28.

© The Author(s), under exclusive license to Springer Nature Switzerland AG 2026
R. P. Ribeiro et al. (Eds.): ECML PKDD 2025, LNAI 16014, pp. 474–491, 2026.
https://doi.org/10.1007/978-3-032-05981-9_28

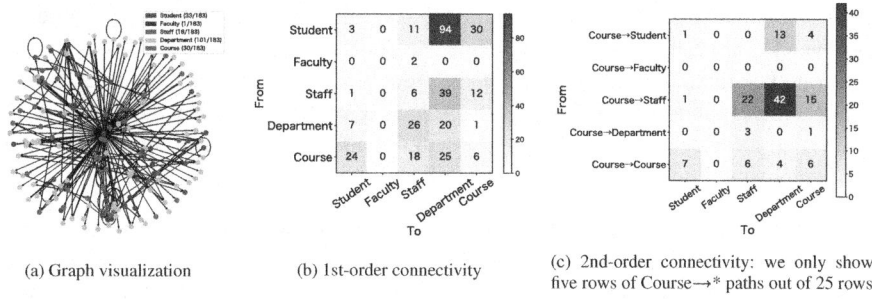

(a) Graph visualization (b) 1st-order connectivity (c) 2nd-order connectivity: we only show five rows of Course→* paths out of 25 rows

Fig. 1. The class label connectivity in the Texas dataset. (a) visualization with five class labels. (b) 1st-order connectivity (#edges) from class label in y-axis to class label in x-axis. (c) 2nd-order connectivity from class label path (e.g., Course→Student) in y-axis to class label in x-axis.

GNNs that capture the characteristics of heterophilous graphs have been actively proposed [1,8–10,22,26,28]. Nevertheless, there are still cases where the accuracy of these GNNs does not surpass that of multilayer perceptrons (MLPs), which rely only on node features without using edges. This result indicates that these GNNs do not fully leverage the structural information of graphs [10].

Motivation. An interesting observation we found on the weakness of current GNNs derived from GCN is that they fail to capture the *higher-order class label connectivity* in graphs, that is, how class labels are connected through multiple hops using directed edges. This weakness is caused by the fact that GCN transforms the node classification problem into a simple classification problem using graph convolution operation: after applying the graph convolution operations, GCN trains the model from embedding space to class label space, so it ignores the class label connectivity among nodes, particularly appeared in the training sets. This limitation also applies to more advanced methods such as [24,26]. While they utilize a class compatibility matrix corresponding to 1st-order class label connectivity, they do not capture higher-order class connectivity.

Strong higher-order class label connectivity often appears in real-world graphs. Figure 1 illustrates such examples in the heterophilous directed graph of the Texas dataset. Figure 1 (a) visualizes the graph with five class labels (i.e., Student, Faculty, Staff, Department, and Course). Figure 1 (b) shows the 1st-order connectivity, depicting the number of directed edges from the class label on the y-axis to the one on the x-axis. We observe that there is strong connectivity from Student nodes to Department nodes, whereas there is no connectivity to Faculty nodes. Similarly, Fig. 1 (c) also reveals strong/weak 2nd-order class label connectivity. For example, the connectivity from Course→Staff class label path to Department nodes is strong, whereas no connectivity to Faculty nodes.

Contribution. In order to capture such higher-order class label connectivity, we propose a novel classifier, Label Context Classifier (LCC), which trains the model using *label walks*, which are sequences of class labels on walks. First, we extract four fundamental types of label walks from a target node: forward walk, backward walk, sibling walk, and guardian walk. They are mutually exclusive, and each walk type captures a different aspect of class label connectivity. We generate *label context embeddings* that capture the label context by training a model using the label walks, an idea inspired by word2vec [13]. Then, we train LCC using the concatenation of node features and the label context embeddings obtained from different types of label walks. Since LCC complements the capability of GNNs, we integrate LCC and any GNN by adaptively learning their importance using validation loss without additional model training.

The contributions of this paper are as follows:

- We propose the Label Context Classifier (LCC), which estimates the class label of a target node by capturing the higher-order class label connectivity across directed graphs. LCC estimates the class label using the label context embeddings generated from four types of label walks.
- We can integrate LCC and any GNN by adaptively learning their importance weights without additional model training.
- Experimental results confirm that our proposal outperforms SOTA methods and the label context embeddings actually enhance node classification performance in heterophilous directed graphs.

The structure of this paper is as follows. Section 2 describes related work, and then Sect. 3 explains preliminary knowledge. Sections 4 and 5 present the details of the Label Context Classifier and how to integrate it and any GNN, respectively. Section 6 conducts experiments to demonstrate the effectiveness of the proposed method for heterophilous directed graphs. Finally, Sect. 7 concludes this paper.

2 Related Work

Traditional GNNs. Since Graph Convolutional Network (GCN) [7] has emerged, numerous methods have been proposed for node classification using graph convolution. The graph convolution ensures 1st-order node proximity, which makes the adjacent node representations similar. Therefore, a family of GCN is suitable for homophily graphs but not for heterophilous graphs.

Graph Attention Networks (GAT) [18] improve accuracy by employing a self-attention mechanism that learns relative weights between connected node pairs. JK-Net [21] is a method that aggregates outputs from multiple layers of a GNN to integrate information at different layer levels. APPNP [4] first transforms the initial node features using an MLP and then applies a personalized PageRank-based iterative propagation mechanism to distribute information among nodes. In addition, sampling-based GNNs [6,23] are scalable methods that compute node representations using subgraphs extracted from the input graph. GraphSAGE [6] samples a fixed number of neighbors uniformly for each node. GraphSAINT [23] samples subgraphs and learns graph representations by combining information from multiple subgraphs.

GNNs for Heterophilous Graphs. Real-world graphs sometimes exhibit heterophily, where nodes of different attributes/classes are more likely to be connected. There have been several GNNs designed for heterophilous graphs [1,8,9,12,22,28]. However, these methods also suffer from the same limitation as the GNNs derived from GCN in the sense that they also transform the node classification problem into a simple classification problem by training the model from embedding space to class label space, so they ignore the class label connectivity.

H2GCN [28], a representative GNN designed for heterophilous graphs, separates the processing of a node's own features from those of its neighbors, utilizes high-order neighborhood information, and employs an appropriate aggregation function to capture complex relationships between nodes. LINKX [9] independently processes node features and adjacency matrix information, learning both in parallel to effectively leverage multiple sources of information. GloGNN [8] combines local node features with global features that capture relationships between distant but structurally similar nodes. Recent studies have further advanced this area. CAGNNs [1] introduce a novel metric based on the distinguishability of neighboring nodes, decomposing node features into representation and aggregation components. A mixer module is then used to adaptively evaluate neighboring information for each node. Adaptive Channel Mixing (ACM) [10] is a GNN framework designed to address heterophily by adaptively combining aggregation, diversification, and identity channels at the node level. ACM allows nodes to learn different weights for each channel, effectively capturing local heterophily without requiring high-order filters or increased computational resources. LG-GNN [22] achieves high-accuracy node classification for heterophilous graphs by adaptively integrating global structural similarity and local feature similarity between nodes. This design effectively considers node relationships during the information aggregation and propagation process.

Other Related Work. There are methods [24,26] that utilize the class compatibility matrix, which corresponds to 1st-order class label connectivity. As a specific example, CPGNN [26] trains the class compatibility matrix using training sets and a prior belief estimator. However, it has a weakness in that it does not capture higher-order class connectivity.

A meta-path is a predefined sequence of node and edge types in order to capture higher-order connectivity and semantic relationships between different entities in heterogeneous information networks (HIN). For example, MetaPath2Vec [2] generates constrained random walks for learning embeddings, while HAN [20] employs attention mechanisms to aggregate multiple meta-paths. Recent studies [19] focus on automatic meta-path discovery to enhance model generalization. These methods assume that all nodes and edges are typed, and meta-paths are defined based on those types. In contrast, our approach is applicable to graphs without predefined types, and we define four types of direction-aware fundamental walks.

node2vec [5] is a method to generate node embedding in order to capture homophily and structural equivalence. Our proposal and node2vec share some common characteristics, such as generating walks and using word2vec. However, there are two major differences. First, node2vec does not use class labels as input and is not designed for directed graphs. Second, the type of walk is limited to only a single type, and the parameters that determine the balance between breadth-first and depth-first search must be manually set by the user. In contrast, in order to capture class connectivity, we define four types of direction-aware class label walks, and their importance is learned automatically without manual intervention.

3 Preliminary

Graph. We consider a directed graph $G = (V, E)$, which consists of a node set V with n nodes and a directed edge set E with m edges. The adjacency matrix $\mathbf{A} \in \{0,1\}^{n \times n}$ is defined such that $a_{ij} = 1$ if $(v_i, v_j) \in E$, and $a_{ij} = 0$ otherwise. Additionally, we define the feature matrix $\mathbf{X} \in \mathbb{R}^{n \times d}$, where each node is assigned a d-dimensional feature vector. Each node v has a unique class label $y_v \in \{1, \ldots, C\}$ (number of classes: C), and the class label vector is denoted as $\mathbf{y}$. For clarity in explanations, we refer to the starting node of a directed edge as the parent node and the ending node as the child node. Additionally, we use the terms, sibling nodes and guardian nodes, which are naturally defined based on the parent-child relationship between nodes.

We define heterophilous graphs after defining edge homophily [28]. The edge homophily [28] is calculated as follows.

$$H(G) = \frac{\sum_{0 \leq i,j < n} a_{ij} \delta(y_{v_i}, y_{v_j})}{m}, \quad (1)$$

where $\delta(y_{v_i}, y_{v_j})$ returns one if $y_{v_i} = y_{v_j}$ otherwise zero. We define graphs with low $H(G)$ as heterophilous graphs. A lower edge homophily indicates a stronger tendency toward heterophily.

Problem Definition (Node Classification). We split a node set V into a training set V_{train}, validation set V_{val}, and test set V_{test}. Given adjacency matrix $\mathbf{A}$, feature matrix $\mathbf{X}$, and node class labels in V_{train} and V_{val}, we predict the labels of the nodes in V_{test}.

4 Label Context Classifier

GNNs fail to capture the higher-order class label connectivity, which often appears in real-world graphs, as we described in Sect. 1. This weakness is caused by the fact that GNNs transform the node classification problem into a simple classification problem: GNNs train the model from embedding space to class label space, so they ignore the class label connectivity among nodes, particularly appeared in the training sets.

To this end, we propose a novel classifier, Label Context Classifier (LCC), which trains the model using various types of label walks in order to capture higher-order class label connectivity. Our method consists of the following steps as illustrated in Fig. 2: (1) extract four types of fundamental label walks: a simple walk (forward walk, backward walk) and a mixture of forward and backward walks (sibling walk, guardian walk). They are mutually exclusive and each walk type captures a different aspect of class label connectivity, (2) generate embeddings that capture the label context by training a model using the label walks, and (3) train LCC using the concatenation of node attributes and the label context embeddings obtained from different types of label walks. This enables the model to appropriately select suitable embeddings for node classification.

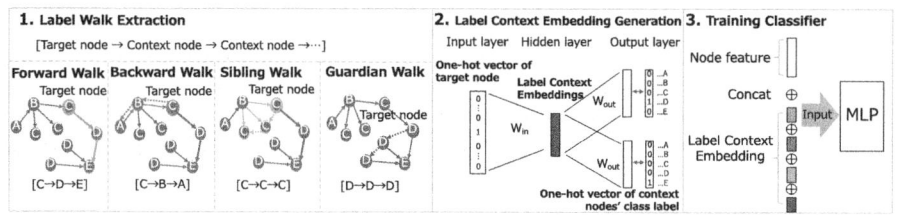

Fig. 2. The framework of Label Context Classifier (LCC). LCC consists of three steps: 1) extraction of four types of label walks, 2) generation of label context embeddings, and 3) training a classifier using the label context embeddings.

Table 1. Summary of label walk types and their characteristics.

Walk type	Description	Traverse edge direction	Class label connectivity order (#hops)
Forward	Depth-first search-based walk	forward only	walk length
Backward	Inverse of forward walk	backward only	walk length
Sibling	Walk on sibling nodes	backward + forward	2
Guardian	Inverse of sibling walk	forward + backward	2

4.1 Label Walk Extraction

A label walk is defined as a walk obtained from a graph where the nodes in the walk are replaced with their labels in the training set. We refer to the first label in the walk as the target label and the remaining labels as context labels. If a node in the walk is not in the training dataset, we use the null label in the label walk, and it is ignored in the label context embedding step.

Table 1 presents a summary of the characteristics of the four label walk types, indicating they are mutually exclusive and each walk type captures a different aspect of higher-order class label connectivity. Step 1 in Fig. 2 shows examples of label walk types: forward walk (C, D, E), backward walk (C, B, A), sibling walk (C, C, C), and guardian walk (D, D, D). The details are described in the following sections.

Forward Walk. The forward walk aims to capture the higher-order class label connectivity directed from a target label down to neighboring context labels. We extract forward walks using the depth-first search that follows the forward direction of directed edges. For the given target node v_0 and the length w of label walk, a forward walk (FW) is formulated as follows:

$$FW(v_0) = (y_{v_0}, y_{v_1}, \ldots, y_{v_w}), \quad \text{s.t.} (v_i, v_{i+1}) \in E, i \in \{0, 1, \ldots, w-1\}. \quad (2)$$

The order of class label connectivity is walk length. For example, it is 1st-order if the walk length is 1 (i.e., 1 hop).

Figure 1 shows an example: the Student nodes are more likely to connect to the Department nodes (1st order connectivity), and those Department nodes are more likely to connect to the Staff nodes (2nd order connectivity).

Backward Walk. The backward walk is the inverse notion of the forward walk. The reason why we introduce the backward walk in addition to the forward walk is that the edge direction is user-defined, so both directions are useful. Also, the backward walk is useful for the sink nodes (i.e., nodes without outgoing edges), because they cannot utilize forward walks. We extract backward walks using the depth-first search that follows the reverse direction of directed edges. Similar to the forward walk, a backward walk (BW) is defined as follows:

$$BW(v_0) = (y_{v_0}, y_{v_1}, \ldots, y_{v_w}), \quad \text{s.t.} (v_{i+1}, v_i) \in E, i \in \{0, 1, \ldots, w-1\}. \quad (3)$$

Figure 1 shows an example: the Department nodes are more likely to be connected from the Student nodes (1st order connectivity), and those Student nodes are more likely to be connected from the Course nodes (2nd order connectivity).

Sibling Walk. In addition to the simple forward/backward walks, we introduce the sibling walk, our new idea which is a mixture of forward and backward walks. The motivation for introducing sibling walks is that sibling nodes (the child nodes connected to the same parent node) often share the same class label for certain target nodes. We extract sibling walks by 1) traversing backward to a parent node of the target node v_0, and then 2) repeatedly traversing forward to its child nodes until reaching the desired label walk length w. A sibling walk (SW)[1] is formulated as follows:

$$\begin{aligned} SW(v_0) &= (y_{v_0}, y_{v_1}, \ldots, y_{v_w}) \\ \text{s.t.} \quad &\exists p \in \text{parents}(v_0), \quad v_1, \ldots, v_w \in \text{children}(p) \setminus \{v_0\}. \end{aligned} \quad (4)$$

where parents(v) and children(v) are parent nodes and child nodes of v, respectively. The order of class label connectivity is 2 regardless of the walk length, because the target node and the sibling nodes are 2-hops apart.

Figure 1 shows an example: the sibling walk captures the connectivity between the nodes labeled as Student whose parent nodes are labeled as Course.

Guardian Walk. The guardian walk is the inverse notion of the sibling walk. Similarly to the sibling walk, the motivation for introducing guardian walks is that guardian nodes often share the same class label for certain target nodes. Compared to the general walks based on depth-first or breadth-first search, the sibling walk and guardian walk extract only siblings and guardians, which mitigates the noisy effect on the downstream classifier. Indeed, our experiments in Sect. 6 verify that the sibling walk and guardian walk significantly improve the accuracy. We extract guardian walks by 1) traversing forward to a child node of the target node v_0, and then 2) repeatedly traversing backward to its parent nodes until reaching the desired label walk length w. A guardian walk (GW) is defined as follows:

$$\begin{aligned} GW(v_0) &= (y_{v_0}, y_{v_1}, \ldots, y_{v_w}) \\ \text{s.t.} \quad &\exists c \in \text{children}(v_0), \quad v_1, \ldots, v_w \in \text{parents}(c) \setminus \{v_0\}. \end{aligned} \quad (5)$$

---

[1] Since a sibling walk traverses multiple sibling nodes without edges, it does not strictly follow the "walk" definition in the graph theory.

Algorithm 1. Label context embedding matrix generation

Input: adjacency matrix $\mathbf{A}$, class label $\mathbf{y}$, embedding dimension d', label walk length w, number of label walk k, epoch T
Output: label context embedding matrix $\mathbf{Z} \in \mathbb{R}^{n \times d'}$
1: ### Initialize ###
2: Initialize the label context embedding $\mathbf{z}_v \in \mathbb{R}^{d'}$ of node $v \in V$ to a random value
3: Create an one-hot vector ℓ_v of class label for node v from $\mathbf{y}$
4: ### Extract label walks ###
5: **for** $v \in V$ **do**
6:    **if** label walk is forward / backward walk **then**
7:       **for** $i = 1, \ldots, k$ **do**
8:          Extract label walks (forward, backward walks) for v
9:       **end for**
10:   **else if** label walk is sibling / guardian walk **then**
11:      Extract a label walk (sibling, guardian walk) for v
12:   **end if**
13: **end for**
14: ### Train the model for label context embedding ###
15: **for** $t = 1, \ldots, T$ **do**
16:   **for** each label walk **do**
17:      Calculate output embedding $\hat{\ell}_v = \mathbf{z}_v^\top \mathbf{W_{out}}$
18:      Calculate cross entropy as loss $\mathcal{L} = \sum_{\ell_u \in contexts(v)} \mathcal{L}_{CE}(\hat{\ell}_v, \ell_u)$
19:      Update $\mathbf{z}_v, \hat{\mathbf{y}}_v$ and $\mathbf{W_{out}}$ to minimize $\mathcal{L}$
20:   **end for**
21: **end for**
22: ### Output label context embedding matrix ###
23: **return** $\mathbf{Z} = [\mathbf{z}_v]_{v \in V}$

Figure 1 shows an example: the guardian walk captures the connectivity between the nodes labeled as Student whose child nodes are labeled as Department.

4.2 Label Context Embeddings

We generate embeddings that capture the label context using the label walks. Our purpose is to verify the effectiveness of leveraging label walks for capturing higher-order class label connectivity, so we use a simple two-layer MLP to train the model to predict the context labels using the target node as input. The idea is inspired by the Skip-gram model of word2vec [13]. Extending our framework to use more advanced techniques, such as transformers, is part of future work. Specifically, the target node is represented as a one-hot node vector in the input layer, and the context labels are represented as a one-hot label vector in the output layer. The model is trained to minimize the loss between the estimated output and the ground-truth context labels, ensuring that the internal layer represents the embedding for a given input node.

Step 2 in Fig. 2 shows an overview of generating label context embeddings. Let $\mathbf{Z} \in \mathbb{R}^{n \times d'}$ be the label context embedding matrix obtained in the hidden layer for each node where d' represents the dimension of the embedding vector. The output layer

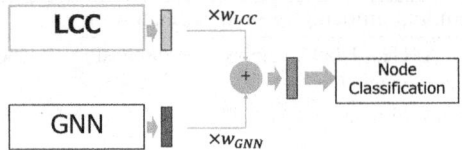

Fig. 3. Integration of LCC and any GNN. The final prediction is computed by average outputs from LCC and GNN weighted by their importance.

embedding $\hat{\ell}_v$ is obtained by multiplying the label context embedding $\mathbf{z}_v$ of the target node v by a weight matrix $\mathbf{W_{out}} \in \mathbb{R}^{d' \times C}$.

$$\hat{\ell}_v = \mathbf{z}_v^\top \mathbf{W_{out}} \tag{6}$$

Then, the cross-entropy loss $\mathcal{L}_{CE}$ is computed with respect to the one-hot vector ℓ_u of the ground-truth context label. The total loss $\mathcal{L}$ over all pairs of $\hat{\ell}_v$ of target node v and its context label ℓ_u is formulated as follows:

$$\mathcal{L} = \sum_{\ell_u \in contexts(v)} \mathcal{L}_{CE}(\hat{\ell}_v, \ell_u), \tag{7}$$

where $contexts(v)$ are context labels in the label walk starting from the target node v. Finally, the model is trained to update $\mathbf{Z}$ and $\mathbf{W_{out}}$ to minimize the loss $\mathcal{L}$. Remember that the context label is null if its corresponding node is not in the training set. We ignore the null label in the model training. In addition, when the context node is the same as the target node in a label walk, we exclude it from the loss computation to prevent information leaks. Algorithm 1 presents the details for generating label context embeddings.

4.3 Training Classifier Using Label Context Embeddings

To perform node classification, we finally train a node classifier (LCC) that predicts the class label of the target node using its label context embeddings. Since different types of label walks capture different aspects of class label connectivity, we train the MLP classifier using the concatenation of node features and all label context embeddings obtained from different types of label walks.

5 Integration of LCC and GNN

LCC captures the higher-order class label connectivity that GNNs fail to capture. Therefore, LCC complements the capability of GNNs. Since there are several GNNs designed for heterophilic graphs, such as H2GCN, LINKX, and GloGNN, we integrate LCC and one of these models and adaptively learn the importance of both LCC and GNN to achieve high accuracy. An overview of integration is illustrated in Fig. 3. Since our integration does not need additional training for both LCC and GNN, it does not require additional training costs.

Algorithm 2. Integration of LCC and any GNN

Input: Adjacency matrix $\mathbf{A}$, Feature matrix $\mathbf{X}$, Class label $\mathbf{y}$,
Trained node classification models (LCC, GNN), Temperature T
Output: Ensemble output $\mathbf{Y}^{GNN+LCC}$
1: ### Calculate model outputs ###

$$\mathbf{Y}^{LCC} = \text{LCC}(\mathbf{A}, \mathbf{X}, \mathbf{y}), \mathbf{Y}^{GNN} = \text{GNN}(\mathbf{A}, \mathbf{X}, \mathbf{y}).$$

2: ### Calculate model weights ###
3: Calculate the validation loss of each model using Eqs. 8 and 9.
4: Calculate temperature-adjusted model weights using Eqs. 10 and 11.
5: Calculate ensemble output using Eq. 12.
6: **return** $\mathbf{Y}^{GNN+LCC}$

Specifically, after independently training both LCC and GNN on the training set, we determine the importance weights of LCC and GNN using validation loss. The reason we use the validation loss is to prevent overfitting to the training data. The losses $\mathcal{L}_{LCC}$ and $\mathcal{L}_{GNN}$ of each model are calculated as the cross-entropy loss $\mathcal{L}_{CE}$ between the predictions $\hat{y}_v^{LCC}$, $\hat{y}_v^{GNN}$ and the ground-truth label y_v in the validation set.

$$\mathcal{L}_{LCC} = \sum_{v \in V_{val}} \mathcal{L}_{CE}(\hat{y}_v^{LCC}, y_v), \quad (8)$$

$$\mathcal{L}_{GNN} = \sum_{v \in V_{val}} \mathcal{L}_{CE}(\hat{y}_v^{GNN}, y_v), \quad (9)$$

Since models with lower validation loss are considered more reliable for node classification, we compute the importance weights w_{LCC} and w_{GNN} as the reciprocal of the validation loss as follows:

$$w_{LCC} = \frac{\exp\left(\frac{1}{\mathcal{L}_{LCC}} \cdot \frac{1}{T}\right)}{\exp\left(\frac{1}{\mathcal{L}_{LCC}} \cdot \frac{1}{T}\right) + \exp\left(\frac{1}{\mathcal{L}_{GNN}} \cdot \frac{1}{T}\right)}, \quad (10)$$

$$w_{GNN} = 1 - w_{LCC}, \quad (11)$$

where T is a temperature parameter to adjust the importance weights.

Finally, the prediction $\mathbf{Y}^{GNN+LCC}$ is computed by weighting the predictions $\mathbf{Y}^{LCC}$ and $\mathbf{Y}^{GNN}$ of the two models with their respective importance weights.

$$\mathbf{Y}^{GNN+LCC} = w_{LCC} \cdot \mathbf{Y}^{LCC} + w_{GNN} \cdot \mathbf{Y}^{GNN} \quad (12)$$

In this way, we can integrate LCC and any GNN without additional training and effectively complement their limitations. Algorithm 2 presents this integration algorithm.

Table 2. The statistics of datasets

dataset	#nodes	#edges	#attributes	#class	edge homophily
Cornell	183	298	1,703	5	0.131
Texas	183	325	1,703	5	0.108
Wisconsin	251	515	1,703	5	0.196
Chameleon	2,277	36,101	2,325	5	0.235
Squirrel	5,201	217,073	2,089	5	0.224
Roman-Empire	22,662	44,363	300	18	0.044
Amazon-Ratings	24,492	113,276	300	5	0.382

6 Evaluation Experiments

We evaluate our proposal, the integration of GNN and LCC (GNN+LCC), to answer the following four questions:

Q1: Does GNN+LCC contribute to improving the accuracy of existing GNN designed for heterophilous graphs?
Q2: Are label walks effective for node classification?
Q3: Which label walk types are important for node classification?
Q4: Does the length of the label walk affect performance?

Our code can be found at https://github.com/TakahashiTakutooo/GNN_LCC.

6.1 Experimental Setup

Datasets. We use seven heterophilous directed graph datasets: Cornell, Texas, Wisconsin, Chameleon, Squirrel, Roman-Empire, and Amazon-Ratings [14,15]. Cornell, Texas, and Wisconsin represent category-based connections in university web pages. Chameleon and Squirrel are networks focused on specific topics from Wikipedia. Roman-Empire represents word connections in Wikipedia articles about the Roman Empire, while Amazon-Ratings represents product connections frequently purchased together on Amazon. Table 2 shows the statistics of the datasets.

Data Splitting. We split each dataset into training, validation, and test sets using five different split methods provided by PyG[2]. For each split method, we perform node classification and compute the average accuracy. The data split ratios are as follows: For Cornell, Texas, Wisconsin, Chameleon, and Squirrel, the train/validation/test split is 48%/32%/20%. For Roman-Empire and Amazon-Ratings, the split is 50%/25%/25%.

Hyperparameters. For our proposed method, we perform a grid search using the validation set to determine the hyperparameters: label walk length, number of label walks, label context embedding dimension, and temperature parameter. The search ranges for each parameter are as follows: label walk length: {1, 2, 3}, number of label walks: {3, 5, 7}, {8, 16, 32}, temperature parameter: {0.01, 0.02, ..., 0.09, 0.1, 0.2, ..., 1.0}.

---
[2] https://github.com/pyg-team/pytorch_geometric.

Table 3. Node classification accuracy (%) on the test data. For GNN+LCC (H2GCN+LCC, LINKX+LCC, GloGNN+LCC), the accuracy differences (Δ) from the respective GNN model and LCC are also indicated. The highest accuracy for each dataset is highlighted in bold.

	Cornell	Texas	Wisconsin	Chameleon	Squirrel	Roman-Empire	Amazon-Ratings
GCN	43.24 ±4.8	56.22 ±4.6	53.33 ±4.8	62.76 ±0.50	44.36 ±2.7	47.24 ±0.84	45.92 ±0.96
GAT	46.49 ±10	53.51 ±11	48.24 ±4.4	65.22 ±2.3	42.56 ±5.9	55.34 ±1.1	44.75 ±0.97
H2GCN	74.05 ±4.3	80.54 ±7.5	80.00 ±2.8	67.46 ±2.0	55.41 ±2.0	79.09 ±0.65	45.58 ±0.13
LINKX	66.49 ±9.1	64.32 ±5.5	79.22 ±6.1	63.99 ±0.7	58.94 ±2.6	52.35 ±0.71	53.70 ±1.8
GloGNN	75.14 ±3.1	77.84 ±4.6	**85.1** ±2.3	68.2 ±1.5	58.48 ±0.78	58.24 ±0.87	49.94 ±0.44
LCC	73.51 ±5.7	77.84 ±3.1	78.43 ±5.4	56.01 ±1.6	44.36 ±1.4	81.05 ±0.44	52.17 ±0.48
H2GCN+LCC	**78.92** ±2.0	**84.32** ±3.1	83.53 ±4.7	68.25 ±1.2	55.14 ±1.0	**84.10** ±0.41	52.09 ±0.60
ΔH2GCN	+4.87	+3.78	+3.53	+0.79	−0.27	+5.01	+6.51
ΔLCC	+5.41	+6.48	+5.10	+12.24	+10.78	+3.05	−0.08
LINKX+LCC	76.76 ±6.0	77.84 ±3.9	78.82 ±3.3	66.93 ±2.0	**61.56** ±1.0	81.11 ±0.15	**57.03** ±0.28
ΔLINKX	+10.27	+13.52	−0.40	+2.94	+2.62	+28.76	+3.33
ΔLCC	+3.25	0.00	+0.39	+10.92	+17.20	+0.06	+4.86
GloGNN+LCC	76.76 ±3.2	81.62 ±4.6	**85.1** ±2.9	**69.96** ±2.1	61.31 ±1.4	80.56 ±0.3	54.42 ±0.24
ΔGloGNN	+1.62	+3.78	0.00	+1.76	+2.83	+22.32	+4.48
ΔLCC	+3.25	+3.78	+6.67	+13.95	+16.95	−0.49	+2.25

6.2 Experimental Results

Q1: Does GNN+LCC Contribute To Improving the Accuracy of Existing GNN Designed for Heterophilous Graphs? To evaluate whether LCC enhances existing GNNs for heterophilous graphs, we integrate LCC with H2GCN, LINKX, and GloGNN (denoted as H2GCN+LCC, LINKX+LCC, and GloGNN+LCC) and compare their performance. Additionally, we compare with standard GNN baselines, GCN and GAT.

Overall. Table 3 shows the experimental results. The most important observation is that the highest node classification accuracy is achieved by one of GNN+LCC for all datasets. In addition, integrating LCC and GNN actually improves accuracy compared to each model alone in most cases (see ΔH2GCN, ΔLINKX, ΔGloGNN, ΔLCC). This result confirms that 1) LCC and GNN capture different graph properties and complement each other, and 2) our integration scheme effectively learns the importance weights of both LCC and GNN.

Analysis for Exceptional Cases. We also observe that there are only four exceptional cases out of 21 cases. GNN alone achieves slightly higher accuracy than GNN+LCC in two cases, **case1**: H2GCN+LCC for the Squirrel dataset (H2GCN is 0.27 higher) and **case2**: LINKX+LCC for the Wisconsin dataset (LINKX is 0.40 higher). Also, LCC alone achieves slightly higher accuracy than GNN+LCC in two cases, **case3**: H2GCN+LCC for the Amazon-Ratings dataset (LCC is 0.08 higher) and **case4**: GloGNN+ LCC for the Roman-Empire dataset (LCC is 0.49 higher). The three cases above can be explained by investigating the importance weights between GNN and LCC: the integration does not work well when one of the model weights is extremely

Table 4. The importance weights of each model and temperature parameter in H2GCN+LCC, optimized using grid search.

	LCC weight	H2GCN weight	temperature parameter
Cornell	0.587	0.413	0.20
Texas	0.482	0.518	0.70
Wisconsin	0.632	0.368	0.30
Chameleon	0.102	0.898	0.09
Squirrel	0.084	0.916	0.08
Roman-Empire	0.502	0.498	1.00
Amazon-Ratings	0.925	0.075	0.02

Table 5. Node classification accuracy (%) on the test data for vanilla MLP and LCC. The higher accuracy for each dataset is highlighted in bold, and the accuracy difference between LCC and vanilla MLP is indicated as *gain*.

	Cornell	Texas	Wisconsin	Chameleon	Squirrel	Roman-Empire	Amazon-Ratings
MLP	$72.97_{\pm 4.5}$	$76.22_{\pm 5.7}$	$77.25_{\pm 3.6}$	$44.04_{\pm 2.7}$	$31.24_{\pm 1.3}$	$64.98_{\pm 0.23}$	$41.00_{\pm 0.41}$
LCC	$\mathbf{73.51_{\pm 5.8}}$	$\mathbf{77.84_{\pm 3.2}}$	$\mathbf{78.43_{\pm 5.4}}$	$\mathbf{56.01_{\pm 1.6}}$	$\mathbf{44.36_{\pm 1.5}}$	$\mathbf{81.05_{\pm 0.45}}$	$\mathbf{52.17_{\pm 0.48}}$
gain	+0.54	+1.62	+1.18	+11.97	+13.12	+16.07	+11.17

high. Table 4 shows the learned importance weights of LCC and H2GCN. The H2GCN weight (0.916) for the Squirrel dataset (**case1**) and the LCC weight (0.925) for the Amazon-Ratings dataset (**case3**) are extremely high. We observe the same phenomena for the LCC weight (0.881) for the Roman-Empire dataset (**case4**). This result implies that there is room for further revision of the weight control mechanism.

Importance Weights of the Two Models in Integration. Table 4 shows the importance weights and temperature parameters for H2GCN+LCC. We omit the results for LINKX+LCC and GloGNN+LCC due to space limitations. Overall, the importance weights are relatively balanced across datasets, except for the Chameleon, Squirrel, and Amazon-Ratings datasets. These results confirm the effectiveness of our weight control mechanism for the LCC and GNN integration. As examples of imbalanced weights, for the Chameleon and Squirrel datasets, H2GCN significantly outperforms LCC (see Table 3), resulting in very high H2GCN weights (0.898, 0.916, respectively). Similarly, for the Amazon-Ratings dataset, LCC significantly outperforms H2GCN, leading to a very high LCC weight (0.925).

Q2: Are Label Walks Effective for Node Classification? To verify the effectiveness of using label context embeddings, we compare the accuracy between a vanilla MLP and LCC. The MLP takes only node features as input whereas LCC additionally takes label context embeddings obtained from four different label walks.

Table 5 shows that LCC outperforms the vanilla MLP in all datasets. This result confirms that the label context embeddings successfully capture class label connec-

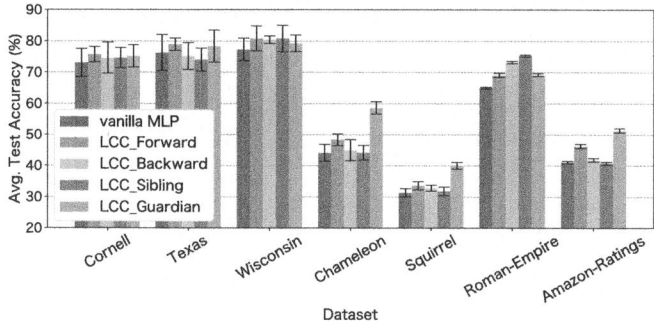

Fig. 4. Node classification accuracy of LCC variations using each label walk type.

tivity and the label walks contribute to improving the node classification accuracy. In particular, the accuracy is improved by more than 10% for the Chameleon, Squirrel, Roman-Empire, and Amazon-Ratings datasets. In particular, the accuracy improvement is significant for the Roman-Empire dataset, more than 16%, which may be due to the large number of classes and the low homophily ratio of the dataset.

Q3: Which Label Walk Types Are Important for Node Classification? To evaluate the importance of each of the four types of label walks, we compare LCC variations which concatenate node features with the label context embedding generated from a single type of label walk: LCC_Forward (using forward walks), LCC_Backward (using backward walks), LCC_Sibling (using sibling walks), and LCC_Guardian (using guardian walks). We also compare with the vanilla MLP as a baseline.

Figure 4 shows that the most important label walk varies across datasets. It is quite interesting to observe that, for the Chameleon, Squirrel, and Amazon-Ratings datasets, the guardian walks contribute the most to improving accuracy and the gain is quite significant. Since the guardian walk captures class label connectivity between guardian nodes, we conjecture that these datasets exhibit strong such connectivity. In contrast, for the Roman-Empire dataset, the sibling walks contribute the most to improving accuracy. The result confirms the significant effectiveness of using different label walks, particularly the guardian walk and sibling walk.

Q4: Does the Length of the Label Walk Affect Performance? To investigate the impact of label walk lengths, we examine the performance of LCC_Forward, LCC_Backward, LCC_Sibling, and LCC_Guardian by varying the label walk length to 1, 2, and 3.

Overall, the result in Fig. 5 indicates that the higher-order class label connectivity is crucial for improving the accuracy, as demonstrated by performance improvements when we increase the walk length for forward/backward walks (the class label connectivity order is walk length) or we use sibling/guardian walks (the class label connectivity order is 2). Also, the trends vary across datasets and the type of label walks, highlighting

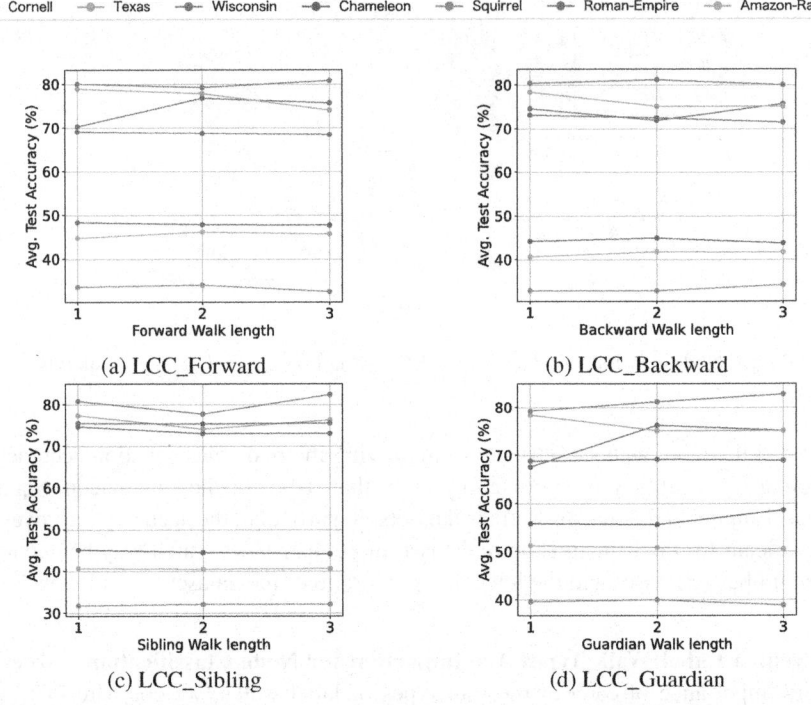

Fig. 5. Node classification accuracy (y-axis) when we change label walk length (x-axis).

the importance of tuning the label walk length as a hyperparameter using a validation set.

For forward walks in the Cornell dataset, the accuracy is significantly improved when increasing the walk length from 1 to 2 and 3, while in the Texas dataset, the accuracy is decreased significantly when the walk length is increased to 3. For backward walks in the Squirrel and Amazon-Ratings datasets, the accuracy is improved with longer walk lengths, whereas the accuracy is decreased for the Texas and Roman-Empire datasets. For sibling walks, the accuracy of Wisconsin drops significantly when increasing the walk length from 1 to 2 but improves again when the walk length is increased to 3. For guardian walks, the accuracy improves with longer walk lengths in the Cornell, Wisconsin, and Chameleon datasets.

7 Conclusion

In this paper, we focused on the fact that conventional GNNs are designed in a way that does not effectively utilize structural information between class labels. The proposed method consists of two key components: (1) the development of a node classifier, LCC, which estimates the class label of a target node based on the neighboring class labels that constitute directed label walks, and (2) the integration of LCC with GNN, enabling both models to complement each other by capturing different graph characteristics. The experiments demonstrated that the proposed method improves node classification accuracy across seven heterophilous graphs.

Acknowledgments. This work was supported by JSPS KAKENHI Grant Numbers JP20H00583 and JP25H01117 and JST ASPIRE Grant Number JPMJAP2328.

A Analysis of Sibling Walk and Guardian Walk

Figure 6 illustrates the sibling and guardian class label connectivity in the heterophilous directed graph of the Texas dataset. Figure 6 (a) shows the sibling class label connectivity. According to this, Department nodes have strong connectivity to Department nodes, while nodes of other class labels also show relatively strong connectivity to Department nodes. In contrast, Fig. 6 (b) shows the guardian class label connectivity, revealing that nodes with Student nodes, Department nodes, and Course nodes have strong connectivity to the same class label nodes. This indicates that guardian walk is crucial for the Texas dataset. Furthermore, our experimental results (Q3) corroborate the effectiveness of guardian walk on this dataset.

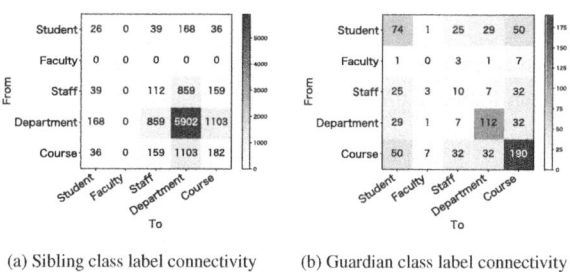

(a) Sibling class label connectivity   (b) Guardian class label connectivity

Fig. 6. The class label connectivity in the Texas dataset. (a) sibling class label connectivity from class label in y-axis to class label in x-axis. (b) guardian class label connectivity from class label in y-axis to class label in x-axis.

We also report the 1st-order connectivity and the sibling and guardian class label connectivity for other datasets, Cornell, Wisconsin, Chameleon, Squirrel, Roman-Empire, and Amazon-Ratings in the Supplementary Material.

B The Best Hyper Parameters of GNN+LCC

For our proposed method, we perform a grid search using the validation set to determine the hyperparameters: label walk length, number of label walks, label context embedding dimension, and temperature parameter. The search ranges for each parameter are as follows: label walk length: $\{1, 2, 3\}$, number of label walks: $\{3, 5, 7\}$, $\{8, 16, 32\}$, temperature parameter: $\{0.01, 0.02, \ldots, 0.09, 0.1, 0.2, \ldots, 1.0\}$. The best hyperparameters for each dataset are reported in Table 6.

Table 6. The best hyperarameters.

(a) Label Walk parameters (Forward, Backward, Sibling, Guardian) of LCC

	Forward			Backward			Sibling		Guardian	
	Len.	Num.	Dim.	Len.	Num.	Dim.	Len.	Dim.	Len.	Dim.
Cornell	3	5	8	1	3	8	1	8	3	8
Texas	1	7	8	2	7	8	2	16	1	8
Wisconsin	3	5	32	1	5	16	1	16	1	16
Chameleon	1	5	8	2	3	8	3	8	3	16
Squirrel	1	3	8	2	7	16	1	32	2	32
Roman-Empire	1	3	32	1	3	16	2	16	2	16
Amazon-Ratings	2	5	8	2	7	8	1	16	1	8

(b) Best temperature parameters for GNN + LCC models

	H2GCN + LCC	LINKX + LCC	GloGNN + LCC
Cornell	0.2	1.0	1.0
Texas	0.7	0.3	1.0
Wisconsin	0.3	1.0	1.0
Chameleon	0.09	0.05	0.1
Squirrel	0.08	0.1	0.2
Roman-Empire	1.0	0.09	0.2
Amazon-Ratings	0.02	0.2	0.1

References

1. Chen, J., Chen, S., Gao, J., Huang, Z., Zhang, J., Pu, J.: Exploiting neighbor effect: Convagnostic gnn framework for graphs with heterophily. IEEE Trans. Neural Netw. Learn. Syst. (2024)
2. Dong, Y., Chawla, N.V., Swami, A.: metapath2vec: scalable representation learning for heterogeneous networks. In: KDD (2017)
3. Duvenaud, D.K., Maclaurin, D., Iparraguirre, J., Bombarell, R., Hirzel, T., Aspuru-Guzik, A., Adams, R.P.: Convolutional networks on graphs for learning molecular fingerprints. In: NeurIPS (2015)
4. Gasteiger, J., Bojchevski, A., Günnemann, S.: Combining neural networks with personalized pagerank for classification on graphs. In: ICLR (2019)
5. Grover, A., Leskovec, J.: node2vec: scalable feature learning for networks. In: KDD (2016)
6. Hamilton, W.L., Ying, R., Leskovec, J.: Inductive representation learning on large graphs. In: NeurIPS (2017)
7. Kipf, T.N., Welling, M.: Semi-supervised classification with graph convolutional networks. In: ICLR (2017)
8. Li, X., et al.: Finding global homophily in graph neural networks when meeting heterophily. In: ICML (2022)
9. Lim, D., et al.: Large scale learning on non-homophilous graphs: new benchmarks and strong simple methods. In: NeurIPS (2021)
10. Luan, S., et al.: Revisiting heterophily for graph neural networks. In: NeurIPS (2022)

11. Maekawa, S., Noda, K., Sasaki, Y., et al.: Beyond real-world benchmark datasets: an empirical study of node classification with gnns. In: NeurIPS (2022)
12. Maekawa, S., Sasaki, Y., Onizuka, M.: A simple and scalable graph neural network for large directed graphs. arXiv preprint arXiv:2306.08274 (2023)
13. Mikolov, T., Chen, K., Corrado, G.S., Dean, J.: Efficient estimation of word representations in vector space. In: ICLR (2013)
14. Pei, H., Wei, B., Chang, K.C.C., Lei, Y., Yang, B.: Geom-gcn: geometric graph convolutional networks. In: ICLR (2020)
15. Platonov, O., Kuznedelev, D., Diskin, M., Babenko, A., Prokhorenkova, L.: A critical look at the evaluation of GNNs under heterophily: are we really making progress? In: ICLR (2023)
16. Reiser, P., et al.: Graph neural networks for materials science and chemistry. Commun. Mater. **3** (2022)
17. Sanchez-Gonzalez, A., Godwin, J., Pfaff, T., Ying, R., Leskovec, J., Battaglia, P.: Learning to simulate complex physics with graph networks. In: ICML (2020)
18. Veličković, P., Cucurull, G., Casanova, A., Romero, A., Liò, P., Bengio, Y.: Graph attention networks. In: ICLR (2018)
19. Wan, G., Du, B., Pan, S., Haffari, G.: Reinforcement learning based meta-path discovery in large-scale heterogeneous information networks. In: AAAI (2020)
20. Wang, X., et al.: Heterogeneous graph attention network. In: WWW (2019)
21. Xu, K., Li, C., Tian, Y., Sonobe, T., Kawarabayashi, K.I., Jegelka, S.: Representation learning on graphs with jumping knowledge networks. In: ICML (2018)
22. Yu, Z., Feng, B., He, D., Wang, Z., Huang, Y., Feng, Z.: LG-GNN: local-global adaptive graph neural network for modeling both homophily and heterophily. In: IJCAI (2024)
23. Zeng, H., Zhou, H., Srivastava, A., Kannan, R., Prasanna, V.: Graphsaint: graph sampling based inductive learning method. In: ICLR (2020)
24. Zhong, Z., Ivanov, S., Pang, J.: Simplifying node classification on heterophilous graphs with compatible label propagation. Trans. Mach. Learn. Res. (2022)
25. Zhou, J., et al.: Graph neural networks: a review of methods and applications. AI Open **1**, 57–81 (2020)
26. Zhu, J., et al.: Graph neural networks with heterophily. In: AAAI (2021)
27. Zhu, J., Yan, Y., Heimann, M., Zhao, L., Akoglu, L., Koutra, D.: Heterophily and graph neural networks: past, present and future. IEEE Data Eng. Bull. (2023)
28. Zhu, J., Yan, Y., Zhao, L., Heimann, M., Akoglu, L., Koutra, D.: Beyond homophily in graph neural networks: current limitations and effective designs. In: NeurIPS (2020)

A QUBO Framework for Team Formation

Karan Vombatkere[1(✉)], Theodoros Lappas[2], and Evimaria Terzi[1]

[1] Boston University, Boston, USA
{kvombat,evimaria}@bu.edu
[2] Satalia, London, UK
theodoros.lappas@satalia.com

Abstract. The team formation problem assumes a set of experts and a task, where each expert has a set of skills and the task requires some skills. The objective is to find a set of experts that maximizes coverage of the required skills while simultaneously minimizing the costs associated with the experts. Different definitions of cost have traditionally led to distinct problem formulations and algorithmic solutions. We introduce the unified TEAMFORMATION formulation that captures all cost definitions for team formation problems that balance task coverage and expert cost. Specifically, we formulate three TEAMFORMATION variants with different cost functions using quadratic unconstrained binary optimization (QUBO), and we evaluate two distinct general-purpose solution methods. We show that solutions based on the QUBO formulations of TEAMFORMATION problems are at least as good as those produced by established baselines. Furthermore, we show that QUBO-based solutions leveraging graph neural networks can effectively learn representations of experts and skills to enable transfer learning, allowing node embeddings from one problem instance to be efficiently applied to another.

Keywords: Team Formation · Quadratic Binary Optimization (QUBO) · Graph Neural Network (GNN) · Combinatorial Optimization

1 Introduction

The team formation problem is commonly defined as follows: given a set of experts, each possessing a set of skills, and a task that requires specific skills, the goal is to identify a subset of experts best suited to complete the task. A vibrant stream of literature has been dedicated to algorithmic solutions for addressing an ever-expanding universe of variants of this problem [1,2,13,16,18,24,34,35].

The fundamental requirements in most team formation problems is that the selected experts maximize the *coverage* of the required skills while minimizing their *cost*. Existing work on this problem combines these two requirements, by setting one as a constraint and the other as the objective. The cost of a team has many different definitions with each leading to a different problem formulation. Common cost functions include a linear sum of individual expert costs or a

---

Supplementary Information The online version contains supplementary material available at https://doi.org/10.1007/978-3-032-05981-9_29.

© The Author(s), under exclusive license to Springer Nature Switzerland AG 2026
R. P. Ribeiro et al. (Eds.): ECML PKDD 2025, LNAI 16014, pp. 492–510, 2026.
https://doi.org/10.1007/978-3-032-05981-9_29

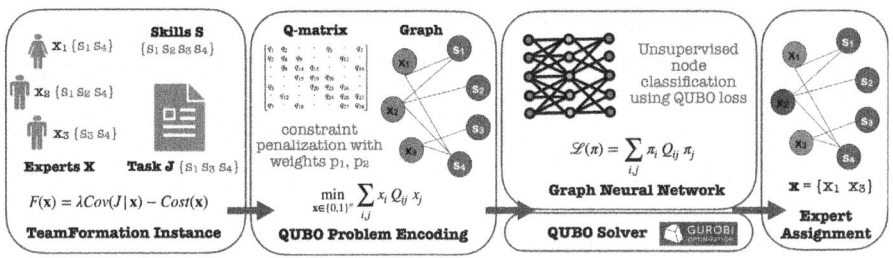

Fig. 1. High-level flowchart of our QUBO framework for TEAMFORMATION.

network-based cost that accounts for the structural connectivity of the selected experts within an underlying social graph.

Inspired by recent work [25,34], we integrate both the coverage and cost objectives aiming to find a team $\mathbf{x}$ for task J such that $\lambda Cov(J \mid \mathbf{x}) - Cost(\mathbf{x})$ is maximized. We call this general problem TEAMFORMATION. In this formulation, λ is a normalization factor that balances the two components of the objective. This formulation is general and can incorporate direct costs associated with experts or more complex cost functions, e.g., coordination costs.

In this paper, we examine three variants of the TEAMFORMATION problem resulting from different cost functions, and show that they can be expressed as quadratic unconstrained binary optimization (QUBO) problems. This perspective enables us to frame team formation as an energy minimization problem, drawing parallels with physics-based combinatorial optimization techniques.

We explore two classes of solution methods: one using QUBO solvers [12] and another leveraging graph neural networks (GNNs) [29]. QUBO solvers provide exact or near-optimal solutions. However, they operate as black-box solvers that do not provide any insight into the underlying space of experts and skills, and their computational complexity grows significantly with problem size.

Motivated by these limitations, and inspired by recent work on deep learning for combinatorial optimization problems [6,30], we introduce a GNN-based approach. This approach models the problem as an unsupervised node classification task; the classification process assigns each expert a binary decision (selected or not selected in the team) and the GNN learns to classify the experts by optimizing a QUBO-based loss function that corresponds to maximizing the TEAMFORMATION objective. Apart from learning good solutions, the embeddings learned by the GNN provide a semantic representation of the expert-skill space, where node proximity reflects relationships between skills and experts.

To the best of our knowledge, we are the first to provide a unified QUBO-based framework (see Fig. 1) for team formation, enabling a consistent algorithmic approach across different TEAMFORMATION variants. In our experimental evaluation, we utilize real-world datasets from diverse domains, including collaboration networks of artists and scientists, and online labor market data. Our results demonstrate that our general algorithms consistently find high-quality solutions, often outperforming combinatorial baselines designed specifically for certain problem variants. Furthermore, our experiments highlight the potential for transfer learning, where GNNs trained on one problem instance can be effectively used to solve related instances with minimal additional computation.

2 Related Work

Our QUBO-based formulation for the TEAMFORMATION problem applies to all variants requiring a balance between coverage and cost. In this way, our work generalizes a lot of existing work on team formation, relates to work on balancing submodular objectives with other objective functions, and extends ideas from QUBO combinatorial optimization and deep learning.

Algorithmic Team Formation. Early work in team formation focused on algorithmic methods to select experts to collectively cover *all* the skills required by a single task, while collaborating effectively within a social network [16,18]. Related work considered forming multiple teams of experts to cover the skills of multiple tasks while bounding the workload or coordination cost across experts [1,2]. Follow-up works then considered more flexible problem variations that aim to balance partial task coverage with expert cost, maximum workload, and coordination cost. These works primarily employ established algorithmic methods, such as integer programming and greedy heuristics [24,25,34,35].

More recent literature has expanded beyond such methods to leverage deep learning for various team-formation variants. For instance, deep neural networks have been used to recommend new teammates to optimally compose high-performance teams [8,28]. In another relevant example, a variational bayesian neural architecture was used to learn representations for teams whose members have collaborated in the past, enabling the selection of top-k teams of experts that collectively cover a set of skills [13].

Our TEAMFORMATION formulation generalizes several prior formulations by incorporating task coverage and a flexible cost definition into a single objective. Furthermore, our GNN-based method is distinct from the deep learning methods used in prior work.

Submodular Maximization. The coverage function is monotone and submodular, which is useful within discrete objective functions, as it encodes a natural diminishing returns property and also comes with an extensive literature on optimization techniques [9,10,17]. The greedy algorithm achieves a $1 - 1/e$ approximation for maximizing a nonnegative monotone submodular function subject to a cardinality constraint [23]. There is also work involving maximizing submodular minus modular or linear functions, where no multiplicative approximation guarantees are possible in polynomial time due to potential negativity [14,15].

The $Cov()$ function in our TEAMFORMATION objective is nonnegative monotone submodular, and depending on the definition of $Cost()$ used, variants of our general problem relate to balancing submodular and other functions. However, our solution framework is general and it does not rely on the fact that our functions have these properties.

Combinatorial Optimization and QUBO. Many NP-hard combinatorial optimization problems have been formulated as QUBO problems [11,19]. More recently, QUBO has been used as a framework for mapping discrete optimization problems to quantum and classical solvers. Methods for encoding problem constraints, such as unbalanced penalization and slack variable techniques, enable the transformation of constrained combinatorial optimization problems into QUBO [3,22,27,33].

We borrow ideas from prior work to formulate TEAMFORMATION problems as combinatorial optimization using QUBO, and use the unbalanced penalization technique [22] to make our formulation more efficient.

Deep Learning for Combinatorial Optimization. Neural combinatorial optimization has gained traction as an alternative to traditional optimization methods, and recent work in reinforcement learning has explored policy-gradient methods and graph-based architectures [4,7]. Neural networks have also been used to learn representations of discrete sets effectively, enhancing the performance of models in tasks involving set-structured data. [32,37].

GNNs have been used to augment existing solvers by identifying smaller sub-problems to reduce the search space for NP-hard problems such as Set Cover [31]. More closely related to our work, GNNs have been used to solve QUBO-formulated combinatorial optimization problems such as Maximum Independent Set and Maximum Cut, by leveraging their ability to encode graph structures and learn meaningful representations [30].

We extend ideas from the deep learning combinatorial optimization literature to design our GNN architecture to solve the TEAMFORMATION problem.

3 Technical Preliminaries

3.1 Team Formation

Experts, Tasks and Skills. Consider a set of n experts $\mathcal{X} = \{X_1, \ldots, X_n\}$, and a single task J. We assume a set of m skills S such that the task J *requires* a set of skills (i.e., $J \subseteq S$) and every expert X_i *masters* a set of skills (i.e., $X_i \subseteq S$).

Assignments. We represent an *assignment* of experts to a task J using $\mathbf{x} \in \{0,1\}^n$; $\mathbf{x}(i) = 1$ (resp. $\mathbf{x}(i) = 0$) if expert X_i is (resp. not) assigned to J.

Task Coverage. Given an assignment $\mathbf{x}$, we define the *coverage* of task J, denoted by $Cov(J \mid \mathbf{x})$, as the number of skills required by J that are covered by the experts assigned to J. That is, $Cov(J \mid \mathbf{x}) = |(\cup_{i \in \mathbf{x}} X_i) \cap J|$, with $0 \leq Cov(J \mid \mathbf{x}) \leq |J|$. We denote the *size* of $\mathbf{x}_i$, i.e., the assignment for task J_i, by $z_i = ||\mathbf{x}_i||_1$. This corresponds to the sum of 1-entries in $\mathbf{x}_i$.

Expert Costs. The cost of an assignment $\mathbf{x}$, denoted by $Cost(\mathbf{x})$, encodes the cost of hiring the experts chosen in $\mathbf{x}$. Inspired by prior related research, we consider the following established definitions of cost:

Cardinality Cost: It is often necessary to constrain the *size* of the team, such that the total number of assigned experts is less than or equal to a specified size constraint k. This can be encoded as:

$$Cost_k(\mathbf{x}) = \begin{cases} 0 & \text{if } |(\cup_{i \in \mathbf{x}} X_i)| \leq k \\ \infty & \text{otherwise.} \end{cases}$$

Linear Cost: The linear cost is based on ideas first introduced by Nikolakaki et al. [25]. In this case, each expert X_i is associated with a cost κ_i, representing the cost of hiring that expert. The total cost of an assignment $\mathbf{x}$ is the sum of costs of the individual experts in the assignment:

$$Cost_L(\mathbf{x}) = \sum_{i \in \mathbf{x}} \kappa_i.$$

Network Coordination Cost: When a set of experts is hired, then there is coordination cost among the experts. We model this by assuming that there is a graph $G = (\mathcal{X}, E)$ between the experts (nodes) and that their pairwise coordination costs are encoded in the weights of the edges between them. We thus assume that $d(X_i, X_j) : E \to \mathbb{R}_{\geq 0}$ encodes the coordination cost between two experts. The relevant literature has suggested multiple definitions of coordination cost based on such underlying graphs [2,18,34]. Inspired by prior work, we define the total coordination cost of an assignment $\mathbf{x}$ as the sum of pairwise costs of experts in the assignment:

$$Cost_G(\mathbf{x}) = \sum_{(i \in \mathbf{x}, j \in \mathbf{x})} d(X_i, X_j).$$

3.2 Quadratic Unconstrained Binary Optimization

Quadratic unconstrained binary optimization (QUBO) is a mathematical optimization framework used to model combinatorial problems where variables take binary values. For a vector $\mathbf{x} = (x_1, x_2, \ldots, x_n)$ of binary decision variables ($x_i \in \{0, 1\}$), the objective function is represented as a quadratic expression of these binary variables:

$$\min_{\mathbf{x} \in \{0,1\}^n} \mathbf{x}^T Q \mathbf{x} = \min_{\mathbf{x} \in \{0,1\}^n} \sum_{i,j} x_i Q_{ij} x_j, \qquad (1)$$

where Q (i.e. the Q-matrix) is an $n \times n$ symmetric matrix, with entries Q_{ij}. The Q-matrix encodes problem-specific interactions between variables. QUBO is an NP-hard optimization problem [21].

Solvers. Classical solvers, such as Gurobi's QUBO optimizer and CPLEX, use mixed-integer programming (MIP), branch-and-bound, and specialized heuristic methods to find optimal or near-optimal solutions to QUBO problems [12].

Linear Programs as QUBO. A linear program (LP) with binary variables $\mathbf{x}$ can be represented as QUBO by reformulating equality constraints using quadratic penalty terms [11,27]. Consider an LP of the form $\min \mathbf{c}^T\mathbf{x}$ subject to equality constraints $A\mathbf{x} = \mathbf{b}$, where $\mathbf{x}$ is any length-n binary vector, A is a $(m \times n)$ matrix and $\mathbf{b}$ is a length-m vector. Denoting $C = \text{diag}(\mathbf{c})$, and for an appropriate scalar penalty p we have the following equivalence:

$$\min_{\mathbf{x}} \mathbf{c}^T\mathbf{x} \text{ (s.t. } A\mathbf{x} = \mathbf{b}) = \min_{\mathbf{x}} \mathbf{x}^T C \mathbf{x} + p(A\mathbf{x} - \mathbf{b})^T(A\mathbf{x} - \mathbf{b})$$
$$= \min_{\mathbf{x}} \mathbf{x}^T Q \mathbf{x} + p\mathbf{b}^T\mathbf{b}.$$

The optimal solution to the LP $\min_{\mathbf{x}} \mathbf{c}^T\mathbf{x}$ subject to $A\mathbf{x} = \mathbf{b}$ corresponds to the optimal solution to $\min_{\mathbf{x}} \mathbf{x}^T Q\mathbf{x}$, where $Q = C + p(A^T A) - 2p\,\text{diag}(A^T\mathbf{b})$ is the Q-matrix of the QUBO encoding, and we dropped the additive constant $p\mathbf{b}^T\mathbf{b}$.

Unbalanced Penalization. To transform an LP with inequality constraints, typically slack variables are introduced as follows: given a constraint $\sum_i a_{ij} x_i \le b_j$, where $a_i, b_j \in \mathbb{Z}$ for every $j = \{1, \ldots, m\}$, a non-negative slack variable encoded as a sum of binary variables $\hat{s} = \sum_k 2^k s_k$ (where $s_k \in \{0,1\}$), is added so the constraint becomes $\sum_i a_i x_i + \hat{s} = b_j$. The reformulated equality is then enforced in the objective function using a quadratic penalty term $p(\sum_i a_i x_i + \sum_k 2^k s_k - b_j)^2$, where p is a sufficiently large penalty coefficient.

The primary drawback of slack variables is the increase in dimensionality of the LP – and the size of the Q-matrix – by $\log \lceil b_j - \sum_i a_i x_i \rceil$ for each inequality constraint. Consequently, for the problems in this paper, we eliminate the need for slack variables by incorporating unbalanced penalization [22]. This technique encodes an asymmetric penalty function (directly into the QUBO objective) which is small when a constraint is satisfied and increases significantly when violated, without increasing the problem's dimensionality.

We provide all mathematical details to use unbalanced penalization to formulate team formation LPs into QUBO in Sect. 4.

4 QUBO Framework for Team Formation

In this section we introduce the general TEAMFORMATION problem, and detail three variants, which we then formulate using QUBO.

4.1 The TEAMFORMATION Problem

Given a set of experts $\mathcal{X}$, and a task J, we define the general TEAMFORMATION problem as follows: find an assignment $\mathbf{x}$ that *maximizes* the objective

$$F(\mathbf{x}) = \lambda Cov(J \mid \mathbf{x}) - Cost(\mathbf{x}). \tag{2}$$

The above function balances the coverage of task J achieved by a specific team with the cost of the team. Parameter λ is application dependent and can be used to tune the importance of the two components of the objective.

We now define three instantiations of the TEAMFORMATION problem, which have different cost functions. We express each of these problems using constrained linear programming and apply the unbalanced penalization technique (see Sect. 3.2) to construct the corresponding Q-matrix.

Throughout this section we use the vector $\mathbf{y} = \mathbf{s} \parallel \mathbf{x}$ which represents the solution to our problems. We call $\mathbf{y}$ the *solution vector*. This vector is of size $(m + n)$ and is the concatenation of $\mathbf{s}$ and $\mathbf{x}$, where $\mathbf{s}$ is a binary vector that encodes whether a skill i is covered (resp. not covered) by $\mathbf{s}$ when $s_i = 1$ (resp. $s_i = 0$). We also use the $(n \times m)$ skill-membership matrix E such that $E(i, j) = 1$ (resp. 0) if expert i has (resp. not) skill j.

Due to space constraints, we omit several mathematical details and refer the reader to the supplementary material for derivations of the QUBO formulations.

4.2 MAX-K-COVER

*Problem 1 (*MAX-K-COVER*).* Given a set of n experts $\mathcal{X} = \{X_1, \ldots, X_n\}$, a task J, and a cardinality constraint k, find an assignment $\mathbf{x}$ of experts such that the following is maximized:

$$F(\mathbf{x}) = \lambda Cov(J \mid \mathbf{x}) - Cost_k(\mathbf{x}). \tag{3}$$

QUBO Formulation Sketch. Let $\mathbf{y} = \mathbf{s} \parallel \mathbf{x}$, be the $(m + n)$-size solution vector we described above. Now let $\mathbf{c}$ be another $(m+n)$ vector such that $c_i = \lambda$ if $i \leq m$ *and* skill $i \in J$, and $c_i = 0$ otherwise. Then, the MAX-K-COVER problem can be expressed by the following linear program:

$$\text{maximize } \mathbf{c}^T \mathbf{y},$$
$$\text{such that } \sum_{i=1}^{n} x_i \leq k$$
$$s_j - \sum_{i=1}^{n} E(i,j) \cdot x_i \leq 0 \quad \text{for all } 1 \leq j \leq m, \text{ and}$$
$$s_i, x_i \in \{0, 1\}.$$

We derive penalty matrices P_k and P_C corresponding to the LP constraints. Then the $(m+n) \times (m+n)$ square matrix $Q = -\text{diag}(\mathbf{c}) - P_k + P_C$ provides a QUBO formulation of MAX-K-COVER, where minimizing $\mathbf{y}^T Q \mathbf{y}$ corresponds to maximizing $F(\mathbf{x}) = \lambda Cov(J \mid \mathbf{x}) - Cost_k(\mathbf{x})$.

4.3 COVERAGE-LINEAR-COST

*Problem 2 (*COVERAGE-LINEAR-COST*).* Given a set of n experts $\mathcal{X} = \{X_1, \ldots, X_n\}$ with their corresponding individual costs $\{\kappa_1, \ldots, \kappa_n\}$, and a task J, find an assignment $\mathbf{x}$ of experts such that the following is maximized:

$$F(\mathbf{x}) = \lambda Cov(J \mid \mathbf{x}) - Cost_L(\mathbf{x}). \tag{4}$$

QUBO Formulation Sketch. Let $\mathbf{y} = \mathbf{s} \parallel \mathbf{x}$, be the $(m + n)$-size solution vector we described above. Now let $\mathbf{c}$ be another $(m+n)$ vector such that $c_i = \lambda$ if $i \leq m$ and skill $i \in J$, $c_i = -\kappa_{i-m}$ if $i > m$; recall that κ_i is the cost of hiring expert i (see Sect. 3). Then COVERAGE-LINEAR-COST can be expressed as:

$$\text{maximize } \mathbf{c}^T \mathbf{y},$$
$$\text{such that } s_j - \sum_{i=1}^{n} E(i,j) \cdot x_i \leq 0 \quad \text{for all } 1 \leq j \leq m, \text{ and}$$
$$s_i, x_i \in \{0, 1\}.$$

We create penalty matrices P_1 and P_2 to capture the constraints in the LP. Then, the $(m+n) \times (m+n)$ square matrix $Q = -\text{diag}(\mathbf{c}) - P_1 + P_2$ has the property that minimizing $\mathbf{y}^T Q \mathbf{y}$ corresponds to maximizing $F(\mathbf{x}) = \lambda Cov(J \mid \mathbf{x}) - Cost_L(\mathbf{x})$.

4.4 COVERAGE-GRAPH-COST

*Problem 3 (*COVERAGE-GRAPH-COST*).* Given a set of n experts $\mathcal{X} = \{X_1, \ldots, X_n\}$ with a corresponding distance function $d(\cdot, \cdot)$ between any pair of experts, and a task J, find an assignment $\mathbf{x}$ of experts such that we maximize:

$$F(\mathbf{x}) = \lambda Cov(J \mid \mathbf{x}) - Cost_G(\mathbf{x}). \tag{5}$$

QUBO Formulation Sketch. We consider the following constrained linear program that encodes the COVERAGE-GRAPH-COST problem:

$$\text{maximize } \lambda \cdot \sum_{i=1}^{n} s_i - \sum_{(i,j)} d(i,j) \cdot (x_i x_j)$$
$$\text{such that } s_j - \sum_{i=1}^{n} E(i,j) \cdot x_i \leq 0 \quad \text{for all } 1 \leq j \leq m, \text{ and}$$
$$s_i, x_i \in \{0, 1\}.$$

For the QUBO formulation we need the solution vector $\mathbf{y}$, we defined above. We also need the $(m+n)$ vector $\mathbf{c} = (c_1, \ldots, c_{(m+n)})$, such that $c_i = \lambda$ if $i \leq m$ and skill $i \in J$, and $c_i = 0$ otherwise. Then we compute the $(n \times n)$ matrix D of pairwise distances such that $D(i,j) = d(X_i, X_j)$ and add it to the lower-right $(n \times n)$ submatrix of $\text{diag}(\mathbf{c})$ to obtain $\hat{D} = \text{diag}(\mathbf{c}) + \begin{bmatrix} \mathbf{0}_{m \times m} & \mathbf{0}_{m \times n} \\ \mathbf{0}_{n \times m} & D_{n \times n} \end{bmatrix}$.
Now, $F(\mathbf{x}) = \mathbf{y}^T \hat{D} \mathbf{y}$ encodes the COVERAGE-GRAPH-COST objective. We create penalty matrices P_1, P_2 to capture the LP constraints; the $(m + n) \times (m + n)$ square matrix $Q = -\hat{D} - P_1 + P_2$ provides a complete QUBO formulation of COVERAGE-GRAPH-COST; that is, minimizing $\mathbf{y}^T Q \mathbf{y}$ corresponds to maximizing $F(\mathbf{x}) = \lambda Cov(J \mid \mathbf{x}) - Cost_G(\mathbf{x})$.

All three TEAMFORMATION problem variants are hard to solve and approximation and heuristic algorithms exist in the literature [14,17,25].

5 Solving TEAMFORMATION Problems

In this section, we describe two different general-purpose methods that leverage the QUBO formulation to solve TEAMFORMATION problems.

5.1 QUBO Solver

We use a QUBO solver implemented by Gurobi [12]. The solver takes the Q-matrix corresponding to a QUBO problem as input, and applies mixed-integer programming methods with specialized heuristics to solve the QUBO instance. We use Gurobi's QUBO solver with the Q-matrix corresponding to the TEAMFORMATION problems, and refer to this method as `Qsolver`.

5.2 Graph Neural Networks

Combinatorial optimization problems are formulated as QUBO [30] and represented as a graph $G = (V, E)$, where each vertex $i \in V$ corresponds to a binary decision variable $y_i \in \{0, 1\}$. The objective function is defined by a Hamiltonian $\mathbb{H}(\mathbf{y})$, which represents the system's energy. The binary state y_i is relaxed into a continuous representation $\pi_i \in [0, 1]$, allowing gradient-based optimization to be applied. The architecture employs multiple layers of message-passing neural networks to iteratively update node representations. At each layer l, the hidden state $\pi_i^{(l)}$ of node i is updated based on its current state and information aggregated from its neighboring nodes $\mathcal{N}(i)$: $\pi_i^{(l+1)} = \sigma \left(W^{(l)} \pi_i^{(l)} + \sum_{j \in \mathcal{N}(i)} W^{(l)} \pi_j^{(l)} + \mathbf{w_0}^{(l)} \right)$ where $W^{(l)}$ and $\mathbf{w_0}^{(l)}$ are the weight matrix and bias vector for layer l, and σ is a nonlinear activation function. The loss function is based on the relaxed Hamiltonian $\mathbb{H}(\pi)$, such that the network is trained to minimize the energy. After training, the continuous node states π_i are projected back to binary y_i, yielding a feasible solution to the original combinatorial optimization problem.

GNNs for TeamFormation. We perform unsupervised node classification using a GNN to solve the QUBO formulation corresponding to TEAMFORMATION. Given the Q matrix that encodes a problem, the goal is to find the $(m+n)$-size solution vector $\mathbf{y} = \mathbf{s} || \mathbf{x}$ that minimizes $\mathbf{y}^T Q \mathbf{y}$, with $\mathbf{x} = (y_{m+1}, \ldots, y_{m+n})$ being the desired solution assignment to the TEAMFORMATION problem.

Graph Creation. We create a graph $G = (V, E)$, where each vertex $i \in V$ corresponds to a binary decision variable $y_i \in \{0, 1\}$; vertices $(1, \ldots, m)$ correspond to the set of all skills, and vertices $(m+1, \ldots, m+n)$ correspond to the experts in the TEAMFORMATION problem instance. For every skill each expert has, we create an unweighted edge in G between the corresponding expert and skill vertices, i.e. $E = \{(i, j) : s_i \in X_j\}$. For COVERAGE-GRAPH-COST, we add weighted edges between expert vertices to encode the pairwise network coordination costs.

Loss Function and Regularization. Since $\mathbf{y}^T Q \mathbf{y}$ is not differentiable and cannot be used as such within the GNN training process, we follow the approach of Schuetz et al. [30] to relax each binary variable $y_i \in \{0,1\}$ such that $y_i \to \pi_i \in [0,1]$, where these π_i can be viewed as selection probabilities, i.e. small π_i implies y_i is not selected, and large π_i implies y_i is selected. We then generate the following differentiable loss function used for backpropagation:

$$\mathcal{L}(\pi) = \sum_{i,j} \pi_i \, Q_{ij} \, \pi_j + \alpha \cdot \sum_i \pi_i \, (1 - \pi_i).$$

We include the regularization term $\alpha \cdot \sum_i \pi_i \, (1 - \pi_i)$ to encourage the GNN to converge to binary solutions, where α is a tunable hyperparameter.

We randomly initialize node embeddings for each of the expert and skill nodes, where the dimension of the embeddings is given by the hyperparameter d_0. We denote the set of $(m+n)$ embeddings by $H^{(0)} = H_S^{(0)} \parallel H_X^{(0)}$, where $\parallel$ represents concatenation of the m skill embeddings and n expert embeddings.

Graph Convolution. Vertices in G represent skills *and* experts, and thus we have two different types of edges: between experts and skills, and between two experts. To ensure message-passing during GNN training occurs over valid edge types, we adopt a two-layer (heterogeneous) graph convolution network (GCN) architecture, with forward propagation given by $H^{(1)} = \sigma_1 \left(\sum_{r \in \mathcal{R}} \Theta_r^0 H^{(0)} \right)$ and $H^{(2)} = \sigma_2 \left(\sum_{r \in \mathcal{R}} \Theta_r^1 H^{(1)} \right)$, where $\mathcal{R}$ is the set of different edge types. $H^{(0)}$ represents the input node embeddings of size d_0, and $H^{(1)}$ and $H^{(2)}$ are the hidden and output layer representations of sizes d_h and $(m+n)$, respectively. Θ_r^0 and Θ_r^1 are trainable weight matrices specific to r, allowing the GNN to learn different transformations per edge type; σ_1, σ_2 are non-linear activation functions, applied element-wise; we use ReLU for σ_1 and a sigmoid for σ_2.

We add batch normalization after the first graph convolutional layer to normalize activations and stabilize training. We also introduce dropout after the ReLU activation by randomly setting p_d fraction of neurons in the GNN to zero.

We call our method QUBO-GNN and visualize the model architecture in Fig. 2. QUBO-GNN is parametrized by several hyperparameters; Table 1 provides a summary of the hyperparameters of the QUBO-GNN model, and heuristic ranges of values to grid-search. The model hyperparameters d_0, d_h, p_d, α and β can be set heuristically or optimized in an outer-loop using grid-search.

Capturing problem constraints effectively in a QUBO formulation requires the selection of suitable scalar penalties p_1, p_2. In practice, we observed for our problems that the unbalanced penalization scheme yields good solutions for a wide range of values of p_1, p_2. However, to enable convergence to better near-optimal solutions we implement a grid search for p_1, p_2 over the range of heuristic values shown in Table 1.

Projection Rounding and Output. At the end of unsupervised training, the σ_2 sigmoid activation layer outputs probabilities π_i associated with each node which we can view as soft assignments. We apply a simple rounding scheme: $y_i = \text{int}(\pi_i)$ to project these probabilities π_i back to binary assignments $y_i \in \{0,1\}$.

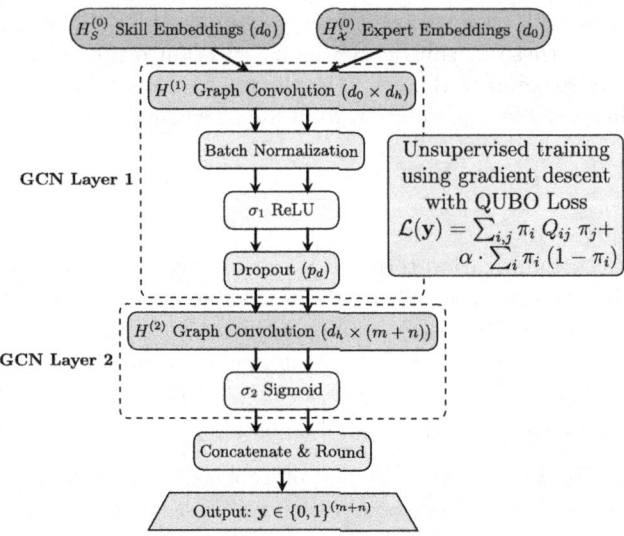

Fig. 2. QUBO-GNN model architecture for solving TEAMFORMATION problems.

Table 1. Description of QUBO-GNN model parameters.

Parameter	Description	Heuristic range
p_1	QUBO penalty 1	$[10^{-1}, 10^2]$
p_2	QUBO penalty 2	$[10^{-1}, 10^2]$
λ	Normalizing coefficient	$[1, 10^2]$
d_0	Size of node embeddings	$[(m+n)^{1/2}, (m+n)/2]$
d_h	Size of hidden layer	$[(m+n)^{1/2}, (m+n)/2]$
p_d	Dropout probability	$[0.1, 0.3]$
α	Binary regularization weight	$[1, 10]$
β	Learning rate	$[10^{-4}, 10^{-2}]$

6 Experimental Analysis

6.1 Experimental Setup

Datasets. We evaluate our methods on several real-world datasets also used in past team formation papers: *Freelancer, IMDB, Bbsm* [1,24,25,35]. We follow the method of [2] and create social graphs with expert coordination costs for our datasets. We provide summary statistics of the datasets in Table 2. Detailed descriptions and pre-processing steps of each dataset are available in the supplementary material.

Baselines. For each of the TEAMFORMATION variants, we evaluate the performance of QUBO-GNN and Qsolver against some problem-specific baselines, which have the same principles across problem variants. We describe those below.

Greedy: For MAX-K-COVER the Greedy baseline iteratively picks the expert with the maximum marginal skill coverage. For COVERAGE-LINEAR-COST, Greedy implements the Cost-Scaled Greedy algorithm introduced by Nikolakaki et al. [25]. For the COVERAGE-GRAPH-COST problem, Greedy picks the expert that maximizes the ratio of coverage over coordination cost at each iteration.

Topk: This is an objective-agnostic algorithm that ranks the experts based on their Jaccard similarity with the input task and then picks the top-k most similar experts, where k is determined by the size of the Greedy (or Qsolver) solution.

Implementation Details. We used single-process implementations on a 14-core 2.4 GHz Intel Xeon E5-2680 processor for all our experiments. We implement our QUBO-GNN architecture in Python using PyTorch [26] and Deep Graph Library [36], and fine-tune model hyperparameters using grid search. For each dataset, we train separate QUBO-GNN models for up to 100 different tasks. For the normalizing coefficient we set $\lambda = 50$, which yields a reasonable balance between weighting coverage and cost for our TEAMFORMATION variants. To aid reproducibility, we report the full set of model parameters used in the supplement, and make our code[1] available online.

6.2 Quantitative Comparison

We evaluate our algorithms against the baselines with respect to our overall objective (and the corresponding coverage, size and cost). Due to space constraints, we only show detailed results for COVERAGE-LINEAR-COST, and provide experimental results for MAX-K-COVER and COVERAGE-GRAPH-COST in the supplement. Note that the general experimental patterns observed were similar across all three TEAMFORMATION variants.

Table 2. Summary statistics of our datasets.

Dataset	Experts	Tasks	Skills	Skills/expert	Skills/task	Average path length	Average degree
Freelancer-1	50	250	50	2.2	4.3	2.6	4.5
Freelancer-2	150	250	50	2.2	4.4	2.4	10.4
IMDB-1	200	300	23	3.3	5.0	3.0	0.4
IMDB-2	400	300	23	3.8	5.3	7.1	0.9
IMDB-3	1000	300	25	4.5	5.2	6.2	2.3
Bbsm-1	250	300	75	12.5	5.5	5.9	1.9
Bbsm-2	500	300	75	13.0	5.5	2.6	9.4
Bbsm-3	1000	300	75	13.1	5.5	2.6	13.3

---

[1] https://github.com/kvombatkere/Team-Formation-QUBO.

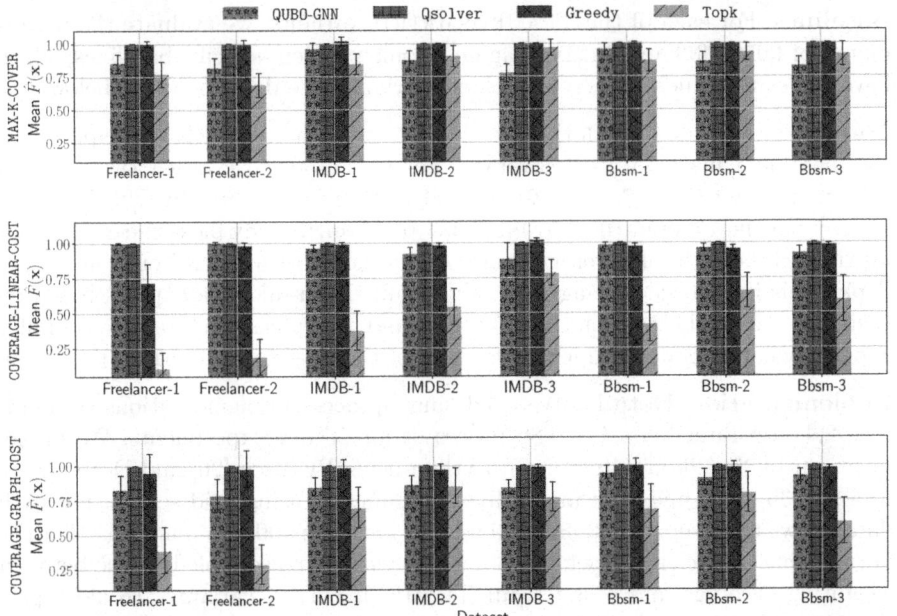

Fig. 3. Bar plots showing the mean Qsolver-normalized objective, $\hat{F}(\mathbf{x})$ of QUBO-GNN, Qsolver, Greedy and Topk, across all training task instances for all three TEAMFORMATION variants.

We observe that Qsolver has the best performance for all datasets, and consequently analyze the objective of our methods by first normalizing by the corresponding Qsolver objective and then taking the mean across all training tasks. We denote the normalized objective by $\hat{F}(\mathbf{x})$.

Aggregate Performance Evaluation. Figure 3 presents the mean $\hat{F}(\mathbf{x})$ across all training tasks returned by QUBO-GNN, Qsolver, Greedy, and Topk across our datasets. We observe that Qsolver consistently achieves the highest normalized mean objective values (i.e., values equal to 1): it outperforms the other methods across all datasets for all three TEAMFORMATION variants. We observe that Greedy performs slightly worse than Qsolver, and Topk consistently has the lowest $\hat{F}(\mathbf{x})$. For most datasets, QUBO-GNN achieves solutions with objective values that are comparable (but slightly worse) than Qsolver. Overall, this is expected as Qsolver finds the optimal solution for the same problem that QUBO-GNN tries to solve. Moreover, the success of both QUBO-based algorithmic solutions demonstrate that our QUBO formulation is appropriate for solving the original team formation problem.

We use $\overline{Cov} = \frac{1}{t}\sum_{i=1}^{t} Cov(J_i|\mathbf{x})$ to denote the mean coverage, and $\overline{z} = \frac{1}{t}\sum_{i=1}^{t} z_i$ to denote the mean solution size, across training tasks $J_1, \ldots, J_t$. We observe from Table 3 that all three methods find solutions yielding high coverages for *IMDB* and *Bbsm*. However, QUBO-GNN and Qsolver often find assignments

Table 3. Mean task coverage, $\overline{Cov}$ and solution size, $\overline{z}$ of QUBO-GNN, Qsolver and Greedy across all training task instances for COVERAGE-LINEAR-COST.

Dataset	Mean Task Coverage, $\overline{Cov}$			Mean Solution Size, $\overline{z}$		
	QUBO-GNN	Qsolver	Greedy	QUBO-GNN	Qsolver	Greedy
Freelancer-1	0.88	0.89	0.48	2.8	2.9	1.4
Freelancer-2	0.98	0.98	0.92	3.2	3.2	2.9
IMDB-1	0.99	1.00	0.99	2.3	2.4	2.1
IMDB-2	0.98	1.00	1.00	2.5	2.3	1.8
IMDB-3	0.88	1.00	1.00	2.5	3.2	1.2
Bbsm-1	1.00	1.00	1.00	3.1	2.7	2.0
Bbsm-2	0.97	1.00	1.00	2.8	2.6	1.6
Bbsm-3	0.98	1.00	1.00	1.8	4.2	1.7

with a larger solution size (and larger cost) than Greedy. These assignments – particularly for *Freelancer* – lead to higher coverages resulting in superior objective values. This tradeoff highlights the ability of the QUBO formulation to balance cost and team effectiveness better than greedy approaches. Finally, even though Greedy was the fastest algorithm in terms of running time, QUBO-GNN and Qsolver converged to good solutions within a few seconds, even for the largest datasets (i.e. *IMDB-3* and *Bbsm-3*).

Individual Task Evaluation. Figure 4 presents a scatter plot of the objectives F for each training task instance (for each dataset) for COVERAGE-LINEAR-COST; the tasks are sorted in decreasing order of F. We conclude that QUBO-GNN is competitive with Greedy and even outperforms it in multiple cases, demonstrating that GNN-based approaches can achieve strong performance even without explicit heuristic tuning. Furthermore, for the *Freelancer-1* dataset, both QUBO-GNN and Qsolver outperform Greedy by over 30%. In our experiments, QUBO-GNN consistently selects experts based on their skill relevance and almost never violates the constraints of the underlying LPs; thus QUBO-GNN can identify well-balanced teams without the need for additional filtering mechanisms.

Investigating Node Embeddings. Figure 5 shows two scatter plots of skill and expert node embeddings projected to 2D using t-SNE [20]. Each set of embeddings was generated by a QUBO-GNN model for COVERAGE-LINEAR-COST after training on a task from *Freelancer-1*. This figure is representative of the patterns observed in node embeddings for all instances of TEAMFORMATION. We observe that the embeddings corresponding to task skills and relevant experts (i.e. experts who have at least one required skill) differentiate themselves from other skills/experts by forming an outer perimeter and occupying distinct regions of the plot. Experts with similar skills often cluster together, and their embeddings are often similar to those of their common skill(s). This

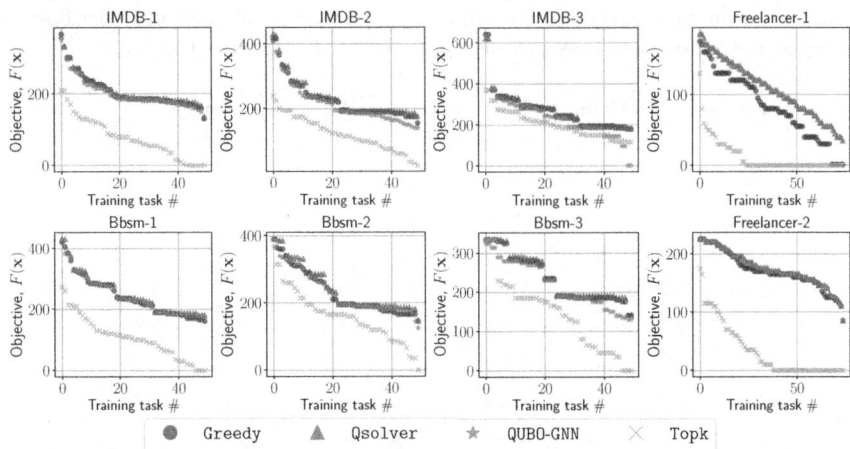

Fig. 4. Comparative performance of QUBO-GNN, Qsolver, Greedy and Topk, across individual training tasks, in terms of the sorted objective $F()$.

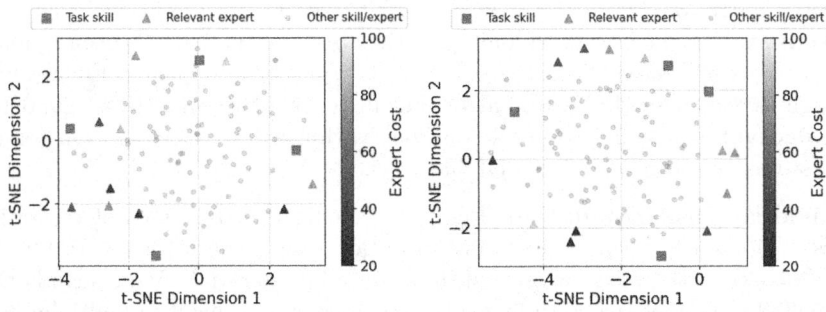

Fig. 5. Scatter plots of skill and expert node embeddings projected to 2D using t-SNE. Each set of embeddings was generated by a COVERAGE-LINEAR-COST QUBO-GNN model after training on a task from *Freelancer-1*.

indicates that QUBO-GNN successfully learns representations between skills and experts and is able to correctly identify sets of experts that are important for covering a task.

6.3 Transfer Learning

Intuitively, we expect a QUBO-GNN model $\mathcal{M}$ to learn node embeddings that result in good assignments for new tasks that are similar to the tasks $\mathcal{M}$ was trained on. Consider t QUBO-GNN models that have been trained on their corresponding tasks $J_1, \ldots, J_t$. Given an unseen task J', we first compute the Jaccard similarity of J' with each of $J_1, \ldots, J_t$, and select the QUBO-GNN model $\mathcal{M}'$ corresponding to the task that is most similar to J'. Next, we initialize the new TEAMFORMATION instance for J' with the pre-trained node embeddings corresponding to $\mathcal{M}'$, and

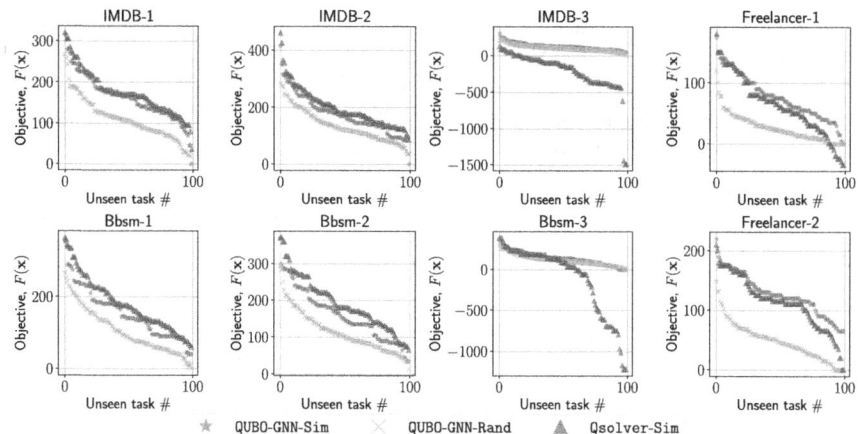

Fig. 6. Evaluation of transfer learning on 100 new tasks across each dataset for COVERAGE-LINEAR-COST in terms of the sorted objective $F()$.

use model $\mathcal{M}'$ to perform a single forward pass to obtain an assignment $\mathbf{x}$ for J'. We refer to this method QUBO-GNN-Sim. For each dataset, we evaluate it against the following two baselines on 100 new tasks.

QUBO-GNN-Rand: We use a random sample of 3 pre-trained QUBO-GNN models. We perform a single forward pass using each model and select the assignment $\mathbf{x}$ that yields the best objective.

Qsolver-Sim: Given a new task J', we use the solution of Qsolver corresponding to the task (from $J_1, \ldots, J_t$) that has the highest Jaccard similarity to J' to compute the objective for J'.

Figure 6 shows a scatter plot of sorted objectives F of QUBO-GNN-Sim and the two baselines for 100 new tasks across each dataset for COVERAGE-LINEAR-COST. The results for the other two problems are shown in the supplement.

We note that QUBO-GNN-Sim outperforms Qsolver-Sim for *Freelancer* and *IMDB-3* and *Bbsm-3*, while the two methods have comparable performance for *IMDB-1*, *IMDB-2*, *Bbsm-1* and *Bbsm-2*. QUBO-GNN-Rand has poor overall performance. This was expected, since using node embeddings of a random task would not necessarily aid solving of a new problem. QUBO-GNN-Sim often finds solutions with high coverages, indicating that the learned node embeddings from the original model can capture useful relationships between skills and experts that can then be leveraged for other tasks. We also find, intuitively, that the efficacy of using node embeddings from a QUBO-GNN model (trained on task J_i) for a new task J_j, correlates strongly with the Jaccard similarity of J_i and J_j.

7 Conclusions and Future Work

In this paper, we introduced a unified QUBO-based framework for the general TEAMFORMATION problem, enabling a versatile algorithmic approach across problem variants that balance task coverage with expert costs. We then evaluated our framework using both a QUBO solver, and a GNN method that maximizes the TEAMFORMATION objective by optimizing a QUBO-derived loss function. In our experimental evaluation on real-world datasets from diverse domains, we demonstrated that our methods consistently find expert assignments with high objectives, often outperforming combinatorial baselines designed specifically for certain problem variants. Finally, we highlighted the potential for transfer learning, where learned representations from one problem instance can be effectively used to solve other related instances.

Future Work. Finding optimal penalty parameters for our QUBO formulations is challenging, consequently opening up an avenue for future work on efficient methods to tune these penalties. A natural extension of our work could consider multiple input tasks and explore more (complex) expert cost functions based on workload, team diameter, etc. Finally, there is scope for fine-tuning the QUBO-GNN model architecture to improve performance.

Acknowledgment. This work was supported by gifts from Microsoft and Google.

References

1. Anagnostopoulos, A., Becchetti, L., Castillo, C., Gionis, A., Leonardi, S.: Power in unity: forming teams in large-scale community systems. In: ACM Conference on Information and Knowledge Management, CIKM, pp. 599–608 (2010)
2. Anagnostopoulos, A., Becchetti, L., Castillo, C., Gionis, A., Leonardi, S.: Online team formation in social networks. In: Proceedings of the 21st International Conference on World Wide Web, pp. 839–848 (2012)
3. Ayodele, M.: Penalty weights in QUBO formulations: permutation problems. In: Pérez Cáceres, L., Verel, S. (eds.) EvoCOP 2022. LNCS, vol. 13222, pp. 159–174. Springer, Cham (2022). https://doi.org/10.1007/978-3-031-04148-8_11
4. Bello, I., Pham, H., Le, Q.V., Norouzi, M., Bengio, S.: Neural combinatorial optimization with reinforcement learning. arXiv preprint arXiv:1611.09940 (2016)
5. Benz, D., et al.: The social bookmark and publication management system BibSonomy. VLDB J. **19**(6), 849–875 (2010)
6. Cappart, Q., Chételat, D., Khalil, E.B., Lodi, A., Morris, C., Veličković, P.: Combinatorial optimization and reasoning with graph neural networks. J. Mach. Learn. Res. **24**(130), 1–61 (2023)
7. Caramanis, C., Fotakis, D., Kalavasis, A., Kontonis, V., Tzamos, C.: Optimizing solution-samplers for combinatorial problems: the landscape of policy-gradient methods. arXiv preprint arXiv:2310.05309 (2023)
8. Dashti, A., Samet, S., Fani, H.: Effective neural team formation via negative samples. In: Proceedings of the 31st ACM International Conference on Information & Knowledge Management, pp. 3908–3912 (2022)
9. Feige, U., Mirrokni, V.S., Vondrák, J.: Maximizing non-monotone submodular functions. SIAM J. Comput. **40**(4), 1133–1153 (2011)
10. Feldman, M.: Guess free maximization of submodular and linear sums. Algorithmica **83**(3), 853–878 (2021)

11. Glover, F., Kochenberger, G., Du, Y.: Quantum bridge analytics i: a tutorial on formulating and using QUBO models. 4or **17**(4), 335–371 (2019)
12. Gurobi Optimization, LLC: Gurobi OptiMods (2023). https://github.com/Gurobi/gurobi-optimods
13. Hamidi Rad, R., Fani, H., Bagheri, E., Kargar, M., Srivastava, D., Szlichta, J.: A variational neural architecture for skill-based team formation. ACM Trans. Inf. Syst. **42**(1), 1–28 (2023)
14. Harshaw, C., Feldman, M., Ward, J., Karbasi, A.: Submodular maximization beyond non-negativity: guarantees, fast algorithms, and applications. In: International Conference on Machine Learning, pp. 2634–2643. PMLR (2019)
15. Hochbaum, D.S.: Approximating covering and packing problems: set cover, vertex cover, independent set, and related problems. Approximation algorithms for NP-hard problems, pp. 94–143 (1997)
16. Kargar, M., An, A., Zihayat, M.: Efficient bi-objective team formation in social networks. In: ECML PKDD (2012)
17. Krause, A., Golovin, D.: Submodular function maximization. Tractability **3**(71–104), 3 (2014)
18. Lappas, T., Liu, K., Terzi, E.: Finding a team of experts in social networks. In: Proceedings of the 15th ACM SIGKDD International Conference on Knowledge Discovery and Data Mining, pp. 467–476 (2009)
19. Lucas, A.: Ising formulations of np problems. Front. Phys. **2**, 74887 (2014)
20. Van der Maaten, L., Hinton, G.: Visualizing data using t-sne. J. Mach. Learn. Res. **9**(11) (2008)
21. Mehta, V., Jin, F., Michielsen, K., De Raedt, H.: On the hardness of quadratic unconstrained binary optimization problems. Front. Phys. **10**, 956882 (2022)
22. Montanez-Barrera, A., Willsch, D., Maldonado-Romo, A., Michielsen, K.: Unbalanced penalization: a new approach to encode inequality constraints of combinatorial problems for quantum optimization algorithms. arXiv preprint arXiv:2211.13914 (2022)
23. Nemhauser, G.L., Wolsey, L.A., Fisher, M.L.: Analysis of approximations for maximizing submodular set functions. Math. Program. **14**, 265–294 (1978)
24. Nikolakaki, S.M., Cai, M., Terzi, E.: Finding teams that balance expert load and task coverage. CoRR **abs/2011.04428** (2020)
25. Nikolakaki, S.M., Ene, A., Terzi, E.: An efficient framework for balancing submodularity and cost. In: Proceedings of the 27th ACM SIGKDD Conference on Knowledge Discovery & Data Mining, pp. 1256–1266 (2021)
26. Paszke, A., et al.: Pytorch: an imperative style, high-performance deep learning library. In: Advances in Neural Information Processing Systems, vol. 32 (2019)
27. Quintero, R.A., Zuluaga, L.F.: QUBO formulations of combinatorial optimization problems for quantum computing devices. In: Encyclopedia of Optimization, pp. 1–13. Springer, Cham (2022)
28. Sapienza, A., Goyal, P., Ferrara, E.: Deep neural networks for optimal team composition. Front. Big Data **2**, 14 (2019)
29. Scarselli, F., Gori, M., Tsoi, A.C., Hagenbuchner, M., Monfardini, G.: The graph neural network model. IEEE Trans. Neural Netw. **20**(1), 61–80 (2008)
30. Schuetz, M.J., Brubaker, J.K., Katzgraber, H.G.: Combinatorial optimization with physics-inspired graph neural networks. Nat. Mach. Intell. **4**(4), 367–377 (2022)
31. Shafi, Z., Miller, B.A., Eliassi-Rad, T., Caceres, R.S.: Graph-scp: accelerating set cover problems with graph neural networks. preprint arXiv:2310.07979 (2023)

32. Skianis, K., Nikolentzos, G., Limnios, S., Vazirgiannis, M.: Rep the set: neural networks for learning set representations. In: International Conference on Artificial Intelligence and Statistics, pp. 1410–1420. PMLR (2020)
33. Verma, A., Lewis, M.: Penalty and partitioning techniques to improve performance of QUBO solvers. Discret. Optim. **44**, 100594 (2022)
34. Vombatkere, K., Gionis, A., Terzi, E.: Forming coordinated teams that balance task coverage and expert workload. Data Min. Knowl. Disc. **39**(3), 1–37 (2025)
35. Vombatkere, K., Terzi, E.: Balancing task coverage and expert workload in team formation. In: Proceedings of the 2023 SIAM International Conference on Data Mining (SDM), pp. 640–648. SIAM (2023)
36. Wang, M., et al.: Deep graph library: a graph-centric, highly-performant package for graph neural networks. arXiv preprint arXiv:1909.01315 (2019)
37. Zaheer, M., Kottur, S., Ravanbakhsh, S., Poczos, B., Salakhutdinov, R.R., Smola, A.J.: Deep sets. In: Advances in Neural Information Processing Systems, vol. 30 (2017)

Enhancing Graph Transformers with SNNs and Mutual Information

Ziyu Wang[✉]

The University of Tokyo, Tokyo, Japan
sltdwzy@outlook.com

Abstract. Although the integration of Graph Neural Networks (GNNs) and Transformers has demonstrated promising performance across various graph tasks, it remains computationally expensive. In contrast, brain-inspired Spiking Neural Networks (SNNs) offer an energy-efficient architecture due to their unique spike-based, event-driven paradigm. To address the high computational cost issue of Graph Transformers while maintaining the effectiveness to the maximum, in this paper, we propose a novel framework CSSGT, which leverages both the strength of Transformers and the computational efficiency of SNNs for graph tasks, trained under the graph contrastive learning framework. CSSGT comprises two key components: Mutual Information -based Graph Split (MIGS) and Spike-Driven Graph Attention (SDGA). MIGS is designed for sequential input of SNNs, splitting the graph while maximizing mutual information and minimizing redundancy. SDGA, tailored for graph data, exploits sparse graph convolution and addition operations, achieving low computational energy consumption. Extensive experiments on diverse datasets demonstrate that CSSGT converges within two epochs and outperforms various state-of-the-art models while maintaining low computational cost.

Keywords: Graph Neural Networks · Spiking Neural Networks · Transformers · Mutual Information · Graph Contrastive Learning

1 Introduction

The integration of Graph Neural Networks (GNNs) and Transformers have achieved remarkable success across various graph tasks [3,6,19,20,24,33]. Additionally, this combination demonstrates high biological plausibility. GNNs are closely aligned with biological systems, while Transformers parallel current hippocampus models and recapitulate spatial representations found in the brain [23]. However, despite their success, the combination of GNNs and Transformers remains computationally expensive, especially when dealing with large-scale datasets [28].

Supplementary Information The online version contains supplementary material available at https://doi.org/10.1007/978-3-032-05981-9_30.

© The Author(s), under exclusive license to Springer Nature Switzerland AG 2026
R. P. Ribeiro et al. (Eds.): ECML PKDD 2025, LNAI 16014, pp. 511–526, 2026.
https://doi.org/10.1007/978-3-032-05981-9_30

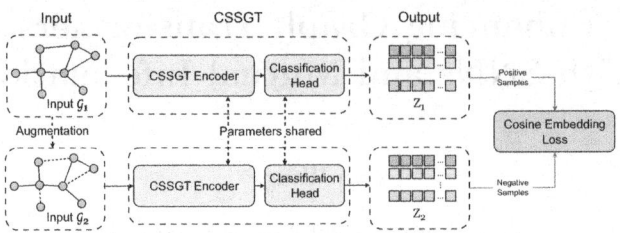

Fig. 1. Overview of CSSGT, trained under the graph contrastive learning paradigm. The detailed architecture is shown in Fig. 2.

Brain-inspired spiking neural networks (SNNs), considered the third generation of neural networks [11], possess superior energy efficiency and biological plausibility due to the unique event-driven processing paradigm and the binary nature of spikes [15]. In SNNs, neurons generate sparse and events-driven binary spikes (0 or 1) to communicate. Thus, during inference, the sparse and event-driven nature of spikes in SNNs eliminates the need for multiplication and significantly reduces computational cost, showing the outstanding energy-saving and memory-saving advantages when deployed on neuromorphic hardware [4, 8, 12]. Moreover, SNNs exhibit memory capabilities due to their intrinsic temporal dynamics and the requirement for sequential input [14, 17]. Given these characteristics, it is attractive to further incorporate SNNs to improve efficiency while developing highly biologically plausible models.

There has been research on incorporating SNNs into Transformers. Most Transformer-based SNNs prioritize maximizing performance instead of fully utilizing the energy efficiency of SNNs, often relying on Multiply-Accumulate (MAc) operations introduced by the vanilla Transformer architecture [5, 36, 37]. [31, 32] use the spike-driven paradigm, which only involves sparse Accumulate (Ac) operations, thus utilizing the advantage of SNNs to further reduce the computational cost. However, none of these works have incorporated GNNs or involved graph tasks. Efforts have also been made to combine SNNs and GNNs. The main challenge is how to fully exploit the benefits of SNNs for processing sequential input. [39] employs a strategy in which the graph is repeated multiple times to sequence the input, resulting in a large amount of redundant information without informative content, thereby limiting the performance of SNNs. Despite these efforts, the advantages of SNNs have yet to be fully exploited.

Our Contributions. In this work, We propose Contrastive learning -based Split Spiking Graph Transformer (CSSGT). We develop a novel mutual information-based graph split method (MIGS), which maximizes mutual information with class labels while minimizing redundancy between subsets. We theoretically proved that MIGS is guaranteed to fa within the range of optimal methods. Inspired by [32], we propose spike-driven graph attention (SDGA) specifically designed for graph data, which improves performance while maintaining low computational cost by adopting the spike-driven paradigm. To advance our work, we train CSSGT under the graph contrastive learning framework, further enhancing its biological plausibility and generalization ability to various datasets.

We conduct comprehensive evaluations on diverse node classification tasks, ranging from citation networks to Wikipedia networks. Experimental results indicate that CSSGT converges within just 2 epochs, achieving performance surpassing various state-of-the-art (SOTA) models from different perspectives, while maintaining low energy consumption across various datasets. The main contributions of this work can be summarized as follows:

- We propose MIGS and SDGA tailored for SNNs in graph tasks. SDGA achieves significantly lower energy consumption compared to vanilla self-attention [19].
- Based on MIGS and SDGA, we develop CSSGT. CSSGT is trained under the graph contrastive learning framework, further enhancing its biological plausibility and generalizability.
- We conduct comprehensive evaluations on diverse datasets. The results demonstrate that CSSGT converges within two epochs and outperforms various SOTA models while maintaining low energy consumption.

2 Related Work

Spiking Neural Networks. SNNs benefit from the integration of deep learning and neuroscience. Many key SNN designs are inspired by various biological mechanisms [11,15,16,26]. However, the traditional backpropagation training algorithm cannot be applied directly to the discrete spikes, an alternative we adopt is surrogate gradient learning [9,25]. It avoids the non-differentiability of spike signals and approximates the backward gradients of the hard threshold function using a smooth activation function during backpropagation.

Efficient Transformers. Deploying Transformers with limited resources remains challenging due to their high computational cost [18]. Typical optimizations include token [34], attention [2], and multi-head [13] approaches. Due to the attention mechanism's high computation scale, its optimization is a key focus. Removing softmax and modifying the operation and value of query, key, and value components are common methods for the optimization. Spiking Transformers typically follow this direction, incorporating SNNs and various computational orders into Query, Key, and Value components. However, most Spiking Transformers adopt MAc operations, limiting their efficiency benefits [5,36,37]. [32] and [31] adopt the spike-driven paradigm, which involves only sparse Ac operations to further reduce the computational cost.

3 Method

In this section, we present CSSGT. We first briefly introduce the notation, mutual information, and spiking neuron layer, then present the overall architecture and the details of each component of CSSGT.

Notations. Let $\mathcal{G} = (\mathcal{V}, \mathcal{E}, \boldsymbol{X})$ denote a graph with n nodes and f features, where $\mathcal{V} = \{v_i\}_{i=1}^{n}$, $\mathcal{E}$ and $\boldsymbol{X} \in \mathbb{R}^{n \times f}$ represent the set of nodes, the set of edges, and node feature matrix, respectively. Let $\boldsymbol{X}^{(i)}$ be the i-th partition of $\boldsymbol{X}$ after applying MIGS. Let $\boldsymbol{H}^{(i)}$, $\boldsymbol{Z}$, and $\boldsymbol{Y}$ denote the node feature matrix in the hidden layers of the input partition $\boldsymbol{X}^{(i)}$, the final output of CSSGT, and the class labels, respectively.

Mutual Information. Mutual information is a measure of shared information between variables. Given two variables A and B, mutual information $\boldsymbol{I}(A;B)$ can be understood as the reduction in uncertainty of B with the knowledge of A. Formally, $\boldsymbol{I}(A;B)$ is defined as: $\boldsymbol{I}(A;B) = \text{H}(A) - \text{H}(A|B) = \text{H}(B) - \text{H}(B|A)$ where $\text{H}(A), \text{H}(B)$ are marginal entropies, and $\text{H}(A|B), \text{H}(B|A)$ are conditional entropies.

Spiking Neuron Layer. As a fundamental component of SNNs, the spiking neuron layer (SN) receives input signals, accumulates membrane potential and compares it with the threshold to determine whether to fire a spike. By default, we adopt the Parameterized Leaky Integrate-and-Fire (PLIF) neuron model in our work, whose dynamics can be described as:

$$U[t] = H[t-1] + X[t],$$
$$S[t] = \text{Hea}(U[t] - u_{\text{th}}),$$
$$H[t] = V_{\text{reset}} \cdot S[t] + \beta U[t](1 - S[t]),$$
$$\beta = \exp(-\Delta t / \tau)$$

where t denotes the time step of the input sequence, and $U[t]$ denotes the membrane potential produced by combining the spatial input $X[t]$ and the temporal input $H[t-1]$. PLIF model extends the LIF model by making key neuronal parameters learnable during training. Specifically, membrane constant τ, threshold u_{th}, and reset potential V_{reset} are all learnable parameters. When the membrane potential exceeds the threshold u_{th}, SN fires a spike (denoted by $S[t] = 1$); otherwise it does not (denoted by $S[t] = 0$). We use the Heaviside step function $\text{Hea}(\cdot)$ to describe this mechanism, $\text{Hea}(x) = 1$ when $x \geqslant 0$, and $\text{Hea}(x) = 0$ otherwise. $H[t]$, V_{reset}, and $\beta < 1$ denote the temporal output, the reset potential, and the decay factor, respectively.

3.1 Overall Architecture

The architecture of CSSGT is shown in Fig. 1 and Fig. 2. The implementation of each component is detailed in Appendix C. The input is first split into T groups $\{\mathcal{G}_i\}_{i=1}^{T}$ using MIGS. Each group $\mathcal{G}_i$ then passes through a graph convolution block, Spiking Graph Position Encoding, and SDGA in order. Residual connections are incorporated in SGPE and SDGA. The outputs $\{\boldsymbol{H}_i\}_{i=1}^{T}$, are concatenated into $\boldsymbol{H}$, which is fed into a classification head and trained under the standard graph contrastive learning paradigm. The model can be written as

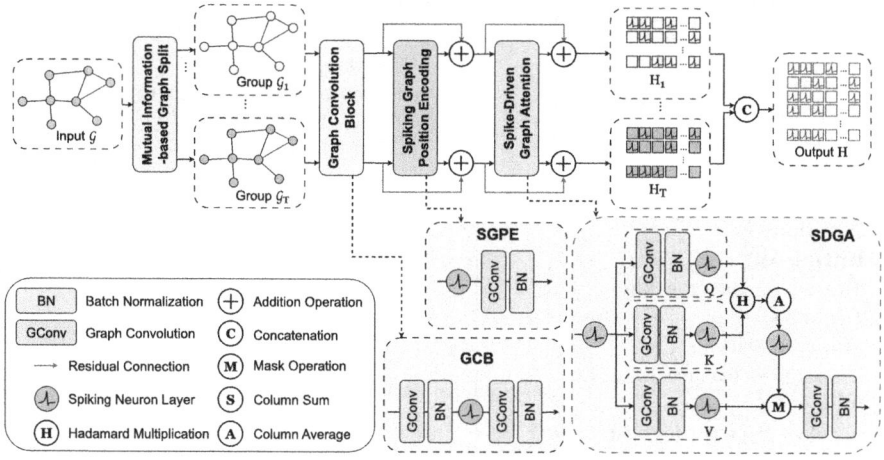

Fig. 2. The detailed architecture of CSSGT encoder.

follows:

$$\{\boldsymbol{X}^{(i)}\}_{i=1}^{T} = \mathrm{MIGS}(\boldsymbol{X}), \qquad \boldsymbol{X}^{(i)} \in \mathbb{R}^{n \times f_i}, \boldsymbol{X} \in \mathbb{R}^{n \times f}$$

$$\boldsymbol{H}_{\mathrm{GCB}}^{(i)} = \mathrm{GCB}(\boldsymbol{X}^{(i)}), \qquad \boldsymbol{H}_{\mathrm{GCB}}^{(i)} \in \mathbb{R}^{n \times h}$$

$$\boldsymbol{H}_{\mathrm{SGPE}}^{(i)} = \boldsymbol{H}_{\mathrm{GCB}}^{(i)} + \mathrm{SGPE}, \qquad \boldsymbol{H}_{\mathrm{SGPE}}^{(i)} \in \mathbb{R}^{n \times h}$$

$$\boldsymbol{H}^{(i)} = \boldsymbol{H}_{\mathrm{SGPE}}^{(i)} + \mathrm{SDGA}, \qquad \boldsymbol{H}_{\mathrm{Att}}^{(i)} \in \mathbb{R}^{n \times h}$$

$$\boldsymbol{H} = \mathrm{Concat}(\{\boldsymbol{H}^{(i)}\}_{i=1}^{T}), \qquad \boldsymbol{H} \in \mathbb{R}^{T \times n \times h}$$

$$\boldsymbol{Z} = \mathrm{CH}(\boldsymbol{H}), \qquad \boldsymbol{Z} \in \mathbb{R}^{T \times n \times c}$$

where h is the hidden dimension, T is the number of partitions, n is the number of nodes and f_i is the feature dimension of the i-th partition. CH is classification head, which is implemented using a linear layer.

3.2 Mutual Information-Based Graph Split

We address the challenge of processing graph data to meet SN's requirement for sequential input. A common approach is to split the graph into multiple groups along the feature dimension, ensuring a uniform distribution of nodes across these groups. This reduces inter-group variability, simplifies further processing, and lowers computational complexity. The key challenge, as mentioned earlier, is organizing the feature distribution to allow SNs to effectively integrate information over time while minimizing information loss.

We propose MIGS, a graph splitting method based on information theory. Along the feature dimension, we split $\boldsymbol{X}$ into T disjoint subsets $\{\boldsymbol{X}^{(i)}\}_{i=1}^{T}$, such that each subset $\boldsymbol{X}^{(t)} \in \mathbb{R}^{N \times F_t}$ maximizes the mutual information $I(\boldsymbol{X}^{(t)}; \boldsymbol{Y})$

Algorithm 1. Mutual Information-based Graph Split

Input:
Feature matrix $X \in \mathbb{R}^{n \times f}$
Class labels $Y \in \{1, 2, \cdots, C\}^N$
Number of partitions T
Regularization parameter λ
Output:
Partitions $\{X^{(i)}\}_{i=1}^T$
Initialize:
Mutual information $I(x_i; Y)$, $I(x_i; x_{i'})$
Empty partitions $\{X^{(i)}\}_{i=1}^T$
Unassigned features $U = \{x_i\}_{i=1}^f$
for $t = i$ to T **do**
  Select x_f with highest $I(x_f; Y)$
  Assign x_f to partition $X^{(i)}$
  Remove x_f from U
end for
	while U is not empty **do**
	  for each unassigned feature $x_f \in U$ **do**
	    for each partition $i = 1$ to T **do**
	      Calculate mutual information gain
	      $\Delta I_{\text{label}}^{(i)}(x_f) = I(x_f; Y)$
	      Calculate redundancy
	      $\Delta I_{\text{rdd}}^{(i)}(x_f) = \sum_{x_{f'} \in X^{(t)}} I(x_f; x_{f'})$
	      Compute net gain $\Delta I^{(i)}(x_f)$
	      $= \Delta I_{\text{label}}^{(i)}(x_f) - \lambda \Delta I_{\text{rdd}}^{(i)}(x_f)$
	    end for
	    Assign x_f to partition
	    $t^* = argmax_i \Delta I^{(i)}(x_f)$
	    Remove x_f from U
	  end for
	end while

with the class labels Y, ensuring that the most discriminative features are preserved and propagated through the network. The partition also ensures each subset minimizes the redundancy between subsets, reducing information overlap.

We start by formulating the optimization problem (proved in Appendix B.1):

Proposition 1. *Maximizing the mutual information $I(Z; Y)$ between Z and Y is equivalent to solving the following optimization problem, where λ is a regularization parameter:*

$$X^{(t)} = argmax \sum_{t=1}^{T} I(X^{(t)}; Y) - \lambda \sum_{t \neq s} I(X^{(t)}; X^{(s)}), \forall t, s \in \{1, 2, \cdots, T\}$$

We employ a greedy feature partitioning algorithm to solve this optimization problem. The algorithm begins by computing the mutual information between each feature and the class labels $I(x_f; Y) = \text{H}(x_f) - \text{H}(x_f|Y)$, as well as the mutual information between all pairs of features $I(x_f; x_{f'}) = \text{H}(x_f) - \text{H}(x_f|x_{f'})$. Each partition $X^{(i)}$ is initialized with the feature that has the highest $I(x_f; Y)$.

At each iteration, we assign a feature to the partition that yields the maximum net gain $\Delta I^{(t)}(x_f) = \Delta I_{\text{label}}^{(t)}(x_f) - \lambda \Delta I_{\text{rdd}}^{(t)}$, where $\Delta I_{\text{label}}^{(t)}(x_f) = I(x_f; Y)$, $\Delta I_{\text{rdd}}^{(t)}(x_f) = \sum_{x_{f'} \in X^{(t)}} I(x_f; x_{f'})$. By selecting the partition that maximizes the net gain for each feature, the algorithm ensures that each partition contains highly informative and minimally redundant features. This method effectively constructs feature subsets that, when processed through SNs, minimize information loss and enhance performance by providing diverse and complementary information across partitions. A comprehensive description is provided in Algorithm 1.

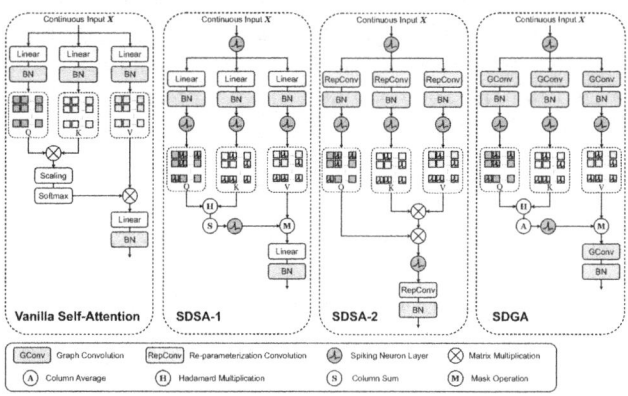

Fig. 3. Comparison between Vanilla Self-Attention (VSA) [19], Spike-Driven Self-Attention-1 (SDSA-1) [32], Spike-Driven Self-Attention-2 (SDSA-2) [31], and our Spike-Driven Graph Attention (SDGA). The key differences are: (**a**) we use graph convolution layer instead of re-parameterization convolution layer and linear layer to process graph data; (**b**) we use column-wise average operation instead of column-wise sum operation.

We further conclude that the greedy algorithm is guaranteed to fall within the range of optimal solutions, as shown in Proposition 2 (proved in Appendix B.2).

Proposition 2. *The greedy algorithm given above approaches the optimal solution. Specifically, For the maximization optimization of the objective function f in Proposition 1, the greedy algorithm partition solution S_{Greedy} and the optimal solution S^* satisfy:*

$$f(S_{Greedy}) \geq (1 - \frac{1}{e})f(S^*)$$

3.3 Spike-Driven Graph Attention

In this section, we present the architecture of SDGA. The detailed energy analyses are provided in Sect. 4.5 and Appendix A.

Given the input $\boldsymbol{X} \in \mathbb{R}^{n \times f}$, to leverage the computational efficiency, we first apply SN to the input:

$$\boldsymbol{X}_s = \mathrm{SN}(\boldsymbol{X})$$

Instead of using the convolution layer employed by Spike-Driven Self-Attentions [31,32], or the linear layer adopted by the Vanilla Self-Attention, SDGA employs graph convolution to obtain the query $\boldsymbol{Q}$, key $\boldsymbol{K}$ and value $\boldsymbol{V}$:

$$\boldsymbol{Q} = \mathrm{BN}(\mathrm{GConv}_Q(\boldsymbol{X}_s)),$$
$$\boldsymbol{K} = \mathrm{BN}(\mathrm{GConv}_K(\boldsymbol{X}_s)),$$
$$\boldsymbol{V} = \mathrm{BN}(\mathrm{GConv}_V(\boldsymbol{X}_s))$$

where $Q, K, V \in \mathbb{R}^{n \times h}$, GConv_Q, GConv_K, GConv_V are graph convolution layers, BN is batch normalization layer, h is the hidden dimension. Since X_s is a sparse binarized matrix, the computation cost of graph convolution remains low. Then we apply SN again:

$$Q_s = \text{SN}(Q), \ K_s = \text{SN}(K), \ V_s = \text{SN}(V)$$

Inspired by SDSA-1 [32], we compute the Hadamard product between Q_s and K_s. This operation can be regarded as energy-free, as the Hadamard product between spikes is equivalent to the element-wise mask operation:

$$\alpha = Q_s \odot K_s, \ \alpha \in \mathbb{R}^{n \times h}$$

Given that the threshold of SN is in the range $[0,1]$, instead of column-wise sum operation, we use column-wise average operation before SN, ensuring the input is scaled appropriately within the range $[0,1]$. We then compute the mask operation with V_s:

$$\overline{\alpha} = \text{SN}(\text{Average}(\alpha)), \ \overline{\alpha} \in \mathbb{R}^{n \times 1}$$

$$V_{\text{mask}} = \text{Mask}(\overline{\alpha}, \ V_s), \ V_{\text{mask}} \in \mathbb{R}^{n \times h}$$

Finally we apply graph convolution to V_{mask} to obtain the SDGA:

$$\text{SDGA} = \text{BN}(\text{GConv}(V_{\text{mask}}))$$

We outline the architecture of SDGA and compare it with other attention mechanisms (see Fig. 3). The intuition behind SDGA is that graph convolution is better suited for graph data, with energy consumption comparable to MLP, significantly lower than traditional convolution. Therefore, we integrate graph convolution into the attention mechanism, and the column-wise average operation ensures the input is appropriately scaled within the range $[0,1]$.

It is important to note that the single-head SDGA can be easily extended to multi-head SDGA (MSDGA). After the first graph convolution, we split the query Q, key K, and value V into H multiple heads: $Q = (\hat{Q}_1, \hat{Q}_2, \cdots, \hat{Q}_H)$, $K = (\hat{K}_1, \hat{K}_2, \cdots, \hat{K}_H)$, $V = (\hat{V}_1, \hat{V}_2, \cdots, \hat{V}_H)$ Where $\hat{Q}_i, \hat{K}_i, \hat{V}_i \in \mathbb{R}^{n \times h/H}$. Then we apply SDGA on each head and concatenate the outputs to obtain the final output MSDGA:

$$\text{MSDGA} = (\text{SDGA}(\hat{Q}_1, \hat{K}_1, \hat{V}_1), \cdots, \text{SDGA}(\hat{Q}_H, \hat{K}_H, \hat{V}_H))$$

3.4 Graph Convolution Block

The graph convolution block (GCB) contains two graph convolution layers (GConv) and two batch normalization layers (BN):

$$\hat{H}_{\text{GCB}}^{(i)} = \text{BN}_1(\text{GConv}_1^{(i)}(X^{(i)})), \ i \in \{1, \cdots, T\}$$

$$H_{\text{GCB}}^{(i)} = \text{BN}_2(\text{GConv}_2(\text{SN}(\hat{H}_{\text{GCB}}^{(i)})))$$

Different graph subsets are processed sequentially by GCB. For each input subset, the first graph convolution layer $\text{Conv}_1^{(i)}$ has different inputs but identical output dimensionality. The second graph convolution layer Conv_2 has the same input and output dimensionality with parameters shared for different input subsets.

3.5 Spiking Graph Position Encoding

In spiking graph position encoding, similar to SDGA, we first apply the spiking neuron layer to reduce computational cost, followed by graph convolution to encode the position information. Specifically, for the input X, spiking graph position encoding (SGPE) can be expressed as:

$$\text{SGPE} = \text{BN}(\text{GConv}(\text{SN}(X)))$$

3.6 Graph Contrastive Learning

We follow the conventional graph contrastive learning framework for training. To generate two different views, we apply edge dropout and cosine loss [1] on the final outputs:

$$\text{loss}(x, y) = \begin{cases} 1 - \cos(Z_1, Z_2), & \text{if } y = 1 \\ \max(0, \cos(Z_1, Z_2) - \text{margin}), & \text{if } y = -1 \end{cases}$$

where Z_1, Z_2 are the final output pairs, $x = (Z_1, Z_2)$ represents a pair of graph representations, and y determines whether the pairs are positive or negative. Cosine loss maximizes the similarity between positive pairs and minimizes it for negative pairs by computing the cosine similarity.

4 Experiments

In this section, we first present the experimental settings (Sect. 4.1). We then evaluate the test accuracy and convergence performance of CSSGT on node classification tasks across diverse datasets, comparing it with various models (Sects. 4.2 and 4.3). We also conduct ablation studies on SDGA, MIGS, and the impact of hyperparameters, including spiking threshold, the number of GNN layers, and the type of SNs (Sect. 4.4). Finally, we provide the analysis of energy efficiency across various attention mechanisms and models (Sect. 4.5). Implementation details and additional experiment results are provided in Appendix C and Appendix E.

4.1 Setup

Datasets. The experiments are conducted on six commonly used graph datasets: *Cora, Citeseer, Pubmed, Chameleon, Squirrel,* and *obgn-Arxiv*. The first three are medium-sized citation networks with high homophily ratios. *Chameleon* and *Squirrel* are Wikipedia networks and identified as heterophilic graphs. *obgn-Arxiv* is a well-known large-scale graph. The details are provided in Appendix D.

Baselines. We compare CSSGT with a wide range of SOTA baselines from various perspectives. In terms of classical supervised GNNs, We compare against GCN [7], GAT [21], and an advanced GNN, JKNet-GAT [29], in which GAT is used as the backbone of JKNet. In terms of unsupervised models, we compare with SOTAs including DGI [22], GRACE [38], and CCA-SSG [35]. In terms of spiking-based models, we compare against GC-SNN [30], GA-SNN [30], and SpikingNet [10]. In terms of Transformer-based models, we compare with various SOTAs including NodeFormer [24], Graphormer [33], GraphTrans [27], and SGFormer. Since the original Graphormer and GraphTrans are too large to scale on all datasets, we compare with the small-sized versions, Graphormer$_{small}$ (3 layers and 8 heads), GraphTrans$_{small}$ (3 layers and 4 heads), Graphormer$_{ultrasmall}$ (2 layers and 1 head), GraphTrans$_{ultrasmall}$ (2 layers and 1 head).

4.2 Node Classification

Table 1 reports the results of all the models. Results demonstrate that CSSGT effectively handles both homophilic and heterophilic graphs, consistently outperforming all competitors across every dataset. Notably, CSSGT achieves its highest improvements on *Citeseer* over Transformer-based models, and on *Pubmed* over classical and unsupervised models. Since both of these datasets have high feature dimensions, a possible explanation for the significant improvement of CSSGT is that MIGS splits the high-dimensional input into multiple lower-dimensional inputs, which helps to reduce information loss from the input data.

4.3 Convergence Analysis

We further study the convergence performance of CSSGT in node classification task. To ensure the clarity of the figures, we report the accuracy curves on *Cora*, *Pubmed*, *Chameleon*, and *Squirrel*, comparing CSSGT with NodeFormer, GAT, JKNet-GAT, and GCN. The results are presented in Fig. 4. Results demonstrate that, across all the datasets, CSSGT consistently converges within two epochs and achieves the highest accuracy. In contrast, on medium-sized datasets *Cora* and *Citeseer*, competitors require at least 30 epochs to converge. On larger datasets *Chameleon* and *Squirrel*, the performance of competitors barely improves after 30 epochs. A possible explanation is that the combination of MIGS and SDGA effectively leverages the advantages of SNs for processing sequential data, as the input data in each epoch is split into multiple partitions, serving as sequential input to the SNs.

Table 1. Node classification test accuracy. U, S, T, and OOM stand for unsupervised, spiking-based, Transformer-based, and out of memory, respectively.

Methods	U	S	T	Cora	Citeseer	Pubmed	Chameleon	Squirrel	obgn-Arxiv
GCN				81.5±0.1	71.3±0.2	79.0±0.2	54.3±3.0	38.6±1.8	71.8±0.3
GAT				83.0±0.7	72.5±0.7	79.0±0.3	51.2±3.1	35.6±2.1	72.1±0.1
JKNet-GAT				83.3±0.4	72.7±0.3	79.9±0.5	51.5±1.3	40.1±1.5	72.3±0.2
DGI	✓			82.3±0.6	71.8±0.7	76.8±0.6	60.3±0.7	39.4±1.1	70.3±0.2
GRACE	✓			81.9±0.4	71.2±0.5	80.6±0.4	58.1±0.9	41.4±0.7	71.5±0.4
CCA-SSG	✓			84.0±0.4	73.1±0.3	81.0±0.4	57.4±1.4	42.2±1.0	71.2±0.5
GC-SNN		✓		80.7±0.6	69.9±0.9	OOM	53.1±1.4	39.4±1.1	66.4±0.3
GA-SNN		✓		79.9±0.6	69.1±0.5	OOM	54.6±0.9	38.7±1.3	66.7±0.2
SpikingNet		✓		82.6±0.5	71.4±0.5	78.6±0.3	55.7±1.9	40.7±1.8	67.5±1.8
Nodeformer			✓	83.2±0.9	72.5±1.1	79.9±1.0	49.6±4.1	38.5±1.5	59.9±0.4
Graphormer$_{small}$			✓	75.8±1.1	65.6±0.6	OOM	54.9±2.8	40.9±2.5	OOM
Graphormer$_{ultrasmall}$			✓	74.2±0.9	63.6±1.0	OOM	54.2±2.4	33.9±1.4	OOM
GraphTrans$_{small}$			✓	80.7±0.9	69.5±0.7	OOM	55.7±3.3	41.0±2.8	OOM
GraphTrans$_{ultrasmall}$			✓	81.7±0.6	70.2±0.8	77.4±0.5	55.2±2.9	40.6±2.4	OOM
SGFormer			✓	84.5±0.8	72.6±0.2	80.3±0.6	56.9±3.9	41.8±2.2	72.6±0.1
CSSGT (ours)	✓	✓	✓	**87.3±1.2**	**77.6±1.0**	**86.9±0.8**	**60.7±1.2**	**42.6±1.9**	**73.2±0.7**

4.4 Ablation Study

We proceed to conduct ablation studies on MIGS, SDGA, SGPE, and the impact of hyperparameters, including spiking threshold, number of GNN layers, and type of SNs. Due to space limitations, we present the figures of accuracy curves and the table of results on dataset *Chameleon*, *Squirrel*, *Cora*, and *Citeseer*. The implementation details and additional results are provided in Appendix C and Appendix E.

Mutual Information-Based Graph Split. Figure 5a presents the accuracy curves of CSSGT with varying numbers of split groups, ranging from 1 to 100. The results consistently indicate that CSSGT is relatively insensitive to the number of groups when the number is greater than 20. However, when the number of groups is less than 20, both performance and convergence speed improve as the number of groups increases.

Table 2. Ablation on SDGA and SGPE

Model	Cora	Citeseer	Chameleon	Squirrel
w/o SDGA	85.4	73.8	60.5	40.0
w/o SGPE	85.4	75.4	59.6	38.2
1-head	87.2	**76.5**	61.2	**41.3**
2-head	87.5	76.3	61.2	40.6
4-head	87.3	**76.5**	**61.4**	**41.3**
8-head	**87.6**	**76.5**	61.2	40.8

Spike-Driven Graph Attention and Spiking Graph Position Encoding. Table 2 presents the accuracy comparison of CSSGT with varying numbers of attention heads, from 1 to 8, without SDGA, and without SGPE. The results demonstrate that, both SDGA and SGPE consistently enhance the performance

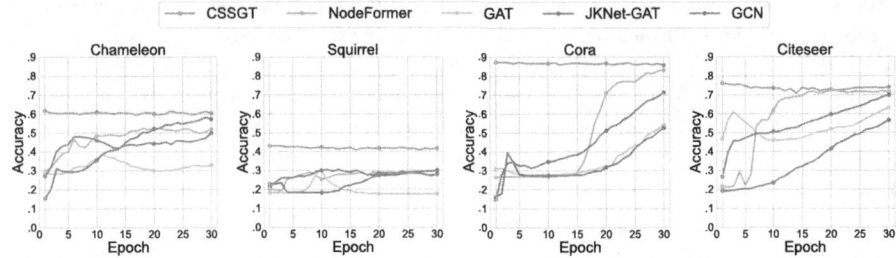

Fig. 4. Node classification accuracy curves comparison on *Chameleon*, *Squirrel*, *Cora*, and *Citeseer* datasets. CSSGT consistently converges within two epochs and achieves the highest accuracy.

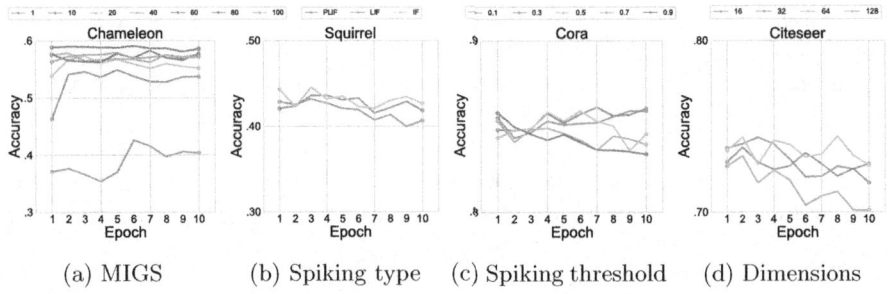

(a) MIGS (b) Spiking type (c) Spiking threshold (d) Dimensions

Fig. 5. Ablation studies. **(a)** MIGS with different number of partitions; **(b)** type of the spiking model type in SNs; **(c)** threshold of SNs; **(d)** hidden dimension of all graph convolution layers.

of CSSGT. The 4-head SDGA achieves the best performance, surpassing CSSGT without SDGA by 3.7% on *Citeseer* and CSSGT without SGPE by 3.3% on *Squirrel*.

Impact of Spiking Type and Hyperparameters. Figure 5b, c, and d present the accuracy curves of CSSGT with different types of SNs: Parameterized Leaky-and-Integrate (PLIF) model, Leaky-and-Integrate (LIF) model, and Integrate-and-Fire (IF) model; different spiking thresholds: 0.1, 0.3, 0.5, 0.7, 0.9; and different hidden dimensions: 16, 32, 64, and 128, respectively. The results indicate that CSSGT is relatively insensitive to spiking type and hyperparameters. Nevertheless, a spiking threshold of 0.7, and hidden dimension of 64 outperforms other settings.

4.5 Efficiency Analysis

Attention Analysis. We calculate the complexity, total number of operations, and energy consumption of SDGA compared with VSA, SDSA-1, and SDSA-2. We assume the input matrix is of size $n \times h$. The results are summarized in Table 3, and the detailed calculation process is provided in Appendix A. The

Table 3. Comparison of the number of operations and energy consumption between different attention mechanisms. The results are presented in the form of operations/energy.

Architecture	Complexity	Cora	Citeseer	Chameleon	Squirrel
VSA	$O(hn^2)$	994 M/4.57 mJ	1491 M/6.86 mJ	707 M/3.25 mJ	3608 M/16.60 mJ
SDSA-1	$O(h^2n)$	559 M/0.50 mJ	655 M/0.59 mJ	571 M/0.51 mJ	1202 M/1.08 mJ
SDSA-2	$O(h^2n)$	581 M/0.52 mJ	687 M/0.62 mJ	610 M/0.55 mJ	1265 M/1.14 mJ
SDGA (ours)	$O(h^2n)$	**198M/0.18 mJ**	**232 M/0.21 mJ**	**203 M/0.18 mJ**	**426 M/0.38 mJ**

Table 4. Comparison of the number of operations and energy consumption between CCA-SSG, SGFormer, and CSSGT. The results are presented in the form of operations/energy.

Architecture	Cora	Citeseer	Chameleon	Squirrel
CCA-SSG	4.40 B/20.08 mJ	13.12 B/60.24 mJ	5.76 B/26.48 mJ	11.84 B/54.64 mJ
SGFormer	0.57 B/2.62 mJ	1.67 B/7.66 mJ	0.74 B/3.39 mJ	1.53 B/7.03 mJ
CSSGT (ours)	0.93 B/**0.84 mJ**	2.09 B/**1.88 mJ**	1.16 B/**1.04 mJ**	2.38 B/**2.14 mJ**

results show that SDGA achieves the lowest number of operations and energy consumption across all datasets, with up to 43.68× lower energy consumption compared to VSA, and around 3× lower energy consumption compared to SDSA-1 and SDSA-2.

Model Analysis. We further compare the number of operations and energy consumption of CSSGT with CCA-SSG and SGFormer, two of the most efficient architectures in contrastive learning-based and Transformer-based models. The results are presented in Table 4, with detailed calculations provided in Appendix A. The results show that CSSGT is significantly more efficient compared to CCA-SSG. Although CSSGT has a larger number of operations compared to SGFormer, since the operations are Ac in CSSGT, while CCA-SSG and SGFormer rely on MAc, the energy consumption of CSSGT is even 3× lower.

5 Conclusion and Discussion

In this paper, to address the high computational cost issue of Graph Transformers during inference, we aim to achieve effective performance while fully leveraging the efficient nature of SNNs. Therefore, we first propose the novel MIGS minimizing the information loss to ensure effectiveness, supported by solid theoretical foundations. We then incorporate SNNs globally in Graph Transformers a spike-driven paradigm to ensure efficiency, which is also, to our best knowledge, the first study in this direction. This incorporation consists of SDGA, SGPE, and GCB. We train the network under GCL and name it CSSGT.

Discussion on Performance. A possible explanation for CSSGT's great performance lies in the combination of SNNs and MIGS. In CSSGT, we introduce an SN before each graph convolution operation, which sparsifies the data and limits the operations to simple Accumulate operation (detailed in Appendix A), significantly reducing energy consumption. While some information loss is inevitable, this approach introduces two key advantages beyond efficiency: a temporal dimension, along which MIGS encodes the information of the input; and the accumulation dynamics of SNs, which provide memory of previous inputs.

Discussion on Experiments. Given the theory of GCL and the linear evaluation protocol used for evaluation, which is a simple linear classifier on top of the frozen representations for a specific downstream task, as detailed in the implementation details section, the model's representations will generalize to various downstream tasks, even with a minimal and task-agnostic evaluation setup. Thus, it is standard practice to use the node classification evaluation task as a proxy to assess the representation of the model. We note that CSSGT can potentially be extended to other graph tasks such as dynamic graph node classification and graph classification.

Discussion on GCL. The key insight of using Contrastive learning is that SNNs inherently introduce the temporal dimension into the graph data, resulting in additional information and relevance in the time domain. However, the binary nature of SNNs causes the loss of information for the supervised-based method, which makes it hard to handle the relevance of data. Contrastive learning provides a framework to explicitly leverage temporal correlations, fully aligning with the SNNs' strength in processing sequential data. Moreover, since the spikes generated by SNNs often exhibit high sparsity (please refer to Appendix E.6), contrastive learning can handle the sparse data well by enhancing the ability to utilize the relevant information. Lastly, Contrastive learning improves robustness, which can be crucial given SNNs' binary nature.

Limitation. Although the calculation of mutual information in MIGS is required only once for a given dataset, it remains relatively computationally expensive.

Acknowledgement. My heartfelt thanks go to my parents, whose constant support has been my quiet anchor, and to my advisor, Dr. Watanabe, whose kindness and support have lit the path forward. Without you, this paper would have been a steeper climb. May this be not just an end, but a hopeful beginning to a journey of exploration. This work has been supported by the Mohammed bin Salman Center for Future Science and Technology for Saudi-Japan Vision 2030 at The University of Tokyo (MbSC2030) and JSPS KAKENHI Grant Number 23K25257.

References

1. Chen, T., Kornblith, S., Norouzi, M., Hinton, G.: A simple framework for contrastive learning of visual representations. In: Proceedings of the 37th International Conference on Machine Learning (2020)
2. Choromanski, K.M., et al.: Rethinking attention with performers. In: International Conference on Learning Representations (2021)

3. Dwivedi, V.P., Bresson, X.: A generalization of transformer networks to graphs. In: Methods and Applications, AAAI Workshop on Deep Learning on Graphs (2021)
4. Furber, S., Galluppi, F., Temple, S., Plana, L.: The spinnaker project. Proc. IEEE **102**, 652–665 (2014)
5. Han, M., Wang, Q., Zhang, T., Wang, Y., Zhang, D., Xu, B.: Complex dynamic neurons improved spiking transformer network for efficient automatic speech recognition (2023)
6. Hu, Z., Dong, Y., Wang, K., Sun, Y.: Heterogeneous graph transformer. In: Proceedings of The Web Conference 2020 (2020)
7. Kipf, T.N., Welling, M.: Semi-supervised classification with graph convolutional networks. In: International Conference on Learning Representations (2017)
8. Krestinskaya, O., James, A.P., Chua, L.O.: Neuromemristive circuits for edge computing: a review. IEEE Trans. Neural Netw. Learn. Syst. **31**, 4–23 (2020)
9. Lee, J., Delbrück, T., Pfeiffer, M.: Training deep spiking neural networks using backpropagation. Front. Neurosci. (2016)
10. Li, J., et al.: Scaling up dynamic graph representation learning via spiking neural networks. In: Proceedings of the AAAI Conference on Artificial Intelligence (2023)
11. Maass, W.: Networks of spiking neurons: the third generation of neural network models. Neural Netw. **10**, 1659–1671 (1997)
12. Merolla, P.A., et al.: A million spiking-neuron integrated circuit with a scalable communication network and interface. Science **345**, 668–673 (2014)
13. Michel, P., Levy, O., Neubig, G.: Are sixteen heads really better than one? (2019)
14. Ponulak, F., Kasiński, A.: Introduction to spiking neural networks: information processing, learning and applications. Acta Neurobiol. Exp. **71**, 409–33 (2011)
15. Roy, K., Jaiswal, A.R., Panda, P.: Towards spike-based machine intelligence with neuromorphic computing. Nature **575**, 607–617 (2019)
16. Schuman, C., Kulkarni, S., Parsa, M., Mitchell, J., Date, P., Kay, B.: Opportunities for neuromorphic computing algorithms and applications. Nature Comput. Sci. **2**, 10–19 (2022)
17. Tavanaei, A., Ghodrati, M., Kheradpisheh, S.R., Masquelier, T., Maida, A.: Deep learning in spiking neural networks. Neural Netw. **111**, 47–63 (2019)
18. Tay, Y., Dehghani, M., Bahri, D., Metzler, D.: Efficient transformers: a survey. ACM Comput. Surv. (2022)
19. Vaswani, A., et al.: Attention is all you need. In: Advances in Neural Information Processing Systems (2017)
20. Veličković, P., Cucurull, G., Casanova, A., Romero, A., Liò, P., Bengio, Y.: Graph attention networks. In: 6th International Conference on Learning Representations (2017)
21. Veličković, P., Cucurull, G., Casanova, A., Romero, A., Liò, P., Bengio, Y.: Graph attention networks. In: International Conference on Learning Representations (2018)
22. Veličković, P., Fedus, W., Hamilton, W.L., Liò, P., Bengio, Y., Hjelm, R.D.: Deep graph infomax. In: International Conference on Learning Representations (2019)
23. Whittington, J.C.R., Warren, J., Behrens, T.E.: Relating transformers to models and neural representations of the hippocampal formation. In: International Conference on Learning Representations (2022)
24. Wu, Q., Zhao, W., Li, Z., Wipf, D., Yan, J.: Nodeformer: a scalable graph structure learning transformer for node classification. In: Advances in Neural Information Processing Systems (2022)

25. Wu, Y., Deng, L., Li, G., Zhu, J., Xie, Y., Shi, L.: Direct training for spiking neural networks: faster, larger, better. In: Proceedings of the AAAI Conference on Artificial Intelligence (2019)
26. Wu, Y., et al.: Brain-inspired global-local hybrid learning towards human-like intelligence. CoRR (2020)
27. Wu, Z., Jain, P., Wright, M.A., Mirhoseini, A., Gonzalez, J.E., Stoica, I.: Representing long-range context for graph neural networks with global attention. In: Proceedings of the 35th International Conference on Neural Information Processing Systems (2021)
28. Wu, Z., Pan, S., Chen, F., Long, G., Zhang, C., Yu, P.S.: A comprehensive survey on graph neural networks. IEEE Trans. Neural Netw. Learn. Syst. **32**, 4–24 (2021)
29. Xu, K., Li, C., Tian, Y., Sonobe, T., Kawarabayashi, K.i., Jegelka, S.: Representation learning on graphs with jumping knowledge networks. In: Proceedings of the 35th International Conference on Machine Learning (2018)
30. Xu, M., Wu, Y., Deng, L., Liu, F., Li, G., Pei, J.: Exploiting spiking dynamics with spatial-temporal feature normalization in graph learning. In: IJCAI (2021)
31. Yao, M., et al.: Spike-driven transformer v2: meta spiking neural network architecture inspiring the design of next-generation neuromorphic chips. In: The 12nd International Conference on Learning Representations (2024)
32. Yao, M., et al.: Spike-driven transformer. In: 37th Conference on Neural Information Processing Systems (2023)
33. Ying, C., et al.: Do transformers really perform badly for graph representation? In: Advances in Neural Information Processing Systems (2021)
34. Yuan, L., et al.: Tokens-to-token vit: Training vision transformers from scratch on imagenet. 2021 IEEE/CVF International Conference on Computer Vision (ICCV) (2021)
35. Zhang, H., Wu, Q., Yan, J., Wipf, D., Yu, P.S.: From canonical correlation analysis to self-supervised graph neural networks. In: Advances in Neural Information Processing Systems (2021)
36. Zhang, J., et al.: Spiking transformers for event-based single object tracking. In: Proceedings of the IEEE/CVF Conference on Computer Vision and Pattern Recognition (CVPR) (2022)
37. Zhou, Z., et al.: Spikformer: when spiking neural network meets transformer. In: The 11th International Conference on Learning Representations (2023)
38. Zhu, Y., Xu, Y., Yu, F., Liu, Q., Wu, S., Wang, L.: Deep graph contrastive representation learning. In: ICML Workshop on Graph Representation Learning and Beyond (2020)
39. Zhu, Z., Peng, J., Li, J., Chen, L., Yu, Q., Luo, S.: Spiking graph convolutional networks. In: IJCAI (2022)

PipeQS: Pipeline-Based Adaptive Quantization and Staleness-Aware Distributed GNN Training System

Donghang Wu[1], Lian Shen[1], Changzhi Jiang[1], Yanhao Li[1], and Xiangrong Liu[1,2,3(✉)]

[1] Department of Computer Science and Technology, Xiamen University, Xiamen, China
xrliu@xmu.edu.cn
[2] National Institute for Data Science in Health and Medicine, Xiamen University, Xiamen 361005, China
[3] Xiamen Key Laboratory of Intelligent Storage and Computing, Xiamen, China

Abstract. Graph Neural Networks (GNNs) have emerged as the state-of-the-art method for graph-based learning tasks. However, training GNNs at scale remains challenging, limiting the exploration of more sophisticated GNN architectures and their application to large real-world graphs. In distributed GNN training, communication overhead and waiting times have become major performance bottlenecks. To address these challenges, we propose PipeQS, an adaptive quantization and staleness-aware pipeline distributed training system for GNNs. PipeQS dynamically adjusts the bit-width of message quantization and manages staleness to reduce both communication overhead and communication waiting time. By detecting pipeline bottlenecks caused by synchronization and utilizing cached communication to bypass message delays, PipeQS significantly improves training efficiency. Experimental results validate the effectiveness of PipeQS, showing up to an 8.3× improvement in throughput while maintaining full-graph accuracy. Furthermore, our theoretical analysis demonstrates fast convergence at a rate of $O(T^{-\frac{1}{2}})$, where T is the total number of training epochs. PipeQS achieves a well-balanced trade-off between training speed and accuracy, significantly reducing training time without compromising performance. The code is available at https://github.com/suupahako/PipeQS-code

Keywords: Distributed GNN Training · Quantization · Staleness-Aware · Pipeline

1 Introduction

Graph Neural Networks (GNNs) have become an advanced technique for handling graph-structured data [10], demonstrating exceptional performance in

---

D. Wu and L. Shen—These authors contributed equally to this work.

tasks such as node classification [23], link prediction [27], graph classification [10], and recommendation systems [25]. However, training on large-scale graphs remains complex and challenging [10], as the growth in the size of the graph can quickly consume memory and computational resources due to the vast number of node features and the enormous adjacency matrix. This limits the exploration of more complex GNN architectures and practical applications on large real-world graphs.

To address the challenges of training on large-scale graphs, researchers have developed sampling-based methods such as GraphSAGE [5] and VR-GCN [1], which reduce the full graph to mini-batches through neighbor sampling, or by extracting subgraphs as training samples, like Cluster-GCN [2] and GraphSAINT [26]. Although these methods reduce computational resources, they introduce approximation errors and suffer from gradient variance problems, where the randomness in sampling leads to unstable gradient estimates, slowing convergence and reducing model accuracy, especially as graph data scales.

In addition to sampling-based methods, distributed full-graph training has emerged as a promising approach for handling large-scale graph training. This method partitions a large graph into smaller subgraphs, each capable of fitting into a single machine, and communication occurs between these machines to train the partitioned subgraphs. Early works such as NeuGraph [12], ROC [8], CAGNET [18], and Dorylus [17] have demonstrated the significant potential of distributed GNN training. Although distributed full-graph training can retain complete full-graph structural information, it requires frequent information exchange between partition nodes, which leads to a significant increase in communication traffic and seriously affects training efficiency. Additionally, the computation of the local nodes needs to asynchronously receive messages from the remote nodes, which causes unnecessary waiting times during communication phases, further degrading overall throughput. Communication overhead and latency have become the major bottlenecks of distributed full-graph training.

Some studies have explored ways to improve distributed full-graph training to address the above bottlenecks, including message quantization and stale-based methods. For the first bottleneck, BNS-GCN [20] reduces communication time by sampling boundary nodes. AdaQP [19] and EC-Graph [16] apply quantization techniques to compress node features, significantly reducing communication volume. However, the compression error introduced is not conducive to the scalability of these methods. Staleness-based methods have been used to solve the second problem, such as SANCUS [15], which provides a strategy to improve training efficiency by allowing stale updates to replace fresh communication. PipeGCN [21] introduces a pipeline mechanism that uses feature staleness and gradient staleness to reduce communication waiting times. Since stale features are used, these methods require longer training time to ensure the convergence rate of the model. The above methods cannot address both issues at once and often face a trade-off between communication efficiency and convergence stability. Therefore, achieving a balance between minimizing communication overhead and maintaining convergence in distributed full-graph training remains a challenge.

In this work, we propose PipeQS, a novel distributed GNN training method that, for the first time, integrates quantification and staleness within a pipeline framework. To address the potential convergence degradation typically associated with these techniques, we introduce an adaptive adjustment mechanism for bit-width and the number of staleness iterations. Our method effectively reduces communication overhead and solves the communication waiting problem, striking an ideal balance between convergence stability and communication time. PipeQS achieves excellent communication efficiency while maintaining a basic convergence rate of $O(T^{-\frac{1}{2}})$, making it a robust solution for large-scale distributed GNN training.

Our main contributions are summarized as follows:

- We propose PipeQS, a distributed GNN training method that innovatively integrates quantification and staleness within a pipeline framework, addressing the challenges of communication overhead in large-scale GNN training.
- We introduce an adaptive mechanism for adjusting bit-width and the number of staleness iterations, ensuring that the convergence rate is maintained at $O(T^{-\frac{1}{2}})$. This allows the method to achieve strong communication efficiency while preserving the basic convergence rate.
- Our theoretical analysis and empirical evaluations confirm the effectiveness of PipeQS in achieving efficient GNN training while maintaining convergence stability, even as graph size increases. PipeQS achieves significant speedups across datasets, reaching up to 5.06x on Ogbn-products and 4.51x on Reddit.

2 Related Works

2.1 Graph Neural Networks (GNNs)

Graph Neural Networks (GNNs) take graph-structured data as input and aim to learn feature vectors (embeddings) for each node in the graph. At each layer, GNNs perform two core operations: neighbor aggregation and node update, which can be expressed as:

$$z_v^\ell = \phi^\ell(\{h_u^{(\ell-1)} | u \in N(v)\}), \tag{1}$$

$$h_v = \psi^\ell\left(z_v^\ell, h_v^{(\ell-1)}\right), \tag{2}$$

where $N(v)$ represents the neighbor set of node v, h_v^ℓ is the learned embedding of node v at layer ℓ, z_v^ℓ is an intermediate feature computed through an aggregation function ϕ^ℓ, and ψ^ℓ is the function that updates the node's feature. In this work, our proposed method, PipeQS, builds upon GCN as the baseline model. In the original GCN model [10], the aggregation function ϕ^ℓ uses a weighted average, and the update function ψ^ℓ is defined as a single-layer perceptron, $\sigma(W^\ell(z_v^\ell))$, where $\sigma(\cdot)$ denotes a non-linear activation function, and W^ℓ is the learnable weight matrix.

2.2 Distributed GNN Training

GNNs excel in tasks like node classification and link prediction by aggregating neighboring features to update node representations [10,23]. However, scaling GNNs to large graphs with millions of nodes poses challenges due to increasing memory and computational demands [7]. Distributed GNN training mitigates this by partitioning large graphs into subgraphs, training them in parallel while exchanging boundary node features. Early works such as NeuGraph [12], AliGraph [24], ROC [8], and Dorylus [17] pioneered this approach but face the persistent challenges of communication overhead and communication waiting. As partitions increase, the number of boundary nodes grows, inflating communication costs. BNS-GCN [20] reduces communication via boundary node sampling but introduces gradient variance, destabilizing training.

2.3 Quantization-Based Methods

Quantization is another effective strategy to reduce communication overhead, especially in large-scale graphs. AdaQP [19] dynamically adjusts the bit-width of messages, significantly lowering communication delays. Other techniques, such as SGQuant [3], use hierarchical quantization to minimize memory and bandwidth needs. However, these methods introduce update variance due to quantization errors, impacting convergence stability, especially for large graphs with high-dimensional features.

2.4 Asynchronous Distributed Training Methods

Asynchronous training methods aim to reduce communication waiting times by using stale gradients or features. In deep learning, systems like Hogwild! [13], SSP [6], and MXNet [11] have employed asynchronous updates to hide communication costs. For GNNs, PipeGCN [21] performs parallel communication and computation, utilizing stale features to reduce synchronization delays. However, it assumes a balance between communication and computation time, which may not always hold, limiting its efficiency gains. SANCUS [15] and EC-Graph [16] similarly reduces communication by allowing stale updates, caching embeddings, and skipping communication when possible. While effective in reducing communication, balancing communication efficiency and convergence stability remains a challenge in such staleness-based methods.

In contrast, PipeQS integrates quantization and staleness into a unified framework. It dynamically adjusts bit-width and staleness to achieve a convergence rate of $O(T^{-1/2})$, significantly reducing communication overhead and maintaining high training efficiency and model accuracy across various graph sizes and complexities.

3 The Proposed Framework

Overview. In this section, We propose a novel strategy, PipeQS. PipeQS utilizes a pipeline approach that parallelizes communication and computation as much as possible. It applies quantization to features and gradients to reduce the communication costs associated with boundary nodes. Furthermore, PipeQS incorporates features/gradients staleness, allowing the training process to use stale external node features or gradients when communication is incomplete, allowing that computation continues without waiting. This significantly reduces the overall time required for convergence.

To the best of our knowledge, there has been limited research that integrates quantization in pipeline training for distributed GNNs, and combining both quantization and staleness in distributed GNN training remains relatively unexplored. As a result, proving the convergence of such an approach presents a unique challenge. This work aims to theoretically and empirically demonstrate the convergence of this novel pipeline GNN training method that leverages both quantization and staleness. Additionally, we show that the convergence speed is comparable to GNN training methods that solely rely on staleness. We further propose an adaptive bit-width and staleness adjustment mechanism, providing convergence guarantees for PipeQS.

3.1 Challenges in Partitioned Parallel Training

Table 1. Vanilla method communication overhead

Dataset	Partitions	Comm. Ratio
Reddit	2	94.85%
	4	79.47%
Yelp	2	49.42%
	4	69.82%
Ogbn-products	4	68.53%
	8	76.79%

Large Communication Overhead. In partition-parallel training, each partition contains local inner nodes and boundary nodes from other partitions, which are critical for neighbor aggregation in GNNs. Updating a node's features requires information from neighboring nodes across partitions. As the number of partitions increases, boundary nodes are replicated, often surpassing the number of inner nodes. This leads to significant communication overhead, with more time spent exchanging boundary node data, ultimately reducing training efficiency. As shown in the Table 1, the Vanilla method faces considerable communication costs. As dataset size and partitions grow, communication overhead becomes the primary bottleneck, significantly restricting training speed.

Long Communication Waiting Time. Another significant challenge in partitioned parallel training is the long communication waiting time. As partitions increase, communication phases become more frequent and longer, leading to substantial idle times for GPUs. During these phases, the GPUs are often left waiting for boundary node information to be exchanged, resulting in poor utilization of computational resources. This not only reduces the overall training throughput but also exacerbates the latency between partitions, further slowing down the entire training process. As illustrated in the Fig. 1, whether it is Vanilla or PipeGCN, when communication time significantly exceeds computation time, there is a long interval between the computations of two consecutive iterations, resulting in substantial communication waiting time.

3.2 The Proposed PipeQS Method

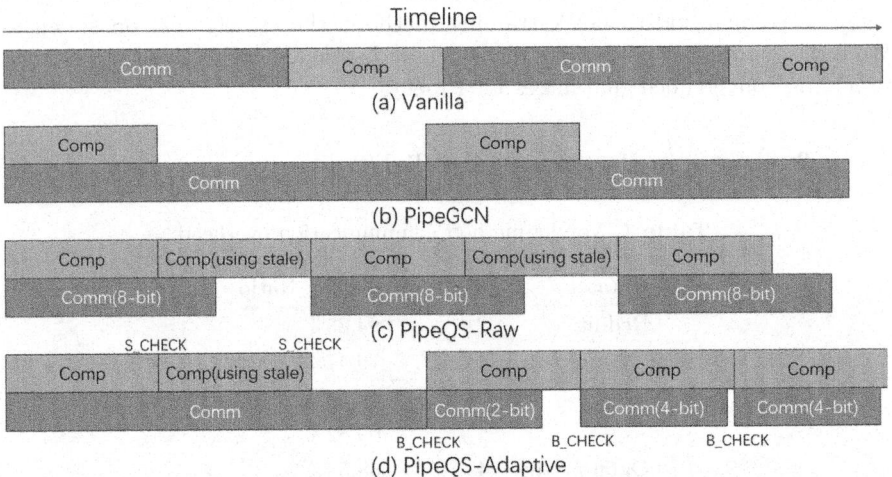

Fig. 1. Comparison of communication and computation for Vanilla, PipeGCN, PipeQS-Raw, and PipeQS-Adaptive on a single layer. The Vanilla method executes communication and computation sequentially. PipeGCN parallelizes them within a layer, but computation still waits for the previous iteration's communication. PipeQS-Raw reduces communication time through quantization and features/gradients staleness, skipping communication when it exceeds computation time. PipeQS-Adaptive dynamically adjusts bit-width and staleness for further optimization. In PipeQS-Adaptive, S_CHECK determines whether communication should be skipped and stale features/gradients should be used, while B_CHECK determines whether communication precision needs to be adjusted.

Figure 1 presents a iteration-level overview of the PipeQS method, which pipelines the communication and computation phases. The figure also compares Vanilla and PipeQS with PipeGCN. Figure 2 illustrates the finer-grained operation of PipeQS at the layer level.

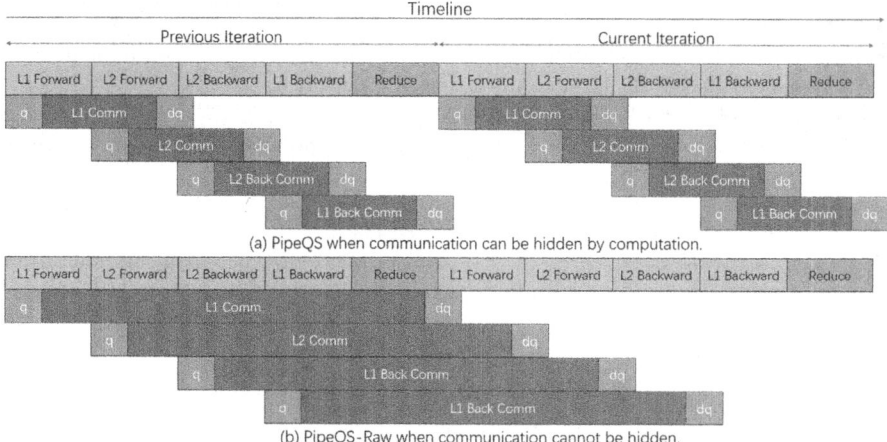

Fig. 2. Fine-grained layer-level operation of PipeQS. (a) shows the operation of PipeQS when communication is hidden by computation. (b) illustrates how PipeQS-Raw uses stale features/gradients for computation when communication cannot be hidden.

PipeGCN breaks the synchronization between communication and computation, allowing each GNN layer's computation to overlap with communication, thereby reducing the heavy overhead seen in vanilla methods. However, for large-scale graph training, communication time often far exceeds computation time, leaving a significant portion of communication time uncovered. Therefore, PipeGCN fails to address the two issues we mentioned earlier in distributed training.

PipeQS addresses the two problems through two key strategies respectively. First, it employs quantization to reduce communication time by decreasing the size of transmitted data. Second, it leverages stale features or gradients while parallelizing communication and computation, allowing training to continue without waiting for communication to finish by using features or gradients from the previous iteration. We refer to the method with fixed quantization bit-width and unlimited staleness as PipeQS-Raw. The implementation is shown in Alg. 1, and the complete process can be found in Alg. D.1 in Appendix D.

While effective, these techniques inevitably introduce certain challenges. Quantization reduces the precision of the transmitted features and gradients, and skipping communication introduces staleness, leading to a mix of up-to-date internal features and gradients with stale boundary features and gradients. To alleviate these effects and ensure convergence, PipeQS incorporates a bit-width and staleness adjustment strategy that dynamically adjusts the bit-width for quantization and determines when to apply staleness, allowing the training process to balance communication efficiency and accuracy.

Algorithm 1 PipeQS-Raw Forward Propagation (Per-Partition View)
───
Require: partition id i, partition count n, graph partition G_i, propagation matrix P_i, boundary node set B_i, layer count L, initial model W_0
Ensure: trained model W_T after T iterations
1: $H_{prev} \leftarrow 0$ ▷ initialize previous communication result
2: **for** $t := 1 \to T$ **do**
3:     **for** $\ell := 1 \to L$ **do**
4:         **if** $t > 1$ **and** $thread_f^{(\ell)}$ not completed **then**
5:             Use H_{prev} ▷ skip communication
6:         **else**
7:             with $thread_f^{(\ell)}$ ▷ communicate features in parallel
8:                 Quantize $H_{S_{i,:}}^{(\ell)}$ to $H_{S_{i,:}}^{(\ell),q}$ with $Q_{S_{i,:}}^{(\ell)}$
9:                 Send $H_{S_{i,:}}^{(\ell),q}$ and $Q_{S_{i,:}}^{(\ell)}$; Receive $B_{:}^{(\ell),q}$ and $Q_{B_{:}}^{(\ell)}$
10:               Dequantize $B_{:}^{(\ell),q}$ with $Q_{B_{:}}^{(\ell)}$; Update H_{prev}
11:         **end if**
12:         $H_{V_i}^{(\ell)} \leftarrow \sigma(P_i H^{(\ell-1)} W^{(\ell-1)})$ ▷ update inner nodes
13:     **end for**
14:     Backward propagation and update model
15: **end for**
16: **return** W_T

3.3 Stochastic Integer Quantization

We adopt a stochastic integer quantization method to reduce communication overhead by converting high-precision floating-point data into lower bit-width integers (e.g., 2-bit, 4-bit, or 8-bit) via scaling and stochastic rounding [4]. In our adaptive approach, each tensor is quantized independently. For every tensor, we first compute its minimum (min) and maximum (max) values to derive the scaling factor:

$$\text{scale} = \frac{2^{\text{bits}} - 1}{\max - \min}, \quad (3)$$

which linearly maps the original floating-point data into the quantized integer domain. The tensor-specific parameters min and scale are stored individually and updated at every training batch to adapt to changes in the data distribution.

The quantization operation is defined as:

$$q(x) = \text{round}\left(\frac{x - \min}{\text{scale}} + \text{noise}\right), \quad (4)$$

where x represents the floating-point input data. The noise term facilitates stochastic rounding to reduce quantization bias. After quantization, the resulting integers are packed into compact bit-streams for efficient communication; the process is highly parallelized using CUDA to ensure scalability with large datasets.

Upon transmission, dequantization is performed using the stored min and scale values:
$$x_{\text{recovered}} = q(x) \times \text{scale} + \min. \tag{5}$$
Leveraging AdaQP-inspired parallel processing [19], our approach minimizes the overhead of quantization and dequantization while preserving model accuracy, thereby enhancing the scalability and performance of distributed GNN training.

3.4 Stale Features and Gradients Utilization

In our distributed GNN communication protocol, we incorporate a staleness mechanism that allows the use of outdated neighbor node features and gradients to reduce communication overhead.

This technique will be used when the current round of computation finishes before the previous communication round completes. When staleness is permitted, rather than waiting for the most up-to-date neighbor features and gradients to arrive, the system proceeds with the outdated data from the previous communication. This enables uninterrupted computation, reducing the idle time spent waiting for communication to complete. By doing so, we effectively skip sending new communication messages for the current round, as the staleness mechanism ensures that previously received data can still be utilized in the ongoing computation.

This approach significantly improves overall efficiency in distributed environments, where communication latency often becomes a bottleneck.

3.5 Bit-Width and Staleness Adjustment Strategy

To balance the trade-off between communication overhead and model accuracy, we propose a bit-width and staleness adjustment strategy. This strategy dynamically adjusts the bit-width for quantization and decides whether to use stale features/gradients at each layer during training.

For each GNN layer ℓ, we measure the difference between the current features/gradients n^ℓ and the previous features/gradients o^ℓ using inverted cosine similarity:

$$d^\ell = 1 - \frac{o^\ell \cdot n^\ell}{\|o^\ell\|\|n^\ell\|} \tag{6}$$

If the difference $d^\ell > E$, staleness is disabled, meaning that stale data cannot be reused ($r^\ell = 0$), and fresh communication must occur. Additionally, to ensure communication precision, we dynamically adjust the bit-width based on d^ℓ. This adjustment is governed by a logistic function:

$$p^\ell = \frac{1}{1 + \exp\left(-K \cdot \frac{d^\ell}{q^\ell}\right)} \tag{7}$$

Here, q^ℓ is a counter tracking the continuous quantization updates and the staleness count, and K is a scaling factor that controls the sensitivity of the adjustment. If $p^\ell > 0.5$, indicating a significant difference between iterations, the bit-width is increased to enhance precision. Conversely, if $p^\ell \leq 0.5$, the bit-width is reduced, thereby speeding up communication to avoid staleness or communication delays.

On the other hand, if the difference $d^\ell \leq E$, staleness is enabled ($r^\ell = 1$), and the previous features/gradients can be reused without adjusting the bit-width, effectively bypassing communication and improving efficiency.

As shown in Fig. 1, the aforementioned strategy is applied during the B_CHECK phase. Additionally, during each computation step, if communication has not yet completed, an S_CHECK is performed. The result of the S_CHECK determines whether to skip communication, based on the staleness flag r^ℓ obtained from the previous B_CHECK.

This adaptive strategy effectively reduces communication time while limiting the error within the threshold E, ensuring convergence and efficient training. The specific code for the strategy can be found in Alg. D.2 in Appendix D. We refer to the version of PipeQS that applies this strategy as PipeQS-Adaptive, with its implementation provided in Alg. D.3 in Appendix D.

3.6 Convergence Guarantee for PipeQS

Due to the quantization and staleness of neighboring node features and gradients, the convergence behavior of PipeQS-Adaptive requires theoretical justification. Unlike traditional full-precision synchronous updates, the presence of quantization noise and staleness error introduces additional challenges in the optimization process.

We establish the following convergence bound for PipeQS-Adaptive:

$$\frac{1}{T}\sum_{t=1}^{T} \mathbb{E}[\|\nabla L(W_t)\|^2] \leq O(T^{-1/2}) + O(\sigma_q^2 + E^2) \tag{8}$$

where $L(W)$ represents the loss function, and σ_q, E denote the quantization noise and staleness error, respectively. The final convergence rate is $O(T^{-1/2})$, but it may be affected by quantization and staleness effects. Hence, an adaptive strategy for adjusting bit-width and staleness threshold is crucial to ensuring efficient convergence while maintaining a reasonable error bound.

The detailed proof of this convergence result is provided in Appendix C.

4 Experiment

4.1 Implementation

We implement PipeQS on top of DGL 2.3.0 [22] and PyTorch 2.3.0 [14]. DGL is utilized for graph-related data storage and operations, while PyTorch's distributed package is employed for initializing process groups and facilitating communication between devices. Before training begins, the graph is partitioned using DGL's built-in METIS algorithm [9]. Each training process is confined to a single device (GPU), and remote node indices—derived from DGL's partition book—are broadcast to create sending and receiving node index sets, allowing processes to fetch the required messages from other devices efficiently.

4.2 Experimental Settings

We evaluated PipeQS on three large benchmark datasets, namely Reddit, Ogbn-products, and Yelp [5,7,26]. The transductive graph learning tasks on Reddit and Ogbn-products involve single-label node classification, while multi-label classification tasks are performed on Yelp. We use accuracy and F1-score (micro) as the performance metrics for these tasks, collectively referred to as accuracy. All datasets follow the "fixed-partition" splits using the METIS algorithm. We train the GCN model [10] for all experiments, ensuring consistency by unifying all model-related and training-related hyperparameters. The model layer size is set to 3, with hidden layers of 256 dimensions, and the learning rate is fixed at 0.01. We employ the Adam optimizer and use the ReLU activation function within the GCN model. For PipeQS using adaptive strategy, we fix the threshold E to 0.1.

Experiments are conducted on a server running Ubuntu 20.04 LTS, equipped with an Intel(R) Xeon(R) Platinum 8362 CPU, 360 GB of RAM, 8 NVIDIA RTX 3090 (24 GB) GPUs and PCIe4.0x16 connecting CPU-GPU and GPU-GPU.

4.3 Comparative Performance Evaluation

In this section, we evaluate the performance of PipeQS-Adaptive in comparison with Vanilla GCN and three other state-of-the-art (SOTA) methods: PipeGCN [21], SANCUS [15], and AdaQP [19]. The datasets used for this comparison include Reddit, Yelp, and Ogbn-products, which provide diverse scenarios for testing both communication efficiency and model convergence.

PipeGCN optimizes training by parallelizing communication and computation, relying on stale features/gradients from the previous iteration to reduce idle communication time. AdaQP focuses on minimizing communication overhead by quantizing the transmitted features/gradients, thereby lowering data transfer costs. SANCUS adopts a staleness-aware strategy, caching and reusing stale embeddings to skip unnecessary broadcasts, which reduces communication while maintaining convergence through bounded approximation errors. Our approach, PipeQS-Adaptive, leverages adaptive methods to dynamically adjust parameters for optimal performance under varying conditions. For a detailed methodological comparison between PipeQS-Adaptive and PipeQS-Raw, as well as an analysis of the impact of bit-width and staleness, please refer to Appendix B.

Training Time and Throughput Comparison. Table 2 compares the training time and throughput of PipeQS against Vanilla GCN, PipeGCN, SANCUS, and AdaQP across three datasets.

Table 2. Training time, throughput, and communication overhead comparison on different datasets

Dataset	Partitions	Method	Comm.(s)	Time(s)	Comm./Time (%)	Throughput (epoch/s)	Speedup (x)
Reddit	2	Vanilla	0.2486	0.2621	94.85%	3.8153	1.00x
		PipeGCN	0.0948	0.1308	72.47%	7.6453	2.00x
		SANCUS	0.0286	0.1887	15.15%	5.2994	1.39x
		AdaQP	0.1488	0.3468	42.90%	2.8835	0.76x
		PipeQS	**0.0729**	**0.1036**	70.37%	**9.6525**	**2.53x**
	4	Vanilla	0.2243	0.2822	79.47%	3.5436	1.00x
		PipeGCN	0.1682	0.2298	73.20%	4.3516	1.23x
		SANCUS	0.3879	0.5246	73.94%	1.9062	0.54x
		AdaQP	0.2157	0.3153	68.42%	3.1716	0.89x
		PipeQS	**0.0186**	**0.0625**	**29.76%**	**16.0000**	**4.51x**
Yelp	2	Vanilla	0.1158	0.2343	49.42%	4.2680	1.00x
		PipeGCN	0.0132	0.1281	10.30%	7.8064	1.83x
		AdaQP	0.0658	0.2238	29.40%	4.4683	1.05x
		PipeQS	**0.0106**	**0.0707**	14.99%	**14.1443**	**3.31x**
	4	Vanilla	0.1422	0.2037	69.82%	4.9092	1.00x
		PipeGCN	0.0723	0.1341	53.94%	7.4571	1.52x
		AdaQP	0.0744	0.1543	48.22%	6.4809	1.32x
		PipeQS	**0.0032**	**0.0468**	**6.84%**	**21.3675**	**4.35x**
Ogbn-products	4	Vanilla	0.5973	0.8717	68.53%	1.1472	1.00x
		PipeGCN	0.2424	0.5791	41.85%	1.7268	1.51x
		SANCUS	1.2423	1.6863	73.67%	0.5930	0.52x
		AdaQP	0.2506	0.4632	54.12%	2.1589	1.88x
		PipeQS	**0.0469**	**0.2827**	16.59%	**3.5373**	**3.08x**
	8	Vanilla	0.5678	0.7394	76.79%	1.3524	1.00x
		PipeGCN	0.3968	0.5743	69.07%	1.7413	1.29x
		SANCUS	1.5913	1.8536	85.88%	0.5394	0.40x
		AdaQP	0.2002	0.3666	54.61%	2.7278	2.02x
		PipeQS	**0.0381**	**0.1462**	**26.06%**	**6.8399**	**5.06x**

As shown in Table 2, on Reddit, PipeQS is 2.53× to 4.51× faster than Vanilla and up to 1.45× faster than PipeGCN. For Yelp, PipeQS achieves a 3.31× to 4.35× speedup over Vanilla and is up to 2.86× faster than PipeGCN. On Ogbn-products, PipeQS shows the most significant improvement, with a 3.08× to 5.06× speedup over Vanilla and up to 3.93× faster than PipeGCN. Overall, PipeQS delivers the best throughput across all configurations.

Communication Overhead Comparison. PipeQS's reduction in training time primarily stems from the decrease in both communication overhead and communication waiting time. Table 2 and Fig. 3 analyze the communication overhead across different methods and datasets. PipeQS consistently reduces communication overhead, especially with increased partitions. For instance, on the Ogbn-products dataset with 8 partitions, PipeQS lowers communication overhead to 26.06% of total training time, compared to 76.79% for Vanilla GCN.

While methods such as PipeGCN, AdaQP, and SANCUS introduce different techniques to address communication issues, they fall short in scalability on larger datasets. PipeGCN hides communication within computation but cannot sustain this as datasets or partition numbers grow, leading to a steep rise in communication overhead. AdaQP reduces communication overhead through

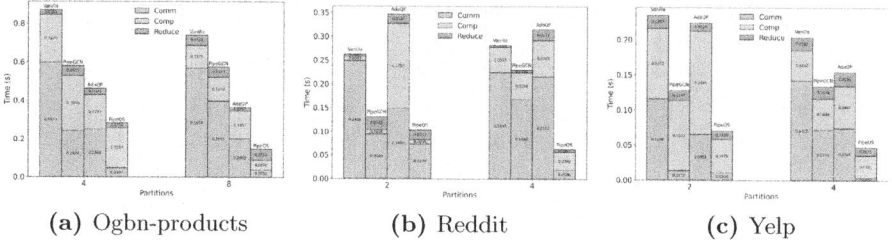

Fig. 3. Training time breakdown of Vanilla GCN, PipeGCN, AdaQP, and PipeQS.

quantization but fails to address communication waiting, resulting in a significant increase in communication time for larger datasets. Similarly, SANCUS leverages staleness to reduce communication waiting time, but its performance deteriorates in larger-scale datasets, as evidenced by the increasing communication time with more partitions.

In contrast, PipeQS not only reduces communication overhead through quantization but also addresses communication waiting by leveraging a combination of pipelining and staleness. This approach ensures consistently low communication time across all datasets and partition sizes, showcasing its superior scalability and efficiency, particularly in large-scale distributed GNN training scenarios where other methods struggle.

Accuracy Comparison. PipeQS reduces training time while still maintaining high accuracy. Table 3 summarizes the final test accuracy of different methods across the datasets. As shown, PipeQS consistently achieves accuracy comparable to that of Vanilla GCN and, in some cases, even surpasses other methods. For example, in the 4-partition setup on the Yelp dataset, PipeQS reaches an accuracy of 47.34%, significantly outperforming Vanilla GCN's 45.19%, which demonstrates the effectiveness of the quantization and staleness adjustment strategies in preserving model accuracy.

Other methods, such as AdaQP, perform well on smaller datasets like Reddit, where communication overhead is lower and the variance introduced by quantization is minimal. However, as the dataset size increases, the variance error caused by quantization begins to hinder convergence, leading to a drop in accuracy. This is particularly evident in larger datasets like Ogbn-products, where AdaQP's performance starts to deteriorate.

In contrast, although PipeQS's accuracy is slightly lower than AdaQP in certain settings on the Ogbn-products dataset, its overall performance remains near-optimal. This confirms that PipeQS effectively balances accuracy and training efficiency, showing resilience in larger datasets.

Convergence Speed Comparison. To evaluate convergence speed, we analyze the relationship between accuracy and the number of epochs for each

Table 3. Accuracy comparison on different datasets

Dataset	Partitions	Vanilla	PipeGCN	SANCUS	AdaQP	PipeQS
Reddit	2	94.85	94.63	94.15	**95.41**	94.78
	4	94.96	94.68	94.17	**95.34**	94.51
Yelp	2	46.15	44.88	-	43.43	**47.11**
	4	45.19	44.63	-	43.38	**47.34**
Ogbn-products	4	76.04	76.36	71.52	75.59	**77.04**
	8	75.47	76.71	71.99	75.24	**76.75**

method. The results indicate that PipeQS generally exhibits better convergence across multiple datasets. As shown in Fig. 4, in the 8-partition setup on the Ogbn-products dataset, PipeQS surpasses 76% validation accuracy within 200 epochs. In comparison, Vanilla GCN and other methods either require more epochs to reach a similar accuracy level or fail to reach it entirely.

In the time-accuracy relationship analysis (Fig. 5), PipeQS demonstrates outstanding training efficiency. Across all datasets and partition settings, PipeQS's accuracy increases significantly faster than that of other methods. For instance, in the 2-partition experiment on the Yelp dataset, PipeQS achieves close to 45% validation accuracy in just under 50 s, whereas other methods requires much more time to approach this level.

These results highlight that PipeQS not only improves training efficiency but also effectively maintains model accuracy, while offering significant advantages in terms of training time.

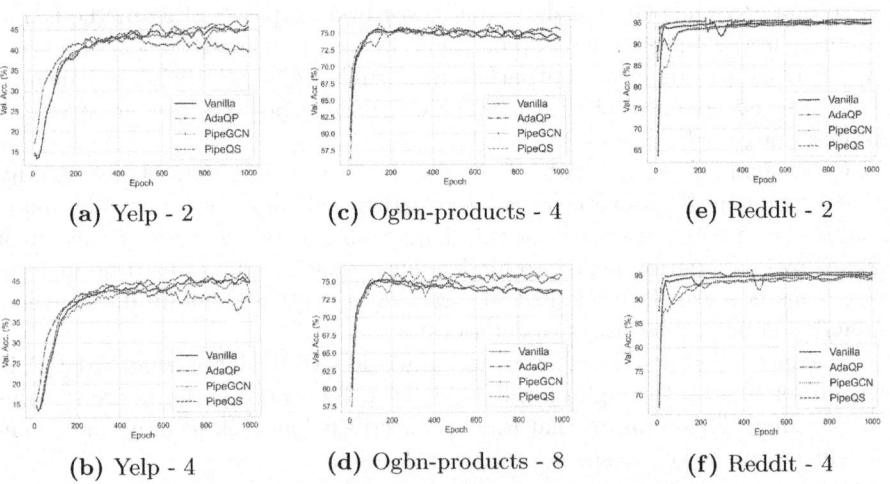

(a) Yelp - 2   (c) Ogbn-products - 4   (e) Reddit - 2
(b) Yelp - 4   (d) Ogbn-products - 8   (f) Reddit - 4

Fig. 4. Epoch-Accuracy curves for different datasets and partition settings.

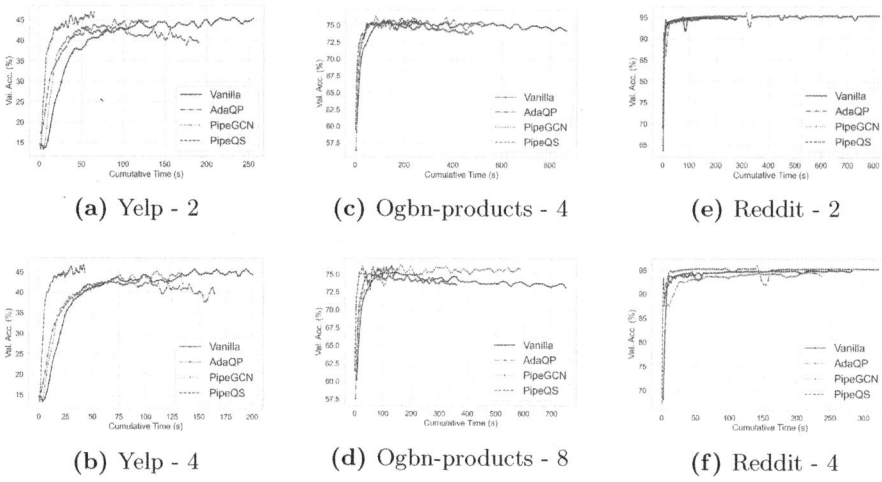

Fig. 5. Time-Accuracy curves for different datasets and partition settings.

5 Conclusion

Training GNNs on large-scale graphs in distributed environments presents a significant challenge, primarily due to the substantial communication overhead and prolonged communication waiting times. Existing distributed GNN training methods, such as sampling and pipelining techniques, partially alleviate these issues but still suffer from high communication costs, synchronization delays, and unstable convergence, especially as the graph size increases and inter-node boundary communication becomes more costly. While recent methods incorporating quantization and staleness have reduced communication volume, they typically sacrifice convergence stability and accuracy, and there remains a lack of effective solutions to fully eliminate communication waiting time.

In this work, we propose PipeQS, a novel distributed GNN training method that integrates quantization and staleness within a pipeline framework. We introduce an adaptive mechanism for adjusting bit-width and staleness iterations, ensuring communication efficiency without compromising convergence stability, maintaining a convergence rate of $O(T^{-\frac{1}{2}})$. Our theoretical analysis and empirical evaluations demonstrate that PipeQS achieves significant improvements in training efficiency across various large-scale graph datasets, while preserving stable convergence. Looking ahead, we plan to extend PipeQS to heterogeneous and temporal graphs, further exploring its adaptability and performance in more complex graph structures.

Acknowledgements. The authors would like to thank the anonymous reviewers for their helpful comments. This work was supported by the National Natural Science Foundation of China (Grant Nos. 62372391, 62072384); the Fujian Provincial Major Science and Technology Project (2022YZ040011); the Wang Deyao Outstanding Graduate Scholarship Program of Xiamen University; and the National Key Research and Development Program of China (Grant Nos. 2023YFF1205600, 2024YFF1206204).

References

1. Chen, J., Zhu, J., Song, L.: Stochastic training of graph convolutional networks with variance reduction. In: Proceedings of the 35th International Conference on Machine Learning (ICML), pp. 942–950 (2018)
2. Chiang, W.L., Liu, X., Si, S., Li, Y., Bengio, S., Hsieh, C.J.: Cluster-gcn: an efficient algorithm for training deep and large graph convolutional networks. In: Proceedings of the 25th ACM SIGKDD International Conference on Knowledge Discovery & Data Mining (KDD), pp. 257–266 (2019)
3. Feng, B., Wang, Y., Chen, G., et al.: Sgquant: squeezing the last bit on graph neural networks with specialized quantization. In: Proceedings of the 32nd International Conference on Tools with Artificial Intelligence (ICTAI) (2020)
4. Gupta, S., Agrawal, A., Gopalakrishnan, K., Narayanan, P.: Deep learning with limited numerical precision. In: Proceedings of the 32nd International Conference on Machine Learning (ICML), pp. 1737–1746 (2015)
5. Hamilton, W., Ying, Z., Leskovec, J.: Inductive representation learning on large graphs. In: Advances in Neural Information Processing Systems (NIPS), vol. 30 (2017)
6. Ho, Q., et al.: More effective distributed ml via a stale synchronous parallel parameter server. In: Advances in Neural Information Processing Systems (NIPS), vol. 26 (2013)
7. Hu, W., et al.: Open graph benchmark: datasets for machine learning on graphs. Adv. Neural. Inf. Process. Syst. **33**, 22118–22133 (2020)
8. Jia, Z., Lin, S., Gao, M., Zaharia, M., Aiken, A.: Improving the accuracy, scalability, and performance of graph neural networks with roc. Proc. Mach. Learn. Syst. **2**, 187–198 (2020)
9. Karypis, G., Kumar, V.: A fast and high-quality multilevel scheme for partitioning irregular graphs. SIAM J. Sci. Comput. **20**(1), 359–392 (1998)
10. Kipf, T.N., Welling, M.: Semi-supervised classification with graph convolutional networks. In: Proceedings of the International Conference on Learning Representations (ICLR) (2017)
11. Li, M., et al.: Scaling distributed machine learning with the parameter server. In: 11th USENIX Symposium on Operating Systems Design and Implementation (OSDI), pp. 583–598 (2014)
12. Ma, L., et al.: Neugraph: parallel deep neural network computation on large graphs. In: 2019 USENIX Annual Technical Conference (USENIX ATC), pp. 443–458 (2019)
13. Niu, F., Recht, B., Ré, C., Wright, S.J.: Hogwild!: a lock-free approach to parallelizing stochastic gradient descent. In: Advances in Neural Information Processing Systems (NIPS), vol. 24 (2011)
14. Paszke, A., et al.: Pytorch: an imperative style, high-performance deep learning library. In: Advances in Neural Information Processing Systems (NeurIPS), vol. 32 (2019)
15. Peng, J., Chen, Z., Shao, Y., Shen, Y., Chen, L., Cao, J.: Sancus: staleness-aware communication-avoiding full-graph decentralized training in large-scale graph neural networks. Proc. VLDB Endowment **15**(9), 1937–1950 (2022)

16. Song, Z., Gu, Y., Qi, J., Wang, Z., Yu, G.: Ec-graph: a distributed graph neural network system with error-compensated compression. In: Proceedings of the 38th IEEE International Conference on Data Engineering (ICDE), pp. 648–660 (2022)
17. Thorpe, J., et al.: Dorylus: Affordable, scalable, and accurate gnn training with distributed cpu servers and serverless threads. In: 15th USENIX Symposium on Operating Systems Design and Implementation (OSDI), pp. 495–514 (2021)
18. Tripathy, A., Yelick, K., Buluç, A.: Reducing communication in graph neural network training. In: SC20: International Conference for High Performance Computing, Networking, Storage and Analysis, pp. 1–14. IEEE (2020)
19. Wan, B., Zhao, J., Wu, C.: Adaptive message quantization and parallelization for distributed full-graph gnn training. Proc. Mach. Learn. Syst. **5** (2023)
20. Wan, C., Li, Y., Li, A., Kim, N.S., Lin, Y.: Bns-gcn: efficient full-graph training of graph convolutional networks with partition-parallelism and random boundary node sampling. Proc. Mach. Learn. Syst. **4**, 673–693 (2022)
21. Wan, C., Li, Y., Wolfe, C.R., Kyrillidis, A., Kim, N.S., Lin, Y.: Pipegcn: efficient full-graph training of graph convolutional networks with pipelined feature communication. In: Proceedings of the 39th International Conference on Machine Learning (ICML) (2022)
22. Wang, M., Yu, L.: Deep graph library: towards efficient and scalable deep learning on graphs. In: ICLR Workshop on Representation Learning on Graphs and Manifolds (2019)
23. Xu, K., Hu, W., Leskovec, J., Jegelka, S.: How powerful are graph neural networks? In: Proceedings of the International Conference on Learning Representations (ICLR) (2019)
24. Yang, H.: Aligraph: a comprehensive graph neural network platform. In: Proceedings of the 25th ACM SIGKDD International Conference on Knowledge Discovery & Data Mining (KDD), pp. 3165–3166 (2019)
25. Ying, R., He, R., Chen, K., Eksombatchai, P., Hamilton, W.L., Leskovec, J.: Graph convolutional neural networks for web-scale recommender systems. In: Proceedings of the 24th ACM SIGKDD International Conference on Knowledge Discovery & Data Mining (KDD), pp. 974–983 (2018)
26. Zeng, H., Zhou, H., Srivastava, A., Kannan, R., Prasanna, V.K.: Graphsaint: graph sampling based inductive learning method. In: Proceedings of the International Conference on Learning Representations (ICLR) (2020)
27. Zhang, M., Chen, Y.: Link prediction based on graph neural networks. In: Advances in Neural Information Processing Systems (NeurIPS), vol. 31 (2018)

Author Index

A
Abghari, Shahrooz 331
Angelova, Milena 331

B
Bao, Runxue 3
Berti-Équille, Laure 259
Bezirganyan, Grigor 259
Birke, Robert 173
Boeva, Veselka 331
Brefeld, Ulf 70
Bronnec, Florian Le 222

C
Chen, Ge 139
Chen, Haoqi 239
Chen, Ke-Jia 457
Chen, Lydia Y. 173, 384
Chen, Shouzhi 294
Chevaleyre, Yann 222

D
Damke, Clemens 403

E
Eliasof, Moshe 420
Epema, Dick 173

F
Fan, Chenrui 384
Fischer, Asja 310
Fournier, Sébastien 259
Frasca, Fabrizio 420

G
Galron, Yaniv 420
Geng, Rushan 139
Gregorová, Magda 190, 206
Guo, Bin 278

H
Hahn, Paul 20
He, Rongshen 156
Herde, Marek 20
Hino, Hideitsu 52
Hong, Chi 173
Huang, Jiyue 173
Huang, Zhixin 20
Hüllermeier, Eyke 403
Huseljic, Denis 20
Hüttel, Frederik Boe 36

I
Ickin, Selim 331
Inane, Ahmed Mehdi 222
Ishibashi, Hideaki 52

J
Jiang, Changzhi 527
Jiang, Jiahui 350

K
Kikuchi, Ryosuke 474
Kong, Lingxiao 350
Kottke, Daniel 20
Kumar, Dibyanshu 190, 206
Kutsukake, Kentaro 52

L
Lai, Siqi 367
Lan, Xiaoyu 331
Lappas, Theodoros 492
Li, Ruixuan 350
Li, Yanhao 527
Liang, Hefei 278
Liu, Bin 294
Liu, Fan 367
Liu, Hao 367
Liu, Jiaqi 278
Liu, Kelin 294

Liu, Xiangrong 527
Liu, Zheng 457
Lu, Quanchao 3
Lukovnikov, Denis 310
Luo, Cuicui 139
Luo, Jiaqi 156

M
Ma, Changsheng 156
Malan, Abel 384
Maron, Haggai 420
Matsui, Kota 52
Mitani, Takahiro 474

N
Nakayama, Itsuki 474
Negrevergne, Benjamin 222
Neubauer, Kai 70
Ning, Yansong 367

O
Onizuka, Makoto 474

P
Paassen, Benjamin 206
Peleška, Jakub 438
Pereira, Francisco 36

Q
Qin, Taoyang 457

R
Rauch, Lukas 20
Riis, Christoffer 36
Rodrigues, Filipe 36
Roos, Stefanie 173
Rudolph, Yannick 70

S
Sasaki, Yuya 474
Šír, Gustav 438
Sellami, Sana 259

Shankar, Aditya 384
Shen, Lian 527
Sick, Bernhard 20
Soi, Zhi Wen 384
Su, Hanjing 294

T
Takahashi, Takuto 474
Terzi, Evimaria 492
Ting, Kai Ming 87
Treister, Eran 420

V
Vaeth, Philipp 206
Väth, Philipp 190
Verine, Alexandre 222
Vogt, Stephan 20
Vombatkere, Karan 492

W
Wang, Haozhao 350
Wang, Ziyu 511
Wojciechowski, Szymon 119
Wu, Donghang 527
Wu, Lei 350

X
Xu, Yang 87

Y
Yan, Qiao 104
Yang, Qinru 156
Yu, Song 239
Yu, Xiaohui 104
Yu, Zhiwen 278

Z
Zakari, Abubakar 156
Zhang, Wendong 239
Zhang, Yanfu 3
Zhou, Yao 294
Zyblewski, Paweł 119

Made in the USA
Monee, IL
03 May 2026

49438649R00345